W9-BFD-128

All Things Austen

All Things

Austen

An Encyclopedia of Austen's World

Volume I

A–L

Kirstin Olsen

Greenwood Press

Westport, Connecticut • London

Library of Congress Cataloging-in-Publication Data

Olsen, Kirstin.
  All things Austen : an encyclopedia of Austen's world / Kirstin Olsen.
    p. cm.
  Includes bibliographical references and index.
    ISBN 0–313–33032–8 (set : alk. paper)—ISBN 0–313–33033–6 (vol. 1 : alk.
  paper)—ISBN 0–313–33034–4 (vol. 2 : alk. paper)
    1. Austen, Jane, 1775–1817—Encyclopedias.   2. Novelists, English—19th
  century—Biography—Encyclopedias.   3. Women and literature—England—History—
  19th century—Encyclopedias.   I. Title.
  PR4036.A275 2005
  823'.7 B—dc22   2004028664

British Library Cataloguing in Publication Data is available.

Library of Congress Catalog Card Number: 2004028664
ISBN: 0–313–33032–8 (set)
      0–313–33033–6 (vol. I)
      0–313–33034–4 (vol. II)

First published in 2005

Greenwood Press, 88 Post Road West, Westport, CT 06881
An imprint of Greenwood Publishing Group, Inc.
www.greenwood.com

Printed in the United States of America

The paper used in this book complies with the
Permanent Paper Standard issued by the National
Information Standards Organization (Z39.48–1984).

10 9 8 7 6 5 4 3 2 1

All line illustrations, except where otherwise noted, credited to Kirstin Olsen.

For Eric

Contents

Acknowledgments

I would like to thank the staff at the Lewis Walpole Library, particularly Sue Walker and Brian Parker, for their invaluable assistance with many of the illustrations for this book. They truly went above and beyond the call of duty, and I am extremely grateful. I am also thankful to the many people who shared their enthusiasm and expertise, including Eunice and Ron Shanahan, who graciously provided photographs of franked and crossed letters and advised me about the history of postmarks; Eliot Jordan, tea buyer for Peet's Coffee and Tea, who helped me track down information about historical tea varieties; David Lisot of Heritagecoin.com, who granted permission for the use of photos from his company's Web site; and Neil Handley of London's College of Optometrists, who patiently explained turnpin-temple spectacles to me. Any errors in these departments are not theirs but my own. I am indebted to my family for their constant support and their patient pretense of interest when I come to the dinner table overflowing with newly acquired information about tea urns, court plaster, or chamber pots.

Introduction

Jane Austen is normally thought of as avoiding richly detailed settings and confining herself almost entirely to the development and interactions of her characters. Certainly, she is a restrained author, eschewing unnecessary details and emphasizing the revelation of character through dialogue, but this is not to say that historical detail does not occur in her works and does not require explanation. If anything, the details she uses require more explanation rather than less, for she chose them with great care and with an expectation that her readers would understand their full significance.

Astute modern readers can grasp the basics of many of her references through context. It becomes evident, for example, that barouches, phaetons, curricles, and post chaises were all carriages of some kind. For Austen's contemporary audience, however, these vehicles were as different from each other in form, purpose, and connotation as sports cars, minivans, and rental cars today. One misses a great deal of what she says about character and fails to appreciate the truly elegant economy of her language without a full comprehension of the objects and ideas to which she refers.

This book, therefore, attempts to provide the background material that makes her work more fully comprehensible. It discusses types of carriages and the associations they elicited, the value and size of certain coins, the difference between a pelisse and a spencer, and hundreds of other areas in which obsolete or unfamiliar terms distance us from Austen's original intentions. The result is a compilation of the available scholarship on everything from the history of food to the composition of Tunbridge ware and takes us through the dawn of tourism, the discovery of chemical elements, the development of the barometer and the thermometer, and the politics of the sugar trade.

There are six principal components of this book, other than the index, to help readers of Austen navigate through her world. One is the alphabetized series of more than 150 articles, ranging from a few sentences to chapter length, depending on the complexity of the subject and its relevance to Austen's work. The second, embedded in the articles, is a system of abbreviations guiding readers to passages in Austen's writings that pertain to the articles' subject matter. These abbreviations refer to the page numbers of the *Oxford Illustrated Jane Austen* (3rd edition), edited by R.W. Chapman, which is the standard text for Austen scholarship. Most scholars, however, have tended to abbreviate all of Austen's Juvenilia and fragmentary novels with the simple notation "MW," for the "Minor Works" volume in the series. I have chosen to be somewhat more specific, and readers will find a prefix such as "*Visit*" or "*L&F*" before citations from the Minor Works volume. (See the List of Works and Abbreviations.) Thus, a parenthetical notation such as (*L&F, MW* 105) means the juvenile fragment *Love and Freindship* [*sic*], Minor Works volume, p. 105. In some cases, including all references to a particular subject (such as instances of the word "servant") would have been unwieldy; therefore, unless otherwise stated, the references are representative and not exhaustive.

The third major source of information is the illustrations, most of them from the Lewis Walpole Library. They are richly informative in their present state, but the Lewis Walpole Library also has an excellent Web site where the pictures can be viewed in color and in greater detail. Each caption has the LWL call number, which can be entered into a search engine on the Web site for easy access to a specific image. In-text references to illustrations that are found in other articles give a short form of the illustration title followed by the article title in parentheses.

The fourth guide for readers is the Guide to Related Topics, which separates the articles in this encyclopedia by broad topic. For example, the category "Business, Work, and Finance" contains the articles on Agriculture, Alehouse, Enclosure, Income, Inns, Lodgings, Money, Servants, Shops, and Taxes. This listing can serve as a study guide for readers interested in a particular aspect of Austen's works. A fifth important resource is the Timeline, which tracks the achievements and movements of the Austen family alongside contemporary events in the realms of politics, culture, religion, science, and medicine. Under the articles "Places," "Bath," and "London," readers will find maps of most of the locations mentioned by Austen (with the exceptions, noted in the text, of a few far-flung places easy to locate without help, such as Russia and America).

Readers will learn the origin of the term "box office" and will investigate the mystery of exactly what sort of spectacles Frank Churchill was fixing at the Bateses'. They will discover why opera girls were so scandalous and why William Price could not get promoted from midshipman to lieutenant without help. They will discover how a servants' bell worked, what a calling card looked like, and how the games of casino, lottery tickets, and loo were played. Crucially, they will learn how terms still used today, such as "public place," "toy shop," "hobbyhorse," and "pocketbook," differ in their usage from the same terms in Austen's day.

List of Articles

Guide to Related Topics

Jews
Marriage
Widow
Witch

Plants and Animals

Animals
Samphire

Reading and Writing

Franking
Gothic
Newspaper
Pen
Pencil
Post
Reading
Writing

Religion

Angels
Bells
Clergy
Jews
Parish
Religion

Riding and Hunting

Horses
Hunting

Science, Medicine, and Technology

Barometer
Bathing
Clubs
Medicine
Pregnancy and Childbirth
Science
Spectacles

Teeth

Time and Place

Bath
Holidays
London
Places
Public Places
Valley of Tempé
West Indies

Transportation and Travel

Barouche
Bathing
Carriages and Coaches
Carts and Wagons
Chair
Chaise
Gig
Inns
Landau
Phaeton
Places
Travel

Wording

Bon Mot
Brickbat
Compts
Condescension
Devoirs
Hobbyhorse
Quiz
Spleen
Ton
Ult.
Under-hung

List of Works and Abbreviations

Minor Works (abbreviation followed by MW)

Amelia	*Amelia Webster*
Beaut Desc	*A Beautiful Description of the Different Effects of Sensibility on Different Minds*
Cass	*The Beautiful Cassandra: A Novel in Twelve Chapters*
Cath	*Catharine or the Bower*
Clifford	*Memoirs of Mr. Clifford*
Col Let	*A Collection of Letters*
Curate	*The Generous Curate*
E&E	*Edgar & Emma*
Evelyn	*Evelyn*
F&E	*Frederic & Elfrida*
First Act	*The First Act of a Comedy*
H&E	*Henry & Eliza*
Harley	*The Adventures of Mr. Harley*
Headache	*On a Headache*
History	*The History of England*
J&A	*Jack & Alice*
L&F	*Love and Freindship*
Lesley	*Lesley Castle*

LS	*Lady Susan*
Mount	*Sir William Mountague*
Mystery	*The Mystery: An Unfinished Comedy*
Ode	*Ode to Pity*
Plan	*Plan of a Novel*
Popham	*On Sir Home Popham's Sentence, April 1807*
Sand	*Sanditon*
Scraps	*Scraps*
3S	*The Three Sisters*
Visit	*The Visit: A Comedy in 2 Acts*
Watsons	*The Watsons*

Novels

E	*Emma*
MP	*Mansfield Park*
NA	*Northanger Abbey*
P	*Persuasion*
P&P	*Pride and Prejudice*
S&S	*Sense and Sensibility*

References to the Kotzebue play *Lovers' Vows,* included by R. W. Chapman in his edition of *Mansfield Park,* are indicated by the abbreviation *MP, LV.*

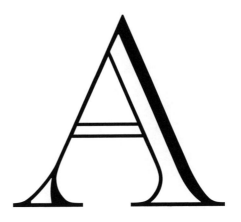

Agriculture

Urban population was increasing in the late eighteenth and early nineteenth centuries, but the vast majority of people still made their living, in one way or another, from the land. Even London was still surrounded by fields and farms (*E* 100), and it was rare to find a person outside the metropolis who was unfamiliar, as was Mary Crawford (*MP* 58), with the cycles of the agricultural year. In the spring, some crops, including barley, were sown, with the youngest children enlisted to frighten birds away from the newly planted seeds. Other crops were weeded. Fallow fields—fields left empty of crops to rejuvenate the soil—were plowed in the spring and periodically throughout the year. Newborn animals such as lambs were tended.

In the summer, children continued to chase birds away from ripening grain, using wooden clappers and running up and down between the rows. Kitchen gardens yielded vegetables, herbs, and medicinal and decorative flowers. Orchards produced fruit of all kinds. Plowing of fallow land continued, and wheat and barley were harvested. Cattle, sheep, and goats produced their richest milk in spring and summer, when they fed on new grass, and the cheese and butter produced from their milk had a rich golden color.

In the early fall, plowing (*First Act, MW* 172) and harvests continued, with hay being laid up in haycocks (haystacks—see *H&E, MW* 33, 39) as winter fodder; some hay would also be stored in ceiling racks in the barns and stables and scratched out with pitchforks as needed. The harvest was a hurried time (*MP* 58), as untimely rain could ruin the crop, and it was important to bring in the crops at the time of optimum ripeness. Accordingly, neighbors tried whenever possible to stagger their harvests, and careful farmers secured contracts with the best laborers well in advance of the season. William Ellis wrote in 1750 that in Hertfordshire,

> we hire harvest-men long before harvest, by way of security, that we may not be at a loss for them when we most want them; and give each man thirty or six and thirty shillings for his month's service, besides victualling and lodging them in the house all that time, for then they are ready early and late to do our work.

Wages would have been even higher by Austen's time, and Ellis wrote that harvesters and haymakers (*H&E, MW* 33; *Sand, MW* 364–65) compared not only the wages from farm to farm but also the accommodation and food provided, preferring, apparently, a diet of "beef, bacon, or pickled pork, beans, pease, puddings, pyes, pasties, cheese, milk, with other culinary preparations, and with well brew'd strong and small beer and ale." A large farm might hire in eight to twelve men, or even more, for harvest.

Wheat (*E* 100) was gathered into sheaves, loaded onto large wagons (*MP* 58), and taken to barns to be threshed—beaten with flails—to separate the grain from the stalks. The grain was then winnowed (sieved) to separate the heavier grain from the lighter chaff. The end of the harvest was often marked by a festival of some kind, with feasting, music, and the garlanding of the last wagons to come in from the fields, and often of the animals who pulled them. Stephen Duck, the "thresher poet," wrote of the celebrations a few decades before Austen's birth:

> The Bells, and clashing Whips, alternate sound,
> And rattling Waggons thunder o'er the Ground.
> The Wheat got in, the Pease, and other Grain,
> Share the same Fate, and soon leave bare the Plain:
> In noisy Triumph the last Load moves on,
> And loud Huzza's proclaim the Harvest done.

Much later, Jane's brother James wrote a poem to his son, describing autumn as the time "When corn is housed, & fields are clear." Once the fields were reduced to stubble, the poor were permitted to come onto the land and "glean"—that is, collect the scattered grains that had fallen onto the ground during the harvest. They did not get a great deal this way, but it meant a few extra loaves of bread, and they were glad to get it.

Pigs were also fattened and slaughtered during the fall, whereupon they were converted into hams, bacon, and brawn for the winter months. The stubbled fields were plowed under once more (*P* 85) and then left alone until spring. The farm was a relatively quiet place through the winter, as little work could be done in the fields. It was a time for repairs—repairs to harnesses, stables, plows, and so on. Wooden bowls and spoons could be carved by the fireside, and saddles and horse collars could be made. The family survived principally on what it had managed to preserve through salting, smoking, drying, and pickling. Root vegetables and apples, which kept well if stored properly, were eaten.

The Parts of a Farm

Farms today often tend to focus on the production of a single cash crop, with relatively little of the land devoted to the sustenance of the family that runs it. Corporate farms, of which there are more and more, need not consider individual sustenance at all but focus entirely on large-scale growth of single crops. In Austen's day, however, a farm was expected to supply virtually all the food needs of the family who ran it; only luxurious imported items, such as citrus fruit and tea, were bought elsewhere. Families and friends traded surplus produce back and forth; for example, a family living near the sea might send fish as a gift and receive in exchange game birds or apples. However, the bulk of one's needs came directly from the land. If you did not plant it, you did not eat it.

Therefore, a farm had many different divisions, both in the fields and in the farmyard, to meet these miscellaneous needs. The fields, in an age of aggressive enclosure, would be newly surrounded by fences (*E* 100), ditches, and hedgerows (*Wat*, *MW* 321; *P* 86). Some of these fields would be planted with grain, while others would lie fallow or, in a relatively recent innovation, be planted with nitrogen-fixing crops to improve the soil. In the mid-eighteenth century, increasing numbers of farmers had followed the example of Lord Townshend (1674–1738), nicknamed "Turnip" Townshend, in rotating their crops. The classic rotation was wheat, then turnips (*E* 100) as winter fodder, then barley, and then clover (*E* 361), a nitrogen-fixing crop, to feed animals and to fertilize the soil.

Interspersed with these fields of crops were meadows (*P* 90) of tall grass for use as hay and areas of so-called wasteland (*Sand*, *MW* 377; *NA* 111). Wasteland did not, in fact, go to waste. It was simply nonarable land that was used for a variety of other purposes, providing, depending on the nature of the terrain, deadwood for fuel, habitat for game birds, berries for cottagers, or pasturage for animals. The enclosure and conversion of wasteland to arable fields throughout the eighteenth century were a matter of controversy, as wasteland often provided subsistence for poorer families who could not otherwise afford to pasture a cow or feed a pig.

Large fields of single-crop vegetables were far less common than fields of grain. Near ravenous London, suburban farmers grew large quantities of such crops as asparagus, but elsewhere, people grew enough to feed themselves in kitchen gardens, the size of which varied according to the size of the household. Large estates might also possess "plantations" (*S&S* 343; *MP* 432) of trees that would be harvested periodically for timber, forming one of the most important cash crops in a country starved for wood.*

Within the farmyard (*MP* 58) were several types of buildings. There were barns for storing grain, hay, and farm tools such as plows and scythes. Stables held horses and oxen, if oxen were employed in plowing. The stables might be relatively small for a small farm, extensive and well managed for a large estate where there were not only draft horses but hunters and riding horses as well. Special structures were constructed for different types of animals: folds for sheep, sties for pigs, special hard-floored pens for boars being fattened, and poultry houses (*MP* 141) for chickens, ducks, turkeys, and geese. Most farms of any size had a dairy, where cows were milked and the milk allowed to settle. Churning and cheese making were both done in the dairy, which was under the supervision of the lady of the house and her dairymaids, if she had them. The farm might also possess a bakehouse with a bread oven, a brewhouse for the large-scale produc-

---

*"Plantations" could in fact be any sort of plantings, but the most common usage was in reference to woods.

The Farm Yard, 1786. A typical farm scene shows a barn or other outbuilding, a neat white cottage, haystacks in the background, and, in the foreground, a woman feeding poultry. Care of domestic fowl and dairy cattle was women's work and was done either by the wife or a female servant. Courtesy of the Lewis Walpole Library, Yale University. 786.4.29.1.

tion of beer and ale, a laundry, and storehouses or sheds. An orchard, usually surrounded by a wall (*S&S* 196–197), yielded fruit, while dovecotes (*S&S* 197) encouraged the roosting of pigeons, which could be captured and eaten. If no natural lake or river existed on the land, a stew-pond (*S&S* 197; *E* 361)—an artificial fishpond—could be created and stocked with freshwater fish. The flavor of such fish was thought inferior to freshly caught saltwater fish, but in inland areas a stew-pond could be a significant convenience.

Improvements

There was strong interest in improving land, an interest that strengthened a great deal during the Napoleonic Wars, when poor harvests, high prices for crops, and interrupted shipping all combined to disrupt food supplies. Crop rotation, improved fertilization, and the enclosure of fields had done much to improve the yields of land, and tools such as seed drills (*E* 473) had decreased the amount of time necessary to perform such tasks as sowing seeds. Men formed agricultural societies to discuss and study the latest methods of agriculture (*E* 150, 361); about fifty such societies had been established by 1800. Some printed magazines, while others offered prizes for refinements in equipment. The result was a dramatic increase in productivity. Corn production rose about 21 percent between 1770 and 1800, as farmers raced to capitalize on higher grain prices.

Despite their best efforts, however, farmers could not control the weather. There were bad harvests in 1795, 1796, 1800, 1809, 1811, and 1812, which worked to the disadvantage of consumers, who paid higher prices for their bread. The poor harvests hurt farmers less, because high prices compensated them for low yields. As real incomes dropped and prices rose, workers grew discontented, and there were riots in various parts of the country in the 1810s over high prices, perceived price-gouging by millers and bakers, the shipment of grain to other parts of the nation, and the use of threshing machines, which rural workers saw as a threat to their livelihood. Machines were destroyed, and hayricks were burned. An excellent harvest in 1813 was followed soon afterward by Napoleon's defeat, and prices dropped precipitously, causing relief among consumers but great anxiety among landowners (and among clergymen, whose tithe values depended on agricultural prices). *See also* Animals; Enclosure; Food.

Alehouse

In the centuries preceding Austen's birth, English drinkers had been entertained at a variety of establishments, which fell into the general categories of alehouses, taverns, and inns. In theory, taverns specialized in serving wine; alehouses, in ale and beer; and inns, in food and accommodation. In practice, however, the three types of businesses overlapped in the services that they provided, and by Austen's day the divisions were especially murky. Alehouses, for example, often provided lodging for travelers (*Evelyn, MW* 180) or for drovers on their way to market; they might even provide temporary pasturage for the drover's livestock. Alehouses, taverns, and inns alike served alcohol, including wine, beer, and spirits. Certain alehouses, aspiring to the more fashionable categories, might call themselves taverns or inns when in fact they were principally purveyors of beer.

Let us then begin with the classic definition of the alehouse, without complications, before we wade into the confusion of terms. The alehouse was, for much of the eighteenth century, the center of provincial and urban social life. It was the place where laborers went after their work and before their evening at home. It was where local festivities and meetings of clubs were held. People ate simple meals, morris dancers capered, fiddlers played, businessmen brokered deals, and drunkards fought. Particularly early in the eighteenth century and before, especially in the countryside, it might be a seasonal or part-time business, run by a woman (*Evelyn, MW* 180, 190) who brewed her own ale and pursued by-employments. The ideal publican might also be a former servant, who had learned the habits of quick, deferential service, or, in urban areas, a prizefighter whose notoriety graced his establishment with reflected fame. The alehouse itself was a private dwelling adapted for hospitality, and the drinkers congregated in the house's kitchen, nuzzling prostitutes and emptying tankards around the kitchen fire while potboys ran back and forth to the cellar to draw beer from the massive kegs. Order was maintained and standards upheld by the local magistrates, who issued licenses and imposed penalties on keepers of disorderly establishments.

In reality, most of these characterizations were false or oversimplified by Austen's lifetime. The alehouse or "public house" (*Evelyn, MW* 190) was still in many ways the social hub of a community, but the community it served was changing. Population was rising steeply as real income plummeted during the French Wars, and an increasing cultural divide emphasized class stratification. The result was a loss in business for alehouses: there were more potential drinkers than ever, but the cost of beer remained constantly high, while duties on tea were slashed, making it a cheap alternative; those who could easily afford their tankard of beer, the gentry, increasingly stayed home to drink or joined private clubs.

Beer Consumption per Capita in England and Wales, in Gallons per Year

1800–1804	33.9
1805–1809	32.8
1810–1814	30.2
1815–1820	28.0 (from Burnett, *Plenty and Want*, p. 27)

Many alehouses failed, and those that survived were viewed with suspicion by an increasingly religious and politically paranoid nation. The charge of promoting disorderly conduct had always been leveled against alehouses (e.g., John Scott, writing in 1773, called them "the infernal mansion where the demons of avarice, extravagance, fury and prophaneness hold their perpetual residence"), but to this old tune, reformers set a new lyric: alehouses were meeting places for dangerous reformers, trade unionists, and radicals, so-called Jacobins who planned to tear down church and crown, just as the real Jacobins had destroyed the monarchy in France. Repression followed, as local communities toughened licensing standards, shortened hours, raised license fees, and cracked down on Sabbath-breaking.

Before 1784, the annual license fee for a public house was one guinea; by 1804, it had doubled. A 1792 London policy closed alehouses that permitted meetings of radicals; publicans had to worry both about being put out of business by the government and about being attacked by pro-government mobs. The situation was worst in urban areas, where there was more fear of unrest, and for smaller alehouses, which were seen as more troublesome than larger, more prosperous establishments. Citizens expressed concern not only about small, licensed public houses but also about "hush shops," unlicensed alehouses, which formed about 10 percent of the total number of establishments in George III's time. Proprietors of hush shops, it was felt, had little to lose by hosting all manners of customers.

At the same time, publicans were suffering, like the rest of the population, from economic hardship and high taxes. Duties on beer, malt, and hops continued to rise—excise and license fees could total as much as £15 for an average-sized London alehouse in the 1810s. The price of beer stayed relatively constant—the 4d. a quart charged in 1799 was typical of the whole period—which meant that the alehouse-keepers' profits fell. Additional taxes were levied on the sale of liquor and on the building itself and its supplies: windows, land, candles, and so on. Then there were the ordinary hazards of doing business: customers continued to get drunk and break things, and theft was a constant problem. Excisemen had to be bribed with drink or presents. Then there were the extraordinary costs of getting into business in the first place. A would-be alehouse-keeper had to find a suitable building to lease and had to pay not only the rent itself—about £30 a year for a middling London establishment in the 1790s—but a substantial "premium" or bonus to the landlord; this could be as high as £2,000 in London for a prime site. The previous publican would expect a payment as well, usually in the neighborhood of £20, in exchange for ensuring the goodwill of the patrons as the alehouse changed hands. The movable goods inside the alehouse also had to be purchased from the previous tenant, at a cost of perhaps £100 to £300. Then there were servants and potboys to be paid. To make matters worse, England's wars, which were the cause of the higher taxes, meant that there were more soldiers who needed to be quartered somewhere, and the burden of billeting them often fell on alehouse-keepers who could ill afford the trouble and expense of these parasitical boarders.

Victualing was a hard way to earn a living, but judging from the number of servants who seem to have gone into the trade, it was better than domestic service. Furthermore, there were ways to work the system. Specialist brokers helped aspiring publicans to find a lease in their price range and also matched them with brewers who would offer generous loans in exchange for an exclusive contract to provide the alehouse with its beer. An alehouse that had made such a bargain, tying its fortunes to those of a particular brewer, was called a "tied house." In this arrangement, the publican got a reliable supply of beer, financial assistance with renovations and improvements, and help from the brewer in dealing with the local magistrates. In return, he gave up much of his control over his business. The brewery decided what beverages would be sold and at what prices, which customers would receive credit, and whether the current tenant was doing a good enough job of keeping order and avoiding the unwelcome attention of the authorities. In some cases, beginning at the end of the eighteenth century, the breweries gained even greater control, buying alehouses outright and installing managers of their own choosing. Whitbread's, a pioneer in the tied house trade, controlled loans or leases for 82 percent of its customer establishments by 1805.

Increasingly, the small brewer-publican was being squeezed out by big brewers whose economies of scale allowed them to endure the higher malt and hop duties. London had 165 brewing victuallers in 1750, 127 in 1800, and only 56 in 1823. In contrast, production at the twelve biggest breweries soared, with some producing 200,000 or even 300,000 gallons a year by 1820; these twelve giants, including Truman's and Barclay Perkins, made three-quarters of the strong beer consumed in London from 1800 to 1830. The tied house phenomenon was strongest in London, weakest in the north, with the south of England falling somewhere in between. Urban areas were much more likely to be supplied by the large firms, while rural alehouses were more likely to be serving locally brewed beer.

The brokers, the consolidation of power in the hands of large breweries, and the currying favor with officials are not the sorts of forces that come to mind when looking at a cozy, sentimentalized engraving of a turn-of-the-century alehouse. Nonetheless, alehouses could be festive places, particularly for the prosperous artisans they increasingly tried to attract. It was not only the unionists and radicals who met at alehouses; peddlers, grain merchants (especially before 1800), and auctioneers sometimes conducted sales at alehouses, and tradesmen often struck deals there. Wedding parties convened there for celebrations after the festivities; Samuel Bamford witnessed one such gathering in the Midlands, where "the landlady brought in a posset of spiced ale for the feast and a fiddler played a jig that set all the lads acapering." On village wake days, the gathering of rushes might well be interspersed by stops at each local alehouse and finished off by a great bout of drinking at one of them. Customers sang songs, told stories, danced, and played games both inside and outside the alehouse: dice, skittles, draughts, dominoes, shove-halfpenny, quoits, and billiards, to name a few. There might also, on any given night, be a club of some sort meeting at the local public house. Most of these clubs had only male members, but there were a few female "friendly societies," too; respectable women would not normally enter the alehouse as customers, but on festive occasions or for club meetings, they could go in without having aspersions cast upon their virtue. This sexual double standard is, of course, why there are so few references to alehouses in Austen's works. As a woman and a member of the gentry class, she would have had little or no exposure to the inside of an alehouse; such an establishment was beneath her notice. Accordingly, then, her only alehouses are in the Juvenilia—specifically, in the fragment *Evelyn* (*MW* 180, 190)—and even then there are no female customers, only a female alehouse-keeper who comically appears as the hostess in two separate alehouses. In the later works, Austen sticks purely to inns, which were far more respectable and with which she would have been far more familiar.

Her use of a female alehouse-keeper harmonizes with the old-fashioned, medieval and Renaissance notion of the alewife, but it was not typical by the late eighteenth century for the proprietor to be a woman. It was certainly not unheard of; women were 12 percent of Bedfordshire publicans in 1822, 14 percent of Gloucester's in 1823, and 18 percent of Leicestershire's in 1825, and similar numbers could be dredged up for other counties. They were not the norm, however, and they tended to be widows or daughters of alehouse-keepers rather than entrepreneurs who had chosen and entered the profession with no familial connections. Then again, many alehouse-keepers, both male and female, were born and married to people in the same line of work; there was a tendency to keep the business in the family and to marry a man or woman similarly brought up to the alehouse trade.

The archetypal alehouse was run by a male publican, wearing a clean white apron, bustling about, and running the place with the assistance of his wife. In smaller alehouses, the children helped as well; in larger ones, servants did the bulk of the work. Almost every alehouse had at least one servant girl to do the cleaning and flirting and at least one potboy to fill the mugs, drum up business outside, and deliver orders to neighbors; each of these male and female servants made a few guineas a year, plus tips. If there were a stable attached to the alehouse, there would be an ostler to look after the horses. The smaller the business, the more likely that the publican or his wife would engage in by-employments—jobs that supplemented the primary business. Common by-employments included shopkeeping, farming, crafts such as blacksmithing or carpentry, and coal selling.

In these small, marginal alehouses, there might be the convivial kitchen atmosphere celebrated in some popular prints or the rough, seedy quality satirized in others: doxies nestled against clients, flattering them, or picking their pockets, or both; shirtless men engaging in wrestling matches outside, while spectators drank and watched, and a couple of patrons urinated against the outer wall; potboys emerging from the cellar with overflowing tankards, headed for customers whose feet were warmed by the roaring fire. Samuel Bamford visited one of the more primitive houses in 1816—a thatched-roof building with one low table, "two candles in clay sockets," a fog of tobacco smoke, and eight or ten laborers "seated in various parts of it, some on stools, some on piled bricks, whilst others occupied empty firkins, . . . or any other article offering a seat."

However, all of these aspects of the alehouse were in the process of disappearing. Like the deals with brokers and brewers, the atmosphere of the alehouse was falling under the sway of the modern business model. Most alehouses had chased away the prostitutes for fear of running afoul of the authorities; others were beginning to address the outdoor-urination problem in light of new, stricter standards of public decency. The potboys' cellar trips, too, had vanished into history, as freestanding kegs were replaced by "beer engines"—kegs attached to manually operated taproom pumps by a network of lead pipes. Even the architectural layout and interior furnishings were changing. The converted private house, with the kitchen as its focus, was giving way to purpose-built alehouses, glorified by shoplike front windows and augmented by private rooms for club meetings, a taproom where laborers drank at lower prices, and a parlor where the better-off paid higher prices and sat on better chairs around mahogany tables. Within a few years after Austen's death, the alehouses would be modernized in yet another way: brewers would begin to post advertising signs outside, notifying passersby that this house served Barclays or Whitbread or Boddington.

Food and lodging were never the primary focus of alehouses, but a meal and a bed could be had at many of them, nevertheless. Alehouse rooms tended to be sparsely furnished; they cost 6d. or 7d. a night, a price high enough to discourage the very poor. The publican and his family typically lived in the alehouse, taking their meals in the taproom. Francis Place, whose father Simon ran a London alehouse, noted that his family dined with the customers and that the customers expected to serve themselves while the hosting family ate. The food offered to patrons was simple: bread and cheese or bread and butter were common offerings. Many alehouses no doubt lacked the staff or facilities to cook large, fancy meals for the multitudes, and in truth there was little motive to try. Plenty of other businesses offered food for sale, from inns and taverns to street hucksters and confectionery shops.

The focus of the alehouse was the beer, which actually changed a good deal over the course of the eighteenth century. At the century's beginning, beer and ale were divided into two categories: "strong" and "small," depending on alcohol content. (An 1806 letter written by Jane's mother at Stoneleigh describes the mansion's "strong beer" and "small beer" cellars.) A third category, "table beer," was added in 1782. All three types had different rates of duty, and the exciseman would travel from one public house to another, measuring the alcohol content of various brews using an instrument called a "saccharometer." This device was also in use by brewers during Jane Austen's lifetime; its use was first described by John Richardson in *The Philosophical Principles of the Science of Brewing* (1784). Richardson also recommended the use of another instrument, the thermometer. His suggestion resulted in more consistent brewing, but the modernization was resisted by brewery employees, who may have feared change, the devaluation of their artisanal expertise, or independent, scientific verification of their skill (or lack thereof).

Quality and taste varied mostly according to the scrupulousness of the brewer and the quality of the local ingredients. The choices available included a cheap brown ale, a more heavily hopped brown ale, and an expensive, high-quality pale ale; when the three types were mixed together in one glass, the resulting concoction was known as "three threads." A very dark, heavily hopped, bitter, high-alcohol beer was introduced in 1722; soon thereafter, it became known as "porter" because of its popularity with London porters. It was popular with brewers, too, because the dark color and strong taste hid impurities. They built enormous production vats; the Meux brewery, in 1795, had a vat that could hold 20,000 barrels (almost 750,000 gallons). Much to the brewers' chagrin, in the late eighteenth century, pale ales came back into fashion; the brewers resisted the change, the publicans searched for alternate suppliers, and the brewers, panicking, began the first great wave of buying up leases and offering loans. The tied house phenomenon, then, was the result of a shift of the English palate from darker beer to lighter. *See also* Beverages; Coffee; Inns; Tea.

Angels

Austen makes reference to only two of the nine orders or "choirs" of angels—the cherubim and seraphim (*Visit, MW* 52). The nine orders were broken into three triads of increasing power and closeness to God, with the cherubim, seraphim, and thrones occupying the uppermost triad. Archangels and angels, by comparison, are members of the least powerful triad.

Animals

The England of Austen's day was still very much a rural, farming world, and animals of one kind or another were nearly always about—the horses that drew the plow or carried the huntsmen; the dogs that herded sheep or pursued foxes for sport; the sheep, pigs, oxen, and goats that populated the farmyard; the dairy cows; the poultry. Some of these animals were raised in relatively small numbers on individual farms, while others were fattened commercially by graziers (*P* 202) and driven to market by drovers. Austen's literary realm is more likely to be the drawing room or the ballroom than the farmyard or the hunt, but she does mention animals here and there in her works.

Occasionally, she makes reference to wild animals—usually in a rather detached manner. Thus, in the silly, stylized "Ode to Pity," she mentions the songs of birds:

> While Philomel on airy hawthorn Bush
>   Sings sweet & Melancholy, And the thrush
> Converses with the Dove. (*Ode, MW* 74)

The birds themselves are relatively meaningless, except that the reference to "Philomel" is deliberately comic. The point of this literary exercise is not the particular choice of birds but a parody of the pastoral poetry so popular throughout much of the eighteenth century. The pastoral, with its celebration of the simple lives of idealized shepherds, was thick with sentimental references to the wonders of nature. Austen's lines could almost have been lifted from any of the pastoral poets; merely one example of a similar style can be found in John Cunningham's "Morning" (1761), whose third verse also invokes Philomel:

> Philomel forsakes the thorn,
>   Plaintive where she prates at night;
> And the lark, to meet the morn,
>   Soars beyond the shepherd's sight.

Cunningham's poem also pays tribute to the sights and sounds of bees, a rooster "the shepherd's clock!," swallows, daisies, and the huntsman's horn. In his verses, as in Austen's, the birds are chosen merely to evoke a mood.

Austen's other references to wild animals are few and have little to do with the specific habits or characteristics of the animals themselves. Gulls are mentioned briefly in *Sanditon* to evoke the seaside (*Sand, MW* 396), and a tradesman's daughter is taunted in another of the minor works when a cruel woman calls her late father "as poor as a Rat" (*Col Let, MW* 158). One gets the sense that either animal could be exchanged for a similar creature without much loss to the text.

Yet this is not the case when Austen mentions cows (*Evelyn, MW* 181; *S&S* 293; *P&P* 163) or poultry (*S&S* 293; *P&P* 163, 216, 222; *MP* 41), and with good reason. The dairy and the poultry yard were part of woman's sphere, tended to by the housewife, by any daughters capable of being useful, and by one or more female servants. Along with the kitchen garden, it was one of the two outdoor departments that were traditionally under female supervision. The establishment might vary a great deal in size, ranging from one or two cows and a small flock of hens to a sizable herd of dairy cattle, with a custom-built, well-ventilated, tiled dairy building, and flocks not only of hens (*S&S* 303, *MP* 106) but also of geese, ducks, turkeys (*Visit, MW* 53–54; *E* 483), and even pheasants (*MP* 90, 91, 104, 106). The Rushworths' establishment represents the more extensive end of the scale, while the prosperous yeoman farmer Mr. Martin (or rather his mother and sisters) fall somewhere in the middle, with their "eight cows, two of them Alderneys, and one a little Welch cow, a very pretty little Welch cow, indeed" (*E* 27), plus geese (*E* 28–29) and presumably chickens. Austen's family had a slightly smaller stock at Steventon Rectory, where Mrs. Austen kept two Alderneys in 1770 and three years later proudly described herself as "worth a bull and six cows" and different kinds of poultry.

Mrs. Austen's enthusiastic dairying was no doubt partly enforced by the combination of eight children and a comfortable, but still very moderate, income. Yet women from many walks of life involved themselves in caring for cattle and birds, taking an active role in providing the household with fowls, butter, cheese, milk, and cream. Evidence of their involvement can be seen in contemporary cookbooks, which often feature a section on the care of poultry. Sarah Harrison's *The House-keeper's Pocket-book; And Compleat Family Cook* (1748), for example, offers advice on breeding, feeding, and housing of fowls:

> Usually ducks begin to lay in *February*, if your Gardener is diligent in picking up Snails Grubs, Caterpillars, Worms and other Insects, and lay them in one Place, 'twill make your Ducks familiar, and is the best Food you can give them. Parsley sowed about the Ponds or River they use, give their Flesh a pleasant Taste; be sure to have a Place for them to retire to at Night. Partition off their Nests, and make it as nigh the Water as possible, and always feed them there, it will make them love Home, being of a roaming Nature.

She offers detailed instructions for the care not only of ducks and chickens but also of geese, turkeys, pigeons, and rabbits. Charles Millington's *The Housekeeper's Domestic Library; or, New Universal Family Instructor* (1805) also directs the housewife in her running of the poultry and dairy, waxing especially specific in the types of pans that should be used in the latter:

> The utensils should invariably be made of wood, the cream-dishes must not be more than three inches deep, but they may be made wide enough to hold from four to six quarts of milk. They should be well washed every day in warm water, and afterwards rinced in cold, and must be entirely cool before they are used. If, however, any kind of metal vessels are improperly retained in the dairy, they must be scalded every day, and well scrubbed and scoured.

Millington and Harrison, like most cookbook authors who included dairy instructions, are far more inclined to describe the care of birds than of cows, leading one to believe that housewives were seldom to be found feeding, herding, or doctoring their cattle. Farm servants probably performed these chores, and thus the cookbook authors begin their discussions of women's duties with milking, but the day-to-day upkeep of the chickens and ducks was definitely performed by women; contemporary prints often show a pretty young daughter or dairymaid scattering grain for the birds.

Just as the cookbook authors draw a veil over the more strenuous parts of cattle herding, Austen draws back from describing farm animals in great detail. Once she leaves the precincts of the dairy and poultry yards, she is trespassing on the world of men, but she cannot ignore animals entirely, as her world was so full of them. Moreover, animals would have been a subject of frequent discussion by the men in her life, many of whom no doubt became interested in improving their livestock.

The eighteenth century saw the dawn of planned, large-scale animal breeding and cross-breeding, with the result that farm animals in 1800 were almost uniformly superior to their counterparts in 1700. Sheep (*P* 73) were bred to produce more wool (*E* 28); cattle and oxen increased in size (*E* 473); pigs (*E* 172), which at the beginning of the century still looked rather like wild boars, were cross-bred with fatter Chinese pigs to produce an animal like the one we know today. New breeds, such as Hereford and Shorthorn cattle, were introduced, and existing breeds were enlarged. In 1710, for example, the average ox sold at London's Smithfield Market weighed 370 pounds; by 1795, the average weight was 800 pounds. Over the same period, calves sold at Smithfield tripled in weight from 50 to 150 pounds, while sheep more than doubled, rising from 38 to 80 pounds. In part, these efforts were facilitated by a general interest in doing everything scientifically, but to a large extent they were supported by new methods of pasturage and fertilization that increased the supply of winter fodder and made it unnecessary to kill most of one's livestock before the onset of winter. *See also* Agriculture; Horses; Hunting; Philomel.

Architecture

From the beginning of the eighteenth century until Jane Austen's birth in 1775, English architecture was dominated by a classical revival. New construction tended to be in Greek or Roman styles, with symmetrical façades, pedimented windows, and, sometimes, porticoes and columns reminiscent of ancient temples. Lines were simple, and floors were constructed according to a mathematical formula, with the tallest rooms on the ground floor. Sometimes a line of stone or brick indicated the change in floors from outside, and this might be accentuated by a slight change in window style.

During the last quarter of the century, however, several new fashions took root. One of these was the Gothic style (*NA* 177), an imitation of medieval architecture that featured turrets, buttresses, crenellated parapets, mock moats, and, most commonly, pointed-arched windows. Uvedale Price, a leading proponent of the Picturesque style in art and landscape, found Gothic windows charming, a "triumph of the picturesque," full of "extreme richness and intricacy." It is chiefly the windows of Northanger Abbey that Catherine Morland notices (*NA* 161, 162), as they are almost the only remnant, from the outside, of the genuine medieval abbey that forms the basis of General Tilney's massive country house.

Where original Gothic ruins (*NA* 141–142) did not exist, it was necessary to invent them. Landowners invited architects to design faux-Gothic ruins for their gardens, complete with rubble and artfully planted moss; Gothic guesthouses, lodges, pavilions, and gatehouses; and, eventually, entire Gothic mansions. Adlestrop Park, a magnificent house owned by Mrs. Austen's rich cousins, had been demolished in the 1750s and replaced with a grand Gothic mansion with a renowned southwest façade, ashlar buttresses, and fretted balustrades. Newly built parsonages were sometimes designed in the Gothic style, as there seemed to be a pleasing harmony between a clergyman's house and an architectural style reminiscent of churches and cathedrals. Sometimes, a Gothic look was achieved on the cheap by remodeling and installing pointed-arched windows, while leaving the rest of the building untouched. Gothic wallpapers were also available from about the 1760s.

The rage for what Uvedale Price called the "splendid confusion and irregularity" of the Gothic led to a general willingness to make houses asymmetrical (*E* 358). Even houses in other styles could now adopt a lopsided, patched-together profile and remain fashionable in their informality. Accordingly, owners added all sorts of wings and special-purpose rooms, without concerning themselves about balancing the additions on the other side of the house. Conservatories, greenhouses, servants' halls (*MP* 141), wings that contained suites of bedrooms for the family, and other useful or ornamental structures sprouted on the sides of country manors.

At the same time, drawing rooms, dining rooms, and other public areas of the house were drifting down to the ground floor (*Evelyn, MW* 189; *E* 476). Historically, they had been located on the next story up (called the first floor in Britain, the second floor in America). Now they were relocated downstairs, closer to the gardens, which could be seen through large windows or even accessed directly through French doors (*Sand, MW* 395).* To compensate, the bedrooms moved upstairs.

A relaxation of symmetry and of the boundary between interior and exterior space was reflected in a sudden interest in cottages (*Ode, MW* 75; *L&F, MW* 79; *S&S* 29, 72, 75, 251–252, 260; *MP* 57, 195, 375). It became desirable to have a picturesque cottage somewhere in view (*NA* 214), either occupied by an actual laborer (*Sand, MW* 366; *MP* 82; *E* 83, 86) or vacant and preserved for its rustic appearance. Conscientious landlords might also build "model cottages" for their laborers or tenants, and these were fairly simple dwellings for which pattern books were available. They resembled the older cottages of farms and villages (*L&F, MW* 100; *Sand, MW* 383; *NA* 212) but were newer and usually cleaner. The ideal model cottage, according to a 1797 report by the Board of Agriculture, had a main downstairs room about twelve feet by twelve feet, used as the multipurpose living room, workshop, and kitchen. A second room might serve

---

*Older mansions, with formal balconies and terraces (*MP* 103) overlooking the gardens, joining the two areas with large, imposing flights of stone steps, now came to seem stodgy and old-fashioned.

as a bedroom, while smaller areas provided storage space for food, linen, and tools. A second story above contained one or two bedrooms, one of them heated by a fireplace. The windows, one per room, would be casement windows, which were less fashionable than double-hung sash windows; the relative lack of windows was not an attempt to deprive the poor of light but a realistic recognition of the fact that windows were not only expensive in themselves (*P&P* 161) but also taxed (*MP* 85) and therefore that every window implied an ongoing expense. Walls could be made of any cheap and readily available local material: mud, wood, brick, and so on. No plumbing was included; the closest pump or well was the water source, and a privy in back of the house was the only toilet.

However, not all cottages belonged to people of the working class. Some people who could afford to live in any sort of home they liked chose to live not in massive stone mansions (*L&F, MW* 79; *P&P* 265; *MP* 243; *P* 36, 123) but in "cottages" (*NA* 120, 141). These, however, were not dingy workers' shacks but carefully designed *cottages ornées* (*Sand, MW* 377; *S&S* 376), the plans for which could be selected from a pattern book. These were built to look rustic from the outside but were often quite comfortable and extensive, with modern conveniences and modern furnishings inside. The Musgroves' "cottage" at Uppercross (*P* 83, 123), "with its viranda, French windows, and other prettinesses" (*P* 36), is one of these modern houses in disguise, described by historian Mark Girouard as fostering "the simple life, lived in simple luxury in a simple cottage with—quite often—fifteen simple bedrooms, all hung with French wallpapers." Lady Elliott's cottage in *Sense and Sensibility* contains a dining parlor, a drawing room, a library, and a saloon (252), while Barton Cottage has a sitting room (*S&S* 342) and four bedrooms. Austen's description of it gives a good sense of its size while mocking the demands of picturesque rusticity placed on cottages by genteel enthusiasts:

> A small green court was the whole of its demesne in front; and a neat wicket gate admitted them into it.
>
> As a house, Barton Cottage, though small, was comfortable and compact; but as a cottage it was defective, for the building was regular, the roof was tiled, the window shutters were not painted green, nor were the walls covered with honeysuckles. A narrow passage led directly through the house into the garden behind. On each side of the entrance was a sitting room, about sixteen feet square; and beyond them were the offices and the stairs. Four bed-rooms and two garrets formed the rest of the house. (*S&S* 28)

The references to tile and honeysuckle reflect a popular prejudice in favor of deeply thatched cottages drowning in climbing vines, a prejudice so strong that Humphry Repton was obliged to remind his clients not to add so much ivy that it blocked off the chimneys. Nonfictional cottages had the same sorts of amenities as some of Austen's creations: numerous bedrooms, halls, parlors, withdrawing rooms, music rooms, billiard rooms, boudoirs, conservatories, studies, dining rooms, and even, in some cases, baths and water closets.

A villa (*NA* 120) was another type of relatively informal country house, but it tended to be much grander in scale and design than a cottage. There was little effort expended to make the house seem rustic and tumbledown, and rooms for large parties were standard, as were conservatories, balconies, breakfast parlors, dressing rooms, and so on. Whereas a cottage, as noted above, might contain some or all of these rooms, in a villa they were considered positively necessary. In short, they were the richer and more elegant cousins of cottages.

In towns, the architectural trends were somewhat different. Here, it was difficult to create a crenellated ruin; though the marquis of Lansdowne, the Austens' landlord in Southampton, had built a short-lived castle in that town, he was very much in the minority. In towns, uniform blocks of townhouses, united to form one gigantic façade, were the norm. London spread out to the west in blocks and circles, with mansionlike rows of town houses (*S&S* 160; *MP* 416) planting themselves in neat geometric arrangements, looking like the building blocks of some enormous child. They often employed the pedimented windows and demarcated floors of the classical style, with the central and most imposing townhouse being distinguishable from the others in some way, often by a large pediment at the roof line. In Bath, this formula was imitated, with terraces (*Sand*, *MW* 384) climbing one above the other, each occupied by a wall of homes joined together to make a uniform front. The crowning achievement of Bath was its Royal Crescent, a gracefully curving structure that inspired imitators in other towns (*Sand*, *MW* 380). Detached town houses may be seen in the illustration in the article about Debt.

Types of Rooms

The number of rooms and their specificity of purpose depended on the wealth of the owner. The houses of the Herefordshire yeomanry, according to a letter in the *Gentleman's Magazine* in 1819, had "a large culinary sitting-room, through which the visitor passes to a parlour." The "culinary sitting-room" has the sound of a multipurpose room, and in many smaller houses one room was made to serve various needs. It might be a parlor for receiving visitors, a sitting room for the women of the family, a breakfast room, and a supper room. In larger houses, different roles were assigned to various rooms, and one person might have several rooms dedicated to his or her use.

The public rooms, in the sorts of houses Jane Austen visited, usually included a dining room (*Visit*, *MW* 53; *Evelyn*, *MW* 189; *NA* 165–166, 213; *S&S* 143, 252; *P&P* 65, 158, 168, 246, 289, 317, 340, 351, 352–353; *MP* 52, 226; *E* 116, 207, 220, 298, 364, 424; *P* 7), in which dinner was

eaten. In smaller houses, breakfast would also be served here. In larger
houses, there was a separate breakfast room (*Evelyn*, *MW* 189; *LS*, *MW*
283, 284; *NA* 173, 175, 228; *S&S* 96; *P&P* 32, 41, 75, 113, 301, 304,
315, 317, 346; *MP* 74, 127, 298, 357, 362; *P* 128), which might double
as a morning sitting room (*E* 272); there was very seldom a room dedicated to supper (*NA* 222), even in the largest houses; supper, if it was
eaten at all, was generally served wherever the family happened to be congregated, as was also the case with evening tea and coffee.

Most of the day was passed by women in sitting rooms (*Sand*, *MW* 427;
S&S 28, 30, 69, 292, 342; *P&P* 168, 250, 352; *MP* 41, 151–152, 168;
E 69, 240, 453), drawing rooms, and parlors (*E&E*, *MW* 32; *Visit*, *MW*
50; *Mystery*, *MW* 56; *L&F*, *MW* 84, 107; *Col Let*, *MW* 151; *Cath*, *MW*
197, 214; *LS*, *MW* 291; *Watsons*, *MW* 323, 327, 344, 351, 355; *NA* 116,
240; *S&S* 29, 60, 73, 75, 77, 96, 106, 107, 348; *P&P* 73; *MP* 377–378,
381, 444; *E* 27, 28, 247; *P* 40, 114, 154), all of which are names given
to rooms for engaging in leisure activities and receiving guests. An 1818
painting by Turner shows the rectangular drawing room of a large Yorkshire home; a fireplace with a coal grate stands at one end, with groups of
sofas and chairs nearby, while scattered around the room are tables, chairs,
statuary, and a harp. Tall windows with festoons of drapery hung around
their edges let in a good deal of light, and the high, arched ceiling, painted
in soft blue and white, is decorated with plaster reliefs in classical designs.
The room is so large that it requires no effort of the imagination at all to
picture sixteen or eighteen pairs of country dancers lining up in the center after a grand dinner.

The drawing room (*Visit*, *MW* 51; *Watsons*, *MW* 350, 357, 358; *Sand*,
MW 394, 395, 413; *NA* 34, 91, 102, 118, 161, 180, 187, 203; *S&S* 29,
110, 114, 143, 175, 203, 252, 257, 274, 294, 311, 316, 334; *P&P* 37, 47,
75, 152, 168, 310, 341, 345, 352–353; *MP* 14, 15, 18, 52, 69, 71, 84, 125,
176–177, 180, 183–184, 205, 206, 223, 224, 272, 273, 336, 387, 447; *E*
27, 117, 124, 213, 215, 219, 302; *P* 7, 10, 37) was where the evening
began and ended. Guests for dinner were shown into this room as they arrived (*NA* 165), and from the drawing room, the entire company paraded
to the dining room to eat. In large homes, the drawing room and dining
room would be separated by a few rooms (*MP* 84) to give the assembled
company the feeling of being in a grand procession. After dinner, the men
remained in the dining room to smoke, drink, and talk (*MP* 334–335), while
the women paraded back to the drawing room to chat (*P&P* 37, 54, 163,
341). When the gentlemen joined them, tea, coffee, cards, music, and dancing ensued. Some homes had multiple drawing rooms (*P* 138, 216, 219,
220, 242, 245) for different times of the day, different levels of formality, or
different sizes of parties; others had to make do with only one. During the
day, the drawing room was primarily the province of women, and the gentleman of the house received his guests in his study, if he had one.

Bedrooms (*Evelyn*, *MW* 186; *Cath*, *MW* 193; *LS*, *MW* 286; *Watsons*, *MW* 351, 353; *Sand*, *MW* 401; *NA* 163, 181, 192, 193; *S&S* 28, 29, 39, 155, 294; *P&P* 250; *MP* 125, 182, 312, 387; *E* 57, 243, 412; *P* 114, 154) were scattered throughout the house, mostly upstairs (*P&P* 352). Bedrooms for servants might be located in a separate wing of the house, in the basement, in the attic (*P&P* 310; *MP* 9–10, 15, 387) or garret (*S&S* 28, 29), or in a combination of these places. Ladies' maids sometimes had rooms adjacent to, or at least near, the apartments of their mistresses. Other upper servants, such as butlers and housekeepers, also sometimes had special rooms of their own (*E* 204).

In large households, the wife and husband would either share a bedroom or have separate bedrooms, with a study (*P&P* 168) and dressing room (*S&S* 259; *MP* 218; *P* 57, 127) for the husband and a dressing room (*F&E*, *MW* 6; *E&E*, *MW* 31; *Col Let*, *MW* 151; *Evelyn*, *MW* 181–182; *Cath*, *MW* 214; *LS*, *MW* 276, 281, 287; *NA* 194; *S&S* 340; *P&P* 333, 345, 358, 377; *MP* 370–371) or sitting room for the wife. The dressing room, which at various times had been a semipublic space, in which certain visitors might be received (*Evelyn*, *MW* 189), was developing into a place to sit and sew, read, or draw; Austen wrote in December 1798 that she and her mother "live entirely in the dressing-room now, which I like very much; I always feel so much more elegant in it than in the parlour." Many houses also had a state bedroom for important guests, though this bedroom, like almost all bedrooms, was moved upstairs from its traditional place on the ground floor. Another specialized type of bedroom was the nursery (*LS*, *MW* 275; *MP* 9; *P* 122), reserved for small children and the servants who cared for them.

The more important bedrooms in large homes might also have water closets, still a relative novelty and quite a luxury. The water closet was patented in 1778 by Joseph Bramah, who claimed to have sold 6,000 of them by 1797. This convenient device, where it occurred, was reserved for the family; the servants still had to use chamber pots and privies. The early water closets were operated by piped or pumped water or by cistern-stored rainwater and were not, by modern standards, reliable. Bathtubs were somewhat more common than water closets, but they were usually cold-water plunge baths. Preheated piped water was still only a wistful fantasy, and water for hot baths had to be heated over the fire; most people only took warm or hot baths when visiting a spa such as Bath. Instead of a bathroom sink with piped water, most people used a basin, filled from a pitcher, both of which stood on a nightstand in the bedroom.

Some houses had special rooms for certain kinds of activities. Libraries (*L&F*, *MW* 95; *Cath*, *MW* 232; *S&S* 252, 304; *P&P* 9, 37, 55, 71, 111, 112, 305, 344, 349, 361), often containing thousands of books, could be found in larger homes, while smaller houses resorted to scattered bookcases in bedrooms and studies. Saloons (*S&S* 252; *P&P* 267, 270) were large downstairs rooms, either in a line with the wide entrance hall (which was a room in itself) or elsewhere on the ground floor; the saloon could be used as an art gallery (*Lesley*, *MW* 127; *NA* 85, 162, 171, 185–186, 191, 194; *P&P* 250) or a ballroom (*MP* 275), but unlike most rooms designated "galleries," it tended to be more square than rectangular. Another downstairs room was the conservatory (*E* 306), found in large homes; this was a room with enormous windows, sometimes with nothing but windows on at least two sides, giving it the look of a greenhouse. It did not feature the damp atmosphere of many greenhouses, but it did include specimens of plants that could be enjoyed and examined by family and guests alike; for a picture of a conservatory, see the illustration *Regency Fete* (Dishes). Older mansions sometimes had chapels (*MP* 86) that had been designed for the private worship of the family and staff.

Some homes had a special music room, but most placed the instruments in the drawing room, where they would be handy for after-dinner concerts. (Mary Bennet's appears to be placed upstairs, perhaps in a dressing room—see *P&P* 344–345.) A billiard room (*MP* 125, 127, 182) was an increasingly common luxury, but not every house with a billiard table placed it in its own room. It might occupy a portion of a hall, library, or gallery, or be ensconced in a bow-windowed alcove of a parlor. Two competing trends battled each other: on the one hand, people liked the status value of being able to say they could afford to have a music room, several drawing rooms, a billiard room, and so on; on the other hand, there was that yearning for informality that made hosts want to break their crowds of guests into little groups, together in the same room, yet occupied in small groups with different forms of amusement. Humphry Repton advocated the building of "living rooms," which, by their easy connections to nearby rooms, or by the creation of numerous smaller spaces within a single room, broke up the stiff old conversational circle and allowed pairs and small groups to play music, read, examine plants, or talk—all at the same time. Fanny Burney, taking note of this latter trend in 1782, described a hostess trying valiantly "to prevent a circle," moving chairs and arranging her guests with "dextrous disorder." This hostess would have been in perfect sympathy, no doubt, with Austen's Musgrove sisters, trying to liven up their parents' "old-fashioned square parlor . . . the proper air of confusion by a grand piano forte and a harp, flower-stands and little tables placed in every direction" (*P* 40).

In some cases, there would be a secondary house, known as a lodge (*P&P* 210; *P* 123). The lodge might be rented out to tenants or allotted to guests. Lodges arose from the habit of building small homes on large estates, usually at some distance from the main house, to be used as a base for hunting parties. Many lodges in Austen's day, however, were quite close to the main house and were sometimes the medium by which landowners experimented with new architectural trends.

Conversazione, Henry Bunbury and William Dickinson, 1794. This bored and
uncomfortable-looking group is clustered in exactly the way that architects were now
trying to avoid. Instead of this forced circle of chairs, planners such as Humphry Repton
wanted to incorporate the outdoors and create small, mobile groups attracted to special
areas of interest within a room. Courtesy of the Lewis Walpole Library, Yale University.
794.4.1.2+.

Some rooms, the "offices" (*NA* 195; *S&S* 28, 393), were used chiefly by
the servants. They included the kitchen (*Watsons, MW* 354, 360; *S&S* 72;
P&P 65; *MP* 379, 385, 392; *E* 236); the butler's pantry (*E* 204; *P* 127);
other sorts of pantries (*Lesley, MW* 114) and storerooms (*Lesley, MW* 113;
MP 31) for food, beer, linen, and other supplies; cellars; laundries; and so
on. The family noticed the size, proportion, and decoration of drawing
rooms, while the servants cared about the efficiency and cleanliness of the
offices and made their objections known if these rooms were inadequate.

One room that might be found in almost any part of the house was the
"closet" (*Visit, MW* 54; *Scraps, MW* 176–177; *S&S* 274, 316; *E* 239).
This was not, as it is now, a storage cabinet crammed full of clothes, sports
equipment, shoes, umbrellas, and so on, but a small room that could be
used for a variety of purposes. There were closets for getting dressed in
the morning, adorned with pictures and mirrors. There were closets that
were essentially pantries. There were closets full of collections of artwork
and scientific specimens. There were Bramah water closets, some of them
quite ornately decorated and hidden behind mirrored panels.

Austen was acquainted with houses of all sizes, from those with rooms doing double and triple duty to those with a room for everything, and several rooms left over, just in case. Steventon Parsonage, the house in which Austen was raised, was neither a mansion nor a cottage. It had a square front and was symmetrically designed, with a door in the middle, two windows to the right of the door looking into the kitchen, and two on the left (*Watsons*, *MW* 322) looking into the better of the two parlors, which also doubled as the dining room (*P&P* 168). The entryway was actually the second-best parlor (*MP* 377–378) rather than a wide hall (*Cath*, *MW* 220; *NA* 161; *S&S* 334; *P&P* 65, 251, 317, 352, 371; *MP* 172, 194, 233, 357; *E* 189, 346–347, 411) or a narrower vestibule (*Cath*, *MW* 220; *S&S* 316; *P&P* 112, 315; *MP* 206, 215; *P* 79). Also downstairs were Mr. Austen's study, with had a south-facing bow window overlooking the garden, and pantries of various sorts. On the floor above were seven bedrooms, including the one shared by Jane and Cassandra and the one they converted into a dressing room in 1798; the latter held Jane's piano and books. In the garret were three more bedrooms, which were at times used by the pupils whom Mr. Austen boarded and tutored. There was no separate servants' hall.

Chawton Cottage, where Jane lived from 1809 until just before her death in 1817 and where she wrote or revised most of her novels, was smaller than Steventon and more closely resembles *Sense and Sensibility*'s Barton Cottage. An L-shaped house, it had an entrance hall, to the right of which was a dining room where Jane did her writing and to the left of which was a drawing room. The offices were also downstairs; six bedrooms and two garret rooms lay upstairs, one of them reserved as a "state" or "best" bedroom and the others in use by the family and the three servants. The cottage was small, with walls that were sometimes damp, and must have presented the occupants with few options for hosting guests. Even Steventon had been so small that guests had had to wait until the school holidays, when Mr. Austen's pupils went home. Other members of the lower gentry had similar difficulties finding room for visitors (*Watsons*, *MW* 351; *MP* 28; *E* 126; *P* 113); Parson Woodforde, when his friends Mr. and Mrs. Jeanes slept over, was forced to displace his niece Nancy in order to find them a suitable bed. When "Mrs. Jeans, two Daughters and Nurse" slept there again in 1792, "Mrs. Jeans slept with Nancy in the best Chamber, with Miss Jeans on a Mattress on the floor of the same Room, and the youngest about 7. Months old with her Nurse, Susan Harrison in the Attic Story."

By contrast, Stoneleigh, a house in Mrs. Austen's family, was a quadrangular mansion based on the remains of a twelfth-century Cistercian abbey. A symmetrical baroque wing with forty-five windows was added to the west side of the house in the early eighteenth century, making the house look entirely modern when approached from that side. The offices were in the old abbey, while the newer portions held a dining room, break-fast parlor, multiple drawing rooms decorated in "rather gloomy brown wainscot and dark crimson furniture," according to Mrs. Austen. There were also two galleries for pictures and prints, two small parlors, a billiard room, and twenty-six bedrooms in the new wing alone, including a state bedroom, Mrs. Austen added, "with a high dark crimson bed, an *alarming* apartment just fit for a heroine."

Interiors

The appearance of rooms, like their use, was evolving. The dark wain-scot (wall paneling—see *E* 187) of earlier centuries was removed or painted in light colors; open-beamed ceilings were stuccoed or plastered to hide the beams and given delicate texture by slightly raised plaster ornaments in the shapes of vines, urns, medallions, and leaves (*S&S* 108; *MP* 183; *E* 81). Lighter colors—white, pale blue, gold—gained favor, while the "dark crimson" Mrs. Austen noted at Stoneleigh was considered very old-fash-ioned (*NA* 158). Huge fireplaces built of dark brick were contracted to small coal fire-grates surrounded by elegant mantelpieces (*Sand, MW* 413; *NA* 162; *S&S* 75, 160, 332; *P&P* 75, 144, 190, 247; *E* 46, 69) in wood or marble, carved in simple, classically influenced styles.

An increasing emphasis on light and an effort to create the feeling of greater space focused attention on windows (*Cass, MW* 46; *Watsons, MW* 322; *Sand, MW* 413; *NA* 34, 82, 91, 122, 162, 163, 167, 172; *S&S* 121, 190, 203, 281, 360; *P&P* 9, 73, 121, 162, 333; *MP* 212, 243; *E* 90; *P* 79). Leaded casement windows (*S&S* 105; *E* 437), with their small panes, were replaced with large double-hung sash windows (*Evelyn, MW* 180; *E* 252, 437). French doors or windows, as noted above, were installed in rooms that overlooked the gardens, admitting more light and allowing easy access to the outdoors (*P* 36). Among the windows that did not open as doors were tall, multipaned windows that stretched almost the full height of the tall downstairs rooms and reached all the way down to the ground (*NA* 213; *MP* 65, 69); "bow" windows that had two short sides extending outward from the house at an angle, joined by a long wall of glass divided into panes (*NA* 213); and Venetian windows, which had a large center panel with a narrower panel to either side (*Sand, MW* 384). Window seats (*NA* 167) allowed people to lounge in the natural light, talking, reading, or taking in the view.

One of the ways of introducing color into a room was changing old vel-vet hangings (*NA* 158, 159, 163, 214) in dark, somber colors for new bed draperies, valances, and curtains (*NA* 167; *E* 83, 252; *P* 179) in lighter shades. Another technique was installing a floor carpet in a fashionable color and pattern. Examples of carpets and window curtains can be seen in the illustrations *A Master Parson with a Good Living* (Clergy), *Advantages of Wearing Muslin Dresses!* (Dishes), *Temperance Enjoying a*

Frugal Meal (Food), *Miseries of Human Life* (Housework), and *Harmony before Matrimony* (Music).

Another strategy was to hang wallpaper (*NA* 163, 214; *S&S* 374; *E* 253), which increasingly replaced old tapestries (*NA* 158, 163) and wainscot. Wallpaper, one of the many commodities that was taxed by the government, could be decorated with stamps or stencils on white or colored backgrounds. Some papers were flocked by making shapes with varnish and then allowing colored lint to stick to the varnished areas. English-made wallpapers tended to be fairly drab, and it was the French wallpapers, with their beautiful colors and floral designs, that were truly fashionable. Papers that were decorated with birds, nonflowering plants, and classical motifs were also popular. Wallpaper manufacturers, also called "paperstainers," were sometimes consulted on the choice of other furnishings, so that upholstery and drapery would harmonize with the paper. The paper hanger then assembled the sheets of paper, cutting them to size, gluing them together, and mounting them on wooden frames nailed to the walls. The paper was not hung directly on the walls until later in the nineteenth century, perhaps because the dyes were seldom colorfast and might have run if exposed to too much glue, or perhaps to make the paper easier to replace if fashions changed. *See also* Furniture; Gardens and Landscapes.

Army

For a hierarchical organization, the army of Austen's day had a remarkably complex and fragmented command structure. At the head of the army was, nominally, the king, who in practice had little to do with the army's administration. This was instead the task of a set of cabinet members, whose identities and titles changed over the years and whose duties and interest sometimes overlapped and conflicted. In wartime, there was a commander in chief, but in peacetime this post was vacant, and the duties of the commander in chief were performed by an official called the secretary at war. The secretary at war was supposedly a mere functionary of the commander in chief, when there was one, but in the absence of a commander in chief, or in the service of a weak one, the secretary at war wielded enormous power. The command structure was altered in 1794, when Prime Minister Pitt created a new cabinet position, secretary of state for war, who shared administrative duties with the secretary at war and the commander in chief. This new secretary for war, however, had no authority over troops in the Americas until 1798, when he became secretary of state for war and the colonies. He now had full control over the size of the military, while the secretary at war controlled financing, and the commander in chief controlled deployment and strategy. Influence over all their decisions, however, was still exerted from time to time by the prime minister, cabinet, king, and royal family.

The commander in chief's staff included the adjutant general, in charge of personnel; the quartermaster general, in charge of supplies; and the military secretary, who handled correspondence and exerted great influence over promotions. Also ranking high, but not necessarily involved with campaigns or administration, were the generals (*NA* 139; *P&P* 312). They rose by strict seniority, which meant that they could be utterly inactive, on half pay, and still creep up the ladder rung by rung. (This was similar to the navy, where a post-captain, even if he had no ship, would rise by the deaths of those above him to an admiral's rank, provided he didn't die first himself.) There were grades of rank among the general officers, from field marshal (Wellington's rank at Waterloo), down through full general, lieutenant general, and major general. Some critics have remarked that it is strange that *Northanger Abbey's* General Tilney, along with other military officers, seems uninvolved in the wars that were being waged as Austen wrote her works, but in 1812, there were 518 generals, of whom only 200 were on active service. Similarly, in 1814, there were 659 general officers, but only 25 were actually present at the Battle of Waterloo. Some were active on other duties elsewhere, but there was definitely a surplus of generals on hand, and General Tilney's idleness is therefore eminently believable.

As if the command structure of the army were not already involved enough, certain important departments were separate from the main branch of the army. The Board of Ordnance, for example, which supplied the army, navy, and marines with ammunition, was its own department, not subject to the commander in chief. Ordnance also controlled all artillery units, the Royal Engineers (who made up the officer corps of the engineers), and the Royal Sappers and Miners (the rank-and-file engineers who were, just to make things slightly more confusing, part of a different organization entirely from their officers).* Other ordnance duties included the building and maintenance of barracks, defense works, and military jails; the administration of the Royal Observatory, Royal Military Academy, Royal Laboratory, and Royal Carriage Works; and military cartography. Local militias, too, ran according to different rules and were empowered by different acts of Parliament, with the result that the militias competed for manpower with both the army and the navy, often to the detriment of the regular military.

Regimental Structure

The basic unit of the army was the regiment. Most regiments (*Watsons,* *MW* 337; *NA* 152; *S&S* 206; *P&P* 60, 229, 318) were founded as single-

---

*The corps was known as the Royal Military Artificers and Labourers until 1797, when its name changed to the Royal Military Artificers. The name changed again to the Corps of Sappers and Miners in 1812.

battalion units, though many acquired second or even third battalions in later years. When a regiment had more than one battalion, one battalion was supposed to remain out of combat as a garrison force while the other battalion took the field. In wars of long duration, however, such as the wars that Britain fought through most of Austen's life, it often became necessary to send both battalions to the front.

The head of the regiment was the colonel (*Col Let*, *MW* 163; *Scraps*, *MW* 175; *P&P* 24, 28, 29, 170, 229; *E* 104, 163; *P* 139), who was often not a colonel in rank at all, but a general (*P&P* 312), a peer, or a private landowner. He received permission from the government to raise a new regiment and was given allotted sums for recruitment and maintenance, in return for which he received a salary, the money from purchased commissions (of which more will be said later), and the difference between his allotments and the actual cost of providing for his troops. As each regiment was thus run under private contract, there were always suspicions of abuse. When food was spoiled or uniforms shoddy, the colonel's greed was blamed, but it appears that while there were certainly occasional instances of shameless profiteering, most colonels made no profit at all until they had been in command for at least two years, and many not only made no profit but paid a portion of their own salaries to secure adequate supplies. Until 1751, the regiment bore the colonel's name, and it often took the facing color of its uniforms from the colors of his family arms.

Infantry battalions were divided into companies, whose number and complement varied over time. Ten companies per battalion was the norm, two flank companies of 112 soldiers (*MP* 91; *P* 20) each, and eight center companies of 86, for a total of 912, which, combined with miscellaneous personnel such as officers, drummers and other musicians, and the surgeon and his assistants, brought the total troop complement to 950. One of the two flank companies was composed of grenadiers, generally the largest and most skilled of the battalion's men. These grenadiers no longer threw the ceramic-skinned explosive grenades that had given them their name long ago, but they remained an elite company, distinguished from the rest of their battalion by special uniforms topped by tall bearskin hats. The other flank company was composed of light infantry, specially trained skirmishers. Some regiments, such as the renowned 95th, contained only light infantrymen specifically trained as marksmen and issued better firearms and less conspicuous uniforms than other units.

There were no permanent units smaller than the company in an infantry unit. Platoons existed, but they were temporary units formed for a specific purpose and reabsorbed into the larger company once the purpose had been achieved. Companies were also divided into squads for billeting in towns, each squad being assigned to a particular location in the town and placed under the supervision of a noncommissioned officer (NCO). These divisions, too, were temporary and were subject to change whenever the soldiers were relocated to another town.

An infantry regiment also had a hierarchy of officers below the colonel. Each company of up to 100 men had a captain (*P&P* 29; *NA* 113, 131), a lieutenant (*E* 163), and an ensign (in some regiments designated a "second lieutenant" rather than an ensign). Ensign (*P&P* 29, 312) was the lowest commissioned rank; major lay between captain and colonel. Below ensign were the NCOs, usually at least two sergeants, three corporals, and, as of 1813, a color sergeant to carry the company colors. NCOs were chosen by captains and approved by the regimental colonel; as NCOs had great responsibility for training the men and inspecting their barracks and messes, they tended to be among the brightest, best trained, and most senior of the soldiers. William Cobbett, later a noted political radical, began life as a soldier in the 54th Foot and quickly rose through the non-commissioned ranks. He was pleased to be promoted to corporal, "a rank which," he wrote, "however contemptible it may appear in some people's eyes, brought me a clear twopence per diem, and a very clever worsted knot upon my shoulder too." He was raised not long afterward to sergeant-major and took pains to work so hard that none of his companions would begrudge him his good fortune.

A typical regiment would also have its own quartermaster, surgeon (who held the rank of captain), two surgeon's assistants (who held the rank of lieutenant), and a paymaster who distributed wages (usually a lieutenant or a captain). NCOs included the armorer and the pioneer corporal, who had staff of ten "pioneers," who did various types of construction and the digging of mines and trenches. Their symbols of office were the ax and shovel each carried. In addition to these men, each colonel had a regimental agent, who engaged in various kinds of business on his behalf, including the receipt of money from the government for the paying and outfitting of soldiers. Until 1796, many regiments also had their own chaplains, but in that year the process of providing religious services to the men was restructured, and military chaplains became based in garrisons or field camps, rather than in the headquarters of a particular regiment. Sometimes religious services were offered by civilian clergymen as well, at a rate of £25 per year.

Each battalion had a band, composed of French horns, bassoons, oboes, fifes, and sometimes cymbals. Great pride was taken in these bands, but they were not merely for display at reviews. They were also functional. They provided the music that taught men the three marching cadences—ordinary step, quick step, and quickest step. Drummers and buglers were also crucial to success in battle, for when the smoke was too thick to see through, and the clamor of shouts, gunfire, and screams made orders too hard to hear, a sophisticated system of drumbeats and bugle calls issued orders through the chaos. There were numerous calls for all sorts of circumstances; when there could be any possible doubt as to which unit was being addressed by a bugle call, a musical prefix identified the company and, if necessary, the regiment.

Cavalry regiments were similar in most respects to infantry regiments, except that they were smaller and were divided into units called "troops" (*NA* 113) rather than companies. Each regiment carried a supposedly descriptive designation, such as dragoons, dragoon guards, or hussars, but the differences between these units were mostly ones of costume and history. By the early nineteenth century, they were all skilled horsemen who fired rifles but relied more heavily on their swords. Dragoons or light dragoons (*NA* 113) were originally light cavalry units, trained in the use of firearms and capable of fighting on foot, while dragoon guards were the descendants of heavy cavalry. Hussars were an imitation of the original Hussars of Hungary; they dressed in heavily braided jackets, tall fur hats, and gaudy, fur-trimmed pelisses that hung from one shoulder. Not all Britons were enamored of this foreign-looking uniform. An 1813 item in *The Public Ledger* lamented that "the ingenuity of our army milliners . . . should be exerted for the purpose of rendering the appearance of our brave fellows ridiculous" and concluded "that the fribbling ornaments with which they are attired would better become an equestrian performer on one of our inferior stages, than a hardy veteran, when equipped for the field."

Cavalry units had most of the same personnel as infantry regiments, but because they had horses as well, they required certain additional specialists. A farrier had to be on hand to shoe the horses, and each regiment, from 1796, was permitted to have a veterinarian on staff as well. The regiment would have its colonel, two majors, an adjutant, the surgeon and his assistants, and trumpeters to play the military calls and orders while the regiment was in its regular quarters. (In the field, the trumpeters were usually replaced by buglers.) The regiment had six to ten troops, of varying strength; in 1776, troops in the 16th Light Dragoons each had one captain, one lieutenant, one quartermaster, two sergeants, two corporals, one trumpeter, one farrier, and twenty-five mounted privates. After 1810 the troop quartermasters were replaced by a regimental quartermaster. The single captain and lieutenant per troop fielded by the 16th were fairly typical, but the number of NCOs and privates often varied over time and by regiment. Some troops fielded three sergeants, four corporals, and fifty to sixty men.

Artillery companies, known as brigades, were larger than cavalry troops but smaller than regiments of either cavalry or infantry. There were brigades of foot artillery and of horse artillery, and their principal challenge, outside of the demands of battle, was the transportation of their heavy guns from one battlefield to another. The logistics of transport were always tricky, not only for the artillery pieces but for the ordinary baggage and supplies that an army required. Accordingly, the army instituted a wagon transport service that, between 1799 and 1814, grew to contain some 2,000 men. These workers, using infernally creaking carts and an assortment of mostly locally hired pack and draft animals, were jeeringly known as the "Newgate Blues" because of their blue jackets and the supposedly criminal class from which they were drawn.

A few prestigious regiments were referred to as either Foot or Horse Guards. They were considered the personal bodyguard of the royal family, but they were occasionally sent overseas and into combat. There were three regiments of Foot Guards and three of Horse Guards (*Scraps, MW* 175). The latter consisted of the 1st and 2nd Life Guards and Royal Horse Guards Blue, known popularly as the Blues (*MP* 361) because of the color of their uniforms. Royal blue was associated with all the units styled "Royal," "King's," or "Queen's," and typically appeared on the collars and facings of uniforms in those units; the Blues were unusual (though not unique) in having all-blue jackets.

Recruiting

When the French Revolutionary and Napoleonic Wars began, Britain's standing army numbered a mere 40,000. By 1813, two years before the wars ended, the regular army alone had over a quarter of a million soldiers, but the regular army was not the only organization seeking to vastly increase its size. At the same time, volunteer and militia (*P&P* 28; *E* 16) units were recruiting, as were the navy and the marines. Meanwhile, as fighting on land intensified, more and more soldiers were lost to injury, death, and disease. The result was a crisis of manpower, with battalions that should have been fielded at full strength going in undermanned by as much as 50 percent. It was not unusual, near the end of the wars, to see a cavalry regiment that ought to have had 905 men going into the field with only about 500.

Colonels resorted, therefore, to a host of tactics to find more men, some of them perfectly legitimate, others underhanded. In theory, there was no draft in Britain, as there was from 1793 in France, but the navy employed press-gangs to seize unemployed sailors; the militia was levied by ballot, and the only way of escaping service was by hiring a substitute for a sizable bounty (a stratagem well within the means of wealthy landowners but out of the question for the poor); and army recruiters often used devious techniques to ensnare the unwary. The trick was to get a young man to accept "the King's shilling" by any means and then convince him that, having taken the king's money, he was now in the army for life, whether he liked it or not.

The easiest way to accomplish this was to get him drunk. (Even the duke of Wellington himself admitted that the "principal motive for our soldiers

to enlist is the propensity of the class from which we take them to drink.")
A successful recruiting sergeant later explained how it was done. If singing
the praises of the army did not work,

> your last recourse was to get him drunk, and then slip a shilling into his
> pocket, get him home to your billet, and next morning swear he enlisted,
> bring all your party to prove it, get him persuaded to pass the doctor. Should
> he pass, you must use every means in your power to get him to drink, blow
> him up with a fine story, get him inveigled by the magistrates, in some shape
> or other, and get him attested, but by no means let him out of your hands.

An even sneakier ploy was that of a Westminster recruiting sergeant, who
in 1795 convinced a young man to do him a favor. Take this shilling, he
said, and go buy some tobacco from that shop over there. When the boy
returned with the tobacco, the sergeant claimed that, having taken the
shilling, the boy was now a soldier; when the boy protested loudly, a crowd
gathered, separated the two, allowed the boy to escape, and dunked the
sergeant under the nearest pump.

Others became soldiers with only a slight pretense on the government's
part that their choice was voluntary. Debtors, prisoners convicted of capital crimes, and vagrants could be forced to join, on the theory that they
had gotten themselves into their predicament, and so this was merely the
outcome of their own poor choices earlier in life. Yet attempts to widen
the net were met with stiff popular resistance. An 1803 Additional Forces
Act too closely resembled a draft and met with low returns and high rates
of desertion.

The army was therefore required to make itself look attractive to what
Wellington called "the scum of the earth." Chief among its lures was the
bounty, a signing bonus that allowed new recruits to buy their required
supplies and possibly have enough left over to get drunk for a few days.
The bounty varied according to a number of factors, including how well
the war seemed to be going, how much longer it seemed likely to last,
and how desperate the army was for manpower. The bounty was £7 12s.
6d. in 1803, for example, and 12 guineas in 1805. At rates like these, a
colonel could be forced to dig deep into his own pockets to find enough
men, but the bounty itself was not his only expense, for he had to pay the
recruiting sergeant 16s. per man, the recruiting party as a whole 15s., and
the "bringer," if there was one, £2 12s. 6d. This bringer was whoever had
made the recruitment possible, for example, a publican who had helped
to get the young man drunk. Even this was sometimes not enough, for
militia companies offered much larger bounties than the regular army. The
army was paying only to get men, whereas the gentry and tradesmen
tapped by the militia were paying to avoid service, and, prompted by this
very personal motivation, they offered substantial sums, often as much as

£25 or £30. Militia service also offered benefits that the army could not: enlistment for only five years, instead of for life; parish help for dependents; and service guaranteed to be closer to home.

Still, the army managed to recruit thousands of soldiers a year. Some joined for the uniform. Some were lured by advertisements that promised excitement and the respect of the nation. An 1811 poster for the 69th Foot called for "[a] few dashing, high spirited young men, whose hearts beat high to tread the patch of glory." In a similar vein, the 7th Light Dragoons announced, in 1814,

> Young fellows whose hearts beat high to tread the paths of Glory could not have a better opportunity than now offers. Come forward, then, and Enrol Yourselves in a Regiment that stands unrivalled, and where the kind Treatment the men experience is known throughout the whole Kingdom.

Some no doubt "enrolled themselves" on the strength of such promises, but others joined for more practical reasons. Men who were extremely poor often felt they had no other recourse; the war had dramatically increased the cost of food, and at least in the army they would be able to eat. Others joined because they were artisans who could immediately step into a respectable NCO rank such as master saddler.

The militia, as much as it penalized the regular army with its bounties, served the interests of the army in the end. It gave men a certain amount of basic military training and then offered them the chance to earn a second bounty by switching over to the regular army (*P&P* 312). Recruiters would show up at a militia camp and sing the praises of their particular regiment, citing its glorious history and its distinct advantages to an ambitious and patriotic young man. Then they would offer the bounty. If not enough men enlisted, the militia officers would oblige the recruiters by intensifying drills and duties until the miserable militiamen transferred in order to escape their newly onerous situation.

Officers and Promotion

Finding officers was always easier—and more lucrative. The army was a gentlemanly profession if one were an officer (*S&S* 102; *MP* 109), so it was a good place to send younger sons who were not destined to inherit the family estates. Militia officers could find a post relatively easily. They merely had to be chosen by the lord-lieutenant of the county whose militia they wanted to join and to demonstrate that they owned land in that county. In one of those bizarre genteel loopholes characteristic of the period, it was not necessary to actually own the property in order to demonstrate ownership. Instead, as Jane's brother Henry did, one could find a local landowner willing to devote his own land, in name only, to the militia enrollment. Thus, Henry, who owned no land in Oxfordshire, was able to join the Oxford Militia in 1793, becoming its adjutant and captain in

1797 and remaining with the regiment until about 1802. The militia offered fewer prospects for long-term career advancement than did the regular army, making it cheaper to join for impoverished gentlemen like Henry Austen and the fictional George Wickham (*P&P* 72, 79, 206).

A commission in the regular army, particularly a good commission in a "good" regiment, was harder to come by and cost a great deal more to obtain. A good regiment was one with a low number; the lower the number, the greater the unit's seniority and the less likely it was to be disbanded after the war was over. A commission in a regiment, or a transfer at the same rank to a better regiment, cost a substantial sum of money in most cases. There were a few commissions for which there was no charge, and there were more of these after reforms by the duke of York, who was named commander in chief in 1795. Some commissions were offered as political patronage (*MP* 109), but the recipients of such commissions were often the sort of young men who could have afforded to purchase commissions themselves. The few commissions handed out as rewards for bravery in the field tended to involve transfers to places like the West Indies where fear of disease made it hard to fill posts by normal means. However, posts vacated by death or cashiering (loss of rank due to court-martial) were filled according to seniority, and this, particularly in wartime, added to the number of commissions that were granted free of charge.

All other commissions were purchased by their occupants (*P&P* 318, 324). When a regiment was first formed, the price of each commission was paid directly to the colonel; thereafter, the commission was the officer's property and could be sold as he liked, the money from the sale being usually applied to his purchase of a higher rank. When a promotion occurred, for example, the rise of a troop captain to major, the captain was obliged to offer his commission to the most senior lieutenant in the regiment. If the lieutenant opted not to buy his superior's commission, the post was advertised for sale outside the unit. However, if the lieutenant did decide to buy, all the other lieutenants moved up automatically in seniority, and the most senior ensign was offered the chance to buy in as the newest and most junior lieutenant. Accordingly, some junior officers would contribute funds to help their superiors buy an increase in rank, as this gave them an opportunity to rise as well.

The price of commissions varied by time period, by rank, and by the seniority of the regiment. An ensign's commission in 1770, for example, cost about £400, £450 in a regiment designated "Royal." A lieutenancy in the 16th Light Dragoons, by comparison, cost £997 10s. in 1812. In addition to these fees, a new officer had to buy an appropriate uniform, which could cost hundreds of pounds, and an assortment of essential supplies, such as a camp bed and tent.

An officer learned his profession on the job, instructed by his superiors in his duties and not permitted to leave the regimental headquarters until he had mastered the basics. He could, if he chose, begin by attending the Royal Military College (as distinct from the Royal Military Academy at Woolwich, which trained artillerymen and engineers), founded in 1801 by the duke of York and located at High Wycombe, Great Marlowe, and finally, after 1812, at Sandhurst. However, few chose to take this route. Like the Royal Naval College at Portsmouth, the academy was never full during Jane Austen's lifetime. Most officers preferred to invest their money in commissions rather than education and to begin accruing seniority right away. Their duties as subalterns included serving as officer of the guard, double-checking the sergeants' night inspections of the barracks, and checking to make sure that the men and their uniforms were clean.

After the duke of York was named commander in chief, he attempted some limited reforms of the commission-for-purchase system. In addition to adding more free commissions, he increased the minimum age for officers to sixteen and established service requirements for various levels of promotion. Two years' service was now required to rise to the rank of captain, six years for major. The requirements were increased in 1809 to three years for captain and eleven years for major.

Pay

The pay of the rank and file was lower than in most jobs in the civilian world. It was only 8d. a day for infantrymen until 1797, when it went up to 1s. per day, a level that was to remain unchanged for the rest of Austen's life. A dockyard worker, by comparison, made 4s. a day in 1806. From the soldier's already low pay, the cost of part of his uniform was deducted. Another portion of his wages—2d. per day in the 8d.-a-day wage era— was retained by the regiment to pay for the soldier's clothing and supplies. Any surplus in this fund, once the bills had been paid, was kept as profit by the colonel. The remaining sixpence had to provide the soldier with drink, food, and entertainment. If he lived in a barracks, the money was paid to him, and he bought food with it, cooking his meals in common with a few others. If he were quartered in an inn, the money was paid directly to the innkeeper, who supplied the soldier with meals. Further deductions were made for hospital treatment, the maintenance of Chelsea Hospital (a facility for aged and infirm soldiers), damage to barracks or equipment, and the services of the regimental agent.

Money was paid by the army's paymaster-general to each regimental agent, who made the necessary deductions for clothing and passed the remainder to the regimental paymaster, who was one of the regiment's officers who performed this service as an additional duty. He then doled out money to the captains of troops or companies. The captains, in turn, paid the troops, always holding back two months' wages (called arrears). Wages differed somewhat between types of regiments. Guards made more than

Full and Half-Pay Officers, 1786. The exaggeratedly nattily dressed full-pay officers on the right are contrasted with the maimed half-pay veterans in the foreground on the left. (Note that even the dog has a peg leg.) The regimentals of the officers are either blue with red collars and cuffs or red with blue. The fate of soldiers who had been grievously wounded and then cast aside by their nation was a common theme of prints and poems.
Courtesy of the Lewis Walpole Library, Yale University. 786.3.1.2.

regular infantrymen, and cavalry troops received an additional sum called "grass money" to allow them to buy the extra supplies their horses required. Soldiers serving in India, which already had a lower cost of living, received a field allowance called *batta* in addition to their wages. Therefore, though service in the East Indies (*S&S* 206) had many disadvantages in the eyes of the troops—long distance from home, strange languages and customs, and tropical diseases—it had pecuniary advantages as well.

Salaries for officers were much higher than for men. These, like most details of military service, varied from time to time and from place to place, but a colonel's salary, exclusive of whatever profit he managed to generate from his running of the regiment, was in the hundreds of pounds. In peacetime many lesser officers were removed from active duty and placed on half pay (*Sand, MW* 401), sometimes a sum too small to sustain a genteel lifestyle. Generals were voted a salary when on active duty in wartime, but peacetime generals received no salary unless they were also colonels.

Pay could be augmented by various means. Soldiers, like sailors, could earn prize money for victories; like sailors, they received larger shares at higher ranks, and, as in the navy, awards could take a very long time making their way through the prize courts. Soldiers in India could be awarded additional *batta* for meritorious service, and officers in some places, chiefly the West Indies, might be granted lucrative colonial governorships. Some soldiers took the matter of compensation into their own hands, seizing loot from captured towns and farms, but this was always a risky venture, as discovery was sure to be followed by punishment.

Duties and Training

Members of the infantry (*E* 163), who made up the majority of the army, were trained mostly to march, to line up in formations, and to handle their weapons. Until the late eighteenth century, marching had been done at a pace determined by each regiment, and this state of affairs could lead to difficulty when regiments attempted to maneuver together in battle. From 1792, David Dundas' *Rules and Regulations for the Formations, Field Exercise, and Movement of His Majesty's Forces* standardized marching speed into three gaits, each based on a pace of 30 inches. "Ordinary step" required 75 steps per minute. According to Dundas,

> The recruit must be carefully trained . . . to maintain it for a long period of time together, both in line and in column, and in rough as well as smooth ground. . . . This is the slowest step which a recruit is taught, and is also applied to all movement on parade.

"Quick step," used for moving from a line of battle to a marching column, from a column to a line, or, less commonly, for short periods of ordinary marching over smooth ground, was 108 paces per minute, and "quickest step," used for wheeling or for passing obstacles, was 120 paces per minute. Recruits were taught to march with a military bearing and a stiff-kneed gait copied from Frederick William I's Prussian soldiers. They were assisted in their efforts to keep the marching time by the regimental musicians, principally the fifers.

Next, beginning in small groups, the soldiers were taught how to move and arrange themselves in formations such as the "hollow square," a formation with ranks of soldiers on four sides and an empty space in the middle. They were also taught how to "lock up" in preparation for firing their muskets. In locking up, the front rank of soldiers dropped to one knee, and the second and third rank (later reduced to a second rank only) staggered themselves, packed elbow to elbow, so that they could fire over the heads of the first rank.

Infantrymen also learned how to handle their muskets and bayonets. They learned to load and fire, but not necessarily to aim, as the "Brown Bess" musket was notoriously inaccurate, especially at ranges of more than 100 yards. The key, from the army's perspective, was getting all the soldiers to perform each stage of the firing process simultaneously and rapidly. The emphasis on speed is intuitive; he who fires fastest fires most and thus kills more of the enemy. The emphasis on simultaneity is perhaps less obvious. Uniform action was important because the front rank could not stand up to reload its muskets unless it was sure that the rear ranks had finished firing. Many a soldier misjudged his timing and died—or killed a comrade—as a result.

Target practice with live ammunition was rare in peacetime, with soldiers being issued as few as four live cartridges per year. It was far more common during war, but even then it served principally to demonstrate how inaccurate a weapon the army musket was. For the most part, soldiers used blanks called "squibs" in training. An exception to this rule was the Experimental Rifle Corps, raised in 1800 and later made into the 95th Regiment. The soldiers in this regiment were issued superior Baker rifles and taught to aim carefully and to steady the weapon, for example, by lying on the back, crossing the right ankle over the left knee, and resting the barrel on the right ankle.

Cavalry troops trained on foot, like infantry, for the four months of the year in which their horses were turned out to pasture. For the rest of the year, they trained on horseback, first learning to ride with skill and confidence, later learning to ride in formation, to charge, and to handle the finer points of horsemanship. They also had to care for their own horses, feeding them and grooming them during regularly scheduled stable hours. Tails and manes were brushed, hooves were inspected, and the horses were exercised once a day and ridden twice a week. At the same time that they were learning to care for their mounts, the cavalrymen learned a host of specific bugle calls. The Assembly call, for example, ordered them to meet at regimental headquarters; if preceded by the call Boots and Saddles, it meant that they were to arrive with their horses.

Cavalrymen were generally somewhat better educated and more genteel than their infantry counterparts. They took pride in this and in their own daring, at times, perhaps, proving a little *too* eager to demonstrate their valor. The duke of Wellington complained of his cavalry troops that they went around "galloping at every thing, and . . . galloping back as fast."

Daily Life

The soldier's day was a long one, with periods of drilling alternating with breaks for meals from early in the morning until nine or ten at night. The men were awakened at 5:00 A.M. in summer or 7:00 A.M. in winter by the sergeant's cries of

> By Bob's rattle the sun's burnin' holes in your blankets. Rouse about, you insanitary frequenters of the casual ward. Turn out, you gutter rats, you unchristened sons of mendicants. Bless your eyes! Bless your souls!

Each change of activity was signaled throughout the day by a drumbeat or a bugle or trumpet call, from reveille in the morning to tattoo at 9:00

or 10:00 P.M., the latter of which told the men to return to their quarters for a final roll call before bedtime. Half an hour after tattoo was played, a patrol inspected all the alehouses in the area to make sure no stragglers were left drinking.

These same alehouses and inns were often the homes of the soldiers, for England's barracks were entirely inadequate to house the troops. This was by design. Citizens and government alike feared the concentrated power of soldiers in barracks, so upon arriving at a new town (*P&P* 28), the military authorities met with the local civilian authorities, in the form of the magistrates, to select quarters for the soldiers and set prices for food and housing. The available accommodations were divided according to troop or company, so that men of the same unit might live near each other, and NCOs escorted the men to their temporary homes. Quartering (*Cath, MW* 240; *P&P* 79) could not be forced upon Englishmen in their private homes—though it could be forced upon innkeepers and upon the Scots, the Irish, and, until the Revolutionary War, Americans. Though some English homeowners opted to admit soldiers into their homes for a fee, most soldiers were quartered in inns and fed at agreed-upon rates.

The quartering system was only slightly less popular than barracks in the public mind. If not within memory, then certainly within the limits of remembered family history, forcibly quartered soldiers had wreaked havoc during England's civil war, debauching young women and stealing what they liked. Accordingly, the subject of proper payment was a sensitive one, and regiments took great care to make sure that their debts were settled— if not by the individual soldier, then by the regimental purse. This extreme caution not to offend the local populace makes Wickham's casual profligacy all the more egregious (*P&P* 324). Quartering troops was always a balancing act, for if soldiers seemed too oppressive a presence in a town, citizens might complain, and if the soldiers became overly friendly with the locals, they might join in food riots or refuse to fire on rioters. If too many were housed in inns, publicans might grow testy—a very real threat that resulted, grudgingly, in the building of many town barracks from the 1790s.

The barracks that existed housed a total of about 20,000 men and were not especially comfortable. They allotted very little space to each man and seldom had beds. Instead, the soldiers slept on straw mattresses or in wooden boxes filled with straw.

In some cases, multiple regiments of soldiers were brought together in camps (*P&P* 237) to practice large-scale maneuvers, the formations of the new 1792 *Regulations*, and mock battles. Reviews by high-ranking officers and by members of the royal family often took place in camps. During Austen's lifetime, these camps were assembled at Shorncliffe and, as she correctly notes in *Pride and Prejudice*, Brighton (*P&P* 219, 229, 232).

Despite the understandable nervousness of the fathers and innkeepers

THE CHARMS of a RED COAT.
London, Publish'd 1.st Nov.r 1787. by Rob.t Sayer, 53 Fleet Street.

The Charms of a Red Coat, 1787. A flirtatious army officer in the old style of uniform woos a young lady while her friends dine in a soldier's tent. He wears clocked stockings rather than dark gaiters, so one may assume this to be a peacetime scenario. Courtesy of the Lewis Walpole Library, Yale University. 787.11.1.1.

of the various towns that hosted regiments, the young women of a town were often very glad to see the soldiers. From the prostitutes who hoped to make extra money to the tradesmen's and gentlemen's daughters who hoped to ensnare an officer as a husband, the enthusiasm for red coats was genuine. Soldiers were widely known to be heavy drinkers, a positive virtue in this era. They were sociable (*NA* 95), and the officers were genteel enough to make good guests at dinners and parties (*Watsons, MW* 315; *P&P* 233). Even Austen, who lacks the enthusiasm for the army that she demonstrates for the navy, acknowledged the appeal of an officer to the average young woman, and her assessment is borne out by the testimony of the officers themselves. William Thornton Keep, upon joining the 77th in 1808, reported to his mother that he regularly attended the assemblies at Winchester, paying a fee of 3s. 6d. for "tea, dancing and cards." "The brilliancy of the scene is greatly enhanced by the red coats, I can assure you," he wrote, "and when the country dances are forming a line of them has a splendid effect by candlelight." The Prince of Wales, too, was a fan of the army, and he was joined by hosts of others after Waterloo, when the glory of that victory seemed to contemporaries to efface all other military triumphs throughout history. Commemorative souvenirs of all kinds featured Wellington and Waterloo in one way or another, and even new construction was named for the battle; the Strand Bridge, begun in 1811, was rechristened the Waterloo Bridge in 1816.

Still, one can understand Mr. Bennet's lack of delight in Wickham as a son-in-law; it is not hard to believe that, even after Waterloo, he would retain a lifelong animosity for this cad. Many fathers, even without the provocation offered by Wickham, would have agreed, for the life of a soldier's wife was not an easy one. The wives of officers had to become accustomed to moving from one town to another, and they had to be as adept as their husbands at knowing the fine gradations of rank, for their rank among the wives was identical to their husbands' rank among the officers. It was possible for them to live relatively comfortably as long as their demands were not excessive, but if their husbands remained stationed at home with little chance of prize money or promotion, and if they had a large number of children, life could be difficult and money scarce. The wives of NCOs and privates led much harder lives. NCOs were generally allowed to marry, but privates were only rarely granted permission, and many, for this reason, married secretly and kept their names off the Married Roll.

Only wives on the Married Roll, however, were permitted to sleep in the barracks or billets with their husbands, and in exchange for this favor, they were expected to wash clothes for the men, nurse the wounded and sick, and subject themselves to a military discipline that fell almost as hard on them as it did on the soldiers. If they complained too much or otherwise made a nuisance of themselves, they could be drummed out of the barracks. Only a small number of wives were permitted to accompany the troops overseas, so when a deployment occurred, there was a lottery to see which wives would be permitted to sail, followed by tearful farewells between couples parted by bad luck. Women allowed to accompany the troops were given half the ration allotted to a man; any children received a quarter ration. Women with numerous children were forbidden to travel in the regiment's keeping at all. Of course, some women followed their husbands unofficially, and then they had to take in washing or do some other work in order to make money to feed themselves.

Food

Officers like Wellington and the fictional Wickham ate well enough, but the ordinary soldier's diet was bland and monotonous. A typical daily ration was one pound of beef or pork, one pound of dark and badly baked bread, one ounce of butter or cheese, one pound of peas, and one ounce of rice. Sauerkraut, spruce beer, or vinegar might be provided to ward off scurvy, and small beer, a barely alcoholic barley brew, was the beverage on most days. Food for those quartered in inns may have been a little better, but one suspects that innkeepers kept strictly to the requirements of the service and charged extra for anything beyond the standard allotment. Soldiers in barracks were assigned to a mess, a group of five to eight men of the same rank who pooled their food and took turns acting as cook. Officers inspected each mess two to three times a week to make sure that the quality and quantity were adequate, and officers had messes of their own (*NA* 153) to attend to.

Troops being transported overseas got an additional allowance of suet and raisins, with which they made a much-beloved pudding called "figgy duff." In the field, they used their "subsistence"—the portion of their wages devoted to food—to buy food from a civilian sutler who accompanied the army and sold basic supplies. Troops in the field might also receive a ration of 1⅓ to 1½ gills of rum per day, as consumption of spirits was believed to prevent certain tropical diseases. Some troops had access to potatoes or oatmeal.

Cooking methods were unadventurous. Most messes boiled their beef or pork in one pot and their potatoes, if they had them, in another. Then the meat broth might be drunk as it was or mixed with oatmeal to make a porridge called skilly. Breakfast was bread and beer or bread and saloop, a tea of milk, sugar, and sassafras.

Military Discipline

An anonymous 1791 poem, "The Volunteer," summed up the miserable plight of the British soldier:

> He's packed in a transport on every state quarrel,
> More tightly than biscuit and beef in a barrel;
> In torrents each summer-shower streams through his tent,
> In barracks more dismal December is spent;
> In damp rotten bedding the moment he's laid,
> To the rage of whole armies his rear is betrayed;
> In health he infallibly more than half-starves,
> In a fever he's used as a rascal deserves. . . .
>   And when for his King thirty years he has toiled,
> In Canada frost-bit, in Africa broiled;
> Has been thrice a week handcuffed for drinking his pay,
> Got nine thousand lashes for running away.

The "nine thousand lashes" were an exaggeration of the severity of military discipline, but not by as much as might be suspected. Some officers, such as Sir John Moore (who died, unlamented by Austen, at Corunna), were in favor of kinder treatment for the men. Others, such as the far more influential duke of Wellington, thought kindness would be interpreted as weakness. The only thing that carried weight with the British soldier, he believed, was "the fear of immediate corporal punishment."

So, while punishments like running the gauntlet and the whirligig (a cylindrical cage in which the offender was spun until sick) had become obsolete by the early nineteenth century, flogging was still a common method of discipline. Flogging (*P&P* 60) was not abolished in peacetime until 1868, and in wartime was retained for several years afterward. A soldier could be flogged for drunkenness, as the anonymous poet noted. He could also be flogged for leaving the line of march to urinate without a ticket of permission from his commanding officer, for minor alterations to his uniform, or for capital crimes that for one reason or another had not drawn the death penalty.

A man to be flogged was ordered to strip to his shirt and lashed down, while his regiment watched, to an iron triangle (in the case of infantrymen) or a ladder (in the case of cavalrymen). The infantry drum major or cavalry farrier produced a cat o'nine tails from a green baize bag, a portion of the ritual that is the origin of the saying, "the cat's out of the bag." A hospital orderly and the regimental surgeon stood by in case the prisoner required medical attention, and the flogging began, continuing with fresh floggers and cats as necessary until the prisoner fainted or until the sentence was complete. Nine thousand lashes would not have been administered at once, but a thousand was not unknown.

Milder punishments included confinement, extra duty, and public reprimand. For severe crimes, the death penalty was imposed. The method used was usually ei-

Etching by Thomas Rowlandson, 1790 (detail). A recruiter and drummer coerce or cajole a bumpkin into joining His Majesty's service. For many young men, the thrill of the uniformed men and drummers marching into town was enough to stir them to enlist. Courtesy of the Lewis Walpole Library, Yale University. 790.6.27.1.

ther hanging or shooting, with the former being considered more shameful than the latter.

Service in the Field

A host of dangers and discomforts awaited soldiers in the field. Battle itself was relatively rare, but the combination of crowded quarters, filth, parasites, and exposure to unfamiliar regions of the world resulted in a high incidence of disease (*E* 163). Soldiers suffered from malaria, typhus, typhoid, cholera, and dysentery. The West Indies were considered particularly deadly; an estimated 43,750 NCOs and men died there, on their way there, between 1793 and 1801 alone. Soldiers were so terrified of the yellow fever common in the West Indies that they would sometimes desert or purposely injure themselves to avoid being shipped to the Caribbean. They were equally afraid of military hospitals, which they feared concentrated disease and exposed them to all sorts of ridiculous experiments at the hands of doctors.

Medical care was indeed very primitive. Hospital orderlies were notoriously incompetent. There was no anesthesia, so men scheduled for surgery or amputations were forced to rely on huge quantities of alcohol. Treatments for venereal disease—one of the most common complaints of soldiers—were rudimentary and often poisonous.

Even the everyday activities of a soldier's life could be grueling. He was sent into frigid climates where even his government-issued greatcoat was insufficient; more commonly, he was sent to tropical colonies, where he sweated and stewed in his red wool jacket. Officers, even infantry officers, typically rode on the march, but the average soldier struggled along under up to sixty pounds of baggage in an unwieldy knapsack with a wooden frame. In July 1809, in a blazing Spanish summer, Edward Costello saw two men shoot themselves rather than walk any farther under the load. Costello himself carried

> Knapsack and straps, two shirts, two pairs of stockings, one pair of shoes, ditto soles and heels, three brushes, box of blacking, razor, soap-box and strap, and also at the time an extra pair of trousers, a mess-tin, centre-tin and lid, haversack and canteen, greatcoat and blanket, a powder flask filled, a ball bag containing thirty loose balls, a small wooden mallet used to hammer the ball into the muzzle of our rifles; belt and pouch, the latter containing fifty rounds of ammunition, sword-belt and rifle, besides other odds and ends that at all times are required for a service-soldier.

The alternative was a shortage of supplies and food, which was no better.

Equipment

Costello's list was a fairly typical assortment of belongings for an infantryman. The soldier's most important piece of equipment was his musket—or, if he were a marksman, his rifle. The musket was long, heavy, complicated to fire, and inaccurate at distances of more than 100 yards. The army's strategy, therefore, was to get as many men as close together as possible and have them all fire at once, on the theory that if a lot of bullets all flew approximately the same way at approximately the same time, they were reasonably sure to hit something.

To fire a musket, the soldier used his teeth to tear open a cartridge—a paper packet containing gunpowder and a .75-inch bullet—while trying not to get the powder inside in his mouth or eyes. He poured a little powder into the flash pan of the gun and closed this compartment, then poured the rest of the powder and the shot down the muzzle of the gun, using a thin metal ramrod to pound the wadded paper after it. If he were thinking clearly, he then removed the ramrod; many a soldier forgot this in the heat of battle and inadvertently fired his ramrod at the enemy. He then cocked his gun and fired by pressing a trigger that released the cock, tipped with a flint. The flint hit steel and made a spark that lit the powder in the flash pan, which in turn lit the main charge in the barrel of the gun.

This is assuming that all went well, and a good many things could go wrong. If the powder were wet, it might not light. Muskets were therefore almost no good at all in the rain, and efforts to shield them with greatcoats or the wide lapels of military jackets were not very successful. Parts in the mechanism could become worn, causing the gun to go off at half-cock. Frequent polishing with wet brick dust could eat away at the metal in the barrel, making it more likely to explode. Or the flint, which lasted for only twenty to thirty uses, might suddenly fail, leaving the hapless soldier to unscrew the flint and install a new one—assuming he had a new one—while the enemy bore down on him, firing their own muskets at him. Under the best possible conditions, he might be able to load and fire four times a minute, but in most circumstances he would be able to fire only twice or three times a minute, especially if his regiment were firing in simultaneous volleys rather than at will.

The Baker rifle distributed to the 95th and 60th was a much more accurate weapon, reliable at 150 yards. It was, however, not without difficulties of its own. It was still a flintlock and therefore had all the difficulties of flints and powder inherent in the musket. Its barrel grooves also tended to collect residue after being fired, so that bullets had to be hammered into the barrel with the sort of wooden mallet carried by Edward Costello.

Soldiers also carried bayonets that could be fixed to the musket muzzle and used for stabbing, but the bayonet was actually much more useful as a general-purpose tool in camp. Bayonets were used to cut branches for the fire, to dig, and even to hold candles. Cavalrymen and officers carried swords, the style of which changed from time to time; officers were required to buy their own swords and pistols.

An army was followed by a long string of carts and wagons hauling all sorts of equipment: tents (*P&P* 232), wine for the officers, flour, produce foraged from nearby farms, meat, ammunition, and various types of iron or brass cannon. One cart could convert into a forge, complete with fireplace, water trough, bellows, and tools. The band carried its instruments, and the pioneers carried their shovels and axes, while the ordinary soldiers labored along under their heavy packs, and ensigns carried the regimental and company or troop colors, immense square or oblong flags that helped soldiers to find their unit in the chaos of battle. The colors, each of which was consecrated before being given to the regiment by a member of the royal family, were considered in some ways the soul of the regiment, and it was a great disgrace to lose them. Accordingly, the colors were aggressively defended, and some of the fiercest fighting typically took place around these flags. A typical flag measured 6' by 6'6" and flew from a pike almost ten feet long.

A cavalryman's most important piece of equipment, besides his sword, was his horse. It had long been the tradition for cavalry horses to be black, but by Austen's time this rule had been relaxed, and horses of many colors could be found in the army, though many troops tried to keep the colors of their horses as uniform as possible. Thus, one troop might be mounted on all (or mostly) bays, another on chestnuts, another on the traditional black horses, another on gray. Cavalry horses had to meet certain height standards, and officers had to provide their own mounts. The horses ate a tremendous amount, and feeding them the eighteen pounds of hay and eight pounds of corn they each required on campaign was a huge logistical issue.

Uniforms

Thomas Cochrane, a naval captain in the Napoleonic Wars and later an admiral, began not as a sailor but at, his father's insistence, as a soldier. He hated it, and most of all, he hated the uniform:

> My hair, cherished with boyish pride, was formally cut, and plastered back with a vile composition of candle-grease and flour, to which was added the torture incident to the cultivation of an incipient *queue*. My neck . . . was encased in an inflexible leathern collar or stock . . . ; these almost verging on strangulation. A blue semi-military tunic, with red collar and cuffs, in imitation of the Windsor uniform, was provided, and to complete the *tout ensemble*, my father, who was a determined Whig partisan, insisted on my wearing yellow waistcoat and breeches; yellow being the Whig colour.

Cochrane, miserable in this outfit, was teased by "a troop of ragged boys" and rushed home, begging his father to release him "from the degradation of floured head, pigtail, and yellow breeches. . . . the reply was a sound cuffing."

Most of those who wore an army uniform took delight in its glamour but nonetheless had some aspect of it that they detested. The stock or collar was a favorite target of the soldier's hatred; stiff and cutting, it was profoundly uncomfortable on the throat and chin, and many a soldier was flogged for shaving a little height off his stock. Many would have chosen the famous red coat as their least favorite part of the uniform, not because of its color but because of the heavy wool cloth of which it was made. Soldiers serving in the Caribbean, India, Africa, or Spain often wished for a coat of lighter weight.

Soldiers were already widely known as "redcoats," and indeed most army uniforms were red (*Watsons, MW* 337; *S&S* 103; *P&P* 64, 232). For most of the eighteenth century, the coat was long, with two tails folded and pinned to show the facing color. Breeches and waistcoats were usually white, and the hat was a black felt tricorne (a triangular cocked hat). Grenadiers, drummers, and pioneers wore miter-shaped hats. White leather belts, periodically re-whitened with pipe-clay, crossed the chest diagonally and carried the soldier's bayonet, canteen, and cartridge box. The lining of the coat, along with collar, cuffs, and lapel facing, was a different color from the rest, and this facing color varied by regiment. It was blue for royal regiments, with other regiments adopting such colors as white, green, or buff. The 56th, in 1799, was known as the Pompadours because its purple facings were said to be Madame de Pompadour's favorite color (or, as some regimental wits claimed, the color of her underwear). Footwear was typically tall jackboots for the cavalry, shorter boots or shoes and gaiters for the infantry. These gaiters were tight coverings that buttoned up the leg; they took the place, visually, of stockings, but were much more durable. They were white when the regiment was stationed at home, gray or black when the unit was in the field. The whole ensemble was known as "regimentals" (*P&P* 29, 72), because it showed not only that the wearer was a British soldier but also, to the trained eye, to what regiment he belonged.

Some units, particularly those populated primarily by foreign soldiers, had uniforms that deviated from this pattern, and variations from one regiment to another were quite common. Light dragoons at times wore blue rather than red, and rifle regiments wore dark green so that they would be less conspicuous when stalking the enemy. The Brunswick-Oels Corps, raised in 1809, wore black uniforms with skull-and-crossbones badges.

The first major change to uniforms came in 1797, when the rank and file lost the long-tailed coat and adopted a short, fitted jacket. Shortly after the turn of

Polonius, Isaac Cruikshank, 1795. A set of regimentals in the period of rapid changes in uniform. The round jockey cap was, in some regiments, a transitional form of headgear between the tricorne and the shako. This individual still wears a wig and a long-tailed coat with the tail facings pinned together, both of which are remnants of the old style of uniforms. His coat is red with buff facings, but regimentals differed so much from one unit to the next that some artists created a print and colored different impressions of it in different colors. Courtesy of the Lewis Walpole Library, Yale University. 795.11.7.1.

the century, infantrymen were ordered to abandon the tricorne hat as well, receiving in its place a shako, a tall cylindrical hat with a shallow brim in front, a brass regimental badge, and festoons of braid in colors that varied from one regiment to another. Officers' uniforms, however, remained largely unchanged; they continued to wear long coats and bicorne hats with cockades (*Watsons, MW* 326). In 1812, this, too, was altered, and officers were required to adopt the short jacket and shako—a move that was greeted with mock horror by some, who claimed that fat generals would look terrible in the jackets, and with genuine horror by others, who pronounced the new style of uniform too "French." At about the same time, the cavalry switched from hats to helmets, often with a plume of worsted or fur. White breeches, too, were replaced in many cases by more practical gray overalls.

A rifleman of the 60th Foot in 1812, then, did not at all resemble the popular image of the redcoat. He wore his tight gray overalls, decorated with a red stripe along the outside of each leg, and black gaiters that reached halfway up his calves. His waist-length jacket was dark green with red collar, cuffs, and shoulder straps. On his head was a black shako with a short stiff plume and a festoon of braid, and around his waist was a black belt. His hair, too, was short. Powdering of soldiers' hair had been banned in 1795, and the queues or pigtails of which Thomas Cochrane had complained had been shorn off, all at once, in 1808.

Most of the distinctive pieces of a soldier's uniform were provided by the regiment. The colonel, out of the money held back from soldiers' pay, was supposed to provide the coat, waistcoat, breeches or overalls, gloves, helmet, cloaks, boots, and, in the case of the cavalry, spurs. The intervals at which these items were replaced varied by the type of clothing; a soldier got a new coat every year, for example, but received a helmet once every four years. All the rest of the soldier's clothing—shirts, underwear, stockings, and gaiters—had to be bought by the soldier out of his small wages. *See also* Marines; Navy.

B

Barometer

The barometer (*NA* 82), an instrument for measuring atmospheric pressure, was invented in the mid-seventeenth century by two pupils of Galileo; it was one of these pupils, Evangelista Torricelli, who had discovered in 1643 that mercury inside a tube rose when atmospheric pressure was low and fell when atmospheric pressure was high. For the next 100 years or so, most barometers were of a simple cistern type, not very different from the first barometer. The cistern barometer consisted of an open vessel that held a fixed quantity of mercury, a closed tube leading up out of the cistern, and register plates—a sort of ruler for reading the height of the mercury—placed at the upper end of the tube and measuring increments between 28 and 31 inches. It was not usual to mark any heights outside this scale, as on most days the mercury fell within this three-inch range. A rough correlation was noted between pressure and weather; days of low pressure tended to be accompanied by rain or cloud, and days of high pressure tended to be sunny. Therefore, the scale of inches was often accompanied by categories of weather: from highest pressure to lowest, these were usually Very Dry, Set. Fair, Fair, Change, Rain, Much Rain, and Stormy.

A slight variation on the cistern barometer, the siphon barometer, had a large, closed tube and a second, smaller tube that extended from the cistern and curved upward, its end open to the atmosphere. The difference was primarily one of location—the location at which atmospheric pressure acted on the mercury. In the cistern barometer, air pushed on the mercury in the open vessel and forced it up into the closed tube. In the siphon barometer, the atmosphere pushed through the upturned end of the open tube. There was also a resulting difference in the way pressure changes were read. In both cases, both the change in height in the tube and in the vessel or siphon had to be measured. With cistern barometers, this reading varied according to the size of the cistern and the quantity of mercury in it. The siphon barometer was easier to use, since one merely added the change in height in the upper tube to the change in height in the siphon.

Another very different-looking style of barometer was the diagonal barometer, in which the tube rose straight up and then bent to the side at an angle. This solved one problem in reading the mercury height—the difficulty of reading the exact height of the mercury on a tiny register plate. The angled tube spread the mercury out, expanding the scale of the reading. However, this spreading of the mercury's surface also made it harder to take a reading in the first place, since it was harder to know exactly which part of the expanded surface to measure. As a result, diagonal barometers never became very popular.

The problem of taking an accurate reading therefore remained trouble-some. Changes in air pressure were often very slight, and a three-inch range made it difficult to see these small shifts. One answer was the vernier scale, which slid up and down the register plate. By lining up the vernier scale with the register plate and the mercury, the normal divisions into tenths of an inch could be refined to hundredths of an inch.

By Austen's day, the barometer had moved from being an uncommon instrument, owned only by people whose business or hobby was science, to being a standard appliance in middle-class and upper-class households. Like a clock or a small useful table, it became part of the furniture of the drawing room, and its design changed as a result. Part of the change was functional. While there were still long stick barometers being made, with their tall tubes of mercury and their small register plates (almost always, by this point, augmented by a vernier scale), there was an increasing tendency toward wheel barometers, in which the register plate was replaced by a dial. The advantage of the dial was that it made the exact height of the mercury much easier to read by enlarging the scale of the register plate. Now the range between 28 and 31 inches could be spread over a large circle similar to a clock face. The wheel barometer did have a tendency to stick and often needed to be tapped lightly to free the needle and bring it up to date with the prevailing air pressure, but this was actually an advantage. Predicting the weather relied not only on the absolute height of the mercury but also on the direction of the shift in air pressure, up or down. Tapping the glass and the resulting self-adjustment of the needle showed whether atmospheric pressure had risen or fallen since the last reading.

Barometers also sprouted extra features for additional utility. Barometers of Austen's time might have a Fahrenheit thermometer. Some barometers also had a hygrometer, a device for measuring humidity, which was a charmingly low-tech contrivance. It was simply a beard of wild oats glued at one end to the barometer case and at the other to a straw pointer. As moisture levels changed, the tiny oat fiber curled or uncurled, pointing as a result either to "Damp" (or "Moist") or "Dry" on a dial. It was a clever domestication of nature, but the oat fiber was so fragile that the hygrometer was often useless after a few months. Many barometers also contained a spirit level, an indicator to make sure the barometer was level when hung on the wall. Others incorporated a clock.

Some changes were decorative. As the barometer became a common household item, its old utilitarian style was adapted to the prevailing fashion. They were made of fine wood such as mahogany or rosewood and bore, at various times, classical reeding, Masonic symbols, or horticultural motifs such as thistle or acanthus. The top of the case might be rounded or might have a classical-style pediment. Barometers may be seen in the illustrations *Very Slippy-Weather* (Shops) and *Matrimonial-Harmonics* (Music).

Barouche

The barouche was the supremely desirable vehicle for summer or for fair-weather travel around town. Two seats, one facing backward, one facing forward, accommodated a total of four persons comfortably (*P* 174, 176), and the box (*MP* 75, 91, 105) held two more—usually a driver and a footman, for unlike a coach, the barouche had no rear step on which a footman could ride. This made a total of six people, and six, of course, is the exact number carried on the outing to Sotherton in *Mansfield Park* (*MP* 74), although the "coachman" is Henry Crawford himself, and the footman's place is occupied by Julia Bertram (*MP* 80). Austen also makes a point of selecting a barouche for the outing rather than a chaise, which was enclosed and did not have a retractable top:

> "But why is it necessary," said Edmund, "that Crawford's carriage, or his *only* should be employed? Why is no use to be made of my mother's chaise? . . ."
> "What!" cried Julia: "go box'd up three in a post-chaise in this weather, when we may have seats in a barouche! No, my dear Edmund, that will not quite do."
> . . . . "And my dear Edmund," added Mrs. Norris, "taking out *two* carriages when *one* will do, would be trouble for nothing." (*MP* 74)

Mrs. Norris makes a valid point; a chaise seated passengers facing forward only, while a barouche seated them facing both ways. Therefore, a barouche can hold the entire party all by itself.

The barouche had a long, shallow, curved body with a single hood that could be raised to cover the back passenger seat only—hence its unsuitability for rainy weather. A cover could also be unfolded to shield the rear passengers' legs from the rain, but this was an expedient for emergencies only. Typically, it was drawn by two horses only, although in processions, four or even six horses might be used for aesthetic reasons, and in this event a postilion would be seated on one of the horses to help guide the carriage. The body rested on springs that determined not only how smooth the carriage's ride was but also how high above the wheels the body sat. The higher the body, the better the view, but high-bodied carriages were top-heavy and thus more likely to overturn. The educator Dr. Edgeworth condemned the trend toward high-sprung vehicles in 1817, writing, "Carriages have risen to a preposterous elevation. That private phaetons and barouches should be mounted out of the town dust, and above the country hedges, is a dangerous luxury." One suspects that Henry Crawford's carriage was exactly as tall as the height of fashion demanded.

That Crawford's carriage should be a barouche (*MP* 59, 62, 222–223) is peculiarly appropriate. It is a fair-weather conveyance, and he turns out to be a fair-weather gentleman, unable to bear real hardship or frustration to win Fanny's love. It is not a vehicle made for long trips in doubtful weather, but then, as a wealthy young man without strong attachments that might make emergency journeys necessary, he can simply wait for the weather to clear and travel when it suits him. The barouche's lack of storage for luggage or cargo, similarly, would not have troubled him; he could simply have his baggage sent behind him by a less fashionable vehicle, such as a wagon.

In addition, the outing to Sotherton and the use of his barouche provide Austen with an opportunity, often overlooked by critics in their analysis of his character, to show him in yet another of his roles. Like the actor he is by nature, Crawford tries on a number of personas throughout the novel, in some cases abandoning them before a single conversation is through. Most notably, he plays at being an actor, at being smitten by Julia and Maria, and at being Fanny's sincere lover, but he also daydreams about being a parson or a sailor, and the Sotherton episode show him in still another role, that of coachman.

The flighty Mrs. Palmer, too, owns a barouche (*S&S* 164), and in her case, too, it seems an appropriate choice. The barouche made a good second carriage, and the Palmer household can certainly afford to keep two. Furthermore, the Palmers spend part of the year in London, where the use of a barouche would fashionable and not terribly impractical. In contrast to both Mr. Crawford and Mrs. Palmer, however, stands Edward Ferrars, who is resolutely serious, unambitious, and unfashionable, and has "no turn for great men or barouches" (*S&S* 16). His mother's hopes of seeing him driving such a carriage are doomed to be unfulfilled. *See also* Carriages and Coaches.

Bath

Visiting Bath (*J&A, MW* 24; *Clifford, MW* 43; *Cass, MW* 48, 49; *L&F, MW* 78–79; *Lesley, MW* 112; *NA* 56, 70–71, 155–156, 226, 238; *MP* 192, 193, 435; *E* 140, 189; *P* 13, 28, 33, 35, 42, 105, 107, 138, 188) in August 1791, novelist Fanny Burney wrote that the city was "beautiful and wonderful through-out." She remarked, as many later visitors would, on the terraces of buildings marching up the town's steep hills:

> The Hills are built up and down, and the vales so stocked with streets and Houses, that in some places, from the Ground floor on one side a street, you cross over to the attic of your opposite neighbour. The White stone, where clean, has a beautiful effect, and even where worn, a grand one. . . . in truth,—It looks a City of Palaces—a Town of Hills, and a Hill of Towns.

She was an enthusiast where Bath was concerned, writing in 1815 that every time she visited she saw some new marvel to enchant her. It was, even then on her fourth visit, "in a state of luxurious beauty that would baffle description, and almost surpass even the ideal perfection of a Painter's fancy." She liked it even with all of its construction, noise, and chaos, and she was not alone. French visitor Louis Simond, viewing the town in 1810, found it "very beautiful" and admired the vast fronts of the mansionlike town houses, all carved from the same local limestone. "This town looks as if it had been cast in a mould all at once," he wrote; "so new, so fresh, so regular." Hester Thrale Piozzi, a close friend of Samuel Johnson's, called Bath "the head Quarters of Pleasure and Gayety."

Thousands of visitors every year agreed with Burney, Simond, and Piozzi, but the verdict on Bath was not unanimous. Charles Dibdin, writing in 1787, declared that the place was "like a Frenchman's shirt—the ruffle is very fine, but the body very coarse. . . . In short, all is either splendidly dull or dirtily vulgar." Four years later, James Beattie remarked on Bath's situation in a valley, which deprived it of fresh breezes and made "the air much more close and stifling than that of London." (Even Hester Piozzi admitted that Bath could be a "stewpot" at times.) Beattie gave the architecture of Bath his lukewarm approval but complained of the chalk soil, which generated huge amounts of dust in dry weather and similar amounts of mud when it rained (*NA* 84). Overall, he concluded, "it is an irregular and very inconvenient town." Uvedale Price, one of the leading writers of the time on landscape and art, condemned the town even more harshly as that worst of all things, un-picturesque.*

Jane Austen seems to have been in Dibdin's and Beattie's camp on the subject of Bath. She visited the town in 1797 and 1799 and possibly at other times as well, eventually coming to dislike it so heartily that, upon being informed that her family was moving there in 1801, she reportedly fainted from the shock. Much like Anne Elliot, "She disliked Bath, and did not think it agreed with her—and Bath was to be her home" (*P* 14). She found it rainy (*NA* 83; *P* 135), gloomy, and, after the decline of the public assemblies, dull. The doctors, she thought, were too quick to write prescriptions, and the price of certain commodities was too high. Any pleasant associations that might have remained vanished when, in 1805, her father died and was buried in Bath, and she moved away from the city the following year with feelings of joy and relief.

Bath's development was directed by two natural phenomena—the hills that surrounded it and the mineral springs that had made it a spa since Roman times. The older parts of the city were located in the valley, while newer houses crept up the hillsides and across the River Avon. About 5,000 houses were built there from the 1720s to 1800, with especially fre-

---

*J. C. Ibbetson disagreed with this verdict. In *A Picturesque Guide to Bath* (1793), he offered advice about the best times of day to sketch the town, favoring clear mornings and all evenings. In the evening, he insisted, "the Crescents are then seen to the utmost advantage; their situation, their concave form, which catches a variety of light, and their tone of color, are then peculiarly adapted to the pencil."

netic periods of construction in the 1760s and from 1788 to 1793; about 1,000 houses were built in the second period alone. The building of the Circus was followed by that of the Royal Crescent, a huge curved row of thirty houses, completed in 1775. The composer Franz Joseph Haydn described its appearance in 1794:

> The curve extends for 100 fathoms, and there is a Corinthian column at each fathom. The building has 3 floors. Round about it, the pavement in front of the houses is 10 feet broad for the pedestrians, and the street is wide *a proportione*; it is surrounded by an iron fence, and a terrace slopes down 50 fathoms in successive stages, through a beautiful expanse of green; on both sides are little paths, by which one can descend very comfortably.

Lansdown Crescent, Somerset Place, and St. James's Square followed in the 1780s and 1790s. Camden Place was begun in 1788 and was intended to be a grand crescent on the pattern of those that had preceded it, but landslides made it clear that the ground was not stable, and only part of the development was built. Its grand portico, intended to stand in the center of the structure, was therefore left unbalanced.

Fanny Burney's 1791 visit occurred in the middle of one of Bath's building booms, and she was overwhelmed by the mania for construction. "This City is so filled with Workmen, dust, and lime," she wrote in September,

> that you really want two pair of Eyes to walk about in it. . . . They are now building as if the World was but just beginning, and this was the only spot on which its Inhabitants could endure to reside. Nothing is secure from their architectural rage. They build upon the pinnacle of Hills that only to look up to breaks ones neck,—and they build in the deepest depths below, which only to look down upon makes one giddy. . . . Their plans seem all to be formed without the least reference to what adjoins or surrounds them, they are therefore high, low, broad, narrow, long, short, in manners their Houses are placed so zig-zag, in and out, you would suppose them built first, and then dropt, to *find* their own *foundation*.

The second boom ended abruptly with the outbreak of war with France in 1793; many people failed to travel at all because of the war, while others shifted their allegiance to different spas. As late as 1801, unfinished houses still lined the London road. Building eventually began again, but with less frantic enthusiasm.

Aristocrats had once flocked to Bath in order to drink or bathe in its waters, but by Austen's day the aristocrats had gone elsewhere. Bath was instead a haven for the gentry, professionals, and tradesmen. It continued to draw large numbers of visitors from these classes, however—an estimated 10,000 people came every year, staying for weeks or even months at a time—and the town prospered. West Indian planters came with dozens of relatives and servants straggling behind them; adventurous men and professional gamblers came to play for high stakes, until most games of chance were banned in 1749. Prostitutes came to ply their trade, and speculators came to start new mineral wells or sell patent medicines. Increasing numbers of people came not as visitors but as new residents, and by 1815 Bath was one of the nation's dozen most populous towns.

Bath's star, however, was gradually declining in spite of all this activity. There were riots in 1800 and 1812. The once-famous assemblies at Bath's Upper and Lower Rooms drew fewer and fewer participants, and those who came tended to be of a lower social class, which in turn made members of the gentry less likely to attend. Tourists became fascinated by the sea, and some opted to spend their holidays by the ocean rather than at the inland spas. By 1817, Bath was, according to one visitor, "incredibly dingy and wretched."

Bath as a Medical Center

The ostensible reason for Bath's existence was its waters, which were piped into pump rooms or into an assortment of hot, cold, and warm baths. People in ill health (*J&A*, *MW* 26; *Scraps*, *MW* 170; *S&S* 208–209; *E* 275, 307) went to take the waters, either internally or externally, as recommended by their doctors. In the pump rooms, people paid to drink glasses of the warm water (*NA* 71; *P* 146). Rates were posted from 1804 onward; there was a charge of 7s. for the first week's water, followed by a guinea a month for the invalid and 10s. a month for the rest of his family. Pumpers of water could not ask for tips, but they could receive them if offered. Many patrons would begin the day with a bath between 6:00 and 9:00 A.M., then proceed to the Pump Room for a glass of mineral water.

In the baths (*P* 152), people of both sexes immersed themselves with the help of an attendant. In order to preserve everyone's modesty, men had to wear drawers or a waistcoat while bathing, women had to wear a shift, and male attendants had to wear a special cap to identify themselves. Suitable attire could be rented for sixpence if the bather did not wish to get his own clothes wet. The baths were supposedly of great help to people with joint or limb pain; they were recommended, for example, in cases of arthritic complaints or gout (*LS*, *MW* 295–296, 298; *Sand*, *MW* 374; *NA* 17; *MP* 425; *P* 163–164). Mrs. Austen's brother, James Leigh-Perrot, for example, spent half of every year in Bath for the treatment of a gouty foot, and the reason Jane went to Bath in 1799 was that her brother Edward was traveling there to relieve his own gouty symptoms. For those too crippled to come to the baths, the baths, in a sense, came to them. Tubs in which to soak one's feet could be filled with the hot bathwater and brought to one's lodgings for a fee.

The baths were open every day of the year except Christmas and Good Friday; they opened early in the morning and offered discounted rates to the poor. There were public baths, such as the King's Bath and Hot Bath,

The Pump Room, 1804. Immediately to the right of the Pump Room is the colonnade where Anne Elliot observed Mr. Elliot talking with Mrs. Clay. Library of Congress.

and private baths, which were increasingly patronized by the wealthy. Private baths, of course, cost more; one facility charged 2s. 6d. for a private bath and a shilling less for a public bath in 1810. This same facility offered medical treatments based on magnetism and electricity as well as lectures on science and bottled mineral water.

The presence of crowds of invalids gave Bath a peculiar appearance. There were an unusually high number of medical personnel, for instance, and an abnormally large number of crutches and wheelchairs. Wheelchairs were also manufactured there. There were also a disproportionate number of medical professionals. According to a trade directory of 1799, there were sixty-three physicians, surgeons, and apothecaries in the town.

Bath as a Social Center

Not everyone who came to Bath, however, was ill. Even the people seeking medical treatment, unwilling to leave their families for weeks at a time, brought wives, husbands, children, servants, and family friends in tow. These friends and family quite naturally wanted something to occupy their time other than watching invalids soak in hot water, so businesses of all kinds evolved to entertain the hangers-on. There was always something to do in Bath (*NA* 78–79).

There were bookstores and circulating libraries for those who liked to read (*P* 146). William Frederick's library at 18 The Grove had an inventory of 9,000 books in 1770; Bull's Library, the descendant of Bath's first circulating library, was run first by its founder John Leake, then by Lewis Bull, who renamed it after himself, and from 1792 by Lewis' son John. William Frederick's establishment passed, after his death in 1776, to Joseph Sheldon and William Meyler. James Marshall ran an especially fashionable library in Milsom Street, with 1,753 subscribers from 1793 to 1799. By the time of Jane Austen's first visit to Bath in the 1790s, the town had nine circulating libraries. Subscribers paid a fee for the year or the quarter and could then borrow as many books as they liked. This fee changed over time, but in 1789 six of the libraries agreed on rates of 15s. per year and 5s. per quarter.

Those who preferred newspapers to books could subscribe to reading rooms that took in a number of papers, including the local Bath paper (*NA* 206). They could also go to one of Bath's coffeehouses and read the paper there. The newspapers were considered important not only for their coverage of political and financial events but for their advertisements and their lists of new and notable visitors lately arrived in town.

Music lovers had plenty of options. Amateurs could join the Bath Catch Club, which from 1784 held weekly meetings to sing all sorts of songs, or the Harmonic Society, which was giving occasional Friday-evening concerts in the Lower Rooms by 1812. There was music at the Pump Room and at the assembly rooms, paid for by the patrons of the various rooms; as the musicians were crucial for balls, there was always much anxiety over whether they were being paid enough. The Pump Room band, which played music from 1:00 to 3:30,* was paid £50 8s. per season in 1795. This was considered adequate payment at the time, but by 1801 a total of £130 8s. for the bands at the Upper and Lower Rooms was thought so little that the number of performances had to be scaled back.

There were also weekly concerts (held on Wednesdays at the Upper Rooms in 1812–1813), special benefit concerts for distinguished performers (*P* 180), and musical evenings at private homes. From 1782 to 1810, Italian singer, keyboardist, and composer Venanzio Rauzzini directed the New Assembly Room Band and thus controlled the content of the weekly concerts; after his death, the post was filled by a flutist, Mr. Ashe. The concerts, like most public events in Bath, were funded by subscription. Patrons became, in effect, season ticket holders, with the right to attend all concerts in a given season in exchange for a fairly substantial fee. In 1819, according to Pierce Egan, this ranged from £2 12s. 6d. to £5 15s. 6d. for one to three tickets to each concert; the tickets could be transferred "to ladies only." Smaller fees could be paid to subscribe to a limited number of concerts, and a single concert could be attended for 8s.

Those who preferred the outdoors could walk (*NA* 35, 68, 80, 97) or

*In 1819 (P. Egan, *Walks through Bath*).

View from Beechen Cliff. Bath had expanded somewhat by the later nineteenth century, when this photograph was taken. The area in the right foreground, for example, was largely empty when Catherine Morland could have stood in this spot and taken in this view. Yet much of the city—the Abbey Church, the houses rising crescent and row above each other—remains the same as what Austen and her fictional characters would have seen. The bridge at the south end of the town can be seen in the left foreground, and a small curve of the Avon can be seen on the right. Library of Congress.

ride. There were several good walks around Bath, including that to the summit of Beechen Cliff (*NA* 106, 111) on the south side of the Avon. Jane, an avid walker, recorded, shortly after her family had moved to Bath, taking a brisk walk with a similarly determined lady named Mrs. Chamberlayne. The two ladies walked so fast, she informed Cassandra, that they would have been entirely alone "after the first two yards, had half the inhabitants of Bath set off us." Equestrians (*NA* 35) and carriage drivers (*P* 168) could ride or drive up any of the numerous nearby hills, such as Claverton Down (*NA* 61), near the burial place of Bath notable Ralph Allen, or Lansdown Hill (*NA* 47), a hill just north of town where a Civil War battle had been fought in 1643. The route to Claverton Down afforded good views of the Royal Crescent, and the Down itself, 400 feet above the town, boasted extensive views in all directions and, according to Pierce Egan, a "beautiful extensive level of velvet turf." If one traveled north past Lansdown, one arrived at Wick Rocks, an area of rugged scenery and cliffs up to 200 feet tall. Patrick Egan, writing about Bath and its environs in 1818, insisted, "Persons visiting either Bath or Bristol ought not to omit viewing the rocks at *Wick*, if they possess in the slightest degree any taste for geology, painting, or romantic natural scenery." For those who preferred not to ride so far afield, there was "Hyde Park," a riding ring on the common.

Other Bath visitors simply enjoyed spending time with friends. Some people came year after year to Bath, meeting friends and family who lived in other parts of the country (*P* 170, 178). They dined at each other's houses or met in the evenings to play cards (*MP* 203).

Bath was also known for its theater (*NA* 195, 217), which became the first Theater Royal in the provinces when it was constructed in 1768. This Orchard Street theater attracted top performers from London, making Bath, for many years, the second-best theater city in the kingdom. The theater building itself, however, was small and inconveniently located in the older part of town that still featured narrow medieval streets. In 1805, it closed and was replaced by a newer, larger theater located in Beaufort Square, midway between the Upper and Lower portions of Bath. Elaborately decorated in red and gold, it cost £20,000 to build and contained twenty-six private boxes, beautiful ceiling paintings, and magnificent chandeliers. Austen is known to have attended a performance at the Orchard Street theater, and it seems likely that she saw others there. It is also possible that she saw plays at the new theater, although she moved away from Bath only a few months after its completion.

Some visitors wanted a little bit of everything, and this they found at Bath's pleasure gardens. These included Spring Gardens (1735–1796), which hosted public breakfasts, teas, and music, in addition to pleasant walks on garden pathways. Villa Gardens (1782–1790) had a more working-class appeal and may have failed for that reason; almost everyone in Bath wanted to believe that they might be rubbing elbows with peers. The queen of Bath's gardens was Sydney Gardens, referred to as "the Vauxhall of Bath." Sydney Gardens, which opened in May 1795, featured elegant landscaping, cast-iron bridges, a faux castle, and outdoor public entertainment such as concerts and breakfasts. Four or five times a year, there were especially large nighttime events lit by as many as 5,000 oil lamps. Austen's first home in Bath was located near the gardens, and she attended events there. In 1799, she made a reference in one of her letters to the public breakfasts, but it is not known if she attended them.

Assembly Rooms

The quintessential Bath diversions, however, were the balls (*NA* 33; *E* 156) held at the town's various assembly rooms (*NA* 130, 195, 201; *E* 156). The oldest of these (*Watsons, MW* 325) in Austen's day was the Lower Rooms (*NA* 89), a cluster of assembly rooms located in the lower, older part of the town. The proprietors hired a master of ceremonies (MC—see *E* 156), who welcomed new visitors to the town and gave those who needed it a little discreet advice on the standards of behavior expected at assemblies. Those who opted to partake of the balls paid a subscription fee admitting them for the season.

The expansion of the town uphill, however, made traveling down to the Lower Rooms and back an annoyance for those living on the heights. Accordingly, in 1771 another set of rooms was built closer to the newly constructed homes. This collection of assembly rooms, known as the New Rooms or Upper Rooms (*NA* 20, 21), drew fashionable customers away from the Lower Rooms, eventually eclipsing them altogether. Much of its success was due to its convenient location, but part was also due to its amenities. Its ballroom, lined with forty Corinthian columns, was 105 feet long, just over 42 feet wide, and a few inches over 42 feet high. It also boasted a tearoom (*NA* 22) with a raised gallery for musicians and a 48-foot-wide octagonal card room (*NA* 20, 51) through which the concertgoers pass in *Persuasion* (181, 190).

At first both sets of rooms had a single MC, but in 1777 separate MCs were elected, and in 1787 they developed two sets of rules, one for the Lower Rooms, and one (more explicit and numerous) for the Upper Rooms. Balls at the Lower Rooms began at 6:00 P.M., while those at the Upper Rooms began at 7:00, but both ended promptly at 11:00, even in the middle of a dance. Subscribers paid a fee, varying from time to time, that admitted them (and sometimes one or two guests) to the season's formal dress balls and a separate fee to be admitted to the fancy balls (cotillions); there were usually about twenty-five to thirty of each kind of ball each season. Patrons of the Upper Rooms had to pay as well for the right to walk around the rooms: 10s. 6d. for annual promenading rights for men, 5s. for ladies. On Sunday evenings, this particular form of discrimination was reversed; the rooms opened for tea-drinking then, with men paying only 6d., while ladies paid 1s.

Attempts were made to keep the two sets of assembly rooms from competing too aggressively with each other. The MCs tended to work out a schedule that allowed each set of rooms to reign supreme on chosen nights. On Mondays, the Upper Rooms held their formal dress ball. On Tuesdays, the Lower Rooms hosted a cotillion. The Upper Rooms held its cotillion on Thursdays, and the Lower Rooms held its formal dress ball on Fridays. The schedule was somewhat different by the season of 1812–1813; by that time, there were balls at the Upper and Lower Rooms, respectively, on Mondays and Tuesdays; concerts on Wednesdays at the Upper Rooms; another ball at the Upper Rooms on Thursdays; and theater performances on most other nights, except for Sundays.

On occasion, an MC was ousted or chose to take a job in another spa town, and then an election was held for a new MC. Candidates did a fair amount of campaigning among the subscribers, who often grew quite excited about the process. Fanny Burney witnessed such a scene in April 1780, when the Lower Rooms were filling a vacancy. She found the rooms "violently Crowded, and parties running very high for the various Candidates." The winner of this particular election was Richard Tyson, who was to remain MC of the Lower Rooms until 1785, when he moved to the Upper Rooms and was replaced by James King, whom the playwright Richard Brinsley Sheridan described as "a very genteel fashionable looking young Man." In 1801, King took a second job as the MC of Cheltenham, and in 1805, he imitated Tyson by moving to the Upper Rooms, retaining his post at Cheltenham and doing his best to preside over their very slightly overlapping social seasons. His successor at the Lower Rooms was Charles Le Bas, an unsuccessful promoter who never seemed able to generate much interest in events there.

He was replaced in 1810 by Francis John Guynette, who fought as well as he could against the gradual drift toward the Upper Rooms. Guynette's job was made all the more difficult by a new trend in Bath life. The gentry, dismayed at the increasingly plebeian patronage of assemblies, was retreating from such public events altogether and resorting to private parties to maintain exclusivity (*MP* 203; *E* 290; *P* 180, 227). Guynette, unable to attract sufficient numbers of subscribers, was replaced in 1815, and the Lower Rooms never again attained the fashionable status they had earned in the mid-to-late eighteenth century.

A third important site, the Guildhall, hosted balls as well, but it does not feature in Austen's writing. This is because its dramatic usefulness would have been limited by the fact that only residents of Bath could attend balls there. As the purpose of assemblies, for the participants as well as for Austen, was to bring together potential marriage partners from different parts of England (*E* 275), balls restricted to local residents did not hold much appeal.

The assemblies, like almost everything else in Bath, were seasonal. For a resort town, Bath had an unusually long season, or rather, two seasons. The first lasted from the end of the hunting season until the combined heat of Bath and desire to visit one's country estate drove visitors away—that is, from February to June. After the "stewpot" had cooled a little, people came back for a second season from September until late December; as the Christmas holidays approached, many visitors returned home to be with family. As time went on, however, many people began staying for part or all of the winter (*Sand*, *MW* 374; *E* 183; *P* 14, 42, 206), making a third Bath season. Haydn, in 1794, wrote that "in Summer one sees very few people; for the people taking the baths don't come till the beginning of October, and stay through half of February. But then a great many people come, so that in the year 1791, 25,000 people were there."

Amenities

Bath's leaders realized very early in the eighteenth century that the tourist trade was its chief hope of worldly glory, and they made efforts to make the city as comfortable for visitors as possible. Standard rates for lodgings were set to avoid gouging renters, and lists of available lodgings made it easy for new arrivals to find a place to live. Little could be done about the streets in the old part of town, which still bore its medieval footprint, but the streets in the upper town were broad and attractive, with sidewalks (*P* 178–179) to help ladies keep their dresses clean. Drainpipes were mandatory from 1757 to keep rainwater from sheeting off the roofs onto pedestrians below, and reservoirs to meet seasonal water demand were built at Beechen Cliff and two other locations in 1765, 1790, and 1799. From 1801, the streets were lit at night by 960 lamps.

On Sundays, visitors could choose to worship in one of the many proprietary chapels built specifically to accommodate visitors and funded, like everything else, by subscription. These included the Octagon Chapel (1767) in Milsom Street, at which Austen is believed to have worshiped, the Kensington Chapel (1795) in Walcot, Laura Chapel (1796) in Bathwick, and All Saints Chapel (1794) in Lansdown Place. The proprietary chapels were a necessity, as the Church of England was very slow to build new churches (and, in the process, split existing clergymen's livings) under any circumstances. Building new churches for temporary residents was quite out of the question. There were, however, traditional churches for local residents, including Walcot Church (*NA* 46), where Jane's father married her mother in 1764 and was buried in 1805.

The most prized amenity in a hilly town was the presence of licensed "chairmen," pairs of men who would carry an individual in a sedan chair. These chairmen were especially necessary at the Orchard Street theater, as the crowded streets in that part of town would not admit hordes of carriages. By regulation, thirty pairs of chairmen had to be in place outside the theater by 9:00 P.M., but this was never really adequate, and patrons often had a long wait for a chair. Public concerts also had to have at least thirty sedan chairs ready, and public balls had to have fifty. By 1801 there were 340 pairs of chairmen licensed in Bath; they charged 6d. inside the old city, 6d. for trips up to 500 yards within the "liberties" (adjacent areas), 6d. for trips of up to 300 yards in seven especially steep areas, and 1s. for all other journeys, up to a maximum of one mile. Prices were raised or refined rarely, but by 1819 Pierce Egan could report that the fares were as follows:

For carrying one person any distance not exceeding 500 yards	0s. 6d.
Above 500, and not exceeding 1173 yards	1s. 0d.
Beyond 1173 yards, and not exceeding one mile	1s. 6d.
Beyond one measured mile, and not exceeding in whole one mile and 586 yards	2s. 0d.
Not exceeding one mile 1173 yards	2s. 6d.
Not exceeding two measured miles	3s. 0d.
And for every 586 yards beyond	0s. 6d.

Shops

For many visitors, the chief attraction of Bath was its assortment of shops (*NA* 25, 29, 217; *P* 141), generally agreed to be second only to that found in London. For some visitors, such as Louis Simond, the proliferation of shops was only another sign of the idleness of the place. Bath had, he complained in 1810, "No trade, no manufactures, no occupations of any sort except that of killing time, the most laborious of all. Half the inhabitants do nothing, the other half supply them with nothings." For women from small villages, however, the assortment of fabrics and trimmings was a delight. People accustomed to very little choice in what they bought went to Bath prepared to be dazzled by variety.

There was, for example, plenty of good food. In 1799, 31 percent of Bath's retailers were involved in some way with the provision of food, from the eighty-five grocers and tea merchants and the thirty-seven bakers to the thirty-three butchers and sixteen fruiterers. Many of them were concentrated in the Walcot area in the northeast part of the city. They brought in famously good mutton from Lansdown, freshly made local butter or cheap Welsh butter shipped by the barge-load, a wide assortment of fish, fresh vegetables, and excellent North Wiltshire cheese. Poulterers supplied all the normal types of domestic poultry, plus game of all kinds, including woodcock, snipe, goose, duck, and even larks. Cooks and housekeepers reveled in the marketplace next to the Guildhall, which Robert Southey praised for its "order and abundance." The main market was held on Wednesdays and Saturdays, the fish market on Mondays, Wednesdays, and Fridays. The discerning bought their poultry from a dealer in Wade's Passage and their fish from the fishmongers in High Street or Bath Street.

Sweets sold especially well. Bath got its first ice cream shop in 1774, and the city was renowned for its confectioners. Loiterers of both sexes could step into a pastry shop, such as Mrs. Molland's at 2 Milsom Street (*P* 174), and eat ices, jellies, and cakes. Another famous pastry shop was Gill's, located in Wade's Passage between two buttresses of the Abbey Church.

Another important set of businesses dealt in transportation, enabling visitors to get to Bath quickly and easily. The town had five horse dealers in 1800 and numerous commercial stables (*MP* 193). In 1799, there were four coach makers, nine saddlers, and six farriers, plus drivers of coaches and wagons who hauled people and goods up and down the new turnpike roads. By 1800, 147 vehicles had regular service at least once a week from Bath to London or from London to Bath, and by 1812 this number had risen to 265. Coaches also ran to Exeter, Bristol, Birmingham, Gloucester, and Cheltenham.

Retailers of cloth and clothing (*P* 221) included drapers, milliners, hosiers, mercers, and glovers. In 1800 there were twenty-two milliners and dressmakers, eight shoemakers, fifty-three tailors and habit makers, forty-four hairdressers and perfumers, and nineteen mantua makers. About 21 percent of retailers in 1799 were engaged in the clothing trades. The drapers and mercers sold fabric by the yard, while the mantua makers and so forth made the clothes to patterns specified by the customer. Hosiers sold stockings; glovers, obviously, sold gloves; and milliners sold hats (*NA* 39) and trimmings like lace and ribbons. One such shop was Smith's at Bath and Stall Streets, run by a Mrs. Gregory; it was here that Jane's aunt Mrs. Leigh-Perrot was accused of shoplifting some lace in 1799.

Another large segment of the retail trade was devoted to household goods such as glass and china. Josiah Wedgwood had a showroom in Bath, initially in Westgate Buildings but later in Milsom Street. There were cabinetmakers, ironmongers, and dealers in earthenware. Toy shops sometimes sold toys for children, but most were devoted to trinkets, knickknacks, and clothing accessories such as fans, pocketbooks, decorative souvenir boxes, jewelry, combs, knives, scissors, and cosmetics.

Toy shops were primarily interested in attracting female customers, but it was not only women who succumbed to what Simond called "multitudes of splendid shops, full of all that wealth and luxury can desire, arranged with all the arts of seduction." Parson James Woodforde, visiting Bath in 1793, went to Perrival's, a draper's shop in Milsom Street, where he bought "three Pieces of Muslin ten Yards each Piece and one Yard & half wide—very great bargain, I paid 3.15.0. which was only twenty five Shillings apiece." The next day he went back and bought more muslin as a gift, then visited a draper called Jones in Abbey Church Yard. Men as well as women patronized Bath's wig makers, print shops (*P* 168–169), bookshops, music shops, and goldsmiths.

Notable Sites in Bath

Austen mentions a number of sites in Bath that would have been familiar to any of her readers who had visited there. There are fewer of these references in *Persuasion*, where most of the action has moved into private homes, but even *Persuasion* mentions a few landmarks. One of these is Molland's, cited above; another is the White Hart Inn (*P* 216), a well-known coaching inn that stood opposite the Pump Room and would thus have been seen almost daily by most tourists in Bath. People often stayed there when they meant to stay only a few days in Bath, or they slept there for a night or two while they searched for appropriate lodgings. Parson Woodforde stayed there in 1793, reporting that it was "a very good, very capital Inn, everything in stile." Louis Simond was a guest as well and offered a description of the service:

> [T]wo well-dressed footmen were ready to help us alight, presenting an arm on either side. Then a loud bell on the stairs, and lights carried before us

to an elegantly furnished sitting-room where the fire was already blazing. In a few minutes a neat-looking chambermaid, with an ample white apron pinned behind, came to offer her services to the ladies and show the bed-rooms. In less than half-an-hour five powdered gentlemen burst into the room with three dishes, etc., and two remained to wait. Our bill was £2 11s. sterling, dinner for three, tea, beds and breakfast.

The inn, sometimes styling itself a "hotel" (a more fashionable term), was considered one of the best in Bath.

Northanger Abbey is richer in references to public spaces, as Catherine Morland is far more interested in the traditional entertainments of Bath than Anne Elliot. One of the most commonly mentioned sites is the Pump Room (*NA* 35, 39, 83, 84, 91, 143, 149, 217), where pumpers served glasses of mineral water from a fountain (*NA* 71). The Pump Room was, in some sense, the headquarters of social Bath. New arrivals signed the guest book (*NA* 35, 43) to announce their presence in town to their friends. Visitors walked up and down the room (*NA* 25, 34, 35, 147) in the morning, looking for acquaintances (*NA* 31), studying the latest fashions worn by their fellow walkers (*NA* 71), and getting some indoor exercise on cold winter days. The curious, if they wished to do so, could look out the windows onto the baths below, watching the invalids bob and tiptoe in the water. In the afternoon there was music played by a twelve-member band.

The Pump Room had already been renovated and enlarged once in the 1760s, but by the 1780s the city fathers felt that more changes were necessary. Accordingly, the building was remodeled again in the late eighteenth century, a process that seemed to take forever and that disrupted its business. Even before it emerged from this cocoon as the Great Pump Room, it was a splendid place. A nine-year-old girl, visiting in 1788, marveled at the statue of legendary MC Beau Nash, "the waters sending up their columns of steam," the crowds, and the music. She later recalled that each entrance to the Pump Room was framed by "beautiful green-house plants or artificial flowers" and that silver balls were used as fly traps, though she does not explain how the devices worked.

Nearby was the abbey churchyard, which Austen calls the pump-yard (*NA* 43, 44, 91; *P* 228). This was a paved courtyard, one of the official places where sedan chairmen could wait for customers, and had a view of the abbey; the south front of the Pump Room, with its Greek inscription (translated as, "Water Is Best"); and the low colonnade (*P* 222), to the right as one faced the Pump Room.

Farther away from the city center, one finds the residential districts in which Austen and her fictional characters resided. Some streets were considered far more genteel than others (*P* 165). To the west of the old city, and unfashionably close to it, lay Westgate Buildings (*P* 152–153, 157–158, 192), one of the places that the Austens considered living

Map of Bath, 1804.

Bath Map Key

1. Abbey churchyard (pump yard)
2. Argyle Buildings
3. Avon
4. Baths
5. Beaufort Square theater
6. Beechen Cliff
7. Belmont
8. Bond Street

9. Broad Street
10. Brock Street
11. Camden Place
12. Cheap Street
13. Circus
14. Claverton Down
15. Edgar's Buildings
16. Gay Street

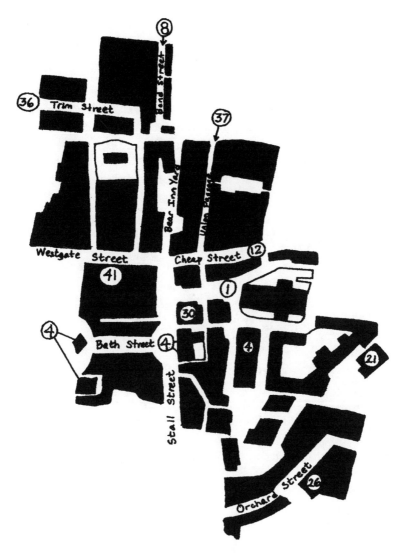

Map of the Lower Town, 1804.

when they moved to Bath. Jane wrote to Cassandra in January 1801 that "Westgate Buildings, tho' quite in the lower part of the Town are not badly situated themselves; the street is broad, & has rather a good appearance."

Little housing was built to the south, but there had been a bridge across the Avon in that direction for many years. In *Persuasion*, Lady Russell's carriage takes Anne "through the long course of streets from the Old Bridge to Camden-place" (135), and indeed this would have been a long, busy, and noisy route. The old southern bridge was about as far south as one could go and existed mostly to bring out-of-town traffic into the city. Camden Place was very far to the north along some of the busiest roads in Bath.

To the northeast, the Avon was spanned by Pulteney Bridge, a lovely arched stone bridge built by Robert Adam in 1770 to 1774 and lined with shops. It led past Argyle Buildings (*NA* 87, 94) to the diamond-shaped Laura Place (*NA* 86; *P* 149, 157), named for Henrietta Laura Pulteney, daughter of one of Bath's landlords and developers. This area was rejected by the house-hunting Austens in 1801; as Jane put it, "The Houses in the Streets near Laura Place I should expect to be above our price." On the other side of Laura Place, Great Pulteney Street (*NA* 19, 51, 80, 86, 149; *P* 178) extended northeast to Sydney Gardens. It was in this neighborhood, at 4 Sydney Place, that the Austens finally settled in 1801. (The neighborhood was to prove too expensive for them, however, and they would be forced to move in 1804 to Green Park Buildings, a rather plain-looking row of three-story houses in the southwest quadrant of the city.)

The northern or "upper" portion of the town contained the Paragon, where the Leigh-Perrots lived at No. 1; Jane disliked this street, which was narrow, busy, and dark. Not too far away lay Queen Square (*P* 42), where she stayed in June 1799. "I like our situation very much," she wrote to Cassandra:

> it is far more chearful than Paragon, & the prospect from the Drawingroom window at which I now write, is rather picturesque, as it commands a perspective veiw [*sic*] of the left side of Brock Street, broken by three Lombardy Poplars in the Garden of the last house in Queen's Parade.

Between Queen Square and the Circus lay 25 Gay Street (*P* 240), where the Austens moved after Mr. Austen's death. By 1806 they had shifted again, to tiny Trim Street just southeast of Queen Square. Milsom Street (*NA* 39, 47, 91, 102, 129, 154, 155, 170, 174, 238) was also very near Queen Square, lying just a few streets to the east. It was originally designed as a residential street, but in later years became famous as a site for fashionable shops. At its northern end stood Edgar's Buildings (*NA* 43, 47, 92, 115, 149), approached by a steep flight of steps.

Just west of the Circus, along Brock Street (*NA* 101), was the Royal

Crescent (*NA* 68, 97, 101), where on pleasant Sundays most of Bath liked to walk. A gravel walk (*P* 241) connected the Circus with the Crescent. On the other side of the Crescent were Marlborough Buildings (*P* 139, 156, 197). A few blocks north of both the Royal Crescent and the Circus was Rivers Street (*P* 136, 215), and still farther north was Camden Place (now Camden Crescent). Camden Place's (*P* 124, 136, 137, 192, 240) construction woes have been mentioned already, but despite its lopsided appearance, its houses offered splendid views. To reach Camden Place, one walked or rode up Broad Street, then turned to the right near the place where Broad Street continued north as the Lansdown Road (*NA* 85).

The upper and lower towns met near the abbey churchyard. Cheap Street (*NA* 44) ran north of the churchyard and eventually became West-gate Street, while York Street ran along the south side and became Bath Street (*P* 217, 228) as it ran westward. To cross from Cheap Street to the upper part of town, one had to walk either through the yards of the Bear Inn or through Union Passage (*NA* 44), a narrow alley that inevitably became choked with traffic at busy times of the day. In the first decade of the new century, the newly constructed Union Street (*P* 175, 239), made possible by the demolition of several buildings, made it much easier to get from one part of town to the other.

Toward its northern end, Union Street was crossed by New Bond Street, a fairly recent development. A wine merchant, Thomas Emery, had begun building houses on the north side in 1805, and a few years later, a carpenter, Joseph Cave, began building on the south side. Soon shops, such as that of a London hairdresser, began opening in the street. The old Bond Street (*P* 141) was one of the southern continuations of Milsom Street. Streets in Bath had a tendency to change names every block or two. For example, High Street ran northward from Cheap Street, then became Northgate Street. It split into two arms, the more westerly of which was Broad Street (*NA* 85). Broad Street then forked again at it ran northward. The eastern branch became Bladuds Buildings, then the Paragon, and Axford Buildings, leading past Walcot Church. The western branch became Oxford Row and Belmont, then Belvidere, then Lansdown Street, and finally left town as the road to Lansdown and Wick Rocks (*NA* 85–86). *See also* Places; Public Places.

Bathing

Health and entertainment had long been linked in the British mind. For centuries, people had been traveling to spots whose waters were supposed to have healthful properties, and as drinking from, or bathing in, mineral springs took time, they generally brought their families along. By the late eighteenth century, leisure activities had been found not only for the patients but for those who accompanied them.

However, in the early nineteenth century, a significant shift occurred in the type and location of water cures and their attendant diversions. An interest in the seaside, nurtured by the Romantic interest in nature and encouraged by the wealth of coastline available in an island nation, shifted public interest from the inland spas to coastal towns. People began traveling to the ocean to witness its beauty and to bathe, tentatively at first, in its waters. Physicians lauded the restorative properties of ocean bathing (*Sand, MW* 367; *P&P* 229; *E* 101, 102), and a few brave souls actually drank seawater, trusting that its purgative properties were cleansing them of what ailed them. Those too ill or too frightened to enter the water (*Sand, MW* 424) could at least benefit, it was thought, from breathing the salt air (*Sand, MW* 367; *E* 101, 105–106). Sanditon's promoter Mr. Parker touted the effects of the sea:

> The Sea air & Sea Bathing together were nearly infallible, one or the other of them being a match for every Disorder, of the Stomach, the Lungs or the Blood; They were antispasmodic, anti-pulmonary, anti-sceptic, anti-bilious & anti-rheumatic. Nobody could catch cold by the Sea, Nobody wanted Appetite by the Sea, Nobody wanted Spirits, Nobody wanted Strength.—They were healing, softing, relaxing—fortifying & bracing—seemingly just as was wanted—sometimes one, sometimes the other.—If the Sea breeze failed, the Sea-Bath was the certain corrective;—& where Bathing disagreed, the Sea Breeze alone was evidently designed by Nature for the cure. (*Sand, MW* 373)

Yet this effusive praise was hardly more rapturous than the testimonials of physician-enthusiasts. Furthermore, after George III partook of the benefits of bathing in 1789 at Weymouth, he gave the practice royal cachet. Thereafter, even the timid were drawn to imitate his example.

The change in preference from spas to seaside happened gradually, but by the last years of Austen's life, the shift was well underway. David Selwyn sees in *Persuasion* the official passing of the torch from one type of "public place" to another, with the pallid joys of Bath being superseded by the romantic power of the coastline. Certainly, Austen found much to observe, enjoy, analyze, and criticize in the vogue for sea-bathing, as she followed *Persuasion* with the incomplete *Sanditon*, which is set primarily in a nascent Sussex resort.

The season in seaside towns was short, confined to the late summer and autumn (*E* 91, 105) months; few people were as bold as Jane's cousin Eliza de Feuillide, who bathed with her chronically ill son at Margate in January and February 1791. Novelist Fanny Burney bathed in November in 1782, and the Austens also bathed in November on one occasion, but they preferred September and October. At Margate, Kent's principal seaside resort, lodging house proprietor William Stone charged 2 guineas a week during May and June, 2½ in July, 3 in August, and 3½ in September and early October. Prices then diminished for the less popular late-autumn, winter, and spring months. Parson James Woodforde's diary, likewise, points to the late summer and early fall as "the Months" (*Sand, MW* 389); on September 5, 1791, he noted that the Barclays, a wealthy Quaker family, "live mostly in London, but generally at this Season of the Year come down from Town for the Benefit of Sea-bathing, and prefer Cromer."

However, there were compensations for the short season. Walks on the beach were pleasant exercise, and children and adults alike enjoyed collecting seashells and even seaweed. Those with an artistic bent enjoyed the visual effects of light, cloud, and waves (*Sand, MW* 396), and those who, like Austen, were put off by the stuffiness of the spa towns could relax in the generally less formal seaside resorts. The seaside was also cheaper than a spa (*Sand, MW* 369); lodgings and fees usually cost less, which must have also appealed to the Austens.

Bathing itself was conducted extremely carefully and never alone. The days of splashing, swimming, and frolicking in the waves lay ahead; in Austen's time, one first "bespoke" or hired a "bathing-woman," as Fanny Burney did in Brighton in November 1782. She rose before dawn and found the water "cold but pleasant. I have bathed so often as to lose my dread of the operation." In order to preserve her modesty, she would have gone out not on foot or by swimming but in a bathing "machine," essentially a small wagon that could be pulled by a horse into the water. She would have disrobed down to her shift inside the machine and exited out the back so that no one from the shore could observe her. Then her "bathing-woman" would have helped her to duck completely under the water several times. The use of bathing machines (*Sand, MW* 424; *P* 96) had at least one effect on the development of likely resorts—the underwater area adjacent to the beach had to have a suitable slope, preferably gradual and predictable, so that the machines could proceed easily into the water.

Other desirable characteristics for a seaside resort were cliffs to block the wind, picturesque scenery nearby to be pursued on walks or rides, and a firm, flat beach. To these natural amenities developers added promenades for afternoon and Sunday strolls, circulating libraries (*Sand, MW* 389; *P* 130), assembly rooms, indoor seawater baths, public gardens, theaters, card rooms, and billiard rooms (*Sand, MW* 384). The building of extensive rows of uniform town houses, which had become a prominent feature of many spa towns, most notably in Bath, was not yet a feature of most of the seaside resorts. Development of extensive crescents and terraces (*Sand, MW* 384) was in its infancy there, and most such towns did not begin speculative building (*Sand, MW* 371) until the 1790s. Even then, it was a risky proposition; Southend's Royal Terrace bankrupted its builders shortly after completion. In many places, lodgers were simply accommodated in existing homes for the short duration of the fashionable season.

Austen would have had a chance to sample many of the facilities of coastal towns, as she lived in Southampton from 1806 to 1809, visited Ramsgate in 1803, and went with her family on seaside holidays to Sidmouth in 1801, to Dawlish and possibly Teignmouth in 1802, and to Lyme in 1803 and again in 1804. However, it was the bathing and scenery rather than the assembly rooms that really interested her; in Lyme, on September 14, 1804, she wrote,

> The bathing was so delightful this morning and Molly so pressing with me to enjoy myself that I believe I staid in rather too long, as since the middle of the day I have felt unreasonably tired. I shall be more careful another time, and shall not bathe to-morrow as I had before intended.

She was suspicious of resorts that had become too fashionable and too extensively developed; Margate, for example, fares badly in her works. Like many "public places," it is full of superficial acquaintances and moral temptations. In 1804, remaining in Lyme while Cassandra went on to Weymouth, she wrote that "Weymouth is altogether a shocking place, without recommendation of any kind," and though she was exaggerating in this instance for humorous effect, she appears genuinely not to have had much affection for the place.

As stated above, Margate was the most popular seaside town in Kent, with Ramsgate and Worthing as lesser attractions, but Kent was not the premier county for sea-bathing. Devon, Dorset, and especially Sussex (*Sand, MW* 368) were more amply supplied with resorts. Devonshire had Dawlish, Teignmouth, and Sidmouth; Dorset had Austen's beloved Lyme, with its often-rebuilt medieval jetty, the Cobb (*P* 96), on which walks could be taken. Sussex, during the last decade of Austen's life, was being heavily promoted and developed as a tourist destination and as a cheap retirement location for military officers on half-pay after the French Wars. Austen's fictional Mr. Heywood found the pace of development disturbing:

> Every five years, one hears of some new place or other starting up by the Sea, & growing the fashion. How they can half of them be filled, is the wonder! *Where* People can be found with money or Time to go to them! Bad things for a Country—sure to raise the price of Provisions & make the Poor good for nothing. (*Sand, MW* 368)

The principal prospects for development were chiefly in southern and western England, with the notable exception of Scarborough in Yorkshire. Scarborough, however, was a special case, as it had begun its life as a spa and had only recently turned to sea-bathing to supplement its amenities. *See also* Medicine; Places; Public Places.

Bells

Bells were used for a wide variety of purposes in Austen's time, though she mentions only a few of them. These fall into three principal categories: church bells (*MP* 82), servants' bells, and doorbells. Of these, the most public were, of course, the church bells, which rang to announce marriages (*Headache, MW* 448; *NA* 252; *E* 267), morning and evening church services, special celebrations (*E&E, MW* 30), and deaths (*Headache, MW* 448). Bells, in this context, served as public notice of an important event. Parson James Woodforde, whose extensive diary describes many of his clerical duties, mentioned being interrupted at his dinner by an unexpected ringing of the church bell, which startled him enough that he "sent to Church to enquire the reason, and word was brought me, that there was a Child then at the Church Gate for Interment." There had been a slipup, and no one had informed him that he was supposed to perform a funeral service, and it was the bell that called attention to the mistake. Funeral bells also punctuated epidemics and served as a shorthand means of alerting a whole village at once that an ailing neighbor had died.

There were rules regarding the tolling of funeral bells. Different numbers of peals, for example, announced the deaths of children, women, or men—a man's death, for example, merited nine bells. The use of the bells was also closely linked to the performance of Protestant rites. Woodforde ruled in 1788 on "a particular Question relating to the tolling of a Bell for a Child that died without being baptized," answering his correspondent "that as the Funeral Service could not be read over it, the tolling of the Bell at any time to be inadmissible."

Pulling on the bell ropes was hard work and an essential community service, so the ringers tended to be tipped or otherwise compensated for their services. On special occasions, the beneficiaries of the bell-ringing might offer money, beer, or both to the ringers (*E&E, MW* 30). Woodforde tipped the village ringers once a year, at Christmastime; on December 26, 1786, he paid them 2s. 6d.

The second type of bell was the servants' bell (*E&E, MW* 32; *Scraps, MW* 172; *Cath, MW* 213; *NA* 165, 187; *S&S* 144, 161; *P&P* 61, 111, 306; *MP* 140–141; *E* 128; *P* 37), an interior bell with two main working parts. The first of these was the bellpull, a cord of some kind that hung in a room. When tugged, it moved a spring-mounted bell in another part of the house, usually the kitchen. The kitchen might have a row of such bells, one for each part of the house likely to need service on call; the bells were not distinguished from each other by sound, but the spring kept the bell jiggling for long enough that the originating room could be determined. The sole purpose of ringing (*Evelyn, MW* 181, 183; *P* 202, 238) this bell was to summon a servant; though servants were often in attendance on the family, they were not always present, and it seemed undignified to many families to have to go running after a servant whenever they needed a message carried, a carriage summoned, or an errand run. It was undignified, in Austen's eyes, for she censures the Price household for not bothering to get its bell fixed (*MP* 379) and for resorting instead to sending children with messages or to shouting (*MP* 392) for a servant.

The third type of bell might also be attached to a board in the servants' quarters. This was the house bell (*Evelyn, MW* 189; *NA* 222) or doorbell (*P&P* 170, 188), whose pull-cord was affixed to the outside of the front door. On occasion, there was a back doorbell as well, and this would usually be distinguished by its tone from the front doorbell; some households eschewed both bells and settled for a door knocker. Visitors would ring the bell (*P&P* 177) and wait to be admitted to the house by a servant (*Sand, MW* 406), who might be a maidservant in smaller homes, a footman in wealthier ones, and a porter in the houses of those with extensive domestic staffs.

Beverages

The beverages drunk by Jane Austen's contemporaries fell into several categories, including milk, hot drinks, wines, beer, and hard liquor. On occasion, these categories overlapped, as in the case of the syllabub, a mixture of wine and milk, or as in the case of chocolate, which was a hot drink made with milk. Water is seldom mentioned as a drink on its own, though it was mixed with wine and heated to make tea and coffee. Water delivery to towns was improving after 1800, as entrepreneurs built piping systems, but prices were high and pipe maintenance erratic. Pollution of water by human, animal, and industrial waste made it often unsafe to drink from the local lake or river. There were places in the country where wells and streams could be trusted, but for the most part, when we hear of people in this era drinking water on its own, they are drinking mineral water in a spa as part of a medical cure.

Milk was drunk on its own and was very much appreciated when it came fresh from one's own farm's dairy. Town milk was far more suspect. Sometimes diluted with water, almost always thin, blue, and dirty, it was made even more unpalatable in places such as Bath by the methods of its production. The cows who yielded the local milk were kept in barn stalls rather than in grassy fields, and their inferior fodder yielded inferior milk. Still, for many people, it was the only option. It was sold in the streets by milkwomen, who carried two pails suspended from a pole across the shoulders, or directly from cows or asses who were milked at the door of each house. Some argued that the working class ought to drink less tea and more milk, but David Davies, in *The Case of the Labourers in Husbandry* (1795), responded that this, while desirable, was impossible:

Were it true that poor people could everywhere procure so excellent an article as milk, there would be then just reason to reproach them for giving preference to the miserable infusion of which they are so fond. But it is not so. Wherever the poor can get milk, do they not gladly use it? And where they cannot get it, would they not gladly exchange their tea for it?

The problem was not that people did not like milk but that good milk was simply too expensive.

The poor often had milk only in their tea, but at the other end of the social spectrum, it was enjoyed in a variety of forms. For wealthy invalids, especially those with tuberculosis, there was asses' milk (*Sand, MW* 393, 401), which had fewer nutrients than cows' or goats' milk but also had less protein and fat and was thus more easily digested. Mixed with cocoa, milk became "chocolate," a luxurious breakfast drink enjoyed at the homes of the wealthy and on special occasions. François de La Rochefoucauld, writing in 1784, explained that in England, "Breakfast consists of tea and bread and butter in various forms. In the houses of the rich, you have coffee, chocolate and so on." A correspondent to the *Gentleman's Magazine* claimed, in 1819, that cocoa was drunk throughout the nation every morning in the homes of the gentry and nobility, but he may have been overstating his case. Parson James Woodforde records drinking coffee and tea on almost every evening social occasion, but chocolate makes a much less frequent appearance in his diaries. It is associated with special occasions; on February 12, 1782, for example, it is served before and after a funeral, along with toast, cake, and wine. Chocolate was heated in special pots, similar to coffeepots, but with an aperture at the top for a stirring rod or mill, which acted like a whisk.

Other Hot Drinks

Like chocolate, other hot drinks were associated with specific purposes or times of day. For example, "caudle" was a warm drink composed of oatmeal, mild spices, water, and wine or ale; it was considered especially appropriate for invalids and for postpartum women. Negus, on the other hand, was associated with late-night parties, particularly balls held during the winter, when dancers might need a warming beverage between periods of activity.* It was made with white wine, red wine, or port mixed with lemon juice, and spices. Maggie Lane states that it was also made without sugar but with calf's-foot jelly and mixed about twenty minutes before serving to allow the jelly to melt; other recipes, such as Mrs. Beeton's from a half century later, leave out the jelly and add the sugar.

---

*Although Parson Woodforde drank white wine negus at an inn in Sherborne at 11 A.M. on August 3, 1789.

Wine

Since wine grapes grew poorly in the English climate, almost all of the nation's grape-derived wine (*S&S* 185; *E* 130, 213, 329) was imported from the Continent. From France came Burgundies, claret (light red wines, specifically those of Bordeaux—see *J&A*, *MW* 18, 23; *MP* 47), champagne,* and Frontignac (a sweet wine from southern France). Port (*P&P* 76) came from Portugal (hence its name), sherry and alicant from Spain, and Chian from the Greek island of Chios. The sweet, expensive Muscat known as Constantia (*S&S* 197) came from South Africa, while Canary sack and Madeira (*MP* 74; *E* 365) were named for the islands that produced them. "Mountain" was a sweet white wine from Malaga, while "Rhenish" hailed from the Rhine region. Many of the favorite wines were fortified with brandy for increased alcohol content. Port, for instance, had just undergone a revolution in the 1770s; new bottling technology allowed it to mature for ten to fifteen years, instead of the previous three or four, and the richer wines that resulted were extremely popular. Marsala, too, a sweet Sicilian wine, was fortified with brandy.†

However, though the English had to import their best grape wines, they themselves produced wines from other fruit, including gooseberries, currants, apricots, orange, elderberries, and quince; the Austens made gooseberry, orange, and currant wines, sometimes from homegrown, sometimes from purchased fruit. Their friend Alethea Bigg was well known for her orange wine, the recipe for which Jane requested in January 1817. Orange wine was typically made in the winter, when Seville oranges were in season, and shifted into casks in the summer. The English also created faux versions of Continental wines—a useful skill when enemy blockades disrupted supply. Contemporary cookbooks feature recipes for mountain wine, Cyprus wine, Frontignac, sack, and champagne, most of which involve steeping imported raisins for several days, then fermenting the strained liquid. Another home-brewed drink, mead, was made by fermenting honey. The Austens kept bees at both Steventon and Chawton, and they were fond of mead, despite the fact that it was losing favor in the nation as a whole. Recipes for mead varied widely; some included the sorts of spices we associate with mulled wine or cider, such as nutmeg, mace, and cloves, while others used green herbs such as marjoram, thyme, or rosemary.

Wine was most often served during dinner, especially during the dessert course (*Watsons*, *MW* 325; *S&S* 355). Neighbors sitting near each other

---

*Champagne, at this date, might be either red or white and was likely to be bubble-free.
†Frederick Accum, in 1820, printed statistics on the alcohol content of various alcoholic beverages. Madeira, he said, averaged 22.27 percent alcohol by volume; port, 22.96; white Constantia, 19.75; red Constantia, 18.92; red Madeira, 20.35; Cape Madeira, 20.51; claret, 15.1; Malmsey Madeira, 16.4; gooseberry wine, 11.84; elder wine, 9.87; mead, 7.82; and brandy, 53.39.

179   *Publish'd Dec.7, 1807, by* LAURIE & WHITTLE, *53. Fleet Street, London.*

THE CONTENTED FELLOW.

CONTENTED I am, and contented I'll be,
For what can this world more afford,
Than a girl that will sociably sit on my knee,
And a cellar that's plentiful stor'd, my brave boys!

See, my vault-door is open, descend ev'ry guest,
Tap the cask, for the wine we will try:
'Tis as sweet as the lips of your love to the taste,
And as bright as her cheeks to your eye, my brave boys!

Sound that pipe, 'tis in tune, and the bions are well fill'd;
View that heap of champaign in the rear;
Those bottles are burgundy; see how they're pil'd,
Like artillery, tier upon tier, my brave boys!

My cellar's my camp, and my soldiers my flasks,
All gloriously ranged in view:
When I cast my eyes round I consider my casks
As kingdoms I've got to subdue, my brave boys!

In a piece of slit hoop I my candle have stuck,
'Twill light us each bottle to hand:
The foot of my glass for the purpose I've broke,
For I hate that a bumper should stand, my brave boys!

'Tis my will, when I die, not a tear shall be shed;
No Hic Jacet engraved on my stone;
But pour on my coffin a bottle of red,
And say that my drinking is done, my brave boys!

The Contented Fellow, Isaac or George Cruikshank, 1807. The song that accompanies this print begins, "Contented I am, and contented I'll be, / For what can this world more afford, / Than a girl who will sociably sit on my knee, / And a cellar that's plentiful stor'd, my brave boys!" This gentleman, wearing fashionable Hessian boots and a frothy cravat, has about him most of the accoutrements of tippling—a tub to serve as a wine cooler, a decanter (on the table at far right), wine bottles, and a cellar full of casks and bottles. Transferring the contents of the casks to bottles would have been the job of a butler. Courtesy of the Lewis Walpole Library, Yale University. 807.12.7.1.

drank toasts together, and the men tended to pour the wine for the ladies. These ladies kept their consumption to a minimum, then retired and allowed the men to get down to the serious drinking, which concluded when they joined the women in the drawing room for tea and coffee. Austen also records in her letters drinking wine at parties and, mixed with water (*MP* 66; *E* 25, 365), after returning home from the theater. Her character Catherine Morland, imitating her creator, drinks "warm wine and water" at bedtime (*NA* 29). The illustration *The Glutton* (Food) shows much of the glassware associated with the serving of wine, as well as a large wine cooler.

It was the sunset of a hard-drinking age; Admiral Lord Thomas Cochrane, looking back on his youthful years in the navy, remembered being a relatively sober youth among bibulous companions. He attempted to keep from getting drunk by tipping some of his wine down his sleeve, was detected, and narrowly escaped the standard punishment of having to drink a bottle all by himself. Men often measured their wine consumption in bottles rather than glasses (*NA* 63, 64; *P&P* 20), and wine—imported wine at least—was usually more alcoholic than it is today. Parson Woodforde records substantial consumption of alcohol at his annual tithe dinners, where he entertained parishioners on a fairly lavish scale in order to console them for having to give him a share of their produce. At a typical dinner, he might have fifteen or so farmers as his guests, who would drink, in the course of the evening, copious amounts of beer, plus four to six bottles of port wine and about eight bottles of rum. As for Woodforde himself, he recorded in August 1790 that he was reducing his personal consumption of port, for health reasons, from a pint a day to a mere "2. or 3. Glasses."

Austen was well aware of the bibulousness of her age. On November 20, 1800, she called her own overindulgence in wine at Hurstborne a "venial error" and mentioned it only because the aftereffects—was she hung over?—seemed to be affecting her handwriting. She also frequently comments in her novels and letters on the drunkenness of others. The most sustained example of drunkenness in her works is *Jack & Alice*, a humorous early work in which the main characters are nearly always three sheets to the wind. They are variously "Dead Drunk" (*MW* 14), "a little addicted to the Bottle" (13), "heated by wine (no uncommon case)" (15), "dead drunk" again (19), overly fond of claret (18, 23), or overly fond of liquor in general (23). Alice's brother Jack dies of drink (25), while her father is "a drunken old Dog to be sure" (25). Most of the humor of *Jack & Alice* comes from the ridiculousness of a family resorting quite so freely to the bottle—no one in Austen's own family could have supposed this a realistic portrait—but imagine a young woman in 1860 or 1880 drawing a light, comic portrayal of alcoholism and its fatal consequences. Such levity would not have been acceptable in Queen Victoria's day, and Austen's casual jocularity says a great deal about how much heavy drinking was tolerated in her own time. Indeed, even as a product of the rowdy Georgian age, she often voices disapproval of drinking (*MP* 426). Fanny Price's father comes in for some of her strongest condemnation; Fanny is "sadly pained by his language and his smell of spirits" (*MP* 380), and the narrator, not pained but simply disgusted, concludes, "he swore and he drank, he was dirty and gross" (*MP* 389).

Wine was sometimes bought in bottles (which were occasionally disguised with a false crust around the neck to simulate age), but it was also bought in large quantities and bottled at home. Parson Woodforde, for example, would buy a quarter of a pipe of port at a time from his wine merchant (*Col Let*, *MW* 158), Mr. Priest. (A pipe equaled 105 imperial gallons, or 131.25 U.S. gallons, so Woodforde was buying enough port to fill a sizable fish tank.) Then it was decanted into a decorative container, and a label made of silver, enamel, or ceramic was hung around the neck of the decanter to identify its contents. This method of labeling wine would last until the late nineteenth century and the advent of printed paper labels that identified the wine and its vintage. If there were a butler in the home, it would be his job to bottle, store, and serve the wine, as well as to care for the decanters and glasses.

Wine was used as an ingredient in food and in mixed drinks such as the caudle described above. Another mixed drink containing wine was the syllabub, a mixture of milk or cream and wine. Traditionally made with milk fresh from the cow and served on the spot, it was by Austen's time a drink prepared beforehand. The frothed milk or cream was separated and allowed to stand and drain, then replaced over the "thin." The contrast between the translucent mixture at the bottom of the glass and the stiff, long-lasting foam at the top was the chief attraction of a syllabub.

Beer

Beer and ale are less present in Austen's works than wine, although beer was, along with tea, one of England's most popular drinks. Historically, it had been brewed at home, supplying much the same place at the table that water would now; servants typically drank at least a quart a day. Mrs. Austen brewed beer at Steventon in the last years of the eighteenth century and at Chawton cottage many years later, but home brewing was slowly being overtaken by commercial brewing. In 1788, a total of nearly 5 million barrels were produced by common brewers and brewing victuallers such as innkeepers and publicans, and 9 million barrels were produced at home. By 1800, commercial and domestic brewers were producing roughly equal volumes, and by 1815 home brewing had fallen behind.

Several types of beer and ale were made. Ale and beer were divided into "strong," "table," and "small" varieties, differentiated from each other by alcohol content*; an 1806 letter written by Jane's mother at Stoneleigh describes the mansion's "strong beer" and "small beer" cellars. Pubs might offer a cheap brown ale, a more heavily hopped brown ale, and an expensive, high-quality pale ale; when the three types were mixed together

---

*Frederick Accum, writing in 1820, estimated the alcohol content of various beers and ales: Burton ale, 8.88 percent alcohol; Edinburgh ale, 6.2 percent; Dorchester ale, 5.5 percent; brown stout, 6.8 percent; London porter, 4.2 percent; London small beer, 1.28 percent. Beer brewed in the countryside tended to be less alcoholic than beer brewed in London.

in one glass, the resulting concoction was known as "three threads." A very dark, heavily hopped, bitter, high-alcohol beer was introduced in 1722; soon thereafter, it became known as "porter" because of its popularity with London porters. It was popular with brewers, too, because the dark color and strong taste hid impurities. They built enormous production vats; the Meux brewery, in 1795, had a vat that could hold 20,000 barrels (almost 750,000 gallons). Much to the brewers' chagrin, in the late eighteenth century, pale ales came back into fashion.

Brewing beer, like baking bread or making wine, was a delicate business subject to the vagaries of bacteria. Since the science of fermentation was poorly understood, brewers had few tools, such the thermometer (in use by commercial brewers from the 1780s) and the saccharometer (which measured alcohol content and thus helped to demonstrate how much fermentation had taken place). However, things could and did go wrong, and most specialized brewing knowledge took the form of damage control. Was the beer cloudy? Add isinglass (a gelatin derived from fish) to "fine" it, that is, to remove impurities. Was the beer sour? Add six special compound balls to each barrel; their marble, oyster shells, or chalk would reduce acidity, while their isinglass and bean flour would act as refining agents. Did it taste bad in general? Add spices. Was it too pale? Toss in some tobacco, treacle, or licorice. Was the head not frothy enough? Add some "beer-heading," a combination of green vitriol, alum, and salt.

Some of these processes were benign. Others were truly dangerous, such as the addition of black extract. This was made by boiling *cocculus indicus* into, in Frederick Accum's words, "a stiff black tenacious mass, possessing, in a high degree, the narcotic and intoxicating quality of the poisonous berry from which it is prepared."* Opium, tobacco, poppy extract, and *nux vomica* were also used to make beer seem stronger; the last of these was a bitter tree seed that contained strychnine. Porter, the easiest of the beers to adulterate, was supposed to be made of browned malt and three pounds of hops to every thirty-six gallons of liquid. The hops added a bitter flavor and also acted as a preservative. However, hops were expensive, and pale malt was cheaper than brown, so commercial brewers made a paler, weaker brew and resorted to various stratagems to disguise it as genuine porter. To color the porter, brewers added caramelized sugar; to give it a bitter flavor, they added poisonous wormwood or quassia, the bitter, narcotic derivative of a Jamaican tree. Capsicum, grains of paradise, ginger, coriander, and orange peel were also used as flavorings. Sulphuric acid was added to "bring beer forward," that is, to simulate eighteen months' aging in much less time.

One form of beer was made neither with barley nor with hops but with

---

Cocculus indicus berries contain a convulsive poison called picrotoxin, which can be used to stun fish and kill lice.

spruce tree needles. This was the spruce beer, more similar in spirit to root beer than to ale, that Frank Churchill copied a recipe for. It was made from the tips of spruce branches, boiled in water, sweetened with molasses, and mixed with yeast.

Spirits

Gin, brandy, and rum were the most widely drunk types of hard liquor (*MP* 4); each, according to Frederick Accum in 1820, was more than 50 percent alcohol by volume. Gin, also known as "Hollands" or "Geneva," was made domestically and had acquired a fairly nasty reputation earlier in the century, when its low price and wide availability occasioned Britain's first major urban drug crisis. Dram shops had advertised that a person could get drunk for a penny and dead drunk for twopence; rooms with straw on the floor were provided for those who wanted to pay a little extra to have a place to sleep off their liquor. The crisis was eventually controlled by the imposition of taxes that raised the price of gin. Taxation made it harder to acquire cheap gin, but not impossible, as illegal distilleries were happy to supply their customers "by moonshine." Parson Woodforde was an avid customer; in 1781 he drank "some smuggled gin which I liked." On 1792 he noted that a local gin smuggler had received a light punishment from some excise officers, and on March 7, 1794, he "Had 2. Tubbs of Geneva brought me this Evening by Moonshine, 4. Gallons each Tub."

Brandy came from abroad, principally from France, and was also a popular item with smugglers. On December 29, 1786, Woodforde recorded,

> Had another Tub of Gin and another of the best Coniac Brandy brought me this Evening abt 9. We heard a thump at the front Door about that time, but did not know what it was, till I went out and found the 2 Tubs—but nobody there.

Rum came from even farther away. It was a by-product of the West Indian sugar industry, and since Britain had quite a number of sugar colonies, rum was fairly cheap. The liquor fermented from leftover molasses formed the basis of grog, the sailor's typical drink afloat, a mixture of rum, water, and lime juice. Ashore, rum was mixed up as punch, a popular drink at all festive occasions, but especially when men got together for club events. Woodforde typically used two bottles of rum to make each large bowl of punch. He also drank rum outside his house; a glass of rum and water (*MP* 387) cost him threepence at a local inn in May 1794. *See also* Coffee; Dishes; Food; Tea.

Bon Mot

A bon mot (*Lesley, MW* 111; *MP* 94) is a clever or witty utterance. The phrase, which derives from French, is pronounced "boh moh," with just a hint of an *n* at the end of the first word. It was one of many French words and phrases that made their way into common use among the gentry and the aristocracy of Austen's time. Another of these expressions was *ton* or *bon ton*, which meant fashion or the fashionable world. *See also* French.

Brickbat

A brickbat (*NA* 113) sounds as if it might be some sort of bricklayer's tool, but it is in fact a fragment of brick—according to the *Oxford English Dictionary* (OED), technically a piece of brick less than half the length of a full brick. In an urban setting such objects made handier missiles than rocks, and they were often used in riots and interpersonal disputes.

Cards

Cardplaying (*Col Let, MW* 160; *Watsons, MW* 343; *S&S* 143; *P&P* 35, 38, 54, 346; *MP* 248; *E* 100, 311, 382) was one of the few forms of entertainment that cut across all classes and both genders. Men of all classes enjoyed blood sports such as cockfighting, but such sports were frequently considered inappropriate for women, either as spectators or as participants. Music was enjoyed by all classes, but not every family could afford a musical instrument for after-dinner amateur concerts. Cards, however, were cheap, widely available, and considered entirely acceptable (except by the most radical religious enthusiasts) for everyone. Contemporary prints show people of all ranks playing cards, and even if the purpose is sometimes to make fun of the pretensions of servants who imitated the card parties of their employers, it also becomes clear that card games had broad popular appeal.

The equipment for card games was mostly the same as today. Decks of cards were not identical throughout Europe, but as the English deck corresponded to the modern deck, with its clubs, diamonds, hearts, and spades, running ace through king, nothing need be said about alternate decks elsewhere. One distinct difference from modern decks, however, was the lack of numbers or letters in the corners of the cards. This was not much of problem with the face cards, which were fairly easily identifiable, but it must have occasioned some confusion with some of the eights, nines, tens, and so on. A certain amount of ongoing pip-counting would have been necessary. Another difference between the decks of Austen's time and those of today was that there was no design on the backs of the cards; they were simply white. The obvious disadvantage of the undecorated back was that it was easy for gamblers to make small marks on the backs of the cards that could be easily detected by alert eyes. Even unintentional smudges could give an advantage to those who wished to cheat. Therefore, a conscientious host or hostess would provide new packs of cards (*E* 290), sealed with a government stamp, to ensure the cleanest possible backs. The cards would be acquired and passed around to the various tables by a servant, who would then receive "card money," or tips, for his trouble. The relatively impoverished Watsons, in Austen's unfinished novel of the same name, cannot afford a new deck for every evening and must rely instead on finding a used but "tolerably clean pack" (*Watsons, MW* 357).

All card games involved a certain amount of gambling, and players often kept track of their winnings not with actual money but with "fish" (*Watsons, MW* 357; *P&P* 84, 166), the eighteenth-century version of the poker chip. Fish were small pieces of ivory that were, indeed, vaguely fish-shaped; if it was necessary to have items marking two different monetary values, then

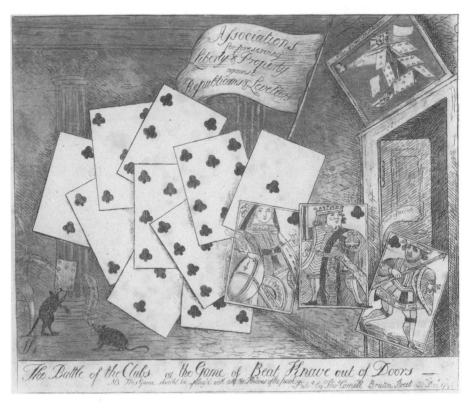

The Battle of the Clubs, Sayers, 1792. This satirical print takes as its subject the formation of anti-Jacobin, conservative associations (the "clubs" of the title) to counter the revolutionary spirit that threatened to make its way from France to England. The "knave" is Charles James Fox, a politician sympathetic to reform. The print shows clearly the style of playing cards of the time, with no numbers on the lower cards and no initials on the face cards. The backs of the cards would have been blank rather than patterned. Courtesy of the Lewis Walpole Library, Yale University. 792.12.21.1.

"counters," a marker with a different shape, were added to the fish. They were kept in piles in front of the players on the card table (*Watsons*, *MW* 332, 357, 359; *S&S* 144, 145, 151; *P&P* 47, 54, 76, 166, 169; *MP* 203, 249), which appears, to judge from contemporary illustrations, to have been covered with a green mat similar to that used on poker tables today. Most card tables were square, but a few tables, earlier in the eighteenth century, had been designed with three-player games in mind and were triangular. Since card games were usually played in the evening, candles were a necessity on the table (*E* 290), and they were ideally placed at the corners of the table so that each player's hand was illuminated without the need to lean forward and possibly expose one's hand. Card tables with candles at the corners may be seen in the illustration *A Rout* (Entertainment).

The usual time for cardplaying was between tea (*S&S* 144, 200; *P&P* 342) and supper (*P&P* 84), that is, in the evening (*S&S* 54), when people amused themselves in various ways. Those fond of music would play or listen; if there were enough people interested in dancing, they might form a set in the drawing room. The majority of the family and their guests, however, would probably not be interested in dancing or in playing music. They needed an alternative form of entertainment, which was usually a card game of some sort. For the servants, relaxing after the efforts of preparing, serving, and washing up after the meal, playing cards was a way of passing the time with fellow servants from other households until the guests were ready to leave. At balls, a special card room (*Cath*, *MW* 221; *Watsons*, *MW* 327, 328; *NA* 20, 52; *E* 254), adjacent to the ballroom, was set up for people who had no interest in dancing. In "public places," such as balls and seaside resorts, the card room was a chief attraction for the older members of a family.

Some people did more than settle on cards as an alternate activity, however. They were enthusiasts who made special efforts to secure fellow players. For women, this meant hosting or attending card parties (*Watsons*, *MW* 350; *E* 20, 156, 290; *P* 245), where no effort was made to provide music or dancing at all. The whole purpose was to play cards and to gamble on the outcome, for higher or lower stakes depending on the participants' income. Men also attended such card parties, but they had another outlet for their interest in the form of card clubs. Clubs of all kinds were popular during the eighteenth and nineteenth centuries—scientific clubs, musical clubs, book clubs, sporting clubs, and card clubs. Card clubs, which were predominantly formed for the purpose of playing the intellectually demanding game of whist, tended to be established and populated by men (*Watsons*, *MW* 324–325; *E* 68, 197).

Card games fluctuated in popularity, even within a single family. In or before 1809, for example, Jane appears to have introduced the game of speculation to her brother Edward's family, and she pretended to be dismayed at its ouster in 1809 by a new game, brag. Parson James Woodforde, an avid card player, went through periods of playing only or mostly quadrille, punctuated by brief flirtations with cribbage and loo. Later, he developed a fondness for whist and commerce, both of which began to appear frequently in his accounts of games played.

Whist

Whist (*Watsons*, *MW* 324–325; *S&S* 166; *P&P* 76, 82, 84, 342; *MP* 119, 227, 239, 246; *E* 96, 325) is the game most commonly associated with the eighteenth and nineteenth centuries, and it was indeed popular. It was similar to bridge, in that it was a game for four players, with tricks taken by partners who remained partners for the duration of the game. Partners were chosen by cutting the cards, with the two highest and the two lowest forming the teams. James Beaufort, in 1775, noted that the "Game of Whist requires great attention and silence, as it chiefly depends on the memory, and derives its name from the taciturnity that should be observed in playing it." It was played by people of both sexes, but it was generally considered to be more popular with men; writing from her brother Edward's house in September 1813, Jane notes that a social gathering included "A Whist Table for the Gentlemen, [and] a grown-up musical young Lady to play Backgammon with [her niece] Fanny."

The ranking of cards was according to the system used in most modern games, with ace high and deuce low, and players were required to follow suit. Trump was determined by the last card dealt, which was dealt faceup and remained there until all but the dealer had played a card on the first trick, whereupon the trump card was added to the dealer's hand. Complex rules of etiquette, mostly involving the unintentional revelation of information about a player's hand, could result in players compelling the offender to play in a certain manner or to reveal information in a formal way; these rules were so numerous and specific that it would be tedious to relate them here.

A rubber (*MP* 240, 246; *E* 81, 326) of whist consisted of three games, the winner of each game being the partnership that first scored five points.* "Book" was six of the thirteen tricks, and each trick (*MP* 245) above book counted for one point; a team that collectively held ace through jack of the trump suit ("honors") scored four points; a team that held three of the honors scored three points. A game might take more than one hand to win. If this were the case, and the leading partnership had four points at the beginning of a new hand, honors were not counted toward winning points.

Once five points were reached and the game won, the actual score became meaningless, except as it determined the value of the victory. A game's value was determined by comparing the score of the victorious team with that of the losing team. A shut-out or "treble" gained the winning team three points; a score of five or more to two or fewer was a "double," worth two points; a score of five or more to the other team's three or four points was a "single," worth one point. Two points were awarded to the winners of the rubber, who, if they won the first two games, did not need to play the third to establish their victory. The losers' winning game points, if there were any, were subtracted from the winners' games to establish the final score.

Scoring Example 1

Team A wins the first game, 5 points to 3. Team B wins the second game, 6 points to 0. Team A wins the third game, 5 points to 2.

---

*Until about 1804 or shortly thereafter, the game was to ten points, with only two points being awarded for three honors.

Game 1	Single	1 point for team A
Game 2	Treble	3 points for team B
Game 3	Double	2 points for team A
Rubber points	—	2 points for team A

1 + 2 + 2 for team A = 5

5 − team B's 3 points = 2 total points for team A; team A wins the rubber.

Scoring Example 2

Team B wins the first game, 5 points to 1, and the second game, 5 points to 4. No third game is played, as team B has already won.

Game 1	Double	2 points for team B
Game 2	Single	1 point for team B
Rubber points	—	2 points for team B

2 + 1 + 2 = 5 total points for team B

It is tempting to read every reference to a "rubber" (*Watsons, MW* 336; *S&S* 145, 151, 178) in Jane Austen's works as a reference to whist, primarily because the term "rubber" is now so strongly associated with bridge, but this assumption would be incorrect. A "rubber" was a grouped series of rounds in a number of types of card games, including casino. It was one of many specialized terms that had to be learned by new card players, and the novelist Frances Burney congratulated herself on having added it to her vocabulary, writing in April 1780, "I returned to finish the Rubber;—don't I begin to talk in a good old Cattish manner of Cards?"

Quadrille

Austen mentions a number of card games by name. Quadrille (*P&P* 88, 105, 166; *E* 21), one of Parson Woodforde's favorites, makes several appearances. Though whist, a forerunner of bridge with very similar rules, was thought of as the quintessential thinker's game, quadrille required every bit as much concentration. Its rules seemed deliberately designed to foil the beginner. Descended from a three-player game, ombre, it was a game for four players and was played with an ordinary pack from which the eights, nines, and tens had been removed. The ranking of cards differed from the modern order in most games and also varied within the game depending on whether the suit was red or black, trump or not. There were also cards that had specific names, based on what suit was trump:

Name	Is This Card	When This Suit Is Trump
Spadille	Ace of Spades	Any suit
Manille	Deuce of Spades	Spades
	Deuce of Clubs	Clubs
	Seven of Hearts	Hearts
	Seven of Diamonds	Diamonds
Basto	Ace of Clubs	Any suit
Punto	Ace of Hearts	Hearts
	Ace of Diamonds	Diamonds

The first three of these, *Spadille, Manille,* and *Basto,* were collectively called *matadores* and had a privilege in play; when a lower trump card was led, the holder of one of these three cards did not have to follow suit. She could play any card she liked. However, if a higher *matadore* was led as the first card in a trick, and the player held a lower *matadore* and no other trump, she was obliged to play it. When clubs or spades were trump, the ranking, from highest to lowest, was as follows:

Trump Suit	The Other Black Suit	The Red Suits
Spadille	King	King
Manille	Queen	Queen
Basto	Jack	Jack
King	7	Ace
Queen	6	2
Jack	5	3
7	4	4
6	3	5
5	2	6
4		7
3		

When hearts or diamonds were trump, the ranking changed:

Trump Suit	The Other Red Suit	The Black Suits
Spadille	King	King
Manille	Queen	Queen
Basto	Jack	Jack
Punto	Ace	7
King	2	6
Queen	3	5

Trump Suit	The Other Red Suit	The Black Suits
Jack	4	4
2	5	3
3	6	2
4	7	
5		
6		

In other words, face cards had the same relative value as in most games today, while the number cards varied, valued either from highest to lowest or lowest to highest depending on the color of the suit. Some cards were always trump, while others took on a special value only if their suit was named trump.

The cards were dealt counterclockwise, beginning with the player to the dealer's right, in three rounds: three cards to each player, another three cards to each player, and four cards to each. Each player began, according to James Beaufort in 1775, with seven *mils* worth of markers—a *mil* being equal to ten fish, and a fish being equal to ten counters. The value of each token was agreed on beforehand. The players also agreed on the number of "tours" to be played, a tour equaling four hands, or one turn for each player to be dealer. Ten tours, or forty hands, was typical.

Before the deal, each player placed a counter into the pool as an opening bet. The dealer also offered a fish, making the total pool equal in value to fourteen counters. Beginning with the eldest hand (the player to the dealer's right), the players each had a chance to bid for the right to name trump. The easiest bid to make was "asking leave," in which the bidder proposed to take six of the ten tricks in partnership with another player. This player was chosen by "calling a king," that is, naming a specific king not held by the bidder and enlisting the holder of that king as a temporary partner.* The partner, however, did not immediately identify herself; the partnership became evident only during the course of play. If no one bid higher, the successful bidder named trump, called her king, and played the hand, following suits and trumping as in most modern trick-taking games, with the exception of the special privileges of matadors and, of course, the unconventional ranking of the cards.

A player with a stronger hand could bid *sans prendre*, offering to take six tricks without an ally. This bid ranked higher than asking leave, but an earlier bidder also ranked higher than a later bidder and was given a chance, if she liked, to up her bid to *sans prendre* and regain control of the hand.

*If the bidder held all the kings, she could call a queen instead. Rarely, for strategic reasons, a player might "call" a king that she held in her own hand, which was perfectly legal but made her, in secret, a player *sans prendre*. The exception to calling a king was the king of trump, which could not be called. Likewise, if the player opted to call a queen, the queen of trump could not be called.

If she declined, the contract went to the new bidder, and play proceeded. At any time between the bidding and the taking of the first six tricks, a player could "declare the vole," announcing that she would attempt to take all ten tricks. If an especially confident bidder chose to bid the vole from the outset, this overruled a bid *sans prendre*. The vole was normally declared, if at all, after the first six tricks were taken, but on occasion the cards justified more confidence. Parson Woodforde, on April 30, 1783, recorded an unusually good hand:

> I played the finest Sans Prendre Vole to Night, that I ever had—Not a loosing [*sic*] Card in hand—It was Mattadores, 9 black Trumps in Spades and the King of Hearts—I was the last Player; after the first Card was played, I declared the Vole.

A player who did not choose to declare the vole, after taking the first six tricks, could simply claim her winnings and stop the hand. If she continued to play, however, she was assumed to be declaring the vole, and each player, including the player trying for the vole, had to ante three more counters to a separate pool. A player who had a partner and was considering trying for the vole had to ask, after winning the first six tricks, "May I?" and wait for her partner to respond yes, or no. A further condition was that, if a king had been called, the king in question had to be played before a vole could be declared.

If no player was willing to bid, the bid became "forced *spadille*." The holder of the ace of spades was obliged to play the hand, calling a king (or a queen if she held all the kings), and naming a trump suit. Play continued in the same manner as for other bids, except that a player playing forced *spadille* was not permitted to declare the vole.

At the end of the hand, the distribution of winnings was nearly as complicated as the ranking of the cards. A player *sans prendre* won the pool, plus the pool for the vole if applicable, plus additional chips from each player.

Condition	*Bonus from Each Player*
Won 6 tricks	Amount in pool
Each *matadore*	1 counter
Each trump in uninterrupted descending order after the three *matadores*, if bidder has all three *matadores*	1 counter for each trump in sequence
Consolation (with a partner)	2 counters
Consolation (*sans prendre*)	5 counters
Consolation (vole)	1 fish

If the bidder had called a partner, the partner split these winnings equally and could also contribute to the collection of *matadores* and *punto*.

The bidder could lose in two ways: by *remise* or by *codille*. *Remise* meant taking only four or five tricks; *codille* meant taking three or fewer. Taking no tricks at all was called *devole* but appears to have borne no special penalties. A player who lost by *remise* doubled the size of the pool—alone if she had played *sans prendre*, with her partner if she had had one. She (or they) then paid to each player the appropriate consolation, plus the amount that the bidder(s) could have claimed for holding *matadores*, had she (or they) won. A player who lost by *codille* paid the same sums, but her partner (if she had called one) did not have to contribute to the losses, and the opposing players, in addition to being paid by the loser, divided the pool between them. If partners lost by *remise*, but the original bidder still failed to take at least three tricks on her own, the called partner was likewise exempted from losses, and the original bidder paid the entire sum. The exception to this rule—there was always an exception in quadrille— was in the case of forced *spadille*, where losing partners split the losses regardless of how many tricks the nominal player of the hand took.

Voles complicated matters still further, as they had the side pool and could be announced at different points in the game. A vole that was bid at the outset, where the bidder took at least six tricks, lost nothing but the side-stake for the vole, which was divided among the opposing players. No one was "beasted" or "basted" (forced to double the size of the pool). A vole declared after the first six tricks were taken, however, was subject to substantial penalties; the player had to pay each opponent what she would have won had she succeeded in her attempt.

To make quadrille even more complicated, the rules varied somewhat by place and time, and there were a host of ways in which a player could be beasted or otherwise penalized, mostly for errors in play that affected the outcome of the hand. The rules for betting were further adjusted according to agreements between the players before the game began. Some players, for example, agreed to pay an additional sum called "premiers" to a team or *sans prendre* player who took the first six tricks in a row. Some households agreed to play for very low stakes; Parson Woodforde, in 1786, mentioned playing quadrille for "1d per fish," which implies that no lesser counters were used. His quadrille winnings or losses on a particular night usually amounted to no more than a shilling or two, which also implies low stakes, remarkably equal levels of skill, or fewer than forty hands played in an evening.

Quadrille seems to have been especially popular with women, although Woodforde played it with men and women alike. It was considered distasteful by some; Charles Lamb, in *The Essays of Elia* (1823), likened it to "the petty ephemeral embroilments of the little Italian states, depicted by Machiavel; perpetually changing postures and connexions; bitter foes today, sugared darlings to-morrow; kissing and scratching in a breath." No doubt the constantly shifting alliances, the potentially high stakes, and the secrecy were what made it appealing to its devotees.

Loo

Loo (*P&P* 37, 47), like quadrille, involved the taking of tricks, but, unlike quadrille, was designed for five or more players. It was thus a "round game" (*Watsons*, *MW* 354, 359; *MP* 239)—a game for a variable number of players, as opposed to games like whist or quadrille, which had a fixed number required. Round games were socially useful, as they accommodated odd numbers of players; Austen's characters with an affinity for whist or quadrille are frequently found scrambling to find a fourth for a game (*S&S* 144, 166; *P&P* 342) or to find occupation for superfluous players (*MP* 239).

Loo arrived in England via France in the mid-seventeenth century and had a three-card and a five-card version. In both versions, players anted a specified number of counters. In each hand, players opted to remain in the game (and pay an additional sum into the pool) or bow out at no charge. Players who remained in had to take at least one trick or add to the pool. There were two schools of thought about how to make this addition. In limited loo, the sort preferred by Parson Woodforde, the penalty was a small, fixed sum. In unlimited loo, the amount was equal to that already in the pool, which meant that if there were successive hands where many players opted to compete, the pool could grow geometrically.* It is probably unlimited loo, then, that was being played at Netherfield, when Elizabeth Bennet declined to play for fear the stakes were too "high" (*P&P* 37).

In three-card loo, the cards were conventionally ranked, with ace highest and deuce lowest, except for the purpose of cutting to see who deals first, in which case ace is low. The deal passed clockwise, and the dealer added three fish to the pool, whether or not it contained leftovers from previous hands. Cards were dealt one at a time, three to each player and three more to a ghost hand called "Miss." The remaining cards were left unused, and the top card was turned over to choose trump. Starting at the dealer's left, players announced whether they would opt out or stay in; the first player in the rotation who chose to do so could stay in and exchange his own hand for "Miss." He could not, however, look at "Miss" before deciding, nor could he choose to drop out of the hand after seeing what he had gotten in exchange. If he made this exchange, and no one else remained in play, he won the pool. If no one stayed in, the dealer won the pool. If only one player stayed in and did not choose to take "Miss," the dealer could either play for himself, winning or losing accordingly, or "defend Miss," playing his own hand to prevent the other player from getting the whole pool, but neither winning nor losing anything for himself. Players won a third of the pool for each trick taken; a

---

*A game whose pool grows in a similar manner is the poker variant known as "Guts." In college in the 1980s, I saw a penny-ante game of guts grow until the pot stood at over $160.00. Small wonder, then, that Elizabeth Bennet shrinks from playing a game where small bets can reach disastrous heights.

Loo in the Kitchin or High Life Below Stairs, 1799. Servants play loo, a "round game." The predictable pun is made by the maidservant who leans flirtatiously close to the be-wigged footman near the center of the table: "I am Lew'd," she informs him. The ample woman in the best chair near the fire is almost certainly the housekeeper. Courtesy of the Lewis Walpole Library, Yale University. 799.6.25.2.

player who remained in and took no tricks had to contribute the agreed-upon amount to the pool. Failure to take a trick was known as "being loo'ed," a term that invited inevitable puns on the word "lewd."

Play was fairly straightforward, with players required to follow suit. The exceptions concerned the play of trump, which was somewhat more complicated, though nothing in comparison with quadrille. The player to the dealer's left led the first trick and was required to lead

the ace of trump

> or, if he does not hold the ace of trump,

the king of trump

> or, if he does not hold the king,

his highest trump card

> if playing against only one opponent, or

any trump card

> so long as he holds more than one.

All players were required to do so if they could not follow suit; if a previous player had already trumped a trick, they were required to play a higher trump card if possible and if they could not follow the original suit. The trick went to the player of the highest card in the original suit or the highest trump card, if trump had been played; the winner led the next trick and had to lead trump if possible.

Five-card loo was similar, except that players competed for a fifth of the pool rather than a third. The ranking of the cards was the same as in three-card loo, except that the jack of clubs always counted as the highest trump card. Nicknamed "Pam," this card derived its name from "Pamphile," a stock medieval character associated with lechery. Choice of dealer and the order of dealing were the same as in three-card loo, though the dealer now contributed five fish to the pool instead of three, and cards were dealt in groups of three, then two, rather than one at a time. There is no ghost hand. The top card of the leftovers was turned up for trump.

The players, as above, announced that they would pass or play. Each player could opt, once, to discard any number of cards from his hand and take replacements from the leftover stack. Before tricks were taken, the holder of a flush could attempt to take the whole pool. A flush was five cards of one suit, as in poker, with Pam acting as a wild card. A flush with Pam was highest, followed by a trump flush, followed by a nontrump flush with the highest top card. High flush took the entire pool, and deal passed to the previous dealer's left, with a new stake of five fish. Sweeping the pool in this manner was called "loo'ing the board."

If no flushes were exposed, play began at the dealer's left and proceeded as in three-card loo, with Pam behaving as a trump card for the purposes of following suit. Anyone leading the ace of trump could call, "Pam be civil," barring the holder of Pam from overtrumping, unless Pam was the only trump in the holder's hand.

Lottery Tickets

Lottery tickets (*P&P* 74, 84), like loo, was a round game. I have been unable to locate rules for its play that are contemporary with Austen's writings, but the OED defines it as a game in which players bet an amount of their choosing and received cards; "winning" cards were then selected randomly, and whoever held the specified cards received a prize. It was, in other words, a game of pure luck, which makes it the natural sort of game to appeal to the brainless Lydia Bennet (*P&P* 76–77).

An 1859 edition of Hoyle gives three different ways to play the game. It is impossible to tell which set of rules was used in the Meryton game. In the first method of play, two full decks of cards were used, with a dealer for each. Each player anted into the pool and then received one card, the "prize," on which she placed a number of fish from the pool, the exact number being left to her discretion. Each player now received from the second deck a "ticket" card, and the prize cards were turned over. If a player had a ticket card that matched a prize card, she got the fish associated with it; any unclaimed fish went back into the pool. It is unclear from the directions given whether the ticket card needed to match the prize card in both suit and rank.

One of the alternate sets of instructions allows half of a single deck to be used rather than two full decks. One red and one black suit are retained, with one suit being used for the prizes and the other for the tickets; in this case, it is evident that only the rank needed to match, so perhaps this was the case in the two-deck version as well. The other alternate set of rules was to deal three cards facedown in the middle of the table from one deck and to use the second deck for tickets. Players paid a set fee per "ticket" and could purchase as many tickets as they liked, with the resulting pool of fish or counters being distributed unevenly on the three cards. As in the first set of rules, unclaimed prizes went back into the pool for the next deal.

Casino

Casino (*Watsons*, MW 332; S&S 144, 175), sometimes spelled "Cassino," could be played by two to four players. The ace was worth 1 point, numbered cards were worth their face value, and the jack, queen, and king were worth 11, 12, and 13, respectively. Each player received four cards, and four were dealt faceup in the middle of the table, while the leftovers were set to one side. Unlike games such as whist, quadrille, and loo, it was not a game that involved taking tricks. The point of the game was to score points by capturing cards from the center section.

Captures were accomplished by equaling the value of one or more cards with cards from one's own hand. For example, if the four faceup cards were a five, a two, a seven, and a jack, player A could use a seven from her own hand to capture *either* the seven *or* the five and the two together. Then she placed the captured card(s) and the card she used to capture them facedown in front of her. If she managed a "sweep," however—a capture of all the faceup cards—the capturing card remained faceup next to her captured cards; this enabled players to keep track of sweeps for scoring purposes. A player who ran out of cards drew four more from the leftovers; if all the faceup cards were removed in a sweep, or if a player could not make a capture, she had to "trail," that is, to leave one of her own cards among the faceup cards in the center.

When all the cards had been dealt and captured, players calculated their totals, using the following formula:

most cards captured	3 points
tie for most cards captured	0 points
Great Cassino (ten of diamonds)	2 points
Little Cassino (two of spades)	1 point
most spades captured	1 point
each ace	1 point
each sweep	1 point

How to Pluck a Goose, Thomas Rowlandson, 1802. The canny old ladies have clearly gotten the better of the callow officer in this print. They are gambling, as gambling was an integral part of all card games at the time, and playing on a typical square card table covered in green baize. Candles, which were often placed at the four corners of such tables, are absent in this picture, implying perhaps that this game is being played in the daytime. The nature of the game is made clear by the lady on the far right, who announces that she has "great Cassino." The officer, incidentally, still possesses his traditional soldier's queue, which he will retain for another few years until the custom is banned. Courtesy of the Lewis Walpole Library, Yale University. 802.6.10.1.

The game, or rubber, was usually to eleven points. Later versions of casino introduced the concept of "building," which allowed players to group cards prior to making a capture in a later turn, but this did not become a uniform part of the game until the twentieth century, and it is not known whether Austen could have been familiar with this variation.

Piquet

Piquet (pronounced "picket") was, like loo, a French import, but it had been known in England, by one name or another, for centuries before Austen's birth. It was played by two people—in Austen's works, by Colonel Brandon with Mrs. Jennings (*S&S* 309), Mr. Woodhouse and Mrs. Goddard (*E* 211), and Mr. Hurst and Mr. Bingley (*P&P* 47). Like quadrille, it was played with a nonstandard deck: thirty-two cards, the six through deuce of each suit being first removed from the pack. Aces were worth 11 points, face cards 10, the others their numerical value.

Players traded the deal back and forth, with the nondealer playing first. The dealer dealt the cards either by twos or threes until each player had twelve cards, leaving the other eight from which to draw. Cards were now exchanged, using the leftover eight cards. The nondealer drew first, discarding up to five of his own cards* and taking replacements; he could glance secretly at any of these top five cards that he left behind. Then the dealer was permitted to exchange for as many of the remaining leftovers as he liked. Before or after drawing cards, either player could declare a "blank"—an absence of face cards—and score 10 points for it; if the nondealer did so, he was not permitted to look at the cards he had drawn until the dealer had drawn cards, the blank had been announced and shown, and the requisite number of cards had been discarded from his hand.

Points were now amassed for special collections of cards within the hand. The player with the longest suit (called "point") received 1 point per card in the suit; if his longest suit and his opponent's longest suit were equal in length, the point values of the cards were added to determine who had the more valuable suit; if the suits were still equal in value, neither scored. Players also received points if they had numerical sequences within a suit, such as queen, jack, and ten of diamonds. As with the longest suits, only the longer sequence scored, the point value of the cards, as represented by the top card in the sequence, was used as a tiebreaker, and, if the sequences were still equal, no points were scored. They also received points for sets (cards of the same rank); only sets of tens, jacks, queens, kings, or aces counted, and again only the best set scored.

Card Group	Points Awarded
Longest suit (point)	1 per card (e.g., 5 points for 7-9-10-J-A)
Sequence of 3 (*tierce*)*	3 points
Sequence of 4 (*quart*)*	4 points
Sequence of 5*	15 points
Sequence of 6*	16 points
Sequence of 7*	17 points
Sequence of 8*	18 points
Set of 3 (*trio*)*	3 points
Set of 4 (*quatorze*)*	14 points

*Only the best sequence or set counts, and only the player with the better sequence or set may score for it.

---

*The nondealer had to exchange at least one card. The dealer had no such requirement.

If one player reached 30 points before the other player had scored any, the first player received an additional bonus of 60 points, known as *repique*. For this purpose, it often mattered that points were scored in order as above—blank, then point, then sequence, then set. At any point in the counting, if one player reached 30 before the other scored, he received the 60 points for *repique*, even if the other player receives points later in the tally.

If neither player earned *repique*, the nondealer could still earn 30 points, or *pique*, if he earned a total of 30 points before the dealer earned any. He could add to his points now, as could the dealer, by leading and taking tricks.

Leading to a trick, including the first trick	1 point
Taking a trick when opponent leads	1 point
Taking the last trick	1 point
Taking 7 or more tricks	10 points
Taking all 12 tricks	30 points (plus the 10 for taking 7 or more)

The game ended at 100 points. As there were a good many points to keep track of, players often used counters or a board, like a cribbage board, to mark their relative scores.

Speculation and Brag

Speculation (*Watsons*, MW 354, 358; *MP* 239–242) was a round game with a conventional deck and conventional ranking, that is, ace high to deuce low. A mid-nineteenth-century description indicates that the object was to acquire the highest trump card. The dealer anted six fish, each other player four fish, and each player was dealt three cards, one at a time, but did not look at them (*MP* 240). After the cards were dealt, the next card was turned faceup. The suit of this card was "trump," though no tricks were taken. Only trump cards counted toward the resolution of the game, and the others were useless except as decoys.

If the revealed trump card was an ace, the dealer immediately won the pool; if not, he could auction it off to the highest bidder or keep it himself. The player to the dealer's left then turned her top card faceup and, if it was a better trump than the dealer's, could keep it or sell it as she chose (*MP* 241, 242–243, 244). If it was not a superior trump card, the next person in clockwise rotation revealed his top card, and so on. If a trump card was revealed and purchased, the player to the purchaser's left was the next to expose a card. The holder of the highest visible trump card was not obliged to turn any cards faceup until all the rest had been uncovered. When all cards had been uncovered, the holder of the highest trump card got the pool (*MP* 243). The players anted again, and the next hand was apparently dealt without shuffling the used cards back into the deck, as the 1847 description advises,

> To play this game well, little more is requisite than recollecting what superior cards of the trump suit appeared in the preceding deals, and calculating thereby the probability of the trump offered for sale proving the highest in the deal.

If no trump were dealt to any player (other than, obviously, the first card turned up at the end of the deal), the fish remained in the pool, everyone anted again, and a new dealer dealt another round of cards. Anyone turning over the ace of trump, of course, won automatically.

Jane Austen was fond of speculation, having introduced it to Edward's family at Godmersham, and several of her letters chart the rise and fall of this game in his home. In December 1808, she writes that "I hope Speculation is generally liked." On January 10, 1809, she responds to a letter that evidently reported the eclipse of speculation by brag, another card game:

> The preference of Brag over Speculation does not greatly surprise me I beleive [*sic*], because I feel the same myself; but it mortifies me deeply, because Speculation was under my patronage;—& after all, what is there so delightful in a pair-royal of Braggers? it is but three nines, or three Knaves, or a mixture of them.—When one come to reason upon it, it cannot stand its ground against Speculation—of which I hope Edward is now convinced.—Give my Love to him, if he is.

A week later, she must have heard that brag, in its turn, had been momentarily ousted by some other game, for she sent a nephew the following verse:

> "Alas! poor Brag, thou boastful Game! What now avails thine empty name?—Where now thy more distinguished fame?—My day is o'er, & Thine the same.—For thou like me art thrown aside, At Godmersham, this Christmas Tide; And now across the Table wide, Each Game save Brag or Spec: is tried."—"Such is the mild Ejaculation, Of tender hearted Speculation."

Brag was a three-card descendant of the fifteenth-century game of "post and pair." Three cards were dealt, the last faceup, and players competed for three stakes. The first stake was awarded for the highest faceup card, the second for the best combination of three cards, and the third for the player whose cards were closest to 31 points without going over. As the game evolved from the early eighteenth century to the mid-nineteenth, it acquired wild cards or "braggers": jack of clubs, ace of diamonds, and nine of diamonds. The second stake was awarded to the holder of the highest pair, or, better yet, the highest pair royal (a set of three, also called a *prial*). By the mid-nineteenth century, additional winning hands had been added, so that, from lowest to highest, hands were ranked as follows:

Pair

Flush (all one suit)

Run (three cards in numerical sequence)

Running flush (all one suit and all in sequence)

Prial

Brag fell out favor not merely in Edward (Austen) Knight's household, but in the nation as a whole. It was in decline already by the first decade of the nineteenth century and was decidedly out of favor by midcentury. It was to acquire new life in the late nineteenth century as a single-stake game related to poker.

Cribbage

Cribbage (*Watsons, MW* 354), like piquet, kept a running total of players' points. An ordinary pack was used, and two players were each dealt six cards, one at a time. Each player discarded two cards facedown into an area on the table called the "crib" (*MP* 283), with the intention of retaining the most valuable combinations. Cards were valued at their face value for this purpose, with face cards worth 10 points each and aces worth 1.

Combination	Point Value
Fifteen (combination of cards with face value of 15)	2 points
Pair	2 points
Prial or pair royal (3 of the same rank, as in brag)	6 points
Double pair royal (4 of the same rank)	12 points
Run (3 or more cards in numerical sequence)	1 point per card in the run
Flush (4 of the same suit)	4 points

The nondealer cut the remaining cards, and the dealer turned the top card, the "starter," faceup. The nondealer then laid down cards one at a time, trying to lay out a sequence that formed a pair, a run, or some other point-scoring group. When he could no longer add to a point-scoring sequence without exceeding a face value of thirty-one points (*MP* 283), he passed the initiative to the dealer, who likewise laid out as many related cards as he could, one at a time, without exceeding 31, tallying points for runs, pairs, and so on as they went, and continuing to lay down cards until they could lay down no more without exceeding a face value of thirty-one points. Additional points were then scored as below:

Condition	Additional Points
Starter is a jack	2 points to dealer
Last card played in revealing runs, etc.	1 point to that player
	2 points if running total equals exactly 31
Hold jack of starter's suit	1 point

Hands were then scored using the starter card as a fifth card in both hands, and the crib was turned over and scored, using the starter as a fifth card, and its points awarded to the dealer. The game was usually to 121 points, and the score was recorded by using a board and pegs. One peg for each player marked the old score, while the other peg marked the new score. Each time points were added, the rear peg was moved ahead the requisite number of holes.

Cribbage appears to have been especially popular at Manydown, home of the Austens' friends the Biggs. In February 1813, Jane wrote to Cassandra that "In a few hours You will be transported to Manydown—& then for Candour & Comfort & Coffee & Cribbage."

Commerce

Commerce was a popular game among the Austens' circle of friends. In November 1800 she wrote to Cassandra, "The three Digweeds all came on tuesday, & we played a pool at Commerce." In October 1808, she informed Cassandra that she had played the game again, for particularly high stakes given her limited income:

> We found ourselves tricked into a thorough party at Mrs Maitlands, a quadrille & a Commerce Table, & Music in the other room. There were two pools at Commerce, but I would not play more than one, for the Stake was three shillings, & I cannot afford to lose that, twice in an even^g—

Novelist Frances (Fanny) Burney also played commerce and, though she rarely gave details about card games, offered a portrait in 1779 of a particularly silly, flirtatious fellow player that reads like an episode in one of Austen's own novels. The offender in this case was Peggy Pitches, the nineteen-year-old daughter of a wealthy merchant:

> When it came to her turn to deal, she mixed the cards, let them drop, tittered, and flung herself into sundry attitudes, and then begged the Captain to shuffle and deal for her.
> Captain Fuller, to Ridicule, I believe, her affectation, took the contrary extreme; he put on an awkward, clownish Countenance, shuffled the Cards with a ludicrous clumsiness, and making various vulgar grimaces, *licked his Thumb* in order to deal!
> This failing, her next attempt was more spirited; she looked over his Hand, and, declaring all cheating was allowable at Commerce, snatched one of his Cards to make her own Hand better.

The Captain, however, had so little gallantry, that instead of regarding this theft as a favour, and offering her her choice of what she pleased, he insisted upon having his Card returned!—and when she resisted, recovered it, in an easy manner, by exposing all her Hand, and then, very composedly, proceeded with the Game without comment.

Commerce was played with a standard fifty-two-card deck, with conventional ranking and with aces either high or low. Players anted a set amount to the pool, and each was dealt three cards. A ghost hand, the widow, was dealt three cards as well. The dealer could exchange his hand for the widow's, and after he had decided whether to exchange or not, players in clockwise rotation opted to exchange a card with one from the widow's hand or not. Exchanges continued until two players had knocked on the table to indicate that they were satisfied with their hands. All hands were then revealed, and the best won the pool.

The ranking of hands was as follows, from lowest to highest:

Point   Highest total face value of the three cards, with aces equaling 11 points, face cards 10, all others their number of pips; ties broken by highest number of cards in a single suit or, if these are equal, proximity to dealer's left

Sequence   A three-card "straight flush"—cards of the same suit and in numerical sequence; aces can be low or high for this purpose, but sequences cannot wrap around; that is, A-K-Q is legal, as is A-2-3, but 2-A-K is not.

Tricon   A set of three cards of the same rank, e.g., three 3s or three kings.

There were variations on the method of exchanging cards. In one version, also known as "trade and barter," new cards could be bought from the dealer or exchanged, blind, for cards from the next player's hand; in this version there was no widow.

Vingt-et-un

The name of this game is simply French for "21," and it is the game known in modern times either as twenty-one or blackjack. Known either as vingt-et-un or vingt-un (*Wat, MW* 358), it was played by the Austens on at least two occasions in January 1801. On Wednesday, January 21, Jane wrote to Cassandra that she dined at Deane and "played at Vingt-un"; five days later, she reported, "We met nobody but ourselves, played at *vingt-un* again, and were very cross."

In vingt-un, the dealer (*Wat, MW* 358) dealt two cards facedown to each player, including himself. Beginning with the player to his left, he offered to deal each player more cards faceup. Each player could refuse to take cards or stop accepting cards at any time. The goal was for all the cards, both faceup and facedown, to total 21 points, or as near as possible to 21 without going over. Face cards counted for 10 points each, numbered cards counted as their number of pips, and aces could be worth either 1 or 11 depending on the player's preference. An ace and a ten or face card, a natural 21, repaid the player double the normal winnings. If he went over 21, he lost his stake immediately.

When all players had ceased to take new cards, the dealer turned over his own cards and attempted to take cards himself until he had the best possible hand. At that point, he won the stakes of all who had equal or lesser hands, and paid out stakes to players with better hands. In some cases, the dealer received a double stake from all players if he himself had a natural 21; some played with the rule that a nondealer with a natural 21 received a forfeit from all players and the right to be the next dealer. Modern blackjack permits a player to "split" identical cards, at the outset, into two different hands, matching the original stake for the second hand. Perhaps this is what Tom Musgrove means when he refers to Lord Osborne "overdraw[ing] himself on both his own cards" (*Wat, MW* 358). Perhaps Lord Osborne has split a pair of fours, or some other pair, into two hands, and gone over 21 on both. *See also* Gambling; Games.

Carriages and Coaches

To modern readers, eighteenth- and nineteenth-century carriages (*Cath, MW* 213, 219–220, 240; *L&F, MW* 85, 90, 107; *H&E, MW* 38; *LS, MW* 275, 291; *Coll Let, MW* 151; *Scraps, MW* 177; *Watsons, MW* 327, 335, 354, 357; *NA* 44, 60, 161, 210, 222; *S&S* 77, 106, 109, 160, 175, 197, 222, 249, 286, 312, 333, 341; *MP* 74, 104, 251, 273, 375; *P&P* 30–32, 84, 102, 194, 219, 257, 281, 286, 315, 353, 358; *P* 50, 123, 135, 163, 176; *E* 19, 110, 112, 187, 213, 217, 230, 323, 374, 451) are something of a mystery. What on earth is the difference between a barouche and a landau, or for that matter between a landau and a landaulette? What makes a vehicle a chair or a chariot, a chaise or a coach, a stagecoach or a post-coach? Why does Austen refer to the same vehicle by different names, calling it here a carriage and there a coach, a chaise, or a curricle (*E&E, MW* 31; *P&P* 166, 293; *NA* 229, 233; *P* 105, 117; *S&S* 67; *MP* 203)?

Interpreting all these terms requires both an understanding of the concrete features that distinguished one type of carriage from another and also a comprehension of the use of, and attitudes toward, the different vehicles. Carriages, though they were owned by a minority of the population, served the same purpose for that population that cars do for today's drivers. Not all cars are the same in shape, use, or emotional subtext, and we have no difficulty recognizing the difference between a little red convertible, a pickup truck, a postal delivery truck, a public bus, and a family sedan. Likewise, Jane Austen's contemporary audience knew what sort of person would drive or ride in a curricle, a dogcart, a mail coach, a stagecoach, and a post chaise.

"Carriage," though it technically meant the lower structure of the vehicle, the part that attached to the wheels, in general usage meant any type of wheeled passenger vehicle. (It was analogous, in other words, to the word "car" today.) Several features then distinguished one type of carriage from another. These included how many wheels it had (two or four), whether it had a roof and whether that roof was retractable, how the lower part was "sprung" (attached to the wheels with springs), how the upper part was shaped, how many horses drew it and whether they were harnessed singly or in pairs, whether there was a "box" or coachman's seat, and whether that seat was attached to the main body, how many people could fit on a seat, what sort of cargo room was available, and whether it had passengers seats facing forward and backward, or only forward.

Coaches: The Stagecoach

A coach, for example, was a large, four-wheeled vehicle with a nonretractable roof, and seats facing both forward and backward. The roof made it a "close carriage" (*Watsons, MW* 315), suitable for driving in all types of weather. It served multiple purposes, though it was unfashionable for private family use. It was more commonly found as a public conveyance: as the stagecoach, running along a specified route with scheduled stops, much like a long-distance bus today; and as the mail coach, carrying mail and a limited number of passengers at high speeds for high prices, much like an express intercity train.

The stagecoach was a decidedly unfashionable way to travel (Austen's brother Frank once prevented her from traveling by stagecoach), though the foreign traveler Parson Moritz found stagecoaches "quite elegant, lined in the inside with two seats, large enough to accommodate six persons; though it must be owned when the carriage is full the company are rather crowded." Part of the stigma attached to stagecoach travel was the lack of freedom. Whereas, in a post chaise, one had control over destination, companions, and pace, in the stage one was subject to external schedules and to the crowding, snoring, dreary conversation, and offensive personal hygiene of one's fellow-travelers. These travelers could be quite numerous. In addition to the six who were crammed rather tightly inside, four were legally allowed to ride on the roof of the coach. The limit of four, however, was routinely exceeded; Moritz saw one stagecoach with at least twelve people riding on top. (Private coaches run by the gentry would hardly have had riders on the roof, which is why Austen's youthful description of a visit by a family of eleven, all crammed into the same coach [*E&E, MW* 31], would have been humorous to the small audience who read it.) Passengers also sometimes rode with the luggage in the rear basket (*L&F, MW* 103, 106) or rumble-tumble, but Moritz found this inconvenient; when the coach went downhill, he was buried in luggage. Outside passengers, who included women as well as men, paid half fare.

The Union Coach

The Union Coach, Isaac Cruikshank, 1799. The political satire in this print may be ig-
nored for the present purpose. However, the basic features of a stagecoach are well represented: the large basket in back, in this case carrying passengers rather than luggage; a
rider on the top of the carriage; the coachman on his box, sitting on a green hammer-
cloth fringed with gold; and the inside passengers crowded together. In the original
print, the box and upper parts of the coach are painted black, the door and lower panels
purple, and the trim yellow; the wheels are orange but may have been intended by the
artist to be the traditional red. The springs from which the compartment was suspended
are visible at front and back as the tall, arched pieces curving in toward the coach.
Courtesy of the Lewis Walpole Library, Yale University. 799.6.4.6.

The advantage of the stagecoach was its price. It cost only 2d. or 3d.
a mile plus tips to the coachman (who expected 2s. to half-a-crown) and
the guard who looked out for highwaymen, as opposed to a post chaise,
which cost 1s. 6d. per mile, plus a 3d.-per-mile tip to the post-boys who
rode and directed the horses, plus sixpence to each inn's ostler for tending to the horses (*Watsons, MW* 349). Nonetheless, the potential savings
are an insufficient attraction for even the poorest of Austen's characters—
at least in the novels. In the Juvenilia, where even the heroes and heroines are seldom taken seriously, there are a few references to the
stagecoach (*LS, MW* 273–274), and these allusions are not calculated to
make the reader think fondly of the experience. A character in *Love &*
Freindship, for example, takes a "Stage-Coach" for Edinburgh and finds
that while it is too dark to count the passengers, one of them is snoring
loudly (*L&F, MW* 102–103). The reference to darkness indicates that this
was a night-coach, the sort that did not even permit its travelers to sleep
overnight in the relative comfort of an inn. Night-coaches were thought
to be the worst of the worst; even the "Stage Waggon" (*F&E, MW* 10),

in which passengers thumped along in a springless, fabric-roofed, glorified farm cart, permitted its passengers to alight for the night at inns. Night-coaches had the worst of everything—the worst coachmen at the worst pay, coaches with rotting harness and moth-eaten cushions, horses half in the grave.

In the Juvenilia, Austen contrasts genteel characters (or those aspiring to gentility) with the inconveniences of the stagecoach for humorous effect. In one comic portrait, Austen depicts a gentleman who has fallen on hard times and turned his last genteel possession, his coach, into a stage traveling every other day between Edinburgh and Sterling. An acquaintance, seeking to help this unfortunate man, forgoes a post chaise and rides repeatedly in the stage, much to the annoyance of his daughter:

> It has only been to throw a little money into their Pockets (continued Augusta) that my Father has always travelled in their Coach to veiw the beauties of the Country since our arrival in Scotland—for it would certainly have been much more agreable to us, to visit the Highlands in a Postchaise than merely to travel from Edinburgh to Sterling & from Sterling to Edinburgh every other day in a crouded & uncomfortable Stage. (*L&F, MW* 105)

In the novels, the stagecoach is used less satirically, though not always without humor. The vulgar Anne Steele dismisses it as a method of travel far beneath her dignity:

> "Well, my dear," said Mrs. Jennings, "and how did you travel?"
> "Not in the stage, I assure you," replied Miss Steele, with quick exultation; "we came post all the way, and had a very smart beau to attend us. Dr. Davies was coming to town, and so we thought we'd join him in a post-chaise; and he behaved very genteelly, and paid ten or twelve shillings more than we did." (*S&S* 218)

Mrs. Norris, like Miss Steele, betrays much about her personality in her attitudes toward the stagecoach. Early in *Mansfield Park*, she suggests that Fanny be conveyed to London by the stage, betraying both her parsimony and her sense that Fanny does not deserve the conveniences automatically accorded to the gentry:

> They may easily get her from Portsmouth to town by the coach, under the care of any creditable person that may chance to be going. I dare say there is always some reputable tradesman's wife or other going up. (*MP* 8)

Austen does not take issue with Mrs. Norris' assumption that only tradesmen and their like would ride the stagecoach; instead, she uses this bit of dialogue to show how unfeeling Mrs. Norris is in expecting a child and a gentlewoan's daughter to ride in a stagecoach, supervised by a stranger. Austen's contemporaries would have considered the demotion to the stagecoach almost as inappropriate as the absence of a family member or family servant as chaperone.

Austen seems to have little animosity for stagecoaches, as long as they are ridden by people of the right sort. Robert Martin, for example, appears to take a stagecoach without any censure from the author, indeed with hardly any comment at all. The vehicle is not specifically identified as such, but Mr. Knightley indicates that Mr. Martin "came down [from London] by yesterday's coach" (*E* 472); the use of "yesterday's" implies a schedule, which in turn implies the stagecoach. Mr. Martin's taking a stagecoach, however, elicits no shock or surprise; he is not, technically, a gentleman, and therefore not used to having the world bend its timetables to suit him.

Those who took the stage had to adjust to a particularly inconvenient timetable, for, in addition to all its other woes, the stagecoach was slow. Because it was large and heavy, and because it might be carrying a large number of passengers and their baggage, it tended to be drawn by four (*L&F, MW* 90–91) or even six horses, but this expedient did not make it speedy. It was slower still when pulled by the "unicorn" arrangement, with a pair of horses near the wheels (one ridden by a post-boy), and a single horse in front. The "flying" coaches, which changed horses frequently, were faster, but the regular coaches simply stopped for hours to "bait," or rest, the same horses.

Still, despite its inconveniences, the stagecoach was an important part of English life. It enabled people of limited means to make long journeys for either business or pleasure, fostering communication between different parts of the nation and stimulating Britain's nascent tourist industry. On festive occasions, the coaches shared in the revelry. Coachmen decorated their vehicles with holly on Christmas, with garlands of flowers on May Day, and with wreaths of laurel after important military victories. While the stagecoach was not an everyday sight in small towns—there were only 400 stagecoaches in 1775, the year of Austen's birth—it was common enough in the large towns. Steventon, where Austen grew up, had no stagecoach stop, but Deane, a nearby town, had departures twice a day to London.

The Hackney Coach

A hack or hackney coach (*Cass, MW* 45) was simply a rented vehicle, which might or might not come with its own coachman; the Parkers, in *Sanditon*, rent a coach but bring their coachman from home (*MW* 364). The hack coach was a step above the stagecoach, but it was still disdained by people who could afford to keep their own carriages. Those with their own coaches typically used their own horses for the first stage; these horses would rest and be sent back to their home stable, while the family traveled on with horses rented at an inn, called hack horses or post-horses (*Sand, MW* 406; *P&P* 351). At the next inn, they would exchange horses again, and so on.

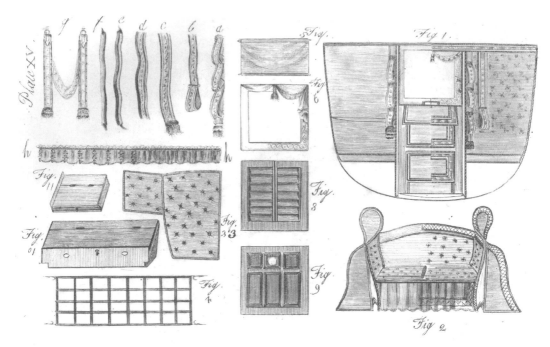

Inside Fittings of a Coach, from William Felton's *Treatise on Carriages*, 1796. Letters a to h "represent the various trimming with which the linings and hammercloths are ornamented":

a. handholds
b. swing-holder—"a long loop for the arm to rest in"
c. glass string or holder to lift the window, "made of a yard of lace, ornamented with a flat tassel at the one end, and nailed on the glass frame at the other; having button-holes worked, by which the glass is hung to any agreeable height."
d. binding-lace or trim
e. pasting-lace "to nail the taped part over the other nailing of the cloth"
f. seaming-lace (more trim)
g. footman-holders—handgrips
h. fringes "which are seldom used but to hammercloths"

The interior is shown half with plain, half with deluxe decoration. "The plain side has the pockets, the falls, and valents, trimmed with a narrow two-inch lace, and the holders with a two and a half. There are many linings used plainer than this; but agreeable to the present fashion, this is as plain as a lining ought to be." The deluxe side has more ornaments and festoon curtains. Figure 3 (shown as 33 above) shows a squab or sleeping cushion, a padded side for the passenger to rest against more comfortably, and Figure 4 depicts a net, which Felton describes as "a convenience sometimes placed across the roof between the doors, for the purpose of containing light parcels free from injury." He shows various kinds of window treatments: spring curtains, festoon curtains, venetian blinds, and common shutters. Library of Congress.

The procedure was the same for hackney coaches, except that all the horses were "hack" or rented (*Cath, MW* 214). There is always something vaguely tacky about hack vehicles in Austen. When she wants to convey a sense of comfortable, sophisticated travel, she uses the phrase "post-chaise" or something similar. Hackney coaches are associated with poverty, disgrace, anonymity, and disappointment. Lydia Bennet's transfer from a chaise to a hackney coach indicates the beginning of her fall into scandal (*P&P* 274–275, 282), and it is two "Hack-Chaises" that bring the laughably small population of the eagerly expected vacationing seminary to Sanditon (*Sand, MW* 414, 420). Likewise, Catherine Morland's return to her home after being expelled from Northanger Abbey takes place not in a string of fashionable phaetons with "three waiting-maids in a travelling chaise-and-four," but in a "hack post-chaise," which "is such a blow upon sentiment, as no attempt at grandeur or pathos can withstand" (*NA* 232).

Like sedan chairs or like taxis today, hackney coaches could be found by chance as they returned from carrying passengers, or they could be found reliably at stands where they waited for customers. Like stagecoaches, they bore painted marks of identification—in this case not nicknames but numbers (*P&P* 293)—and like stagecoaches, they had four wheels. Two-wheeled hackney coaches would come into use in London later in the nineteenth century, becoming a standard symbol of urban life, but Austen would have been familiar with the four-wheeled variety.

The Mail Coach

If one had to travel in a public vehicle with a regular schedule, the mail coach (*MP* 266, 443) was the superior alternative. Invented by John Palmer of Bath in 1784 to take advantage of improving road conditions and to replace post-boys on horseback, the mail coaches delivered the nation's mail with comparative speed and safety. The safety came in part from the presence of a guard on every coach, armed with a cutlass and a blunderbuss with a folding bayonet. Paid only 10s. 6d. a week, the guards nevertheless made a fairly good living by collecting tips and also by surreptitiously carrying parcels in the coach-box for less than the going rate. The latter practice was tolerated by the Post Office except in egregious cases, such as one guard's attempt to privately deliver 150 pounds of meat and ice.

The guards, who between their various sources of income might make a few hundred pounds a year on good routes, became confident, sometimes arrogant, fellows. John Byng wrote of the Shrewsbury Mail guard in 1793, "The guard of the mail coach is one of the grandest and most swaggering fellows I ever beheld, dressed in ruffles and nankeen breeches, and white stockings." Some along the routes complained, too, that the guards, who sat in boredom and isolation at the back of the coach, amused themselves by shooting their blunderbusses at livestock. They had reason to be cocky, for they ruled the mail coach and all in it. Even the coachman was subject to the guard's authority, and the guard could report him for drunkenness, rudeness, or incompetence. The guard determined when the mail would leave each stop, kept an official watch in a locked case inside a pouch (for verifying that the schedules were kept), and turned the watch in to postmasters at intervals for inspection, winding, and repair.

They were responsible for the integrity of the mail, which they kept at the rear of the coach in a locked box; in practice, however, they seem to have been lax about this part of the duty, for guards were regularly reprimanded and fined for leaving their mail boxes open. (The typical fine in 1792 amounted to a week's pay.) If the carriage broke down, the guard had final say over what to do—try to effect repairs, hire a post chaise, or go on ahead himself with the mail on one of the lead horses. If necessary, he was to walk; the mail had to proceed one way or another to its destination. Furthermore, guards had to jump on and off the coach on downhill slopes to set the iron shoe skids that served as brakes and then to replace them on their hook. They helped in some cases to change horses, often in the dark, if the local ostlers were absent or asleep. All of these tasks were performed night and day, in good weather and bad, over forty- to sixty-mile stretches before a quick sleep and a journey of equal length in the opposite direction.

In order to facilitate these various duties, guards had two weeks' training in basic repairs at Millbank, where the "patent coaches" that carried the mail were made. They had to be literate, under thirty years of age, and willing to take an oath of fidelity and to sign the postmaster's "Sheet of Instructions." Two people had to vouch for their character, and each guard had to post a bond of £20. Despite all these requirements and the obvious hardships of the job, there was always a long waiting list for posts. The guard was a little king on the road, chief officer of a vehicle invested with unique prestige. He got to blow a horn that signaled the toll gates to open, and all other coach traffic had to give way before the mail, and, of course, there were the pay, the tips, and the illicit extra money to be made from carrying private letters and packages.

For passengers, the mail coach was nearly as exciting. Author Thomas DeQuincey gushed about the virtues of this mode of travel. Chief among its attractions were speed and, more important to DeQuincey, the sensation of speed. The railroad train, which he was to ride later in life, was nothing compared to it. On the train there was speed without the awareness of speed; it was not at all the same. He liked being one of the three outside passengers, who rode on the roof, rather than one of the four "insiders," though he acknowledged that there were advantages to riding inside. Insiders got to eat in the dining room at inns, for example, while outsiders, who paid a lower fare, had to eat in the kitchen. Writing of the period around 1804 or 1805, he said,

> Up to this time . . . it had been the fixed assumption of the four inside people . . . that they, the illustrious quaternion, constituted a porcelain variety of the human race, whose dignity would have been compromised by exchanging one word of civility with the three miserable delf-ware outsides.

Even to have kicked an outsider might have been held to attaint the foot concerned in that operation, so that, perhaps, it would have required an act of Parliament to restore its purity of blood.

DeQuincey and his comrades, as Oxford students, could afford to sit inside, but riding outside had its delights: "The air, the freedom of prospect, the proximity to the horses, the elevation of seat," and the possibility that the coachman could be bribed to let them drive for a while. He adored the prestige of the mail and the fact that turnpike gates and other travelers alike had to get out of the way:

> Look at those turnpike gates: with what deferential hurry, with what an obedient start, they fly open at our approach! Look at that long line of carts and carters ahead, audaciously usurping the very crest of the road. Ah! traitors, they do not hear us yet; but, as soon as the dreadful blast of our horn reaches them with proclamation of our approach, see with what frenzy of trepidation they fly to their horses' heads.

Some passengers found the speed and the springiness of the mail coach nauseating, with the result that once they arrived at an inn, they were unable to eat anything, but DeQuincey seems not to have suffered from motion sickness. He was intrigued by everything, from the comic sight of a cart of apples or eggs overturned as it struggled to get out of the mail coach's way to the exact amount of time it took to change horses at each stop. In 1804 or 1805, on the Bath road, he estimated that it took just under seven minutes to make the exchange; a decade later he thought it took eighty seconds.

One unique feature of the mail coach was its paintwork. Carriages in general could be any color, though private carriages tended to be painted in sober dark colors—black, brown, or green, for example. The silly fiancée of Austen's youthful work *The Three Sisters* wants her husband's new carriage to be "blue spotted with silver" but he insists on "a plain Chocolate" with unfashionably low springs (*3S, MW* 58). Public conveyances such as stagecoaches tended to advertise themselves by means of bright colors, lots of text, and memorable nicknames: the Flying Machine, the Telegraph, and so on. The mail, by contrast, had a set and undeviating color scheme: red wheels, maroon doors and lower body, black upper body. Each door bore the royal arms, and on each of the four upper panels (one to each side of the door, on both sides of the coach) appeared one of the stars of the principal orders of knighthood: Garter, Bath, Thistle, and St. Patrick. The fore-boot bore a symbolic reference to the current king, and the hind-boot displayed the particular coach's number. As opposed to the stagecoaches, which were heavy with wording, the mailcoaches simply bore the names of the terminal cities of its route and the words "Royal Mail." DeQuincey, unsurprisingly, approved thoroughly:

Once I remember being on the box of the Holyhead mail, between Shrews-bury and Oswestry, when a tawdry thing from Birmingham, some "Tallyho" or "Highflyer," all flaunting with green and gold, came up alongside of us. What a contrast to our royal simplicity of form and colour in this plebeian wretch! The single ornament on our dark ground of chocolate colour was the mighty shield of the imperial arms, but imblazoned in proportions as modest as a signet-ring bears to a seal of office.

This stagecoach compounded its offense of tackiness by daring to race the mail coach; such impromptu races were common enough along the turn-pike roads. The mail coach won—of course.

Because the mail coach was so far superior to the stage, and because it originated in Bath, readers may assume that it is this type of coach that Mr. Elton takes to Bath. Austen says that his baggage was being conveyed "to where the coaches past" (*E* 186). It seems, in light of the way she uses the stagecoach and the mail coach in her novels, that the coaches in ques-tion are mail coaches. Furthermore, it is hard to imagine the haughty and ambitious Mr. Elton stooping to ride in a stagecoach, whereas it is easy to see him as one DeQuincey's "illustrious quaternion."

Private Coaches

However, not all coaches were operated as public vehicles. Many fami-lies had their own coaches (*Cath*, *MW* 197, 225; *S&S* 274), thinking of them in much the same way that people today might think of a van or a minivan: as a serviceable, practicable, but not especially speedy or flashy way to get a large number of passengers from point A to point B. Private coaches could be distinguished from public ones chiefly by their paint-work. No labels indicating destinations were present, nor were the ubiq-uitous symbols of the Royal Mail. Instead, a simple color scheme was usually chosen, with a coat of arms or symbols of nobility if the owner was entitled to them. These arms were generally painted on the door of the coach, below a window or "glass" that could be opened; Mr. Elliot's arms are thus accidentally covered by a greatcoat hung out the window (*P* 106). One presumes that Sir Walter Elliot's carriage had arms painted on it, though no mention is made of it; Lady Russell's certainly does (*P* 158). In the Juvenilia, we encounter a lord's carriage decorated with a coronet (*L&F*, *MW* 91), a kind of heraldic crown depicted in slightly different ways according to rank. Princes, dukes, earls, viscounts, and barons were all en-titled to use coronets above their arms, with the ranks being indicated by varying numbers of leaves or pearls; see the illustration *The Pacific En-trance of Earl-Wolf, into Blackhaven* (Landau) for a carriage decorated with an earl's coronet. Given that only a minority of people could afford to keep a carriage, that of these only some would choose to keep a coach (e.g., rather than a chaise or a gig) and that each coach was custom-made and decorated, it is not surprising that people could often recognize pri-

A TRIP TO BRIGHTON,
OR. THE P— AND HIS REDUCED HOUSEHOLD RETIRING FOR THE SUMMER SEASON.

A Trip to Brighton, Dent, 1786. This satirical print, which shows the Prince of Wales and his wife on their way to Brighton, deliberately portrays them as strapped for cash and thus traveling in less than the highest style. Accordingly, baggage is stowed on top of the coach, while the coachman keeps eggs, meat, and carrots under his seat. Humbler people than the prince, however, no doubt carried belongings in this way when they traveled in their coaches. The print also shows how coaches were decorated with the owner's heraldic symbols. Side glasses, or mirrors, appear above the door and in each upper panel; the one nearest the coachman has the blind drawn. Courtesy of the Lewis Walpole Library, Yale University. 786.7.15.1.

vate coaches and make a guess as to the identity of the occupants (*L&F*, *MW* 108).

The occupants, or at least the owners, were seldom likely to be dashing young men eager to make a good impression. Coaches were stolid family vehicles, a fact reflected in Austen's works. Her fictional coach owners are substantial and often middle-aged: Lady Greville (*Coll Let*, *MW* 158–159), Lady Russell (*P* 157), the Edwardses (*Watsons*, *MW* 314), the elder Musgroves (*P* 50), the Middletons (*S&S* 119), and the decidedly frugal and unfashionable Heywoods (*Sand*, *MW* 373). The Bennets, too, need a coach for its seating capacity; after all, they have five daughters to transport (*P&P* 75, 298). A notable exception, not meant to be taken seriously since he apparently owns one of every type of carriage ever invented, is Mr. Clifford of *The Memoirs of Mr. Clifford*. He travels in his coach and four but also has the choice of "a Chariot, a Chaise, a Landeau, a Landeaulet, a Phaeton, a Gig, a Whisky, an italian Chair, a Buggy, a Curricle

& a wheelbarrow" (*Clifford, MW* 43). As will become clear later in this article, Mr. Clifford would have had to be the king of England to afford so many carriages.

Parts of a Carriage: The Mechanism

Carriages had many different parts, all of which fell into two broad categories: the "carriage" or actual mechanism for moving, and the "body" or passenger-holding compartment. How each part was constructed determined what type of carriage resulted. To avoid confusion, since in common usage "carriage" also meant almost any wheeled vehicle, I use the words "mechanism" and "compartment" to distinguish between the lower and upper halves of the carriage.

The mechanism, which in a typical carriage-building establishment would be constructed mostly by a blacksmith and a woodworker, was based around the "perch," a substantial keel-like piece of timber that ran from front to back. The perch was typically about 9'2" long for a chariot, 9'8" long for a coach. To this, the coach builder (*NA* 61, *S&S* 215) attached two axles: a rear axle that stayed fixed and a fore axle that was attached to the perch by a large iron bolt called the king bolt or perch bolt, allowing it to turn to the right or left. Wheels were slipped onto the axles and held in place with linchpins: pegs that passed through the axle and, in theory, kept the wheels from falling off. In practice, linchpins often came loose, leading to crashes and to various attempts to improve upon this primitive design.

Wheels themselves had undergone a significant improvement not long before Jane Austen's birth. In 1767 a Mr. J. Hunt devised a way of fitting metal bands around the wooden rims, thus extending the life of carriage wheels. These wheels usually had elm naves, oak spokes, and ash or beech felloes (rims); the number of spokes varied according to the size of the wheels:

Wheel Size	Number of Spokes
3'2" diameter	8
4'6"	10
5'4"	12
5'8"	14

The largest wheels could be as tall as an adult. Often brightly painted, they attracted attention with their color, their movement, and their characteristic clatter as they bumped over gravel or cobblestones. However, they were a constant source of worry for the coachman, and not only because of their tendency to fall off.

Braking was always a problem in a coach. Horses could pull uphill reasonably well, though it was sometimes slow going with a heavy load (*MP*

189), but they were less able to manage their speed going downhill. The carriage was connected to the horses' harness by a comparatively delicate set of poles and by padded leather collars. On gentle slopes the horses could brace themselves against the collars, slowing the coach, but on steep hills, the horses and their harness were no match for a heavily laden coach, carrying perhaps ten passengers, a coachman, and hundreds of pounds of baggage. Every descent of this kind was perilous, made more so by the almost complete lack of mechanical brakes on carriages. In most cases, the "brake" was an iron skid shoe, fixed in place against one rear wheel to keep it from turning, then removed once the hill was successfully negotiated. John Besant, inventor of the patent mail coach, introduced a new kind of brake called a band-brake, which supposedly tightened a strap around the wheel nave when traveling downhill, but this innovation was ineffective.

Besant's other inventions included a lock-release for the front wheels. Ordinarily, a lock kept the front wheels from scratching against the carriage body, but in tight turns taken too quickly, this lock could cause the carriage to tip over. Besant gave his mail coaches an emergency pedal to deactivate the lock; this was, like the band brake, probably useless. However, Besant did better when he designed a wheel that was less likely to detach in motion. Instead of simply passing the axle through the wheel and securing it with a washer and linchpin, he designed a fitting that bolted the axle directly to the inside of the wheel nave. The determination of some to infringe on his patent for the "mail-wheel" testifies to its improved safety.

The unit formed by wheels, axle, and perch was attached to three other important components: the horses (*E* 233, 353, 357), the coachman's box (*L&F*, *MW* 103; *MP* 75, 91, 105, 189), and the body of the carriage. The horses, wearing their padded collars and saddles or saddle pads, were "put to" (*E* 475) by attaching leather straps called traces to both the carriage and to the collars and saddle pads. The number of horses harnessed varied by the type of carriage and the need for haste. Heavier carriages tended to be pulled by four or even six horses, while a light gig would require only one. Since traveling over long distances required renting additional horses at every stop, people tended to travel with extra horses only when it was absolutely necessary (*S&S* 316), or when they were so rich that they need not care about the additional expense (*P* 165, 219). Mrs. Elton introduces an example of the latter circumstance to impress upon Highbury how wealthy her brother-in-law Mr. Suckling really is:

> But what is distance, Mr. Weston, to people of large fortune?—You would be amazed to hear how my brother, Mr. Suckling, sometimes flies about. You will hardly believe me—but twice in one week he and Mr. Bragge went to London and back again with four horses. (*E* 306)

Clearly, Mr. Suckling's carriage would normally require only two horses, but he is so rich that he can trade economy for speed. For travel near one's home, however, considerations of cost were trumped by those of inconvenience. There was no extraordinary need for speed in paying visits or running errands, and it was unnecessary to put the servants to the extra trouble of harnessing four horses when two would do. When the Hartfield party goes to Randalls at Christmas, for example, John Knightley refers to their using "four horses and four servants" for the purpose. As they ride over in two carriages, clearly only two horses are being used for each (*E* 113).

Sometimes, however, four horses were required. In the case of a coach and four, the two wheel horses (those closest to the carriage) would be put to first, each one on one side of a long pole extending forward from the carriage. The traces would be drawn through the sides of the saddle pads and on to the collar, while the pole itself would be attached to the bottom of the collar by a chain. Next, the lead horses were put to; their traces were attached to a crossbar that then hooked onto the long pole, and reins (*P* 92) were passed through their saddle pads and bridles. Finally, each pair of horses was harnessed together with coupling-reins. This is only an abbreviated version of the harnessing process, which in any case had to be double-checked for safety's sake. Mail coach drivers were allowed five minutes for the entire procedure, from the time they stopped at an inn until the time the new horses were ready to set forth. Private coachmen had longer to put their horses to, but even at a relatively leisured pace, it was far more laborious than getting into a car and turning a key. The knowledge of what was involved makes some of Austen's characters reluctant to put their coachmen to this trouble without a good reason (*E* 8; *MP* 221).

The second carriage component attached to the mechanism was the coachman's box. On early carriages, this attached directly to the mechanism, without springs to cushion the ride. It must have been intensely uncomfortable. By Austen's day, the box was in most cases part of the upper body, or at least mounted on its own set of springs. The box had a seat, covered with a decorative hammer-cloth, and an outward-turned lip on which the coachman could rest his feet.

The body of the carriage, often including the box, was suspended above the mechanism by springs. In the early part of Austen's life, these were either the long, slightly curved springs known as whip springs, or elbow springs, which were made by joining pairs of whip springs at their narrower ends. In the first years of the nineteenth century, however, methods of springing changed. The older forms were replaced by the C-spring, so named because it resembles the letter C, and the elliptic spring, invented in 1804 by Lambeth coach maker Obadiah Elliott. The result was a smoother ride, though ruts and bumps still flung passengers from side to side, and carriages still had to be built to more stringent standards if they were to be used in town, where cobblestones unmercifully rattled all the moving parts.

Parts of a Carriage: The Body

The body of a carriage, for the most part, distinguished it from other types of vehicle. Though wheels and springs mattered—gigs, for example, had only two wheels and often a special type of spring called a grasshopper or horizontal spring—it was the body that was most often the defining element. The coach, for example, as has already been described, had a rigid body, a fixed roof, and seats facing backward and forward. The seats were four feet wide inside, on occasion a couple of inches wider, allowing room for three people to sit on each. The chariot was identical to the coach except that it had only a forward-facing seat and thus accommodated three people instead of six. The elder Mrs. Rushworth, Mrs. Jennings, and John and Fanny Dashwood all own chariots (*MP* 202; *S&S* 184, 275), and so does Mr. Clifford of the Juvenilia—but then the redoubtable Mr. Clifford owns one of everything (*Clifford, MW* 43). The post chaise was very similar to a chariot, but it had no coachman's box—in lieu of a coachman, a postilion rode one of the horses—and had a 3'5" seat (*NA* 163) that accommodated only two passengers.

Carriages with retractable roofs had different names: a landau was essentially a coach with a roof that folded in two sections, while a barouche was a coach with a roof that unfolded to protect only one side. A phaeton had no roof at all. Neither did a dogcart, which was distinguished from other types of carriages by having a louvered compartment under the seat for transporting hunting dogs. Gigs and chairs, too, had no roofs; it is a gig that is referred to in *Northanger Abbey* as an "open carriage" (*NA* 47, 61, 84, 104). Austen is not specific about the "open carriages . . . to be employed" for the proposed outing in *Sense and Sensibility* (62), but one presumes they were gigs, phaetons, or the like.

A carriage body began with drawings of the sides and top. Then the coach maker built wooden pattern pieces and built the frame out of ash, the paneling of mahogany or cedar, and the floor, lining, and roof interior of deal. The roof exterior, if there was one, was made of leather stretched over the frame while wet. Windows were made of glass (*E* 114), and some could be opened; the number of windows varied depending on the type of carriage. Stagecoaches, for example, had only two windows—one on each side, over the door (*P&P* 217, *MP* 376). Private coaches, however, might have three "side glasses" (*P&P* 316) on each side—the one over the door, plus one in each side panel. A 1786 print of the Prince of Wales' coach shows a rectangular window over the door and two curved windows in the side panels, one of which is covered with a shade or blind (*P&P* 222). A carriage that had only forward-facing seats, such as a chariot or a post chaise, would have had a "front glass," a forward-facing window, as well; such a window is mentioned in *Love and Freindship* (*MW* 89).

From start to finish, a fine carriage, also sometimes called an "equipage"

Malagrida, Driving Post, James Gillray, 1792. The two-horse chariot closely resembles a post chaise, but unlike the post chaise, it has a box for the coachman, who is dressed in the same livery as the footmen clinging to the chariot's back. Courtesy of the Lewis Walpole Library, Yale University. 792.3.16.3.1.

(*Watsons, MW* 338; *Sand, MW* 382; *NA* 64, 65; *P* 158), would require the skills of wheelwrights for the wheels, carriage makers for the mechanism, body makers for the coach body, blacksmiths for the manufacture of springs and iron hardware, a woodcarver for decorative trim, upholsterers and embroiderers for the interior, curriers for the leather components, painters for the colors and arms, more painters for the many coats of varnish (*MP* 74), lamp makers for the lamps or "moons" that provided a feeble illumination (*S&S* 316), glaziers for the glass windows (*E* 357), and perhaps a locksmith for door locks and a gilder for additional decorative touches. The carriage was a master work of art and was recognized as such; coach maker William Felton bragged that, by 1790, "the art of Coach-building had been in a gradual state of improvement for half a century past, and had now arrived at a very high degree of perfection, with respect to both the beauty, strength, and elegance of our English carriages." So exceptional was English work, he claimed, that the export of carriages "to foreign nations is become a profitable and considerable branch of British commerce."

Felton, in 1796, provided a detailed diagram and description of the internal conveniences of a carriage. These included handholds—a real necessity in a jolting vehicle traveling over bad roads without seatbelts, decorative trim, pockets (*NA* 235) and nets to hold personal belongings, a box under the seat for additional storage, and curtains, blinds, or shutters for the windows. He noted that closed carriages were generally lined with light-colored cloth, that open carriages usually had dark linings, and that scarlet or crimson lining made "an addition of exactly one-third in the price of the cloth." Exterior trimmings included the hammer-cloth, handgrips for the footmen, different types of steps for getting into and out of the carriage, and lamps. Of these last he wrote,

> Lamps were originally used as necessary conveniencies to a carriage, but are now principally used for ornament. . . . There have been some few lamps used of the patent principle for burning oil, but the smoke they create renders their use objectionable; the hard spermaceti candle is the best to burn. The lamps are frequently smothered, or the lights go out, for want of sufficient openings at the bottom and top to receive the air, and to discharge the smoke.

The material used for the lamps was most frequently tin. Again and again, he notes that there is a wide difference in the price of a carriage based on the elegance and expense of the trimmings. Just as, today, a car can be made more expensive by adding options such as leather seats or entertainment systems, the carriage could be furnished in a very basic style or in a profusion of lace and fancy paintwork that proclaimed the individual owner's wealth.

Not all carriages, however, were purchased by individuals. Some were retained by the coach maker and used as rental vehicles. John Thorpe and James Morland visit a coach maker before they go out driving with Catherine and Isabella (*NA* 61). Inns also purchased vehicles with the intention of renting them; artist Thomas Rowlandson drew a sketch of himself hiring the first post chaise for a long journey in a busy inn yard. A sign hanging from the inn's balcony advertises "Post Chaises Saddle Horses . . . Phaetons Whiskeys Gigs to lett."

Staff: The Coachman

The care of all this English excellence required specialized servants. A coachman (*F&E, MW* 6; *MP* 375) was an absolute necessity, and postilions or post-boys might be required as well. A large household would also have one or more under-coachmen, stable boys to help groom the horses and tend to their feed and bedding, and footmen to ride at the back of the carriage to look splendid in their matched livery and to assist the passengers upon arrival.

Of all these servants, the most important was the coachman. He was in many ways the public face of the household and therefore was expected to exhibit "sobriety, steady conduct, and respectable appearance," according to an 1825 manual for servants written by Samuel and Sarah Adams. The ideal coachman, in the Adamses' opinion, was a careful driver and scrupulous in his dealings with coach makers, farriers, and horse dealers. He was to inspect the carriage frequently, buy fodder for the horses, supervise the other stable workers, make basic repairs, consult with a blacksmith or a coach maker if he thought more extensive repairs were warranted, clean and grease the carriage mechanism, and clean and polish the harness. He must drive expertly and in all weather, day and night, perched on a high box as the carriage rocked and jolted (*MP* 189, *E* 126).

On an ordinary day, the coachman would rise early and spend the morning supervising the care of the horses. By breakfast, or shortly after, he would turn to the inspection and cleaning of the harness, brushing it "with a dry hard brush" and polishing the brass or silver bits. Then he washed the carriage (*Sand, MW* 386) and wheels with mop and brush, blackened the leather parts, polished the decorative metal, greased the works, and checked the security of the linchpins on the wheels. Then he turned to the inside of the carriage, brushing the upholstery, wiping the windows, cleaning the lamps, and trimming the lamp wicks. If the family owned more than one carriage, there would be a separate coachman for each, with each performing these tasks on the carriage assigned to him.

If the carriage were to be used that day, the master or mistress would probably already have delivered orders to that effect. People certainly called for their carriages with little notice, but this was the exception rather than the rule. Much had to be set in motion to bring out a coach-and-four. The horses had to be physically ready, the coach itself washed, the harness dry and clean, and the coachman dressed in his uniform and wig (*MP* 189). Once all was ready, the coachman made a final inspection, took his whip in his left hand, mounted the box, and drove around to the house. It was a complicated business.

For this reason, carriages in Austen are "ordered" (*Watsons, MW* 341; *L&F, MW* 89; *E* 127, 392; *P&P* 307) or "spoken for" (*E* 128) hours or even days in advance (*Cath, MW* 236; *NA* 224; *E* 210; *MP* 221); it is rare indeed for a spontaneous demand to be made. Even when a character is on a visit (*Watsons, MW* 359; *P&P* 45), and the order is expected, it takes time to bring the carriage around to the front door (*Evelyn, MW* 183; *P&P* 220–221; *E* 362; *S&S* 178). On long visits, the horses would have been removed from their harness and fed in the host's stable (*E* 8); they would then have to be "put to" again at departure time, which could cause a few minutes' delay. Then the coachman must make himself ready again, perhaps breaking off in the middle of a friendly meeting with servants from other houses. Perhaps, as Jonathan Swift suggested in the mid-eighteenth century in his small, satirical volume of *Directions to Servants*, the coachman must interrupt his tippling:

Let your horses be so well trained, that when you attend your lady at a visit, they will wait until you dip into a neighbouring ale-house, to take a pot with a friend. . . .

If your master dines with a country friend, drink as much as you can get; because it is allowed, that a good coachman never drives so well as when he is drunk, and then shew your skill, by driving to an inch by a precipice, and say you never drive so well as when drunk. . . .

Get a blackguard-boy to watch your coach at the church door on Sundays, that you and your brother-coachmen may be merry together at the ale-house, while your master and lady are at church.

If the party were especially large—the ball in Fanny's honor at Mansfield Park comes to mind—it would take extra time simply to match up the proper coachmen with the proper horses, and each must get in line and wait his turn to gather his passengers (*P&P* 342). Delays in bringing the carriage were so customary that Austen uses the phrase "till the Carriage is at the door" to mean "until the very last minute" (*Sand, MW* 367). For the coachman, waiting around for departure time could be pleasant enough, as long as he had a comfortable place to sit and other servants with whom to socialize. When he was in a city, however, waiting for his employers was less amusing. There was sometimes nowhere to wait but in the street, and this could lead to crowding and ill-temper. In the *Bath Herald* of June 15, 1799, for example, merchants complained that their shops were being obstructed by the carriages of doctors and brewers and that when they requested that the offending carriages be moved, they were subjected to "unwarrantable insolence" from the servants holding the horses.

When the coachman finally got his employers safely home, he returned the carriage to the stable or coach house, unhitched the horses and saw to their care, washed and sponged the harness and hung it up to dry, put his whip away, and did as much of the next morning's cleaning as he could. If he had been out late on his duties, for example while taking his employers to and from a ball, he was allowed to sleep in late the next morning; it is partly because of this customary privilege that Emma Watson is told that she cannot expect to be taken home in the morning by the Edwardses' carriage, which took her to a ball on the previous night (*Watsons, MW* 340). However, the prejudice against use of the horses on the day after the ball was based on more than the coachman's convenience; it was difficult, though not impossible, to put everything in readiness again so quickly.

The coachman was paid, in 1825, between 25 and 36 guineas a year, plus, in the words of the Adamses, "two suits of livery—a box coat once in two or three years, two hats, and two pair of boots; also one or two stable dresses, consisting of overalls, jackets, waistcoats, and undress frock coat." An under-coachman made from £20 to 24 guineas, with a similar clothing allowance. Some, no doubt, found them overpaid at such rates. Swift found coachmen not only drunken but also unwilling to perform more than the basic necessities of their position: driving when they felt like it, in good weather, and exerting themselves not at all. Austen's characters, however, seem to be extremely fond of their coachmen. The Bennets' and Bertrams' coachmen are both singled out for punctuality (*P&P* 219; *MP* 222); Mrs. Norris is very fond of Wilcox, or at least professes to be (*MP* 189, 251); and no one but Emma, perhaps, could exceed James in Mr. Woodhouse's estimation (*E* 133, 210). James and most of the others appear only indirectly, but Wilcox himself makes an appearance when he rides out with the timid Fanny and comments approvingly on Mary Crawford's ability at riding. An upper-coachman in a baronet's household would have had a great many duties, and Wilcox could certainly have assigned a groom to the task of accompanying a young lady on horseback. It appears from his conversation with Fanny, however, that he has often worked as her groom. We are not told that he was ordered to do so by Sir Thomas, so we may assume that he has stooped to this duty out of kindness or fondness for Fanny, a fact that somewhat softens his praise of Mary (*MP* 69). Certainly, his tone, as he recalls Fanny's first horseback ride, is the fond and nostalgic tone of an old friend.

Admittedly, Austen coachmen can be opinionated, but their occasional fits of pique are not censured because their concern is for the safety and property of their masters. Wilcox, the coachman at Mansfield Park, resists driving to Sotherton, not because he is lazy but because "of the narrow lanes scratching his carriage" (*MP* 74). The Parkers' coachman grumbles and seems to drive deliberately badly, but this appears to be because he recognizes the poor quality of the road, a judgment borne out by the overturning of the carriage and by a local gentleman's surprise that anyone should attempt to negotiate such a terrible road in a carriage at all (*Sand*, *MW* 364).

Staff: Postilions, Post-Boys, and Ostlers

Some carriages could not be driven by a coachman. Some were intended to be driven by the owner, while post chaises had no box for a coachman, and other carriages required both a coachman and additional attendants. In the last two instances, the near horse or horses were ridden by a man who was usually called a postilion (*L&F, MW* 85, 90; *F&E, MW* 8; *H&E, MW* 38; *P&P* 293) when he was employed by the passenger's household and might be called either a postilion or a post-boy (*Watsons, MW* 349; *NA* 232; *S&S* 354) when he was hired along with a post chaise. In *Mansfield Park*, Mrs. Norris reveals the name of a postilion, Charles, when she reassures the ailing coachman that "Charles has been upon the leaders so often now, that I am sure there is no fear" (*MP* 189). Presumably, Charles has been accustomed to ride the near lead horse, in which capacity he

RETURN FROM BRIGHTON,
OR A JOURNEY TO TOWN FOR THE WINTER SEASON.

Return from Brighton, Dent, 1786. Here, note the post-boys, with whips, mounted on the near wheeler and near leader. Passengers are shown facing both forward and backward inside the coach. Running from front to back beneath the coach, the perch is clearly visible. Courtesy of the Lewis Walpole Library, Yale University. 786.10.23.1

would help to control the horses as they pulled the carriage and serve as a groom when they stopped or were stabled.

Readers seldom fail to assume that postilions were adult men, but they often misinterpret the term "post-boy." A post-boy was usually not a boy at all but a grown man, indeed often a middle-aged man. He was based at an inn (*S&S* 354; *E* 383), from which he was hired by passing travelers. He made threepence a mile to ride in all weathers, wrestling recalcitrant horses, negotiating roads in fatally bad repair, and deferring to often spoiled or unreasonable customers. Some post-boys became so disenchanted with their occupation that they conspired with local highwaymen to rob their passengers; others simply drank to excess.

The ostler was the public equivalent of the stableboy. An employee of the local inn, he tended to the horses, whether hired or owned, that were brought in by travelers. In theory, he was supposed to feed, water, and tend to the hot and weary animals; in practice, or at least in the published complaints of the day, he was all too often dishonest or lazy. Ostlers, it was claimed, gave the horses inferior fodder and pocketed the difference. Or, some claimed, they were asleep on the job, forcing the post-boys, coachmen, or guards to do their work instead. Austen steers clear of these controversies. Her token ostler is "old John Abdy's son . . . head man at the Crown" (*E* 383) and struggling to make ends meet and maintain his invalid father. We know little about him, except that he seems to fill a variety of posts at the inn and that he appears to have one post chaise available for rent (*E* 383). An ostler who, unlike Abdy, was hired by the publican would make most of his money from tips or "vails." Good ostlers were very much in demand and might move from one inn to another if they were offered better wages.

Carriage Costs

Though carriages seem to be everywhere in Austen's writing, they were actually rather uncommon in the England she inhabited. They were simply too expensive for most people to keep. It was not merely the expense of buying a carriage, though this was significant; a chariot for use in town cost about £91 in 1801. Nor was it the upkeep, though this, too, added up: there was the coachman's salary; fodder, shoeing, and doctoring for the horses; maintenance of the coach; and perhaps additional wages for a groom or two. All these costs would have been daunting in themselves, but to them was added a burdensome and entirely new level of taxation. England's wars with France came at a cost, and one of the expedients to which the government resorted was a tax on private carriages. In 1790, this tax amounted to £3 17s. per year on two-wheeled carriages (12s. for basic gigs or carts that bore the words "taxed cart") and £8 16s. per year for four-wheeled carriages. Additional carriages cost increasing amounts: the second four-wheeled carriage cost £9 18s., and the third, fourth, and so on cost £11 each. This is why Austen's fictional Mr. Clifford, who keeps at least twenty-two carriages, is so funny. Keeping one close carriage was a sure sign of comfort; keeping two was a sign of wealth (*E* 277); keeping three was evidence of opulence (*P&P* 157). Keeping twenty-two was simply ridiculous.

Not everyone could afford to keep even one carriage. Jane's father George Austen did so, despite having to maintain eight children, but he also died without being able to leave his wife and two daughters enough to live on comfortably. At any rate, his carriage could not have been used frequently, as the horses that pulled it were also the draft animals on his small farm, and he was forced to sell it in 1798 to save money. Jane, much later, depicted in the Heywoods a family similarly endowed with good property but forced to economies by the demands of a large family: they had "enough for them to have indulged in a new Carriage & better roads, an occasional month at Tunbridge Wells, & symptoms of the Gout and a Winter at Bath;—but the maintenance, Education & fitting out of 14 Children demanded a very quiet, settled, careful course of Life" (*Sand*, *MW* 373–374). The Heywoods, as a result of their extreme fecundity, had not purchased a new carriage since their marriage. George Austen, likewise, put his family first; when he gave up his carriage, it was because he was turning over the curacy of Deane to his eldest son, James.

James also kept a "close carriage" during his first marriage, when he was merely a country curate living on his small stipend and his wife's allowance from her father—an income that totaled £300 per year. The consensus is that he was living well beyond his means and would have been better off dismissing the carriage until his income improved. Another of Jane's brothers, Edward, had been adopted by a wealthy family and could afford to keep more than one carriage, and there were certainly many Austen acquaintances and relatives who also kept carriages, but Jane herself was more like Harriet Smith or Jane Fairfax than like Emma Woodhouse, more likely to be given a ride in someone else's carriage than to be able to offer a ride in her own. The constant borrowing and lending of carriages in her novels no doubt reflect her personal awareness of the value of such a convenience (*P&P* 59; *S&S* 40, 248, 293; *P* 39, 169; *MP* 206, 266; *E* 159, 185, 223, 244, 283, 319–322, 390, 418). She was not the only person of her class put in the position of borrowing a carriage; Parson James Woodforde frequently noted in his diary that, when dining with the local squire, the squire's carriage was employed to bring him to dinner and to send him home again.

To put carriage ownership in perspective, in 1801 the entire population of England was about 8 million. Thirteen years later, there were 69,200 taxed carriages in Great Britain: 23,400 four-wheeled carriages, 27,300 two-wheeled carriages, and 18,500 "tax-carts," extremely basic, springless vehicles such as carts and rib-chairs. Only 3,636 private carriages were built in 1814. Not all vehicles were taxed, and surely some people managed to evade the tax, but the exempted vehicles were not of a nature to carry ladies to genteel morning calls, and the loud complaints about the tax from across the nation imply that most carriages were eventually subjected to it. We can at least say with safety that fewer than 1 in 100 people owned a carriage and that fewer than 1 in 160 owned the sort of private carriages that we associate with Austen's characters. Even if we add public vehicles to the tally, there were still relatively few carriages on the roads; there were only 80 mail coaches when the service began in the 1780s and only 700 by 1835.

We can therefore assign modern approximations to different types of carriages: the phaeton and curricle were the convertible sports cars of their day, driven by young people eager for speed and admiration; the dogcart was not unlike a pickup truck, with its dogs riding under the seat rather than in the bed; the post chaise was similar to a taxi or limousine but hired for long distances; the coach was a minivan, the chariot or landau a family sedan; the stagecoach was analogous to an intercity train, and the wagon to an intercity bus. However, we should not carry the analogy too far. Wheeled vehicles were far less common than they are today. One should imagine not only the purpose and connotations of each vehicle but also their rarity. Imagine, for example, that in a given year there were only

4,000 or so new cars purchased in Los Angeles. Who would be able to buy them? Certainly, not the modern corollaries to "old John Abdy" or Mrs. Ford. Laborers would have gone their whole lives without riding in a private carriage, and merchants had to rise above a certain level of income before they could even aspire to a post chaise. Even in Austen's fictional gentry "neighborhoods"—by which she means not all the people of the town but only those with whom it was appropriate to socialize—not everyone is blessed with a carriage (*NA* 88–89). In those close-knit, highly interdependent neighborhoods, it is perfectly natural that there should be a great deal of carriage-lending, because society as its inhabitants knew it could not proceed unless people could get to each other's houses. Sheer boredom, if not good nature or Christian charity, would have stimulated the offering and receiving of rides.

Again and again in Austen's works, the keeping of one or more carriages is a measure of wealth. Mrs. Bennet assesses the value of her daughters' marriages according to the sorts of jewels, clothes, and carriages they will be able to afford (*P&P* 376, 378), while the sensible Elinor Dashwood laughs at Marianne's plans of keeping two carriages (*S&S* 91) and motivates their mother to sell their carriage because it will be too expensive to keep (*S&S* 12, 26). The Edwardses, in the incomplete novel *The Watsons*, are introduced as "people of fortune who lived in the Town & kept their coach" (*Watsons*, *MW* 314), and Anne Steele assures Elinor Dashwood that her friends the Richardsons "are very genteel people. He makes a monstrous deal of money, and they keep their own coach" (*S&S* 275). In *Emma*, the Jane Fairfax subplot turns at one point on a reference to the town's apothecary, Mr. Perry, planning "to set up his carriage." The genial Mr. Weston, hearing of it, remarks, "I am glad he can afford it" (*E* 345), though, as it turns out, Mr. Perry *cannot* afford it and abandons the plan. In such circumstances, when one of the leading citizens of Highbury has to dismiss keeping a carriage as too expensive, it is no wonder that the town is agog at Mrs. Elton's brother-in-law, who keeps "two carriages!" (*E* 183).

Driving

Some carriages were meant to be driven by a coachman, but not all. Well-to-do young men enjoyed showing off their prowess with the whip and reins (*NA* 65, 87), and therefore some carriages, such as gigs, curricles, and phaetons, were intended to be driven by the owner. The light weight of these carriages made them fast; the high springs, particular toward the end of the eighteenth century, made them top-heavy and likely to tip over if driven poorly. In other words, they were deliciously dangerous.

However, not all the drivers were men. A 1776 engraving entitled *Phaetona, or Modern Female Taste*, shows a woman with hair and headdress that stand half as tall as she does, perched on a phaeton as tall as a grown man, whipping horses so tiny that they seem about as large as beagles next to the exaggerated woman and her exaggerated vehicle. (One thinks of Miss De Bourgh and "her little phaeton and ponies" [*P&P* 67, 168].) Another print, *A Lesson Westward—Or a Morning Visit to Betsy Cole* (1782), shows a woman taking a driving lesson from "Tom Longtrot," whose cart sign advertises that he will teach young ladies to drive in a fortnight. Evidently, Julia Bertram was not the only woman who wished to learn to drive a carriage (*MP* 80). Indeed, we see Mrs. Croft driving with absolute fearlessness and a good deal more skill than her husband (*P* 84, 92), and Emma Watson's older sister Elizabeth does not scruple to drive the family chair (*Watsons, MW* 315). It is not clear that Mrs. Jennings drives; her carriage is a chariot, which would have had a coachman. However, she uses a driving metaphor when she taunts her son-in-law with the fact that he cannot get rid of his silly wife Charlotte: "you have taken Charlotte off my hands, and cannot give her back again. So there I have the whip hand of you" (*S&S* 112). In other words, she has an advantage, just as the driver has over his (or her) horses.

All drivers had to exercise caution, for there were plenty of hazards on the road. Speeds were low, but the quality of the roads was extremely poor, and many so-called roads were nothing more than a succession of bumps, ruts, and cavernous potholes. Turns, which often had been designed with riders, walkers, and livestock in mind, could be perilous in a carriage (*E* 133); while overturning or crashing a carriage was not an everyday event, it was an ever-present danger (*Sand, MW* 363–365, 370; *NA* 65; *E* 126; *P* 84, 92). Austen's school friend and cousin Lady Williams (née Jane Cooper) was killed in August 1798 when a carriage she was driving collided with a runaway horse. A fatal carriage crash also features prominently in the plot of Henry Fielding's novel *Tom Jones*. Nevertheless, people probably thought of the danger of overturning in much the same way we think of car accidents, as a very real possibility but one that only a timorous person like Mr. Woodhouse would consider every time he stepped into a vehicle.

Less serious hazards abounded. Coach springs were still quite primitive, and when combined with the state of the roads, the resulting ride was anything but smooth. Passengers were flung about in the compartment or simply rattled until they became motion-sick (*P&P* 222). Driving in the dark was especially dangerous, because obstacles often went unseen. Travel at night was therefore avoided, especially in carriages like gigs that were not normally equipped with lamps (*NA* 116), and if one had to travel at night, one tried to time it so that the moon was full or nearly so. Then there were the effects of weather. Though Mr. Elton praises the innovation of a sheepskin blanket for warmth (*E* 115), the carriages were not heated inside and must have been quite chilly on cold days. Open carriages would have been even less comfortable, to the point of being unusable for much of the winter, and if a sudden shower took the passengers by surprise, their clothes could be ruined. Clothes also suffered, as Mrs. Allen points out, from the dirt of open carriages (*NA* 104). Gigs and chairs were open in the front, and if the road were dusty or muddy, the horse's hooves, and the wheels themselves, would kick up a fair amount of filth. *See also* Barouche; Carts and Wagons; Chair; Chaise; Gig; Horses; Landau; Phaeton; Travel.

Carts and Wagons

Carriages and coaches were the glamorous vehicles of the Regency, but carts and wagons did the practical work of the nation. Along with canal barges and oceangoing ships, they hauled goods from one place to another, carried the heavy luggage that lumbered behind swiftly traveling upper-class tourists (*E* 186), brought in the harvest (*MP* 58), and made

Unloading a Waggon, Thomas Rowlandson, 1813. The distinctly working-class clientele of the stage wagon disembark to a probably unenthusiastic reception at an inn. The passengers include a Jewish peddler (recognizable by his beard), a half-pay officer in the center of the print (recognizable by his uniform as an officer and by his gaunt appearance as one on half-pay), and several unfashionably stocky women—one holding a basket, another holding the arm of a gouty man, and the third holding a toddler. The inn, named the "Flying Waggon," advertises "Entertainment for Man and Horse." Courtesy of the Lewis Walpole Library, Yale University. 813.9.12.1.1.

commercial deliveries within towns (*NA* 44; *P* 135). They were much more common than fine carriages, a fact that Mary Crawford notices without managing to grasp its significance (*MP* 58). Edmund Bertram understands; moving a harp is not necessary to the life of the nation, but getting in the harvest is, and for that the humble wagon trumps a phaeton or a barouche. For the English, nervous about revolution and dictatorship across the Channel, "the heavy rumble of carts and drays" (*P* 135), noisy as it no doubt was, was the music of commerce.

Drays were exclusively commercial vehicles; they were two-wheeled vehicles without sides and often carried large barrels, for example, the barrels of brewers. Carts and wagons, however, might also carry passengers. Some small passenger vehicles were called carts, and there were larger, two-wheeled carts that were designed to carry people. Wagons had four wheels. When they carried hay or other produce, they were typically uncovered, but when they carried baggage or passengers, they were covered with arched, tubular cloth covering, making them look like the Conestoga wagons of the Old West. The passenger wagon, or "Stage Waggon" (*F&E*, *MW* 10), was the humblest of public conveyances—crowded, slow, but cheap and less likely to be targeted by highwaymen. Its patrons were tolerated rather than welcomed when they stopped at an inn for the night, and contemporary engravings show passengers who look rather the worse for their long, bumpy trip. *See also* Carriages and Coaches.

Chair

"Chair" is a problematic term in Austen's works because it means two different conveyances. One of these usages occurs only in the Juvenilia, the other in the novels, but readers unfamiliar with either meaning can find use of the term confusing. In the Juvenilia, the word refers to a kind of simple, two-wheeled, springless carriage, similar to a gig. A 1799 print, *One Inconvenience Attending a Low Chair*, shows a tiny carriage body with no top or front, looking very much like a wide wicker armchair, seating two people facing forward and with only one horse in harness. The print, which shows the driver being kicked by his own horse, demonstrates one of the chief problems with the chair, which was that the view was chiefly of the horse's back end, with all of the discomforts associated with being directly behind and below the horse.

The chair is found, along with both grander and humbler vehicles, in the comic list of carriages owned by Mr. Clifford in the *Memoirs of Mr. Clifford*:

> He traveled in his Coach & Four, for he was a very rich young Man & kept a great many Carriages of which I do not recollect half. I can only remember that he had a Coach, a Chariot, a Chaise, a Landeau, a Landeaulet, a Phaeton, a Gig, a Whisky, an italian Chair, a Buggy, a Curricle & a wheelbarrow. (*MW* 43)

By an "italian Chair," Austen may mean specifically a kind of Italian gig or chair that had a seat for only one person; a seventeenth-century example of such a chair is in the collections of the Museums at Stony Brook, Long Island, New York. A "chair" is also found in a more serious context in *The Watsons*. Here, a family so impoverished that it just barely manages the appearance of gentility keeps a chair as its only carriage. This "convenient but very un-smart Family Equipage" (*Watsons, MW* 338) is driven either by a servant or by one of the Watson sisters and carries the girls to the nearest town to do their shopping and to go to balls. The most genteel of the Watsons, Emma, who has had an education superior to that of her sisters, is taken aback by the idea of traveling in such a basic vehicle at night to a ball (*Watsons, MW* 319), and, to be sure, a low open carriage would have exposed its riders not only to possible bad weather but also to dirt flying up from the horse's hooves—not a very attractive prospect to a girl with a limited number of good ball gowns.

Despite its disadvantages, however, the chair was a popular vehicle in provincial towns. One variation, the "rib chair," had a semicircular wooden seat connected to a semicircular upper rail by a row of small wooden rods. It was simple to make, cost only £12 to purchase, and, if the words "taxed cart" were painted upon it, had only a 12s. annual tax levied on it, versus the £3 17s. annual tax for fancier two-wheeled carriages. For a gentry family that simply wanted a quick, practical way to get from point A to point B, the attractions of the rib chair were obvious. Jane Austen's brother Edward, who as the wealthy owner of Godmersham could certainly afford any sort of carriage he wanted, owned a chair for just such purposes; on visits to Godmersham, Jane wrote of Edward taking another gentleman "to Canterbury in the chair" and of going herself "in the chair" to tour the Canterbury Gaol.

The other type of chair, the sedan chair (*NA* 24, 81, 96), was found in towns such as London and Bath and was both wheel-less and horseless. A descendant of the ancient and medieval litter, it was a vertical, enclosed, windowed box with a seat inside (see the illustration *The Successful Fortune Hunter* [Marriage]). The box was suspended from two poles that extended before and behind and were held by two "chairmen." These chairmen picked up the box and carried the passenger to her destination. Eighteenth-century Londoners, dismayed by the increasing size of the city, bemoaned the lot of the poor chairmen who had to convey heavy passengers through the ever-lengthening streets, and no doubt it was hard work. Austen's examples come not from London but from Bath, where, due to the town's steep hills, chairmen were also probably very weary by the end of their labors. Chairmen also worked in the rain, while their passengers sat in the closed box and stayed dry; in both *Persuasion* and *Northanger Abbey* there are references to keeping dry in a sedan chair (*P* 177; *NA* 83), though there would have been no protection for the chairmen in such cases.

In Bath, the chairmen, who wore blue coats, congregated mostly in the abbey churchyard, which Austen calls the pump-yard. However, it would have been possible on certain occasions to find a chair headed back to the center of town after dropping off a passenger. In special circumstances, such as when concerts or plays let out, chairs would be waiting for fares outside the building, though there were fewer sedan chairs than theatergoers, and people had to wait their turn (*NA* 95). If one was on

Etching by Thomas Rowlandson, 1790 (detail). A sedan chair carried by two chairmen. Courtesy of the Lewis Walpole Library, Yale University. 790.6.20.1.

the street on one's own, it was perfectly acceptable to go in search of a chair (*P* 177), but at home, or anywhere else where servants were present, a servant would be sent on this errand (*P* 238). *See also* Carriages and Coaches; Gig; Travel. *For indoor chairs, see* Furniture.

Chaise

The chaise* (*Clifford, MW* 43; *Lesley, MW* 110; *Cath, MW* 225; *NA* 163, 229, 233, 235; *S&S* 318, 354–355; *P&P* 152, 286; *E* 383; *P* 121) was a closed (*MP* 74), four-wheeled carriage that could be thought as a half-coach. Whereas a coach had seats facing both front and back, each holding up to three passengers (*NA* 232), the chaise had only the forward-facing seat and thus accommodated only three (*P* 116). Admittedly, it was more comfortable for two; Parson James Woodforde remarked in his diary in 1785, after two people called for his niece in a post chaise, that he "did not like that Nancy should crowd into the Chaise with them and for no Purpose whatever." However, because it did seat three, the chaise offers Austen a final chance to highlight the selfishness of Lucy Steele; Lucy could easily have taken her sister Anne away from London on her way to her honeymoon with Robert Ferrars, but instead she borrows or steals all of Anne's money, leaving the elder Miss Steele no way to hire a post chaise of her own (*S&S* 370–371).

In most respects, including the number of passengers, the chaise was identical to a chariot, the chief difference being the location of the driver. In a chariot, the driver sat on a box, while a chaise had no box. A driver

---

*Chaise was also, somewhat confusingly, a term applied to a large, one-horse, two-wheeled carriage with whip springs at the rear and elbow springs in front.

The Gilpin Whigs Return to Rochester without Their Candidate, Cruikshank, 1790. Two views of the front and side of a post chaise. Note the absence of a coachman's box and substitution of a post-boy mounted on one of the horses. Courtesy of the Lewis Walpole Library, Yale University. 790.5.20.2.

would ride one of the horses if there were two horses in harness, and postilions would ride the near wheeler and the near leader if there were four horses (*NA* 131, 212, 232; *Cath, MW* 213, 214; *P&P* 3; *P* 7). (The wheelers were the horses adjacent to the carriage wheels, while the leaders were the horses in front. The near horses were those on the left side if one were seated in the carriage facing forward, and the off horses were those on the right.) Four horses were not strictly necessary; artist Thomas Rowlandson's drawings of his tour in a post chaise routinely show two horses harnessed side by side. However, four were preferable if either speed or show were desired (*P* 115). Thus, Elizabeth Elliot and Sir Walter are loath to part with two of their four carriage horses, not because they cannot do without them, but because they are used to going faster and looking richer (*P* 13, 35).

An extension in the back of the carriage held luggage (*P&P* 216) and additional servants. The disadvantage of the chaise versus the coach was the loss of passenger and baggage room. The advantage was additional speed, as the weight of passengers, baggage, and the carriage itself was less. For this reason, it was the predominant choice of fashionable travelers, who either bought their own chaises (a typical model cost £93 in 1801) or hired them (as did Rowlandson). All in all, the chaise was a practical, yet not stodgy, vehicle; it seems appropriate that it is what the jovial, earthy, sensible Mrs. Jennings uses (*S&S* 153, 341). It also seems to be the right vehicle for Mr. Rushworth—straightforward, fashionable enough not to make him ashamed of it, yet not fashionable enough to rival Henry Crawford's elegant barouche (*MP* 84, 203). Mr. Bingley, too, a man of good nature and few pretensions, owns a chaise (*P&P* 30, 34).

There was some overlap in how the terms "post" and "chaise" were used. The hired or "hack" chaise (*Sand*, *MW* 414, 420; *P&P* 19; *MP* 377), which came with its own staff to drive and manage the horses, was usually called a post chaise (*F&E*, *MW* 8; *NA* 232; *S&S* 218; *Watsons*, *MW* 355). This kind of conveyance could frequently be hired at an inn (*P* 114). "Post" (*S&S* 65) or "traveling post" (*MP* 266, 372) was a somewhat more general term; it meant traveling with control over route and stops, rather than in a public stagecoach or hackney coach, and stopping as necessary to exchange horses; this could take place in any kind of carriage, attended by one's own servants or by rented ones (*L&F*, *MW* 90). Thus, a privately owned chaise could also be called a post chaise (*MP* 74) if it were used for posting. Henry Crawford, for example, travels post in his own carriage (*MP* 266).

Whether the servants were one's own or hired for the journey, a driver of some kind was a necessity. The chaise was not the sort of fashionable carriage driven by the gentry for fun. Therefore, in Austen's youthful work *Catharine, or the Bower*, we are meant to find it funny that "a Gentleman [arrives] in a Chaise & 4," but "he has not a single servant with him, and came with hack [i.e., rented] horses" (*Cath*, *MW* 214). The superiority of the private post chaise to the hackney coach, a cheaper public vehicle, also provides the alert reader with another clue to Lydia Bennet's imminent ruin, for in Clapham Wickham removes her "into a hackney-coach and dismisse[s] the chaise that brought them from Epsom" (*P&P* 274, 282). *See also* Carriages and Coaches; Travel.

Chaperones

Society following the French Revolution was looser in dress, conversation, and (some would say) morality than either the early Georgian era that preceded it or the starchy Victorian age that would follow it. However, even a period of plunging necklines and nearly transparent muslin dresses took at least nominal precautions to safeguard the virginity of its young women. When a young, unmarried woman went out into "public"—to public balls, for example, or to the theatre, or to dinner parties at the homes of acquaintances (in short, anywhere that she might be subject to the attentions of men)—she was required to take a chaperone (*Col Let*, *MW* 156; *Cath*, *MW* 206; *Watsons*, *MW* 328; *S&S* 110; *E* 370). This was usually a respectable woman who had to be either beyond marriageable age or, preferably, a married woman (*P&P* 99) who understood the sexual undertones of courtship and flirtation.

In theory, a chaperone served her young charge by offering advice and by acting as a visible deterrent to unscrupulous men. In practice, the chaperone seems to have been more of a tour guide and social director in unfamiliar settings and something of a token of decency in more familiar surroundings, such as a local public ball. In the latter case, her presence served to advertise that the basic precautions were being taken to ensure the good character and modesty of the girl under her protection. Presence alone seems to have been enough in most cases; chaperones appear to have spent a fair amount of time amusing themselves by playing cards or sitting by the fire (*MP* 117) chatting with friends. Certainly, Mrs. Norris views her duties not as a sacred trust but as an opportunity to expand her own social horizons (*MP* 35), and when Austen herself, in an 1813 letter, mentions acting as "a sort of chaperon," it is to point out that her post allows her some cherished personal comforts: "I am put on the sofa near the fire and can drink as much wine as I like."

Even if a chaperone did not confine herself to sipping wine by the fire, she was not necessarily very useful. Austen saw clearly that not every married woman was, by virtue of her acquaintance with sexual intercourse, automatically endowed with wisdom or even common sense. The idea of Lydia Bennet (who is herself to be undone by the lax oversight of a married woman) chaperoning her sisters "about to all the balls" (*P&P* 221) is a ghastly one, and the petty Mary Stanhope of *The Three Sisters* does not seem likely to be a model chaperone either; she, too, thinks only of the relative power and consequence that her position will give her and thinks of it as a worthy excuse to get married (*MW* 58). Mrs. Allen is neither vicious nor especially negligent, but her shallowness and her preoccupation with dress make her a poor role model for a young woman (*NA* 20). One of the worst, perhaps, is the Bath "lady" suggested by Mrs. Elton to Emma as "the very person for you to go into public with" (*E* 275). Emma judges—and Austen gives us no reason to doubt her judgment in this instance—that the "lady" in question is probably "some vulgar, dashing widow, who, with the help of a boarder, just made a shift to live" (*E* 275–276).

However, these antichaperones merely underscore the perceived necessity of a careful, responsible woman to look out for the welfare of marriageable girls. The consequences of failed stewardship are obvious in the fate of Lydia Bennet and in the near-disaster that befalls Georgianna Darcy. There are hints of near peril in other novels and fragments, too. Elinor Dashwood, always the voice of reason and the moral establishment, is shocked that her sister would drive away from a group outing and tour a country house "with no other companion than Mr. Willoughby" (*S&S* 68). In that case, very definite harm results from Marianne's rejection of conventional notions of propriety. In the fragment *Catharine*, we have less information about the results of Edward Stanley's assaults on Kitty's expectation that a chaperone will always be present. When he arrives unexpectedly from his travels and accompanies her, otherwise unattended, to a ball, it is neither strictly correct nor strictly taboo. He is her cousin, which renders him partially "safe"; yet he is previously unknown to her and could legally marry her, which makes him less safe than a brother or a father. Kitty (also referred to as Catharine or Catherine) is well aware that to alight from a carriage and appear in public with a man unknown to almost all the ballgoers will seem scandalous, at least until (and possibly after) his identity is revealed, and Stanley, too, understands the effect that their appearance will create:

> "if we go in together, we shall be the whole talk of the Country— . . . and why should you object to entering a room with me where all our relations are, when you have done me the honour to admit me without any chaprone [*sic*] into your Carriage? Do not you think your Aunt will be as much offended with you for one, as for the other of these mighty crimes."
>
> "Why really said Catherine, I do not know but that she may; however, it is no reason that I should offend against Decorum a second time, because I have already done it once." (*Cath, MW* 219)

Later, he manages to walk with her "in the Garden . . . without any other companion for nearly an hour in the course of the Evening" (*Cath, MW* 230). Kitty's aunt, of course, disapproves of his tactics, but she is an unusually scrupulous—even paranoid—chaperone, who refuses her niece many social opportunities because of "the recollection of there being young Men in almost every Family" in the neighborhood (*Cath, MW* 196). Given the treatment of other charming, morally slippery young men in Austen's other works, it seems likely that the aunt's judgment in this case is, for once, a case of a chaperone performing her most essential function.

Charity

The eighteenth century saw the birth of many types of charitable organizations, founded for many purposes. Some trained poor children for work in trades or domestic service, while one prominent charity trained boys as sailors. Several focused on the sexual habits of working-class women, either by attempting the reform of prostitutes or by providing obstetrical care for the poor. Some were religious charities, founded to spread the word of God by distributing Bibles at home and abroad or by educating the nation's children in Sunday schools. These were only the new funnels for assistance; the traditional means of support for the poor, a tax (the "poor rate") levied in each parish for the relief of the local community, was still Britain's principal social safety net. Personal giving from individual to individual also remained extremely common.

For members of Austen's social class, the giving of charity was an essential part of one's religious life and neighborly duty. Austen herself spent a great deal of time sewing clothes for the local poor. The diary of parson James Woodforde, who as a man did not sew smocks or shirts, notes many occasions on which he gave small cash gifts to poor people who either entertained him, performed some service, or simply touched him with a hard-luck story: "To a poor old Man with a Dulcimer gave 0.0.6. [sixpence]." "To some Children opening the Gate gave 0.0.6." "To a very poor Weaver with a large Family and a Wife and can get no Work whatever gave last night 0.1.0." "This being St Thomas Day [December 21], I gave to the poor of my Parish that came to my House at 6^d each 1.7.0." Such contributions were a regular part of life for the gentry; the anonymous author of *The Mirror of the Graces* (1811) defined one of the duties to "our inferiors" as "our kindnesses in their exigencies." *Persuasion*'s Mrs. Smith, indeed, maintains her fragile claim to continued membership in the gentry by continuing to make charitable donations even in her straitened circumstances (*P* 155).

However, it is worth noting that in the case of a well-read family like Austen's, charity would also have an important dramatic and literary aspect as well. In many of the novels of manners read by the Austens, such as the works of Frances (Fanny) Burney, a timely act of charitable generosity or sensitivity to the plight of the poor is an important turning point. Kindness to the *deserving* poor—those made miserable by misfortune rather than by unlawful or immoral conduct (*H&E*, *MW* 38)—is an essential characteristic of both hero and heroine and sometimes forms the basis of their first attachment to each other. Such episodes are often highly sentimental, and Austen wisely eschews the dramatic value of single, highly visible acts of giving in favor of long-standing patterns of generous behavior. Thus, Emma's "charitable visit . . . to a poor sick family" (*E* 83), in itself, does not induce Mr. Knightley to fall in love with her, but it is part of a pattern of noblesse oblige that makes her an exemplary member of her class and thus places her in the pool of appropriate partners.

Similarly, Mr. Darcy's housekeeper's certainty that he will be "just as affable to the poor" as his father (*P&P* 249) speaks to his good character; Miss Bates' generosity despite her limited income reinforces her continuing respectability (*E* 85, 383); and the Rushworths' building of almshouses attests to their family's adherence to traditional gentry values (*MP* 82). In each case, specific instances of charity are not the focal point of episodes but details that combine with others to form a flattering portrait of worthiness. In the cases of the Darcys and Rushworths, both wealthy families, the mention of charity almost fades into the background, for by doing their class duty, both families have done nothing exceptionally noteworthy but have merely come up to the expected mark. Only in Miss Bates' case is her charity considered to be really shining and laudable, because it is so genuine, so constant, and so near to the maximum her income will support.

In a few instances Austen uses charity to delineate a negative character. Mrs. Norris, for example, resents the demands placed upon her by the expectation of charitable giving (*MP* 30). This may be evidence that despite the fact that she and her sister have "married up" into the top reaches of the gentry, she still retains a vulgar interest in money. However, Elizabeth Elliot of *Persuasion* has no such excuse, and she apparently feels that personal extravagances are more important than "unnecessary charities" (*P* 10). Austen takes a different approach to negative characterization through charity in the incomplete novel *Sanditon*; here, Mr. Parker's casual and genteel interest in getting Lady Denham's support for a poor woman is contrasted with his sister's officious and insistent demands that Lady Denham make large contributions to three additional causes (*Sand, MW* 423–424). However, in this instance, as in the cases of Mrs. Norris and Miss Elliot, giving is part of a pattern of behavior. Mr. Parker gives because he has a generous nature and a sense of his position; Diana Parker gives—or, rather, organizes the giving of others—because it makes her feel important.

Children

Children (*S&S* 31; *P&P* 152; *MP* 41, 50; *E* 79, 80–81, 98–99, 233, 476; *P* 37, 133) occupied a less prominent place in social life in the late eighteenth and early nineteenth centuries than in later periods, but they were present in certain parts of daily life. Jane Austen has often been accused by critics and biographers of having little patience with children and perhaps even disliking them, but the truth is that she probably liked *good* children quite a bit, and they seem to have liked her. It is the bad characters in her novels who dislike or neglect children (*Lesley, MW* 124; *Watsons, MW* 350; *P* 22) or who merely pretend to like them in order to ingratiate themselves (*LS, MW* 244; *S&S* 119, 120, 122). Characters meant to be viewed in a positive light, however, are fond of children and devoted to their care (*Sand, MW* 407; *S&S* 304; *P&P* 325; *E* 113, 435; *P* 43, 49). The one exception is Emma, who feels that, knowing what children are like, five times a governess' normal salary would be "dearly earned" (*E* 382). Emma, however, is a deliberately flawed heroine, and many of her opinions are not what Austen's authorial voice espouses.

It was badly behaved children that she found tiresome (*S&S* 4; *MP* 381–383, 387, 391, 439; *P* 38, 79–80). Noisy, disobedient, troublesome children irked her, as they do many sensible people, but she had no difficulty getting along with her own nieces and nephews, with whom she cheerfully played games and to whom she read aloud. It was to Jane and Cassandra that their little niece Anna was entrusted after the death of her mother, and it was to Jane that certain of Edward's sons were consigned after the death of Edward's wife, Elizabeth. Having a great many interesting and apparently well behaved children among her relatives, Jane had little patience for those who spoiled their children and allowed them to show no consideration for their fellow creatures. Mrs. Weston's fondness for her baby (*E* 476) is not ridiculed or condemned, but Lady Middle-

THE ——— NURSERY or NINE MONTHS AFTER

Published 9ᵗ May 1786 by S.W.Fores at the Caricature Warehouse Nº3 Piccadilly

The Nursery or Nine Months After, 1786. This attempt to depict the Prince of Wales as a devoted husband and father after the birth of his one legitimate child failed in the long run, as his martial troubles were fodder for all kinds of public scandal. Nonetheless, the emphasis on his connection to an infant child not only encouraged support for the monarchy but fed into the increasing importance placed on good parenting. Courtesy of the Lewis Walpole Library, Yale University. 786.5.9.1.

ton's negligent discipline of her rowdy offspring is (*S&S* 32, 34, 120, 121), as are Mary Musgrove's ineffectual attempts to bring her sons into line (*P* 43–45). One suspects that the author is speaking through John Knightley when he summarizes his instructions for tending to his children: "do not spoil them, and do not physic them" (*E* 311).

Austen was born at a time when attitudes toward children were evolving. Previous generations had thought of children as miniature, but defective, adults, incapable as yet of rational thought and therefore well advised to be quiet and sit still until they were old enough to be married to the family's advantage. They addressed their parents only when spoken to and used a respectful form of address such as "Sir" or "Madam." Parents and caregivers were alert for any signs of the original sin that lurked in children's hearts and punished lapses promptly and severely. Corporal punishment was used both as a corrective measure and to make children generally tougher. The punishments employed included the beatings, confinement, and dunking in ice-cold water. The water treatment was supposed to make children stronger, but the poet Robert Southey recalled with sympathy how his little sister had been subjected to a forcible dip in well water every morning on awakening: "the shock was dreadful, the poor child's horror of it every morning when taken out of bed even more so." He blamed her early death on the practice and never forgot her suffering.

Austen, too, had an example of severe discipline among her circle of acquaintances, though discipline in her own family was always mild. She was very fond of their neighbor Mrs. Lloyd, mother of three daughters (two of whom eventually married brothers of Jane's, and of whom, Martha Lloyd, lived with the Austen women for much of her adult life). Mrs. Lloyd's mother had been the notorious Mrs. Craven, who beat, starved, and imprisoned her daughters until they escaped her power by marrying. Many critics assume, probably rightly, that the character of Lady Susan is based in part on Mrs. Craven.

However, influenced in part by the philosophy of Locke and Rousseau, parents were beginning to think of their children as inherently innocent and potentially rational. Mothers in particular were encouraged to bond with their children in a variety of ways, for example, by breast-feeding them rather than farming them out to wet nurses, and by spending time in educating them morally and intellectually. Joanna Baillie, writing in 1790, described the deep satisfaction of observing one's own baby:

Small understanding boasts thy face,
Thy shapeless limbs nor step nor grace;
A few short words thy feats may tell,
    And yet I love thee well.

Enjoying this new fondness for their children, parents bought them expensive toys (*S&S* 119), took a serious interest in their education, commissioned expensive portraits of them, and took them on walks, foxhunts, and trips to public pleasure gardens. Terrifying bedtime stories meant to frighten children into good behavior were replaced by educational books and collections of nursery rhymes. Children learned "Baby Bunting," "Baa, Baa, Black Sheep," "Little Boy Blue," and "A Doleful Ditty":

I.

Three children sliding on the ice
    Upon a summer's day,
As it fell out they all fell in,
    The rest they ran away.

II.

Oh! had these children been at school,
    Or sliding on dry ground,
Ten thousand pounds to one penny,
    They had not then been drown'd.

"Mama" and "Papa" replaced "Sir" and "Madam" in many families, and discipline went out the window. Loose clothes replaced the tight swaddling of earlier decades, which had confined babies in tight wrappings for the first several months of their lives.

Parents, in the name of raising their children "naturally," allowed them to become not-so-noble savages. Henry Fox, for example, father of the statesman Charles James Fox, was an extremely lax disciplinarian. When his older son, against Henry's wishes, grew his hair long, Henry did not order him to cut it but wheedled, claiming he would be "much obliged" if his son would yield. When young Charles James threw his father's watch on the floor, Henry observed, "If you must, I suppose you must." One can only imagine what fun Austen would have made of this response.

Although many mothers were convinced to breast-feed their children themselves, not all did so. Many women, Jane's mother included, farmed out their infants to local caregivers. The Austens were all raised until they could walk and talk by John and Elizabeth Littleworth, and Mr. and Mrs. Austen tried to visit them once a day. Mrs. Austen mentioned having personally nursed Cassandra for the first three months before turning her over to the Littleworths, and this may have been her practice with her other children as well.

Other genteel families followed a similar pattern, handing the very young children either to a cottage family or hiring servants who lived in the house. People wealthy enough to do so hired a battery of servants to care for the children—nurses to raise them (*E* 91–92), maids to dress them (*Watsons*, *MW* 350), governesses and tutors to educate them as they got older. Charles and Mary Musgrove think nothing of traveling to Bath without their children, because they can leave them entirely in the care of servants (*P* 123). Children were brought to the parents at intervals throughout the day, especially after dinner (*E* 219), but it was the servants who woke, dressed, fed, and cleaned them, and put them to bed. Middle-class families, who could afford fewer servants, raised their children more personally. Siblings, unmarried aunts like Jane and Cassandra, and grandparents might be asked to shoulder some of the responsibility or give parents a break now and then (*P* 122), and servants might be expected as part of their duties to take the children for some amount of time each day, but most of the job of raising children fell on the mother. Austen takes it for granted that a mother ought to be involved in raising her children. In her fiction, she approves of parents who take a serious interest in their children's welfare and who spend large amounts of time with them (*LS*, *MW* 275), conversely condemning those who neglect their duties (*Watsons*, *MW* 350; *MP* 19–20; *P* 56–57, 163).

Among working-class families, third-party child-rearing was out of the question. Children were cared for by the mother and, to some extent, by older siblings (*MP* 381). If the family had a maid-of-all-work, she, too, would be enlisted to do some amount of child care (*MP* 391), although her duties would be extensive enough already, and she would not have exclusive care of the child. As soon as the child was old enough to work, he would be given farm chores, put to work in the family shop, sent out to do factory work, or apprenticed to an artisan of some kind.

Etching by Thomas Rowlandson, 1790 (detail). Children playing blindman's buff. Courtesy of the Lewis Walpole Library, Yale University. 790.6.20.1.

Birthrates were high (*Gen Cur, MW* 73; *Sand, MW* 374; *S&S* 276; *MP* 4), especially among the upper class, who could afford to hire wet nurses and so lost the contraceptive benefits of breast-feeding. Jane, who was one of eight children herself, makes fun of this tendency toward fertility in *Edgar and Emma*. In this short juvenile work, the Willmots bring nine of their children on a visit, mention eleven others, including "Sam at Eton . . . Jem & Will at Winchester, Kitty at Queen's Square . . . Hetty & Patty in a Convent at Brussels. Edgar at college, [and] Peter at Nurse" (*E&E, MW* 32–33). Then, unable or unwilling to name an unspecified number of additional children, they simply call them "the rest" (32). Elizabeth Austen, Edward's wife, bore eleven children before dying in childbirth; the fictional Catherine Morland is one of ten children (*NA* 13), and Austen suggests that this enormous number of children was relatively common (*Cath, MW* 203). *See also* Games; Pregnancy and Childbirth; Toys.

Clergy

The Church of England was governed, in name at least, by the king. Below him stood the two archbishops, the archbishop of Canterbury and the archbishop of York, and twenty-seven English and Welsh bishops (*Cath, MW* 203, 206). Then came archdeacons and deacons and then, finally, the numerous parish clergy (*Gen Cur, MW* 73–74; *Cath, MW* 193; *Watsons, MW* 329; *Sand, MW* 401; *NA* 30; *S&S* 102, 296; *P&P* 101, 200–201; *MP* 21, 30, 91–92, 93, 145, 289), called parsons or priests, with whom Austen mostly concerns herself. These were divided into three classes: rectors, vicars, and curates. The difference between them was not their duties but their source of income.

Income

Tithes (*Plan, MW* 429, 430; *S&S* 293, 368; *P&P* 101) were a percentage of produce, typically 10 percent, paid in specified installments by the local farmers to the parson. The great tithe included grain, and the small tithe included livestock and vegetables. The difference between rectors and vicars was that rectors (*F&E, MW* 5; *P&P* 101, 364; *P* 78) received both the great and small tithes, while vicars (*E* 21, 66) were entitled to the small tithe only (*E* 35). A curate (*Visit, MW* 49; *Gen Cur, MW* 73–74; *Cath, MW* 203; *Plan, MW* 428; *NA* 221; *S&S* 61, 273, 275; *MP* 110; *P* 23, 73, 76, 78, 103) received no tithe at all. He was paid either by the legitimate holder of the "living" (the job of caring for a particular parish—see *Cath, MW* 203; *NA* 135; *P&P* 328; *MP* 3, 109, 241) or else by a layman whose ancestors had managed to secure the right to the tithes for themselves. These "lay impropriators" were far from being a majority, but by one estimate, in 1836 they held 20 percent of the tithes collected. They tended to favor the more lucrative great tithes, holding these in perhaps as many as 50 percent of parishes and making them, technically, the rectors of the affected parishes. Some impropriators were clergymen and did the duties of the parish; most, however, hired a vicar or curate to do the duties for them.

So far, this seems fairly straightforward, yet nothing was perfectly simple or uniform in Georgian England. Agreements made decades or even centuries before could complicate the payment of tithes in a particular parish. Some farmers or parishes had made arrangements to pay a fixed sum, called a modus, instead of a tithe, which kept the accounting somewhat simpler. In many cases, however, it merely shifted the complexity of tithe collection by forcing the parson to tally hens instead of eggs or pennies instead of pigeons. John Law, the vicar of Brotherton, wrote in his diary of the collection of moduses, in terms that make it clear that a modus did not necessarily simplify payment. Each pigeon house, he recorded, earned him a payment of 1s. 3d. per year, each dovecote half a crown,

> a new milch cow two pence halfpenny, a ship't cow three-halfpence, a foal four pence, every house ninepence halfpenny, a swarm of bees two pence. . . . The Marsh Mill pays an old modus of 2s 6d yearly; and tho' I have agreed to take the same for the Windmill, yet my successor is not obliged to do the same.

A modus was a source of grief to the parson in prosperous years and to the farmer in lean years. Some farmers chose to make a composition instead of a tithe; this was similar to a modus and had the same advantages and disadvantages but was calculated by the acre. In some parishes, the clergy had agreed to accept "commutation," a gift in exchange for tithes, often presented either as a sum of cash or as a plot of land to be farmed by the parson himself. Even in areas where the 10 percent tithe was the norm, certain types of land were exempted from tithes.*

---

*Exempt lands included barren land; crown forests; land tithe-free since "time immemorial" (which, in legal terms, meant since 1189); land owned before 1215 by Cistercians, Templars, or Hospitallers; land owned tithe-free at the Dissolution of Catholic institutions by Henry VIII; and the parson's own glebe.

Tithes could be collected either as cash or as a percentage of the actual produce of each farm. The latter method was referred to as "tithing in kind" and served as the subject matter for a popular print, occasionally dusted off and reissued during Jane Austen's lifetime. Entitled *Tithing in Kind,* or a variation on that title, it showed a fat parson running from a grinning farmer who was making his tithe payment with exactly one-tenth of an angry swarm of bees. Tithing in kind had been replaced in many places by tithes in cash, but it was still common in many English counties in the 1790s, including Cheshire, Lancashire, Durham, Shropshire, Berkshire, Buckinghamshire, Kent, Surrey, Wiltshire, Somerset, Cumberland, Westmorland, and Austen's own Hampshire. John Law, again, offers a sample of how complex the collection of tithes could be and what a headache it was for the clergyman who had to assess them:

> Everyone above the age of sixteen pays two pence as a comminicant. Turnips are paid for according to their value, or as they are let. Potatoes are paid in kind if not compounded for. The tythe of Orchards, Pigs and Geese are also paid in kind, if not compounded for. Rape and all new species of vicarial tythes are to be paid in kind unless compounded for, but Hemp and Flax must be paid according to Statute. . . . The new Shelling Mill built last year . . . is also titheable, after it has been so long employed as may be fairly supposed to reimburse the proprietor the expense of the building. N.B. If Clover and Saint Foin stand for seed the Tythe thereof belongs to the vicar, but if it is cut or made use of for Hay, the Tythe belongs to the Appropriators, or Lessee of the Dean and Chapter.

In all, Law had to collect 347 separate payments from 132 parishioners, and his was not an isolated case. The efforts of clergymen like Law were further complicated by a Byzantine set of rules that governed which produce was titheable. Bees, for example, were subject to tithe, but honey was not. Fallen apples were titheable, but not certain trees in certain types of woodland. In other cases, acorns were titheable, but not the trunks and branches of the trees themselves.

A large amount of time was spent by parsons in calculating tithes, collecting them, and storing the produce in the case of tithes in kind. Farmers did not necessarily make the process any easier. They were not especially eager to offer the fruits of their labors, and some went out of their way to make collection more difficult, specifying inconvenient times for pickup or requiring that the parson collect ridiculously small amounts at frequent intervals. Others simply lied about how many animals they had or how good the harvest had been; a parson needed to be vigilant, and the more vigilance he exercised, the greater the local resentment grew (*Cath, MW* 195). Compositions, as stated above, made things simpler and eased tensions, as a set fee per acre could be specified throughout the parish, but farmers with poorer land then felt cheated, as they paid the same rate as those with exceptionally fertile acres. Farmers who invested in improvements to their land felt cheated as well, because it seemed to them that they were working hard to enrich the parson. Constant negotiation and a careful assessment of how many years each composition agreement should last were necessary to make the system run smoothly.

Commutation was extremely popular with the clergy, as it accelerated their rise among the gentry. It was also a common solution to the tithe problem in Austen's time, because many communities opted for the enclosure of common land. Since parsons typically had a stake in the use of common land, their consent was usually required for the passage of an enclosure act. Their support was therefore purchased by a gift of land, written into the enclosure act. Commutation, however, did not solve all the problems of tithe collection, for enclosure did not always affect the whole parish.

A particular clergyman's income (*Gen Cur*, *MW* 73) was affected by tithe arrangements, by the number of arable acres in his parish, and by the fertility of the local soil (*S&S* 368). Income could also depend on the number of parishioners he served. In many cases, like John Law's, he received a small payment per parishioner, and he could also augment his income by means of "surplice fees," fees paid for his services at marriages, christenings, and funerals. Parson James Woodforde, whose parish lay near Norwich, received set payments from some, plus about £250 to £300 in tithes per year, and surplice fees that varied according to the occasion and the income of the parishioner. He typically charged a shilling or sixpence for churching a woman after the delivery of a baby, but on March 20, 1791, he recorded waiving his fee: "Being a poor Woman I took nothing for churching her." He received £1 1s. for a wedding in 1794, double that amount (a sum he considered "very handsome") for another wedding in 1788. A funeral in 1790 brought him £1 1s., and in 1780, he received "a Norwich Bank Note of five Guineas" for baptizing one of the squire's children. Sometimes he waived his fee out of personal attachment to the people involved; when his maid Anne Kaye got married in 1791, Woodforde took the fee that her new husband paid and gave it as a present to the bride.

No one was really happy about the tithe system. Farmers felt they paid a great deal in exchange for very little, as William Cowper indicated in his poem "The Yearly Distress":

> Quoth one, "A rarer man than you
>   In pulpit none shall hear;
> But yet methinks, to tell you true,
>   You sell it plaguy dear."

Clergymen newly posted to parishes often felt that their predecessors had not done enough to increase the tithes, while clergymen as a group felt

that they were being cheated of their due. Vicars complained that they held "not livings but leavings," and curates could hardly find words to express their hopelessness and indignation.

Total incomes varied widely, with many clergymen falling below what most gentry families would have thought of as the poverty line. Elinor Dashwood rejected out of hand the idea of living on a mere £350 a year, but in 1802, an estimated 1,000 livings (out of a total of about 12,000) earned their incumbents less than £100 a year, while another 3,000 brought incomes of £100 to £150. Curates, in some regions, could earn as much as £75 per year, but most scraped by on about £35 to £50 in the 1790s. Austen's brother Henry, after a free-spending life as a militia officer and banker, was reduced to a curacy in his later life and in 1818 had an income of only £54 12s. William Jones, a curate with nine children, never made more than £60 a year from his curacy at Broxbourne. Some parsons who hired curates allowed these poor fellows to keep the Easter offerings or the surplice fees, but this never

A Master Parson with a Good Living, 1782. A common theme in popular prints was the contrast between clergymen blessed with advantageous tithe arrangements and those stuck in dead-end curacies with meager stipends. This parson's comfortable family can afford a footman, mirrors, wax candles, a fine tablecloth, good curtains, a sizable dining room carpet, and fashionable wigs. Courtesy of the Lewis Walpole Library, Yale University. 782.6.25.1.

amounted to very much. Many curates, along with the rectors and vicars of inconsequential parishes, were forced to teach school in order to make ends meet; Austen's father, though his income was quite respectable, took in pupils (at £35 to £65 per year each) to pay for the upbringing of his eight children.

Clergymen faced a unique set of social and financial pressures as they neared retirement. Unless they had managed to save a substantial sum over the years, they could not hope for any sort of retirement in the conventional sense. Curates could not hope to retire at all, and rectors and vicars could retire only by subcontracting their jobs to others (*P* 78, 103). Parson Woodforde, for example, when he became too infirm to perform his duties, hired a curate for £30 plus surplice fees, a fraction of the amount of the parish tithes. Austen's father (*Mystery*, *MW* 55) did the same, hiring his eldest son, James, as a curate for Steventon and retiring

A JOURNEYMAN PARSON with a BARE EXISTENCE.

A Journeyman Parson with a Bare Existence, 1782. This poor clergyman, probably a curate, lives in a simple cottage with the bed and the dining table in the same room. His wig is ill-fitting, his dinner plain, his furniture mismatched, and his tablecloth unfashionably short. The scanty bookshelves and patched door advertised this room as not only the bedroom and dining room but the foyer and library as well. Courtesy of the Lewis Walpole Library, Yale University. 782.6.25.2.1.

for a few years on the difference between the income of his living and the £50 he paid James. For any elderly cleric, there was always an uncomfortable awareness that someone—the patron of the living, a young and ambitious divinity student, perhaps even his own son or nephew—was calculating, consciously or subconsciously, how much longer it would be until the living was vacant, in other words, until the current incumbent died (*MP* 473). A shortage of available livings, especially good livings, meant that the sharks were always circling. Once a clergyman died, his widow and children had to leave the parsonage and yield it to the next incumbent, which often meant real hardship (*Cath, MW* 194–195, 203).

Efforts were made from time to time to improve this situation. Queen Anne had, early in the eighteenth century, introduced a program to purchase land to augment the poorest livings. It was a successful initiative, but it was able to assist only a portion of those clergymen who needed help. The gap between the bottom of the scale, represented by men making less than the average member of Parliament's upper servants, and the top of the scale, represented by the archbishop of Canterbury's £7,000 a year, was huge.

Pluralism

One way of improving a clerical income was to become a pluralist, a holder of more than one living (*NA* 13). Estimates of the number of pluralists vary by date and source, but perhaps a third of all clergymen held more than one living. In some cases the two or more livings were close enough to each other that it was possible for one man to perform the duties of both parishes, but in many cases it was necessary to hire a curate for the parish in which the clergyman did not reside. Not every living with a curate, however, was held by a pluralist. Some incumbents, like Parson Woodforde in his later years, had handed their duties to a curate so that they could live in retirement. In other parishes, there was no rector or vicar at all, merely a "perpetual curate" salaried by the owner of the living. In still others, there was no parsonage for the incumbent to live in, or there was a parsonage in such ill repair as to be uninhabitable, so the parson lived somewhere nearby, but necessarily in the same parish.

According to a statute of 1604, a would-be pluralist had to hold a master's degree, reside in each living for "some reasonable time in the year," and depute a curate to perform any duties he could not manage on his own. The livings also had to be within thirty miles of each other (as were Mr. Austen's livings at Deane and Steventon). This law was not fundamentally revised before 1800, but it was much abused. Bishops could grant dispensation from the thirty-mile limit, and well-connected clerics managed to garner multiple valuable livings, rather than reserving pluralism for their poorer brethren. The result was a gradual drop in residency, so that by the 1820s only two-fifths of country incumbents actually resided in, and did the duties of, their own parishes.

Pluralism was never popular, but it was defended on the grounds that many clergymen needed more than one parish in order to make a decent living. Only as the Evangelical movement took hold in the first decades of the nineteenth century did pluralism come to seem disreputable (*MP* 248–249). Austen's works are full of pluralists, and no wonder; her father held two livings, and her brother James held three. Even her most scrupulous fictional clergyman, Edmund Bertram, may also be a pluralist. At the end of *Mansfield Park*, he inherits the living at Mansfield, but there is no indication that he yields the living at Thornton Lacey. Literary critics disagree as to whether or not he retains both livings, but Austen does not make an issue of it either way, which would seem to indicate that the question held little moral weight for her.

Parsonage and Glebe

The value and comfort of a living depended to a great extent on the property that came with it. This property, which was held only for the lifetime of the incumbent and could not be willed to his heirs, consisted of the parsonage and the glebe. The parsonage* (*F&E, MW* 5; *S&S* 296; *P&P* 88, 155, 172; *MP* 8, 23, 82, 205, 222, 241) was provided by the parish, but there was no guarantee as to the quality of the building or the attractiveness of its furnishings. Its upkeep, moreover, was the responsibility of the incumbent (*P&P* 101), and if he allowed it to fall into disrepair, his heirs could be sued by the next tenant for "dilapidations" (*MP*

---

*A parsonage occupied by a rector was a rectory (*S&S* 282; *P&P* 63); if inhabited by a vicar, it was known as a vicarage (*E* 113, 280, 305, 455).

55). However, if he did not live in the parsonage to begin with, an incumbent was extremely unlikely to spend money to repair it, and this perfectly understandable reluctance led to the worst parsonages falling deeper
and deeper into disrepair. Worse still, as late as the nineteenth century, an
estimated 3,000 parishes had no parsonage at all.

Austen was certainly acquainted with parsonages at all points in the spectrum (*MP* 242–243). The parsonage at Deane, her father's first parish, had
uneven floors and ceilings so low that they prevented tall people from standing up straight (*S&S* 292). Henry Austen's Chawton parsonage was considered "exceedingly bad" in 1796. Steventon parsonage, in which Jane was
brought up, was somewhat better, with an attractive, if simple, façade, two
parlors, a study, seven ordinary bedrooms, and three attic bedrooms. Yet
James Edward Austen-Leigh, Jane's nephew, thought the kitchen and the
servants' quarters entirely inadequate and the walls and ceilings unfashionably bare. The building was eventually demolished, some years after Jane's
death, when her brother Edward built a better parsonage with the hope of
installing one of his sons there. Other friends and relatives of the Austens
had better parsonages (*NA* 175–176; *P&P* 328; *E* 204); the rectory at
Wrotham and the parsonage at Ashe, for example, were elegant houses.

Some parsons remodeled their houses to suit their own tastes (*S&S* 372,
374; *MP* 241–242), putting up wallpaper, planting extensive gardens, and
even building bowling greens. Others moved into quarters they liked better and let the parsonage remain empty. Most clergymen liked to live near
the local squire or lord of the manor (*S&S* 197, 290; *MP* 82), and, in
cases where the magnates had moved away from the village or town, a parsonage was sometimes built near the large country houses rather than near
the church.

The glebe (*S&S* 368), like the parsonage, was an important aspect of
any living. The glebe was land affiliated with the living that could be
farmed by the parson. The Steventon glebe was fairly small, only three
acres, but George Austen also rented 200 acres at Cheesedown and was
able to add as much as 50 percent to the value of his living by farming
this land. Many parsons were forced to do likewise, as the glebe was often
too small to be very useful; others simply gave up and rented the glebe to
someone else with adjacent lands. Legislative efforts were made to improve
the situation. A 1776 Act of Parliament allowed parsons to take out government loans to add to the glebe, and an 1802 act struck down a centuries-old statute that barred clergy from renting the glebe to others, the
latter law a ratification of a practice already widely adopted. Enclosure also
enabled many to add to the glebe.

Church and Vestry

Though the parsonage and the glebe were the clergyman's responsibility, the upkeep of the church (*Watsons, MW* 321, 350; *S&S* 273, 374;

P&P 319; *MP* 82, 86, 203, 241; *E* 204) and churchyard (*NA* 178) was the duty of the parish, as represented by the vestry, or governing body (*E* 455). An annual meeting of the vestry was held anytime within a month of Easter and, with a greater or lesser degree of contentiousness, depending on the mood of the parish, elected overseers of the poor, made a report to the local magistrates, and levied taxes as necessary to maintain the church. Membership in the vestry and thus the right to attend this meeting were typically extended to all landowners and to the incumbent priest or his delegate, who presided over the parish meeting.

In theory, the vestry was responsible for all parts of the church except the chancel. This included the pews (*E* 175, 270), roof, font, pulpit (*MP* 93, 341), altar (*P&P* 107), and such basic supplies as Bible, prayer book, and communion vessels. In practice, there were complaints that churches and their property were in poor repair. William Cowper complained that too many churches had "scarce any other roof than the ivy." A number of churches, including the little church at Steventon, were quite old, with plain windows, no heating, and perhaps some rushes on the floors. The walls and floors of some churches were decorated with carved plaques in honor of deceased local dignitaries; a monument of this type would eventually be placed in Winchester Cathedral in memory of Jane Austen herself and can still be seen there today.

Education and Job Placement

In order to join the clergy, it was necessary for a young man to complete a course of study at one of the universities (*P&P* 79, 200). This automatically eliminated most poor boys, though the majority of candidates appear not to have come from the gentry and aristocracy. Over the course of the eighteenth century, the number of upper-class clergy increased, but it was still only perhaps 20 percent by Austen's time. Austen's writings tend to leave the impression that all clergymen were born gentlemen, but this was not in fact the case, and for many families, putting a son into the clergy was a way of rising in social status.

There were general trends in university matriculation. Southern parishes tended to favor Oxford graduates, for example. Patrons with an Evangelical bent might choose a candidate from Cambridge, where the Evangelical movement was especially strong. Austen's family were of the Oxford camp; Mr. Austen, James, and Henry all attended St. John's College, Oxford, which one of the family forebears had founded. As "founder's kin" they all received scholarships. The university education might begin at quite an early age—James Austen enrolled at age fourteen—although ordination (*L&F, MW* 82) could not take place until the age of twenty-three. The studies were not especially arduous, nor was the process of ordination (*S&S* 274, 275, 291; *P&P* 62, 200; *MP* 89, 255, 341), which in many cases was a mere formality. The requirements for ordination were a university degree, a testimonial from the candidate's college, and a brief examination by a bishop. Ben Lefroy, who married one of Jane's nieces and was ordained in 1817, was asked no questions about Scripture or the liturgy, but only whether he knew Jane's father, whom the bishop in question remembered from years past.

The ordination over, newly minted clergymen began the really difficult work of finding a living. In some cases, this was no more work than Ben Lefroy's ordination had been. Wealthy family members might save a living for a worthy relative, installing a curate in the post until the prospective candidate was of age (*P&P* 79; *P* 217). This appears to be the plan followed by Sir Thomas Bertram in *Mansfield Park* (23, 109), but financial pressures force him to yield one of the two livings being saved for his son Edmund. He gives up the living of Mansfield to an incumbent in exchange for a cash payment; this was a common practice, and landowners and clergymen alike were well aware of the going rates for a living (*S&S* 294–295; *MP* 23). The owners of advowsons (rights to employ clergy for particular benefices) based the price on both the value of the living and the life expectancy of the current incumbent. Sir Thomas, like Colonel Brandon in *Sense and Sensibility*, need not worry about a current incumbent and can sell the occupancy of the living at a good price.*

Those who could not get a living right away tried to settle for a curacy, but there was a glut of applicants for these posts as well. Those with relatives or friends among the senior clergy might apply for curacies in their parishes (*S&S* 275); those with indirect influence exerted it (*S&S* 149; *MP* 109; *P* 76); the rest advertised for posts in magazines and newspapers. Those who failed to find anything resorted to teaching school or to poorly paid naval chaplaincies (*Harley*, *MW* 40; *MP* 111). Everyone, even those already gifted with a living, scrambled to ingratiate himself with the people who could provide a benefice, a second benefice, or a better benefice (*P&P* 169). These patrons were of various types.

There were, in the middle and later years of Jane Austen's life, about 11,600 livings available, spread through 10,500 parishes and staffed by as many as 15,000 clergymen of all ranks. About 2,500 of these livings were in the gift of church patrons, such as bishops (*Cath*, *MW* 206; *P* 76). Another 600 or so could be distributed by the universities and the prominent public schools; these went primarily to masters and fellows of the various institutions and were generally awarded by election after a competitive debate between rival candidates. The crown owned about 1,100 livings, which were given out to political supporters and their relatives by the prime minister. Most of the remaining livings, about 5,500, were in

---

*The right to hire the next incumbents of both Deane and Ashe were purchased by Mr. Austen's uncle Francis Austen in 1770; Deane was awarded to Jane's father, George Austen, and Francis resold the presentation of Ashe to another, who installed George Lefroy in the post.

the gift of private landowners (*S&S* 149, 282–283, 289; *P&P* 79) who either sold the posts or gave them away to friends and relatives. On occasion, a landowner who was himself ordained might take the post himself, keeping the tithes and hiring a curate to perform the day-to-day duties. More rarely, the landed occupant performed the duty himself (*NA* 135).

There was constant pressure to please one's patron (*P&P* 383), both because parson and patron often lived in the same village and because there was always the hope of something better. Tom Fowle, a former pupil of George Austen's, became engaged to Jane's sister Cassandra while holding a small living at Allington, Wiltshire. He had hopes of a better living from his patron, Lord Craven, and to please his lordship, signed on as chaplain on a naval expedition that Craven was sending to the West Indies. While on his mission, Fowle died of yellow fever, a casualty of the race for a better post. Few paid so high a price, but all sought rich livings and prestigious appointments, such as cathedral "stalls" (positions as canons, who cared for the cathedral and elected its bishop—see *MP* 469).

Austen's Clerical Connections

Austen's familiarity with the clergy was not limited to Tom Fowle, her father, and her brothers. She had too many relatives and acquaintances in the profession to name, but they included Mr. Lloyd of Ibthorpe, two of whose daughters married Austen sons; Samuel Blackall, who showed matrimonial interest in Jane; Jane's godfather Samuel Cooke, the husband of one of her mother's cousins; Thomas Leigh, another of her mother's cousins; George Moore, eldest son of the archbishop of Canterbury and a relative of Edward Austen's by marriage; and John Rawstone Papillon, vicar of Chawton, whom Jane joked about marrying when she moved into the neighborhood:

> I am very much obliged to Mrs Knight [Edward's mother-in-law] for such a proof of the interest she takes in me—& she may depend upon it, that I will marry Mr Papillon, whatever may be his reluctance or my own.

There were Ben Lefroy, the neighbor whom Anna Austen, James' daughter, married, and Michael Terry, another clergyman to whom Anna was briefly engaged. Jane's friend Catherine Bigg married a clergyman, Herbert Hill of Streatham. She had ample opportunity, in other words, to observe the habits and foibles of a number of clergymen, which is undoubtedly why so many of them appear in her works and why she takes such an unsentimental view of their habits.

She found many of them to be exceedingly dreary. Her cousin Edward Cooper had too much of an Evangelical bent, in her opinion, and she was much amused, or provoked, or both, by the pretensions of James Stanier Clarke, a naval chaplain who was patronized by the Prince of Wales and, on the prince's behalf, escorted Jane on a tour of the Carlton House library. Thereafter, he pestered her to write a book according to his own suggestions, suggestions that made it clear that the book he had in mind was a fictionalized biography of himself:

> Do let us have an English Clergyman after *your* fancy—much novelty may be introduced—shew dear Madam what good would be done if Tythes were taken away entirely, and describe him burying his own mother—as I did—because the High Priest of the Parish in which she died—did not pay her remains the respect he ought to do. I have never recovered the Shock. Carry your Clergyman to Sea as the Friend of some distinguished Naval Character about a Court—you can then bring foreward . . . many interesting Scenes of Character & Interest.

Austen demurred, whereupon he urged her to write a "historical Romance illustrative of the History of the august house of Cobourg," and she again politely refused. Afterward, she mocked him privately in her *Plan of a Novel, according to Hints from Various Quarters*, in which the virtuous father describes his life in a long aside to his daughter, detailing his adventures in an almost word-for-word repetition of Clarke's ridiculous outline (*Plan, MW* 429). Clarke's flattery of her, combined with his absolute failure to understand the nature of her work, is the sort of unwittingly revealing juxtaposition so often used to illuminate Austen's fictional clergymen.

Clerical Duties

Austen offers allusions to, rather than detailed descriptions of, the professional duties (*MP* 248–249, 394) of clergymen, but her readers should not therefore assume that a parson's time was entirely taken up in hunting, riding, and eating large dinners. True, parsons enjoyed a good deal of leisure in comparison to artisans or day laborers, and their enthusiasm for good food was considered axiomatic (*MP* 110, 111, 469), but they were not idle. Bishops—not all of them as lax as the one who interrogated Ben Lefroy—conducted ordinations (*S&S* 275), sat in Parliament, and were nominally responsible for the parochial "visitations" that were supposed to ensure compliance with church rules. Archdeacons took on most of the actual duties of these visitations, and deacons, just coming into a period of great activity in the second decade of the nineteenth century, made inspections of church repairs, schools, charities, and so on, reporting on their findings to the bishops.

Parish priests were supposed to offer both a morning (*P&P* 60) and an evening service (*NA* 190) each Sunday, though this schedule was routinely adhered to in only about half of all parishes. This, however, was not necessarily the fault of the clergy. There is some evidence that the clergy were merely acceding to the wish of the people, many of whom appear to have been content with one service. In some cases, it was a matter of necessity; pluralists with closely spaced parishes often tried to do the duty in both, which meant a morning service in one parish and an evening service in the other. "Double duty," with both morning and evening services offered in the same parish, was generally more common in the north and Wales, less common in the south and east. The frequency with which communion was offered followed a similar pattern. Communion was offered once a month by a few scrupulous parsons, usually in the north and west, but most parsons offered it only the required minimum of three times a year: at Easter, at Christmas, and once more at their discretion, usually with at least a week's notice.

The parson's most important duty, if public enthusiasm is to be believed, was his Sunday sermon (*P&P* 66, 328; *MP* 226, 227, 249, 341; *E* 75). Parishioners loved to hear good preaching (*MP* 93, 340–341), and they were disappointed if the parson failed to preach on a particular Sunday, or if he preached badly. They would at times travel to a different parish to hear an especially good speaker or to hear any preaching at all if they knew in advance that there would be no sermon that day at their own parish church. Parsons were given extra credit in the public mind if they wrote their own sermons (*P&P* 101; *MP* 92); it was not exactly considered cheating to use one of the many books of prewritten sermons, such as those written by Scottish rhetoric professor Hugh Blair (*MP* 92) or Jane's own cousin Edward Cooper, but neither was it considered laudable. The rabble-rousing enthusiasm of later preachers was viewed with suspicion in Austen's time; instead, formality, audibility, and sincerity of expression were prized (*Watsons, MW* 343–344).

Clergymen were also expected to officiate at the rites of passage of the community. They baptized newborn children (*P&P* 64), sometimes publicly, sometimes privately in the parents' home. This was done right away in the case of sickly infants but was sometimes delayed for healthier children, to allow far-flung godparents (*NA* 63; *P&P* 79, 199; *MP* 387; *P* 6) time to arrive for the ceremony. Austen herself, who was born in December, was not christened (*E* 79) until the following April, as the guests were not expected to travel in the unusually harsh winter of 1775–1776. Shortly after the baptism, the mother was "churched," which meant she was symbolically reintroduced to the full community as she gave thanks for her safe deliverance from the potential dangers of childbearing. Churchings and most christenings, along with weddings (*S&S* 296; *P&P* 64; *MP* 89; *E* 482–483), could be scheduled in advance, but deaths might occur at any time, and funerals (*P&P* 64) and emergency baptisms required clergymen to be flexible about their schedules. A clergyman may be seen officiating at a wedding in the illustration *The Wedding* (Marriage).

When they were not composing sermons, conducting services, or performing ceremonial duties, clergymen taught children the catechism and visited the sick (*P* 20). Once a year, often at Shrovetide, they administered communion to those too sick to leave their beds. Some parsons also held

A Christening, Thomas Rowlandson, 1790. Clergymen received "surplice money" for special ceremonies such as christenings, weddings, and funerals. Courtesy of the Lewis Walpole Library, Yale University. 790.0.18.

weekday services and officiated at special occasions, such as services of thanksgiving on patriotic holidays. Increasingly, parsons were also serving as justices of the peace, though they were a minority on the bench. They might be consulted on questions of religion or on issues of public importance, and they were often asked to lend credibility to some new venture by their presence or participation.

Clergymen sometimes assisted each other in their duties. They took turns, for example, helping each other to perform sick communion, and they might step in for a neighboring priest in an emergency (*P&P* 63). James Woodforde noted on March 25, 1785, that Mr. Mattishall, a nearby parson, was "very ill" and that he had accordingly agreed to handle Mattishall's Easter Sunday evening service. Parsons who intended to preach a sermon on a particular Sunday also consulted with the clergy in neighboring parishes, trying to make sure that no one's sermon conflicted with anyone else's, so that the populace could attend more than one sermon in a single day. *See also* Income; Religion.

Clocks and Watches

Clocks (*Cath*, *MW* 218; *Watsons*, *MW* 322, 359; *NA* 83, 189, 193; *P&P* 33; *E* 189) took many forms. There were longcase clocks of mahogany or oak, the kinds of pendulum clocks often called grandfather clocks today. On these clocks, as on most clocks and watches of the time, the hours were marked in Roman numerals, with "IIII" replacing the correct "IV" because it seemed more aesthetically harmonious with the "VIII" on the opposite side. Minutes were typically marked in Arabic numerals and might appear on a concentric circle with the hours, or as a completely separate ring. From the mid-eighteenth century, the trend was toward minute and hour hands of matching style. Seconds, which had not been of any concern in previous centuries, were now considered important enough to merit a dial or ring of their own. The roughly triangular areas between the round dial and the square edges of the case were the "spandrels," and they were usually made of sand-cast brass and gilded. Typical designs included cherubs' faces, flowers, or depictions of the four seasons.

Minutes, hours, and seconds were not the only features tracked on elaborate longcase clocks. Some of these clocks had dials that told the calendar date or the phases of the moon. Others indicated the state of tides or the position of the sun in the zodiac.

Some clocks were designed to stand on tables or fireplace mantels (*P* 144); originally built with square dials, they might have round dials instead from about the mid-eighteenth century. The dial was protected by a hinged glass door that could be opened to reset the clock by manually adjusting the position of the hands. Wall clocks were out of favor for much of the eighteenth century but became fashionable again, in round or octagonal forms, at the beginning of the nineteenth. One especially characteristic type of wall clock was the tavern clock, which appears in many prints and paintings of the day. It had an exceptionally large dial, sometimes as much as two or three feet in diameter, and had a minute hand, an hour hand, and a pendulum to mark the seconds. Tavern clocks came into their own from 1797 to 1798, when Prime Minster Pitt imposed a tax of five shillings a year on watches and clocks—ten shillings for gold watches—that induced some people to relinquish their watches and keep time by occasional peeks into the local tavern. A device that increased foot traffic so effectively

A MAIDEN EWE, DREST LAMB FASHION.
"The end of these things is Death"
Published 15th Sept 1796, by LAURIE & WHITTLE, 53, Fleet Street, London.

A Maiden Ewe, Drest Lamb Fashion, 1796. The title of this print plays on the double meaning of the word "dressed," which could mean either dressed in clothes or, with reference to food, prepared for the table. Cookbooks of the time often contained recipes for one meat "dressed" as if it were another. In this case, the old "ewe" is dressed in the latest fashions, which emphasized the willowy figures of young women, or "lambs." The waist is exaggeratedly high, but the custom of hanging a pocket watch from the sash is valid and can be seen in a number of prints from around this time. Courtesy of the Lewis Walpole Library, Yale University. 796.9.15.1.

was naturally popular with tavern keepers, who prized their "Act of Parliament" clocks and competed to have the handsomest and most accurate clock in town. Two wall clocks may be seen in the background of the illustration *Billiards* (Games).

Watches (*NA* 45, 67, 155, 162, 165, 171; *MP* 95, 218, 279; *E* 246) were "pocket" watches, although they were not always kept in the little watch pockets that formed a feature of many waistcoats. Many were worn suspended from belts or sashes, so that their beautifully ornamented covers could be admired by acquaintances and passersby. Like clocks, they might well have separate dials for minutes, hours, and seconds. Inside the cover, the owner might place a "watch paper"—a decorative cloth or paper lining; Parson James Woodforde, a contemporary of Austen's, visited Norwich in November 1784 and met there a girl who

> had no Hands or Arms, and yet wonderfully cleaver with her Feet. She cut out a Watch Paper for me whilst I was there with her Toes she opened My Watch and put it in after done. Her name was Jane Hawtin, about 22 years old. She talks very sensible and appears very happy in her Situation—She uses her Toes as well as any their Fingers. I gave her for cutting the Watch Paper 0.1.0.

Woodforde, whose tithes equaled about £300 a year, in 1794 owned two "eight day Clocks" and the aforementioned pocket watch.

Clothing

The clothing (*E&E*, *MW* 30; *L&F*, *MW* 107; *Cath*, *MW* 198; *Sand*, *MW* 421; *NA* 20, 33, 216; *S&S* 119; *P&P* 160–161, 222, 376; *MP* 14, 282–283, 444; *E* 321; *P* 43, 142–143) of Jane Austen's childhood was much as it had been throughout the eighteenth century. For women, this meant voluminous silk dresses, open at the front to reveal ornate matching petticoats; tall, powdered clouds of hair; low bodices with the exposed flesh covered by lightweight bits of fabric called handkerchiefs, fichus, or modesty pieces. For men, this meant heeled shoes and white stockings; powdered wigs in a bewildering assortment of styles; and a three-piece suit of knee breeches, knee-length, full-skirted frock coat, and waistcoat (vest), with all three pieces often made of the same fabric. By the time she began publishing her novels in 1813, fashion was entirely different, and only the most old-fashioned people, usually elderly men, wore anything like the styles they had worn thirty years before.

Men's Clothing

Men's clothing began to evolve in the 1790s in response to three enthusiasms. One of these was vogue for classical literature, art, and architecture, which led men to adopt Roman-style short haircuts and fashions that echoed the lines of Greek statuary. A second was sympathy for the egalitarian sentiments of the French Revolution—not a common sentiment in England but quite common in France, which developed simpler Republican styles of dress designed to bridge the differences between the classes; these fashions then crossed the Channel and influenced English costume. The third was an interest in hunting and equestrian sports, which in some men bordered on obsession. These gentlemen had taken to wearing their informal shooting jackets (*S&S* 43; *MP* 138–139) and high-top boots almost everywhere, and their example was imitated by men who longed, even indoors, for the comfort of hunting attire.

In response to these influences, both the color and cut of men's clothes

A MEETING *at* MARGATE, *or a* LITTLE MISTAKE.

(A Polite Bow from both Parties) Lord. *"Sir your face is quite familiar to me, I must have seen you somewhere before, will you do me the honor to tell me your name".* Taylor.*"Yes my Lord, I have had the honor — I..I made your Breeches"—"Oh! Oh! Major Bridges, I am very happy to see Major Bridges."* Publish'd Jan'.1.?1803. by LAURIE & WHITTLE, 53, Fleet Street, London.

284

A Meeting at Margate, or a Little Mistake, 1803. The new features of men's fashion can be clearly seen in this print: the newly short hair, the round hat, the long, tight breeches or pantaloons, and the diminishing tails of the coat. The women wear high-waisted (but full-skirted and thoroughly opaque) dresses. Courtesy of the Lewis Walpole Library, Yale University. 803.1.1.4.

changed. Parsons still continued, for the most part, to wear black, and some men persisted in wearing old-fashioned bright colors (*F&E, MW* 8; *J&A, MW* 13), but most men shifted their allegiance from suits all of one color (or from those where the breeches and coat, at least, matched) to a coat (*Cath, MW* 222; *Watsons, MW* 353; *MW* 445; *S&S* 86; *P* 49) of one color, breeches (*NA* 172) of another, and waistcoat (*L&F, MW* 98; *MW* 445; *NA* 172; *S&S* 38, 378) of still another. The frock coat was usually blue (*F&E, MW* 8; *P&P* 9, 319) or black, double-breasted, with large buttons, only the bottom few of which were fastened. The remainder were left undone so that an increasingly large expanse of white could be seen at the throat: white shirt, white waistcoat, and white cravat. Then buff or black breeches and boots or shoes and stockings completed the picture. The breeches were replete with buttons. They fastened in front with a vertical row of buttons, with a small horizontal flap at the bottom of this fly fixed in place by two or three more buttons. Then there were buttons at each knee, on the outside of the leg.

As the new style evolved, both the coat and the breeches underwent additional refinements. Knee breeches and boots, for example, were a poor match; there was always just a little bit of boot stocking showing between the two. One solution, adopted around 1800, was to add short gaiters to the tops of the boots, allowing them to be buttoned above the knee. A more common solution was to extend the breeches well below the knee so that their bottoms were entirely hidden by the boots. From this move it was just a short step to pantaloons, tight-fitting trousers that were made of stockinette (a knitted fabric) or doeskin. Some of these pantaloons were so tight-fitting, in fact, that they had to be worn with a lining in their upper part to prevent young ladies from getting a premature education in male anatomy. A fashion for somewhat lower boots lengthened the line of the leg, and the buff color enhanced the illusion of classical nudity. Later in Austen's lifetime, black pantaloons became increasingly popular, a trend that was to lead to the sober three-piece suits of the Victorian era.

The frock coat lost its voluminous skirts and, like the pants, hugged the body. It was cut either straight across or with a curve, frequently exposing the bottom of the waistcoat, and cut away sharply to the side and back. A little coattail was left on the sides of the body, but not much. The lapels and collar off the coat gradually expanded, focusing attention on the cascades of white linen at the throat and chest, and the collar was stood up a bit in back.

There were, of course, exceptions to this pattern of dress. Old men stuck to the comfortable, roomy coats they had known in their youth. Some younger men favored buff waistcoats rather than white, or single-breasted coats rather than double-breasted. Evening dress, worn from dinner on, was always different and far more formal (*Watsons, MW* 327, 357; *E* 114; *P* 55, 99). A description of proper evening attire in the April 1811 edition of *Ackermann's Repository*, a popular fashion magazine, instructed men to wear either blue coat with gilt buttons, single-breasted waistcoat, and cream-colored kerseymere knee breeches, or black coat and black silk knee breeches. Court attire was still fancier and far more old-fashioned; there it was not out of place to wear an old-style green velvet (*P* 40) suit with a white waistcoat embroidered in gold, and boots at court were quite out of the question.

The standard outer garment for men was the greatcoat (*Watsons, MW* 356; *Sand, MW* 407; *NA* 83, 131, 155, 210; *E* 58; *P* 106). This, unlike the frock coat, did not shrink appreciably in size. It remained a large, comparatively shapeless garment and was worn at any time when an additional layer was deemed necessary for warmth or protection from rain. Coachmen favored a style that had multi-layered capes below the lapels, and for a time in the late 1790s this was adopted by fashionable men as well (*NA* 157). The court, however, and the prince regent's arbiter of sartorial taste, George Bryan "Beau" Brummell, rejected the coachman's greatcoat.

Shirts (*NA* 172) were relatively plain around the turn of the century, reacquiring ruffles in about 1806 for evening wear. Daytime shirts remained plain, and more and more of the shirt began to show in the gap between cravat and coat. The other principal item of underwear was drawers, long and sometimes footed when worn with pantaloons, knee-length or just above when worn with breeches. They buttoned down the front and sometimes had tapes or strings in the back to perfect the fit. The pantaloons themselves were held up with leather braces (suspenders), which came into common use around 1800.

The cravat (*NA* 28, 172, 240) or neckcloth was a square of clean white linen, at least 40 to 45 inches square. It was folded in half diagonally. The folded edge was placed around the throat, near the chin or sometimes, to judge from some illustrations, up around the ears. This left a deep triangle to be tucked into the shirt and two loose ends, which were wrapped around the back of the neck and brought to the front again, where they were tied together in a variety of patterns. Some had discreet little knots, while others produced waterfalls of puffs and folds. The tying and arranging of the ends were the tricky part. As the author of *Neckclothitania* wrote in 1818,

> My neckcloth, of course, forms my principal care,
> For by that we criterions of elegance swear,
> And costs me each morning, some hours of flurry,
> To make it *appear* to be tied in a *hurry*.

The cravat was often stiffly starched, making it rub uncomfortably against the throat and jowls, and a man in a properly tied cravat was almost incapable of moving his head. To look around, he had to swivel his whole upper body.

At night men wore long, baggy linen nightshirts and sometimes caps as well. When they lounged around indoors, they might wear a dressing gown—a loose, long, comfortable garment with a shawl collar—in place of the frock coat. This could serve as a general-purpose indoor garment and could also be worn to protect the clothes during the powdering of hair (*P&P* 300). An example may be seen in the illustration *Miseries of Human Life* (Housework).

Women's Clothing

Women's clothing (*P* 215), like men's, underwent a process of streamlining and simplification. The 1780s and early 1790s had featured full, round skirts, slightly puffed out at the back, though not sporting the wide panniers that had spread the skirt far to the sides in the middle of the eighteenth century. As if to compensate for the bulge behind, generously sized fichus had covered the bosom, puffing out in front. As France's Republican and classical styles spread across the Channel, however, the bulk of the

Too Much and Too Little, George Woodward, 1796. The lady on the left, garbed in Elizabethan ruff and farthingale, debates fashion with the lady on the right, dressed in a fashionably sheer and low-cut gown that reveals most of her breasts and clearly reveals the height to which her stockings rise. The latter woman's fashion statement is exaggerated for humorous effect, but Woodward's print, by emphasizing these features, shows us what people found new and shocking about the classical style of dress. The tall feather headdress was also popular at the end of the eighteenth century, creating problems at court, where feather-wearing women in the process of curtseying were a nuisance to those they faced. Courtesy of the Lewis Walpole Library, Yale University. 796.2.8.2.

skirt gradually diminished; it took ten yards to make a dress in 1796, but only seven yards in 1801, when Jane asked Cassandra to buy "Seven yards for my mother, seven yards and a half for me" to make dresses. The number of supporting petticoats (*E* 225) diminished, too, until some women were wearing only one, or even none at all (to the scandal and shock of moralists and the secret delight of lascivious men). In the fashions of earlier decades, the petticoat had been a prominent part of the dress, highly decorative and so visible between the folds of an "open robe"—a dress that parted in the front—that it often appeared to be part of the dress itself. Now the petticoat retreated under the gown (*P&P* 36), and even gowns that still opened in the front wrapped completely and fastened in place. Now the petticoat, if it showed at all, showed only as an ornamental band at the bottom of the dress.

In addition to the petticoat, many women now took to wearing drawers. These were quite long—long enough that Lady de Clifford pointed out to Princess Charlotte that hers were visible every time she got into or out of a carriage. Unimpressed, the princess replied, "the Duchess of Bedford's are much longer, and they are bordered with Brussels lace." There was, as the princess implied, little effort taken to hide the drawers, which came into fashion around 1806.

Above the petticoat, a chemise was worn. This was a knee-length linen or cotton shirt, often with a frill of some kind at the neckline and short sleeves. It was usually, but not always, worn beneath a dress. If it were worn, part of it, for example, the decorative neckline, often peeked from underneath the dress.

As the silhouette slimmed, the waistline rose, until it ended just under the breasts. The dress itself was rather loose and was pulled into classical

"Monstrosities" of 1799—Scene, Kensington Gardens, James Gillray, 1799. The features of the latest fashions are wildly exaggerated, emphasizing the details that Gillray found odd—the tasseled Hessian boots, the sheerness of the classically inspired muslin dresses, the deep brims of straw bonnets, the diminishing tails of men's coats, and the gathers at the shoulders of men's coat sleeves. As in many prints of the time, the transparency of muslin dresses is exaggerated. The lady at the left of the picture is fairly modest, showing only an outline of nipple, but the lady on the right has a very low neckline, especially for daytime, and the line of her left garter can be perceived through her dress. A lady walking in the background of the image has her whole figure visible through the thin veil of her dress. Courtesy of the Lewis Walpole Library, Yale University. 799.6.25.3.

folds of drapery, often by tightening drawstrings at the neckline and artificial waistline. Beneath this apparent ease and lightness, many women retained the stays they had worn for centuries. These were corsets made of heavy cotton fabric or silk and stiffened with whalebone. They were sometimes assisted in front with a "divorce," a triangular piece of padded metal that separated the breasts. Their height fluctuated from short to long in about 1800, then back to short again in about 1811, but they generally came either to the top of the hips or to just below them. An 1807 advertisement for a stay maker (*L&F, MW* 106) promised that his stays would "give the wearer the true Grecian form." Stays could cost about three or four guineas.

Necklines were very low and revealed a great deal of the bosom, so many women retained the modesty pieces of earlier decades, tucking a gauzy

A FASHIONABLE BELLE.

A Fashionable Belle, Williams, 1816. The shift away from classical styles toward the end of Austen's life can be seen in this print. Her costume is more gaudily ornamented, from the trim at the hem of her walking dress to the ribbons, slashed sleeves, and lace collar of her pelisse. Her bonnet, like most fashionable hats of the time, is tall, and she wears tiny half-boots. Courtesy of the Lewis Walpole Library, Yale University. 816.0.9.

piece of fabric around the back of the neck and into the top of the gown, sometimes crossing the ends of the fabric in front. During the day, women wore what was known as "morning" or "walking" dress (*Cath, MW* 211), which covered almost all of the skin. They wore long sleeves and, if they went outside, gloves and bonnets. The fichu covered the chest, and often a jacket of some sort was worn. Indoors, before a woman went out, she might wear a dressing gown (*P&P* 344), not the voluminous and decorative indoor coat of the same name worn by men but a loose and comfortable gown appropriate for wearing while the rest of her toilette was completed. Morning gowns were often white, a difficult color to keep clean and thus a silent advertisement for the leisure that women of Austen's class enjoyed. (Thus, Mrs. Norris is pleased that the Sotherton housekeeper has fired maids for their pretensions in wearing impractical white gowns—*MP* 105–106.) Walking dresses, which were meant to be worn outdoors, were similar to morning gowns but were more frequently colored in order to hide dirt. Jane Austen, at various times, owned pink, brown, and yellow-and-white dresses.

At dinnertime, women changed into evening dress (*NA* 162–165, 195; *S&S* 193; *MP* 141), a process that could take anywhere from half an hour to upwards of two hours. They traded their colored walking dresses for evening gowns in white (*NA* 91; *MP* 222; *E* 178) or very pale colors. The anonymous author of *The Mirror of the Graces* (1811) suggested white above all for evening gowns, as "White is becoming to all characters," but if a large woman ("a lady of majestic deportment," as the author tactfully put it) chose to wear colors, she should adhere to "the fuller shades of yellow, purple (*NA* 218), crimson, scarlet, black, and grey."

The evening gowns were exclusively short-sleeved until about 1814. In March of that year, Jane wrote to Cassandra from London with the radical intention of adopting the new fashion of wearing long sleeves at night (*P&P* 140): "I wear my gauze gown today," she explained, "long sleeves & all; I shall see how they succeed, but as yet I have no reason to suppose long sleeves are allowable." In the end, it was all right; a family friend, Mrs. Frances Tilson, informed her that they were indeed "allowable." "Mrs Tilson had long sleeves too," Jane reported, "& she assured me that they are worn in the evening by many. I was glad to hear this." Later that same year, again in London, she confirmed that "long sleeves appear universal, even as *Dress*."

Fichus were set aside in the evening, and women displayed their low necklines to full advantage. Gloves that reached above the elbow were kept handy; they would be taken off for dinner and replaced for the evening, especially if dancing was planned. Evening gowns had trains for the first few years of the century, losing them by the time Austen began publishing. Those who planned to dance would gather up the train (*NA* 37) before lining up in the set; those who preferred to play cards could leave their trains to sweep grandly along the floor. No doubt this is part of Mrs. Allen's concern in the assembly rooms at Bath. She is extremely glad to walk through the crowded ballroom without "injury" (*NA* 22).* Dresses for balls were especially grand (*Col Let, MW* 156; *Cath, MW* 216; *MP* 254, 257); women brought out their best and most flattering attire on such occasions.

Progress of the Toilet.—The Stays, James Gillray, 1810. A lady, assisted by her maid, gets dressed for the evening. She has already washed at least her face and hands, as is hinted by the presence of a basin and pitcher in the left foreground. She inserts a busk, a stiff front piece, into her stays while her maid laces the stays at the back. The petticoats of former days have been replaced by drawers, and her stockings have discreet white-on-white clocks. The maid's costume is a simple blue dress, white apron and modesty piece, and white cap with lappets that are presumably tied under the chin, although Gillray does not show a knot or a bow. Courtesy of the Lewis Walpole Library, Yale University. 810.2.2.6.1.

One example of a ball gown, from an 1801 issue of the *Gallery of Fashion*, is a "robe" (*NA* 26). A robe was a descendant of the open-fronted gown that exposed the petticoat, and this particular example still belongs very much to the eighteenth century. The skirt of the white muslin petti-

---

*As *Northanger Abbey* was written in 1790s and only minimally revised, it retained the anachronistic train when it was finally published after Austen's death. The other example of a train comes from *The Watsons* (*MW* 327), presumed to have been written in 1804, when trains were still common on evening wear.

Progress of the Toilet.—Dress Completed, James Gillray, 1810. The lady, having put on her dress and chosen her jewelry, is ready for dinner in a low-necked, short-sleeved gown. Courtesy of the Lewis Walpole Library, Yale University. 810.2.2.6.3.

coat is full and plain, with a narrow band of trim near the hem. The black velvet robe, trimmed with gold braid, is actually quite small in comparison to the rest of the dress. Trimmed with gold lace, it drops very low at the neckline and is cut quite high at the front of the skirt, leaving only a tiny horizontal band that is laced like a medieval bodice. There are no sleeves to the robe, only shoulder straps; the sleeves are instead part of the under-dress or part of the chemise. From the sides, the back of the robe falls away rapidly from the front, leaving at least half the circumference of the petticoat exposed, and trails away into a train. Another example of a robe from the *Gallery of Fashion*, this one from June 1798, shows a white robe for day wear. It is more typical of the eighteenth-century robe, in that both sides slope toward the waistline, meet there, and then divide to expose a triangular panel of equally white petticoat. In later years, the robe became a "chemise robe," with one side crossing completely over the other in front and the petticoat entirely covered except at the bottom.

Just as a "robe" meant a very specific kind of dress, so did "frock" and "gown" (*Watsons, MW* 323, 327, 353; *NA* 28, 52, 70, 73, 74, 91, 93, 104, 118, 165, 238; *S&S* 249; *P&P* 13, 36, 214, 238, 292; *MP* 99–100, 146, 222, 272; *E* 178, 271, 302, 324; *P* 142). From the front, these two kinds of dresses looked very similar. They presented the appearance of a single tube of fabric, gathered at the waist if necessary and given sleeves (*NA* 70) as appropriate. The difference between them was in the back, where the gown was still uninterrupted, while the frock was open at the back, at least nominally, and gathered together with pins or other fastenings. Austen uses the term "gown" almost universally, referring to "frock" only in relation to children's clothing (*Lesley, MW,* 111; *MP* 13), so it may be that the people she knew used the term in a general, rather than technical, sense.

She may also have used the term "gown" to refer to dresses that opened

A Shrewed Guess or the Farmers Definition of Parliamentary Debates, 1813. Working-class costume is illustrated here. The farmer's wife wears a long, serviceable apron, a simple mob cap or biggin with a blue ribbon, and a plain red dress. The farmer wears a loose, comfortable coat, much like the shooting dress worn by gentlemen. His top boots can be seen hanging from a peg on the wall behind him. His son, sitting in an old-fashioned, large fireplace, wears the customary working costume of agricultural laborers, the farmer's smock. Courtesy of the Lewis Walpole Library, Yale University. 813.0.11.

in front, not in the manner of a robe, but in the manner of a "stomacher" (*E* 86). The stomacher had a front flap made either of part of the skirt or part of the skirt and the front panel of the bodice. The wearer got into the gown and, in the case of stomachers that incorporated part of the bodice, pinned or buttoned this portion at the shoulders. Then a drawstring in the waist of the flap was pulled to cinch in the waist and tied in a bow in back. In the case of stomachers where the flap was only part of the skirt, the flap was tied around the waist using a string that was part of the flap. Then the bodice was closed by wrapping, lacing (with a shirt underneath to cover the gap under the crossed laces), or buttoning down the middle.

Like the robe, the frock or gown could be adapted with equal ease to morning or evening wear. One 1807 example of an evening frock, for example, has a square neckline, short sleeves, and a relatively smooth front of sprigged muslin; all its fullness is gathered at the back and allowed to cascade down as a train. An 1808 walking frock, however, has no train and is worn with long gloves, a jacketlike vest, a shawl, and a straw bonnet. This careful covering of almost all exposed skin would have met with the approval of the author of *The Mirror of the Graces*, who advised the cautious woman that

> morning robes should be of a length sufficiently circumscribed as not to impede her walking; but on no account must they be too short; for when any design is betrayed of showing the foot or ancle [*sic*], the idea of beauty is lost in that of the wearer's odious indelicacy.

Not only the ankle should be covered, she wrote, but also "the arms and the bosom, nay, even the neck."

As with men, there were exceptions to every rule for dress. Older women tended to be better than older men at keeping up with the latest fashions, but they were expected to modify their dress to reflect their more advanced years. Accordingly, they retained the fichus and tuckers that partially covered the bosom, kept to more old-fashioned hairstyles that relied on powder, frizzing, and sausage curls, and wore long sleeves more frequently than younger women, even at night. Court dress, as always, was behind the times and retained old-fashioned fitted bodices, hoop petticoats, and powdered hair.

Outer Garments

The thinness of the classical garments worn in the first years of the nineteenth century left women in a somewhat uncomfortable position, as the English climate was rather different from that of Greece or Rome. Therefore, women needed a variety of garments to keep them warm. One of the most popular of these accessories, used as a decorative quasi-classical drapery as well as serving as a warm wrap, was the shawl.

The shawl (*MP* 212, 251; *E* 48, 322, 346, 349; *P* 117) was a large rectangle of fabric, initially of cashmere from Tibetan mountain goats and made in India. It often came in bright or deep colors and featured decorative borders with repeated patterns such as spades, so-called pinecones (actually bunches of flowers), or paisley swirls. Other shawls featured borders with Greek motifs. The shawl was typically allowed to drape over both shoulders, with its loose ends hanging in some cases almost down to the ground.

Shawls quickly became popular in England, so popular that several unsuccessful attempts

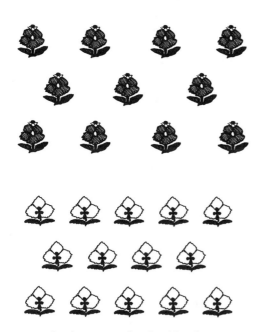

Spade patterns for shawl borders.

were made to introduce Kashmir goats to the British Isles. Despite the repeated failures, British manufacturers in Norwich, Edinburgh, and Paisley began making machine-woven shawls in the 1780s and 1790s, but these remained inferior to the Indian originals (*MP* 305), which were handwoven, slowly crafted, and often sewn back-to-back to make them equally soft on both sides. Unpatterned, solid-color Indian shawls were so fine and light that they could be passed through a ring and were known as "ring shawls." Nonetheless, British manufacturers eventually produced shawls that were interesting in their own right. A silk example from about 1810 to 1820 reproduces the outline of the "pinecone," but instead of fanciful eastern flowers, it fills the space with roses, acorns, ears of wheat, and other British flora. Some women sewed their own shawls; Parson Woodforde, in 1781, gave his niece Nancy some muslin for this purpose.

The shawl remained primarily decorative in nature, but other garments were more practical. The spencer (*E* 173) was a jacket with long sleeves, cut very short to end at the false waist of the dress. Jane Austen had one in 1808, which she wore for walks on June evenings.

The pelisse (*LS, MW* 27; *Cath, MW* 211; *Watsons, MW* 341; *NA* 32; *MP* 395; *P* 142) was a warmer garment, almost a dress in itself. It wrapped with one side over the other or met in the middle and frequently covered the dress almost entirely. Like the spencer, it had long sleeves. An example of a pelisse from *The Gallery of Fashion* for March 1799 is a bright pea-green with purple lining, collar, and cuffs, with dark fringe at the collar and cuffs. Another pelisse shown in the same magazine in 1803 was crimson with brown fur at the neck edges, waist, and hem and a row of gold cord frog closures up the front. Novelist Fanny Burney used a pelisse in 1795 to go to the theatre in disguise for the opening night of her tragedy *Edwy and Elgiva*; hidden in a box "wrapt up in a Bonnet and immense Pelice," she was no doubt grateful for the voluminous folds, because the play was not well received. Pelisses could be lined or unlined for winter or summer wear.

A relative of the shawl was the tippet (*NA* 51; *E* 328), a small scarf with the ends worn loose in front. It was almost too small to qualify as an outdoor garment, being more of an accessory, but it kept the neck and chest warm. The cloak (*NA* 28, 40) was a relatively shapeless wrap with slits for the arms. Styles popular in 1801 in-

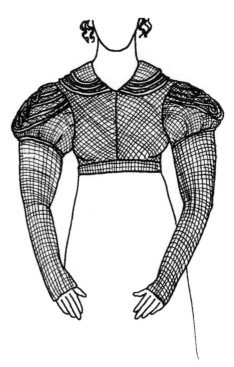

Spencer, 1815. The original was made of rose and cream-colored satin with cream-colored piping.

cluded Hungarian silk cloaks of scarlet trimmed in black; varieties from 1810 included triangular mantles with hoods that could be tied under the chin. On the latter type of cloak, the arm slits could be buttoned closed. Short cloaks came into fashion in 1812, and in Austen's last years mantles with capes appeared. In her youth, Austen owned a muslin cloak, or so it would appear from her dedication of *Frederic and Elfrida* to Martha Lloyd "for your late generosity to me in finishing my muslin Cloak."

Accessories

Streamlined clothing did not give women many places to carry extra belongings, but they might store a fan, a handkerchief, or a bottle of scented water in a reticule. Handkerchiefs could be pocket handkerchiefs, used for blowing noses and wiping eyes (*NA* 28, 98, 229; *S&S* 75, 121, 133, 182), or they could be somewhat larger and used to tie a hat to the head. Jane is known to have made cambric pocket handkerchiefs for her friend Catherine Bigg, sending a poem along with the gift (*MW* 446). In Austen's childhood, "handkerchief" had also meant a large muslin scarf whose ends were crossed in front and tucked into the skirt or sash (*S&S* 120; *P&P* 344; *MP* 14); in other words, it was yet another variation on the fichu. It is probably in this more old-fashioned sense that Jane refers to a handkerchief in a letter of November 1800, where she reports that she "wore my aunt's gown and handkerchief." The sash into which handkerchiefs were often tucked was worn tied around the waist like a belt; it had been an important element in defining the rising waistline from the 1780s on.

Ribbons (*Sand*, *MW* 426; *NA* 114; *E* 235, 237; *P* 8, 221) were used to trim almost everything. They were folded into rosettes and added to shoes and hats or braided and used as trim at necklines and hems (*NA* 26). In March 1814 Jane wrote to Cassandra from London,

> I have determined to trim my lilac sarsenet with black sattin ribbon just as my China Crape is, 6^d width at bottom, 3^d or 4^d at top.—Ribbon trimmings are all the fashion at Bath, & I dare say the fashions of the two places are alike enough in that point, to content *me*.—With this addition it will be a very useful gown, happy to go anywhere.

A few days later she confessed, "I have been ruining myself in black sattin ribbon with a proper perl edge; & now I am trying to draw it up into kind of Roses, instead of putting it in plain double plaits." Ribbons were also used, especially at the turn of the century, to pull women's hair into Greek-style curls bound close to the head. They appeared as straps on sandals and ties for bonnets. Their versatility made them a near-necessity for female attire; Parson Woodforde recorded buying "4 Yards of Ribband for my 2 Maids" for 2s. in 1782, while his niece Nancy bought the same quantity for herself.

Aprons (*MP* 146), reinvented as gauzy, decorative swatches of expensive fabric, had been a fashionable accessory for much of the eighteenth century. By Austen's time, however, they were usually purely practical items, worn by working-class women and servants.

In cold weather, even the gloves habitually worn by women outdoors were not enough to keep their hands warm. For this purpose, they often carried fur muffs (*S&S* 168), which could be quite enormous—a foot or more in diameter. Usually they were all of one color of fur, but at least one fashion plate from the period shows alternating diamonds of tan and black fur.

Fabrics

All fabrics used during the period were weaves or knits of four natural fibers: linen, cotton, wool, and silk. Up until the time of Austen's birth, linen, wool, and silk had reigned supreme—linen for sheets (*E* 306), table-cloths, and napkins (*Lesley, MW* 113; *Watsons, MW* 347; *S&S* 13, 26, 225, 355; *E* 24), shirts, chemises, and similar items; wool for anything that needed to be warm or especially durable; and silk, in the form of satin (*MP* 180; *P* 40), velvet, or brocade, for the most expensive and stylish clothes. However, during Austen's lifetime, all three of these fabrics were ousted by cotton (*F&E, MW* 6), imported from India or America and manufactured by an increasingly mechanized and efficient process. By the early nineteenth century, British cotton fabrics were considered so superior that even Empress Josephine and her daughter wore English cotton, lying to Napoleon when he questioned them about the fabric's origin and claiming that it was French linen. Wool, linen, and silk were still in use, but their share of the market diminished steadily. Even bedclothes such as sheets and counterpanes (*NA* 164) were, by Austen's time, often being made of cotton.

Cotton manufacture took several steps. George Crompton described the washing and carding of the cotton fibers in the 1780s, when he was just a child:

> My mother used to bat the cotton on a wire riddle. It was then put into a deep brown mug with a strong lye of soap-suds. My mother then tucked up my petticoats* about my waist and put me in the tub to tread upon the cotton at the bottom. When a second riddleful was batted, I was lifted out and it was placed in the mug, and I again trod it down. This process was continued until the mug became so full that I could no longer safely stand in it, when a chair was placed beside it and I held on the back. When the mug was quite full, the soap-suds were poured off and each separate dollop of [cotton] wool well squeezed to free it from moisture. They were then placed on the broad rack under the beams of the kitchen loft to dry. My

*Little boys wore skirts and petticoats like their sisters until they were four to six years old, when they were "breeched," or put into their first pair of knee breeches.

mother and my grandmother carded the cotton wool by hand, taking one of the dollops at a time on the simple hand cards.

The carded cotton was then spun into thread, sometimes by hand, sometimes with a machine called a "spinning jenny," and woven on hand or machine looms. The completed fabric might be dyed, bleached, or printed using copper plates or cylinders.

The principal cotton fabric in use for women's clothing was muslin (*NA* 22; *P&P* 72, 292, 307, 310; *E* 233, 235), a lightweight and semitransparent woven fabric. Indian muslin (*F&E*, *MW* 6; *NA* 28) was especially soft and opaque, while mull (*NA* 74) was similar to Indian muslin, but not quite as silky in texture. Some muslins were "figured" (*E* 235); that is, they bore a pattern of some kind. Sprigged muslin (*NA* 26, 105) was decorated with tiny sprigs of leaves or flowers. Spotted muslin (*NA* 68, 73, 74; *S&S* 276) was decorated with dots rather than with sprigs. Tamboured muslins (*NA* 73) were those decorated with embroidery; the tambour was a kind of rectangular embroidery frame. Muslins varied widely in price according to their quality. As *The Mirror of the Graces* indicated,

> A pretty muslin gown may be bought by the village girl for ten shillings; while a robe of the same material, but of a finer quality, cannot be purchased by a lady of rank for less than as many guineas. Indian muslin wrought with gold or silver is nearly as costly as the stately brocades of our ancestors, but it is infinitely more elegant.

Parson Woodforde bought muslin on several occasions, but he does not always indicate the price he paid or separate the cost of the muslin from the other things he purchased at the same time. In July 1793, however, on a visit to Bath, he bought three pieces of muslin at Perrival's in Milsom Street. Each piece was ten yards long and a yard and a half wide and cost 25s., or 2s. 6d. a yard. He considered it a "very great bargain," and he was probably right.

Austen usually refers to muslin as a fabric for dresses, but it could be put to other purposes as well. As Henry Tilney points out, it was used in the making of caps and cloaks (*NA* 28–29). It was also used for fichus, aprons, shawls, and veils.

Other cotton fabrics differed from muslin chiefly in their weight. Cambric was very light, lawn lighter still, to the point of being almost entirely transparent.* Jaconet (*NA* 74) was a lightweight cotton fabric, lighter than many muslins but a little heavier than the cambric used for handkerchiefs. Calico (*P&P* 307), whose name, like the name jaconet, was a corruption of the name of a town in India, was originally imported from India and

---

*Parson Woodforde bought some cambric for handkerchiefs in 1794 for 6s. a yard. They must have been enormous handkerchiefs. He claimed that the 4¾ yards he bought would "make me five good handkerchiefs, and a small one for Nancy besides."

later made in England. Calicoes, heavier than muslins, were usually printed with some sort of design. Dimity (*NA* 194) was a kind of cotton with a raised pattern, often tiny dots.

Silks remained important for evening dresses, particularly in the winter. Both satins and velvets were worn in the winter. *The Mirror of the Graces* listed a number of appropriate winter fabrics:

> The materials for the winter dresses of majestic forms, and lightly-graceful ones, may be of nearly similar texture, only differing, when made up, in amplitude and abundance of drapery. Satin, Genoa velvet, Indian silks, and kerseymere, may all be fashioned into as becoming an apparel for the slender figure as for the more *en bon point*; and the warmth they afford is highly needful to preserve health during the cold and damps of winter.

Sarsenet (*NA* 118) was a lighter silk appropriate for summer wear. Linen, too, was still in use for underclothes and bed and table linens, but it was being rapidly displaced by cotton. Wool and wool blends were comfortable in the winter, but they were not usually fashionable. Baize, for example, was a cheap, coarse wool fabric with a nap; it is no doubt chosen as the curtain fabric for the *Mansfield Park* play because of its low cost and quality (*MP* 195). If well made, however, wool fabrics were perfectly acceptable. Poplin (*E* 302), a wool and silk blend with a fine corded texture, had a respectable reputation. Women wore a good many other fabrics; bombazine (a silk-worsted blend) and China crape (a thick silk) are only two of those mentioned in Austen's letters.

Buying and Making Clothes

Clothes might be made at home or by a person hired to do the job. Relatively few items were sold ready-made, even at the end of the period in question. A few things, such as caps, cloaks, aprons, skirts, and jackets, most of them designed for middle- and working-class consumers, could be bought in the "warehouses" (*NA* 68; *S&S* 215; *P&P* 288) of large cities, which often sold fabric by the yard as well, but coats, dresses, and other substantial items of clothing could be bought ready-made only if they were bought secondhand. Most women of Austen's class selected fabrics personally from a linen-draper (who sold linen and cotton fabrics—*E* 56), a mercer (who sold silks), or a woolen-draper (who sold wool). They took the fabric they had bought to a dressmaker (*E* 178), sometimes called a mantua-maker, and specified how they wanted the garment to be made. If they had skilled housemaids (*MP* 130, 254), they might also hand the fabric over to them to be turned into a gown, a pelisse, or some similar garment. Rarely did they make an entire garment from start to finish. They confined almost all of their needlework to simple clothes for the poor and to decorative embroidery on small pieces such as handkerchiefs and workbags.

It was not possible, therefore, to purchase a dress on short notice (*NA* 73). The selection of the fabric alone could take quite a while. If a woman lived far from good shops, for example, as the Austen women did for most of their lives, she would have to wait until she or a friend or relative traveled to someplace with a wider selection, such as London or Bath (*P* 217, 221). London visits were especially useful, as not only did they afford the largest selection, but the streets and houses of the city presented the alert consumer with walking models of the latest fashions.

Patterns (*Cath, MW* 207; *S&S* 120; *E* 86) were devised either from a paper pattern or, more commonly, from studying existing garments. Friends and even shops were usually willing to lend a pattern garment (*E* 235) so that it might be examined and copied. For example, Mary Austen, James' wife, borrowed such patterns for children's clothes from Edward Austen's family at Godmersham. Innovations to the existing design might then be made after a careful consultation of fashion magazines, of clothes worn by acquaintances, and of opinions from those who were considered especially tasteful or well informed about current trends.

Some items were bought not from shops but from traveling salesmen. Parson Woodforde, living in a small village, was fairly regularly visited by peddlers who offered to sell his household a wide variety of textiles. In 1782 he bought an assortment of shirt linen, cambric, lace edging, and ribbon from "One Mr. Aldridge who carries about Cottons, Linens, Muslins, Lace, Holland, &c. in a Cart and comes round regularly this way once in ten Weeks." The following year he bought pea green and light blue fabric from "a Man who comes from Windham and carries about stuffs for Gowns &c." However, he also went into Norwich from time to time. In 1784, apparently, his niece Nancy had been buying too much on credit, for he "Called at Brownsmith's Silk Mercer, and there paid a Bill for Nancy for Silk, for a Gown &c. 6.1.0. I talked to them of their Behaviour to Nancy, in trusting her."

Men had their coats, waistcoats, and breeches made by tailors or specialist breeches makers. Their linen, however—shirts, cravats, and so on—was often made by female relatives. *See also* Army; Clocks and Watches; Cosmetics; Fan; Gloves; Hair; Hats; Jewelry; Navy; Pocketbooks and Reticules; Servants; Shoes; Spectacles; Stockings; Umbrellas and Parasols.

Clubs

The hallmark of a gentleman, thought Samuel Johnson, was that he was "clubbable"—the sort of fellow one could invite to join a gentleman's club. Although gentlemen of the eighteenth and nineteenth centuries dearly loved their clubs, it was not only the genteel, and not only men, who enjoyed forming and attending clubs. Clubs had grown, perhaps, out of the coffeehouses of the seventeenth and early eighteenth centuries, which had grad-

ually developed clientele of specific occupations or interests. There had been
coffeehouses for Whigs, for Tories, for
lawyers, for writers, and so on, and the
men who congregated in such places
still yearned for companionship even
after the heyday of the coffeehouse had
passed. Meeting in alehouses, in inns,
and occasionally in private homes, they
met chiefly to drink and eat but also to
discuss whatever their collective passion
might be.

[Lilliputian Figures], 1799. The meeting of a men's
club, complete with those requisites, the pipes and
punch bowl. Courtesy of the Lewis Walpole Library,
Yale University. 799.7.12.4.

There were clubs devoted to almost
every topic of interest. There were
agricultural improvement societies,
musical societies, and political soci-
eties. Tradesmen and artisans formed clubs to look out for their business
interests. Workers banded together to form welfare groups that paid benefits in case of death or injury and agitated for better wages. Gentlemen
met to play whist (which was perfectly respectable—see *E* 197) or the dice
game called hazard (which was risky and disreputable). There were clubs
for golfers and cricketers, gamblers and womanizers, art lovers, and religious reformers. There were staid gentlemen's clubs (*S&S* 143; *NA* 210),
where genteel conversation reigned, and Freemasons' chapters, reveling in
their secrecy and in the fact that most male members of the royal family
were Masons. There were clubs for homosexuals and clubs for men who
liked to be beaten during sex. Africans, Welshmen, and Scots had social
clubs. Patriotic associations suppressed sedition, amassed rewards for
heroic military officers, and sent proclamations of loyalty to the king.
Newspaper clubs banded together to buy papers from all over and share
them among the members. Debating societies developed political skills and
helped people to form (or confirm) opinions. Mathematical and scientific
societies discussed the latest developments in their fields and sometimes
held competitions for new ideas. Birmingham and Manchester, for example, had notable scientific clubs. London had an archery club, the Tox-
ophilite Society, founded in 1781, and fashionable men's clubs, like
White's and Almack's, where there was a good deal of high-stakes gambling. Oxford had clubs devoted to fossils, antiquities, and botany.

Most clubs existed for only a few years before disbanding, and most
were almost purely social in nature. The drafting of rules, the meeting
times, and the nominal purpose of the club were almost beside the point.
The main goal was to get in a room with one's friends, drink moderately
to heavily, and get away from the womenfolk.

Most clubs were for men only, and a few were for women only. Women were especially fond of book clubs and musical clubs (*E* 277); Jane Austen herself belonged to at least two book clubs during her life. Very few clubs admitted both men and women, though charitable societies for the benefit of orphans, soldiers, sailors, and so on were a notable exception.

Coffee

Coffee, a drink once almost unknown outside the Middle East, became the beverage of choice in much of Europe during the seventeenth century. It conquered England as well in the late 1600s, and coffeehouses sprang up all over London to meet the demand. In 1700 there were about 2,000 of these establishments in London alone, and in time each coffeehouse developed its own self-selected clientele—lawyers, Whigs, Tories, actors, importer-exporters, stockbrokers, and so on. The coffeehouse that attracted shipping merchants became the basis for the marine insurance company Lloyd's of London; another house, patronized by stockbrokers, developed into the Stock Exchange.

However, a variety of factors combined to topple coffee from the throne of fashion. Chief among these was the rise of the East India Company, which was the only licensed importer of tea. Furthermore, most of England's coffee came from the West Indies—in 1788 half the world's supply was grown in San Domingo alone—and the West Indies were inexorably moving to a monocultural economy based on sugar, the most profitable crop grown in the islands. On a smaller, more personal scale, tea was simply easier to make. It could be stored for longer than coffee without losing its flavor, did not need to be roasted or ground, was cheaper, and could be easily mixed by unscrupulous dealers with a long list of adulterants. Coffee lost its ascendancy, and most of the old coffeehouses were gone by 1730. In their place arose public gardens where people could drink their tea in three-sided, roofed cubicles before strolling the elaborately landscaped grounds in search of romance and panoramic views.

Coffee did not disappear from the English table, however. It merely moved into the home, where it could be enjoyed by men and women alike. It became a common drink at breakfast and at teatime (*NA* 215; *S&S* 233; *P&P* 37, 163, 173; *MP* 104), though never as popular as tea. Jane's mother, writing in 1806 of the lavish breakfasts at Stoneleigh, a relative's house, mentioned the appearance of "chocolate, coffee and tea, plum cake, pound cake, hot rolls, cold rolls, bread and butter, and dry toast for me." Among the immediate Austen family, it appears that Jane's brother Edward was fondest of coffee; Jane wrote that he would need the use of a coffee mill while visiting the family home at Steventon, because he was in the habit of taking coffee every day with his breakfast. Edward, like the owner of Stoneleigh, was wealthy, and according to French traveler

François de La Rochefoucauld, coffee was a beverage chiefly enjoyed by the well-to-do. "Breakfast," he wrote in 1784, "consists of tea and bread and butter in various forms. In the houses of the rich, you have coffee, chocolate and so on."

The coffee itself, like tea, sugar, citrus fruit, spices, and similar imported luxuries, would have been purchased from a grocer (*Col Let, MW* 158). The beverage was considered harder to adulterate than tea, though Frederick Accum noted that it was sometimes mixed with "pigeon's beans and pease," a practice banned by an act of

Coffee service.

1803. Contemporary illustrations of people drinking coffee show a tall, tapered coffeepot with a narrow, curved spout and a long handle with a wide, ridged grip, attached to the back of the coffeepot at an angle. The pot's lid is a shallow dome with a knob on top. Coffeepots were sometimes made of a layered metal called "Sheffield plate"—copper coated thinly with silver on the outside and with tin on the inside. Ceramic coffeepots, however, were rare. Cups (*P&P* 341) might or might not have handles. The coffee, once made and set on the table, was served by the hostess (*P&P* 76, 341). Afterward, fortunes were sometimes read in the leftover grounds, in much the same way that some people read tea leaves.

Though tea continued to reign supreme throughout Austen's lifetime (*E* 323), coffee was about to experience a resurgence in popularity. Import duties on coffee were lowered in 1808 and 1825, and coffeehouses began to make a comeback. There were only a dozen in London in 1815, but they multiplied rapidly in the 1820s, and there were almost 1,800 by 1840. Selling coffee, tea, spruce beer, and ginger beer and providing access to a wide variety of newspapers, they became important gathering places once again.

Collections

Large and often surprisingly varied collections were common in gentlemen's homes throughout the eighteenth and early nineteenth centuries. Don Saltero's early-eighteenth-century coffeehouse, London's first public museum, featured carvings on cherry stones, a dead cat found in the walls of Westminster Abbey, a giant's tooth, Native American wampum, snakes, and the horns of a chamois. Sir Hans Sloane, former physician to the governor-general of Jamaica, amassed a monumental collection of coins, medals, seeds, live plants, butterflies, manuscripts, stuffed and mounted animals, and a fetus. His collection of nearly 80,000 objects, on display in London in the first half of the eighteenth century, evolved after his death into the British Museum. The Knightley collection in *Emma* is nowhere near this large but is equally miscellaneous (*E* 362–364).

Some collections were primarily artistic in nature, consisting of prints, paintings, cameos, statuary, medals, miniatures, and fine pieces of porcelain. Other collections tended to focus on the natural world: unusual animal specimens, drawer after drawer full of beetles and butterflies mounted on pins, plants from around the world kept alive in specially built greenhouses. William Hunter, a prominent London surgeon, had the latter type of collection, rich in minerals, fossils, and shells, while his brother John had a collection of skeletons and similar items that eventually opened as a museum devoted to comparative anatomy. The Hunterian Museum eventually acquired 13,682 items, differing from the typical gentleman's collection principally in size and in being open to the public. In private homes, nonliving collections were usually kept in "cabinets" (*E* 362)—not pieces of furniture but small rooms devoted to housing books, important papers, and, eventually, collections of interesting objects.

Complexion

There were generally understood to be four types of complexion (*F&E*, *MW* 4; *MP* 198; *E* 39, 199, 478; *P* 104): sallow, ruddy, brown, and fair. The sallow skin (*F&E*, *MW* 8; *NA* 42) had a yellowish cast. The ruddy skin (*J&A*, *MW* 17; *Col Let*, *MW* 159; *P* 48) was inclined to redness and was generally attributed to overexposure to sun and wind (*P* 19, 22). Brown skins (*Watsons*, *MW* 337–338, 357; *NA* 42; *S&S* 46; *P&P* 270; *MP* 44) are what today we might call olive, or approaching olive; the term is also used simply to indicate that a person has dark hair and eyes and a skin coloration consistent with the hair and eye color. Fair skins (*Watsons*, *MW* 357; *NA* 42; *E* 478) were pale, at times almost translucent, with just a faint blush to the cheeks; this skin tone was most often associated with blonds.

To Austen's contemporaries, the important thing was that the skin be even in tone, without blotches or blemishes, and that the skin be expressive. *The Mirror of the Graces* (1811) stresses the importance of an expressive complexion:

> It is complexion that lends animation to a picture; it is complexion that gives spirit to the human countenance. Even the language of the eyes loses half its eloquence, if they speak from the obscurity of an inexpressive skin. . . . the effect [of a good complexion] is, an impression of loveliness, an attraction, which fills the beholder with answering animation and the liveliest delight.

An expressive skin was clear enough of makeup that blushes and the glow of exertion could be clearly detected by observers; it was supposed to reveal thoughts and emotions, portraying its occupant in a true and natural state. This was a novel concept, for during most of the eighteenth century, fashionable women had buried their faces under layers of white makeup, adorned these white canvases with tiny black fabric patches, drawn artificial blue veins to simulate the translucency of a very fair skin, and otherwise taken great pains to disguise their natural complexions.

Yet the period associated with Regency style—though it is not really contiguous with the actual, political Regency—was characterized by an interest in what was "natural" in behavior, dress, education, and personal appearance. Some found the thin, flowing gowns that women adopted in this period scandalous, a mere step away from nudity, but the Regency woman was naked in a way that her mother and grandmother had not been. She exposed far more flesh to public view, not only on her face but on her arms, neck, and chest. Daytime costume was still fairly modest, with the arms and throat covered, but evening dresses were often short-sleeved and low-necked, and women began to worry about how their skin looked all over. According to *The Mirror of the Graces*, they were right to worry:

> Women, according to the fineness of their skins and proportions, must accept or decline the privileges which modesty grants. It is preposterous for her who is of a brown, dingy, or speckled complexion, to disarray her neck and arms as her fairer rival may. A clear brunette has as much liberty in this respect as the fairest; but not so the muddy-skinned and ill-formed.

Women were suddenly being inspected and judged in ways that were unfamiliar to them, and they naturally felt insecure. Books such as *The Toilet of Flora* offered recipes to remove freckles (*P&P* 22; *P* 34, 146), wrinkles, and warts. Pastes and creams to improve the complexion could be homemade or bought in well-stocked shops. With a little assistance, women were promised, they could withstand the scrutiny to which their "natural" selves were subjected. *See also* Cosmetics.

Compts

"Compts" (*Cath, MW* 237; *Evelyn, MW* 186; *Coll Let, MW* 159), which appears only in the Juvenilia, is an abbreviation for "compliments."

Condescension

Though today the word "condescension" (*F&E, MW* 8; *H&E, MW* 35) connotes a somewhat insulting, patronizing attitude, in Jane Austen's time it had precisely the opposite meaning. In a world in which the gentry and aristocracy had very definite privileges, condescension was the setting aside of one's right to formal deference. It was, in short, treating social inferiors as if they were equals, or at least as if the social distance were smaller. Novelist Fanny Burney, who was for a few years a member of the Court in the service of Queen Charlotte, repeatedly praised the queen's "condescendsion," especially at their first meeting, when Burney was joining the royal household:

> The condescendsion of her efforts to quiet me, and the elegance of her receiving me, thus, as a visitor, without giving me the smallest employment, without naming to me a single direction, . . . struck me to shew so much delicacy, as well as graciousness, that I quitted her with a very deep sense of her goodness.

The anonymous author of the conduct manual *The Mirror of the Graces* (1811) uses the word in this same sense when she describes the social order. A deep sense of the justice and order of a firmly class-based society, she says,

> gives us dignity with our inferiors, without allaying it with the smallest particle of pride; by keeping them at a due distance, we merely maintain ourselves and them in the rank in which a higher Power has placed us; and the condescension of our general manners to them, and our kindnesses in their exigencies, and generous approbation of their worth, are sufficient acknowledgements of sympathy.

Clearly, there are distance and hierarchy, but condescension is meant to set others at ease, not to emphasize the gap between the classes.

Of course, awareness of condescension implies that the differences in social standing were never fully forgotten by either party, but the word is always meant as a compliment, even when the object of the description doesn't really deserve the praise. Lady Catherine de Bourgh, for example, is praised for her condescension (*P&P* 157), but the sting of the remark lies not in the meaning of the word but in Mr. Collins' failure to use it properly. He uses it, unwittingly, in its modern sense—a mode of address that rudely reminds the auditors of their inferiority while pretending to do just the opposite. To a modern reader, it seems odd that he should praise her for such behavior, but the humor, for Austen's contemporary audience, lay in his inability to distinguish true from false condescension.

Cosmetics

During Jane Austen's lifetime, the English attitude toward cosmetics shifted dramatically. At her birth, heavily powdered white faces were the norm; by the time of her death, the appearance of artificiality in the skin was abhorrent, a sign of bad taste and poor judgment. Throughout most of the eighteenth century, women achieved a pale complexion through the use of face paint and powder (*F&E, MW* 7; *Cath, MW* 218), whose chief ingredient was poisonous white lead. Then they enhanced this pallid mask with rouge (*Lesley, MW* 119, 127, 137) and tiny velvet patches (*F&E, MW* 7) pasted on the face to draw attention to particularly attractive features. The effect was completed by a towering hairstyle, plastered into place with pomade (*F&E, MW* 7; *Cath, MW* 218) and sprayed with white or gray powder.

This toilette (*Sand, MW* 390; *P&P* 289; *MP* 34) was time-consuming and uncomfortable to achieve and maintain, and it was therefore natural that, when an alternative was offered, women would seize it eagerly. The alternative arose in 1789, when the French Revolution caused Europeans to question every assumption they had hitherto held. Everything from political systems to hairstyles came under reasoned appraisal, and the gigantic headdresses, the pallid face, and the stiff women's clothing with its voluminous skirts all fell victim to the Revolution. There was a vogue for seeking what was natural in human behavior and dress, and simpler styles of clothing and cosmetics followed.

The white face paint was an early casualty, not merely because it had come to seem ridiculous but also because it was discovered to be poisonous. The anonymous author of *The Mirror of the Graces*, writing in 1811 when the fashion was all but dead, expressed the new attitude toward the complexion:

> No eye that is of the commonest apprehension can look on a face bedaubed with white paint, pearl powder, or enamel, and be deceived for a minute into a belief that so inanimate a "whited wall" is the human skin. No flush of pleasure, no shudder of pain, no thrilling of hope, can be descried beneath the encrusted mould; all that passes within is concealed behind the mummy surface. Perhaps the painted creature may be admired by an artist as a well-executed picture; but no man will seriously consider her as a handsome woman.

However, rouge (*P* 215) survived, and the same author even advocated its limited use for the "delicate woman, who, from ill-health or an anxious mind, loses her roses," but it must never appear to be artificial color, nor must it cover the whole cheek, nor must it lose translucency, so that a natural blush may be noticed by observers. "A violently rouged woman," she writes, "is one of the most disgusting objects to the eye. The excessive red on the face gives a coarseness to every feature, and a general fierceness to the countenance, which transforms the elegant lady of fashion into a vulgar harridan." She recommends, instead, a light dusting of carmine powder for brunettes and the same powder lightened with hair powder for the fair-skinned. Coloring the lips, drawing false veins to give the impression of translucent skin, and penciling the eyebrows are all dismissed as "clumsy tricks" worthy of "contempt."

Even this author, however, provides recipes for far more than simple pow-

The Finishing Touch, James Gillray, 1791.
A lady applies rouge at her dressing table.
Courtesy of the Lewis Walpole Library,
Yale University. 791.9.29.1.

der rouge. It took more than one substance to achieve the appearance of unadorned natural beauty, and many contemporary manuals for housewives and servants give instructions for compounding a wide variety of cosmetics. There are perfumes, lotions, creams, washes for the face, potions for the hair, tooth powders, lip salves, wart removers, depilatories, breath fresheners, wrinkle creams, hair dyes, and preventives against fleas and lice. Oils, ointments, and soaps abound.

Many of these concoctions had multiple purposes. Lavender water (*NA* 77) and orange-flower water, for example, could be used on their own as perfumes (*P* 192) or in concert with other ingredients for a variety of purposes. *The Toilet of Flora*, for example, includes a remedy for toothache that consists of rinsing the mouth daily with a teaspoon of lavender water mixed with a teaspoon of warm or cold water. The same book's recipe for making lavender water (*NA* 77; *S&S* 177) is as follows:

Fill a glass or earthen body two thirds full of Lavender Flowers, and then fill up the vessel with Brandy or Melasses Spirits; let the Flowers stand in infusion eight days, or less if straitened for a time, then distill off the Spirit, in a water bath with a brisk fire, at first in large drops or even a small stream, that the Essential Oil of the Flowers may rise with the Spirit; but as this can't be done without the phlegm coming over the helm at the same time, the Spirit must be rectified. The first distillation being finished, unlute the still, throw away what remains in the body, and fill it with fresh Flowers of lavender, in the proportion of two pounds of Lavender Flowers to one pint of Spirit; pour the Spirit already distilled according to the foregoing directions, on the Lavender Flowers, and distill a second time in a vapour bath.

The Toilet of Flora also includes a second recipe for lavender water, one that eliminates the need for distillation:

put two or three drops of Oil of Spike, and a lump of Sugar, into a pint of clear Water, or Spirit of Wine, and shake them well together in a glass phial, with a narrow neck. This Water, though not distilled, is very fragrant.

Other perfumes were used to add fragrance to gloves or to soap.

Books that included cosmetic recipes often offered several types of creams for the skin. Hannah Glasse's *The Art of Cookery Made Plain and Easy* described a "*Nun's Cream*" made of "One ounce of pearl-powder, twenty drops of oil of Rhodium, and two ounces of fine pomatum" and a *"Cold Cream"* compounded of "one pint of trotter-oil, a quarter of a pound of hog's-lard, one ounce of spermaceti, [and] a bit of virgin-wax" warmed with rose water. *The Toilet of Flora* included *"An excellent Cosmetic for the Face"* made of hartshorn, rice powder, ceruse, "Powder of dried Bones," frankincense, gum mastic, gum Arabic, and rose water. The author of *The Mirror of the Graces* no doubt disapproved of this compound, as she specifically prohibited cosmetics made with ceruse (another name for white lead). *The Toilet of Flora* also contained a recipe for whitening the skin, made from a distillation of "the Roots of Centaury and the White Vine, a pint of Cows Milk, and the crumb of a White Loaf." This recipe, like so many others for cosmetics, sounds more like alchemy than chemistry or cooking. In a simpler mood, presaging the era of the clean, unwhitened face, the author recommends washing the face frequently to "remove the kind of varnish that covers the skin, and thus render perspiration more free, which is the only real cosmetic for the skin."

She (or he) also advises rinsing the face with "Virgins Milk," a ubiquitous lotion whose creation is described in almost every book that touches on the subject of cosmetics. So standard was this item on the dressing table that the author of *The Mirror of the Graces* acknowledges that a book about beauty "would certainly be looked upon as an imperfect performance, if we omitted to say a few words upon this famous cosmetic." She continues with the recipe:

> It consists of a tincture of Benjoin, precipitated by water. The tincture of Benjoin is obtained by taking a certain quantity of that gum, pouring spirits of wine upon it, and boiling it till it becomes a rich tincture. If you put a few drops of this tincture into a glass of water, it will produce a mixture which will assume all the appearance of milk, and retain a very agreeable perfume. If the face is washed with this mixture, it will, by calling the purple stream of the blood to the external fibres of the epidermis, produce on the cheeks a beautiful rosy colour; and, if left on the face to dry, it will render it clear and brilliant.

The miraculous "milk" was also said to remove spots, freckles, and pimples.

In addition to face and skin creams, women used soap, often scented soap, to wash their faces, arms, and hands. Full immersion in a bathtub was extremely rare, but Englishwomen liked to keep their visible parts clean. Accordingly, books of the time are replete with recipes for "washballs," or soaps. There are tinted wash-balls, almond wash-balls, "Windsor soap" scented with caraway oil, white soap, and honey soap. *The Toilet of Flora*'s white soap "is made with one part of the Lees of Spanish Potash and Quick-lime, to two parts of Oil of Olives or Oil of Almonds." Its honey soap, like many similar concoctions, is promised to whiten the skin; a fair skin was almost always considered desirable.

For the reddening of the cheeks, several methods were advised. One was the carmine powder mentioned above. Other rouges used alkanet root, red wine, sandalwood, or Brazil wood to achieve the desired shade; one particularly unusual technique involves wetting a red ribbon and rubbing it against the face.

One wonders, however, whether the average woman hovered over a still, with an alchemist's array of potions and wood shavings and loaves of white bread. It seems likely that most women left the mixing and decocting to others and simply bought such products ready-made. Most cosmetics were available in well-stocked stores, to judge from a 1786 tax imposed on beauty aids. The act listed, under the category of taxable goods, hair powder, tooth powders, perfumes and perfumed goods, pomatums and ointments for the hair, rouge, white paint, creams, and pastes. Several brand names were listed specifically, including Pomade de Nerole, Duchess pomatum, Powder of Pearl of India, and a wash called Venetian Bloom. Sir Walter Elliot's Gowland's Lotion (*P* 145–146), though not listed in 1786, was by 1814 at least an actual product available for sale, not an invention of Austen's. Like most of the face and skin lotions of its day, it optimistically promised to heal all problems of the skin and sold for 8s. 6d. a quart.

Many of these beauty products and their exotic ingredients, far from being made at home, were imported from as far away as the East Indies and the Levant. Indeed, it seems likely, from the sheer number of products available for sale, that most women did not manufacture their own cosmetics unless they lived far away from a reliable supplier.

Court

The royal court was officially known as the Court of St. James's (*P&P* 25, 122) even though it was often held not at St. James's Palace but at other palaces such as Kew and Windsor. It had a set of complicated rules of behavior that emphasized the social distance between the royal family and its subjects. Novelist Fanny Burney, who served for five years as one of the personal attendants to Queen Charlotte, found these rules by turns baffling, silly, or provoking. In 1785, before she began serving the queen, she was "presented" (*P&P* 67), or introduced, to the king and queen. Presentation was a serious affair; it was permitted only to peers, gentry, very accomplished persons, professional men, military officers, and the sons, daughters, and wives of extremely wealthy tradesmen (but not the tradesmen themselves). Knights were presented (*P&P* 18), often for the first time, when they received their knighthoods; on at least two occasions, men received illicit knighthoods by insinuating themselves into the royal presence on days when knighthoods were to be conferred.

Burney described the restrictions placed on those in the royal presence:

Directions for Coughing, sneezing, or moving before the King and Queen.

In the first place, you must not Cough. If you find a cough tickling in your throat, you must arrest it from making any sound: if you find yourself choacking with the forbearance, you must choak: But not cough.

In the 2d place, you must not sneeze. If you have a vehement Cold, you must take no notice of it; if your Nose membranes feel a great irritation, you must hold your breath; if a sneeze still insists upon making its way, you must oppose it by keeping your teeth grinding together; if the violence of the repulse breaks some blood-vessel, you must break the blood-vessel: But not sneeze.

In the 3d place, you must not, upon any account, stir either hand or foot. If, by chance, a black pin runs into your Head, you must not take it out: If the pain is very great, you must be sure to bear it without wincing; If it brings the Tears into your Eyes, you must not wipe them off; If they give you a tingling by running down your Cheeks, you must look as if nothing was the matter. If the blood should gush from your Head by means of the black pin, you must let it gush; If you are uneasy to think of making such a blurred appearance, you must be uneasy; but you must say nothing about it. If, however, the agony is very great, you may, privately, bite the inside of your Cheek, or of your lips, for a little relief; taking care, meanwhile, to do it so cautiously as to make no apparent dent outwardly. And, with that precaution, if you even gnaw a piece out, it will not be minded, only be sure either to swallow it, or commit it to a corner of the inside of your mouth till they are gone,—for, You must not spit.

I have many other Directions, but no more paper.

As she was to learn later during her service in the court, it was similarly forbidden to wear spectacles (a severe torment to the nearsighted Burney), to pass the open doorway of a room in which the king or queen was sitting, to speak to the king or queen without being spoken to first, to sit without being invited to do so, to contradict, or to introduce a new subject of conversation.

Burney's diaries and letters reflect her astonishment every time Queen Charlotte said or did anything that mitigated this social boundary. She was, for example, almost overcome by the queen's kindness in offering her two tickets to the trial of Warren Hastings. Austen, it seems, would not have been so awestruck, judging from her tone when Sir William Lucas interprets ordinary politeness as a mark of great consideration and condescension. Invited to tea and cards at Rosings, Lady Catherine de Bourgh's home, he remarks that "About the Court, such instances of elegant breeding are not uncommon" (*P&P* 160). Austen also appears to have been unimpressed by her own brush with royalty; shown around the Prince of Wales' Carlton House library by James Stanier Clarke and offered the opportunity to dedicate *Emma* to the prince regent, she took the royal suggestion (one she could hardly decline) but displayed no enthusiasm.

Afterward, she mocked Clarke privately by writing a *Plan of a Novel* (*MW* 429) that ridiculed his suggestion that her next work be either a thinly veiled biography of himself or a German historical romance.

There were certainly aspects of the court's reputation that deflated any pretensions to superhuman virtue. George III was a faithful and devoted husband, and Queen Charlotte was by all accounts a sensible and affectionate wife, but the early history of the court had been plagued by debt and by the freehanded distribution of sinecures. George Wickham's interest in obtaining such a post is therefore not completely without foundation, but the salary that Lydia Wickham proposes—"three or four hundred a year" (*P&P* 386)—would have been more than was made by most royal servants, including the English tutor to the royal children and the royal wet nurses. In the second half of the eighteenth century, salaries in this range went to people like the master of the ceremonies and the master of the jewel office.

George III was endeared to the public by his domestic virtues, his frugality later in life, and his obvious patriotism; unlike the earlier Hanoverians, he thought of himself as English rather than German, but he went mad twice, once for about a year, and again for nine years, from 1811 until his death in 1820. His place was supplied during the Regency by his son, the later George IV, who was known to the public as a spendthrift, a libertine, and an aesthete. Very nearly his first act as regent was to throw a gargantuan dinner party at shocking expense. His brothers were scarcely less respectable in the public mind. Two of them married commoners, while a third carried on for years with the actress Dorothea Jordan.

Coxcombs and Dandies

There were all sorts of unflattering characterizations of men in Austen's day. The macaronis, rakes, and fops of the earlier eighteenth century had given way to rattles, coxcombs, and dandies, led in their foolish posturing and shallow concerns by the Prince of Wales (later the prince regent) and his on-again, off-again friend Beau Brummell. George Bryan Brummell (1778–1840) was famous for his vicious wit, his spotless linen, and his sense of personal style. He ruthlessly mocked those who did not meet his standards of behavior, talked insolent nonsense, and took every opportunity to display his own finery. For Brummell, how one opened a snuffbox was far more important than what books one had read. He was fearless, even with the prince regent (whose dandyism took a far more drunken and lascivious turn than Brummell's). Once, when the two were having a tiff, they appeared at a party together, and the prince regent "cut" Brummell—in other words, refused to acknowledge his presence. Brummell, unfazed, turned to one of the prince's companions and asked him to introduce his "fat friend." Burdened by debt, Brummell fled to

France in 1816, was thrown into debtors' prison in 1835, and died in a lunatic asylum.

Dandies adored the company of women, or at least professed to do so. It has been suggested by Roger Sales that Austen intends Henry Crawford as a portrait of the Regency dandy, but she is not fond of the word "dandy." Instead, she uses other words to describe men negatively, chiefly "coxcomb" and "rattle." A coxcomb (*NA* 217; *S&S* 148, 250; *E* 150, 212; *MP* 297) was originally the cap worn by a jester, and by Austen's time it had come to mean a man who was unintentionally a fool, usually because he took inordinate pride in some superficial accomplishment, such as his ability to dress well, or because he affected to know more than he really did. A coxcomb was typically young, silly, and showy. A "puppy" (*E* 321, 372) was a coxcomb with an additional fault—impertinence. A "rattle" (*LS*, *MW* 276; *NA* 50, 65, 134; *P&P* 249), too, was similar to a coxcomb, but his chief characteristic, not always a negative one, was his ability to keep up a constant, lively flow of chatter.

Crime

Though moral crimes abound in Austen's works, actual crime is rare. Even the infamous Gypsies of *Emma* are not really guilty of any crime (*E* 333). Crime appears mostly for humorous effect, and the more serious the crime, the more likely it is to be used in this manner. The antiheroines and antiheroes of her outlandish juvenile compositions, for instance, often prove their lack of worth by murder (*J&A*, *MW* 28; *Scraps*, *MW* 175) or theft (*H&E*, *MW* 34; *L&F*, *MW* 96), while the more mature works feature prosaic crimes, such as the theft of Mrs. Weston's "turkies" (*E* 483).

It is worth recalling, however, that even relatively minor thefts in Austen's time carried heavy penalties. A philosophical concern over the sanctity of private property was heightened by the frequency of theft. In crowds at fairs, at the theatre, and on the street, pickpockets stole watches, pocketbooks, and even wigs. On the turnpike roads, highwaymen—not especially common, but common enough to be a constant source of worry—might stop a carriage and rob all the occupants (*NA* 19). No one was entirely safe from this sort of attack, except those who looked as if they had nothing worth stealing; even Henry Dundas, secretary of state, reportedly lost £150 to a highwayman in 1793. Petty criminals stole from shops. Poachers stole game from nearby estates. Even the government was at risk, for counterfeiters and smugglers indirectly stole from the state.

The fear of being robbed or defrauded led to a truly extraordinary number of capital crimes being placed on the books. Fifty capital offenses existed in 1689, a number that rose to 223 by 1819. France, by contrast, considered only six crimes worthy of execution in 1819. Pickpocketing goods worth 1s., shoplifting goods worth 5s., vandalizing turnpikes or

SHOP-LIFTER DETECTED. 147
London, Printed for R. Sayer Printseller Nᵒ 53 Fleet Street; as the Act directs 10 Aug 1787

Shop-Lifter Detected, 1787. This lady, like Jane's aunt Mrs. Leigh-Perrot, is being accused of shoplifting a piece of lace. Mrs. Leigh-Perrot, however, was not subjected to such a search, as her "stolen" piece of lace was wrapped up with another she had legitimately purchased. Courtesy of the Lewis Walpole Library, Yale University. 787.8.10.2.

fishponds, sending threatening letters, firing a gun at a gamekeeper while in the act of poaching, and stealing a sheep all carried the death penalty, as did stealing goods worth 40s. from a house, associating with Gypsies, cutting hop-binds, and impersonating a Chelsea Pensioner. An attempted murderer, curiously, was not threatened with execution, but a servant who stole from his master was. Forgery (*Scraps, MW* 175) and counterfeiting were considered very serious crimes, because they affected credit and trade; perjury (*Scraps, MW* 175), by comparison, was a minor offense, punished by seven years' imprisonment and two stints in the pillory.

The harsh character of the English system of justice made itself felt in the Austens' extended family in August 1799, when Jane's aunt, Mrs. Leigh Perrot, was accused of shoplifting from a Bath lace shop. A bit of lace that she had not bought was wrapped together with a bit that she had actually purchased, and it appears that the shop owner had done this deliberately, in order to extort money from her husband. The indignant Leigh Perrots refused to pay blackmail, and Mrs. Leigh Perrot was confined to jail for several months before being acquitted in a sensational trial. Had she been found guilty, she could have been executed or, more likely, transported.

Transportation to America—later, when the American colonies had been lost, to Australia—was a lesser sentence for theft and some of the other more serious crimes. The transported party had to stay away from England for some period of years or face the death penalty. This, although unpleasant, was certainly better than being hanged, and many judges, sensing the cruelty of the system, advised juries to undervalue stolen goods in order to allow more lenient sentencing. Only children under seven were exempt from the death penalty; children between the ages of seven and fourteen could be sentenced to death, but they had to wait until they were at least fourteen to be executed, and some were reprieved in the interim.

Reprieves were in fact quite common. Judicial practice seems to have been based on Russian roulette: the death penalty was a deterrent, but it could be just as good a deterrent if it were imposed somewhat randomly. The tendency toward mercy strengthened near the turn of the century, with nearly 80 percent of those convicted of capital crimes in the 1790s receiving remitted sentences. A lesser sentence, such as transportation, branding, or whipping, was usually imposed instead. Public branding, usually on the hand, was supposed to be a dramatic example of the state's power, but the wielder of the branding iron could often be bribed not to heat the iron or not to heat it very much. Whipping might take place either in private or in public. The pillory, too, was sometimes imposed for minor crimes; the severity of this sentence depended entirely on public opinion of the criminal and his crime. If there was public sympathy for him, his ordeal might be nothing but a day's inconvenience. If, however, he had done something that met with profound public disapproval, the pillory could actually be fatal. Crowds would stand nearby, jeering the victim and pelting him with any handy object, including stones, mud, and human waste. One man confined in the pillory in 1780 died, and Ann Marrow, pilloried in 1777 for masquerading as a man and marrying three women, was blinded.

Those who received no reprieve were usually sent to the gallows (*J&A, MW* 29) to be hanged (*Sand, MW* 424). London hangings, which had the atmosphere of a public holiday, were described most fully by contemporaries. For most of the eighteenth century, the hangings, which took place about every six weeks, were preceded by a procession from Newgate Prison to Marble Arch, where "Tyburn tree," the three-legged gallows, stood. In the morning, usually on a Monday, the prisoners said farewell to their families and climbed aboard carts, where each sat next to his or her own coffin. A chaplain read prayers, to which the prisoners pointedly pretended not to listen, while the carts rattled through the streets along the three-mile route. Crowds of sightseers, pickpockets, and ballad-sellers followed the procession through the streets, while others watched from their windows. The prisoners often acted as if they were riding in triumph, and sometimes the parade would stop at taverns along the way to allow the condemned men and women to get drunk. The carts drove up directly under one of the three crossbeams of the "tree," while crowds that might number up to 20,000 sat on wooden grandstands, ate food, argued, and bought copies of the dying men's speeches, conveniently composed and printed before they had even been spoken. Then, according to French observer Henri Misson, the executioner

> fastens to that ill-favour'd Beam one End of the Rope, while the other is round the Wretches Neck; This done, he gives the Horse a Lash with his Whip, away goes the Cart, and there swing my Gentlemen kicking in the Air; The Hangman does not give himself the Trouble to put them out of their Pain; but some of their Friends or Relations do it for them: They pull

the dying Person by the Legs, and beat his breast, to dispatch him as soon as possible.

Without such helpers to hasten death, hanging was an extraordinarily slow and painful way to die. There was no trapdoor to create a sudden snap and break the spine; instead, the condemned men and women slowly suffocated, a process that took at least twenty or thirty minutes. Afterward, surgeons might try to claim the bodies for medical dissection. Those who had committed certain types of crimes had their bodies mutilated or displayed in some way. The corpses of highwaymen, for example, were sometimes hung in chains along the turnpike roads they had prowled. Pirates, mutineers, and deserters were strung up along the Thames as gruesome reminders of naval power. Hawkers, meanwhile, bargained for sections of the hanging ropes; a murderer's rope was said to possess magical properties, and sections of the ropes of particularly notorious criminals could be sold as souvenirs at 6d. an inch. Sensitive souls objected to all these proceedings, and in 1783 the processions to Tyburn were abolished. Tyburn tree was torn down, and hangings thereafter took place at Newgate, still observed by large crowds.

Hanging was by far the most common method of execution, but it was not the only one. Beheading was still used in rare instances as the final upper-class privilege, and the scaffold (*Hist Eng*, *MW* 144) was last employed in 1820. Traitors might be drawn and quartered, and women convicted of treason (a category of crime that included not only plotting against the state but also such offenses as counterfeiting coins and murdering a husband) were burned at the stake until 1789. *See also* Law; Prison.

Dance

Dance (*Lesley, MW* 111; *Col Let, MW* 158; *Watsons, MW* 330; *NA* 37, 103, 130, 134; *S&S* 44–45, 47, 171; *P&P* 13, 25, 92; *MP* 250, 252; *E* 229, 245, 247, 258, 328, 333; *P* 43, 72) was an important element of society and courtship, allowing young people to mingle with the opposite sex in a controlled environment, displaying their charms to potential marriage partners (*MP* 39). It was also, for those who enjoyed it, a tremendous amount of fun. The music, the challenge of learning new steps and figures, the subdued competition and necessary cooperation with the other dancers, and the physical exercise could all be exhilarating. There were few things that people enjoyed as much as a ball (*3S, MW* 58; *Lesley, MW* 133; *Cath, MW* 193; *Watsons, MW* 315, 321, 323; *MW* 444; *NA* 79, 89; *P&P* 6, 300, 317, 349; *MP* 35, 250, 251, 270; *E* 191, 276), and both men and women looked forward to such events. Austen herself was an avid dancer; so was her brother Charles. They would probably have agreed with Thomas Wilson, the dancing teacher who wrote *An Analysis of Country Dancing* (1808):

> how delightful, after a tedious journey, to mingle in the sprightly Dance, to associate with those most dear to us in amusement that at once delights and benefits its votaries; that while it gives joy on the one hand, promotes health on the other; where we are pleased with ourselves, and see others pleased; to meet at every circlet of the figure some beautiful female whose animated countenance bespeaks the pleasure she enjoys.
>
> In short, Dancing is the most enchanting of all human amusements, it is the parent of joy, and the soul and support of cheerfulness; it banishes grief, cheers the evening hours of those who have studied or laboured in the day, and brings with it a mixture of delightful sensations which enrapture the senses.

Jane was always proud of herself when she could dance all evening without running out of partners and without getting tired. She lost her relish for balls only in the last few years of her life, when it seemed to be more trouble than it was worth. However, many older people who no longer danced (*E* 327) enjoyed a ball, for it was a chance to meet with friends, talk, and play cards. A separate room was usually provided for those who played cards, so that they could talk and concentrate on their whist hands without too much interference from the music.

The Ball

There were two types of ball: public and private. Public balls were given by subscription, which meant that anyone who could afford the fee could attend all the balls in a given season. The peak season was winter, when outdoor activities were harder to engage in and when people felt trapped indoors. Rural areas and small towns tended to hold their balls once a month at the full moon, a time chosen to make nighttime traveling easier. In small towns, public balls (also called "assemblies"—*Watsons, MW* 314; *P&P* 6; *MP* 249) were often held in inns (*E* 197–198, 250–251), which usually kept a ballroom for this very purpose. The assemblies at Basingstoke, which Jane attended when she lived at Steventon, were held in the Town Hall, with smaller gatherings using the ballroom at the Angel Inn and semiannual "club balls" sponsored by a local gentleman's club using either the Maidenhead Inn or the Crown Inn; the public balls in Southampton were held at either the Dolphin Assembly Rooms in High Street or the Long Rooms near the West Quay.

In Bath and other resort towns, there were one or more assembly rooms in which balls were given, and there might very well be a master of ceremonies. His job kept him extremely busy. He had to greet new arrivals to town and instruct them, if necessary, on the conduct expected of them at the assemblies. During the balls, he was to maintain the proper atmosphere, enforce rules of behavior and dress, introduce suitable partners to each other, and arrange the dancers for each dance. A couple, having agreed to dance together, would approach the master of ceremonies and ask him for permission to join the next dance. Once he knew the identities of the dancers, he could establish which couples belonged at the top and which at the bottom of the set, arranging them according to social class and precedence. Just before the dance began, he would consult with the top couple and confirm their choice of dance, ascertain to the best of his ability whether they could call it successfully, and ensure that it was not a dance that had been chosen already that evening. Then he would instruct each set, if necessary, about how to perform the dance.

Private balls were usually much less formal. The guests tended to know one another and their relative precedence already, so there was no need for help in arranging themselves (*Cath, MW* 223–224; *P&P* 90; *MP* 275; *P* 7). Repetition of the same dance in a given evening was still frowned upon, but among close friends it would have been overlooked. The number of couples dancing was also usually smaller, resulting in less initial confusion and instruction but also making each dance shorter in duration, as we will see below. An advantage of the private ball (*P&P* 91) was that the guest list could be carefully controlled (*Watsons, MW* 350), ensuring a congenial gathering; a disadvantage was that one tended to see the same people at all such occasions, and this could grow tiresome.

The hostess of a private ball (*Col Let, MW* 155; *Cath, MW* 202, 203, 207, 219; *NA* 209; *S&S* 33, 53, 99, 152, 171; *P&P* 45, 46; *MP* 210, 252–254) would first establish that she had a room large enough for dancing (*S&S* 252; *P&P* 91; *MP* 253). There needed to be room not only for

A Master of the Ceremonies Introducing a Partner, Thomas Rowlandson, 1795. Dancers at assembly rooms had to be introduced to each either by mutual acquaintances or by the master of ceremonies, who knew all the subscribers to the assembly rooms and had a fair idea of their level of gentility. Courtesy of the Lewis Walpole Library, Yale University. 795.11.24.1.

the couples to line up but also for them to make the set wider, as some figures required. They also needed room to move forward and back. Once a proper room had been chosen, the hostess compiled a suitable guest list and sent out invitations (*P&P* 55, 86), either handing them out in person or, more commonly, sending a servant around to all the houses in question.

The guests arrived at, or a little after, the starting time (*Watsons, MW* 319, 327, 328); some people liked to arrive late in order to make an entrance. Only girls who were "out," that is, who were officially on the marriage market, could attend (*Col Let, MW* 150; *Cath, MW* 226; *MP* 51, 275; *P&P* 122, 165), and the first attendance of a particular girl at a ball was likely to generate some interest (*MP* 267), especially if she were an heiress or considered to be particularly beautiful. The dancing began and went on for two or three hours, and then refreshments were served. Dancers tended to become overheated, and they needed plenty of liquids. At public balls, participants took tea (*Watsons, MW* 329, 332; *NA* 25–29); at a private ball, there would be a full supper (*MP* 278, 282; *E* 248), with soup (*Watsons, MW* 315; *P&P* 55), several other dishes, and a variety of

An Election Ball, George Cruikshank, 1813. This print features most of the essential features of a ball, though it is missing the card room. Musicians play in a gallery above the ballroom, ladies in the vestibule remove pattens and cloaks, couples dance, and the older people chat. Courtesy of the Lewis Walpole Library, Yale University. 1813.4.28.1.

beverages, including wine, negus, and orgeat. It was customary for the gentlemen to sit at tea or supper with the woman they had just been dancing with (*Watsons*, *MW* 332; *NA* 59); hence, Henry Crawford tries to arrange to dance with Fanny just before supper, so that he will have an excuse to be near her through the meal (*MP* 278). Likewise, Mr. Elton's snub of Harriet is all the more cruel and pointed because it occurs just before supper is due to begin (*E* 326). The entertainment then continued until late at night (*Col Let*, *MW* 157)—or rather, early the next morning. Fanny's debut ball at Mansfield Park is still going on at 3:00 A.M., when she goes up to bed (*MP* 279), and Austen herself attended a ball in 1800 at which the dancing began at 10:00 P.M., the supper began at 1:00 A.M., and she was not back until 5:00 A.M.*

Of course, not all balls were this elaborate. Sometimes impromptu dancing occurred after dinner (*S&S* 54; *MP* 117; *E* 208, 229–230; *P* 47, 71), when guests or family members felt like dancing and some member of the company was willing to play some music. Parson James Woodforde recorded such an occasion in July 1785, when he had had some company

---

*Some public balls ended earlier; those in Bath ended at 11:00 P.M., even in the middle of a dance, but a public ball at Tunbridge Wells in 1787 went on until at least 2:00 A.M.

for dinner. "After Tea the Ladies and Gentlemen got to dancing and danced and sang till Supper Time," he wrote in his diary. "About 12 o'clock this night we all got to dancing again."

The Dance

In all balls, however, public or private, planned or proposed on a whim, it was the men who sought partners and the women who could merely accept or refuse. If they refused, it was incumbent on them to avoid looking as if they refused that particular gentleman. Even if a woman found the gentleman who asked her to dance repulsive or clumsy, she had to spare his feelings by refusing to dance with anyone, usually for the rest of the evening (*P&P* 102). Austen herself resorted to this tactic at a private ball at Kempshott Park, where, she told Cassandra, "One of my gayest actions was sitting down two Dances in preference to having Lord Bolton's eldest son for my Partner, who danced too ill to be endured." A woman who wished to avoid dancing could claim fatigue or disinclination, the two most common excuses, but under no circumstances could she refuse one man and then stand up immediately with another. Most women who liked to dance, therefore, maneuvered around the room in the hope of avoiding unsavory partners, while positioning themselves conveniently close to men with whom they wished to dance. They also frequently chose to dance with bad dancers in order to keep themselves available for dancing for the rest of the evening. All too often, women had the opposite problem: too few partners (*Watsons*, *MW* 315; *MP* 267).

Fewer men than women generally wished to dance, and so it was considered a kind of civic obligation for eligible young men to make themselves available as partners as often as possible (*P&P* 10–11, 175). Jane wrote to Cassandra after a ball in November 1800, "There were only twelve dances, of which I danced nine, & was merely prevented from dancing the rest by want of a partner." At some balls, the host solved the problem of partners and choices by simply drawing lots and assigning partners at random. At times, women might dance with each other if there were simply not enough men to go around.

In earlier years, a woman had been committed to one partner for the entire evening, and this made it all the more important to be asked by the right person (*NA* 131). By Austen's day, the rules had relaxed somewhat. Dances were grouped in pairs, and when a gentleman asked a lady to dance, he did so for two dances (*Watsons*, *MW* 335, 336; *MP* 278–279; *E* 250, 326). He could "engage" her before the ball even started, requesting that she save two dances for him, and she was obliged to accept or not dance at all (*Cath*, *MW* 214; *Watsons*, *MW* 328, 330; *NA* 50; *P&P* 292; *MP* 256, 268, 272, 274; *E* 250). However, dancing more than twice with the same partner in the same evening was frowned upon (*Watsons*, *MW* 334; *S&S* 54), except in the case of engaged or married couples (*MP*

117). Even dancing twice with the same partner (*Cath, MW* 224; *Watsons, MW* 320; *P&P* 12–13; *MP* 278) indicated a marked romantic preference, so a woman could legitimately refuse to dance a second pair of dances with a given gentleman on the grounds of decorum; in this case she could still accept other partners and keep dancing (*NA* 57, 76). The most serious offense of all was to agree to dance with two men for the same pair of dances; earlier in the eighteenth century, this sort of gaffe could ruin a woman's reputation and even lead to a duel. The fact that Miss Osborne, in *The Watsons*, offers this insult to young Charles Blake is a sign not only of her own selfishness but also of her inability to see the boy as a human being with rights and feelings (*Watsons, MW* 330).

The dancers, who had removed their gloves to eat dinner, now put them on again (*Col Let, MW* 157; *Watsons, MW* 331) and, in the case of a country dance, lined up "longways," two by two, with the line of men facing the line of women, each gentleman across from his partner. If there were a great many dancers, this arrangement, called a set (*Watsons, MW* 331, 340; *NA* 52, 80; *E* 328), would be divided into smaller sets (*NA* 55) within the line that would interact with each other as well as with the larger group. Alternatively, as in large assemblies, there might be completely separate sets dancing at the same time. The couple at the top (*MP* 118)—which was usually the end of the line closer to the musicians—selected the dance and called the figures in the proper order. Ideally, the dance was chosen with reference to the level of skill of all the dancers and the nature of the tune, but as dancing teachers were fond of pointing out, this could be a tricky task, and no doubt many a young man or woman stood nervously hoping that he or she could complete the dance without making any serious mistakes. It was customary for the musicians to play the tune once through before the dancers began, to give the dancers a chance to refamiliarize themselves with the tune, run through the figures in their heads, and accustom themselves to the tempo. Dancers who joined the set after the dance began, regardless of their social standing, had to enter at the bottom of the set (*NA* 80). When the next dance began, the second couple (or the first couple in the second set, if there was one) called the dance.

The dancers moved through a variety of figures, including the hey (a figure in which the dancers wove in and out of their respective lines) and hands across (*NA* 133). Hands across was a figure for four dancers, two men and two women; each person held out his or her right hand and took the hand of the person diagonally across the set, forming a little circle with four right arms extended into the center. All four then walked or danced around the circle halfway, so that they stood where their diagonal opposites had stood a moment before. The right hands were released, and the dancers did the same movement in the other direction, joining left hands and dancing back to place. Some figures called for the dancers to move sideways along their own line, while others called for partners to move together, either down the middle of the set or in parallel along the outside. Not all of the figures utilized all of the dancers, and couples at the end of the line might be standing idle for a few minutes while they waited for their opportunity to move again. This was a perfect time to talk, flirt, and look around the room (*P&P* 91; *MP* 278).

As the dance progressed, the top couple gradually moved down the set, taking the place of the second couple, then the third, while the displaced couples moved up toward the top. The second couple would follow them, and then the third, and so on (*E* 327), so that the relative arrangement of the dancers was constantly shifting. One could suddenly come into proximity to a person who had been very far away at the beginning of the dance. When all the dancers had had a turn at the top, the dance was over. A small set, therefore, meant a short dance (*NA* 131), while a large set meant that each dance took a good while to complete. Elizabeth Bennet mentions "half an hour" (*P&P* 91) as a typical length for a dance, and this seems to have been average, though as Thomas Wilson pointed out, a dance could last anywhere from five minutes to an hour, depending on the size of the set. Many ballgoers, Jane Austen included, measured the success of a ball by the number of "couple" who stood up to dance (*Watsons*, *MW* 340; *S&S* 171; *P&P* 91; *MP* 117, 253; *E* 230, 248, 325); more dancers was almost always considered better. Austen considered a ball with seven couples "a very small one indeed" and one with eight "a very poor one." She considered "seventeen couple" a respectable number. Her cousin Eliza de Feuillide considered a large set fairly challenging; at a ball in Cheltenham, she bragged that she "danced every dance, which was taking a tolerable degree of exercise considering there were above thirty couple."

The music for impromptu dancing might be provided by a single pianoforte played by the hostess, one of her daughters, or a female guest (*P* 47, 72). In the case of Fanny Price's first "ball," the music is played by a violinist from the servants' hall (*MP* 117); the ability of a servant to play music for such occasions was a valuable skill and often contributed to finding a good place. At public assemblies, there was a full band (*Watsons*, *MW* 328), which might consist of anything up to about twelve musicians. Sometimes the musicians were placed on a dais; at other times, they were housed in a balconied gallery above the ballroom floor. As opposed to dances at home, where the keyboard was the dominant instrument, music at larger balls tended to be heavy on the stringed instruments, especially violins (*Watsons*, *MW* 327; *S&S* 171; *MP* 275). The nature of the music varied. Minuets were slow and sedate, while "Scotch and Irish airs" (*P&P* 25, 511) were lively. Most English country dances fell somewhere in between.

The musicians must have had a hard time of it. They were not especially well paid, and they worked long hours. Moreover, people who failed to call the dance well often blamed the musicians. In one instance, related in an 1816 dancing manual, a nineteen-year-old nobleman, failing to set figures to a dance he had called, seized the bow from a violinist, who grabbed it back and shook the "puny little lord," breaking his quizzing glass in the process. Far from blaming the musician, the author of the dancing manual praised him for standing up to the rude young man.

Good dancing (*NA* 72), like good behavior, was prized wherever it was found. It was not always easy to come by (*P&P* 90), as different types of dance required very different movements and styles; cotillions and quadrilles, for example, could be safely embellished with balletic postures, while the country dance was to be performed easily and gracefully without any quasi-professional airs or attitudes. The author of *The Mirror of the Graces* (1811) believed firmly in the importance of dancing well, especially for women:

> Nothing is more ugly than a stiff body and neck, during this lively exercise. The general carriage should be elevated and light; the chest thrown out, the head easily erect, but flexible to move with every turn of the figure; and the limbs should be all braced and animated with the spirit of motion, which seems ready to bound through the very air. By this elasticity pervading the whole person, when the dancer moves off, her flexile shape will gracefully sway with the varied steps of her feet; and her arms, instead of hanging loosely by her side, or rising abruptly and squarely up, to take hands with her partner, will be raised in beautiful and harmonious unison and time with the music and the figure; and her whole person will thus exhibit, to the delighted eye, perfection in beauty, grace, and motion.

However, she did not believe in a dance education for all, only for the upper classes; "girls of the plebeian classes," she wrote, should stick to learning "how to manage a house, how to economize and produce comfort at the least expence at their father's frugal yet hospitable table."

Learning to dance was considered an essential part of the education of any young lady or gentleman (*Lesley, MW* 119–120; *P&P* 39; *MP* 276), and responsible parents hired dancing masters to teach their children to move elegantly. To judge from the number of satirical prints whose titles turn on the phrase, "Hold up your head" seems to have been the most common advice offered by these dancing masters. When the dancing teachers were not present, families practiced the steps (*Cath, MW* 212; *MP* 273) of old dances to keep them well memorized and learned new ones together. The quadrille, a complicated dance, appears to have been one of the ones that required copious drawing-room rehearsal. Dancers also kept themselves up-to-date by buying books that came out annually and featured the dances that were currently most popular. Dancing also formed part of the curriculum in many boarding schools. Charles Austen was taught to dance at the Naval Academy at Portsmouth. His report for

Bobbin about to the Fiddle—A Family Rehearsal of Quadrille, 1817. Courtesy of the Lewis Walpole Library, Yale University. 817.5.0.1.

February 1792 noted, "Dances tolerably," but he must have improved, because by 1793–1794 the assessment had changed to "Dances very well."

Types of Dances

The most formal and old-fashioned of the dances that was still performed with any frequency was the minuet. It had different variations, one of which was the minuet de la cour mentioned in *Love and Freindship* (*MW* 78). It was a demanding dance with small steps in which posture, timing, and graceful positioning of the limbs were essential, and it was usually performed by only two people at a time. It was rarely danced in private balls or in impromptu dances at home, but it was still danced at the major assembly halls, such as Almack's in London and the Upper and Lower Rooms at Bath. Balls at Bath were divided into two types, "dressed," and "undressed" (or "cotillion" or "fancy") balls (*NA* 35, 73); the references to clothing were because the minuet had a stricter dress code than other dances. Dressed balls began with minuets, then proceeded to other types of dances, chiefly country dances, after tea. The minuet lost favor fairly steadily over Austen's lifetime; by 1811, *The Mirror of the Graces* could state that the "*minuet* is now almost out of fashion."

The cotillion's (*NA* 74) name derived from the French word for "petticoat," and as a French-derived dance, it, too, was more formal than country dancing. A contemporary manual for performing sixteen cotillions describes the dance as being for four couples, sometimes with minuet steps, sometimes with hand clapping, and with a set that sometimes arranged itself longways and sometimes reshaped itself as a circle. It did not require nearly as much skill as the minuet and replaced the minuet at the beginning of cotillion balls. Yet it was praised in *The Mirror of the Graces* for its "rapid changes," which were "admirably calculated for the display of elegant gaiety." By the early nineteenth century, it had become a five- or six-figure dance known as the quadrille, first introduced in public by Lady Jersey, who danced it at Almack's in 1815. The quadrille does not appear in the novels but crops up in the letters, when in February 1817 she thanked her niece Fanny Knight for sending her some quadrille music. However, she reserved the time-honored right of the older generation to disapprove of innovation. She was "Much obliged" for them, she wrote; they were "pretty enough, though of course they are very inferior to the Cotillions of my own day."

The most popular type of dance for most of Austen's lifetime was the country dance (*Lesley, MW* 129; *NA* 74, 76–77; *E* 229, 245; *P* 47), an undemanding form of dance that required chiefly that the dancers be able to carry themselves gracefully. Thomas Wilson, who approved strongly of country dancing when it was done properly, wrote that the "general character of this style of Dancing is simplicity, ease, freedom, and liveliness, rather inclining to the mirthful than the graceful, and to cheerfulness than elegance." *The Mirror of the Graces* concurred: "The characteristic of an English country-dance is that of *gay simplicity*. The steps should be few and easy; and the corresponding motion of the arms and body unaffected, modest, and graceful." This was the dance with the longways sets "for all who will" described above. It was the easiest dance for the relatively unskilled, as they could watch the top couples before they had to perform the same maneuvers themselves. The steps were simple, consisting mostly of a step-hop forwards or backwards.

Scottish dances (*Cath, MW* 212) such as reels (*MW* 448; *P&P* 52) were even more informal than country dances and used considerably more energy. Scottish and Irish reels, jigs, and country dances became extremely popular beginning in the 1790s, with examples such as "New Tartan Pladdies," "Ranting Highlanders," and "Limerick Jig" appearing in books of music and manuals of dance steps. *The Mirror of the Graces* approved of reels, but only in certain circumstances:

> There are no dancers in the world more expressive of inward hilarity and happiness than the Scotch are, when performing in their own reels. The music is sufficient (so jocund are its sounds) to set a whole company on their feet in a moment, and to dance with all their might till it ceases, like

people bit by the tarantula. Hence, as the character of reels is merriment, they must be performed with much more *joyance* of manner than even the country-dance; and therefore they are better adapted (as society is now constituted) to the social private circle than to the public ball. They demand a frankness of deportment, an undisguised jocularity, which few large parties will properly admit.

Edward Topham's *Letters from Edinburgh* (1775) confirmed that the spirit of the dance was a joyful one:

> The young people in England only consider dancing as an agreeable means of bringing them together. But the Scotch admire the reel for its own merit alone, and may truly be said to dance for the sake of dancing. A Scotchman comes into an assembly room as he would into a field of exercise, dances till he is literally tired, possibly without ever looking at his partner. In most countries the men have a partiality for dancing with a woman; but here I have frequently seen four gentlemen perform one of these reels seemingly with the same pleasure and perseverance as they would have done, had they had the most sprightly girl for a partner. They give you the idea that they could with equal glee cast off round a joint stool or set to a corner cupboard.

Other popular dances included contredanse, a square dance for four or eight dancers, and the Boulangere (Baker's Wife—*P&P* 13), a dance in which the dancer turned first one partner and then another. On September 5, 1796, Jane reported from Goodnestone (her brother Edward's first house, before he moved to Godmersham) that "We dined . . . & in the Evening danced two Country Dances & the Boulangeries."

Many dances were imported from the Continent, but while imports like the cotillion and quadrille met with favor, others were deemed too immodest for young British women to perform. The fandango, because it was a solo dance, was thought to attract too much attention to the individual. The author of *The Mirror of the Graces* found it shocking:

> Imagine what must be the assurance of the young woman, who, unaccustomed by the habits of her country to such singular exhibitions of herself, could get up in a room full of company, and, with an unblushing face, go through all the evolutions, postures, and vaultings of the Spanish fandango?

The same author also disapproved of the bolero, a partner dance that an unscrupulous male partner could shift "from gaiety into licentiousness."

The dance that was destined to oust most of these forms, however, was the waltz (*MW* 448). It had just been introduced in the last years of Austen's life, arriving in England in about 1812, but bits and pieces of the dance had been trickling in for years and adopted as figures in other dances, while the music for waltzes was often played, not as accompaniment to the waltz but as the background to country dancing (*E* 229, 242). What was so shocking about the waltz was the degree of physical contact it permitted, even mandated, between the couple, and the first illustrations of the full-fledged dance emphasized its sensuality. Thomas Wilson approved of the dance wholeheartedly by 1816, but the author of *The Mirror of the Graces*, writing a few years earlier, could not give it her endorsement:

> But with regard to the lately-introduced German waltz, I cannot speak so favourably. I must agree with Goetté [*sic*], when writing of the national dance of his country, "that none but husbands and wives can with any propriety be partners in the waltz."
>
> There is something in the close approximation of persons, in the attitudes, and in the motion, which ill agrees with the delicacy of woman, should she be placed in such a situation with any man other than the most intimate connection she can have in her life.

It was not until 1814, when it was performed at Almack's, that the waltz began to gain in popularity. Still, even Lord Byron, not known for his prudery, had reservations:

> Endearing Waltz!—to thy more melting tune
> Bow Irish jig and ancient rigadoon.
> Scotch reels, avaunt! And country-dance, forego
> Your future claims to each fantastic toe!
> Waltz—Waltz alone—both legs and arms demands,
> Liberal of feet and lavish of her hands;
> Hands which may freely range in public sight
>   Where ne'er before—but—pray "put out the light."

It was the arms entwined around partners' waists that truly shocked English observers of this dance. Nor can it have helped that the waltz was associated in many minds with German romanticism, and German sentimental novels and plays had been identified with many of the emotional excesses mocked by Austen. In Goethe's *The Sorrows of Young Werther*, which Austen uses as an emblem of the literature of sensibility, the hero gushes,

> Never had I danced more lightly. I felt myself more than mortal, holding this loveliest of creatures in my arms, flying with her like the wind, till I lost sight of everything else; and—Wilhelm, I vowed at that moment that a girl whom I loved, or for whom I felt the slightest attachment, should never waltz with another, even if it should be my end!

One other type of dance is mentioned by Austen, but this was not a social dance. It was the "figure-dance" (*MP* 124), a showy sort of dance often performed between dramatic pieces at the theater. Each dance had several parts, and each part might be symbolic in some way. Joseph Strutt, in *The Sports and Pastimes of the People of England* (1801), described the dance as "pantomimical representations of historical and poetical subjects, expressed by fantastic gestures." *See also* Bath; Music.

Death

There were relatively few hospitals in the late eighteenth and early nineteenth centuries, and most people died (*Lesley, MW* 114; *MW* 442; *P* 96) at home. If time permitted, they would gather their relatives (and sometimes their servants as well) at the deathbed (*S&S* 54), issue final words of advice, perhaps revise or write a will, and make their wishes known about disposal of certain items of sentimental value.* The doctor might come; frequently, the only time a family hired a physician, whose rates tended to be exorbitant, was when death was already unavoidable. The local parson would show up as well and offer prayers and possibly communion. There was a set formula for prayers at a sickbed, concluding with a prayer whose nature was based on the likelihood of recovery; the prayer for "a sick person at the point of departure" went as follows:

> O ALMIGHTY God, with whom do live the spirits of just men made perfect, after they are delivered from their earthly prisons: We humbly commend the soul of this thy servant, our dear brother, into thy hands, as into the hands of a faithful Creator, and most merciful Saviour; most humbly beseeching thee, that it may be precious in thy sight. Wash it, we pray thee, in the blood of that immaculate Lamb, that was slain to take away the sins of the world; that whatsoever defilements it may have contracted in the midst of this miserable and naughty world, through the lusts of the flesh, or the wiles of Satan, being purged and done away, it may be presented pure and without spot before thee. And teach us who survive, in this and other like daily spectacles of mortality, to see how frail and uncertain our own condition is; and so to number our days, that we may seriously apply our hearts to that holy and heavenly wisdom, whilst we live here, which may in the end bring us to life everlasting, through the merits of Jesus Christ thine only Son our Lord. Amen.

We are told that on her own deathbed, Austen purposely received religious rites while still conscious enough to comprehend the words, so one assumes the above prayer was read for her. When death was sudden, none of this was possible (*E* 387).

Death was a regular visitor in the households of Austen's era. Birthrates were high, and so was infant mortality. Diseases caused by poor hygiene, poor nutrition, and crowding routinely thinned the population of London, which continued to rise only because immigration to the city outpaced the death rate. While some people lived to be genuinely elderly, most died young by modern standards (*S&S* 10–11). It was quite common, particularly given the fact that many women continued to give birth until they

---

*Some property was "entailed" (*LS, MW* 256; *P&P* 28, 164, 308)—that is, its inheritance was limited by earlier family wills and had to pass to heirs designated by the entail. This legal device was often used to keep property in the male line of descent within a family.

reached menopause, for a child to grow up without one or both parents (*J&A*, *MW* 16; *NA* 180; *E* 96, 163). Jane's father, George Austen, lost his own father when he was only nine years old, and Jane's cousin Jane Cooper lost her mother to an epidemic when she, too, was just a child.

After the death, the body was cleaned, often dressed in clothing, and then wrapped in a shroud, the material of which was regulated by the government. Wool shrouds had been required by law for centuries in order to support England's wool industry, and until the law was repealed in 1814–1815, those wishing the deceased to be buried in a linen shroud had to pay a fine. The family, or servants hired for the purpose, sat with the body until the time of burial came, a period known as the "wake" (*MW* 444).

The funeral (*Evelyn*, *MW* 189; *S&S* 5; *E* 388) procession walked to the church, the mourners dressed in black robes, the coffin (*NA* 191) covered by a cloth called a pall (hence the term "pallbearers"), and the procession led by a man called a mute who carried a staff topped with a gathered bundle of black crape. Sometimes a tray of black ostrich plumes, called a "lid of feathers," was carried by a "featherman." The pall was usually black with a white cross, sometimes red with heraldic decorations for the rich, and always white for girls in honor of their virginity. Girls' coffins were also decorated with garlands of flowers. The flowers might be real or artificial, and if the latter, might be made of paper, wire, silk, wood, dyed horn, or painted eggshells. A woman's coffin was often borne by female pallbearers; if the deceased were a spinster, these pallbearers would usually wear white. White was also worn at the burials of children.

At the churchyard, the church bell tolled (*MW* 448) to inform the community that someone had died. Three peals were rung for the death of a child, six for a woman, and nine for a man. It was the bell that alerted Parson James Woodforde to his duty on November 22, 1786:

> I buried this Afternoon about 4 o'clock, John Plummer an Infant aged only 5 Weeks. I knew nothing of burying the above Infant till 3 o'clock this Afternoon, then on hearing the Church Bell, I sent to Church to enquire the reason, and word was brought me, that there was a Child then at the Church Gate for Interment—It being my Dinner Time, I went as soon as ever I had finished my Dinner—Some Mistake of my old Clerk or the Father of the Child—in not acquainting me.

(An unbaptized child could not be buried in the churchyard, and no bell was rung to mark its passing.) The procession then entered the churchyard, and here the paths diverged based on class. Paupers were buried in communal graves, while most people were buried in single graves with headstones (*F&E*, *MW* 9) of varying size according to their wealth. The upper classes might be buried in the churchyard, but they preferred to be buried in a tomb (*MW* 442) under the church itself or in a family vault

(*E* 398), a small building that might be located either on the church grounds or on the family estate. If buried in the church, as Jane Austen was buried in Winchester Cathedral, a plaque or other monument (*NA* 190) inside the church would replace the traditional headstone.

Bodies were not usually carried very far by the pallbearers. They traveled most of the way in a hearse, a black carriage drawn by two or four horses. On one occasion in 1785, Parson Woodforde recorded that a child's body was brought to the churchyard by the family carriage. On another occasion in 1782, Woodforde gave a detailed description of the funeral procession of a Mrs. Howes:

> Before we went to Church there was Chocolate and Toast and Cake with red Wine and white. At half past 11 o'clock we went to Church with the Corpse in the following Procession. The Corpse first in an Hearse and Pair of Horses, then followed six Chaises, in the first which was Du Quesnes went Du Quesne and Dr. Thorne, in the second which was Mr. Shelfords went Mr. Shelford and Mr. Smith, in the third which was Mr. Priests, went Mr. Priest and myself, in the fourth which was one from Dereham, went Mr. Potter and Mr. Bodham, in the fifth which was from Norwich went Mr. Priest of Norwich and a Mr. Forster the Undertaker, in the sixth which was Mr. Howes's, went Mrs. Howes's two Servant Maids in deep mourning. The Underbearers and Servants all in Hatbands black closed the Procession and an handsome appearance the whole Procession made—we returned to Mr. Howes's in the same manner as we went from it to Church—Mr. Du Quesne buried her—The Pall-Bearers were Mr. Shelford, Mr. Priest, Mr. Potter, Mr. Bodham, Mr. Smith and myself—we had all black Hatbands and Gloves, but they were white. Poor Mrs. Howes if she had lived till to Morrow wch was her birth Day—she would have been 69 Years. It was as decent, neat, handsome Funeral as I ever saw and everything conducted in the best manner. . . . Mr. Howes, Mrs. Davy &c. kept above stairs all the Time—They desired me to walk up to them which I did after the Funeral, but did not stay long with them—found them low and left them so. After our return from Church we had Cake and Wine and Chocolate and dried Toast carried round. My Servant and all Servants that attended and all the drivers all had Hatbands and gloves given to them.

His reference to refreshments was typical of funerals at the time; cakes, wine, ale, chocolate, and so forth were often served to the mourners either before or after the funeral. Largesse was also sometimes distributed to the poor or to members of the household staff; ladies' maids, for example, could expect to receive some of their mistress' clothes upon her death.

After the funeral, a fee was paid to the officiating clergyman. Parson Woodforde recorded receiving £1 1s. for his services at the burial of a young man in 1790. In 1785, he was given £5 5s. for burying the squire's sixteen-week-old daughter. Gifts, frequently hatbands (*P* 147), rings, black ribbons, or gloves, were distributed to the mourners; at the 1790 funeral, Woodforde received "a black silk Hatband and a pair of Beaver Gloves." If the deceased were a woman, some or all of these "tokens" might be white, as were the gloves Woodforde received at the funeral of Mrs. Howes.

Funeral expenses could be kept down by renting the trappings of mourning. Parishes sometimes had a communal pall that could be rented, and mourning scarves, hoods, and cloaks could be rented from undertakers for the procession. Members of trade guilds and associations often clubbed together to pay for each other's funerals, and this was of great help.

Money could also be saved by dyeing one's garments to make mourning clothes rather than buying new ones. Relatives and servants of a deceased person were expected to wear mourning for a period of time that varied depending on the closeness of the relationship (*Lesley, MW* 130–131). In May 1799, on a journey to Bath, Jane wrote to Cassandra that she had "met a Gentleman in a Buggy, who on a minute examination turned out to be Dr Hall—& Dr Hall in such very deep mourning that either his Mother, his Wife, or himself must be dead."

Mourning clothes would be distributed to the servants (*P* 105, 106), and garments might be dyed black or ordered newly made in dark and somber colors. First mourning was all black (*P* 8), from hat to shoes. Women could wear black silk crape (*P* 147) or bombazine, materials universally approved because they were not shiny, with small touches of white here and there. A sample mourning outfit from a 1799 fashion magazine shows a full-skirted, high-waisted black robe and petticoat with white half-diamond edging along the edges of the robe and the sleeve hems, black gloves, simple black jewelry, a white ruffle at the neck, black ostrich plumes in the headdress, and a white fur muff. Female servants were dressed in black bombazine or in bombazet, a cheaper fabric than bombazine. Men, too, dressed in black for first mourning (*P* 104). Shoes were "shammy"—chamois leather, which like crape had little gloss. People in first mourning were not expected to retreat entirely from society, but they were expected to refrain from riotous or noticeably joyous activity (*MP* 121–123).

After a period of time (usually a few months—*E* 460) had elapsed, the deceased's family began to wear second mourning. Men wore gray at this time, while women wore black, white, and touches of color, especially shades of purple. After a few months of second mourning, life and dress were expected to return to normal (*P* 159). Many people also wore mourning on the death of the king or a member of the royal family, and those at court also wore mourning on the death of foreign monarchs. The duration of mourning in these cases typically depended on the rank of the deceased.

Debt

Debt (*P* 12, 209), never a pleasant thing in any society, is especially in the sink-or-swim commercial atmosphere of Austen's Britain. Generous bankruptcy (*Col Let*, *MW* 158) laws with forgiveness of debt were unheard of; a debtor had to pay every cent he owed, no matter what, or reach a private agreement with every creditor. Creditors who lost their patience could pay to have the local bailiffs arrest the debtor, seize his goods (*L&F*, *MW* 88–89), and throw him into debtors' prison (*S&S* 207). A poem by Joseph Mather, written in the early 1790s, summed up the process:

My creditors may sue me,
And curse the day they knew me;
The bailiffs may pursue me,
   And lock me up in jail.

The Bailiff's Hunt, George Woodward and Thomas Rowlandson, 1809. One of the common formats for satirical prints was the hunting sequence, showing established stages of the hunt—the hounds picking up the scent, the kill, and so on. Often the sequence was used to poke fun at the poor riding skills of the hunters. Here it is used to track the pursuit of a debtor, with the bailiffs as the hunters. The first panel, "Going out in the Morning," shows the two bailiffs setting out; "In Full Scent" shows them finding the debtor's door; "Breaking Cover" shows the debtor, like a pursued fox or hare, fleeing; and "The Pursuit" shows him trying to evade his captors. Courtesy of the Lewis Walpole Library, Yale University. 809.0.53.

A less serious take on the subject was a satirical print that parodied traditional images of the hunt; in this case, however, the hunters are the bailiffs, and the quarry is a debtor on whom they seek to execute a warrant. The "Execution in the House" in *Love and Freindship* is along these lines: not an execution in the sense of putting someone to death, but the execution of a warrant for the arrest of a debtor (*L&F*, *MW* 88). As unpleasant as it was to go to jail for debt, at least it didn't carry the death penalty, despite Sophia's concern that her debtor husband has been "hung" (*L&F*, *MW* 97).

A debtor in jail could not carry on his trade, making it much less likely that the debt could ever be repaid. Furthermore, while in prison, the debtor had to pay for his own sustenance, a situation that led to the pathetic sight of debtors pleading through the windows of the jails for largesse from passersby. The specter of debt haunted anyone at financial risk—families with a son or husband who had a penchant for dice or drink (*S&S* 70; *P&P* 297–98; *MP* 23–24), merchants with cargo-laden ships at sea, a wife whose husband, by law, had complete control of all the couple's finances, no matter how foolish or unscrupulous he might be (*P* 152–153). Often debt was simply a matter of poor spending habits. Gentlemen ran up bills with numerous tradespeople (*P&P* 294; *P* 9), such as tailors and china merchants, relying on generous credit terms, until they found they simply could not pay the bills (*LS*, *MW* 246). Meanwhile, their creditors, unable to collect, frequently found themselves dragged down into debt along with their genteel customers.

There were few ways out once a person was deeply in debt. Landowners who had incoming rents could economize and hope to squeak by until the debts were paid off (*S&S* 194; *P* 13). This was the tack taken by the Austens' friend John Harwood, who inherited nearby Deane House along with massive debts from his father. He sacrificed a great deal to maintain control of the family estate, including marriage to a woman whom he loved but whose dowry was inadequate to rescue him. When a newly widowed woman gave birth unexpectedly in his house, however, he gave up some of the last of his stores of wine to make caudle for her.

Inheritance hurt rather than helped John Harwood, but sometimes inheritance could rescue a profligate son—at least for a time. Marriage to a wealthy woman could also effect a repair of one's fortune (*S&S* 194), as wives brought dowries with them in the form of cash, jewels, land, or goods. On occasion, friends might offer some help in paying creditors (*P&P* 265, 313, 324, 387), but usually only if they could be sure that they themselves would be repaid, or at least that the descent into debt would not be repeated.

Devoirs

"Devoirs" (*NA* 45), which descended from a word meaning "to owe," could mean duty, one's best effort, a service due to someone, or the courteous social attentions that were someone's due. It is in this last sense that Austen uses it. According to the OED, the word was initially pronounced "DEH-verz" and was sometimes spelled as if it were an abbreviation of "endeavours," but by Austen's time it had adopted a modern French spelling and a French-style pronunciation. *See also* French.

Dishes

Until about the seventeenth century, dishes had been fairly limited in both type and composition. The poor ate off wood or cheap earthenware; the "pitcher" owned by the poor family in *Emma* is no doubt a rough earthenware pitcher, for instance (*E* 88). The rich ate off silver plate, and the middling sort might have something in between—pewter, perhaps. The seventeenth and eighteenth centuries, however, saw a revolution in both the materials used for dishes and in the number of kinds of dishes considered necessary for a well-equipped house. The impetus in both cases was trade with the East Indies, which brought regular shipments of tea and of Chinese porcelain (hence the name "china" for porcelain—*NA* 162; *P&P* 75). Drinking tea required "tea things" to drink it out of, and porcelain was such a fascinating new material, so strong, so impervious to heat, that the rich found they *had* to have it.

The catch was that no one quite knew the chemistry behind porcelain's strength and lightweight beauty. They knew that it had something to do with the kind of clay used and with very high heat in the kiln, but it was many years before people discovered European deposits of the special clay—kaolin—and acquired enough skill to exploit it properly. Nonetheless, recapturing some of the money spent on millions of pieces of imported porcelain was a profound incentive. At first, Europeans created fake porcelains that contained no kaolin. These included soft-paste porcelains, such as the early products of Vincennes and Sèvres (the "Sève" of *NA* 175), the so-called porcelain of Chelsea, and faience, a tin-glazed earthenware.

The Germans mastered the new technology first, in a manufactory at Meissen, near Dresden (*NA* 175). This facility flourished due to an influx of royal commissions, a wide range of products, and high artistic quality, but war interrupted its trade somewhat, and manufactories in Vienna, Sèvres, Höchst, and elsewhere were able to capture more of the business. All of these facilities were mixing kaolin, feldspar, water, quartz, and varying additives into a paste, storing it for a while to improve its quality, and then shaping it into dishes or figurines. The shaped pieces were then baked at about 900°C, leaving them dry and porous. They were then dipped in a glaze, also of porcelain, and fired again at a much higher temperature—1350 to 1460°C—which fused the kaolin and feldspar. Then they could be painted and fired a third time, or even a fourth, depending on the number of colors added and whether or not there was gilding. In the early years of porcelain manufacture, all these designs were hand painted, by artists who specialized in a certain type of subject, such as flowers, landscapes, or portraits. The reason they painted on top of the glaze was that the extreme heat of the second firing meant that few colors could be added before glazing, as the kiln would simply burn them away. A handful of colors, however, could survive this process, including cobalt blue, which is why much of the Chinese ware that arrived in Europe was blue-and-white and why so many European manufacturers created blue-and-white dishes.

The royal manufactory at Sèvres was merely the most successful and influential of many French porcelain workshops. French porcelains were much admired, and their artistic decorations were widely copied elsewhere in Europe. In England, the principal workshops were at Chelsea, Bow, Derby, and Worcester, all of which produced soft-paste porcelain; and at Plymouth and Bristol, which made hard porcelain from Cornwall kaolin, the only source in all of England. Most of the items made in Europe were relatively small in size—small boxes, oil and vinegar cruets, needle cases, snuffboxes, thimbles, jugs, ewers, basins (sizable bowls—see *Watsons, MW* 359; *MP* 180), vases, candlesticks, inkstands, clocks, dish covers, and wine coolers.

Then, of course, there were the breakfast (*NA* 175; *S&S* 13) and tea services—teapots (*Sand, MW* 416), coffeepots, chocolate pots, sugar bowls or boxes, creamers, teacups (initially without handles, hence the colloquial phrase, "a dish of tea"—see *MP* 378), saucers, and tea caddies. Twelve teacups was a standard number. Sometimes a service would have separate teacups and coffee cups (*P&P* 341), and some sets had a slop basin and a plate for it to rest on, a spoon tray, and plates (*MP* 413) for bread and butter or cakes. When Austen refers to "tea things" (*Watsons, MW* 357; *Sand, MW* 416; *S&S* 144, 200; *P&P* 342; *MP* 335, 378), she means this sort of set of dishes, plus a board (*MP* 344) or tray (*Sand, MW* 416) on which to carry them; either an urn (*MP* 344) or, in humbler homes, a kettle (*MP* 383), in which to heat the water for the tea; and tongs for the cubes of sugar, all three of which would have been made wholly or partially of some kind of metal. A breakfast service would also have one or two special pieces, such as, perhaps, a toast rack.

Soup tureens, often shaped like animals or vegetables in England and Germany, but rarely in France, were a popular item to be made from porcelain; since the glaze and the core of the item were both made of porcelain, they expanded at the same rate when exposed to heat and thus suffered no cracking in the glaze. They were not the only items to be given whimsical shapes. Sauceboats, too, might be shaped like ducks or like foxes' heads; dram bottles might be shaped like pistols or fish; and mugs might look like a seated man, or like a man's head. Dinner plates (*MP* 171) and bowls, much more sober in their design than these fanciful ves-

Advantages of Wearing Muslin Dresses!, James Gillray, 1802. The tipping table is loaded with the "tea things" so often mentioned by Austen. The large tea urn in the center holds hot water, which is poured from a spout into a teapot on the left side of the table. A cream pitcher is shown in front of the urn, and just behind it and to the right are a sugar bowl and sugar tongs. The footman is entering the room with a china plate that matches the cups and saucers. Courtesy of the Lewis Walpole Library, Yale University. 802.2.15.1.

sels, were often made from porcelain for those who could afford this still-expensive material. Huge platters, however, still had to be imported from China, as no one in Europe as yet could quite figure out how to make such large pieces.

Earthenware and Bone China

For those who could not afford porcelain, there were increasing numbers of attractive, inexpensive alternatives. Two important potteries arose in Staffordshire (*NA* 175) in the second half of the eighteenth century, and these two firms—Spode and Wedgwood—along with many others, were responsible for a sort of small revolution on the tabletop. Josiah Wedgwood (1730–1795), an avid experimenter and a marketing genius, saw that people wanted to imitate the classes above them. He therefore aggressively courted royal and noble favor for his products, then used the information to make his products fashionable. His creamware, for example, earthenware with a warm, pale-yellow glaze, was purchased in the 1760s by Queen Charlotte, and he promptly renamed the style "Queen's Ware."

He opened a London showroom (shown in *Wedgwood & Byerly* [Shops]), streamlined production, made use of the recent improvements in turnpikes and canals to transport his goods with less chance of breakage, and, though he created elaborate art pieces such as vases for the rich, always kept some of his ceramics within the reach of the status-conscious middle class. They answered his call by discarding their old, rough mugs and dishes and replacing them with delicate, beautifully painted creamware.

Meanwhile, he continued to experiment. He embraced the interest in classical design in the 1760s and 1770s, producing vases in imitation of Attic red-figure originals and introducing classical motifs such as laurel leaves and Greek key borders into many of his pieces. He invented, or at least popularized, a clay "body" (a specific mixture of components) called Black Basalt. This had a deep black, satiny finish and was used both for art pieces and for ordinary, useful items such as teapots; Parson James Woodforde bought "a black Tea Pot" in October, 1783, probably either Wedgwood's or an imitator's.

Wedgwood had a fascination with reproducing the colors and textures of nonceramic materials, principally types of stone. Some of his pieces look as if they are made of agate or granite, but he is best known for his Jasper ware, which has the appearance of a cameo, with the background and figures being of two distinct colors. He had a great deal of difficulty developing this technique. Pieces kept shattering in the kilns, some lots showing failure rates of as high as 75 percent, and the cobalt used to color the background was extremely expensive. In 1782, however, he invented a pyrometer for measuring kiln temperature, composed of a series of ceramic rods that could be inserted into a kiln for a specific length of time, after which they were drawn out and compared to the width of a standard tube. Their degree of shrinkage indicated temperature. He also constructed a special kiln just for firing Jasper ware and reduced the amount of cobalt required by making the bulk of the piece of white clay and then dipping it in a thin coating of the blue. By the late 1770s, he was making all sorts of dishes out of Jasper ware, not only in "Wedgwood blue," but in two other shades of blue as well, plus lilac, with gray, yellow, and dark brown used as backgrounds for decorative pieces such as portrait medallions. Another of his inventions was caneware, a yellow ceramic that resembled bamboo; he had difficulty with it as late as 1779, but it was being marketed in his catalogues by 1787. The various clay bodies were used to make all the standard dinnerware and tea items listed above, plus the large plates, bowls, and platters that could not yet be manufactured in porcelain.

Most items corresponded to the sorts of dinnerware we would expect to see on a table today, with a few additions, such as "salts" (small salt dishes), tall pie dishes shaped like the elaborate standing crusts of poultry pies, and custard and ice cups (dessert cups, rather like tea or coffee cups, but with a lid to cover the chilled confection inside). Customers might also buy a pap boat (a sort of cross between a baby bottle and cereal bowl) or a cheese plate, not really a plate at all, but a tall round stand and cover that looked something a small, fancy soup pot. Even simple dinner plates were sometimes much more elaborate than those widely available today. Some of the plates had scalloped rims, pierced rims (with lozenge-shaped sections cut out at regular intervals), or a shell-like edging of tapering grooves.

Josiah Spode Sr. (1733–1797) and his namesake son were also busy innovating. At their pottery in Stoke-on-Trent, which comprised several groups of buildings punctuated by bottle-shaped brick ovens three or four stories tall, they, too, were making punch bowls, tea and coffee sets, plates, mugs, and vases. The younger Spode, in 1798, perfected a recipe for bone china (*S&S* 26), a type of hard porcelain made of ox bones that had been boiled, dried, burned, and powdered; china clay; and Cornish stone.

The process of making earthenware began with amassing the ingredients and allowing the clay to sit outside for several months, exposed to the elements, to remove salts that could injure the finished pieces. Though the Spode works was located in Staffordshire, its clay did not usually come from the immediate area, which was noted for its coarse red clay, but from such places as Dorset, Devon, and Cornwall. The finely ground ingredients were mixed with water into a wet mixture called "slip," which was sieved to remove lumps and passed over a magnet to remove iron. After evaporating much of the moisture from the slip, workers cut it with bronze spades into workable pieces from which they kneaded all the air. A thrower used a potter's wheel, operated by a child apprentice, to shape the pieces, which were now called "green ware." This green ware was dried and arranged in "saggars," large round clay containers that protected the pieces from the kiln's most severe heat. After a thorough baking in a biscuit kiln that could hold 500 to 600 pieces at once and was heated to a temperature of 1100°–1250°C, the dishes or statuettes emerged as "biscuit ware," fired but undecorated and unglazed. At this point, until the mid-eighteenth century, the ware would have been glazed, fired, handpainted, and fired again at a lower temperature, but at midcentury, a new technique drastically expanded the variety of decoration available and simultaneously lowered the cost of production.

This was underglaze printing, which was accomplished by one of two methods: paper transfer or bat printing. In paper transfer, the biscuit piece—let us assume it was a plate—was heated to make it more porous. Meanwhile, a copper-plate engraving, with grooves carved into its face where the lines were meant to be, was also heated. Coloring, called "oil," was applied to the plate, and the excess was wiped away, leaving the oil only in the grooves. A piece of tissue paper, moistened with soap and water to increase its flexibility and decrease its absorbency, was placed over the plate and pressed down with a felt pad. Then it was carefully lifted off and handed to an apprentice—usually a little girl—who cut away the excess paper and cut the parts of the design into separate pieces. These were then rearranged, facedown, on the warm plate, by a worker who pressed the paper against the plate to make the color adhere. The plate was then handed to another worker, who rinsed the plate in water to dissolve the tissue, leaving the color on the surface of the plate.

Bat printing was similar, in that it transferred the design from an engraved copper plate, but this method used not tissue paper but a "bat," a sheet of flexible, dried glue, and the copper plate was impregnated not with coloring but with linseed oil. The oil pattern was transferred to the biscuit plate, and powdered colors were sprinkled over the plate, adhering to the places where oil was present. At the end of the day, the used bats were collected by a worker who reboiled the glue and spread it out to dry on plates; in the morning these recycled bats would be ready for use.

In both cases, bat and paper transfer alike, the colored plate was then taken to a "dipper," who dipped the piece into a solution containing materials that would harden into a glassy coating when heated.* Underglaze printing was adapted with great success to Spode's Chinese-style plates, including two of its earliest and most popular patterns, Mandarin and Willow. (Willow, probably the most famous blue-and-white ware, featured a bridge with three figures on it, a willow tree, a boat, a house, two birds at the center top, and a fence in front of the house and its garden; Mandarin was very similar, but omitted the fence, birds, and bridge.) Spode was, however, not the only pottery to use the underglaze method; it was widely used throughout the industry, as the method drastically reduced costs and allowed potters to decorate their dishes with a wide variety of landscapes, figures, and other motifs, often copied from popular prints.

Not all pottery was decorated with underglaze prints. Some was still handpainted, and Spode, Wedgwood, and others were always anxious to find good painters for their wares. The painting might involve several steps, each followed by a firing. For example, a teapot with a floral design might be painted with a "resist," a liquid that resisted the application of color, everywhere that flowers were intended to be painted. Then a background color would be painted on and the teapot fired. After firing, the resist was removed, the teapot was glazed and fired again, and the first colors of the flowers were hand-painted by a floral specialist. More enamel colors would be applied, and the teapot would be fired as many times as necessary in between applications, this time at a lower temperature of 600°–900°C to avoid destroying the more delicate enamel colors. Finally, gold mixed with mercury and oil would be added as a detail, and the pot would be fired at a still lower temperature to avoid damaging the gold.

*This glaze was often made with lead, and dippers were known to suffer from the effects of lead poisoning.

Though any of the large potteries would seem quaintly unmechanized to a modern factory worker, they were adopting many new methods to make and sell their wares. Spode, for example, invested in an early steam engine for grinding flint and the ingredients in enamel colors, supplementing it in 1810 with a more powerful engine that could also turn the potting wheels. Both Spode and Wedgwood built beautiful London showrooms to whet customers' appetites for their products and sent out salesmen with samples—either on paper in books or in the form of sections of glazed plate rim—that showed the selection of handpainted designs available. Molds were used whenever possible to speed up production, and lathes were employed to create patterns of ridges.

Metal

Some of Jane Austen's acquaintance no doubt had great stores of family "plate" (*S&S* 13, 26; *P&P* 162)—dishes made of silver that gleamed in the candlelight and made a beautiful display at dinner, but even those who did not own much silver might own a few pieces that would make the best possible show for company, such as teaspoons and ladles. It was this kind of acquisitions that the genteelly poor Austens made in 1808. "My Mother has been lately adding to her possessions in plate," Jane wrote in December, "—a whole Tablespoon & a whole dessert-spoon, & six whole Teaspoons, which makes our sideboard border on the Magnificent. . . . A silver Tea-Ladle is also added." An individual item of silverware was also considered a welcome gift, and accordingly, in July 1808, Jane wonders in a letter whether to buy Frank's wife "a silver knife—or . . . a Broche," planning to spend about half a guinea on the present. A silver knife, spoon, or pap boat was also often given as a christening gift (*MP* 386–387, 396–397).

People like the Austen women had to limit themselves to a few pieces, for silver was quite expensive, not only because it was intrinsically valuable but because there were high taxes on its manufacture. By the late 1780s, silversmiths were being charged 6d. per ounce for the silver they used; in 1797, the tax was raised to a shilling an ounce, and by 1815 it had risen again to 1s. 6d. Parson Woodforde considered it "a great Bargain" when, in 1789, he managed to buy twelve tablespoons and six dessert spoons for £10; this was no small outlay of cash for a man whose annual income was in the low three figures. Many people, daunted by the cost of solid silver, resorted to cheaper alternatives, such as pewter or Sheffield plate. The former was an alloy of tin and lead or other metals, while the latter was a copper core plated with silver. In the case of hollowware items such as urns and teapots, both outside and inside might be plated with silver, or the inside might be plated with tin instead, to save money. Items made of Sheffield plate included urns; tea, coffee, and chocolate pots; tea caddies; salt cellars (which would be lined with either gold or blue glass to protect

Regency Fete or John Bull in the Conservatory, Williams, 1811. Despite the elaborate drawings of cookbooks, showing a wealth of dishes placed on the table at once, most dinners included only a handful of dishes. This table is an exception to the rule. Plate gleams on the shelves and table, with covered dishes, ornate decanters, and matching forks and knives arrayed in a long line. Down the middle of the table, in an allusion to the Prince of Wales' notorious first banquet as regent, is a running stream of water flowing along the table. The prince regent's tabletop river was an unusually dramatic centerpiece, but decorations of some kind in the middle of the table were common at great feasts. Courtesy of the Lewis Walpole Library, Yale University. 811.6.29.1.

the silver from the corrosive effects of the salt); mustard pots, also lined with blue glass; cream and sugar containers; punch bowls; toast racks; serving trays (*MP* 65); and various serving utensils, such as fish servers, soup ladles, punch ladles, and cheese scoops. All these items, of course, could be made with solid silver as well.

Another type of metal dish was the entrée dish, which kept food warm—an important consideration when several dishes were served on the table simultaneously—by having a reservoir beneath it which could be kept hot either with a piece of hot iron or, after 1810, by hot water. Deeper breakfast dishes could be heated from below by a spirit lamp. Supper dishes, soup tureens, and a wide variety of forks (*MP* 413, 446; *P* 64), knives (*MP* 413; *P* 64), and spoons were also made of various types of metal. Table knives had blunt tips but were nevertheless often used to pick up food and bring it to the mouth; forks, then as now, were held in the left hand both for cutting food and for conveying it to the mouth. The forks might be all of metal or have handles of a different material, such as mother-of-pearl. The largest forks were the toasting forks, which sometimes had wooden handles to protect the toaster's hand from the conducted heat of the fire. Another type of specialized utensil was the egg scissors, which had spiked blades that neatly cut off the top of a boiled egg.

Silverware would have been kept in the sideboard, which was an all-purpose piece of furniture for the convenience of the servants. Food could be placed here either in preparation for serving or as a supplement to the dishes on a crowded table. The butler could open and pour wine here, and in some cases, basins of water were incorporated for washing the silverware. Atop the sideboard might be a knife box for holding the table knives, while inside were drawers for holding corkscrews, napkins, and flatware and a chamberpot for the relief of the gentlemen after the ladies had departed for the drawing room.

Wood and Glass

Wood was no longer an acceptable material for dishes in fashionable homes, though it could be found occasionally in the homes of the poor. It was used, however, for a few specific items. Tea caddies could be of wood, especially if they were elaborately inlaid or equipped with decorative metal fittings. Implements for serving salad, likewise, could be made of wood without shame; Parson Woodforde mentioned an instance in February 1793, when the local squire's wife gave Woodforde's niece "a large wooden Spoon and a four-pronged wooden Fork for dressing up a Sallad, quite fashion."

Glass was used primarily for the serving of beverages. Wine glasses (*S&S* 197), for example, were an absolutely essential part of any well-equipped household; these were smaller than the average wine glass today and would have been the responsibility of the butler, if the household had a butler. Only in the homes of the wealthy would the table have had the "finger glasses" for washing the fingertips, which fill Susan Price with such anxious anticipation (*MP* 446), but most homes of middle class or above would have had a decanter in which to serve wine. The decanter, then as now, had a narrow neck and a wide base, and in order to identify its contents, the butler or, in less well-staffed homes, a lesser manservant would place a decorative tag around the decanter's neck. These tags might be made of silver or ceramic.

Dishes of various kinds may be seen in illustrations throughout this book. An assortment of table items, including a decanter, may be seen in the illustration *The Glutton* (Food). Mugs, platters, bowls, and a knife are shown in *A Journeyman Parson with a Bare Existence* (Clergy), and cruets, egg cups, a salad bowl, and a salad fork and spoon appear in *Temperance Enjoying a Frugal Meal* (Food). A few dishes may also be observed in the illustration *Nobody's Song* (Servants). *See also* Beverages; Food.

Doge

The doges (*MP* 209–210) were Genoa's nominal rulers from 1339 until the Napoleonic Wars. (Venice also had doges, but, as it turns out, it was not Venice's leader to whom Austen refers.) In theory, they were elected for life, but the competition between factions within the city meant that high turnover, enforced exiles, and unelected doges were, for many years, the norm. The doges, in turn, were controlled by one of a number of stronger European powers that wished to command Genoa's naval and banking expertise. In the seventeenth century, one of the doges was invited to Versailles and asked by the marquis de Seignelai what he found most singular about the palace. The doge's response was *"C'est de m'y voir"*—"Seeing myself in it." The episode is directly referred to in *Mansfield Park* and could have come from one of two sources: Voltaire's *Siècle de Louis XIV*, in which the anecdote was originally related, or Samuel Johnson's collected letters, which first appeared in 1788. The Johnson letter, like Austen's reference, transfers the wonder at finding oneself in an unexpected place to a new traveler. In Austen's case, it is Mary Crawford who finds herself amazed to be in the country. In Johnson's letter, it is Johnson who is astounded at being in Scotland. On September 30, 1773, he wrote to his friend Hester Thrale:

> You remember the Doge of Genoa who being asked what struck him most at the French Court, answered, "Myself." I can not think of many things here more likely to affect the fancy, than to see Johnson ending his Sixty fourth year in the wilderness of the Hebrides.

R. W. Chapman suggests that Austen derived the episode from Johnson, but Austen seems to have read French herself and certainly had French-speaking relatives, such as Eliza, the comtesse de Feuillide, who often traveled back and forth between France and England. If Johnson and Mrs. Thrale had read the anecdote (presumably in an edition of Voltaire's works), then it is also possible that Austen had done the same.

Duels

Given the frequency with which men dueled in the eighteenth century, it is somewhat surprising that these combats of honor do not figure more often in Austen's novels. Particularly for men in public life, who were offered a higher than average number of personal insults, it could be hard to avoid dueling. Many prominent men fought duels or narrowly avoided them, including the duke of York, who fought a Colonel Lennox in 1789; Benedict Arnold, who fought Alexander Lindsay, earl of Balcarres, former governor of Jamaica, in 1801; and Richard Brinsley Sheridan, who fought two duels and whose play *The Rivals* features a famous dueling scene.

Rowlandson Etching, 1790, detail. A duel with swords. Courtesy of the Lewis Walpole Library, Yale University. 790.6.20.1.

Duels arose from one of two principal causes: a verbal insult or an insulting action. The duel between Arnold and Lord Balcarres arose from the former cause; when introduced to Arnold by George III, Balcarres asked, "What, the traitor Arnold?" When a verbal insult of this kind was offered, the utterer was usually offered an opportunity to retract the statement. Alternatively, the offended party, if especially quick-witted, could turn aside the insult with a clever quip that brushed aside the offense without escalating the conflict. If, instead, the utterer of the insult refused to withdraw his comment, the offended party could demand satisfaction and issue a challenge, either orally or in writing. An insulting action could be a physical blow or an attempt to deliver a physical blow. It could also be an offensive action taken against a person who could not legitimately offer to duel, most commonly a woman, and who was morally or legally under the protection of the challenger (*S&S* 211; *P&P* 287, 288, 298). In cases of offensive action, it was harder to avoid a duel, for there was no way to withdraw a blow already delivered or a woman's chastity; though there were means of recompense, they were more difficult than a simple apology.

According to the rules of the Code Duello, the challenged party then had the right to choose the meeting place and the weapons (usually swords or pistols). Each party was required to choose a second, whose job was to mediate between the duelists and attempt to reach a reconciliation and thus avoid the duel altogether. It was also a requirement, in a properly conducted duel, for the parties to arrange to have a surgeon present to tend to any wounds. If all these rules were followed, prosecution for any injuries or deaths was less likely; departures from the rules, such as ambushing one's foe or attacking in the heat of the moment, without a formal challenge and choice of seconds, was likely to bring severe retaliation from the legal system.

Pistols were not always very accurate, but they had the advantage of clarity—once both combatants had fired, the duel was over. It was important, however, not to aim. The combatants were to level their pistols and fire immediately, trusting to chance to vindicate them. This impromptu method of firing also permitted both parties to make a dignified exit from the duel. The duelists could shoot wide of each other on purpose, indicating in this manner that they had the courage to back their words or actions with their lives but disdaining to kill another man over an insult. (Refusal to kill another was not only a matter of morality; it was pragmatic. Though judges were reluctant to hang a man for killing another in a formal duel, arrests and successful prosecutions were not unknown.) In the Arnold-Balcarres duel, the use of pistols allowed Balcarres to show his disdain for Arnold yet again. Arnold took his shot, but Balcarres then turned his back and walked away. To Arnold's indignant query, "Why don't you fire, my Lord?" Balcarres replied coolly, "I leave you to the executioner."

E

Education

Education (*Cath, MW* 193, 203; *Sand, MW* 376; *S&S* 127; *P&P* 139; *MP* 276; *E* 15, 62, 164, 169; *P* 74, 89, 150, 202) was undergoing a revolution in the second half of the eighteenth century, and though even after the changes the educational system was still pervasively flawed, the new theories had a good deal of merit. The most influential thinkers about education were John Locke, whose *Some Thoughts Concerning Education* (1693) exerted influence throughout the eighteenth century and beyond, and Jean-Jacques Rousseau, whose *Émile* (1762) encouraged parents to think of their children as naturally innocent and infinitely moldable. Severe corporal punishment and rote learning were to be discouraged, while good nutrition, healthful exercise, and lessons that made learning pleasant were to be embraced. The poet William Cowper's *Tirocinium: or, a Review of Schools* (1784) expressed the ideal:

> Our parents yet exert a prudent care
> To feed our infant minds with proper fare;
> And wisely store the nursery by degrees
> With wholesome learning, yet acquired with ease. (ll. 115–19)

The number of rules should be reduced and children given more liberty and playtime.

The rise of Locke and Rousseau, however, did not mean the development of an educational system that we would find comfortingly familiar. Almost all aspects of the educational system differed from their modern counterparts, not least the fact that there was no "system" as such. The government did not concern itself with education, and there was no interest in universal education or in using education as a tool to help people rise through the social and economic system. Education was privately purchased or distributed as charity to poor children in the form of Sunday schools.

The Sunday schools made no claim to a full education, nor did they aspire to one. All they strove for was basic literacy, mostly to fit children to become better servants and better Christians. The fact that Sunday schools kept children inside on their one true holiday a week—for most children worked to help feed their families—was an added bonus. If they were not idle, they would not get into trouble. The parish school mentioned in *Emma* (456) is probably a Sunday school, as it is described as being "under the patronage" of two genteel ladies and as being linked in size with its parish—a religious as well as a civil district. Sponsoring of Sunday schools was a relatively common charitable endeavor for upper-class men and women, while support of a mere day school was not.

Working-class children worked themselves, but those in the next tier up might attend a day school in their village or town, run either by a poorly paid clergyman seeking to increase his income or by a woman, depicted in most descriptions as elderly. The latter type of school, called a "dame school" (*Gen Cur*, *MW* 73–74), was considered notoriously inadequate, and popular prints depicted the students as often possessing more knowledge than their supposed instructor. Such schools do not fare well in Austen's works, either. The idea of sending a child to such a school is played for laughs in *The Generous Curate*, and it is clear that the uncouth and impoverished Price boys attend a similar school, as they are released every afternoon (and early on Saturdays—*MP* 381, 388, 391). Children in such schools stayed few years, as a rule, and were lucky to master the hornbook, a wooden and vellum or paper paddle printed with the alphabet, the Roman numerals, and the Lord's Prayer. These rudiments of learning, sometimes supplemented by a didactic verse, were sealed, as Cowper's *Tirocinium* explained, "Beneath a pane of thin translucent horn" (l. 120). The dame schools charged two or three pennies a week and cared for some children who were almost too young to walk; these were tied to table legs or to the teacher's skirts. There was no pretense of teaching these toddlers; they were sent to school merely to get them out from underfoot at home. Slightly superior schools might charge 6d. a week and have real books instead of hornbooks. They taught not only reading and spelling but also, perhaps, a little Latin. Neighborhood schools such as these often accepted female pupils as well as male.

Austen barely touches on these schools except to point out their isolation from the world she inhabited. The school in *The Generous Curate* is resorted to only because of the comic poverty of the curate; the Sunday school in *Emma* is a charitable venture to which the female patrons would never send their own children; and the school to which the Price boys are sent is merely a foil to the lavish education that Fanny Price has received at Mansfield Park. Boys and girls of Austen's class were tutored at home or sent to boarding schools, or a combination of the two. Austen herself was taught at home by her mother and father for most of her life and had tutors for subjects that required specialized knowledge. She had a music teacher and a drawing teacher, for example, but she also went to two different boarding schools for short periods of time: Mrs. Cawley's school in Oxford (later Southampton), where she fell ill in an epidemic and nearly died, and then the Abbey School in Reading, where the head teacher was Mrs. La Tournelle, an Englishwoman with a French name, a cork leg, a wardrobe that never changed from one day to the next, and a passionate devotion to the theater. In all, the years of Austen's boarding school education totaled only about three years, and all the rest of the time she was taught at home.

Tutors and Governesses

This accords fairly well with what we know about the education of most girls. At home, they learned needlework, the rudiments of running a household, and basic literacy from their mothers (*NA* 15, 110; *P&P* 164). If they were lucky and had parents like the Austens, they were also exposed to good books and important ideas. If not, they grew up silly and empty-headed, concerned only with landing a husband and dressing in the latest fashions. Austen must have known plenty of such girls, for she is merciless toward parents who neglect their children's education and toward those of her characters who are incapable of discussing any subject seriously and intelligently. Catherine Morland's haphazard education—a little reading and recitation, some dabbling in music, an incompetent and self-taught bout of drawing, and a smattering of French, writing, and arithmetic (*NA* 14)—was probably more common than most gentry families would have liked to admit. In some cases, this superficial education was actually the intended result. The anonymous author of *Female Tuition* (1784) suggested that mothers keep their daughters busy with housework, make home as attractive as possible to them so that they would be happy in their future destiny as wives and mothers, and teach them "Habits of attention and deference." This was far more important than knowing history or geometry.

In wealthy families, a special full-time tutor called a governess (*J&A, MW* 16; *LS, MW* 244, 251; *Sand, MW* 393; *P&P* 67, 82, 164, 165, 322; *MP* 9, 10, 14, 19–20, 22, 51, 134, 150, 169; *E* 5–6, 37, 164, 278, 299–301, 380, 382; *P* 152) was hired to live in the household and instruct all the young children; in the case of girls who did not go away until boarding school, their duties could last until the girls were in their teens (*J&A, MW* 17). The governess occupied an anomalous position in the home, a status to be explored far more fully after Austen's death in Charlotte Brontë's *Jane Eyre*. The governess was not a member of the family, but neither was she a servant in the traditional sense. She was, after all, hired for her education and her accomplishments—achievements that were often superior to those of the people who paid her salary (*E* 301). She could not therefore be automatically dismissed from consideration the way other servants could or relegated to another class of humanity. This special status often earned her the resentment of the rest of the staff, but it did not buy her full membership in the life of the family. She lived in a kind of social limbo, an existence that would be excruciating to a sensitive woman such as Jane Eyre or Jane Fairfax.

In addition to the governess, "masters" (*J&A, MW* 3; *Cath, MW* 198; *Sand, MW* 420–421; *P&P* 164; *MP* 20), or specialized tutors, might be hired to teach such subjects as music, drawing, and dancing. The author of *The Mirror of the Graces* (1811) had no objection to this practice unless it filtered down to the middle class:

> Were girls of the plebeian classes brought up in the praiseworthy habits of domestic duties; had they learned how to manage a house, how to economize and produce comfort at the least expence at their father's frugal yet hospitable table; we should not hear of dancing-masters and music-masters, of French and Italian masters; they would have no time for them.

Education solely by tutors (*Watsons, MW* 329, 331; *S&S* 130, 250–251) and governesses was more common for girls than for boys, though boys, too, experienced the system. Admiral Lord Thomas Cochrane recalled of his tutor that "my most vivid recollection is a stinging box on the ear, in reply to a query as to the difference between an interjection and a conjunction; this solution of the difficulty effectually repressing further philological inquiry on my part." Cochrane went to sea late and thus missed out on the education doled out to the "young gentlemen" aboard ship by a naval schoolmaster (*P* 52).

Boarding Schools

After a little preliminary education at home, many boys and girls were sent to boarding schools (*J&A, MW* 16; *Lesley, MW* 112; *Cath, MW* 203; *Sand, MW* 393, 420–421; *NA* 31, 68; *S&S* 208; *P&P* 199–200, 201; *E* 21–22, 23; *P* 14, 31, 40, 152). These might be quite small establishments. Mr. Austen, for example, kept a little school in his house, teaching his own sons and taking in a handful of boarding pupils at a time. At the other extreme, they might be England's renowned public schools—a term that often confuses American readers, as public schools in England are what are called private schools in the United States. These included Westminster (*S&S* 251; *MP* 61); Tonbridge School, which Mr. Austen had attended as a boy; Rugby; and Eton College (*E&E, MW* 32; *MP* 21), founded in the fifteenth century and already one of the most prestigious of the public schools.

Boys destined for the military might attend a specialized boarding school. For future naval officers, this was the Royal Academy in Portsmouth (*Gen Cur, MW* 73); for aspiring army officers, it was the Royal Military Academy, which was eventually located at Sandhurst. Austen's brothers Frank and Charles both attended the Portsmouth academy. They were, however, in the minority; most boys simply went to sea at about eleven to thirteen years old and picked up a good deal of practical knowledge plus whatever they acquired from the ship's schoolmaster.

Girls could not attend the public schools, but they were on occasion sent to boarding schools for a polite education. These, like boys' schools, varied widely in size and in reputation. The best schools were considered to be in London (*L&F, MW* 78; *LS, MW* 244, 245–246, 247, 252–253, 266; *S&S* 160), where a young lady could pick up a metropolitan accent and study with the best tutors. Girls' schools in other parts of the country also brought in male tutors for some subjects (*Sand, MW* 412), but they often had to be less selective in their choice of masters. Catholic families sometimes sent their daughters to the Continent to be educated at convents, a strategy used by Austen only in comic circumstances (*L&F, MW* 77).

Children at boarding schools spent most of the year there, coming home only at specified holidays (*MP* 127; *P* 129, 133, 163). At some schools there was only one annual holiday at Christmas, and children were in school the rest of the time. Many students were deeply homesick, including the schoolboy in Cowper's *Tirocinium*, of which Fanny Price keeps thinking while she is isolated in Portsmouth (*MP* 431). Cowper, addressing the father, pleads with him not to wound both parent and child by sending the son away:

> Then why resign into a stranger's hand
> A task as much within your own command,
> That God and nature, and your interest too,
> Seem with one voice to delegate to you?
> Why hire a lodging in a house unknown
> For one whose tenderest thoughts all hover round your own?
> This second weaning, needless as it is,
> How does it lacerate both your heart and his!
> The indented stick, that loses day by day,
> Notch after notch, till all are smoothed away,
> Bears witness, long ere his dismission come,
> With what intense desire he wants his home. (ll. 551–562)

Not all public schools separated boys from their families; a handful were day schools, including Merchant Taylors' (*NA* 32), a school founded in London in the sixteenth century by the Worshipful Guild of Merchant Taylors and given a second campus in Crosby in the seventeenth century. Cowper favored private tuition at home over a boarding-school education. He asserts in *Tirocinium* that boarding schools teach boys to drink, to solicit prostitutes, to revere the disorderly older boys, and to gamble. While acknowledging that fathers felt nostalgia and quite naturally wanted to send their sons to the places where they themselves had been happy, he condemned fathers who would take personal charge of the training of a horse or a dog but not of their own sons. Public schools, he felt, were sure to confirm faults already present and create new ones, resulting in "The pert made perter, and the tame made wild" (l. 346). (He noted the unruly behavior of the students, which was legendary at some schools, but he glosses over the savage corporal punishments.) Austen seems to share Cowper's dim view of public schools, at least judging by her side-by-side portrayals of the conscientious Edward Ferrars (privately tutored, though not at home) and his superficial, immoral brother Robert (sent to a boarding school). She has Robert make the contrast explicit, blaming Edward's "extreme gaucherie" on his private education, while he, Robert, "merely from the advantage of a public school, was as well fitted to mix in the world as any other man" (*S&S* 250–251). The quietly noble Edmund Bertram attends a public school and does not seem ruined by the experience, but perhaps his being sent there is another of the means by which Austen indicts Sir Thomas Bertram's hands-off style of parenting.

Susan Sibbald, who was about eighteen years younger than Austen, wrote a memoir of her life up to the age of twenty-nine. In it, she described the daily life of a girls' boarding school. Each girl had a bed of her own, with several beds to a room and a teacher sleeping in the dormitory to supervise the girls. The students woke at 6:00 A.M., heard prayers in the schoolroom at 7:30, and ate a breakfast of bread, butter, and tea at 8:00. Until noon on Mondays through Fridays, there were lessons; on Saturdays, this period of time was spent doing mending. Dinner depended on the day of the week:

> generally roast beef on Mondays; on Tuesdays and Fridays roast shoulders of mutton, a round of beef on Wednesdays; Thursdays boiled legs of mutton, and stewed beef and pickled walnuts on Saturdays. Then two days in the week we had "choke dogs," dumplings with currents in them, other days rice or other puddings; but after the meat not before, as was the case in some schools. A few of the girls remained a few minutes after the others had gone up to the schoolroom and had a glass of port wine each, for which an extra charge was made.

The girls were forbidden to talk during meals and had a system of hand signals that they used to request extra helpings. Supper was bread, cheese, and beer. In their off-hours the girls walked along the road into the countryside or played games on the terrace. On Sundays they went to church and usually spent the afternoon and evening with local friends or relatives. Sibbald was lucky, for this was an unusually pleasant boarding-school experience. Many schools were much worse, and even this one, humane as it was, does not seem to have stressed academics very strongly. Most schools provided the basic subjects—math, reading, writing, sewing, geography, history—at a standard rate, then charged extra for clothes, tea, sugar, letters received, dancing lessons, French lessons, music lessons, painting lessons, and so on. Charges and options varied by school.

Universities

After surviving the boarding school, many boys proceeded on to one of England's two universities: Oxford (*MW* 447; *NA* 64, 107) and Cambridge (*MW* 447).* Their academic reputation for most of the eighteenth

---

*Scotland had highly regarded universities of its own (*Lesley*, *MW* 118).

century was not stellar, and, like the boarding schools, they were renowned chiefly for their ability to place ambitious boys in close proximity to future peers who could be of use in furthering their careers later in life (*P&P* 70). The two universities had a long-standing rivalry and a slightly different emphasis in curriculum and theology. The rivalry may help to explain why almost all of Austen's "good" university students attend Oxford (*S&S* 362; *MP* 21, 88, 94, 376), while the disreputable ones tend to attend Cambridge (*P&P* 200; *MP* 61); her father was an Oxford man, a distant ancestor had founded St. John's College at Oxford, and her brothers James and Henry were both students there. Oxford graduates predominated in the southern clergy familiar to Austen, which would also perhaps have endeared the university to her, while Cambridge was the home of the Evangelical movement, of which she was suspicious.

Students at university entered a college (*NA* 33; *MP* 376), a collection of buildings where the students dined, studied, and lived. The colleges had been founded over the centuries, often by royal patrons, and had individual histories of which they were proud. Oxford's many colleges included St. John's, with which the Austen family was affiliated; Christ Church (*NA* 46); Balliol, where Mrs. Austen's relative Theophilus Leigh was master; All Souls, where Mrs. Austen's father had been a fellow; New College; and Oriel (*NA* 47).

Boys often entered universities at a much younger age than today. They went, in short, whenever their studies had rendered them ready to attend. James Austen, for example, matriculated at the age of fourteen. Most of those attending went into the church, though a small percentage entered law and medicine. Some went purely to learn a little, to form friendships, and to have a frolic or two before heading off to the Continent for the Grand Tour (*Cath, MW* 196) and the really *serious* partying. Exams at the universities were regularly scheduled but not difficult to pass, especially as the subjects rarely changed and could be studied in advance. A final oral examination, based both on college-specified texts and on three authors of the student's choice, was brief and virtually impossible to fail. It was said that one could get a B.A. at Cambridge by reading only two authors: Euclid and William Paley. Those students who were guaranteed of a comfortable income and an easy life studied very little, leaving the academic drudgery to those who needed to adopt a profession after graduation.

Women were not permitted to attend the universities, though Austen appears not to have pined after a university education. A letter to her brother James' Oxford magazine *The Loiterer*, which may have been written by Jane under the pseudonym Sophia Sentiment, pokes fun at many of the same literary excesses that Austen lampooned in her Juvenilia. It also claims that the author "never, but once, was at Oxford in my life" and was not impressed by it. It was nothing, she claimed, but "so many dismal chapels, dusty libraries, and greasy halls, that it gave me the vapours for two days afterwards."

Curriculum

The subjects studied differed somewhat for boys and girls. Both sexes were expected to be able to read (*Lesley, MW* 129; *Cath, MW* 197; *LS, MW* 273) and write English with fluency, to possess a decent grasp of English grammar (*NA* 120; *S&S* 150; *E* 50–51), to have neat handwriting (*NA* 14), and to be able to perform simple arithmetic (*NA* 14). Recitation aloud formed part of the traditional education (*NA* 14), though not, in Edmund Bertram's opinion, enough of it (*MP* 340–341). A good education also included a solid foundation in religious doctrine, history (*Hist Eng, MW*; *Cath, MW* 230–231; *NA* 108–109; *MP* 18, 22, 419), and geography.

Geography (*MP* 18), in an age of wars and expanding empire, was considered quite important. Students were expected to be knowledgeable in "the use of the globes," as it was called, meaning not only the traditional terrestrial globe but also a celestial globe that showed the positions of the constellations in the night sky. A contemporary geography book, the *Compendious Geographical and Historical Grammar* (1795), goes on for pages and pages in tiny print, explaining thirty-six different problems that a student should be able to solve using a globe:

> Prob. I. To find the latitude and longitude of any given place; and the latitude and longitude being given, to find the place.
>
> Bring the place, by turning the globe to the East side of the brazen meridian; on the meridian you have the latitude, and on the equator you have the longitude. To answer the second part of the problem, seek the given latitude on the equator, bring that point to the brass meridian, and under the degree of latitude on the meridian you have the place.
>
> Prob. II. A place being given, to find all places of the same latitude and longitude.
>
> Bring the place to the brass meridian, and under the meridian you have all the places of the same longitude. Mark the latitude of the place on the brass meridian, turn the globe quite round, and all the places that pass under the mark are of the same latitude.
>
> Prob. III. The time being given, to find the sun's place and declination.
>
> On the wooden horizon seek the month and day, against which is the sign and degree of the sun's place. On the globe bring the sun's place in the ecliptic to the brazen meridian, and directly over it on the meridian is the declination.
>
> Prob. IV. To find the distance between any two given places.
>
> Apply the quadrant of altitude to the two places, and the number of degrees is between them. Multiply the degrees by 60, and the product is the distance in geographical miles, such a mile being a 60th part of a degree. But if you want the distance in English miles, multiply the degrees by 69½.

The problems continue, demonstrating the correct way to "rectify the globe," to find the "angle of position of two places, or the angle formed by the meridian of one place, and a great circle passing through both places," and to "find the Periaeci, Antaeci, and Antipodes to any given place." Students should be able to determine time of day in various places around the globe, locate places where the sun is directly overhead at a given time, and identify all the places where the sun is simultaneously setting. Other geographical texts of the day stressed the places mentioned in classical literature and history, in keeping with the fashionable emphasis on classical learning.

Here the paths for boys and girls diverged. Girls were channeled into the acquisition of "accomplishments" (*Plan, MW* 428; *P&P* 12, 39; *MP* 42; *E* 21–22, 104; *P* 40), a set of mostly artistic skills that were designed to keep them busy in their life of leisure and to enhance the pleasure of those around them. In an age without recorded music, it was considered of the first importance that girls be musical (*J&A, MW* 20; *Lesley, MW* 124; *Cath, MW* 198, 229, 232; *LS, MW* 253; *Plan, MW* 428; *NA* 14, 56; *P&P* 164; *E* 301), so that they could play and sing in the evenings to entertain parents, siblings, husbands, children, and guests. An accomplished woman should also be able to speak French and perhaps Italian as well (*J&A, MW* 20; *Cath, MW* 198; *LS, MW* 253; *Plan, MW* 428; *NA* 14; *MP* 22, 312). She should be able to paint in watercolors and sketch in pencil (*J&A, MW* 20; *Lesley, MW* 124; *Scraps, MW* 176; *Cath, MW* 197, 198, 206, 232; *LS, MW* 253; *NA* 14, 56, 110–111), although prowess in oils was unladylike. She should be adept with a needle (*Cath, MW* 197; *S&S* 160; *MP* 18), not merely for the purpose of sewing and mending clothes, but for the sort of ornamental embroidery that adorned walls, pillows, footstools, slippers, and reticules. Finally, she should be able to dance gracefully (*J&A, MW* 20), so that she could engage in one of the central acts of courtship—the country dance.

The authors to whom parents turned for advice in raising their daughters agreed in the importance of good manners and morals for girls. Hester Chapone thought that academics and accomplishments could be added to these essentials, as long as care was taken not to become too masculine:

> Politeness of behavior, and the attainment of such branches of knowledge, and such arts and accomplishments, as are proper to your sex, capacity, and station, will prove so valuable to yourself through life, and will make you so desirable a companion, that the neglect of them may reasonably be deemed a neglect of duty.

John Gregory, an earlier writer, but one whose *Father's Legacy to His Daughters* was still widely read, stressed modesty and religion far more than academic excellence and in fact cautioned his daughters to avoid wit, which could "create you many enemies," humor, which was relatively innocent but "will never procure you respect," and even the appearance of erudition:

> Be even cautious of displaying your good sense. It will be thought you assume a superiority over the rest of the company. But if you happen to have any learning, keep it a profound secret, especially from the men, who generally look with a jealous and malignant eye on a woman of great parts, and a cultivated understanding.
>
> A man of real genius and candor is far superior to this meanness. But such a one will seldom fall in your way.

His advice seems to confirm Austen's dour appraisal of what attracts men:

> The advantages of natural folly in a beautiful girl have been already set forth by the capital pen of a sister author;—and to her treatment of the subject I will only add in justice to men, that though to the larger and more trifling part of the sex, imbecility in females is a great enhancement of their personal charms, there is a portion of them too reasonable and too well informed themselves to desire any thing more in woman than ignorance. (*NA* 111)

Girls who acquired too much learning and were too eager to show it off risked being stigmatized as "bluestockings"—women so eager to invade masculine realms of study that they neglected the feminine spheres of dress and personal grooming. They became, in short, unmarriageable.

Boys, meanwhile, were expected to grapple with the higher forms of math, such as algebra (*MP* 119) and geometry. They, too, were expected to be able to dance (*E* 328), but the ability to play music or to sing was desirable but unnecessary. The main focus of their education was Greek and Latin, with the emphasis on the Latin. The curriculum at Eton consisted of writing, arithmetic, Euclidean geometry, algebra, Greek and Roman history, a handful of English literary classics such as the works of Pope and Milton, and Latin and Greek grammar. Other schools added geography, navigation, and modern languages. At the Naval Academy in Portsmouth, which two of Jane's brothers attended, the curriculum included geometry, arithmetic, logarithms, French, fencing, writing, drawing, and dancing. Oxford's curriculum was made up of about two-thirds classics and one-third "sciences," where sciences were defined as logic, rhetoric, geometry, morals, and politics. Cambridge stressed classics less and mathematics and moral philosophy more. *See also* Music; Reading; Science; Sewing.

Enclosure

At the beginning of the eighteenth century, English land-ownership and cultivation was a complex arrangement: in some areas, already neatly arranged into blocks of fields separated by hedgerows, in others, still based on the medieval open-field system, in which members of a community tilled strips of land. In the latter system, a family's strips might not necessarily be adjacent to one another, and the sometimes inconvenient locations necessitated much negotiation with neighbors and much redundancy of effort. However, this apparently awkward system came with centuries of accommodation for the poor of the community; common land (*MP* 69–70, *E* 126) was set aside for the use of the whole village—for example, for grazing of livestock—and wasteland, though untilled, provided essential commodities such as firewood.

Over the course of the eighteenth century, however, the English landscape changed dramatically, primarily due to the legal concept known as enclosure (*S&S* 233). A landowner, or a group of landowners, decided to consolidate his holdings so that they formed one or more large parcels. However, this meant, in essence, trading land with one's neighbors to draw new boundaries, and the process could grow contentious at times. In many cases, enclosers attempted to secure common land for themselves (*S&S* 225). Complex and highly localized traditions about rights and duties had to be codified, revised, or even overturned, and almost everyone in the village had a stake in the outcome.

Not everyone, however, had an equal say. In general, at least four-fifths of the affected landowners had to consent to the new arrangement, or the House of Commons would reject the legislation. Still, large landowners had the advantage, not only because they held more local property and had more means of coercion at their disposal but also because enclosure usually involved passing a private act of Parliament, which required a level of expense and political influence not available to average citizens. The local clergy, too, were frequently involved in decisions pertaining to enclosure, because they were often paid in tithes—a percentage of produce from the land. Their right to tithes could not be abrogated willfully, and so an arrangement might be worked out whereby the newly enclosed land was free from tithe and the parson was compensated with a fixed income, a parcel of land, or a lump-sum payment. Local magistrates also became involved to some extent, for landowners wishing to reroute paths and roads (*E* 106–107) and appropriate the old road—perhaps using it as a road to a mansion—had to get the approval of two magistrates; this was usually a formality, as the principal landowners in an area were often magistrates as well and tended to look out for each other's interests.

Enclosure offered landowners many advantages. Economies of scale could be practiced. Livestock could be controlled more easily and pastured in fields that, unlike common fields, had not been overgrazed. Land was cultivated more efficiently and lay fallow for less time. Aesthetics, too, were served, as longer vistas of one's own property could be seen from the manor house; in consequence, landscape gardening flourished to improve the territorial view. For the wealthy, enclosure was an attractive means of improving income, despite the initial outlay involved in getting an act of Parliament, hedging and fencing the new boundaries of one's land, digging ditches, putting up gates, and constructing new outbuildings. The result was a pair of enclosure frenzies. The first peaked before and around the time of Austen's birth, in the 1760s and 1770s. The second occurred during her adulthood, in the 1790s, 1800s, and 1810s, as continued wars with France made increased agricultural productivity a matter not only of profit but also of patriotism and even of survival.

However, enclosure was far from being universally lauded. While it generated a temporary burst of employment among local workers, who were occupied in draining, fencing, and improving the larger fields, it was catastrophic for the marginal poor, who had relied on common land and wasteland for fuel and for pasturage for a cow, a pig, or a few geese. Many who had been able to scrape out a semi-independent farming existence were forced into day labor or domestic service.

Poets were enlisted on both sides of the question. William Whitehead lauded the kindness of Lord Harcourt in moving the entire village of Nuneham Courtney in order to enclose his parkland and improve the view:

> The careful matrons of the plain
> Had left their cots without a sigh,
> Well pleased to shroud their little train
> In happier mansions, warm, & dry.

Oliver Goldsmith, on the other hand, turned the same episode into "The Deserted Village" (1770), a lament for the vanishing way of life centered around the village common:

> Sweet smiling village, loveliest of the lawn,
> Thy sports are fled and all thy charms withdrawn;
> Amidst thy bowers the tyrant's hand is seen,
> And desolation saddens all thy green:
> One only master grasps the whole domain. . . .
>
> . . . The man of wealth and pride
> Takes up a space that many poor supplied;
> Space for his lake, his park's extended bounds,
> Space for his horses, equipage and hounds

John Freeth, rather than relying on third-person narrative, put words directly into a cottager's mouth in "The Cottager's Complaint, on the Intended Bill for Enclosing Sutton-Coldfield" (1782):

> My ewes are few, my stock is small,
>   Yet from my little store
> I find enough for nature's call,
>   Nor would I ask for more!
> That word, ENCLOSURE! to my heart
>   Such evil doth bespeak,
> I fear I with my all must part,
>   And fresh employment seek.

Austen's position in the war of opinion is fairly clear, though she mentions enclosure seldom in her works. It is the greedy, selfish John Dashwood who seeks to enclose common land, and the noble Mr. Knightley who will not move so much as a path on his land "if it were to be the means of inconvenience to the Highbury people" (*E* 106–107). Her sympathies lie not with the enclosers but with the traditional village order.

Entertainment

While the working class had less leisure than they do today, routinely working Saturdays and often working long hours on weekdays, they had many ways of spending their few free hours. The gentry and aristocracy, with many more leisure hours to fill, found even more ways of passing the time pleasantly. One of their most common recreations was giving and attending parties of one kind or another (*E* 276, 290). They ate dinner at each other's houses and after dinner played cards, played and listened to music, or, on occasion, danced. Other parties were formed specifically for dancing, while others featured hired musicians and focused on the quality of the music (*S&S* 248). In 1811, for example, Austen's brother Henry and his wife, Eliza, threw such a party at their house on Sloane Street in London; "above 80 people are invited for next tuesday Even^g," wrote Jane, "& there is to be some very good Music, 5 professionals, 3 of them Glee-singers, besides Amateurs. . . . One of the Hirelings, is a Capital on the Harp, from which I expect great pleasure." On such occasions it was essential to be (or at least to *pretend* to be) an educated listener and a devout music lover. Private parties (*P* 180, 220, 223, 227) began to predominate among the gentry and aristocracy in the later years of Austen's life, partly because many "public places" admitted people of any class with the ability to pay the entrance fee. In order to maintain exclusivity (*E* 116), it was necessary to hide in one's home rather than attending public balls.

Outdoor parties (*S&S* 33, 62; *E* 274, 352, 354), which became increasingly popular between 1790 and 1820, took people by boat or carriage to scenic sites, where they might stroll, take in picturesque views, or eat picnic food. The Austens, when they lived in Southampton, appear to have taken excursions over the water (*E* 160) to nearby places of interest, including Netley Abbey and the Isle of Wight. One suspects that these outings were rather informal, if only because of the Austens' fairly limited income, but some picnics and "exploring parties" could be quite lavish, with fully set tables loaded with dishes by liveried footmen.

A "rout" (*Lesley, MW* 136) was an altogether different kind of party, a fashionable evening party that appears, from contemporary prints, to have been designed chiefly to pack as many people into a house as possible. Guests were crammed into hot, crowded rooms (*S&S* 175), where they

A Rout, 1790. Cards, crowds, and conversation are the essence of this form of entertainment. Courtesy of the Lewis Walpole Library, Yale University. 790.1.2.6.1+.

attempted to talk, play cards, or dance without being jostled, groped, tripped, or otherwise manhandled. Some people no doubt enjoyed the close quarters and the consequent compression of personal space; satirical prints show jokesters playing pranks on their neighbors at such events, while dirty old men lift skirts, look down dresses, or squeeze just a little too close to attractive young women. For others, including, perhaps, the attractive young women, the rout must have been a foretaste of hell.

People of all classes liked to go to exhibitions, many of which were priced to admit a wide cross-section of the population. Parades and processions on public occasions were free of charge, and even servants and apprentices, if given permission, could afford to go. In 1783, Parson James Woodforde took himself and nearly all his servants to watch "the Grand Procession of Bishop Blaize &c." through Norwich. It began at about 11:00 A.M. and featured four trumpeters, characterizations of "Peace" and "Plenty," orators, drums and fifes, forty "Argonauts" surrounding a Golden Fleece and a man impersonating Jason in a four-horse phaeton, the "Bishop's Chaplain in a Phaeton and Pair," "Bishop Blaize in a Phaeton drawn by 6 Horses" and twelve companies of the societies of wool-combers.

Some pleasure gardens, too, charged reasonable admission rates for illuminations, concerts, and fireworks. London had a few museums of curiosities that had low prices, or were free and existed to draw in customers to some other sort of business. Many shows and displays traveled from town to town. Unusual people or animals—dwarfs, giants, accomplished blind men, performing pigs and bears, and so on—were always a hit, particularly in the provinces. Woodforde recorded the arrival of such shows in his diary with much enthusiasm. In 1784, he paid sixpence to see "the Dwarf Man that is at Norwich." In 1785, also in Norwich, he saw the "learned Pigg," wearing a supposedly magical collar, that could spell words by indicating letters on tiles spread before it. This pig was quite famous, was drawn by

Rowlandson, and appeared in the writings of James Boswell and Robert Southey. The pig's show cost a shilling, and afterward Woodforde paid another 2s. 6d. to hear a lecture on astronomy and see an "Eidouranion or transparent Orrery" (evidently some sort of illuminated representation of the movement of the planets). In 1787, the show came to him; a cart with five men drove up to his door, and the leader, "a black with a french Horn," offered to display "a little Woman only 33 Inches high," who came into Woodforde's kitchen and sang two songs for a shilling. In 1788, in Norwich, he "saw the Polish Dwarf, Joseph Boruwlaski," who played the guitar, also for a shilling (though Woodforde gave him an additional 1s. 6d., perhaps because of his class—Boruwlaski was of noble birth).

When Woodforde was in London, he had a wider range of entertainment options. He visited the Shakespeare Gallery, a collection of waxworks in the Strand, and an exhibition of "some very curious wild Beasts." However, Norwich was not without variety. In addition to traveling dwarfs and pigs, there were "Bunns Rural Gardens" and, in 1790, an iron foundry that could be toured by visitors. There were occasional concerts—one in September 1790 featured the renowned opera singer Nancy Storace—and, on the king's birthday, fireworks. In Woodforde's own small parish, more rural entertainment was offered. Usually, it consisted of competitions between working-class people: "smock races" (races run by women, often in various stages of undress, with a smock as the prize), races between men for a shirt, and plowing contests.

Country towns might also be the sites of fairs. Fairs were sometimes primarily intended for business, with stock breeders, farmers, or manufacturers coming together to trade livestock or other commodities. In this case, there was entertainment provided, but it was somewhat incidental to the business at hand. Other fairs, however, had lost almost all of their utilitarian core and were exclusively places to have fun. Puppet shows and pantomimes took the stage; children feasted on gilded gingerbread loaves pressed into fanciful shapes; showmen displayed "raree-shows," boxes with elaborate scenes constructed inside, which could be viewed for a small fee, usually a penny. Lovers bought each other souvenir trinkets such as bowls, cups, and ribbons. Learned animals, animals with extra limbs, and other oddities were on display as well.

Jane Austen, sadly, never takes her readers to the fair. (One yearns to know what she would have thought of the learned pig.) She does, however, take us, if only indirectly, to Astley's (*E* 471–472, 481), one of London's most popular showplaces. Sergeant-Major Philip Astley (1742–1814), who had begun his career as a horse-breaker for the 15th Dragoons, had in 1768 established a riding school that featured periodic performances by himself, the versatile Mrs. Astley, and "the Little Military Learned Horse," who could play dead, set a tea table, jump through hoops, heat a kettle and make tea, play hide-and-seek, do mathematical

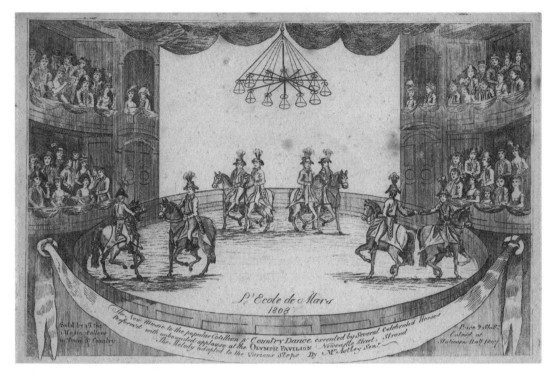

L'Ecole de Mars, 1807. An equestrian performance at Astley's Royal Amphitheatre. Courtesy of the Lewis Walpole Library, Yale University. 807.0.5.

calculations, and fire a pistol. By 1776, the emphasis was entirely on the performances, which included not only trick riding but also tumbling, rope-vaulting, "The Grand Temple of Minerva," and "le force d'Hercule, or the Egyptian pyramids, an entertainment never seen in England." Admission prices were 1s. or 2s., depending on seating. Astley's performance ring acquired a roof in 1779, along with the title "The Amphitheatre Riding-House, Westminster Bridge." A rival establishment, Charles Hughes' Royal Circus, flourished from the 1770s until its destruction by fire in 1805, thanks to such acts as an eight-year-old girl who could ride two horses simultaneously at a full gallop.

Astley kept trying to circumvent the law limiting the number of London theaters by staging pantomimes and other theatrical shows within his walls, but his main focus remained stunts: feats of equestrian skill, animal training, or athletic prowess. A 1788 program featured a broadsword combat between performers dressed as "a British sailor" and "a Savage Chief," tumbling, music, dancing, displays of horsemanship, a transparent painting (illuminated, most likely, from behind), and horses dancing a minuet. It was not only the horses who could dance; Astley's son, according to the enthusiastic spectator Horace Walpole, could dance a minuet himself— while riding three galloping horses.

Astley's first amphitheatre burned down in the early 1790s and was rebuilt; a second fire in September 1803 claimed not only the theatre but Astley's mother-in-law and fifty of his horses. The theater was rebuilt yet again and reopened in 1804, drawing large crowds. It was probably the second theater that Austen visited in 1796, when she was sightseeing in London. She wrote in August, "We are to be at Astley's to night, which I am glad of," but if she described her evening in a later letter, it has not survived.

Etiquette

Etiquette was barely a subject of discussion in the Regency, mostly because a strong distinction was still maintained between the trading middle class and the upper class, containing the gentry and the aristocracy. People of Austen's class were "brought up to the trade" of politeness; they had been reared from birth inside the system and educated year after year by parents, tutors, and peers. Any mistakes they made were swiftly corrected (*Watsons, MW* 332), either by their parents and governesses or by the disapproval of those outside the family. They needed no conduct books or manuals to explain the use of forks or the proper way to make a bow. Their conduct manuals were more concerned with morals and life's major choices: how to think about religion, how to choose a wife or a husband with discretion and wisdom, what books to read, how to converse intelligently and politely. In the Victorian era, a middle class that had chosen to ally itself with the upper class would devour books about the minutiae of daily life, seeking to ape the behavior of those above them in the hopes of joining their ranks, or at least feeling more like them and simultaneously distancing themselves from the ragged poor. This makes it easier for the historian to determine both what the ideal was and in what ways people were failing to live up to it.

For the Regency, it is harder to determine the specifics of polite behavior. There are only hints here and there in novels and diaries of the period, and these are often maddeningly vague or refer only to the incorrect performance of some point of etiquette, not the ideal being sought. There are detailed accounts of court etiquette available, but the court was a world unto itself, with fashions and modes of behavior that applied nowhere else in the kingdom. One can search early Victorian conduct manuals and extrapolate backwards, but this is risky. While some standards of behavior no doubt remained consistent across both periods, others may have evolved. Certainly, the moral and religious climate of the Victorian era was entirely different from that of the Regency, and it is entirely possible that small points of etiquette added themselves over time, like coral accretions that slowly amassed a mammoth structure.

The chief emphasis, when behavior was discussed in the early nineteenth century, was on doing things gracefully (*Lesley*, MW 136; *Sand*, MW 394–395; *NA* 45; *P&P* 39; *E* 99, 278; *P* 143). Movements should be smooth, fluid, and apparently unstudied. Indeed, by the time men and women reached adulthood, these movements *were* unstudied, as they had been practiced for a whole lifetime. Only when there was a shift in fashion—as, for example, when sofas and upholstered chairs became fashionable, and people needed to learn to lounge, rather than to sit stiffly upright in unpadded wooden chairs—did people of the gentry and aristocracy need to study their posture or gestures.

Bowing (*L&F*, MW 94; *Lesley*, MW 136; *Watsons*, MW 333, 335; *NA* 243; *S&S* 108, 110; *P&P* 73, 92, 166, 195; *MP* 51, 193; *E* 82, 192, 195, 206; *P* 36, 59, 181, 188) was to be done elegantly and gracefully, with no extravagant show of humility (*P&P* 162). A "scrape" (*NA* 45), which was a backward sliding of one leg while making the bow, was to be avoided, as it looked clumsy and rustic. The depth and duration of the bow depended on the circumstances, as a short, curt bow, more like a nod, could indicate displeasure or mere formal acknowledgment (*NA* 93), while a long bow could be ridiculous in some situations and lend emphasis to one's words or departure in others. Gentlemen were expected to bow upon taking leave of a lady, rather then simply turning tail and walking away. Bows or tips of the hat were also offered as greetings to women, to social superiors, and to acquaintances seen at a distance. (Laborers without hats, confronted with a member of the gentry, would bob head or upper body in a bow and pull on the hair at the front of their heads to indicate that they would have removed their hats if they had had them.) No doubt there was some relaxation of these rules among close friends and relatives, who would not expect to be constantly acknowledging each other's presence and departure and who would adopt more informal ways of greeting each other (*E* 99–100, 424).

What applied to the bow also generally applied to the curtsey (*F&E*, MW 6; *Cass*, MW 45, 46; *Lesley*, MW 136; *Cath*, MW 215; *Watsons*, MW 333, 336; *Sand*, MW 394–395; *S&S* 175; *P&P* 214, 267, 335; *P* 59, 181). Women used it as a way of formal greeting and farewell, and it had lost the deep knee bend of earlier centuries to become a quick placement of one foot behind the other and a short bend of the knees, along with a brief inclination of the head. For more informal greetings, women could choose to shake hands (*NA* 34; *S&S* 176; *P&P* 214; *E* 99, 261, 444), even with a man, though conduct books indicated that this was a favor to be distributed with care. *The Mirror of the Graces* (1811) offered stern warnings on the subject:

> When any man, who is not privileged by the right of friendship or of kindred, to address her with an action of affection, attempts to take her hand, let her withdraw it immediately with an air so declarative of displeasure, that he shall not presume to repeat the offence. At no time ought she to volun-

teer shaking hands with a male acquaintance, who holds not any particular bond of esteem with regard to herself or family. A touch, a pressure of the hands, are the only external signs a woman can give of entertaining a particular regard for certain individuals. And to lavish this valuable power of expression upon all comers, upon the impudent and contemptible, is an indelicate extravagance which, I hope, needs only to be exposed, to be put for ever out of countenance.

Still less should they allow people to kiss them hello, a custom that had been nearly universal in Shakespeare's day. The author of *The Mirror of the Graces* was sent into paroxysms of disapproval by the mere thought:

> As to the salute, the pressure of the lips: that is an interchange of affectionate greeting or tender farewell, sacred to the dearest connections alone. Our parent; our brothers; our near kindred; our husband; our lover, ready to become our husband; our bosom's inmate, the friend of *our heart's care*; to them are exclusively consecrated the lips of delicacy, and woe be to her who yields them to the stain of profanation!

Among men, the handshake (*Scraps*, *MW* 171; *Evelyn*, *MW* 190; *Watsons*, *MW* 335) was exchanged only between those of roughly equal social class.

Speech was fairly strictly regulated. Conversation (*Col Let*, *MW* 167; *Scraps*, *MW* 171; *Cath*, *MW* 201, 229, 230–231; *Watsons*, *MW* 323; *NA* 25, 56; *S&S* 233; *P&P* 54, 72, 172; *MP* 47–48; *P* 58, 97) should be on subjects considered appropriate for one's age, sex, and class. It would be considered inappropriate, for example, for women of Austen's class to debate fiscal or military policy (*Cath*, *MW* 212), though they could comment on the price of veal or the welfare of their cousins in the army. They should do so, moreover, in quiet and appealing tones of voice (*P&P* 39). Shouting (*MP* 392), arguing (*MP* 379), and even whistling were forbidden. Men, of course, could do all three of these things, but gentlemen did them out of the hearing of ladies. Conversation was to be adapted not only to one's own class but to the class of those with whom one spoke. One's manner to social inferiors was to be polite and considerate but not overly familiar. When speaking to social superiors, it was critical to remember the proper forms of address and to be neither obsequious nor offensively informal. Bragging (*L&F*, *MW* 77–78), mannered or affected speech patterns, and habitual exaggeration were to be avoided, as were monopolizing the conversation (*P&P* 163), indiscretion about family matters, wit at the expense of others, or detailed discussions of any part of the body. These specifics were all aspects of the principal rule, which was to think about the feelings of others. Hester Chapone, author of a consistently popular book of advice for young ladies, put it simply enough, pointing out that "the principles of politeness are the same in all places. Wherever there are human beings, it must be impolite to hurt the temper, or to shock the passions of those you converse with."

Introductions, one assumes, were made much in the same manner as in the Victorian era, when it was customary for the person of lesser social standing to be introduced to the other, as in, "Lady Whateverington, may I present Miss Taylor?" In the case of a lady being introduced to a gentleman, the lady was usually treated as the superior by virtue of her sex. The lady would curtsey and the gentleman would bow. Of course, not all introductions would have been this formal, but a degree of formality was considered necessary, especially when people of very different social standing were to be introduced to each other. Furthermore, it was essential that a third party known to both make the introduction (*Evelyn*, *MW* 187; *NA* 25; *P&P* 6, 256, 351; *P* 141); one did not simply introduce oneself, especially to a social superior (*P&P* 97). Genteel people who had not been introduced simply did not speak to one another (*NA* 22).

An introduction was a matter of some importance, as once two people were introduced, they had to "know" each other for good (*MP* 183; *P* 176), acknowledging each other's presence every time they met and accepting visits back and forth. The only way out of perpetual acquaintance was for one of the two to do something so horrific and unforgivable that the other could "cut" him. A cut was a deliberate failure to refuse to acknowledge an acquaintance. For example, two men are walking in different directions on a sidewalk, gradually approaching each other. Their eyes meet. One tips his hat and nods his head toward the other, wordlessly indicating that he has seen him, knows him, and wishes him well (or at least pretends to). The other, seeing this, walks past without making any sign of greeting. Or, even more directly and publicly, at a social gathering that included both men, one could refuse to shake the other's hand or to speak to him.

The cut was a serious breach and either required serious provocation or a complete lack of manners on the part of the person delivering it. This is the reason that Marianne reacts so dramatically to Willoughby's cold reception of her at a London party (*S&S* 177). It is also one reason that Elizabeth Bennet is disposed to think Mr. Darcy proud and contemptuous; as she has seen nothing in Wickham's manner that would make her think him less than a gentleman, she can only conclude that Mr. Darcy's near-cut of him in Meryton (*P&P* 73) reflects a fault in Mr. Darcy. The cut, in one form or another, appears repeatedly in Austen's novels, because in her social world it was almost as dramatic an incident as could possibly happen. Sometimes it is the fault of the party who is cut—as it is in Wickham's case. Sometimes it is intended to reflect poorly on the one delivering the cut, as it is in Willoughby's case, Sir Walter Elliot's extremely minimal acknowledgment of Frederick Wentworth (*P* 181), and Miss Bingley's return visit to Jane Bennet (*P&P* 148), which in its form and manner is as close as it could come to being a cut without actually being one.

Dinner etiquette was a little simpler than it would be in later years. The

THE HONOR OF PRECEDENCE.

The Honor of Precedence, 1804. In a parody of the quest of ladies for precedence, the artist depicts the wives of a cheesemonger, a tobacconist, and a grocer taking precedence: "when they were taking leave," the caption reads, "the cheesemonger's wife was going out of the room first, upon which the grocer's lady pulling her back by the tail of her gown, and stepping before her. 'No, madam, (says she) nothing comes after Cheese.'—'I beg your pardon, madam,' replies the cheesemonger's wife, putting the tobacconist's lady back, who was also stepping before her, 'after cheese comes tobacco.'" Courtesy of the Lewis Walpole Library, Yale University. 804.10.22.1.

guests often walked into the dining room in couples (*Visit, MW* 53), with the rank of the ladies determining the order in which they entered. Where rank was equal, married women went before single women, and older ladies took precedence over their juniors (*P&P* 317; *E* 298; *P* 7, 129, 250). Where rank, age, and marital status overlapped, there could be confusion and hurt feelings about who went first (*P* 45–46). Once inside the dining room, the hostess sat at the top of the table (*Visit, MW* 52; *Lesley, MW* 121; *P&P* 310), the host at the bottom (*Visit, MW* 52). The pre-eminent male guest was seated on the hostess' right hand, the chief female guest (*MP* 223) at the host's right (*MP* 52). Otherwise, people sat where they liked. They were encouraged to make conversation with their neighbors, and men helped women to the various dishes before them on the table. After dinner, the ladies would drink a glass or two of wine with the men, then retire to the drawing room, again in order of precedence. The men would remain a while in the dining room; in the early part of the period, they had all returned to the drawing room together in a group, but later they were permitted to depart individually.

All then took tea and coffee, signaling by leaving a spoon in the cup or across it when they were done drinking. A cup, once poured, had to be drunk. A contemporary print makes fun of a Frenchman who, not knowing the spoon rule, has his cup refilled over a dozen times before he realizes his mistake.

Fan

Fans (*NA* 75, 77) might have sticks of bone, horn, ivory, wood, tortoise-shell, mother of pearl, or metal. The leaf, or covering, of the fan was usually elaborately decorated on both front and back, and the variety of this decoration was quite surprising. There were, as one might expect, scenes of gardens, or lovers courting, and of episodes and characters from classical mythology. However, there were also fans that showed architects consulting with clients, royal weddings, scenes from popular works of literature, and elements of Chinese or Japanese art. Chapel or church fans were printed with verses from the Bible and commonly used prayers and psalms. Some bore riddles, puns, puzzles, or games. Businesses issued fans as a form of advertising and used them as a medium to promote plays, spas, and coach routes. Vendors in cities such as Rome and Venice made fans painted with pictures of popular tourist sites; these were sold as souvenirs to travelers. A few fans, intended perhaps as the ballroom equivalent of a cheat sheet, included the steps for tricky dances. The designs might be hand-painted or printed; in some cases, the design was purely ornamental rather than pictorial and was worked into the ivory or metal sticks in delicate, lacelike patterns.

The construction of a fan involved several steps. The leaf was made first out of lace, cloth, vellum, or paper. If made of paper, it would be stuck to another sheet with a pliable glue and stretched tightly on a circular frame to dry. Then it would be decorated. Meanwhile, a different craftsman began carving the sticks to the proper size, making them thickest at the bottom, where a rivet would fasten all the sticks together. If the sticks bore decorations of some kind, the stick maker would consult with the leaf decorator to make sure the designs were harmonious. The sticks might be gilded or studded with gems. Then the leaf was placed on a special mold, and a craftsman checked to make sure that the pleats of the fan would fall in an aesthetically pleasing way—for example, never bisecting an important figure. Then folds were marked on the mold and flattened with the fingers. The layers of the leaf were carefully separated at the proper places and the sticks inserted. The sticks were joined with a rivet, and the entire fan was stored either in a small, roughly triangular case, usually of bright green shagreen, or a bag made of silk, satin, or brocade. Images of fans can be seen in the illustrations *A Meeting at Margate* (Clothing), *A Master of the Ceremonies Introducing a Partner* (Dance), and *Conversazione* (Architecture), among others. *See also* Clothing.

Fire

When twenty-first-century readers imagine an eighteenth-century fireside (*L&F, MW* 79; *MP* 188; *E* 22, 113, 303, 461), they usually surmise that the author means a *wood* fire. This is an entirely understandable assumption, since most fireplaces today use either wood or gas for fuel, and gas was not available for this purpose in Jane Austen's day. Furthermore, pictures of stately old houses often show large open kitchen fireplaces, clearly meant to hold sizable logs. (Such a fireplace may be seen in the illustration *A Shrewed Guess* [Clothing].) Therefore, it is eminently sensible to assume that when Austen speaks of a fire (*E&E, MW* 32; *L&F, MW* 100; *Col Let, MW* 167; *Watsons, MW* 319, 343; *S&S* 90, 193, 307; *P&P* 54, 71; *MP* 139, 151, 178, 249, 340, 398, 446; *E* 24, 53, 115, 320, 322, 323, 340, 372; *P* 134), she means a wood fire. However, it is an incorrect assumption. Wood fires were so rare in Austen's time that she makes a special point of mentioning wood as fuel on the rare instances when it appears (*NA* 167).

The reason her fires are not fueled by logs has to do with the rate at which the English were consuming their natural resources. England had once been thickly forested in many places, but a rapacious desire for timber for building houses and ships, coupled with a need for fuel, had decimated the forests. Timber was so valuable that "plantations" of trees were one of the most prized assets on large estates. Austen's wealthiest brother, Edward Austen (later Edward Knight), had multiple plantations designed for periodic harvesting. Trees were simply too expensive to burn, and when they were burned, it was usually to create charcoal for industrial purposes.

Most people burned a more plentiful natural resource: coal (*MP* 379). Coal was stored near the fireplace in a large box and shoveled into a grate (*S&S* 39; *MP* 168) of horizontal bars that kept it from spilling out. The top bar of the grate could, in many houses, move to the level of the second bar, forming a little shelf for pots and pans. Side flaps inside the grate could be moved in or out to expand or contract the size of the fire. An assortment of devices and tools surrounded the fireplace, depending on its location and use; fireplaces in drawing rooms, for instance, might have decorative brass holders for wood or coal, while such adornments would not be found in the kitchen, or in a single-fire home. Many fireplaces also had fenders (*NA* 167), or screens (*P&P* 162; *E* 208), which helped to deflect sparks and excessive heat. A chimney board (*S&S* 274) covered the fireplace in the summer months.

The kitchen usually had the largest fireplace, and here one would find the standard assortment of tools for maintaining the fire—shovel, bellows, poker, and so forth—as well as racks, hooks, cranes, spits, pots, and pans for cooking. The fire also needed a curfew (a metal cover for banking the fire at night), a tinderbox for lighting the fuel, and, in the rare instances when wood was used, irons (*Sand, MW* 387) for moving the logs. Toward the end of the eighteenth century, tin reflector ovens were introduced. These stood in front of the fire and partially surrounded roasting meat, making it easier to salvage drippings and harder for the sizzling fat to land on the floor. Toasting or grilling forks would also be present, and some homes had plate warmers, trivets, gridirons for grilling steaks, and salamanders (irons that were heated and passed over food to brown it). An unusually elaborate arrangement of ovens, stovetop, and fireplace may be seen in the illustration *The Physicians Friend* (Servants). A more typical kitchen fire is that in the illustration *Loo in the Kitchin* (Cards).

Fireplaces in other parts of the house (*Watsons, MW* 327; *MP* 308), such as the parlor (*Watsons, MW* 355, 356) drawing room (*S&S* 175; *MP* 125, 273), or sitting room (*MP* 312, 322; *E* 240), had fewer associated tools and might well be smaller, as they were for heat only, not for cooking large meals. However, even here, some cooking might be done. Toast or cocoa might be heated here during tea (*Sand, MW* 416–417), and some contemporary prints show people cooking more substantial food over a small fireplace in what appears to be a room other than the kitchen. Bedroom fireplaces (*NA* 167; *S&S* 190; *MP* 312) were used for heat throughout the night, and a few coals could be removed slightly before bedtime and placed in a warming pan, a device somewhat like a flat-lidded skillet with a very long handle. The coal-filled warming pan was placed between the chilly layers of bedding to raise them to a comfortable temperature. Fireplaces in various rooms may be seen in the illustrations *A Shrewed Guess* (Clothing), *Temperance Enjoying a Frugal Meal* (Food), and *Advantages of Wearing Muslin Dresses!* (Dishes).

Toasting Muffins, Vide Royal Breakfast, James Gillray, 1791. In this caricature of George III, the monarch toasts muffins by a small inset fireplace. The coal grate and coal are clearly visible. Courtesy of the Lewis Walpole Library, Yale University. 791.11.28.1.

The household fire was much appreciated for its usefulness in cooking and for the comfort it offered on cold days. Invalids and the aged, in particular, were thought to benefit from a seat close to the fire (*Sand, MW* 413, 415; *E* 10, 217, 351, 357), though it was not only the old and sick who delighted in "a good seat by the fire" (*Watsons, MW* 327; *S&S* 247). Austen herself wrote in 1813, after a party at someone else's house, "I find many *douceurs* in being a sort of chaperon, for I am put on the sofa near the fire and can drink as much wine as I like." It is easy to forget in an era of central heating that the internal temperature of a house could easily drop into the forties (Fahrenheit) on winter nights. It is also easy to forget that it was not the master or mistress of the house, typically, who would rise before dawn on frigid mornings to light the family's fires. This task would, in many cases, be performed by a servant (*S&S* 180), who would sweep out the previous day's ashes (*E* 236) and clean the fireplace. According to Eliza Haywood's *A New Present for a Servant-Maid* (1771), this was no simple matter. First the housemaid had "to rub the stove and fire-irons with scouring-paper, and to clean the hearth." Iron and brass fittings could be cleaned with vinegar and ashes, "then with an oily rag, and after that with scouring paper, rotten-stone, or white-brick," or, alternatively, with goose fat. Steel irons had to be oiled, rubbed with emery, and then scoured. The maid then had to fill the grates with coal hauled from a storage area, light the fire with a tinderbox, fan it with a bellows, wash the hearth with hot water and soap, dry it, and then move on to the next fireplace.

Fireplaces were troublesome not only to the servants who tended them. They were, on the whole, extremely inefficient. They tended to heat only a small part of the room and to create a draft in other parts, as air was heated and funneled upward through the chimney. Air circulation was not always sufficient, and in these cases smoke poured back into the room (*P* 128). The fireplace linings were often cast of iron, which absorbed heat rather than reflecting it into the room. In short, the English fireplace was a great deal less useful than it appeared.

However, English consumers repeatedly rejected attempts to woo them away from open hearths toward efficient, enclosed stoves. They felt that limited cool drafts were healthful; that stoves heated rooms too well, requiring open windows and strong breezes that were considered dangerous to health; and that an unevenly heated room allowed various zones of comfort to please those who preferred different temperatures. People believed, in the words of one contemporary "expert," that

> Stoves do not promote a discharge of air from rooms, which yet is every moment more and more replete with vapours dispersed from burning candles, the breath and perspiration of the company, and occasionally from other sources; whence the air inspired becomes noxious.

Some attempts at reform to the design of fireplaces were made by the American Benjamin Thompson, later Count von Rumford (1753–1814), whose hearths were considered the state of the art in warmth and efficiency (*NA* 162). He changed the size of the fireplace opening and tinkered with the height and shape of the flue, moved the fire farther forward, recommended firestone or plastered bricks for the fireplace lining, and introduced a movable tile for easier sweeping. He sought, as much as possible, to send heat into the room rather than up the chimney and to lengthen the time that it took to consume the fuel, so as to generate more heat for less money.

Fishing

Austen makes little mention of fishing (*P&P* 254, 255, 266), but it was a popular way to spend a morning. Some fishing was done with casting nets; it seems that Parson Woodforde used this technique during an extraordinary day of fishing on May 16, 1781:

> We begun at Lenewade Mill and fished down to Morton. And we had the best day of Fishing we ever had. We caught at one draught only ten full Pails of Fish, Pike, Trout and flat fish. The largest Fish we caught was a Pike, which was a Yard long and weighed upwards of thir-

Patience in a Punt, Henry Bunbury, 1792. A fishing excursion. Courtesy of the Lewis Walpole Library, Yale University. 792.5.1.1+.

teen pound after he was brought home. We caught about 20 brace of Pike, but threw back all the small ones—also we caught abt 15 brace of Trout, the largest not marc than a Pound and half—all the smallest we threw back—5 brace also of Perch—one tolerable Tench and I dare say near if not quite five hundred Brace of Roach and Dace. Prodigious sport indeed we had today tho' cold and wet. . . . We eat some cold meat which we carried about one o'clock and returned home to dinner at 4.

Woodforde also records a slight altercation with a landowner who objected to Woodforde's fishing on his land; propertied gentlemen were, indeed, covetous of their fishing rights and protected them almost as zealously as they guarded their hunting rights (*P&P* 258).

Net-casting was not the typical means of catching fish. It was more conventional to use a rod, preferably of hickory, greenheart, or lancewood. Trout rods also had reels for winding the line. Some anglers used artificial worms or flies made of gray horsehair; others used live bait. Woodforde caught trout using grasshoppers as bait, while others caught pike using small live fish, artificial minnows, or, occasionally, live frogs. A small minority of anglers objected to live bait on ethical grounds.

Food

Food in Austen's lifetime differed greatly from food consumed in industrialized countries today. From the methods by which it was brought into the household and prepared, to the timing, elements, and presentation of the meals themselves, the food was—though containing many of the same components as modern food—alien enough that it would surprise a modern diner in many ways. The quality, quantity, and variety of the food depended, like so much else, on economic and social class, and it could be said that in these respects the fare enjoyed by the poor differed as much from that of the rich as both did from modern food. However, some generalizations can be made, especially if we confine ourselves to the sorts of meals likely to have been consumed by Austen's characters.

Acquisition

Food was acquired from various sources, none of them as consistent or as amply supplied as a modern supermarket. Some items were produced on the family farm. There might be livestock that could be slaughtered as needed, a kitchen garden, orchards, fishponds, and fields in which grain was grown. A farm's livestock offered a potential source of fresh meat. In 1798, for example, Jane writes from Steventon of being able "to kill a pig soon," and Mr. Austen also kept sheep, which were sometimes butchered as well.

Some types of meat, particularly among the gentry and aristocracy, would come from the hunting or fishing activities of the family's men. Other items were acquired by purchase from neighbors or by exchanges with family and friends. Those who lived near the sea might send fish to inland relatives and receive, in exchange, a return gift of apples or game birds. Parson James Woodforde, a thorough diarist, also engaged in this sort of friendly, informal barter. On August 24, 1790, he reported sending a dozen apricots from one of his trees to the local squire, Mr. Custance, who "sent us back some fine black Grapes which came from Mackay's Hot House, a Gardner at Norwich." On an earlier occasion, in 1784, he sent three dozen apricots to Custance and received in return a "large Piece of fine Parmesan Cheese"—an imported luxury item that made a handsome gift.

Not all such exchanges were purely friendly. Some were rather more mercenary. Woodforde, for instance, sometimes sold his surplus animals to neighbors or to the local butcher (*Sand*, *MW* 392; *MP* 58; *E* 186; *P* 202). On December 22, 1788, he reported paying his yearly butcher's bill (£39 11s.) and receiving from the butcher, Harry Baker, a refund of £1 15s. 8d. for a calf. It seems likely that most farmers would have engaged in similar deals with tradesmen, offering whatever they had in surplus as partial payment for their purchases.

In all these types of exchange, buyers, sellers, and donors alike were at the mercy of the seasons. Increasingly, throughout the eighteenth century, livestock were able to survive the winter, as improved agricultural methods improved the supply of winter fodder; previously, there had been a mass slaughter in late fall or early winter of animals that would otherwise starve. However, even if meat was more continuously available to those who could afford it, fruits and vegetables were restricted to their own particular seasons. Preserving and pickling could extend their life span, but it was not the same thing as having the fresh items at hand all year long.

Some foods were imported, but these were rarely brought in to extend the season of domestically raised produce. Instead, they were foods that did not grow successfully in England or that were deemed better when processed elsewhere. These items included citrus fruits, spices, tea, sugar, and Woodforde's fine piece of Parmesan. Such foods tended to be expensive, their prices reflecting the additional costs of importation, and their consumption indicated relative affluence and, in some cases, genuine wealth. Their presence was certainly not taken for granted.

Still other foods were available year-round, or nearly so, but were subject to spoilage in an age before refrigeration. Eggs fell into this category, as did milk and some of its by-products. Milk had to be processed immediately: skimmed, strained, preserved as cheese, or the cream churned into butter. Meat, fish, and poultry, too, suffered from storage difficulties. Dr. Grant's green goose (*MP* 212) is Austen's most notable example of the failure of meat to keep as long as one might wish.

One way of avoiding some of the thorniest issues of supply and demand was to purchase one's food from specialist shops: a butcher (*Sand*, *MW* 392; *P&P* 331; *MP* 379) who dealt in meat, in large cities perhaps a poulterer (*MP* 212–213) who specialized in birds, a confectioner for sweets and jellies, a baker (*Sand*, *MW* 392; *E* 233) for bread, a grocer for imported items such as chocolate or tea, a fruiterer for fruit, and so on. Sometimes there was a significant distance between these sorts of specialist retailers and one's home. When the Austen women lived at Chawton, there was a market in nearby Alton, but it was not especially impressive, and most of the marketing was done in Winchester or Farnham. Some items, such as tea, were ordered from as far away as London. In earlier years, at Steventon rectory, the marketing took place mainly in Basingstoke. The principal grocer in Basingstoke, the nearest town to Steventon, advertised in 1794 that his wares included "Old Raisin Wine, Confectionery, Perfumery, Stationery, &c. Oils, fine Westmoreland Hams, Burgess's Essence of Anchovies, Mushroom and India Soy, Sauce Royal, Devonshire Sauce, Lemon Ketchup, Olives, Capers, Vinegar &c." As suggested by this list, shopkeepers could offer a wider variety than farm and friends afforded, and they could offer a more consistent and sometimes fresher supply. In some cases, patronizing shops was not a matter of choice; residents of towns, such and Mr. and Mrs. Austen, Jane, and Cassandra, during the years they lived in Bath, often had no other options. Without a farm or a kitchen garden, they were naturally dependent on shops.

The environment in which one bought food was both like and unlike the supermarkets of today. In a supermarket, food is segregated by type: bread, produce, fish, meat, frozen food, and so on. Similarly, food in Austen's day was distributed into different areas by type. This could happen in one of several ways: the food might be available, as described above, in discrete shops—permanent, fully interior spaces, such as a grocer's shop. These shops, with attractive bow windows filled with goods on display, were increasingly replacing the old-fashioned stalls, which were shops open to the street, with the wares arranged on a counter or hanging from hooks. Then there were markets, which might be permanent or temporary, and which were set up in sizable "market towns" (*E&E, MW* 29; *H&E, MW* 34; *Watsons, MW* 322; *P* 10). At a market (*NA* 68), one or more days of the week were set aside for the display and sale of all kinds of goods. As in the case of shops, the vendors remained specialists. One went to a butcher for meat, to a fishmonger for fish, to a grocer or chandler for tea and sugar, and to yet another vendor, usually a farm woman, for eggs or butter or local cheese. Assembling a meal, especially one of the lavish dinners that the gentry served to company, involved visiting just as many "departments" as going to the supermarket today, but each department required negotiation with a separate sales staff, an inspection of the quality of the goods, a round or two of haggling perhaps, and a financial transaction. Of course, in many cases these multiple errands were simplified by familiarity; the merchant might simply make a notation in his books, rather than demanding cash for every purchase. A merchant might also come to recognize the level of quality demanded by a particular client and make no attempt to deceive or to haggle, and customers learned to avoid merchants whose wares did not suit them. Nonetheless, the process of buying food was far more complex before the days of shopping carts and checkout lines.

The Austens were fortunate in at least one respect. In the years they resided in Bath, the town was blessed with a number of particularly well stocked shops. Aside from the markets, held on Wednesdays and Saturdays (and on Mondays, Wednesdays, and Fridays for fish), there were respected dealers in meat, fruit, vegetables, fish, milk products, and even imported wines. Pastry-cooks sold confections, ices, jellies, and savory snacks that could be eaten in the shop or taken home. Two of the more prominent Bath pastry shops were Molland's in Milsom Street, mentioned in *Persuasion* (174), and Gill's, built between two buttresses of the Abbey Church.

Shops charged a premium for the variety and convenience they offered; bakers in particular were singled out by public opinion as price-gougers. Furthermore, many shops were guilty, intentionally or accidentally, of diluting or adulterating the products they sold. Meat was hard to adulterate, but tainted meat might, by various stratagems, be disguised as fresh. A cask of stale butter might be passed off as fresh by hiding a lump of fresh butter within the cask, and offering tastes from this small lump to prospective shoppers. Bread was whitened with chalk or alum, and many foods, from pickles to milk, ranged from substandard to poisonous in quality. Pickled items were sometimes made in copper vats, which lent color to the food but also made it poisonous. Vinegar was sharpened by the addition of sulphuric acid. Pastry cooks used cherry laurel leaves to lend a bitter-almond flavor to desserts, not knowing, or not caring, that the pleasant almond flavor came from cyanide. Prepared anchovy sauce was colored with a lead compound called "Venetian red," while olive oil was often processed abroad using lead press plates or lead cisterns, and then imported by unsuspecting consumers. Clearly, customers had to be cautious.

Nonetheless, they continued to buy not only from shops and market stalls but from a variety of places serving ready-to-eat food. Large towns such as London had cook shops, which, according to J. P. Malcolm in 1810, sold "baked and boiled meat and flour and pease puddings at a very reasonable rate." Coffee shops and public houses also sold food as well as beverages, and for dessert one might stop at a pastry shop for ice cream, tarts, or gingerbread. Food was also "cried," or sold, in the streets. An 1819 letter in *The Gentleman's Magazine*, intended as a tongue-in-cheek music criticism of street vendors' cries, lists a wide variety of commodities sold door-to-door: potatoes, shrimp, cod, spinach, muffins, periwinkles, smelts, mackerel, radishes "twenty a penny," watercress, salad, cheese, and buns. This list was by no means exhaustive.

Preparation

Even the most casual reader of literature or history must be aware that food preparation (*P&P* 44, 65; *MP* 383) was done in the absence of most modern devices. However, the actual methods of preparation are often something of a mystery to them. What sorts of things were cooked in an oven, and to what extent did it resemble a modern oven? How were dishes cooked over an open fire? What equipment was used? Readers often picture a kitchen fire that is either too early or too late—resembling either the giant open hearths of the Renaissance or the cast-iron stoves of the later nineteenth century.

Regency cooking more closely resembled the former model than the latter, though the huge fireplace with its wood fire had given way to a more compact unit with coal for fuel and a metal grate, consisting of several horizontal bars, to keep the coal from falling out. Cooking at such a hearth could be accomplished in a variety of ways. In many homes, the top bar of the grate could swivel so that it fell into a horizontal plane with the second bar, and on these two bars, pots or pans could be perched. Sometimes they supported a gridiron, a round grating used for broiling steaks and chops. Meat could be roasted on spits or in portable tin reflector ovens, which contained a drip tray and a three-walled spatter guard to keep grease from soiling the rest of the kitchen. Toasting forks in a variety of shapes were used to toast bread, muffins, sausages, and other food, and "salamanders"—named for a mythical beast that lived

Eliza Haywood's *A New Present for a Servant-Maid*, Frontispiece, 1771. Most of the tools of the kitchen staff can be seen in this illustration, and each portion of the engraving represents one of the disciplines of an accomplished cook. The center background is devoted to plain cookery: roasting, stewing, and so forth. Above the hearth are racks of spits in various sizes, a mortar and pestle for grinding spices, candlesticks, and shakers of salt and perhaps flour. Over the large coal fire, a huge kettle of soup simmers, suspended from the swing-out crane; below the kettle, a large bird roasts on a spit. On the left-hand side, a maid works at the second important discipline: baking and pastry making. Her rolling pin is characteristic of the time: gently tapered at each end rather than possessing distinct handles, to prevent the formation of edge lines in the crust. On the right-hand side, another maid holding a skillet consults Haywood's book. She—or at least her part of the kitchen—is probably intended to symbolize preserving and pickling, a crucial area of food preparation in the days before refrigeration. On the table behind her book can be seen two jars of preserves, covered (in the absence of reliable canning supplies) with sheets of thick paper soaked in brandy and tied on with string. Library of Congress.

in fire—were pieces of metal with one flattened end that could be heated in the fire and passed over food to brown it. Most houses would also have had one or more hooks or swing arms from which kettles could be suspended. These kettles were used not only for making soup and broth but also for boiling meat, vegetables, and puddings and for providing hot water for coffee and tea. However, hot water was sometimes made instead in a boiler, an iron or copper container with a lid that stood near the fire and had a tap for drawing off the heated water.

A relatively new enthusiasm for efficiency drove the creation of the boiler, as well as the shallower, smaller fireplace, which saved on fuel. The idea was to capture as much heat as possible from the fire, and to this end, ovens were sometimes built adjacent to the fire. There were at least three ways of heating an oven, none of which allowed for much control over temperature. The first was, as stated, to build the oven right next to the main fireplace, so as to radiate heat through the wall that separated them. Small box ovens were often built into the wall next to the fireplace, but they had the obvious disadvantage of being heated only on one side, and they were typically not large enough or hot enough to bake bread. The second method of heating an oven was to pass a large iron bar through both the fireplace and the oven; the fire heated the bar, which conducted some portion of the heat to the oven. The third method, which was the standard method for detached ovens (such as the ones in the bakehouses of large homes), as well as for many ovens adjacent to fireplaces, was to build and light a fire inside the oven and allow it to burn out. The ashes were swept away, and the food, placed inside, was cooked by the residual heat in the bricks or stones that lined the oven. The effects of this cooking technique can be seen in baking recipes of the time, which sometimes instruct the cook to alternate fire and baking several times for foods that required long periods of heat.

The typical freestanding oven had its bottom about two and a half feet above the floor and had a diameter of two to three feet and a rounded roof about a foot and a half to two feet high. The door was occasionally made of oak strapped with iron, but a fully iron door was more common. At its hottest, the oven was usually used for bread, which was inserted using a "peel," a tool similar to an enormous spatula, made of iron with a wooden handle. Once the bread was removed, items that required lower heat, such as cakes or pies, might be inserted using a peel made entirely of wood. When only a small amount of residual heat remained, the oven might be used for other tasks: allowing dough to rise, drying the icing on a cake, or drying fruit. If none of these tasks needed to be performed, the cook filled the oven with kindling so that the remaining heat would dry out the wood, making the next oven fire easier to light.

Baking was subject to certain limitations: ovens could get only so hot, their temperature was to some extent erratic, their heat could not be kept constant over long periods of time, and they required great effort to operate. Indeed, in most houses, baking was done once or twice a week, if at all; an increasing number of households, particularly among the working classes, chose not to bother with the oven at all but instead bought their bread from bakers' shops. (The Austens, when they lived at Steventon, were not among these families; Mrs. Austen made all her own butter, cheese, bread, beer, and wine.)

Economy of effort extended beyond baking to all the cooking done in the house. There was a tendency to do most of the cooking in preparation for dinner—the most substantial meal of the day—and to use the leftovers from dinner to feed the servants and make up cold suppers. This meant that it was exceedingly difficult to scrape together a dinner at the last minute or to scrap one in favor of an invitation to dine elsewhere. Maggie Lane has pointed out that, while last-minute invitations to tea are common in Austen's writings, her characters know better than to offer a last-minute invitation to dinner when the prospective guest's servants are probably already well advanced in their marketing, cutting, chopping, stewing, and broiling. Austen does refer to impromptu or standing dinner invitations, but these are usually offered to one person at a time—Jane Fairfax (*E* 283) or Mr. Bingley (*P&P* 103), for example—and one person could easily be accommodated by stinting the servants a little and feeding them on plainer fare, or by substituting a different cold dish at supper for the dinner leftovers.

Once the cooking was finished, there still remained one aspect of preparation to be performed at the table. This was the carving of the meat (*P&P* 163, *MP* 34), an important ceremony, since meat was the centerpiece of every dinner among prosperous people. It was customary for the hostess to sit at the head of the table and for the host to occupy the foot. Meat that came to the table whole was brought to the bottom of the table, where the host would slice it and serve it to his guests. Cookbooks of the time usually include a section on carving, which was a delicate business. Charles Millington, author of *The Housekeeper's Domestic Library; or, New Universal Family Instructor* (1805), included instructions and diagrams for carving, including this advice:

> In carving, never rise from your seat, but have a seat high enough to give a command of the table; so not help any one to too much at a time: distribute the nice parts, if possible, equally among the whole, and do not cut the slices too thick nor too thin.

The carving of a turkey, chicken, or beef or pork roast is familiar to many home cooks today, but the Regency host had a wider array of animals to divide. He might be called upon to cut up a saddle of mutton, a hare, a pheasant, a goose, a haunch of venison (*P&P* 342, *MP* 52), or a pig's or calf's head. Small wonder that the timid Mr. Woodhouse usually relinquishes his place at the bottom of the table (*E* 291); one suspects that the daunting task of carving is taken up either by Mr. Knightley or, in his absence, by the servants.

Serving

Many members of the household staff were involved in the preparation and distribution of food. In humble homes, many of the tasks would be performed by a kitchen maid or maid of all work, with the dishes being passed around with little ceremony. However, in most of the homes that appear in Austen's novels, there are servants not only to cook the food but to present it. In houses that could afford to keep male servants (*P* 129), this job would be performed by one or more footmen (*S&S* 233, 355; *P&P* 162; *MP* 180; *NA* 213; *P* 219), who carried in the platters from the kitchen with a great show of bustle and efficiency. The footmen also stood around the table (*MP* 239), ready to assist diners who needed more of anything.

The dishes were delivered all together, with platters and tureens scattered at the top, bottom, sides, and corners (*E* 218) of the table and extra food, along with wine and glasses, placed on a sideboard (*E* 458). This made for a great show of abundance and wealth, but it was not, perhaps, the most convenient way to serve a variety of dishes. Some occasionally went cold before they could be served (*MP* 239), while others might not reach the diners who wanted them. Nonetheless, the attractive display was too enchanting to be forgone, and there would be no substantial change in the method of service until the second half of the nineteenth century. In the more prosperous households, there would be a "second course"— not merely a second type of food as we would use this term today, but a removal of most or all of the platters and bowls from the first half of the meal, followed by a completely new set of dishes (*E* 218)—more meat, vegetables, sauces, tarts, and so forth. Then, after a decent interval, this food was removed, along with the tablecloth (*S&S* 355), and wine and dessert were served (*Watsons*, *MW* 325; *S&S* 355), the latter being not so much sweets or cakes as small finger foods such as nuts (*E* 28, 35; *P* 86), olives, and dried or fresh fruit.

Other meals were less elaborate. Servants were indeed present to bring the food in (*MP* 344), clear it away, and attend to the needs of those who were eating, but there were fewer types of food to serve, and there were less show and ceremony expected. The family took more responsibility for making the tea, the coffee, the sandwiches, or whatever else was at hand, leaving less for the servants to do.

French versus English

French cooking, like the French language and French manners, occupied an ambivalent place in English culture. On the one hand, the aristocracy adored all things French and leapt to pay French "man-cooks" far more than they would pay an Englishwoman. Many people farther down the social ladder then imitated this vogue for France. On the other hand, there was a good deal of patriotic irritation at Francophilia, and this irritation only increased as wars with France dragged on for most of Austen's life.

The battle between French and English only explicitly reaches the dinner table in one of her novels, however. This is *Pride and Prejudice*, in which Darcy's circle is twice identified with French cooking. The first instance brings up the feature of French cooking that was so controversial—sauce. Sauces were integral to French presentation, with the chief meats or vegetables thickly intermingled with their sauce in a ragout. The English style of presentation, on the other hand, was to plop a large piece of meat onto a platter with a comparatively thin sauce spooned around it. To the English, the former method seemed deceptive—*anything* could be hidden in there—and the latter was straightforward and honest. A goose was a goose and looked like a goose. The contrast forms the substance of Elizabeth Bennet's only exchange with Mr. Hurst, Mr. Bingley's brother-in-law, "who when he found her prefer a plain dish to a ragout, had nothing to say to her" (*P&P* 35). With that, Austen dismisses Mr. Hurst from serious consideration, not only because he thinks too much of food, but also because he has chosen the wrong side of the argument.

Yet French cooks remained fashionable, and those who could afford such

French Liberty. British Slavery, 1792. At the height of fears about France's revolutionary fervor spreading to England, caricaturists contrasted the plight of the prerevolutionary French peasants with the prosperity of Englishmen. The French are invariably depicted as gaunt and gnawing on some unappetizing food, while the Englishmen are fat, regaling themselves on bread, beef, and beer. Courtesy of the Lewis Walpole Library, Yale University. 792.12.21.4.

a luxury hired them. Few, indeed, could afford it; French chefs charged their employers handsomely for their services. Mrs. Bennet refers to this practice in one of her assessments of Mr. Darcy's wealth, commenting, "I suppose he has two or three French cooks at least" (*P&P* 342).

Breakfast

The names and timing of meals differed in some respects from their modern forms. Then as now, breakfast (*LS, MW* 284, 285, 286; *NA* 60, 84, 154, 203, 235, 241; *S&S* 63, 83, 96, 164, 172, 201, 202, 369; *P&P* 31, 33, 41, 61, 215, 266; *MP* 156, 445; *E* 10, 50, 237, 258, 259, 293, 472; *P* 58–60, 95, 102, 107, 145, 229) was the first meal of the day, but for the gentry it came late, usually around 9:00 or 10:00 A.M. All meals, as we shall see, were later for the idle and fashionable than for the old-fashioned (*E* 443; *P* 59) and for the working classes. Elizabeth Bennet's uncle Mr. Gardiner, for example, leaves "soon after breakfast" for a fishing excursion that begins at noon (*P&P* 266). Lydia Bennet, staying with her uncle Gardiner later in the novel, notes, "we breakfasted at ten as usual" (*P&P* 318). Early breakfasts tend to have a specific reason for being eaten at an uncivilized hour (*NA* 228; *MP* 280, 282–283, 374). The late hour at which breakfast was served among the gentry, however, should not necessarily be taken as evidence that they were late risers or entirely idle before breakfast. Frequently, they rose fairly early and engaged in some activity before breakfast. Jane played piano before the nine o'clock breakfasts at Chawton, for example, and when staying elsewhere, she might write letters to fill the time. Others took walks to work up an appetite (*S&S* 180; *P* 104). The eldest Austen son, James, did so when he was a curate at Deane, walking a mile on some mornings to visit his father at Steventon.

A healthy appetite was often necessary, for breakfasts could be quite lavish, even if they paled in comparison to the variety and quantity offered at dinner. Breakfast in a substantial home might include cold meat (*MP* 282), cheese, fish, eggs (*MP* 282), coffee, tea (*L&F, MW* 106), chocolate (by which Austen's contemporaries meant the beverage, cocoa, rather than solid chocolate), rolls, toast, bread (*NA* 241) and butter, and, on occasion, freshly prepared steaks or chops. Sometimes, the heartier elements of the meal were eschewed, and the meal consisted mostly of some form of bread or cake accompanied by tea or another hot beverage. The anonymous author of *The Mirror of the Graces* (1811) took issue with even this abridged breakfast menu, which she claimed made women ugly:

> Their breakfasts not only set forth tea and coffee, but chocolate and *hot* bread and butter. Both of these latter articles, when taken constantly, are hostile to health and female delicacy. The heated grease, which is their principal ingredient, deranges the stomach; and, by creating or increasing bilious disorders, gradually overspreads the before fair skin with a wan or yellow hue.

It is unknown whether Englishwomen took her advice and shunned buttered toast (*L&F, MW* 106); one suspects that they continued to indulge.

Luncheon, Picnics, and Dinner

The next meal was dinner (*Visit, MW* 52; *Lesley, MW* 121; *Cath, MW* 229; *LS, MW* 299, 303; *Watsons, MW* 324–325, 339; *Sand, MW* 389; *S&S* 67, 160, 193, 247, 315; *P&P* 45, 54, 342, 344; *NA* 84, 96, 114, 116, 129, 211; *MP* 104, 141, 142, 191, 194, 220–221, 296, 336, 406–407, 412, 469; *E* 6, 14, 50, 108, 209, 213, 226, 290, 303, 344; *P* 39, 54, 95, 98, 137, 140, 219), and it was by far the most significant meal of the day. At one time it had been held around noon, or in the early afternoon, but the association of high status with late mealtimes led to a creeping inflation of the dinner hour. By Austen's day, the upper classes served dinner to their children at about 2:00 or 3:00 P.M., while the adults ate at 5:00 or 6:00. The result was a long period in the middle of the day when no food was served.

Therefore, as the gap between breakfast and dinner widened, with everyone trying to eat later than their neighbors, it became more common to have a little something between breakfast and dinner. However, this meal, known variously as noonshine, nuncheon, or luncheon, did not became standard during Austen's lifetime. Even in families who regularly indulged in sandwiches, cold meat, or some other light fare around noon, the food was seen as refreshments or a "collation" (*H&E, MW* 38; *E* 367) rather than as a full meal. It was eaten in the drawing room, or wherever the family happened to be gathered, rather than in the dining room, which further deprived it of full mealtime status. It might also be consumed on the road at an inn, when travelers were at the mercy of schedules and of inn location. In such circumstances, they ate when they had the chance, regardless of time and fashion. "Lunching" was not an English verb until the 1830s and did not become an acceptable term among the educated until still later.

On occasion, people chose to take their afternoon meal outdoors, in which case the meal might be referred to as "cold meat," a "cold collation," or a "pic-nic." The practice of eating outside with packed lunches was also known as "gipsying." All members of the party were supposed to contribute something to the meal, rather like a potluck dinner today, and the result could either be a good-natured sense of communal purpose or an unpleasant contest of display.

Dinner was not only the largest meal but also an important marker in the passage of time. It officially ended the morning, regardless of when it was scheduled. Morning dress, in which one went walking and paid morning calls, was exchanged for evening dress (*E* 114), which in women's case often meant revealing a little more skin. An invitation to someone's house for dinner (*E* 290) was more intrinsically valuable than an invitation to any other meal, because it was at this meal that the full efforts of the household staff were engaged.

A *Gentleman's Magazine* letter of 1819 about the customs of Herefordshire describes the meal simply enough. Among "the nobility and the

Rowlandson Etching, 1790, detail. A picnic excursion. Courtesy of the Lewis Walpole Library, Yale University. 790.6.27.1.

gentry," dinner is served at 5:00 or 6:00 P.M. and consists of "soup, poultry, butcher's meat, and sweets: the wines, port and sherry." This, the author insists, is true not only in Herefordshire, but everywhere in England. He makes no such claim for the yeomanry, whom he describes as eating "a profusion of butcher's meat" and drinking cider or beer. Laborers ate more or less meat depending on their circumstances. Live-in servants and farm laborers usually ate the same food as their masters, which generally included a fair amount of meat, while poorer tenant farmers and small craftsmen might be able to afford meat only seldom. According to contemporary accounts, in 1794 in Hampshire, live-in farm laborers ate mostly pork and pudding, while in Middlesex in 1795 laborers ate "bread and cheese and pork for breakfast, coarse joints of beef boiled with cabbages and other vegetables, or meat pies or puddings for dinner, cold pork, bread and cheese, etc. for supper; and with every meal, small beer."

At its simplest—that is, when no company was present—dinner even among the gentry was not an especially lavish display, especially by the standards of the day. Parson Woodforde, when dining alone at home, lists very simple dinners in his diary: "Fryed Soals and cold green Goose for Dinner" and "Giblet Soup and Shoulder Mutton rosted" are two typical entries from July 1791. A dinner of similar simplicity appeared on Henry Austen's London table in 1813 when he welcomed his sister Jane, his brother Edward, and three of Edward's daughters—in Jane's words, "a most comfortable dinner of soup, fish, bouillée, partridges, and an apple tart, which we sat down to soon after five."

However, dinners for company tended to be as lavish as the host's budget allowed (*MP* 221, 239). Most dinners consisted of one "course"— that is, one set of dishes, perhaps only three or four, perhaps as many as twelve or fourteen—placed on the table nearly simultaneously. In such cases, the customary formula was for the host to say, "You see your dinner" (*Watsons*, *MW* 354) in order to inform the company that no second course would be forthcoming, and they might eat all they liked of the present dishes without needing to save room for more. In some homes, this first course would be followed by a second course (*P&P* 84, 120, 338). Whether the meal was of one course or two, it was usually followed by dessert (*E* 89, 219). Austen frequently omits a catalog of the dishes at her fictional dinners, but Parson Woodforde was good enough to note down almost everything he ate on visits, and we can gather, from his lists, the sorts of food that appeared at the tables of the gentry.

At a postbaptismal dinner for one of the squire's children, for example, he describes far more than the standard, simple, family fare.

We had for dinner a Calf's Head, boiled Fowl and Tongue, a Saddle of Mutton rosted on the Side Table, and a fine Swan rosted with Currant Jelly Sauce for the first Course. The second Course a couple of Wild Fowl called

Dun Fowls, Larks, Blamange, Tarts etc. etc. and a good Desert of Fruit after amongst which was a Damson Cheese. I never eat a bit of a Swan before, and I think it good eating with sweet sauce.

Woodforde, too, liked to entertain his friends. At a dinner for friends in 1790, his guests received skate with oyster sauce, pea soup, ham, chicken, the boiled leg of mutton with capers, roast turkey, fried rabbit, brawn (a kind of preserved pork—see *P* 134), tarts, and mince pies. He finishes his list with "&c.," so one may safely assume that dessert and wine followed this gargantuan meal.

Few sources are as exhaustive as Woodforde's diary when it comes to food, but other documents of the time confirm his reports of small, private dinners versus large ones for company. The cookbooks of the time consistently offered suggestions for dishes to be served together in small family meals. Susannah Carter's *The Frugal Housewife* (1795) listed several bills of fare for August:

> *Ham* and *fowls* roasted, with gravy sauce: *beans.*
> *Or,*
> *Neck* of *venison*, with gravy and claret sauce: *fresh salmon*, with lobster sauce: *apple pie* hot and buttered.
> *Or,*
> *Beef a-la-mode*: *green pease*: *haddock* boiled, and fried *soals* or *flounders* to garnish the dish.

However, it was more common to provide extensive bills of fare, perhaps on the theory that housewives could manage to throw three or four dishes together without much assistance. *The French Family Cook* (1793) suggests, for a summer dinner for ten, roasted meat in the middle of the table, a "veal tourt," "a fowl between two plates," rabbit hash, and "sheeps tongues en papillotes" for the first course; a "dish of little cakes," chickens, a leveret, peas, cream à la Madeleine, a salad of lettuce, a salad of oranges for the second course; and peaches, cherries, plums, cream cheese, cakes, and mulberries for dessert. Sarah Harrison's *House-keeper's Pocketbook; And Compleat Family Cook* (1748) shows several diagrams indicating not only the dishes to be served but their placement on the table. A typical first-course arrangement shows soup at the top of the table, to be replaced midway through the course by stewed carp; chine of veal at the bottom of the table; salad in the middle; and beans and bacon on one side, fricassee on the other. For the second course, these dishes are replaced, respectively, by partridges or capons, rabbits or wild ducks, tarts, peas or veal sweetbreads, and "Fry'd Patties." On the sideboard, she has neat's tongue or sliced ham, prawns, butter, anchovies, and cheese.

The contrast between this latter type of meal, with its groaning sideboard, and a comparatively simple family dinner (*P&P* 61, 120) is borne out in Austen's brief descriptions. The Coles, true to their delight in showing off their new wealth, invite plenty of company and shower them with a multiplicity of dishes (*E* 88–89), exemplifying the role of dinner hosts. The Grants, too, throw generous dinners (*MP* 239), not so much from a sense of novelty and hospitality as from the demands of Dr. Grant's palate. Small dinners without company, by contrast, are given the briefest mention.

Dinner, even more than breakfast, was subject to fashionable delay, for postponing this meal advertised one's wealth; a later dinner, and the consequent extension of evening activities into the hours after dark, meant extra expenditure on candles. Only the lowliest workmen still ate dinner at noon, therefore, and among themselves, the gentry, aristocracy, tradesmen, and artisans kept tabs on each other to see who reigned supreme at staving off hunger. The difference of an hour or even half an hour was no trivial matter. Comparing the manners of the modest rectory at Steventon to those of her wealthy brother Edward's house in Kent, Jane

Temperance Enjoying a Frugal Meal, 1792. George III and Queen Charlotte eat hard-boiled eggs and salad. Courtesy of the Lewis Walpole Library, Yale University. 792.7.28.1.

wrote in 1798, "We dine now at half after Three, and have done dinner I suppose before you [her sister Cassandra, then visiting Edward] begin. . . . I am afraid you will despise us." Ten years later, she reported, "We never dine now till five."

Some of her characters betray the same awareness of dinner hours. The genteelly poor Elizabeth Watson, in Austen's unfinished novel *The Watsons*, has to apologize to the fashionable Lord Osborne when he makes a "morning" call at 2:55 P.M. (*Watsons, MW* 344) and finds the family's housemaid readying the table for dinner. "I am sorry it happens so," explains Elizabeth, "but you know what early hours we keep" (346).* *The Watsons*, perhaps because it examines the life of a family barely holding on to its gentry status, is the most concerned of all Austen's works with the timing of meals and the social consequences of this timing. The self-consciously trendy Tom Musgrave aspires to "an 8 o'clock

---

*The Watsons had their parallels in the real world. In 1789, novelist Horace Walpole wrote that his unfashionable four o'clock dinners were often interrupted by "morning" calls from acquaintances. Another fictional example occurs in the Juvenilia, where Lady Greville not only interrupts someone else's dinner but forces the unfortunate victim to stand at her coach door in wind and cold (*Col Let, MW* 158–159).

The Glutton, Thomas Rowlandson, 1813. This is a large dinner for one man, though it would have been considered perfectly appropriate for company. Soup and meat are being brought in from the kitchen, and a chicken, some vegetables, and some other little dishes, possibly "made dishes," are already on the table, along with cruets of oil and vinegar, a decanter, and a glass of wine. More wine is being poured into a glass at the sideboard, and several bottles are waiting in a wine cooler at the base of the table. Courtesy of the Lewis Walpole Library, Yale University. 813.0.13.

dinner" (355) and even implies that he might dine as late as nine (356), an absurdly late hour. When he accidentally lingers late enough for supper at the Watsons', he flees, though he has eaten nothing all evening, simply for the pleasure of "calling his next meal a Dinner" (359).

Musgrave is unusually silly about his mealtimes; most of Austen's characters eat, by early nineteenth-century standards, at a much more reasonable hour. The Dashwoods at Barton Cottage eat at 4:00 (*S&S* 74, 361), as do Catherine Morland, General Tilney, and Miss Tilney when they eat at Henry's Woodston parsonage (*NA* 214). Of course, both *Sense and Sensibility* and *Northanger Abbey* are early novels; as the years went by, the dinner hour crept farther and farther into evening. As evidence, Diana Parker, a character in the unfinished late novel *Sanditon*, eats at 6:00 (*Sand, MW* 411), though she is not satirized for any pretense to cutting-edge etiquette. Even within a single novel, however, there may be differences of dinnertime based on social stature, London or provincial residence, and adherence to London or rural manners when in the country. (London dinnertimes were generally later.) Henry Tilney, for example, may dine at four, but his richer and more ostentatious father dines at five (*NA* 162, 165).

Tea

Dinner ended with the withdrawal of any ladies to another room, while the gentlemen remained in the dining room to talk, drink, and smoke. Some eighteenth-century sideboards were even equipped with chamberpots so that the gentlemen could relieve themselves without having to exit the room. When they had finished discussing subjects deemed inappropriate or uninteresting to women—politics, financial matters, hunting, bawdy humor, and the like—they rejoined the ladies in the parlor or drawing room (*MP* 334–335), and here tea was served (*Col Let, MW* 150; *Evelyn, MW* 187, 189; *LS, MW* 269; *Watsons, MW* 354; *Sand, MW* 390–391, 413; *NA* 118; *S&S* 99; *P&P* 166, 344–345, 346; *MP* 104, 177; *E* 8, 124, 347, 382–383, 434).

Tea was, at this point, neither fully a meal nor simply the pouring of a beverage. Its components varied from household to household, but in the homes frequented by the Austens, it included not only tea but coffee as well. The women of the family prepared these beverages, and there was frequently some sort of food offered as well. At its simplest, this was bread and butter, which might take the form of some sort of roll or muffin, toast made in the kitchen, or slices of bread to be toasted at the drawing-room fire (*MP* 383). However, many families chose to provide more than bread. There might be cakes or other sweet offerings.

The time at which tea was served depended on when the family ate dinner. The correspondent who wrote to *The Gentleman's Magazine* about Herefordshire habits in 1819 noted that dinner among the gentry was served at 5:00 or 6:00 and tea at 8:00 to 10:00. The Austen family, when it dined at 3:30, served tea at 6:30, and the fictional Edwardses of Austen's incomplete novel *The Watsons* take their muffin and dish of tea at 7:00 (*Watsons, MW* 326).

Supper

Supper (*F&E, MW* 8–9; *J&A, MW* 23; *Col Let, MW* 167; *P&P* 84, 348; *MP* 267, 283, 376), too, was dependent on dinner for its schedule and even for its very existence. Supper as a formal meal, with hot dishes, the tablecloth laid, and everyone sitting around the table, was virtually nonexistent among the fashionable. Dinner had crept later and later, with teatime following about three hours afterward, and the result was that there was no time before bedtime to go through the full ritual that a sit-down meal demanded. Therefore, "supper," when it was eaten at all, became more of a hearty snack—in the words of *The Gentleman's Magazine* letter cited above, it was merely "a tray of cold meat, or a light thing hot." Some people, who took their dinner and tea especially late, eschewed supper altogether (*Watsons, MW* 351). Upon reflection, Austen herself realized that the Bennets should have been among those who skipped supper; class-conscious Mrs. Bennet, who routinely speaks of serving two-course dinners and who brags that her daughters are ignorant of the work of the kitchen, would probably have followed fashion in this respect, even if her sister Mrs. Philips still likes "a little bit of hot supper" (*P&P* 74). Resigned to her mistake, Jane sighed in a letter that "I suppose it was the remains of Mrs. Bennet's old Meryton habits." More likely, the slip was the result of the Austens' old habits. There are several references to suppers in Austen's letters—a supper of tart and jelly with Edward's wealthy benefactress and adoptive mother Mrs. Knight; another of widgeon, preserved ginger, and black butter served to guests; a third of toasted cheese, served to Jane in 1805 by Edward Bridges because it was her favorite supper food. Clearly, in this respect at least, Austen and some of her circle were content to be well fed and unfashionable.

However, at balls, where the participants might stay active until well after midnight, it was not only acceptable but even obligatory to serve a substantial supper (*S&S* 252; *E* 248, 254–256). Public balls, such as those at Bath's assembly rooms, often served tea (*NA* 21, 25, 59), while private balls tended to have more extensive refreshments. The latter might include cold or hot drinks, as the weather dictated, soup, sandwiches, or more complex dishes. For the guests who merely played cards, sat by the fire, or watched the dancers and gossiped, the supper was a convenience; for those who danced for hours with little intermission, it was a caloric necessity, hence Austen's famous, oft-quoted pronouncement that "[a] private dance, without sitting down to supper, was . . . an infamous fraud upon the rights of men and women" (*E* 254). However, this is not Austen's only word on the subject. Another reference, this time from *Sense and Sensibility*, makes clear that while food of some kind was a constant, its presentation was variable and depended on the preferences of the hosts and the requirements of fashion. A "mere sideboard collation" (*S&S* 171)—that is, a sort of buffet table, at least in its comparative level of informality—will do for the country, but not for London, where a sit-down meal with footmen in attendance is a necessity.

It should be understood, however, that fashion did not reign entirely supreme in the matter of suppers. While suppers at balls were almost universally fancier and more extensive than family suppers at home, the fact that the aristocracy and their imitators had nominally abandoned supper as a meal did not mean that the rest of the country necessarily followed the trend. Suppers in some form were still necessary for those who ate their dinner on the early side, and the dishes served at supper, though presented with less formality and often eaten cold, could, in many homes, rival the complexity of those served at dinners. Hartfield's supper of "minced chicken and scalloped oysters," gruel, wine, boiled eggs, custard, and wine (*E* 24–25) may be unfashionable, but it is not unique. Austen's Juvenilia provide a concrete example of a simple supper united with an implication that the gentry went in for something a little more lavish:

> "Was your Mother gone to bed before you left her?" said her Ladyship. . . .
> "She was just sitting down to supper, Ma'am."
> "And what had she got for Supper?" "I did not observe." "Bread & Cheese I suppose." "I should never wish for a better supper," said Ellen. "You have never any reason" replied her Mother, "as a better is always provided for you." (*Col Let*, *MW* 156–157)

Clearly, Ellen's supper is more akin to Hartfield's chicken and oysters than to Austen's own favorite toasted cheese.

Cookbooks of the time continued to provide bills of fare for suppers, and though dinner remained preeminent, supper was not forgotten by its adherents. Susannah Carter's *The Frugal Housewife, or Complete Woman Cook*

(1795) suggested, in its bills of fare, plans for suppers that sound rather like Hartfield's. One supper includes a "White fricassee of chickens," peas, roast duck, and gravy; another suggests roast chickens or pigeons, asparagus, and artichokes with melted butter. *The French Family Cook* (1793) offers pages of supper menus, including the following "Little Family Suppers of Four Articles":

Boiled Chickens. Cold Beef or Mutton Sliced. Pickles. Scolloped Oysters.

Boiled Tripe. Bologna Sausage sliced. Pat of Butter in a Glass. Hashed Hare.

Gudgeons fried. Biscuits. A Pat of Butter. Rasped Beef. Duck roasted.

Roasted Chickens. Potted Beef. Cheesecakes. Sausages, with Eggs poached.

Whitings broiled. Tongue sliced. Biscuits. Calf's Heart.

Veal Cutlet. Tart. Butter. Radishes. Asparagus.

The anonymous author's suppers increase in size; suppers of four articles are succeeded by those of five, seven, nine, and so on. One of the suggestions for a supper of eleven items is buttered lobster, peas, lemon custard, scalloped oysters, cold chicken, roasted sweetbreads, sliced ham, artichokes, two ducklings, raspberry cream in cups, jellies, and a preserved green orange in the middle of the table. It is had to conceive of this meal fitting on a single tray and harder still to imagine the one seventeen-item menu doing so; one supposes that these suppers were for balls and other special occasions. Sarah Harrison's menus, in the midcentury *House-keeper's Pocketbook; And Compleat Family Cook*, are far simpler. She offers a supper of poultry, potted venison, lobster or crab in the shell, and tarts or cheesecakes, to be replaced at the end of the meal by a selection of fruit.

January Bill of Fare, from Francis Collingwood's *The Universal Cook, and City and Country Housekeeper*, 1801. Soups are at the top and bottom of the first course, indicated by closed tureens. In the second, as was traditional, sweet dishes such as jellies and fruit desserts are served side-by-side with roast meats and vegetables. Library of Congress.

Meat

The constant in all these menus is meat (*Sand, MW* 393; *P&P* 169, 268, 331; *NA* 190, 214; *E* 355, 365; *P* 39), for meat formed the centerpiece of almost every meal. One could get by without it for tea, sometimes for breakfast, and on the occasional solemn religious holiday, but for the Georgians, it just wasn't dinner or supper unless the table held a haunch of something, a small flock of birds, or something's steaming head. Meat equaled food, so much so that "to take one's mutton" was an idiomatic way of saying "to eat" (*NA* 209, *MP* 215, 406). Roast beef (*Lesley, MW* 112–113) in particular was wrapped up with the national identity, celebrated in song and pictorial art as the source of British strength and the evidence of British virtue. (A sirloin of beef dances prominently next to John Bull in the illustration *John Bull and His Friends Commemorating the Peace* [Napoleonic Wars].) It was perceived as simple, straightforward, copious, and lifegiving, as opposed to the Frenchman's little bits of things—frogs and snails and pretentious sauces—that, according to the propaganda of the day, left him dangerously lean and jealous of the fat and jolly Englishman. Even those who could not afford to eat meat very often lauded the Roast Beef of Old England.

Cookbooks of Austen's day, as well as contemporary diaries and letters, reveal the variety of meat consumed. Far more mutton and game (*S&S* 30), for example, was eaten then than is eaten today. A modern cook would expect to see headings for chicken (*Lesley, MW* 114; *S&S* 33; *P&P* 100; *E* 24), turkey (*Visit, MW* 54; *Lesley, MW* 119; *Watsons, MW* 353–354; *MP* 212, 215–216; *E* 483), duck (*Beaut Desc, MW* 72; *Scraps, MW* 173; *P&P* 331), and perhaps even goose (*MP* 215–216, *E* 28–29), but a turn-of-the-nineteenth-century housekeeper would also require recipes for partridge (*F&E, MW* 8–9; *Scraps, MW* 173–174; *Watsons, MW* 344; *P&P* 342), pigeon (*F&E, MW* 8–9; *Lesley, MW* 119, 129; *E* 353), pheasant (*F&E, MW* 8–9; *MP* 104, 105, 171), quail, larks, woodcocks, snipe, and other game birds. Furthermore, cooks drew distinctions that we are less likely to make today: recipes often differed based on whether a duck was wild or domestic and, if wild, to what species it belonged. Even among domestic birds, there were divisions, such as that between a "stubble" goose—old enough to have lived through a harvest and fed off the scythe-cut grainfields (and traditionally eaten in late September, around Michaelmas)—and a "green" goose (*MP* 111), eaten in May, whose name came not from its color but from its youth. Hens, too, were differentiated by age; a "chicken" was technically a hen too young to lay eggs, while a "pullet" (*Lesley, MW* 129) laid eggs but had not yet moulted, and a "fowl" (*Lesley, MW* 113–114; *Watsons, MW* 346; *S&S* 160) was a fully adult hen that had undergone at least one moult. Then there were hares (*Sand, MW* 412), rabbits, and leverets (hares under a year old—see *F&E, MW* 8–9), as well as venison (*Evelyn, MW* 182; *NA* 210; *P&P* 342; *MP* 52). Frequently, several of these types of meat would appear on the table in a single meal.

Nor did variety derive only from the types of animals eaten. It also came from the parts of the animals that made their way onto platters. Few parts of the cow, for instance, went to waste. Diners feasted not only on steaks

(*MP* 379), rumps, and sirloins (*Lesley, MW* 113) but on tongues (*Lesley, MW* 119), udders, necks, ribs, feet (*Visit, MW* 53), sweetbreads (the thymus glands of calves—see *E* 329), hearts, "lights" (testicles), tripe (stomach lining—see *Visit, MW* 53), and even whole heads. Even the bones were not neglected; their marrow went into soups and sauces.

Methods of preparation included roasting (*Lesley, MW* 112–113; *Watsons, MW* 353–354; *E* 172), boiling (*S&S* 160; *E* 177), baking, stewing (*Lesley, MW* 112–113), braising, frying (*Watsons, MW* 341; *E* 172), and grilling, then referred to as "broiling" (*Lesley, MW* 113). In many cases, the meat was boiled or roasted, and its drippings—sometimes referred to as its "gravy"—were combined with mild spices and broth or wine to make a sauce. Common accompaniments to beef (*Lesley, MW* 128; *Scraps, MW* 173) included mustard, horseradish, sauces based on anchovies or oysters, butter, and sauces flavored with onions (*Visit, MW* 53) or a related vegetable such as shallots or leeks. Veal (*Lesley, MW* 121; *S&S* 160; *NA* 68) often appeared in the form of "collops"—small, thin slices—with some sort of accompanying sauce. Both beef and veal might be "forced," which meant being stuffed with some sort of seasoning or with forcemeat, a sausagelike mixture. Both might be layered with other types of meat or forcemeat and then rolled, tied, and cooked.

Leftover meat did not go to waste. Some of it went immediately to the servants' table for their consumption. The remainder was saved and served up again at supper or breakfast, where it might appear cold (*NA* 214), sliced

How to carve a fowl, hare, or goose, from Charles Millington's *The Housekeeper's Domestic Library; or, New Universal Family Instructor*, 1805. Carving was an essential masculine skill; one had to divide the animal into approximately equal parts while accommodating everyone's individual preferences, just as today, but one also had to do it with grace and equanimity, keeping up a flow of genial conversation at the same time. Note the standard presentation of the hare: the jawbones have been taken out and struck through the mouth so that they protrude from the eye sockets. Library of Congress.

and used in sandwiches, or chopped up and reused in a "made dish." Made dishes were more complex than the standard roasted or boiled joint. They used sauces, vegetable ingredients, and interesting methods of presentation to overcome the fact that the meat—the real focus of the dish—was not being eaten in its impressive original form. Made dishes included various kinds of minced, hashed (*MP* 413), rolled, spiced, and sauced meats, as well as meat incorporated into pies (*P&P* 44; *P* 134) and patties. Some made dishes were served hot; others, at room temperature.

In homes attached to farms, where an entire animal would have to be killed in order to supply meat for the household, it was essential to preserve some of the meat for later use. Hannah Glasse's directions for some recipes involve hanging or soaking a joint of meat for several days, even weeks at a time, thus extending the total life of the carcass. Some pieces would be prepared for immediate use on the table, while others would be hung or soaked, and still others would be dried, salted, smoked, potted, or pickled for use in the far-distant future. Potting meat, for example, involved chopping it up into small bits, mixing it with butter, and sealing it into a pot with a cap of clarified butter. Pork (*E* 172, 173, 175, 177), one of the cheapest meats (and thus sometimes less esteemed than beef, venison, and other expensive varieties), kept extremely well when cured into ham (*Lesley*, *MW* 114; *S&S* 33; *P&P* 100) or bacon; Mrs. Austen, on one occasion, cured six hams at Southampton to be sent to sea with her son Frank, a naval officer.* On another occasion, in January 1799, she ordered an entire pig to be killed and cured as shipboard provisions for her other sailor son, Charles.

Making a ham involved several steps. The first was severing the correct section of the leg from the pig. Then this leg was placed in a salting-pan (*E* 173) in a mixture of salt, spices, and saltpeter (potassium nitrate). Sometimes the salt mixture was used as a dry rub, and sometimes it was dissolved in wine or water to make a strong brine. This salting step was essential, as it drew blood out of the ham and allowed bacteria to interact with the saltpeter to complete the curing process. Salting (*E* 172) generally lasted for about ten days to two weeks. Then the ham was hung in a smokehouse and exposed to a small, steady fire for a fixed period of time; one modern recipe uses a rule of two days per pound for hams over ten pounds.

However, even with multiple methods of preservation, many types of meat remained seasonal. For example, while mutton (*L&F*, *MW* 100; *Lesley*, *MW* 113; *S&S* 197; *MP* 215–216; *E* 109, 119, 168), in a wool-producing nation, remained available year-round, the nature of the sheep's reproductive cycle, with a predictable lambing season, meant that lamb (*E* 353) was a seasonal food. The young, tender lambs who were still nursing rich milk from grass-fed ewes were known as "grass lambs" and were available from April to September. A few of these lambs were then kept in pens over the winter and were slaughtered as slightly tougher "house lamb" from November to March.

Two of Austen's references to meat deserve special clarification. The first is a request for "fried Cowheel & Onion" in her play fragment *The Visit* (*MW* 53). Cowheel turns out to be a nearly impossible dish to find in

---

*We think of ham today as being exclusively a pork product, but hams were also made from beef, veal, and venison.

cookbooks of Austen's era, though dishes that sound somewhat similar are easy to come by. Veal knuckles are fairly common, and many of the recipes for veal knuckles include onions. However, Austen's terminology implies that we are in search of a foot, or part of a foot, rather than a joint of some kind. The OED defines cowheel as "The foot of a cow or ox stewed so as to form a jelly," or a dish made from this jelly, but this presents the food historian with a few difficulties. The first, Austen's union of gelatin and onions, is not quite as bizarre as it seems; savory jellies were an old tradition in English cooking, and though they were being superseded in popularity by sweet jellies, it is not necessarily out of the question to unite jelly and onions in a single dish. However, Austen specifically refers to the cowheel as "fried," and fried gelatin is indeed hard to imagine. Furthermore, jellies are almost always referred to as being made from calves' feet, not those of cows or oxen. More importantly, the concept of fried gelatin is simply not present in the cookbooks of Austen's day. Therefore, she must have meant something else.

One has to return to much earlier cookbooks to find the dish Austen intends, with the name she gives it. A recipe for "Cow-Heel" appears in Richard Bradley's *Country Housewife and Lady's Director* (1736), and a somewhat altered recipe, under the name "Fried Ox Feet," resurfaces in John Farley's *London Art of Cookery* (1783). Both versions meet Austen's requirements. They use the feet of adult cattle, rather than calves; they are fried; and they include onions. By Austen's time, this dish was considered humble fare; in fact, much of the humor in this part of *The Visit* comes from the rustic dishes being served at a genteel dinner.

The second dish requiring clarification is "Liver & Crow" (*Visit, MW* 53), which appears in the same scene. This dish presents us with some difficulties, for none of the major cookbook authors of the later eighteenth century seem to have included a recipe for it. Indeed, since they frequently plagiarize from one another, adding a handful of original recipes to enliven a new cookbook and slightly rewording hundreds of others culled from competitive cookbooks, the researcher encounters the same frustratingly similar description over and over. Hannah Glasse writes of bacon hogs, "The liver and crow is much admired fried with bacon; the feet and ears are both equally good soused." Charles Millington and John Farley phrase it in precisely the same words. Clearly, liver and crow was a well-known dish to Austen's contemporaries, so well known that an explanation of its preparation seemed unnecessary.

In order to find a full recipe for the dish, we need to go back to the mid-eighteenth century, to William Ellis' *The Country Housewife's Family Companion* (1750). This volume is only in part a cookbook; in many other respects it is a complete guide to being a farm wife, with extensive sections on keeping the dairy and curing cattle of disease, caring for poultry (*P&P* 222), processing wheat and storing flour, and doctoring the family and servants. There is an explicit emphasis on frugality, and many of the recipes are specifically identified as being for "poor people," while only one is directed at "the gentry." French names for styles of preparation, always an indicator of fashion, are absent, but perhaps the strongest evidence that this was a cookbook for the working classes was the almost total reliance on pork as meat. There are plenty of directions for preparing bacon, brawn, and pig's innards, but only a handful of recipes for beef and mutton, and the references to beef are entirely about using calf guts. The presence of not one but two recipes for liver and crow in this volume confirms that the dishes in *The Visit* were deliberately chosen for their incongruity on a genteel table.

The liver in question was a pig's liver; the "crow" was its intestines or its mesentery (a piece of tissue adjacent to the stomach and intestines). According to Ellis, both pieces, along with the sweetbread (thymus gland), were "the first meat we dress of a hog, for this sort is fit for frying as soon as it is cut out." All three pieces were cut into 2- or 3-inch squares and fried in the fat that melted from the crow, then served with mustard. Ellis also presents a somewhat more complex method as an alternative:

> A second way to fry liver and crow is, to cut the liver into short thick pieces, because being short and thick they will fry the tenderer, but the sweet-bread and crow rather long ways, about the same bigness; then soak the pieces of liver first in scalding water, and while this is doing, make a composition with eggs, water, flower, salt, shred sage, pepper, and grated bread; in which dip all the pieces of meat, and fry them in lard or butter, over a quick fire. For sauce, melt butter, and mix it with sugar and mustard.

In other words, the pieces were chopped slightly differently than in the first recipe and then batter-fried in lard or butter. Either method of preparation was quick and used few ingredients, resulting in just the sort of meal a woman might cook after she had spent a tiring day helping to slaughter a bacon hog.

Seafood

As an island nation, Britain had plenty of access to good fish (*L&F, MW* 79; *P&P* 61; *E* 14). Improving transportation times meant that saltwater fish could maintain their freshness farther and farther inland, much to the delight of the populace. This meant, however, that stewponds (*S&S* 197; *E* 361), where the gentry had bred freshwater fish, fell somewhat out of favor, as it was believed that freshwater fish had a less pleasant taste than ocean varieties. (However, when Mrs. Austen visited Stoneleigh in 1806, she noted that the magnificent estates had, among its other attractions, ponds that produced excellent fish.) Of course, fish could always be salted, in which case perishability was less of a concern, but salt fish were even less desirable than fish from stewponds.

While the variety of game consumed in the eighteenth century might be surprising to modern home cooks, the variety of fish is a little less so, if only because we usually have access to so many kinds of fish in our supermarkets. Hannah Glasse, who tends to be fairly comprehensive on such matters, lists recipes for turbot, carp, tench, cod (*S&S* 160), mackerel, weavers, salmon (*S&S* 160), herring (*Visit, MW* 53), water-sokey, eels, lampreys, pike, haddock, sturgeon, skate, sole, crab, lobster, prawns, shrimp, crayfish, oysters, mussels, scallops, smelts, white-bait, and miscellaneous small and flat fish. John Farley and Elizabeth Raffald follow her lead, though Farley lists trout among his fish.

Seafood was also used frequently in sauces and stuffings. Oysters (*Watsons, MW* 335, 336; *E* 24) often form the basis of "forcemeat" (meat stuffing), sausages, and sauces, while anchovies in small quantities are added to sauces for their intense flavor. Poultry and fish were the dishes most likely to be garnished with seafood-based sauces.

Oysters were beloved in other contexts as well. London cookshops sold cheap oysters to the working classes, just as later in the nineteenth century oysters would be sold by street vendors as a snack. Oddly, during the eighteenth century, it was fashionable to buy green oysters. The oysters of certain Essex rivers developed coatings of algae around September, and when their odd appearance became appealing to diners, oystermen began "breeding" green oysters by catching regular oysters and steeping them in salt marshes for a few weeks until they acquired a dark green tint to their shells. Less reputable dealers saved time and trouble by dyeing the oysters with copperas or other poisonous green dyes.

Dairy and Eggs

In most homes, gentry and working-class alike, women had charge of the dairy (*P&P* 163; *MP* 104) and the poultry-yard (*P&P* 163; *MP* 104). Here, their tasks included milking, cheese making, butter making, feeding chickens or other fowls, and gathering eggs. However, for those women who bought their cheese, eggs, and butter at market, it was important to be a careful shopper. Cheese might be infested with worms, mites, or maggots, and housewives were cautioned to make sure the entire rind of the cheese was intact, "for, though the hole in the coat may be but small, the perished part within maybe considerable." The freshness of eggs (*Clifford, MW* 43; *MP* 31, 104–105, 106, 282; *E* 24) was to be judged by their temperature, by holding them up to a candle to see if the yolk appeared solid and the white clear, or by placing them in cold water, where John Farley assured his readers that an "addled or rotten" egg would float. Eggs could be stored for a while in bran, straw, hay, sawdust, ashes, or salt, but Farley advised that "the sooner an egg is used, the better it will be."

It was always preferable to produce dairy products at home, where their quality could be strictly controlled. Milk (*P* 135), in particular, was valued when it came straight from the cow. However, the milk sold in towns was especially notorious. Watered down, thin and blue (*MP* 439), often contaminated by germs, it was avoided by anyone who had a choice. Mrs. Austen, who had had a small herd of dairy cows at Steventon, no doubt missed them after the family moved to Bath, and then on to Southampton and Chawton. At Chawton, Cassandra lamented, "We have not now so much as a cow."

Most of the milk consumed in the eighteenth century was cows' milk. Earlier centuries had relied to some extent on the milk of goats and sheep, but this dependence seems to have waned by Austen's day. However, the milk of asses was a delicacy treasured by invalids, who found it easier to digest than cows' milk (*Sand, MW* 393, 401). It is worth remembering that pasturage for dairy cows was less consistent than today, and the unfortunate dairymaid might discover, upon milking, that her cows had been eating cabbage, turnips, or certain wild plants, which would give the milk a bad odor.

Many cookbooks offered suggestions about the proper running of a dairy. Charles Millington, in *The Housekeeper's Domestic Library* (1805), provides extensive instructions. According to him, churning was to be done early in the morning, when cool weather would help the butter solidify; this phenomenon could be assisted by keeping a pump churn partially submerged in cold water. When the butter (*Sand, MW* 417; *MP* 31, 383; *E* 89, 168) had formed, it was removed from the churn with the hands and kneaded in cold water. A knife was drawn through it at every possible angle to draw out dirt or hair that might have blown into the milk pans. Finally, the butter was salted and either made into decorative shapes or simply packed into containers. Earthenware pots or wooden casks were preferred in most dairies, and partially filled containers would be layered with salt and filled up the next time butter was made.

Milk for drinking was taken from the pans after the cream had been skimmed off to make butter. The buttermilk that remained in the churn after the butter was made was also drunk as a beverage. Alternatively, the whole or skim milk could be processed with rennet and made into cheese. The rennet was derived from a calf's stomach-bag, pickled in brine or salted, dried, and used a piece at a time as needed. A section of the bag would be boiled to yield the rennet.

Cheese (*Col Let, MW* 156–157) made in the summer, when cows were pastured on fresh grass, was the richest of all. Full of milk fat, it had a yellow hue, and accordingly, housewives shopping for cheese looked for the golden tinge. It did not take cheese makers long to learn how to simulate the appearance of summer cheese; they simply added saffron, annatto, or marigold petals to the mixture. Their deception lives on in the artificial coloring applied to many cheeses, including much cheddar. The same trick was applied to butter sold at markets and in chandlers' shops, using marigold petals or carrot juice as a food coloring.

Domestic cheeses included Stilton (*E* 89), Cheshire, Warwickshire, Gloucester, double Gloucester, north Wiltshire (*E* 89), and Cheddar; imported cheeses, which were more expensive and had to be purchased from grocers and other specialty food dealers, were led in popularity by Parmesan. The cream cheeses mentioned so often by Austen (*Lesley*, *MW* 129; *MP* 104, 105) were then, as now, soft, young cheeses that only took a week or two to cure. Cheese was always well liked at all levels of society, and everyone who could afford to buy it ate it. People of all classes enjoyed toasted cheese (*Beaut Desc*, *MW* 72; *MP* 387), a piece of toast topped with shredded cheese, or a mixture of cheese, wine, mustard, and spices, that was browned before the fire or with a tool called a salamander.

Vegetables and Fruit

Vegetables (*Sand*, *MW* 380) in general were far less popular in Austen's day than they are now. To some extent, this was the result of seasonal availability. Not all vegetables could be preserved beyond their natural season, and most were far less palatable in their preserved state than when fresh. To some extent, the blame lay with the tendency of the English, noted by foreign observers, to overcook their vegetables and to smother them in butter sauce. Primarily, the relative absence of vegetables in the diet was due to the primitive understanding of medicine and diet. No one even knew what a vitamin was, let alone where it might be found or what its impact on health might be. Novelist Frances Burney D'Arblay and her husband were unusual in being "people who make it a rule to owe a third of their sustenance to the Garden."

This is not to say that vegetables were not eaten, merely that they were overwhelmed in quantity by the vast piles of meat consumed on the average upper-class or middle-class table. Vegetables—though they were more commonly referred to at the time as "potherbs" or "garden stuff" (*Sand*, *MW* 380; *S&S* 30)—appeared on their own as side dishes or as accompaniments to meat or eggs. Almost every country home had a kitchen garden, which in the case of large estates might run to several acres. Jane's mother was an avid gardener well into her old age and grew not only flowers but also herbs, fruit, potatoes, peas, and other vegetables. She had a fascination for new plants, judging from the fact that at Steventon she was considered trendy for growing potatoes (*MP* 54), and at Chawton, in 1813, she grew tomatoes for eating long before they were considered edible by most of the rest of the nation.

Parson Woodforde's diary confirms that the full variety of vegetables was available only for part of the year. The majority of his references to eating vegetables are in the spring and summer, particular June to August, while his references to eating vegetables out of those seasons are to the sorts of vegetables that "kept" well for long periods of time. In the spring and summer, he ate green peas, artichokes, beans, asparagus (*E* 329), morels, truffles, stewed mushrooms, radishes, cucumbers, and new potatoes. In the fall and winter he was confined to root vegetables like onions (*Visit*, *MW* 53) and turnips that could be stored in a cool place and to items like olives (*S&S* 193) and peas that could be pickled or dried.

Storage methods varied according to the vegetable in question. Parsnips (*E* 172), for example, could simply be left in the ground over the winter, where their starch would convert to sugar as they froze. Potatoes, carrots (*E* 172), and turnips (*E* 100, 172) could be stored in a cool, dark room such as a cellar. Cookbook author Charles Millington advised keeping beans in jars, alternating layers of beans and salt; peas, he said, should be boiled in salt water and dried. Mushrooms, according to Elizabeth Raffald and others, should be steeped in salt for a while, then drained, baked in an oven at very low temperature, then sealed in jars with the liquid that was yielded by the baking, capped with a layer of suet. Beet root (*E* 89) was sometimes served fresh, but it also lent itself well to pickling; the roots were sliced and often cut into decorative shapes before pickling.

Methods of preparation varied as well; boiling, stewing, broiling, frying, and pickling seem to have been the most common. Peas were usually boiled, sometimes in combination with lettuce. Spinach was often served with eggs, while cucumbers (*L&F*, *MW* 100; *P&P* 219), whose shape and firmness lent them to being filled, were often hollowed out and packed with meat or vegetable stuffings. They were also eaten raw or pickled and might, odd as it sounds to modern ears, be given as gifts. Austen writes of the appropriateness of a cucumber as a gift in May 1801, noting that such a vegetable was worth a shilling, and Parson Woodforde writes of visiting a friend in May 1784, with "a Cucumber in my Pocket" as a present. Salads (*P&P* 219), like cucumbers, might be served raw or cooked; they might be composed of fresh lettuces or of any boiled and cooled vegetable, served with a light sauce as a dressing.

Some vegetables were prepared in ways that seem especially alien today. Celery (*E* 89), for example, which is today used primarily as a flavoring in stuffings and stocks or as a raw vegetable dipped in dressing or mixed into salad, was then cooked in a variety of ways. It might be stewed, batter-fried, or served in a thick sauce as a ragout. Cabbage (*Sand*, *MW* 380; *E* 354) was often boiled as a whole head and served in one gigantic lump, sometimes with interior hollowed out and filled with forcemeat, or with forcemeat layered in between the leaves.

Though the English were not wild about vegetables, they were quite enthusiastic about fruit (*Evelyn*, *MW* 182; *Sand*, *MW* 380; *S&S* 30). The cultivation of orchards had been a hobby of the well-to-do for centuries, and landowners took pride in locating and nurturing the best varieties.

Parson Woodforde was at least as delighted with his Anson apricot as Mrs. Norris was with her husband's Moor Park (*MP* 54).* The ingredients of desserts tended to reflect this pride. Fruit-based confections were quite popular, as was unadorned seasonal fruit and fruit that had been preserved in some way. Fruit found its way into puddings, cakes, jams, marmalades, jellies, dumplings, fritters, wines, pies, tarts, creams, and distilled waters. Preserving (*MP* 54–55), drying, and pickling kept many fruits available (in some form at least) year-round.

Fruit tended to be eaten after meat and its accompaniments. If there was only one course at dinner, the fruit tarts (*Scraps*, *MW* 173; *MP* 13, 54–55; *E* 24–25, 239) or other fruit dish would be placed on the table at the same time as the other food, but if there were a second course, the tarts and such would usually make their appearance then. Dessert was composed mostly of "finger foods" and often had a fruit component, usually something like raisins, other dried fruit (*S&S* 194), or fresh fruit that could be eaten easily without silverware.

Parson Woodforde, once again, provides us with a window into what the gentry actually ate, confirming much of what was printed in contemporary cookbooks. His diaries record fruit as part of pastries and jellies, fruit in sauces to accompany meat, and fruit eaten on its own, almost always as part of a dessert course after dinner. On various days between 1780 and 1795, he ate "Currant Jelly Sauce" as an accompaniment to roast swan; a "Damson Cheese," which was a kind of fruit jelly made with damsons and sugar; applesauce as an accompaniment to pork; apple, currant, gooseberry, raspberry, and grape tarts; apple fritters; strawberry and raspberry creams; apple and raspberry puffs; baked apples; brandied cherries; apple, apricot, and gooseberry pies; and apricot dumplings. Fruit he ate by itself included raisins, pippins, oranges, apricots, strawberries (*E* 354–355, 358–359, 368), black grapes, plums, mulberries, melons, currants (*E* 359), cherries (*E* 359), "Peaches, Nectarines and Grapes"—the last grouping identical in kind, and almost identical in wording, to the assortment of fruit served at Pemberley (*P&P* 268). Contemporary cookbooks also list recipes for desserts based on pears, peaches, pineapples, lemons, mangoes, cranberries, quinces, citrons, barberries, and blackberries.

The more exotic the fruit or the more prized the variety of tree, the more it advertised the wealth and status of its owner. Certain kinds of fruit required special care, and this was especially true of pineapples. A tropical fruit, the pineapple was transplanted to England, where it could grow and produce fruit only in hothouses called pineries (*NA* 178). The plants took a long time to mature, and the care and cost that went into nurturing

*In fact, according to R. W. Chapman's notes to *Mansfield Park*, these were actually the same variety of tree, which was also called Temple's apricot or Dunmore's Breda.

made them a living status symbol. To offer one's guests such a valuable treat was the ultimate gesture of welcome, and the pineapple became a symbol of hospitality. It can still be seen as a motif on everything from cookware to textiles today, where it retains the same meaning, though the symbolism is less widely recognized.

The fruit dish that receives the most attention in Austen's works is the baked apple (*E* 236–238, 240, 328–329), which surfaces repeatedly in *Emma*. Baked apples could be made fairly rapidly in a "quick oven" or in slow stages in an oven that was cooling after being used for other purposes. The Bateses, who are too poor to own an oven of their own, send their apples (and, no doubt, their bread as well) to be baked by the local baker, Mrs. Wallis, who probably charges them a small fee to use her oven. Since the apples are cooked as the oven is cooling, it takes two to three sessions to get them soft enough; Mr. Woodhouse, always careful of his digestion, prefers them cooked three times.

Another apple dessert was the apple dumpling (*E* 237), which was either a very small, cored apple or a segment of a larger apple, wrapped in puff pastry and then wrapped in cloth and boiled. Sometimes, when the cored whole apples were used, the center was filled with marmalade (*S&S* 121). Apples were also made into puddings, pies, and fritters; they were preserved, pickled, roasted, and stewed. Part of the reason for the apple's popularity was that, like root vegetables, it kept well. Apples could be harvested in the fall and laid out in some cool, dry place—often a garret or attic—so that they did not touch each other. With luck, they could be stored (*E* 245) this way for several months, and since they were being used in tarts and pies rather than being eaten fresh, their gradual deterioration of texture was less noticeable.

Bread and Porridge

Since potatoes were not yet a principal part of the English diet, and rice was consumed only rarely, most of the starch on the table came from wheat flour in the form of breads (*Col Let, MW* 157; *MP* 7; *E* 165), puddings, pancakes, and fritters. That it was wheat flour and, whenever possible, *white* flour was a relatively new development in English history. For centuries, white bread had been a delicacy enjoyed only by the upper class, with humbler levels of society dining on fine whole wheat bread, coarse whole wheat bread, bread made of mixed wheat and rye flours, or, at the very bottom of the economic scale, bread made of barley or of barley and peas. However, by Austen's time, the working class had lost its "*rye teeth*," in the words of a description of Nottinghamshire laborers in 1796. A correspondent to *The Gentleman's Magazine* wrote much the same thing of the Herefordshire peasantry in 1819: "Barley bread they do not eat." A large loaf of white bread was considered the right of every man, woman, and child, and people grew extremely cranky when they were forced by necessity to eat anything else, as they were at times during the shortages caused by the Napoleonic Wars.

They did not always bake it themselves. Not all homes had bread ovens, which used expensive wood as fuel. People without an oven either bought ready-made bread from a baker or else made up their loaves at home and took them to the baker to be baked. Making up one's own loaves was time-consuming, but at least it allowed control over the ingredients. Bakers were frequently accused of whitening their bread with additives, chiefly alum. Some bakers also added potatoes to their dough, Accum said: "I have witness that five bushels of flour, three ounces of alum, six pounds of salt, one bushel of potatoes boiled into a stiff paste, and three quarts of yeast, with the requisite quantity of water, produce a white, light, and highly palatable bread." He acknowledged that there was nothing harmful in this practice, but he was miffed that bakers did not pass their savings along to the customers in the form of lower prices. He was more indignant about bakers who used carbonate of magnesia, gypsum, chalk, and even pipe clay in their bread—all without telling the customers what the loaf contained. Accum was ahead of his time; legislation against adulterants in bread would not be passed until 1872.

Those who had an oven of their own, of course, could save money and be sure of the quality of their bread by making it themselves. Baking, because it was so labor-intensive, tended to be concentrated into as few days as possible. An entire household's bread for the week, for example, would be baked in just one day. William Cobbett, in *Cottage Economy* (1821), was unsympathetic about the work involved and railed, "How wasteful, and indeed how shameful for a labourer's wife to go to the baker's shop; and how negligent, how criminally careless of the welfare of his family must the labourer be who permits so scandalous a use of the proceeds of his labour!"

Whether store-bought or homemade, however, bread truly was the foundation of the meal. Many people could not afford to eat meat on a daily basis, but a family was considered truly destitute if it could not buy bread. People ate bread and butter (*MP* 383, 439; *E* 168), buttered toast (*L&F*, *MW* 106; *Sand*, *MW* 416, 417; *MP* 383), and rolls for breakfast; for luncheon they often ate sandwiches (*Evelyn*, *MW* 182; *MP* 65; *E* 254), named for John Montagu, fourth earl of Sandwich, who invented that handy snack in about 1760; for dinner there were starchy meat puddings and sweet fruit puddings, both of which had flour as a chief ingredient; for tea there was more bread or toast or possibly muffins (*Watsons*, *MW* 326–327; *P&P* 76; *E* 170; *P* 135), the bread known today in America as "English muffins" and in England as "crumpets"; and for supper there might be more bread and butter, or bread and cheese, or porridge (*P&P* 24) or gruel (*E* 24, 100, 104–105, 133), a boiled dish made from various types of grain, of varying thickness, and sometimes incorporating spices, fruit, or wine. Another type of porridge suitable for suppertime was made from arrowroot (*E* 391, 403). Arrowroot is a starch derived from the tubers of *Maranta arundinacea*; similar starches can be extracted from other members of the genus *Maranta*. Along with its close relatives, sago, salop, and tapioca, arrowroot was considered an appropriate, nourishing food for invalids, so Emma naturally offers some to the ill and weak Jane Fairfax. It also makes sense that Hartfield would have plenty of arrowroot on hand, since Mr. Woodhouse's digestive system is so sensitive.

At every meal, the quality and quantity of the bread would vary depending on the means of the family. The comfortably well off ate good-quality white bread at each of these meals, and the wealthy might substitute French bread (*NA* 241)—not a baguette but a rich bread made with milk, butter, and eggs—which was substantially more expensive to make. Most people could afford to treat themselves to a smaller, similar kind of bread—buns (*MP* 413)—which also had a rich eggy dough and incorporated caraway comfits, caraway seeds dipped repeatedly in boiling sugar to turn them into candy. Some people also ate a somewhat exotic starchy food—"Maccaroni"—which had been popularized in England by young men returning from the Italian portions of the Grand Tour.*

Pastries and Sweets

Consumption of pastry and confectionery increased substantially during the eighteenth and early nineteenth centuries. It was, after all, the first age in which sugar was abundantly available in Europe, thanks to rapidly multiplying colonies in the West Indies. It was also an age without widespread refrigeration—only the wealthiest people and commercial enterprises such as pastry shops (*NA* 44) could afford to keep icehouses for making chilled desserts. Both these influences had their effect on sweet dishes.

The relative novelty of large quantities of sugar made it the principal flavoring in many dishes. Jellies (*Lesley, MW* 119; *Evelyn, MW* 182; *MP* 283), for example, which were thickened with isinglass, hartshorn, or calves' foot gelatin, often had little flavoring, because the beauty of the apparently frozen liquid was half the fun, and anything sweet was the other half. Cookbooks instructed readers in constructing gelatin models of moons, stars, fishponds, islands, and temples, using specially designed molds and

*Some of these aristocratic young men, in the mid-eighteenth century, formed a club called the Macaroni Club, in which they met to reminisce about the Italian journeys and to calculate how best to shock their parents and the public at large. They adopted outrageous fashions designed to draw comment and succeeded admirably. They and their imitators were satirized and lionized in numerous series of prints, and "Macaroni" became a term for someone who was self-consciously fashionable or truly cutting-edge. This is the reason that the song "Yankee Doodle" contains that odd, apparently nonsensical reference to macaroni. The song was originally sung by British soldiers to taunt the Americans; you are such bumpkins, the message ran, that you stick a stupid feather in your hats and think *that's* fashion.

filling them with appropriate colors of "jelly." The lack of refrigeration meant that puddings, custards (*E* 25), cakes, tarts, and biscuits dominated the national sweet tooth. Ices (in other words, ice cream—see *Cass, MW* 45; *Evelyn, MW* 182; *NA* 116; *E* 290), jellies, and other desserts that needed to be cooled were consumed at the homes of the rich, at specialized shops, or during cold weather, when nature could be enlisted as *sous chef*.

Terminology is also somewhat surprising to the modern cook, especially to American cooks who are often unfamiliar with present-day British usage. "Pudding" in America means a specific kind of dessert, a thick, creamy substance in various flavors. In Britain, it can simply mean "dessert" in any shape and form. In Austen's time, it meant neither of these things. Pudding (*MP* 413; *E* 109) was a specific kind of dish that was by no means always a dessert. It might be a floury confection with fruit and suet (*Visit, MW* 53), tied in a pudding bag and boiled; a meaty center surrounded by pastry, tied in the same bag and boiled; or a custardy mass baked in the dripping tray below a joint of roasting meat. There were lemon puddings and almond puddings, chestnut puddings and carrot puddings, spinach puddings and rabbit puddings. The starch in them most often came from flour, but there were also oat, millet, and barley puddings. Savory puddings were often served with the meat in the first course, while sweet puddings followed in the second course.

"Biscuits" (*MP* 413; *E* 329) in Austen's time were also not quite what might be expected. Biscuits, to current-day Americans, are flaky, not-at-all-sweet breads the size of dinner rolls. In Britain, they are cookies. To Austen, they were small baked treats that usually contained flour, sugar, and eggs, but rarely butter. They might even be as simple as Hannah Glasse's orange biscuits, composed of dried sheets of orange peel and sugar. The common denominator between all biscuits was that they were baked—the root of "biscuit" means "cooked twice"—until they were dry.

Cakes (*P&P* 268; *MP* 344; *E* 156, 213; *P* 45), likewise, differed from their modern counterparts. They might be very small, for eating with tea, or they might be enormous, as they were for special occasions like weddings and Twelfth Night. These gigantic cakes were not cooked in pans, but instead with a large hoop around the dough to keep it roughly in shape. The idea of a specific sort of cake for weddings was just evolving. In general, wedding cakes (*E* 19) were made with a rich batter, into which the cook placed candied citrus peel, nuts, raisins or currants, and some sort of alcohol—wine, brandy, or rum. The gigantic cake was baked, then covered with an almond icing, baked again to brown the icing, then coated with a very white icing to serve as a contrast to the almond layer beneath.

Rout-cakes (*E* 290) were altogether different. These were small cakes dropped onto and baked on a sheet of tin—the eighteenth-century equivalent of a cookie sheet. They were composed of butter, flour, sugar, currants (few cakes seem to have been considered complete unless they included either currants or caraway seeds), eggs, rose- and orange-flower waters, wine, and brandy.

Pastry, too, was sometimes what we imagine and sometimes not. Tarts and small pies often had a crust that is similar to what we use today and were not baked all that differently. Savory pies could be enormous and were baked without pans, in a crust so thick and stiff that it stood alone. Shaped like clay and filled with meat, they were completed in one of two ways. Either the "gravy" would be added before baking, in which case the top crust would be pinched into place atop the pie, or the top crust (the "lid") would be baked without attaching it to the bottom, and the liquid would be poured in after baking. Some pies took an intermediate form; mince pies (*P&P* 44), for example, might contain mostly meat, meat and fruit in roughly equal proportions, or fruit only.

One treat enjoyed by all levels of society was gingerbread (*E* 233). Gingerbread had long been a special treat among the English, and by Austen's time it had evolved from its medieval roots as a dish made with bread crumbs and wine. It could be made as a breadlike loaf or as bite-size gingerbread "nuts." Large cakes of gingerbread were sometimes baked, then pressed into detailed wooden molds, such as molds of kings and queens, and occasionally gilded. Contemporary prints often show rows of such gingerbread hanging from booths at fairs. Gingerbread also appears to have been used at fairs as a target. A piece of gingerbread was spiked on a post, and people paid to throw sticks at it, trying to knock it off in order to win a prize. Other popular treats included sweetmeats (a catchall category that included marmalade and candied citrus peel—see *S&S* 193) and sugar plums (another general category comprising candies or comfits made with boiled sugar—see *S&S* 191).

Soups, Stews, and Curries

Soup (*Lesley*, *MW* 112–113; *Evelyn*, *MW* 182; *NA* 116; *P&P* 342; *MP* 52, 180) was the quintessentially cheap meal, the means by which the poor could turn a lump of unappetizing meat, a few handfuls of grain, and some vegetables into a tasty and nutritious meal. It was a source of unfailing exasperation to reformer Sir Frederick Eden that the poor insisted upon roasting their meat, or boiling it in a mass, rather than chopping it up for soup, which would have been, to his mind, more economical. Yet soup could be dressed up quite a bit beyond this modest presentation. On the tables of the gentry, it might be the sea in which a French roll, a fowl, or a piece of veal rose like an island. It was certainly, if nothing else, an opportunity to display the huge and decorative tureens that formed an essential part of a good china service.

Soups usually started with a broth (*E* 88), to which the cook added herbs, vegetables, and usually some sort of meat. Sometimes it was beef, but it might also be fish, oysters, or eels. Turtle soup was considered highly desirable, but it was also prohibitively expensive, and most people made do with mock-turtle soup made from gravy, Madeira, and calf's head.* To complete the illusion, it was suggested that the cook serve this soup in a turtle's shell.

Generally served as part of the first course, if the meal was grand enough to be divided into courses, the soup was served right away. Once it was finished, its tureen—which usually occupied a place of honor at either the top or the bottom of the table—was removed and replaced with another showy dish. Thus, Jane Austen's uncle James Leigh Perrot wrote of his dinner on July 4, 1806, that he ate "Mackerell at Top, Soup at Bottom removed for a Neck of Venison." Soup was also considered appropriate for suppers at balls (*Watsons*, *MW* 315; *E* 330) and for people returning from an outing, such as a trip to the theater. Austen does not usually specify what type of soup was served, but she does make a reference to "white soup" (*P&P* 55), which was the most elegant type of soup, based on veal broth, cream, and almonds. Its lofty reputation stands in contrast to the humble, everyday "pease-soup" served at Steventon on November 30, 1798. Pease-soup was ubiquitous and without pretensions, a thinner descendant of the centuries-old "pease porridge hot, pease porridge cold, pease porridge in the pot, nine days old."

Stews (*Headache*, *MW* 448) were thicker and more generally full of meat; frequently, they simply consisted of one or more large pieces of meat surrounded by a thick broth. Like soups, they had the advantage of needing little attention from the cook. Once in the pot, they could be left to cook themselves, with only occasional stirring required. Curry (*Lesley*, *MW* 121) was the stew's exotic cousin, which, with "pillau" or "pillaw" made its way into cookbooks via Britain's possessions in the East Indies. Curry is not an individual spice but a mixture of several spices, and by the 1780s this mélange, premixed and ready for use, had found its way into English groceries and kitchens. No doubt its spicing was too strong for some palates—it is hard, for example, to imagine the digestively timid Mr. Woodhouse asking for seconds—but it appealed to many, especially to Britons back in England after military or civil service in India.

Sauces and Spices

It has been claimed that the English of Austen's day had only one sauce, or perhaps only two sauces—brown and white. This is a vast oversimplification. While it is true that the most common sauce for meat was its own juices thickened into a seasoned gravy and that the most common sauce for vegetables was "melted butter" (a combination of butter and flour), there were plenty of other sauces (*Headache*, *MW* 448). There were oyster sauces that were popular with turkey, onion sauces for poultry and rab-

*This is why the Mock Turtle in *Alice in Wonderland* has a turtle's flippers and a calf's head.

bit, celery sauces, and sauces made with hard-boiled eggs. Most sauces were based on either gravy or cullis, strong broths based on browned beef, veal knuckles, fish, or vegetables. Then there were condiments, either home-made or store-bought, that added to the depth of simple sauces: lemon pickle, mushroom ketchup, and mum ketchup (but not tomato ketchup).

The use of spices had declined since the seventeenth century, but Georgian cooks had a wide range of spices available to them, thanks to England's far-flung commercial empire. A well-stocked pantry might have salt, black and white pepper, mustard, nutmeg, mace, cloves, cayenne pepper, Jamaica pepper (allspice), cinnamon, caraway seeds, saffron, and even curry powder. Vanilla was prohibitively expensive, but its place was supplied by rose water and orange-flower water, which lent a subtle flavor to fruit dishes and pastries.

These spices, generally acquired from grocers, were not always thoroughly pure. Frederick Accum's *Treatise on Adulterations of Food* (1820) reveals the sorts of deceptions that were practiced only a few years after Austen's death; one may assume that most of these stratagems were also being employed during her lifetime, as Accum often supplies anecdotal evidence from earlier dates. Mustard, he wrote, was adulterated with capsicum to increase its shelf life and improve its color, or with radish seed and pea flour to save money; both black and white pepper were about 16 percent "false pepper," "made up of oil cakes (the residue of linseed, from which the oil has been pressed), common clay, and a portion of Cayenne pepper, formed in a mass, and granulated by being first pressed through a sieve, and then rolled in a cask." Pepper was perhaps the most adulterated spice. Ground pepper was extended with sweepings from the floors of pepper warehouses, while so-called white pepper was in fact merely black pepper that had been steeped in seawater and urine to remove the dark skin of the peppercorns. As with all food products in an age before protective legislation, the buyer had to be extremely cautious. *See also* Beverages; Dishes; Fire; Housework.

Franking

Most people had to pay postage whenever they received a letter, as postage was typically paid by the recipient. However, there was an exception to this rule. Members of Parliament (MPs) could send mail postage-free, a practice called franking (*S&S* 113; *MP* 16), which made it a stroke of good fortune to be acquainted with an MP. Not only did the letters one received from an MP come free of charge, but the MP could sometimes be persuaded to frank letters when he was not the sender. The Austens had such a friend and made use of his frank whenever they had the opportunity. Franked letters were specially stamped in red by the Post Office; the exact shape and wording of the stamp changed over time, as did regulations regarding the use of the franking privilege.

Franked letters had to weigh less than two ounces and had to be personally addressed by the possessor of the privilege, who was almost always an MP.* There was also a seasonal limit; franking was valid only for forty days before, during, and after sessions of Parliament. Hostility toward franking as an unfair practice increased toward the end of the eighteenth century, and there were repeated attempts to limit abuses of the privilege. In 1764 the privilege was withdrawn from some who had held it, but this reform was later partially rescinded. Letters received by an MP were not free unless sent to his home or to Parliament itself. Another act in 1781

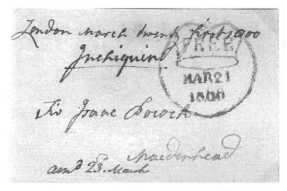

Franked letters, 1800 and 1792. The shape of the franking stamp changed from time to time. Courtesy of Eunice and Ron Shanahan.

mandated that the place and date of posting had to be written on every envelope; a third, in 1795, lowered the legal weight to one ounce and limited MPs to sending fifteen and receiving ten free letters per day. Furthermore, the MP had to be within twenty miles of the place the letters were posted, either on the day they were posted or the day before. Despite these efforts, the volume of franked letters increased dramatically. In 1790, about 180,000 such letters were sent; by 1810, the number had risen to approximately 971,000. The practice would not be abolished completely until 1840. *See also* Post; Writing.

French

The English attitude toward France and all things French was strangely paradoxical. On the one hand, France was the home of all things fashion-

---

*At times Post Office clerks were granted franking privileges, but this was not always the case during Austen's lifetime. Government documents, regardless of the sender, were customarily franked.

able and desirable; on the other hand, it was a traditional enemy of Britain and, in only the most recent war between the two countries, had cost Britain thirteen of its American colonies. The result was a kind of cognitive dissonance; people of good education learned French, spoke French, read French, and aped French fashions in clothing and manners yet condemned the French and all they stood for.

Attitudes were further complicated by the French Revolution, which some in England condemned immediately but which most greeted with enthusiasm. As the Revolution turned more violent, however, and as Britain went to war with France again for the second and third times in Austen's lifetime, attitudes became noticeably more hostile. Even those most influenced by French language and mores felt compelled to offer some explanation; the anonymous author of *The Mirror of the Graces*, an 1811 book of advice on dress and deportment, follows a passage on French behavior with a patriotic gloss:

> My intimacy with the French manners makes me quote these short extracts with greater pleasure; and, as I bear witness to the truth of their evidence, I hope that an amiable ambition will unite in the breasts of the British fair, to be as much superior to their French rivals, in all feminine graces, as our British heroes are to the French on the seas!

Long before this passage was written, however, there was ample resentment against the French. While some women studied Paris fashions and some wealthy men hired French cooks, others bought satirical prints contrasting "British Slavery" and "French Liberty." A common type of popular print, this might vary somewhat in composition but usually expressed the difference in the two nations through food; the "enslaved" and portly Briton dined on a giant platter of roast beef, a huge loaf of bread, and a brimming mug of beer, the emblems of universal prosperity, while the "free" and dangerously gaunt Frenchman made do with a scant portion of garlic, or frogs, or snails. Of course, many of the same people who bought such prints went home to dine on fricassees, ragouts, and other French-inspired dishes, but their spirit was patriotic all the same.

As members of the country gentry, the Austen children would certainly have been expected to be acquainted with French (*LS, MW* 252–253; *NA* 14; *MP* 14, 22, 312), just as any well-educated child today would be expected to know algebra. To what extent they were fluent is not precisely known, but Jane, who attended boarding school for a handful of years, whose parents were both extremely literate, and who was given a book of French stories, probably read it quite well. Her two sailor brothers, Charles and Frank, were required to learn it at the Portsmouth Naval Academy, even if they had received no instruction in it from their father (which seems unlikely). Charles' academic records, for example, report that he was "Very diligent" in French in 1791–1792, "Pretty diligent" in 1793–1794. In the case of the sailor brothers, knowledge of French would have been useful not only as a mark of gentility but also as an essential skill in time of war. Family tradition holds that knowledge of French was also useful to another Austen connection, Eliza de Feuillide Austen, a cousin who married a French count and then, after his execution during the French Revolution, Jane's brother Henry. She and Henry, according to some accounts, were traveling in France during these troubled times, seeking to recover some of her first husband's property, when the order went out to detain all Englishmen. Henry, who appears *not* to have been fluent, kept his mouth shut, while Eliza, who spoke like a native, got them safely back to England.

Austen's works are peppered with French phrases and references, such as "the whole *tout ensemble* of his person" (*J&A, MW* 14), "Finis" (*Hist Eng, MW* 149), "Beau Monde" (*Sand, MW* 387), and "*au fait*" (*P* 155). "Adieu" (often misspelled—see *L&F, MW* passim; *NA* 67, 229; *P&P* 235, 330) and "tête-à-tête" (*NA* 243; *S&S* 294, 369; *P&P* 257; *MP* 35, 210, 234, 363; *E* 129, 360, 417, 422) occur frequently throughout Austen's works, so often indeed that they must have been in common use among her acquaintances. Sometimes they are used by silly characters, but not always, and they seem to have lost some of their explicit Frenchness. They are never italicized in order to call attention to their foreign derivation. More noticeably, French terms, such as *gaucherie*, are often associated with unsympathetic characters, such as Robert Ferrars (*S&S* 250) and the pretentious Tom Musgrave (*Watsons, MW* 340).

Brian Southam, among others, has noted that Jane, as the years progressed, grew increasingly likely to be the sort of person who would purchase a patriotic print. In *Emma* and *Mansfield Park* particularly, French language and manners are associated with duplicity and immorality. Frank Churchill's devious Frenchness is repeatedly contrasted with Mr. Knightley's straightforward manner, to the detriment of the former; the words "espionage" and "finesse," still very much thought of as French words, are used in reference to his conduct. Austen is even more explicit in the discussion of whether Churchill is amiable (*E* 149)—is he *aimable* (smooth and ingratiating in manner) or amiable (carrying in Austen's day a connotation of, in Southam's words, "a quality of thoughtfulness and consideration for others")?

Mary Crawford, too, is associated with French language at a critical moment; she calls her brother Henry's elopement with Mrs. Rushworth merely "a moment's *etourderie*" (thoughtlessness—*MP* 437), when clearly, to everyone in the Bertram household, it is much more significant. Not only her manners and language but even her morality have been infected by a supposedly French willingness to overlook infidelity. However, by this time, she and her brother have already been associated with the French by their liberal use of French phrases: *esprit du corps* (*MP* 47), *menus plaisirs*

(*MP* 226), *exigeant* (demanding—*MP* 361), and lines passionées (*MP* 393). The phrase "à-la-mortal," though used by the narrator, is likewise used in relationship to a Crawford (*MP* 274). Mary thinks highly of the seductive qualities of French women (*MP* 42); Fanny Price, in contrast, "had never learnt French" (*MP* 14) until she arrived at the Bertrams', and Edmund Bertram asserts that he cannot utter "a bon-mot" (*MP* 94), using a French term only in order to distance himself from *l'aimable*. The cases of Frank Churchill and the Crawfords perfectly summarize the English attitude toward French language and manners; they behave badly, but they're so handsome and appealing that one can't help liking them, at least a little. *See also* French Revolution; Greek and Latin; Italian; Napoleonic Wars.

French Revolution

The French Revolution, as many critics have noted, makes virtually no appearance in Austen's works, although it forms an important part of the background to her writing. Her cousin, Eliza de Feuillide, was married to a French count and was thus a direct link between Steventon and the Revolution, and rivalry between France and England was the single most important influence in British foreign policy throughout Austen's lifetime. Reaction to the Revolution evolved over time, as did the practical consequences.

At the very beginning of the Revolution, there was enthusiasm in many quarters. It was felt by some that the French were throwing off the yoke of tyranny and starting down a road to constitutional monarchy—in other words, that they were patterning themselves on England's own Glorious Revolution of 1688 and on the American Revolution. Initial supporters of the Revolution included Charles James Fox, who called the storming of the Bastille "the greatest event that has ever happened in the world, and . . . the best!" The poets William Wordsworth, Robert Southey, and Samuel Taylor Coleridge were also enthusiastic, as were MP Samuel Romilly and the dukes of Bedford and Sussex. The Reverend Dr. Price exulted publicly, "I have lived to see thirty millions of people, indignant and resolute, spurning at slavery, and demanding liberty with an irresistible voice. Their king led in triumph, and an arbitrary monarch surrendering himself to his subjects." Religious Nonconformists were generally more favorably disposed than were members of the Church of England, probably because of the resentment expressed by the French rebels against the established church of their own country.

The general enthusiasm spilled over into a desire for political reform at home. The English system of parliamentary elections, though far superior to the absolute monarchy of France, was far from being perfectly representative. Some districts had a fairly broad electorate, but others, known as "rotten boroughs," had only a handful of electors who could be bribed or intimidated, putting their seats in Parliament into the keeping of a few rich and powerful men. Reformers, who had been hoping to change this system, now saw inspiration in the French Revolution and used it as a symbol of their own fight, adopting Jacobin rhetoric and, at times, waving the tricolor. (This would prove, in time, to be a singularly unfortunate association.) "Corresponding" societies arose to spread the gospel of political reform; the most famous of these was the London Corresponding Society (LCS). In general, the reform organizations called for an end to class privilege, tax reform, and reform or disestablishment of the Church of England. They wanted, in the words of the Sheffield chapter of the LCS, to make "the Slave a Man, the Man a Citizen, and the Citizen an integral part of the State, to make him a joint Sovereign, and not a Subject."

These were demands to chill the heart of conservative and very happily entrenched establishment. Even those who had little stake in the political system sometimes found the reformers' plans for a new Britain terrifying. Statesman Edmund Burke, for example, found the Revolution and its possible domestic consequences a frightening and—pardon the pun—revolting development. He castigated the revolutionaries, finding a receptive audience, especially after Louis XVI and Marie Antoinette had been imprisoned. In a spirited defense of the hierarchical class structure, he defended the English (as opposed to the French) attitude toward the world:

> We fear God; we look up with awe to kings; with affection to parliaments; with duty to magistrates; with reverence to priests; and with respect to nobility.

He encouraged Britons to rally around the king and the established church, and his allies accused reformers, in the wildest terms, of meaning to destroy the entire fabric of British society. Novelist Fanny Burney recorded a conversation with Burke in June 1792, when he laid out his case for her and her father:

> The French Revolution, he said, which began by authorising and legalising injustice, and which by rapid steps had proceeded to every species of Despotism except owning a Despot, was now menacing all the Universe, and all Mankind with the most violent concussion of principle and order.
>
> My Father heartily joined, and I tacitly assented to his doctrines, though I feared not with his fears.
>
> One speech I must repeat, for it is explanatory of his conduct, and *nobly* explanatory. When he had expatiated upon the present dangers even to English Liberty and Property, from the contagion of Havock and novelty, he earnestly exclaimed "*This* it is that has made *me* an abettor and supporter of Kings! Kings are *necessary*, and if we would preserve peace and prosper-

ity, we must preserve *Them*. We must all put our shoulders to the Work! Aye, and stoutly, too!"

It seemed to Burke and his supporters that there could be no order without a king and without an established church. If one of these props collapsed, it appeared that the people would drift helplessly toward lawlessness. He had to convince the populace both of the imminent danger and of the salvation that lay in defending the current social order.

Burke's best assistance came from the French themselves, who were permitting the Revolution to sink further and further into violence and chaos. In 1792, when Austen was writing *Catharine*, France was already at war with its neighbors, and the mood internally was growing uglier by the month. Church property had been seized in 1789, hereditary titles abolished the following year. In June 1791, Louis XVI and his family had been caught trying to flee the country, and the king had been briefly stripped of his powers. The guillotine had gone into service in April 1792, and in June, crowds stormed the Tuileries in an antiroyalist demonstration.

The king and nobility had not stood idly by while all this happened. Louis XVI had been in contact with other monarchs, trying to enlist support for his cause, and various nobles, including the comte de Feuillide, Eliza's husband, had joined an insurgency against the Revolution. Others, fearing for their lives, had emigrated (*S&S* 254) to England.* In response, the French government stripped the emigrants of their property in 1792. In August of that year, a mob again stormed the Tuileries, and the king was deposed. On August 13, the French royal family was imprisoned, and by the end of September, the sale of emigrants' property had begun, divorce had been legalized, the republic had been proclaimed, and more than a thousand Paris prisoners had been massacred for fear that they would join the insurgency. In late September, French orator George Danton proclaimed the Revolution a revolution against all kings, not merely his own nation's.

Most of these events created a sense of outrage in Britain, and the shift from support for the Revolution to anger against it was heightened by the executions of Louis XVI and Marie Antoinette in 1793. Parson James Woodforde noted in his diary entry for January 19, 1793, two days before Louis' execution, that according to Woodforde's perusal of the newspapers, "there appears but very small hopes at present of the King of France long remaining here upon earth, his blood-thirsty Enemies being so wicked and inveterate against him." A week later, he had confirmation of his fears: "The King of France Louis 16 inhumanly and unjustly beheaded on Monday last by his cruel, blood-thirsty Subjects. Dreadful times I am afraid are approaching to all Europe. France the foundation of all of

*One of these emigrants, General Alexandre d'Arblay, married the novelist Fanny Burney.

it." Fanny Burney wrote to her father in late October, after the execution of Marie Antoinette, in a similar strain, blaming neither mob psychology nor political motives but inherent cruelty for French tactics:

> The terrible confirmation of this last act of savage hardness of Heart has wholly overset us again . . . the Death of the Queen could answer *no* purpose, helpless as she was to injure them, while her life *might* answer some, as an hostage with the Emperor.* Cruelty, however, such as theirs, seems to require no incitement whatever; its own horrible exercise appears sufficient both to prompt and to repay it.

Woodforde's and Burney's reactions were repeated in thousands of homes across Britain. Reaction to the executions was amplified by patriotic feeling when, in February, France declared war on Britain. Many in England who had initially supported the Revolution now turned against it, and their numbers swelled as, throughout 1793 and 1794, the Revolution began devouring its own, suppressing the women's political clubs that had been among its earliest supporters, falling out of love with this radical leader or that, and feeding him and all his supporters to the guillotine.

Eliza de Feuillide, who had spent the years prior to the Terror shuttling back and forth between France and England, now remained in England, often visiting one or another of the Austens. She was with them, for example, during the storming of the Tuileries and the September massacres in 1792. In 1793, an acquaintance, the marquise de Marboeuf, was accused of conspiring against the republic, in large part because she had planted nitrogen-fixing clover in a field rather than bread-producing grain. Upset, the comte de Feuillide attempted to bribe a government official to testify for the marquise and suppress some documents, but the official betrayed him to the Committee of Safety, and both the marquise and the comte de Feuillide were guillotined.

Through the newspapers and ties of personal acquaintance, such stories were becoming well known in England. Political and labor dissidents, however, continued to use the rhetoric of the Revolution in literature and public demonstrations. Parliament and others with a stake in the status quo, genuinely terrified of revolution at home, took several types of measures to crush political dissent and turn the tide of public opinion against events in France. Their most direct tack was legal. Habeas corpus, at various times during the 1790s, was suspended to allow the detention of suspected rebels; the LCS was banned in 1799; and the 1800 Combination Act made it a crime for workers to unite in order to force employers to grant better wages or working conditions. Certain towns, including London and Manchester, withdrew licenses from alehouse keepers who permitted radical

*Marie Antoinette was a Hapsburg and thus a member of the family that produced the Holy Roman Emperors.

meetings on their premises. There were high-profile arrests for sedition, including the arrest in February 1793 of John Frost, a leader of the LCS. Booksellers who sold Thomas Paine's political tract *The Rights of Man* were arrested or, in lieu of arrest, forced to issue printed apologies for their "Misconduct." Suspension of freedom of the press was discussed but never enacted, although radical newspaper publishers and distributors were threatened with prosecution for sedition and were harassed by both government officials and the patriotic public.

"Church and king" violence was, for a time, widespread. In 1791, a mob pillaged the house of Dissenter Joseph Priestley, known to be a supporter of the Revolution, an attack that caused Anglican cleric Dr. Samuel Parr to comment angrily, when asked to drink a patriotic toast to "Church and King," "Well, then, gentlemen,—Church and King—once it was the toast of Jacobites; now it is the toast of incendiaries. It means a Church without a Gospel, and a King above the laws." A delivery man for the *Sheffield Register* was beaten in May 1794. In that same year, a mob singing "God Save the King" destroyed the house of a radical bookseller, while elsewhere, another mob sacked a public house known to allow radical meetings within its walls. Paranoia, while perhaps not quite epidemic, was certainly heightened, and spies (*NA* 198) of all kinds—both actual government agents and patriotic busybodies—were ready to inform on anyone who uttered a rebellious speech. Judges were not in a mood to interpret political crimes with lenience. Laughing at troops or saying, "No George, no war," could earn a sentence in the pillory, at hard labor, or aboard a ship as a sailor.

However, voices continued to be heard either in support of the Revolution or in support of traditional English legal rights. While navies and armies fought on sea and land, another war was waged on paper, as radicals stated their case and conservatives countered their arguments. Burke's *Reflections on the Revolution in France* was answered by Thomas Paine's *Rights of Man*. Paine was defended by Mary Wollstonecraft, arguably Britain's first feminist, who wrote a *Vindication of the Rights of Man* by way of support, then followed it with her *Vindication of the Rights of Woman*, a pamphlet that questioned the way women were educated and challenged women to become full participants in society, not merely consumers and appendages. Radical William Godwin, later Wollstonecraft's husband and unfortunately not her equal at composing pithy titles, added his thoughts to the debate in *The Enquiry Concerning the Principle of Political Justice and Its Influence on General Virtue and Happiness* (1793), in which he espoused a political and religious system based not on natural rights or government power but "universal benevolence," the moral impulse to share power and use skills for the good of all. Other pamphleteers, such as schoolteacher Thomas Spence, took advantage of the climate to advocate agrarian reforms. Paine himself, after leaving England

and being prosecuted in absentia for seditious libel, turned to both religious and agrarian reform, publishing his Deist *Age of Reason* from his exile in France and following it in 1797 with *Agrarian Justice*.

Poets, too, took up the cause of liberty. John Wolcot's *Resignation* (1792), an objection to the suppression of workers' combinations (unions), mockingly advised, in the voice of those in power,

> Now go, and learn submission from your Bible:
> Complaint is now-a-day a flagrant libel.
> Yes, go and try to chew your mouldy bread—
> Justice is sick, I own, but is not dead. . . .
> Let dice, and chariots, and the stately thrones
> Be formed of poor men's hard-worked bones.

James Kennedy took up the cause of those persecuted by government spies. In *The Exile's Reveries* (1795), the narrator consoles himself that, in France at least, "Here no rotten spy, / Spider-like, the snare extends."

The government, too, had its enthusiastic propagandists. The anonymous author of a *Proposal to the Ladies of Great Britain* (1794) created the heroine "Mrs. Britannica," who was trying to defend her "estate" from "a set of thieves." Alfred's *Address to the Ladies of England* (1803) urged women to help recruit militiamen. Richard Graves' *Maternal Despotism; or, The Rights of Infants* (1801) satirized Paine, Wollstonecraft, and others who demanded rights, by taking their arguments to an absurd extreme:

> Have I not right to kick and sprawl,
> To laugh or cry, to squeak or squall!
> Has ever, by my act and deed,
> Thy *right* to rule me been decreed?
> How dar'st thou, despot! then control
> Th' exertions of a free-born soul?
> Though now an infant, when I can,
> I'll rise and seize "The Rights of Man."

John Parrish's *The Democratic Barber; or, Country Gentleman's Surprise* (1793), informed the reader:

> The London people all are mad;
> There rages now a sad disorder
> (Amongst the low plebeian order),
> A strange chimera of the brain,
> Occasioned by the works of Paine;
> A disappointed man—quite crazy,
> Best pleased when others are uneasy.

Some of the attacks were extremely vitriolic, particularly the attacks on Wollstonecraft, who challenged dearly held ideas about gender as well as class. A gentler touch was exhibited by Hannah More, who wrote patronizing, but popular, works for the poor. Her poem *The Riot; or Half a Loaf Is Better than No Bread* (1795), takes an approach familiar at the time: the instructive dialogue. Works of this sort were common for teaching children; one character was ignorant of the proper way to do something but willing to learn, while the other was wise, sententious, and patient. Alternately, the one would express some sort of wrongheaded sentiment, and the other would explain why he was wrong and how he ought to think or behave instead. In More's poem, the role of Ignorance is played by Tom Hod (whose surname, meaning a holder for bricks or mortar, indicates that he is a bricklayer), and the role of Wisdom by Jack Anvil, a blacksmith. Tom proposes to rally the townsfolk, who are upset over the price of food due to the war, and "go kick up a bit of a riot." His plan is to attack the mill, a common strategy employed by mobs, who saw the local miller (*MP* 58) and baker as controlling the supply of food or who at least perceived these tradespeople as convenient symbols of famine. Jack replies that such tactics will only alienate the merchants without addressing the root cause and advises that Tom instead place his trust in Burke's favorite people—king, Parliament, clergy, magistrates, and nobles:

> But though poor, I can work, my brave boy, with the best,
> Let the King and the Parliament manage the rest;
> I lament both the war and the taxes together,
> Though I verily think they don't alter the weather.
> . . .
> . . . I'll work the whole day and on Sundays I'll seek
> At church how to bear all the wants of the week.
> The gentlefolks too will afford us supplies;
> They'll subscribe—and they'll give up their puddings and pies.

Other authors encouraged the aristocracy to mend their dissolute ways and set a good example, lest they meet the fate of the French nobility. The gentry, too, were encouraged to make sacrifices to show the poor that all suffered, if not equally, then at least together.

More's advice to the poor was not universally heeded; riots over food, over the war, and over workers' grievances erupted throughout the Revolutionary period. There was a riot in London in 1792, when Eliza de Feuillide was in town, and near the end of that year there were substantial fears of a Bastille-style attack on the Tower of London or the Bank of England. Parson Woodforde made numerous entries on the subject of riots, worrying in 1791 that there would be "bad Consequences" on the anniversary of the fall of the Bastille, and reporting several instances, near the end of 1792, of rumors that "a great Mob" would assemble. By December 29, however, he could report that the backlash was well under way. "Revolution Clubbs every where much suppressed," he wrote, "and Constitutional Societies daily increasing all over the Kingdom. Levelling principles and Equality almost discarded." His anxieties demonstrate that the background of Austen's young adulthood was one of political, economic, and social tension, and "France the foundation of all of it." *See also* Napoleonic Wars; Politics and Government.

Furniture

The furniture (*Scraps*, *MW* 176–177; *LS*, *MW* 250; *Sand*, *MW* 393, 427; *NA* 88, 158, 162, 163; *S&S* 12, 13, 26, 69, 119; *P&P* 65, 75, 133, 156, 246, 249; *MP* 41, 48, 152, 182, 202; *E* 184, 355; *P* 10, 22, 32, 37, 137) of the late eighteenth century and early nineteenth century was influenced by classical, Egyptian, and Gothic styles. The rococo styles of earlier in the eighteenth century, exemplified by the work of Thomas Chippendale (1718–1779), had been replaced by graceful neoclassical pieces by cabinetmakers like George Hepplewhite (who designed Mr. Austen's library bookcase at Steventon) and Thomas Sheraton (1751–1806). From 1810 to 1815, there was a return to interest in French styles of furniture, largely due to the influence of the prince regent. Common design motifs in general included honeysuckle, acanthus leaves, the triple-feather plume of the prince regent, sphinxes, lotuses, Chinoiserie, palm leaves, fluting like that found on Greek columns, and winged Victories. The legs of tables, chairs, and sofas often were carved to resemble animals or had claw feet.

The woods used in furniture-making included native ash, birch, and chestnut. Beech was widely used for painted chairs. Mahogany (*NA* 193; *MP* 84) came into use in the second half of the eighteenth century and quickly became popular for its deep reddish-brown color. Veneers might be of sycamore, bird's-eye maple, and various types of heavily figured imported woods. The types of wood that were imported gave a sense of how far-flung Britain's colonial and trading networks already were. Craftsmen used black-and-yellow calamander and pale yellow satinwood from Ceylon; light-brown amboyna from the West Indies; streaky kingwood, rosewood, and feather-figured partridge wood from Brazil; ebony from east India, purplewood and zebra-wood from Guiana, and golden-brown thuya wood from Africa.

Furniture-making techniques included painting, lacquering, veneering, carving (*MP* 84), gilding (*MP* 84, 434), and inlay. The lacquering was referred to as "japanning" and was often used on pieces that featured Chinese or Japanese scenes. The technique was used in England from the late seventeenth century, when the shellac used was tinted red, green, white, black, or other colors. By the late eighteenth century, the preference was for black on yellow, with the yellow sometimes being mixed with metal dust to give it sparkle. The best japanning (*NA* 201) had at least ten coats of lacquer, carefully rubbed between coats to give the surface a glossy smoothness, while cheaper items had only one or two coats of lacquer and thus had a slightly bumpy feel.

Chairs and Sofas

One of the design elements characteristic of the period was the curve, and chairs in particular seemed to be fond of curving. Some, imitating the curule seats of the ancient Romans, were supported on legs composed of intersecting semicircles, making a kind of "X" at the front and back. Windsor chairs had a top rail that curved around in one continuous line with the arms and a smoothly rounded hollow in the seat for comfort. Window seats and sofas had curved, scrolled sides and armrests, and tables gradually acquired rounded edges.

There were numerous kinds of chairs (*F&E, MW* 8; *Visit, MW* 51; *Evelyn, MW* 187; *Cath, MW* 215; *Watsons, MW* 356; *S&S* 42, 175, 177, 265, 288, 290, 317; *P&P* 162, 341; *MP* 118, 126, 145, 169, 192, 231, 239, 342, 379; *E* 255, 378, 410; *P* 223, 237), some more formal than others. In addition to the Windsor chair and curule chairs, there were Grecian chairs with sweeping curved backs and splayed, tapering, rectangular legs. There were chairs with cane seats and chairs painted to simulate bamboo, complete with carved "rings." There were armchairs with swooping, descending, scrolled armrests and a slight backward tilt to the backrest, making them almost appear to be frozen for a moment in the midst of swift motion. Trafalgar chairs had curves everywhere and were often decorated with rope and cable designs in honor of Nelson's victory at Trafalgar in 1805. Painted chairs were described in the August 1814 Repository as "intended for best bed chambers, for secondary drawing rooms, and occasionally to serve for routs," and indeed a chair of this type does appear in the late Mrs. Tilney's room at Northanger Abbey (*NA* 193). Parlor chairs, as in the dining parlor, were used in the dining room and were generally simpler in design than drawing-room chairs, which were often made of expensive mahogany or of wood that had been painted and gilded. There were many more styles of chairs— so many that in 1822 Richard Brown wrote that they were so various that "it now baffles the most skilful artist to produce any new forms." Chairs in a few of the myriad styles available may be seen in the illustrations *A Master Parson with a Good Living* (Clergy), *A Journeyman Parson with a Bare Existence* (Clergy), *Progress of the Toilet.—Dress Completed* (Clothing), and *Temperance Enjoying a Frugal Meal* (Food).

One special type of chair was the window seat (*NA* 167). This was a wide seat, large enough for lounging or for two people to share. It was designed to be placed in front of the tall windows of grand homes, windows that in fashionable homes stretched all the way down to floor level to let in maximum light. Closely related to the window seat was the sofa (*J&A, MW* 14; *E&E, MW* 31; *Mystery, MW* 57; *L&F, MW* 86, 88; *Lesley, MW* 111; *Evelyn, MW* 189; *Sand, MW* 413; *S&S* 307; *P&P* 54; *MP* 71, 74, 104, 125, 126, 179, 277; *E* 45, 124, 125; *P* 37, 39, 67–68, 78, 79), a larger piece of furniture, either with a padded back and two arms of equal height, or with one tall arm at one end and a short end at the other, with a back panel stretching across only about half the length of the sofa. This latter sofa was designed for stretching out and was an imitation of the Greek and Roman couches used by the diners of ancient times. These pieces often featured classical-style fluting and scrollwork that reflected their origins; the sofa with a full back, after 1812, often had some sort of ornament at the center along the back; leaves, honeysuckle, and shells were common motifs for this sort of carved crest.

Tables

The variety of tables (*L&F, MW* 107; *NA* 158; *S&S* 63, 67, 165, 175, 198, 231, 317; *P&P* 39, 48, 341; *MP* 72, 74, 118, 124, 142–143, 145, 224, 318, 439; *E* 24, 82, 157, 255, 355, 434; *P* 40, 105, 112) was even greater than the variety of chairs, for tables served a great number of purposes. The principal table in a household was the dining room table (*Watsons, MW* 353; *NA* 165; *P&P* 288, 310; *MP* 220–221, 239; *E* 291), which formerly had been a rigidly rectangular affair with monumental carved legs and feet. Now it became a piece of furniture of lighter weight and more versatility, for its huge legs became pillars, each of which splayed out into four claw-footed supports. The right angles at its ends were rounded, and the middle developed leaves so that the table could be made larger or smaller as the occasion demanded. The legs were moved away from the corners and toward the center, with one leg under each leaf. Eventually, the taste for curves led to at least some dining tables being made entirely round (*E* 347, 349), as this did away with hierarchical sitting arrangements and, it was thought, made guests feel more at ease. Circular tables could also be used for breakfast or for playing "round" card games (games that did not confine themselves to a specified number of players). Early in the period, they had a central pillar that divided into four supporting legs (shown in the illustration *The Glutton* [Food]); later, they rested on triangular pedestals. Other circular or octagonal tables were known as drawing-room tables.

Some tables were designed to be used either separately or in conjunction as needed. These included wine tables, which could be pushed together near the fire to hold wine glasses and decanters, and "sets of dining tables" of the kind purchased by Austen's family in November 1800. Jane wrote about them to Cassandra, expressing her delight:

> The Tables are come, & give general contentment. . . . The two ends put together form our constant Table for everything, & the centre piece stands exceedingly well under the glass; holds a great deal most commodiously, without looking awkwardly.—They are both covered with green baize and send their best Love.—The Pembroke has got its destination by the sideboard, & my mother has great delight in keeping her Money & papers locked up.

Messrs. Morgan & Sanders, 1809. A well-equipped London furniture showroom. Courtesy of the Lewis Walpole Library, Yale University. 809.8.1.4.

A set of dining tables was a group of three tables, two that stood on four fixed legs and a third, middle table with two fixed legs and two that could swing out to support flaps. To use them together, the middle table would have its flaps raised and the legs extended; then all three tables would be hooked together with brass clips.

The Pembroke table (*Watsons, MW* 355), which this set had replaced, would also have had flaps. Pembroke tables had four legs and a flap at each short end supported by hinged wooden brackets. At this period these tables were usually rectangular with rounded corners; earlier examples had often been either oval or more strictly rectangular. After 1812, the four legs were sometimes replaced by a central pillar supported by four legs or feet.

Other kinds of tables included pier tables, which stood against the walls between windows (*MP* 153); console tables, which were supported in some way by the wall; and side tables, which stood against the wall but could be moved if necessary. Some tables that appeared to be side tables were actually card tables (*Watsons, MW* 332; *S&S* 144, 145, 151; *P&P* 38, 54, 76, 342; *MP* 119, 203, 239, 249; *E* 290); they resembled a narrow rectangular table and stood against the wall most of the time, but when evening came, they could be pulled away from the wall and the tops unfolded to reveal a square surface covered in baize or leather. Sofa tables (*Sand*, *MW* 413) stood, as their name implies, either in front or in back of a sofa and were used for a variety of purposes as people sat in the drawing room. Work tables (*S&S* 144, 181) had a sliding or lifting top beneath which a pleated silk bag or pouch was suspended. When it was time to do sewing, the top could be lifted and sewing supplies inside the bag accessed.

Library tables were massive affairs, with a wide kneehole between two pedestals containing cabinets. When the size of these pedestals was diminished and filled with drawers (*L&F*, *MW* 95) rather than cabinets, the piece became a writing table (*P&P* 305; *P* 237). Writing tables (*MP* 307) could also be supported by four legs and have their drawers in the "frieze," the level below the tabletop. Some had drawers here as well as in a shallow section atop the table. Also known as a writing desk (*MP* 152; *E* 298, 442), the writing table might have a top that lifted up to provide an angled surface on which to write or draw (*S&S* 104, 105). A dressing table was similar to a writing desk, but it usually had a mirror either sitting on it or incorporated into its structure, and its contents were of course different. Dressing tables may be seen in the illustrations *A Maiden Ewe, Drest Lamb Fashion* (Clocks and Watches), *Progress of the Toilet.—The Stays* (Clothing), *Progress of the Toilet.—Dress Completed* (Clothing), and Hairdressing (Hair).

Other Furniture

Storage pieces included wardrobes (*NA* 158, 193), chests of drawers (*NA* 158), cabinets (*NA* 160, 168, 201), and bookcases (*MP* 127; *P* 99). Cupboards (*P* 170), unlike the rest of these pieces, were hung on, or otherwise affixed to, the walls. Some pieces served multiple purposes; they might have a few shelves for books, a small space for writing letters, and a cabinet at the bottom. Storage could also be accomplished in chests (*NA* 158, 163, 165), though chests and trunks were not as popular as they had been in past years. They tended to be put away in corners rather than prominently displayed.

In the dining room, some items were stored in the sideboard (*P&P* 156; *E* 458), a cabinet longer than it was tall, equipped with drawers and doors. Food and drink were also served from the sideboard, and extra glassware was kept here during the meal. Some sideboards had a top at two levels, with the right and left sides of the top being higher than the middle section. Some sideboards had compartments that could be filled with water for washing dishes or a heated cavity under the stack of dinner plates. Behind the cabinet doors, a chamberpot might be secreted for the use of the gentlemen after the ladies had left.

Beds (*Visit*, *MW* 50; *Scraps*, *MW* 172; *Cath*, *MW* 220; *NA* 49, 158, 159, 168, 172, 193; *S&S* 190, 193, 198, 219, 292, 307; *MP* 13; *P* 113, 154; *E* 378) might be four-posters, preferably of mahogany with turned posts.

Canopy beds often had elaborately carved and painted headboards that were quite tall and supported a canopy that extended outward from the wall. Both of these types of beds had valances and curtains (*NA* 171) that could be closed for privacy and warmth at night. Many contemporary prints show people in curtained canopy or four-poster beds, which were the most popular styles. Less popular were sofa beds (in essence a sofa with a canopy suspended from a dome or rod) and tent beds (the lighter and cheaper form the four-poster, found in servants' rooms and cottages). Portions of beds and their hangings can be seen in the illustrations *A Journeyman Parson with a Bare Existence* (Clergy) and *Nobody's Song* (Servants).

Some homes had small pedestals or tables used to support artwork or vases of flowers (*P* 40). They might also have music stands. Footstools (*P&P* 105; *MP* 152) were similar to chairs in design; they were simply chairs without backs or arms. The poor had joint-stools, simple wooden stools without upholstery that did duty everywhere from the barn to the kitchen, and genteel artists and walkers had camp-stools (*Sand, MW* 383), folding stools that could be taken outdoors. Children had few pieces of furniture that were distinctively theirs; whereas a nursery today might contain a changing table, trash pail, crib, cradle, and playpen, children of Austen's time slept in cradles (*Visit, MW* 51; *P&P* 355) until they were old enough to move to beds.

G

Gambling

Gambling was such a commonplace element of eighteenth- and early nineteenth-century life that its existence was usually denounced only in cases of very high stakes or personal ruin. Religious enthusiasts, to be sure, railed against dice and horse racing, two of the most popular subjects for wagers, but almost everyone gambled to a greater or lesser extent. There was a national lottery (*E&E, MW* 31; *Sand, MW* 372) run by the government (to the great irritation of Evangelicals). Card games, which were among the most popular forms of evening entertainment, were always attended by wagers (*Watsons, MW* 315); the only difference from gathering to gathering was the size of the stakes. Parson James Woodforde even gambled when he played at home with his niece-housekeeper, Nancy, keeping a record in his diary of his winnings or losses, and almost every time he had guests or went to someone else's house for dinner, cards and the attendant gambling ensued. "At Quadrille this evening won 0.4.0," "After Coffee and Tea we got to Cards to Loo at which I had the good Luck to win abt. 0.1.0," and "At Cribbage this Evening with Nancy lost 0.1.0" are typical entries. Neither winning nor losing evenings predominate heavily, which means that Woodforde was a fairly average card player, that many of the games he played were based on luck, or that there was a certain amount of genteel effort in his circle of friends not to win too much too often for fear of being an aggravation.

This sort of gambling was considered perfectly acceptable by all but the most severe reformers. The anonymous author of *Female Tuition; or, an Address to Mothers, on the Education of Daughters* (1784) authorized "Gaming" (*J&A, MW* 14, 23) by women only in moderation:

> It may be adopted occasionally, to prevent the appearance of singularity, for the sake of variety, in complaisance to the humour of a party, to shew good-nature, promote harmony, or preclude scandal. But the least inclination to play, on any other principle, or from any other motive, is ominous, and ought to be checked with steadiness and severity.

There was no suggestion that cards ought to be played for the fun of the game, with no stakes at all; instead, those who could not afford to lose any money chose not to play cards (*P&P* 37).

Gentlemen gambled on cards as well, not only in the drawing room but in the gentlemen's clubs of London and at provincial clubs that met in taverns. In London and in the principal spas, stakes could reach ridiculous levels, and it was to prevent crime and individual financial ruin that Bath outlawed games such as hazard, basset, ace of hearts, EO ("Evens and Odds," a form of roulette), and faro in the mid-eighteenth century. However, these games could be found elsewhere, and wealthy young men were drawn to the excitement they offered. Popular prints often link gambling with the other great temptations, liquor and loose women (*J&A*, *MW* 13), as this trio of vices was supposed to present the greatest threat to virtue. The dangers of gambling to a family fortune were also the subject of many eighteenth- and nineteenth-century novels, and it was a peril that Jane Austen knew within her own circle of acquaintance. The Reverend John Harwood inherited nearby Deane House from his father, who had seriously encumbered the estate with his gambling debts, costing John Harwood his chance at marriage with a relatively poor woman whom he loved. Austen, who took a very traditional view of the responsibilities of landowners, takes a correspondingly dim view of reckless gambling (*Lesley*, *MW* 137; *P&P* 297–298; *MP* 48). Interestingly, one of her case studies in gambling addiction, Tom Bertram, suggests for the Mansfield theatricals *The Wheel of Fortune*, a comedy about a young man who loses his fortune by gambling (*MP* 188).

Unfortunately for men like the real-life Harwood and the fictional Tom Bertram, opportunities to gamble remained all too common. Horse-race meetings were particularly notorious, for there was rampant gambling not only on the races themselves but also on the boxing matches, card games, dice games, and cockfights that often attended such events. Bets on the main race could reach staggering levels; side betting on the Hambletonian-Diamond match at Newmarket in 1799 was estimated at between 200,000 and 300,000 guineas. The lure of easy money drew professional gamblers and cheats, who worked the gambling fever to their own advantage. Some races, therefore, were rigged, as were many of the EO tables that set up temporary shop near the racetracks. *See also* Cards.

Games

Games tended to fall into one of three categories: mental, social, or physical. Physical games were most often played by children, while social games could be enjoyed by all ages, and mental games were especially popular with adults, who took great pleasure in demonstrating their cleverness. The physical games included cricket, trap ball, battledore and shuttlecock, and lawn bowling; of these, only lawn bowling tended to be an overwhelmingly adult pursuit.

Physical Games

Cricket (*NA* 13, 15) had two teams of eleven players. One of these was the bowler, who threw a ball in a strip of ground called the pitch. Sticks called stumps were driven into the ground, in a line, with one batsman next to one stump and another batsman at the other stump directly opposite. The bowler, in between the batsmen, threw the ball overhand toward one of them, who attempted to hit it with a bat. Then the two batsmen attempted to run back and forth, exchanging places as many times as they could before an opponent returned with the ball and tagged one of the stumps with it. The goal was to get safely to a stump before it was hit with the ball. These exchanges of place were called runs, and runs could also be scored by hitting the ball out of bounds or as a penalty when the bowler bowled incorrectly. A batsman could be called out if the ball were caught on the fly, if the bowler hit the batsman's stump while bowling to him, if the stump

[Lilliputian Figures], 1799, detail. Cricketers. Courtesy of the Lewis Walpole Library, Yale University. 799.7.12.4.

were hit with the ball while the batsman was running, if the batsman chose to end his turn voluntarily, or if the batsman made certain types of errors. The game ended when both teams had bowled a specified number of times, or when one team had ten players called out and therefore could no longer field two batsmen.

Trap ball was a similar game, in that it used a bat and a ball, but it was far less complex. A hard wooden ball called a knur was placed in the "trap," a shoe-shaped box with a lever. The knur was placed on top of one end of the lever, and each player used a long wooden stick to hit the other end, flinging the ball into the air. Then the player used the same stick to hit the ball. Scoring was based either on reaching a base of some kind without being tagged out or on the distance traveled by the ball. Poorer children used a brisket bone as a lever and a hole dug into the ground as a trap, while rich children might have special knurs made of stag's horn and lead. The "base ball" (*NA* 15) played by the young Catherine Morland might well have been trap ball, or it might have been stool ball, another bat-and-ball game with bases that dates back to the Middle Ages.

Battledore and shuttlecock was simply an earlier form of badminton, which acquired its present name in the mid-nineteenth century. Austen mentions playing it at Godmersham with a nephew in a letter of August 24, 1805:

Yesterday was a very quiet day with us; my noisiest efforts were writing to Frank, & playing at Battledore & Shuttlecock with William; he & I have practised together two mornings, & improve a little; we have frequently kept it up *three* times, & once or twice *six*.

Bowls was a more sedate sport, played on a stretch of flat, close-cropped lawn called a bowling green (*MP* 90). Wooden balls, deliberately not quite round to give them a curved trajectory, were rolled at a target ball called the jack. It was a popular game for those who could afford to set aside the requisite piece of land and landscape it appropriately. William Cowper chastised parsons, in particular for indulging in the sport:

I could not help wishing that the honest vicar, instead of indulging his genius for improvements, by enclosing his gooseberry bushes within a Chinese rail, and converting half an acre of glebeland into a bowling green, would have applied part of his income to the more laudable purpose of sheltering his parishioners from the weather during their attendance at divine service.

Cowper would no doubt have disapproved, then, of Mr. Du Quesne, a clergyman and a friend of the diarist James Woodforde, who had installed a bowling green on his property; Woodforde "played a Game of Bowls on his Green" in May 1784. Like so many other games, bowls was adapted for friendly gambling; on this occasion, Woodforde lost sixpence to his opponents.

Social Games

All games were to some extent social, since they existed to pass time pleasantly with other people, but some games were specifically designed to be played indoors and to facilitate merriment, rather than to demonstrate mental or physical prowess. They might partake of mental or physical activity or a little of both, but their main attraction was personal interaction. Among these "merry evening games" (*E* 28) were hunt the slipper, snapdragon, bullet pudding, blind-man's-buff, hide-and-seek, and oranges and lemons. In hunt the slipper, participants sat in a circle and passed a slipper around behind their backs. A guesser in the center of the circle then had to guess who held the slipper. Snapdragon was a game in which players snatched currants from a bowl of burning liquor. Bullet pudding, a game often played at Edward Austen's house at Godmersham, used a single bullet hidden in a dish of flour; participants had to find it using their noses and chins only. Edward's daughter Fanny Knight reported that the game turned the players into "strange figures all covered with flour but the worst is that you must not laugh for fear of the flour getting up your nose & mouth & choking you." Blind-man's-buff involved blindfolding one person, who was turned around three times and then attempted to locate the other players. When he managed to catch one, he had to guess who it was without looking from beneath his blindfold; if he succeeded, his captive became the next "blind man." Hide-and-seek was played very much as it is today; oranges and lemons was a game like "London Bridge," in which players passed beneath an arch formed by the hands and arms of two other players and tried to avoid capture at the end of a rhyme:

"Oranges and Lemons,"
Say the bells of St. Clements,
"You owe me five farthings,"
Say the bells of St. Martins,
"When will you pay me?"
Say the bells of Old Bailey,
"I do not know,"
Says the great bell of Bow.

For men, one of the principal social games was billiards (*NA* 96;
S&S 111, 305; *P&P* 180; *MP* 125,
127, 183), a game in which balls
were propelled around a green-
cloth-covered table using "maces,"
the ancestors of today's pool cues.
The sides of the table were cush-
ioned with felt; rubber cushions
and slate-bedded tables would not
be introduced until after Austen's
time. There were six pockets on
the table, just as there are on a
modern pool table—one at each
corner and one in the middle of
each long side; there were also
three balls, one for each of two
players and a cue ball.

Billiards, 1780. Courtesy of the Lewis Walpole Library, Yale
University. 780.0.7.

Mental Games

Mental games were primarily
strategic or creative and were not
necessarily conducive to conversation or socializing. They included chess, backgammon
(*P&P* 69; *E* 9, 329, 377), dominoes, draughts (checkers), nine
men's morris, poetry competitions, charades, and riddles. The
Austen family, well read and in-
ventive, was particularly fond of
these sorts of games. Austen's
works contain several charades (*E*
76, 77, 82), which were riddles
that had to conform to a specific
pattern. Each charade took the
form of a poem whose answer

A Hitt at Backgammon, Thomas Rowlandson, 1810. Courtesy of the Lewis Walpole Library, Yale University.
810.11.19.1.

had to be a two-syllable word. The poem hinted at the meaning of the
first syllable, then at the meaning of the second syllable, then at the meaning of both syllables together. An early Austen charade is included in her
History of England:

My first is what my second was to James 1st, and you tread on my whole.
(*MW* 148)

The poetry is lacking here, but the riddle otherwise follows the classic pattern. The first syllable is "car" (Carr) for Robert Carr, earl of Somerset (c. 1590–1645), who was for a time the favorite ("pet") of James I. The "whole," that is, the two syllables together, form "carpet," which one indeed treads upon. Mr. Elton, too, offers a charade, this time in verse:

> My first doth affliction denote,
>> Which my second is destined to feel
> And my whole is the best antidote
>> That affliction to soften and heal. (*E* 70)

The answers are "woe," "man," and "woman." Elton's next charade (*E* 71), like his first, is a highly intellectual way of flirting with Emma:

> My first displays the wealth and pomp of kings,
>> Lords of the earth! Their luxury and ease.
> Another view of man, my second brings,
>> Behold him there, the monarch of the seas!
>
> But, ah! United, what reverse we have!
>> Man's boasted power and freedom, all are flown;
> Lord of the earth and sea, he bends a slave,
>> And woman, lovely woman, reigns alone.
>
>> Thy ready wit the word will soon supply.
>> May its approval beam in that soft eye!

The answers are "court," "ship," and "courtship." Emma, a clever woman, figures out the charade almost instantly, but Harriet Smith is stumped until Emma explains it to her (*E* 72–73). Three more of Austen's charades are printed in the *Minor Works* (450).

Magazines often published charades and riddles, usually providing the answers in their next issues. *Le Beau Monde* for September 1807 published a group of charades; however, I have been unable to locate the answers for them, and they present an interesting challenge for those who wish to test their mettle against a puzzle from Austen's era.

I.

Take my first from Vagaries; and from your best friend
Take my Second, if ever you money should lend.
But take not my Whole, if you ever for life,
Should take to your bosom a husband or wife.

II.

On the head of my First grows my Second;
    And, bating a little bad spelling,
Join both, and my whole may be reckon'd
    A thing w[h]ere good sense has no dwelling.

III.

My First is a roarer of might and of main;
My Second roars out in a still louder strain;
Of my Whole, if I have but enough in my chest,
Without bills or cash, I might sure be at rest.

IV.

Be my First, and you're hateful by nature;
    Be my Second, and Nature's your friend;
Be my Whole, and there's no human creature
Will e'er for your nature contend.*

Riddles were similar to charades, but they were not strictly limited to two-syllable answers. Mr. Woodhouse's "Kitty, a fair but frozen maid" (*E* 70, 78–79) puzzle is a riddle rather than a charade, and the answer is "a candle." Riddles, charades, anagrams, conundrums, rebuses, and the like were collected by a number of people (*E* 69–70), including an Austen connection, Mrs. Eliza Chute of the Vyne, who amassed about 500 examples. The game with the spelling letters in *Emma* (*E* 348–349) is similar to puzzles involving anagrams, which are words reorganized to spell other words. A conundrum, like a charade, was a specific type of riddle, in which the answer involved some sort of pun. Mr. Weston's conundrum is just this sort of play on words; his "two letters of the alphabet . . . that express perfection" are M and A, which, sounded out, are Emm-a (*E* 371). This is a good enough conundrum in itself, but, as David Selwyn has pointed out, Austen, whose family adores these sorts of puzzles, may have included an extra layer of complexity. Mr. Knightley's commentary on the conundrum, that "*Perfection* should not have come quite so soon" (*E* 371), may be a reference to a theory of eighteenth-century philosopher Francis Hutcheson's, in which perfection of virtue is expressed as a mathematical formula using the letters M and A as variables. Perfection was achieved when M, representing a moment or occasion of good, equaled A, representing the ability of a person to act for the greater good—in other words, when people did all the good that was in their power. As Selwyn points out, when Mr. Knightley makes his observation, Emma is at the Box Hill picnic, acting selfishly and thoughtlessly and therefore not in accordance with moral perfection.

Many types of mental games, other than charades, involved poetry. Mrs. Elton refers to an acrostic (*E* 372)—a poem in which the first letters of the lines, read from top to bottom, spell out words, often a person's name;

---

*My husband and I believe we have solved charades II and III—"coxcomb" and "windfalls." We have yet to solve charades I and IV.

this was one of many ways in which an astute versifier could show off his or her talent.* Other poetic games included bouts-rimés, in which the contestants were given a set of words with which to end their lines; then they had a fixed amount of time, usually half an hour among the Austens, to construct a poem around them. One example, described by Jane's nephew James Edward Austen-Leigh, had to end its lines with the words "Sleep—Creep—Chatter—Turn—Burn—Batter." Sometimes the Austen family would write questions on pieces of paper and nouns on other pieces; then contestants would draw a piece of paper from each pile and have to compose a poem that answered the question while including the specified noun. James Edward Austen-Leigh once composed a quatrain that had to include the word "fox" and answer the question "Do you take snuff?" His poem would have been well liked by the family, not only because it met the requirements of the contest but also because it poked gentle fun at himself and another:

> As seldom take I snuff, alack!
>   As Robert takes a fox;
> Although for show he hunts a pack,
>   And I display a box.

See also Cards.

Gardens and Landscape

Eighteenth-century landowners spent a great deal of time and money remaking the grounds of their estates (*MP* 53, 56–57, 61, 241–243). A series of trends and revolutions altered the formal French-style garden, turning it into a relic and replacing it with the landscape still considered quintessentially English. At first, the formal garden, with its parterres and topiaries, was replaced by an iconic landscape dotted with statues and structures full of symbolic significance. William Kent, a midcentury landscape gardener who invented the sunken fence or "ha-ha" (a glorified ditch—*MP* 96, 100), created this sort of landscape at Stowe.

He was succeeded by Lancelot "Capability" Brown (1715–1783), a revolutionary designer who swept away all remaining traces of the rigidly geometric garden, and, making heavy use of ha-has to open up grand vistas, created vast parks or rolling, grassy plains punctuated by clumps of trees (*S&S* 27; *E* 100). His trademarks, aside from the undulating lawns (*F&E*, *MW* 5; *LS*, *MW* 271; *Sand*, *MW* 406; *S&S* 302; *P&P* 267; *MP* 65, 90; *E* 273, 434; *P* 14), were his use of water and trees. He diverted streams (*F&E*, *MW* 5, 9; *P&P* 245, 253; *MP* 56, 242; *E* 358) in order to make them

---

*Lewis Carroll's *Alice in Wonderland* begins with an acrostic poem spelling out his inspiration's name: Alice Pleasance Liddell.

more attractive and built artificial ponds to reflect the mansions of his employers. Trees were arranged in irregular clumps to create a sense of perspective, with a belt of trees enclosing much of the park to screen out views of any land that did not form part of the estate, and a path formed a circuit winding through this belt. Uvedale Price, a leader of the picturesque movement, hated the Brownian belts. The belt, he wrote in 1796,

> has, indeed, all the sameness and formality of the avenue, to which it has succeeded, without any of its simple grandeur; for though in an avenue you see the same objects from beginning to end, and in the belt a new set every twenty yards, yet each successive part of this insipid circle is so like the preceding, that though really different, the difference in scarcely felt; and there is nothing that so dulls, and the same time so irritates the mind, as perpetual change without variety.
>
> The avenue has a most striking effect, from the very circumstance of its being strait; no other figure can give that image of a grand gothic aisle with its natural columns and vaulted roof, whose general mass fills the eye, while the particular parts insensibly steal from it in a long gradation of perspective. The broad solemn shade adds a twilight calm to the whole, and makes it, above all other places, most suited to meditation. . . .
>
> The destruction of so many of these venerable approaches, is a fatal consequence of the present excessive horror of strait lines. Sometimes, indeed, avenues do cut through the middle of very beautiful and varied ground, with which the stiffness of their form but ill accords, and where it were greatly to be wished that they had never been planted. . . . But being there, it may often be doubtful whether they ought to be destroyed; for whenever such a line of trees is taken away, there must be a long vacant space that will separate the grounds, with their old original trees, on each side of it; and young trees planted in the vacancy, will not in half a century connect the whole together.

Price was reacting too late to save many avenues, for, as he noted, the interest in natural landscaping, begun by Brown and Kent, had replaced avenues with lawns, belts, and clumps. Price was no fan of the clump, either, pointing out dourly that "if the first letter was taken away" the resulting word "would most accurately describe its form and effect." Clumps, he continued, "from the trees being generally of the same age and growth, planted nearly at the same distance in a circular form, and from each tree being equally pressed by his neighbour, are as like each other as so many puddings turned out of one common mould."

Brown's revolution, however, amounted to more than trees and water. He also uprooted all superfluous statuary and decreed against flower gardens, reducing the palette of the landscape to shades of green and brown and the silvered blue of the water. Pemberley's rolling hills, simple stream banks, modified stream, rim of "woody hills," and ten-mile path around the park are characteristic of a Capability Brown landscape (*P&P* 245–246, 253–254). Brown had an enormous aspect on the English landscape, not only because he designed about 150 estates at the enormous cost of 10 guineas a day but also because a generation of imitators adopted his ideas and employed them elsewhere.

Brown's successor was Humphry Repton (1752–1818), who believed in the value of land, first and foremost, as it served the needs and comfort of people. He favored parks over forests and history painting over landscape painting precisely because the former in each pair concerned itself primarily with human activity. Austen stigmatized Repton (*MP* 55) in *Mansfield Park* as a destroyer of the grand avenues (*MP* 56, 82, 103) of old trees (*NA* 177; *MP* 55; *P* 36) that lined paths and roads, and in fact he did recommend doing away with avenues that destroyed the view from the house, but he was actually in favor of preserving most old timber (*Sand, MW* 426; *S&S* 302; *MP* 82, 241). Austen appears to have based her opinion of Repton on the before-and-after views at an estate held by her mother's family, and she may well have seen other examples of his work or heard him discussed in her circle of acquaintances. She knew his practices well enough, at least, to be accurate about his fees: he did, indeed, charge five guineas a day (*MP* 53) plus travel expenses. However, she was wrong about many of his theories, for he actually held many of the same ideas about landscape that she did.

Like Austen, Repton approved of building houses in sheltered valleys rather than at the tops of hills (*Sand, MW* 379–380; *S&S* 28–29); like her, he appreciated flowers and restored them to the monochrome Brownian landscape. He also approved of gravel walks and shade near the house for the sake of comfort, though Brown had done away with many such features in favor of bringing the rippling grass right up to the foundation of the house. Despite the fact that Repton invented the term "landscape gardener" specifically to evoke the connections between scenes on canvas and those in nature, he opposed those gardeners who sought picturesque effects at the expense of utility and comfort. In *Sketches and Hints* (1795), he explained, in a swipe at the doyen of the picturesque, William Gilpin, that he was not designing landscapes "for the residence of banditti." Garden historian John Dixon Hunt has suggested that the description of Donwell Abbey in *Emma* is in fact a Reptonian landscape. Austen describes the farm and its mansion house as snug and practical. She admires

> the respectable size and style of the building, its suitable, becoming, characteristic situation, low and sheltered—its ample gardens stretching down to meadows washed by a stream, of which the Abbey, with all the old neglect of prospect, had scarcely a sight—and its abundance of timber in rows and avenues, which neither fashion nor extravagance had rooted up.—The house was larger than Hartfield, and totally unlike it, covering a good deal of ground, rambling and irregular, with many comfortable and one or two handsome rooms.—It was just what it ought to be, and it looked what it was—and Emma felt an increasing respect for it.

This, Hunt says, is perfectly in keeping with Repton's emphasis on "the propriety of the buildings, the avoidance of overly calculated picturesque vistas, the retention of old timber, and such formal features as avenues, together with the estate's exact appeal to the mind's judgment." He points out that the phrase "It looked like what it was" even unintentionally echoes Repton's own language in his plan for a cottage on the grounds of Blaise Castle: "it must look like what it is, the habitation of a labourer who has the care of the adjoining woods, but its simplicity should be the effect of Art and not of accident."

The difference between them is Repton's understandable value for "Art" in landscape, whereas Austen appears to have wanted to take the inherited landscape, avenues and all, and leave it alone, untouched by "awkward taste" (*P&P* 245). Virtually all remaking of the landscape meets with her disapproval, and Repton's art merely tinkers with, or tries to restore, what should, in her opinion, have been there all along. The description of Donwell rejects all artifice; there is a river, but it can barely be seen from the house, and there is a pond, but it is not a Brownian mirror of water but a utilitarian fishpond (*E* 361, 362).

Parks, Woods, and Shrubberies

Estates with sizable acreage had both a garden and pleasure ground near the house and a vast sweep of grass and woodland (*S&S* 88, 302; *P&P* 245, 267, 301; *MP* 56, 91, 94–95) farther off, known as the park (*Sand, MW* 426; *NA* 178; *S&S* 88, 226, 302; *P&P* 155, 156, 182, 195, 245, 253, 325, 352; *MP* 15, 27, 48, 56, 68, 69, 97, 103; *E* 275). The park, as designed by Brown, Repton, and their imitators, was more than pretty or picturesque. It was also practical. Its swaths of meadow* (*Sand, MW* 379; *NA* 214) could be rented out to the owners of livestock, and it actually brought in more money from grazing than it could have from the planting of wheat. In time, the livestock came to seem decorative and pastoral, but they also raised the park owner's income. Likewise, the fences, hedges (*Watsons, MW* 321; *MP* 208; *E* 83, 189; *P* 86, 87, 90), ha-has, and palings (fences—*Sand, MW* 426; *P&P* 155, 195; *E* 89, 275) used to direct the flow of animal traffic came to be seen as essential features of an attractive rural landscape.

The clumps of shrubs and trees that gave variety to the landscape were likewise useful. Like the fences and ha-has, they controlled the movements of animals. They provided habitat for game birds such as pheasants and thus provided pleasure to the men of the family, and they also provided timber (*S&S* 375) that could be culled periodically. Landowners planted fast-growing softwoods among the valuable hardwoods, forcing the hard-

---

*"Water meadows," mentioned in *MP* 55, were simply meadows that at times were covered by the rising water of rivers or streams.

woods to grow taller and straighter to compete for sunlight. Coppices*
(*NA* 106; *P&P* 253–254), or sections of shrubs and young trees, were
planted specifically in order to be cut occasionally. Some landowners, including Jane's brother Edward, created "plantations" (*Sand, MW* 381; *NA*
250; *S&S* 88, 302, 343; *MP* 54, 191, 218, 432) of trees to be harvested
at maturity, and these stores of timber added materially to the value of an
estate.

Planting trees had another practical benefit—the shade offered to
strollers. Landowners often added a "wilderness" (*P&P* 352; *MP* 90,
94–95, 103) to the pleasure grounds near the house, a grove of trees that,
in its neat gravel paths and conveniently placed seats and benches, bore
little resemblance to a real wilderness. These touches of civilization, however, were not resented by ladies walking in such grounds.

Gardeners planted a wide variety of trees. They planted oak (*NA* 111,
142, 161; *MP* 83, 99, 205) and ash (*S&S* 302) for timber, interspersed
with larch (*MP* 91) or pine (*Ode, MW* 75; *Evelyn, MW* 189) to encour-
age growth. Elms (*L&F, MW* 97, 98) made attractive borders for paths.
Firs (*L&F, MW* 100; *Evelyn, MW* 181; *S&S* 302), though they were used
in combination with chestnuts as a boundary at Steventon, did not earn a
recommendation for this purpose from Uvedale Price. In *An Essay on the
Picturesque* (1796), he observed that their lower trunks did not provide
enough concealment. Yews (*MP* 241) tended to be found in churchyards.†

Some trees and shrubs were grown not for timber or as natural walls
but for their shade (*MP* 91) or appearance. These included lime (*E* 360,
362); laurel (*P&P* 155; *MP* 91, 209), which was admired for its full and
rapid growth; privet, which grew compactly and thus made good hedges;
heath (*MP* 105), in Austen's time any of a number of low, shrubby plants;
Lombardy poplar (*Evelyn, MW* 181; *S&S* 302), which grew into a narrow,
pointed column; and other species of poplar (*F&E, MW* 5), which were
leafier and made a pleasant sound in the wind. Some trees, such as mul-
berry (*S&S* 197), walnut (*Evelyn, MW* 189), apricot (*MP* 54–55), and
apple (*NA* 214; *E* 186) trees, produced fruit or nuts in addition to shade,
and in grounds too small for a separate orchard, these might form part of
the shrubbery (*Watsons, MW* 322; *NA* 176, 214; *S&S* 302, 306, 374;
P&P 86; *MP* 57, 65, 90, 209; *E* 26, 196, 336, 412, 424, 434; *P* 18,
127)—a little area designed for walking (*Evelyn, MW* 184; *LS, MW* 271;
P&P 52, 301, 351; *MP* 55, 208, 322, 323, 346, 357; *E* 196) and sitting
in the shade of shrubs and small trees. In addition to ornamental trees and
bushes, a shrubbery might feature flowers, currant bushes, and raspberry

---

*The "pollard" (*E* 83) also involved cutting, but a pollard was a tree that had been cut down to
force multitude of new branches to sprout from the cut trunk.
†Though, as the tree may have had pagan religious significance, the sites of the trees may have
been co-opted by early churches in order to supplant existing shrines.

canes. A paddock (*Sand, MW* 426; *P&P* 301)—a fenced area near the stables—might also be planted with some trees.

Certain trees, imported from warmer climates, were planted to create an exotic atmosphere. Myrtle (*Ode, MW* 74) and citron (*J&A, MW* 18, 20), for example, evoked the Mediterranean. Warren Hastings, governor-general of India and an Austen family acquaintance, bought back his ancestral home at Daylesford and filled its gardens with a dazzling variety of exotics—acacia (*S&S* 302), tamarisk, and mango— along with myriad native trees. When the grounds at Steventon were being redone in the fall of 1800, Jane wrote to Cassandra that an earlier plan to plant "beech, ash and larch" was in danger of being scrapped. The question was "whether it would be better to make a little orchard of it, by planting apples, pears and cherries, or whether it should be larch, mountain-ash and acacia."

THE LOVE LETTER.

The Love Letter, 1785. This view of a country estate's garden shows shady trees, a bench, and a gardener smoothing the gravel paths with a roller. Courtesy of the Lewis Walpole Library, Yale University. 785.10.11.1.

Gardens

The paths (*NA* 179; *P&P* 53, 327; *E* 360; *P* 90) that ran through gardens, shrubberies, and parks were made of gravel (*Evelyn, MW* 184; *NA* 161; *S&S* 302, 306, 359; *P&P* 42, 353; *MP* 322; *E* 186), which, unlike dirt, did not turn into mud in bad weather. It was time when too much moisture in either the air or the ground was considered bad for health, and the dryness of gravel spoke in its favor. The paths wound through the shrubbery, if there was one, and into the garden, which was often protected by walls (*S&S* 197; *MP* 54) and an ornamental gate (*Watsons, MW* 355; *S&S* 42). In larger gardens, there would be walks intersecting with each other (*P&P* 156); in smaller gardens, one path would make a circuit of the grounds.

A "garden" (*Sand, MW* 379; *Cath, MW* 193, 230; *NA* 13, 176, 240; *P&P* 67, 71, 155, 156, 217; *MP* 27, 191, 241–242, 291, 432; *E* 22, 58,

359; *P* 36) could mean all the planted grounds near a house, encompassing shrubbery, hedge mazes, formal topiary gardens if they still survived, flower gardens, and the kitchen garden. The term could also apply specifically to an area dedicated to growing flowers (*S&S* 226; *MP* 57; *P* 18) or to the kitchen garden (*Sand, MW* 380; *NA* 175–176, 178), which produced food and herbs for household use. In smaller homes, the flower garden and the kitchen garden would be united, and in laborers' cottages the flower garden would be almost entirely sacrificed for the sake of food production (*E* 87). Few people could afford the kind of massive landscaping seen at the fictional Pemberley and the real-world Stowe, so they constricted the park to a little lawn and a few trees and gave the garden most of the available space (*S&S* 28; *MP* 54).

Those who could afford to garden on a grand scale invested not only in a kitchen garden but also in an orchard (*Sand, MW* 379; *NA* 178, 240; *E* 238; *P* 23), a walled enclosure for fruit trees. Those who could not grew fruit in kitchen gardens and shrubberies, as, for example, in Mr. Knightley's strawberry beds (*E* 354, 358) or in the real-life strawberry beds at Steventon. The Austens managed to grow currants, gooseberries, raspberries, and strawberries in their little garden in Southampton, and at Chawton they grew plums, apricots, currants, strawberries, and gooseberries.

A garden was hard work. In great homes, the work was done by servants, but in smaller homes such as the Austens', the labor was performed by the family itself. Mrs. Austen was active in the garden into old age, and novelist Fanny Burney D'Arblay's husband was a keen, though unlucky, gardener. Burney wrote a letter in March 1800 explaining what had happened to their garden during an absence from home:

> M. d'Arblay has worked most laboriously in his garden; but his misfortunes there, during our absence, might *melt a Heart of stone*. The Horses of our next neighbouring Farmer broke through our Hedges, and have made a kind of bog of our Meadow, by scampering in it during the wet; the sheep followed, who have eaten up All our Greens—Every sprout and Cabbage and Lettuce, destined for the Winter—while the Horses dug up our Turnips and carrots, and the swine, pursuing such examples, have trod down all the young plants, besides devouring whatever the others left of vegetables! our potatoes, left—from our abrupt departure, in the Ground, are all rotten or frost-bitten—and utterly spoilt; and not a single thing has our whole Ground produced us since we came home.

An example of the kind of labor gone to waste in D'Arblay's case can be seen in Francis Collingwood's *Universal Cook, and City and Country Housekeeper*, which offers advice on gardening for each month of the year. April's list of tasks is as follows:

> If you omitted to finish your planting or sowing at the latter end of last month, do it at the beginning of this. Sow the main crop of the red and

green borecole, in an open situation, to plant out in May and June, for autumn, winter, and the supply of the following spring. Sow likewise some of the purple and cauliflower sorts of brocoli, to plant out in summer, for the first general autumn crop.

Kidney beans of the early dwarf kinds should now be sown in a warm border, as also some speckled dwarfs, and a large supply in the open quarters, in drills two feet, or two and a half distant. Sow different kinds of lettuce two or three times this month, for succeeding crops.

Great care must now be taken of your melons in hot beds. Train the vines regular, give them air daily, with occasional moderate waterings. Cover the glasses every night, and keep up a good heat in the beds, by linings of hot dung.

Sow full crops of peas for a succession of marrowfats once a fortnight, and also of other large kinds. Sow the seed for all sorts of pot-herbs, and plant aromatic herbs, such as mint, sage, balm, rue, rosemary, lavender, and such like, either by young or full plants.

Continue sowing successional crops of radishes every fortnight, in open situations, in order to have an eligible variety, young and plentiful. Sow a principal crops of savoys in an open situation, detached from walls, hedged, or any other impediment, that the plants may be strong and robust for planting out in summer, to furnish a full crop well cabbaged in autumn, and for the general winter supply, till next spring, this being a most valuable cabbage in autumn and winter.

His instructions for the other months are similarly copious. One task he does not mention, however, is the task on which Parson Woodforde was employed in April 1780, "painting some boarding in my Wall Garden . . . to prevent people in the Kitchen seeing those who had occasion to go to Jericho." "Jericho" was the slang term for an outhouse, and this example gives a good sense of the vast difference between the gardens of huge estates and those of ordinary people. It is hard to imagine Mr. Darcy or General Tilney stooping to concern themselves with the outhouse wall.

Garden Structures

Scattered throughout park and garden were various structures designed for the comfort of those who used the ground. These included seats (*Cath, MW* 231; *P&P* 327; *MP* 57, 94) and benches (*MP* 95, 208; *E* 273) on which walkers could rest, some of which were backed by stone or brick walls to provide shelter from the wind. Other gardens had statuary, fountains, urns, and obelisks that had escaped the clutches of Capability Brown and his followers. These decorative structures sometimes alluded to the history of the family that owned the place and were sometimes intended to look much older than they were. Faux ruins enjoyed a period of popularity in the second half of the eighteenth century, and the only question was how to make a new pile of stone look properly antique, so that it appeared to be the genuine remains of a castle or abbey.

Some landscape designers avoided ruins altogether, favoring brand-new temples (*S&S* 302, 303) and hermitages (*NA* 107; *P&P* 352) in classical or Gothic styles. Despite the austere sound of the word "hermitage," such houses were modern and habitable. These buildings looked ancient, but they concealed comfortable rooms where guests could drink tea or even take a bath. In one case, a Greek façade hid an old and unsightly building that the landowner in question could not bear to tear down because his mother had been fond of it.

Closer to the house, hothouses (*Visit, MW* 54; *Cath, MW* 230; *NA* 178; *S&S* 226, 303) with glass panels and fireplaces could be built at enormous cost. The cost of glazing of such buildings, along with the window tax they involved and the staff required to run them, made them a luxury that only the richest could afford. Inside, exotic flowers bloomed and young plants were cultivated in preparation for transplanting them outdoors when the weather was warm enough. Some hothouses were called "succession houses" (*NA* 178) because there were a number of them at varying temperatures, and plants could be moved from one to another to fool them into bearing fruit out of season. Another type of specialized hothouse was the pinery (*NA* 178), devoted to the growing of pineapples. This was such an expensive and time-consuming endeavor that the pineapple served as an edible symbol of its owner's wealth, and offering pineapple to guests was the ultimate gesture of hospitality. *See also* Agriculture; Public Places.

Gentry

The gentry, the class to which Austen belonged, may be thought of as a kind of upper middle class—not always "upper" in terms of income, but certainly in terms of social status, and often in terms of income as well. The differentiation between the social and the economic definitions of class is an important one, as money was already tending in Austen's time to blur the distinctions between classes, a phenomenon that troubled many.

People of the late eighteenth and early nineteenth centuries had a very clear notion of rank and class. At the top of the hierarchy, of course, was the royal family. Below that lay the nobility, from dukes down to barons. Below that was the gentry, stretching from baronets and knights at the top of the scale down to penurious, but well-educated, clergymen. Members of the professions—law, clergy, medicine, and the upper ranks of the military (*MP* 91)—were considered gentlemen, even though they had to work for a living, but the ideal was the gentleman-farmer, who lived off the proceeds of his land and the proceeds of his investments (*E* 136, 358). Below the gentry were tradesmen (*P&P* 15; *E* 183, 481), prosperous tenant farmers (distinguished from the gentry chiefly by education and family lineage), and successful artisans. Most numerous but lowest in status were the common working people—servants, farm laborers, apprentices, and so on—who might be called anything from "the commons," to "the peasantry," to "the mob."

It was at the fringes of each class that difficulties arose. If a man were a wealthy brewer or shipping merchant or industrialist, to what extent was he a gentleman? If he could not qualify as a gentleman, could his idle wife and children be considered gentry? A physician was clearly a gentleman, but what about a surgeon, who held less professional status, or an apothecary, who held less still? Was a writer a gentleman? What about an architect or an academic?

The answer to all these questions was that it depended on a host of circumstances. Being a gentleman or gentlewoman (*P&P* 106; *E* 213) depended largely on birth (*E* 62; *P* 21) and occupation, but what really cemented class membership was behavior (*E* 278). A good education (*E* 15), good manners, and graceful movements when walking, sitting, and dancing (*E* 328) mattered a great deal (*E* 33). Emma, the most class-conscious of Austen's heroines, is surprised to find a letter written by a mere yeoman farmer free of "grammatical errors" (*E* 50–51), just as the letter of a gentleman might be. In *Persuasion*, Charles Hayter, alone of all his family, can be considered a member of the gentry, and Austen explicitly links his upward mobility to education:

> the young Hayters would, from their parents' inferior, retired, and unpolished way of living, and their own defective education, have been hardly in any class at all, but for their connexion with Uppercross; this eldest son of course excepted, who had chosen to be a scholar and a gentleman, and who was very superior in cultivation and manners to all the rest. (*P* 74)

He is further assisted in his rise to the gentry by genteel connections on his mother's side and by his choice of a religious profession. The three factors together combine to make him a more eligible suitor for a Miss Musgrove. If education and polish could raise a man, however, physical awkwardness, bumptious manners, poor grammar, and a lack of acquaintance with history, geography, or literature carried corresponding social penalties.

Rank within one's profession mattered a great deal. A militia colonel was a gentleman, but a sergeant was definitely not, and a lieutenant might or might not be, depending on his antecedents and deportment. An admiral was a gentleman (*P* 21), and a captain probably was, but the ordinary sailors were not. A physician, who by definition had to have attended one of the universities, was certainly a gentleman, but a surgeon was not. Thus, Mr. Edwards, in the incomplete novel *The Watsons*, discourages his daughter from falling in love with Sam, even though he "is a very good sort of young Man, & I dare say a very clever Surgeon" (*Watsons*, *MW* 324). Bishops were actually peers for the purposes of membership in Parliament, but by birth they might be members of the gentry. Members of the clergy were treated by almost everyone as gentlemen for the purposes of social ranking, although the snobbish Sir Walter Elliot cannot bring himself to regard a curate, the lowest-ranking type of clergyman, as a gentleman (*P* 23).

Another factor was relationship by marriage; marriage into a genteel family could confer a rosy reflected glow onto other members of one's own family, while marriage down the social scale slightly dimmed the family's social status. Thus, it matters very much that Mrs. Bennet is the daughter of an attorney (a less prestigious member of the legal profession), that her sister married a law clerk (lower still), and that her brother is a London tradesman (not genteel at all—*P&P* 28, 37). All of these associations reflect poorly on Elizabeth Bennet's social status and thus her ability to attract a husband from the nobility or even the upper reaches of the gentry.

Personal lineage, too, counted; a writer might be a gentleman if he were born a gentleman and wrote for personal pleasure, as did Horace Walpole, but if he wrote to make a living and had been born the son of a tradesman, he was not a gentleman at all but merely a different sort of artisan. The issue of financial necessity also entered into the class status of tradesmen. A merchant who spent all day, six days a week, engaged in active trade was clearly not a gentleman, while a merchant wealthy enough to delegate most of the day-to-day operations to his inferiors might be fully accepted by genteel society (*E* 33–34).

Money could also be used to buy gentility (*E* 207), at least for the next generation. It could buy a country estate (*E* 16, 310) that reflected some glory on its owner; it could purchase entry by marriage into a genteel or even noble family, by means of a generous dowry; and it could buy expensive educations for one's children, resulting in the kinds of social graces and commonly held opinions that were expected among the gentry. Instances of this sort of social mobility occur in Austen's works: the Bingley sisters, for all their snobbery, are only one generation removed from trade, and their family has yet to buy a landed estate to seal its membership in the gentry (*P&P* 15), and Sir William Lucas, for all his pride in his title, began in trade as well and came to the king's attention through his wealth (*P&P* 18). It should be remembered, however, that origins in trade were not easily forgotten by one's associates; Mrs. Jennings, in *Sense and Sensibility*, is "the widow of a man who had got all his money in a low way" (i.e., trade—*S&S* 228), and Maria Williams, in *A Collection of Letters*, is taunted for having been the granddaughter of a wine merchant (*Col Let*, *MW* 158). Austen, though she was more egalitarian than many of her contemporaries, is not free from all ideas of class, and she scorns those who think that money alone determines gentry status (*S&S* 275).

There was another aspect to the interrelation of money and social class. Since the Middle Ages, it had always been a problem when a person of genteel birth and upbringing was impoverished to a point at which he could no longer maintain the style of living expected of his class. Without luck or external intervention, he was almost certainly doomed to have his children and grandchildren slip to the class below. This is a danger faced by several of Austen's characters, most famously Mrs. Bates, Miss Bates, and Jane Fairfax, whose relative poverty means they can afford to keep only one servant. In the course of one generation, their family has sunk to a fingernail grip on gentility, with the threat of sending Jane Fairfax into service looming over them all. Less prominently, William Walter Elliot has faced a similar situation; Anne's friend Mrs. Smith notes that when he was young, he was poor, "and it was as much as he could do to support the appearance of a gentleman" (*P* 199). Hospitality was one way of spending money to reinforce status; expenditure on fine clothing was another; hiring multiple servants, especially menservants, was a third (*E* 30).

Finally, gregarious necessity played some role in deciding who was and was not a member of the gentry. There was only so much isolation that a country family could bear; sooner or later, they had to have *someone* over to dinner, and if it were someone a bit below them, simply for lack of any neighbors on an equal footing, then so be it. A lonely clergyman might invite a surgeon to his home, and the surgeon thus gained a measure of gentility. Thus, a certain amount of socializing takes place in Highbury among "the gentlemen and half-gentlemen of the place" (*E* 197); those on the boundaries of gentility are included as a matter of convenience. However, a need for companionship only went so far; Mr. Woodhouse may think the world of his apothecary's medical opinion, but he never invites him to dinner.

Many people disapproved of these blurrings of class boundaries (*E* 310). A cartoon by Gillray, c. 1808, displays the pretensions of a tenant farmer, Farmer Giles of Cheese Hall, whose daughter Betty is being trained in the genteel graces, including music. The contrast between the physical rusticity of the farmer's family and their aspirations to higher rank is portrayed as a joke on Farmer Giles; he is unaware that by imitating his social superiors, he emphasizes how little he belongs in their world. With considerably more earnestness and less humor, the anonymous author of *The Mirror of the Graces* (1811) voiced the concerns of many who feared to lose their social advantage over ambitious inferiors. She criticized the "fashion of educating all ranks of young women alike," in which "the brazier's daughter is taught to sing, dance, and play like the heiress to an earldom." Girls "of the plebeian classes," she insisted, should limit their education to the study of economical housekeeping. (She would have found a kindred spirit in Mrs. Norris, who thought Fanny Price's reluctance to learn music and drawing contemptible, but in perfect keeping with what Mrs. Norris thinks of as Fanny's class—*MP* 19.) At all times, she went on, social class was to be kept in mind. To inferiors, one should be dignified but not proud, helpful but not overly intimate. One should praise when appropriate and serve as a good example. To superiors, deference was the watchword, and how much deference depended entirely on rank:

> Deportment to superiors must ever carry with it that peculiar degree of ceremony which their rank demands. No intimacy of intercourse with them, no friendship and affection from them, ought ever to make us forget the certain respect which their stations require. Thus, for a mere gentlewoman to think of arrogating to herself the same homage of courtesy that is paid to a lady of quality, or to deny the just tribute of precedence, in every respect, to that lady, would be as absurd as presumptuous. Yet we see it; and ridicule from the higher circles is all she derives from her vain pretensions.

As a helpful guide to women in their quest to know their place in society, she provides a list of precedence, which reads to a more egalitarian society as comically complex:

> Queen. Then Princesses. Then follow, in regular order, Duchesses, Marchionesses, Countesses. The Wives of the Eldest sons of Marquisses. The Wives of the Younger sons of Dukes. Daughters of Dukes. Daughters of Marquisses. Viscountesses. Wives of the eldest sons of Earls. Daughters of Earls. Wives of the younger sons of Marquisses. Baronesses. Wives of the eldest sons of Viscounts. Daughters of Viscounts. Wives of the younger sons of Earls. Wives of the eldest sons of Barons. Daughters of Baronets. Wives of the younger sons of Viscounts. Wives of the younger sons of Barons. Wives of Baronets. Wives of Privy Counsellors, Commoners. Wives of Judges. Wives of Knights of the Garter. Wives of Knights of the Bath. Wives of Knights of the Thistle. Wives of Knights Bachelors. Wives of Generals. Wives of Admirals. Wives of the eldest sons of Baronets. Daughters of Knights according to their fathers' precedence. Wives of the younger sons of Baronets. Wives of Esquires and Gentlemen. Daughters of Esquires and Gentlemen. Wives of Citizens and Burgesses. The Wives of Military and Naval Officers of course take precedence of each other in correspondence with the rank of their husbands.
>
> This scale, if every young lady would bear in mind and conform to it, is a sufficient guide to the mere ceremony of precedence; and would effectually prevent those dangerous disputes in ball-rooms about places, and those rude jostlings in going in and out of assemblies, which are not more disagreeable than ill-bred.

A simpler, but equally traditional, view of the social world was proposed by the statesman Edmund Burke, who, in laying out his arguments against the French Revolution, described the English attitude toward class and society. "We fear God," he wrote; "we look up with awe to kings; with affection to parliaments; with duty to magistrates; with reverence to priests; and with respect to nobility." Austen at times echoes these sentiments; the estimable Mr. Knightley warns of spoiling Harriet Smith for her sphere in life, which is destined to be somewhere below the gentry (*E* 38). Austen herself pats Mrs. Jennings on the back for restricting her circle of friends to people whom a young gentlewoman can "know" without lowering herself (*S&S* 168). In these sentiments, she was perfectly in line with one of the principal authorities of the age, Mrs. Hester Chapone, whose *Letters on the Improvement of the Mind* (1772) were frequently reprinted. Her letter "On the Regulation of the Affections" reads like advice intended specifically for Emma Woodhouse, advising young women to "avoid intimacy with those of low birth and education," because their "servile flattery and submission . . . will infallibly corrupt your heart, and make all company insipid from whom you cannot expect the same homage."*

Yet Austen does not subscribe unquestioningly to the traditional hierarchy. In the same passage that she reassures her readers that Mrs. Jennings "visited no one, to whom an introduction could at all discompose the feelings of her young companions," she expects these readers to approve of Mrs. Jennings' loyalty in not dropping "a few old city friends"—friends from the mercantile districts of London—despite pressure from her more class-conscious daughter (*S&S* 168). Austen's Robert Martin (*E* 65) receives much more sympathetic treatment than Gillray's Farmer Giles, and her titled characters are often pretentious fools—Lady Catherine de Bourgh, "the Dowager Viscountess Dalrymple, and her daughter, the Honourable Miss Carteret" (*P* 148), Lord Osborne of *The Watsons*, and Sir Walter Elliott come to mind (*P* 166, 248). Invariably in her works, obsession with rank is equated with pettiness; Emma, in order to become a laudable woman, must learn to discard her youthful scrupulousness about class (*E* 29, 198, 214). Perhaps the best example of Austen's attitude is Captain Wentworth and all his associates in *Persuasion*; in the naval profession, she shows us, comradeship and merit are more important than birth and elegant posture while sitting. She is far from disdaining genteel education or manners, ridiculing the ignorant at least as much as the snobbish, but she seems to believe in a kind of natural gentility, an elite selected by intellect and decent behavior rather than by title or occupation. *See also* Titles.

Gig

The gig (*Clifford, MW* 43; *Sand, MW* 425; *NA* 65, 88; *P* 73) was merely one member of a large family of two-wheeled vehicles that included the curricle (*Clifford, MW* 43; *NA* 155) and the whisky. Carriages in this group were distinguished from each other not so much by the shape of the car-

---

*In the preceding paragraph, Chapone offers another piece of advice that echoes Anne Elliot's famous description of "good company" in *Persuasion* (150): "When I speak of the best company," Chapone writes, "I do not mean in the common acceptation of the word,—persons of high rank and fortune,—but rather the most worthy and sensible."

[Boy Bringing Round a Citizen's Curricle], Thomas Rowlandson, 1787. This carriage, identified as a curricle by the British Museum catalog, appears rather to be a gig, as it is drawn by only one horse. Courtesy of the Lewis Walpole Library, Yale University. 787.12.15.1.

riage body as by the way it was suspended above the wheels or hitched to a horse. In the body, the differences were subtle at best. The curricle seems to have been more likely than the gig or the whisky to have a folding leather hood, while the whisky might be missing part of the lower panel beneath the seat. All three had seats that were chair- or sleighlike, open in front, with room for one or two occupants, and often with arms that flared outward to protect the passengers from mud flung up by the wheels. Some of these two-wheeled vehicles had a platform in the rear on which a servant could ride (*Sand, MW* 425; *NA* 44); on one version, the so-called "suicide gig," this seat was especially high and precarious.

The most obvious difference between the gig and the curricle, other than the hood, was in the number of horses used. The curricle was typically pulled by two horses who were separated by a pole, while the gig was typically a one-horse vehicle (*NA* 44). It can be extremely difficult to tell the difference between the two, however, as spring designs changed over time, and the curricle closely resembled the one-horse cabriolet that was introduced into England early in the nineteenth century. John Thorpe adds to the reader's confusion by pointing out that his gig is "Curricle-hung" (*NA* 46) by which he means perhaps that the rear springs are "C" springs (shaped like the letter), which became common on curricles. Rear springs on gigs might be C springs or might instead be "whip" springs, which had a gentle overall curve and a small arc at one end.

William Felton, whose *Treatise on Carriages* (1801) is the standard reference to turn-of-the-century vehicles, confirms that the main difference is the number of horses but concedes that from that point the variations are nearly endless:

> There are two descriptions of two-wheeled carriages; the curricle which is used with two horses, and the chaise that is used with one horse only. The one-horse chaises are of different patterns, and are distinguished by a variety of names, but mostly by the gig and the whiskey, in which there is a material difference; but both the curricle and chaise, like other carriages, are finished in various fanciful ways.

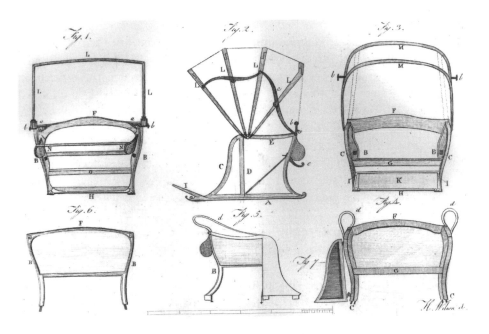

Gig, from William Felton's *Treatise on Carriages*, 1796. Library of Congress.

One of these "fanciful ways" of varying the two-wheeled carriage was the "changeable curricle, or curricle gig," which was light enough to be drawn by one horse but was "longer in the carriage than a common gig," and so "makes the appearance more uniform with that of a curricle, when used as such"—that is, when drawn by two horses. Thorpe's carriage might possibly be of this variety.

Thorpe goes on to brag about the features of his gig: "seat, trunk, sword-case, splashing-board, lamps, silver moulding, all you see complete; the iron-work as good as new, or better" (46). The seat is self-explanatory. The "trunk" would have been Thorpe's own traveling-trunk, strapped between the rear wheels above the axle; what he is really asking Catherine Morland to notice is that his carriage has a space for his trunk. The sword case was exactly what it sounds like, though it seems to have been a feature of the post chaise or chariot, where it formed a horizontal, tubular protuberance on the back of the carriage body. Contemporary engravings do not tend to show a sword case at the back of the gig, so perhaps Thorpe had improvised something. The splashing-board could have meant the flared panels at the top of each side of the gig, which minimized the dirt thrown up by the wheels, but since it is singular, it probably refers to a board in front of the driver's feet to block dirt stirred up by the horse's hooves. Illustrations from the early 1790s show extremely small footrests in front of the driver, while later gigs and curricles exhibit tall rectangular splash-boards that look rather like large cookie sheets balanced on one long edge. Depending on when this innovation reached Austen's circle of friends, the addition of this detail of Thorpe's equipage may have been one of her later revisions. As for the lamps, these were oil lamps which were not, to judge from contemporary drawings, a standard feature on all gigs at this time. By the 1830s, they were hung below the side splash guards, just above and inside the wheels. Thorpe is perhaps justifiably proud of this extra luxury, though the gig was not a vehicle that was ideal for night driving, so the lamps may also be intended as an example of his general silliness. The "silver moulding" is, however, consistent with the fancier gigs and curricles of the day, which were often fitted out with silver trim.

Many of these details would have been identical or nearly so on a curricle, making it all the more difficult to tell the two apart. The one-horse whisky, fortunately, can be distinguished from both the gig and the curricle by the manner in which the springs were attached. On the gig and curricle, the carriage body hung from the top ends of the springs, whose bottom ends were in turn connected to shafts or poles. The shafts were then fixed to the axles at one end and ran along the sides of the horse or horses, where they connected to the harness. On the whisky, the process was reversed: the seat was fixed instead to the shafts, and the shafts were then connected to the axles by the springs. In Austen's works, the whisky appears only in *The Memoirs of Mr. Clifford*, where she seems to have made an effort to list every type of carriage then in use and very nearly succeeds (*Clifford*, *MW* 43).

Gigs and curricles, however, make far more than a cameo appearance in her works. The crucial aspect of the gig and curricle, as they relate to Jane Austen, is how they were both used. Gigs—to speak now of the entire family of vehicles—were fast, fashionable, and driven not by a professional coachman but by the owner, for pleasure. Because they were carefully balanced and sprung, they provided a pleasant ride on fine days; because they were lightweight and inclined to tip, they required skill to handle. Because the owner himself drove, he got all the credit (or blame) for his handling of the horse or horses (*NA* 44, 157). In other words, curricles and gigs provided drivers with an opportunity to show off, to test their skill, and to experience, in a very direct way, an exhilarating sense of speed. It was this combination of advantages that allowed these vehicles, around the time Jane Austen reached adulthood, to supersede the phaeton as the height of style.

The curricle was more desirable than the gig, for reasons that are not quite clear. It appears to have had something to do with the way it drove; no doubt at least part of its attraction was that it was only slightly heavier than the gig but was driven by two horses and thus could travel somewhat faster (*Watsons*, *MW* 339; *NA* 156–157). For whatever reason, it became the must-have vehicle for fashionable young men (*NA* 35), and though a gig was nothing to be really ashamed of, a curricle was considered better. This may be why Thorpe hastens to point out that his gig is "curricle-hung"; if he cannot have the real thing, he can at least have the next best, and he still feels that he must offer some apology for not having a real curricle. He had "pretty well determined on [buying] a curricle" (*NA* 46), he says, but bought a gig instead because the opportunity arose. In fact, in *Northanger Abbey* carriage ownership serves as a subtle hint about Catherine Morland's proper mate; John Thorpe has the faux curricle, but Henry Tilney owns the real thing. She claims to "know so little about such things" (46) that she cannot judge whether Thorpe's gig was a bargain, but by the time she joins Henry in his curricle, she has decided "that a curricle was the prettiest equipage in the world" (156). Her opinion of carriage and man, in both cases, are in sync—indifferent on the one hand, enamored on the other.

Elsewhere, the ownership of a gig or a curricle is not necessarily as significant. The fawning Tom Musgrave drives a curricle, it is true (*Watsons*, *MW* 338, 339), as do the false Mr. Elliot (*P* 105) and Mr. Willoughby (*S&S* 52, 67, 75, 194), but so does William Goulding, a neighbor in *Pride and Prejudice* of whom the reader hears almost nothing (*P&P* 316) and the stupid, but decent, Mr. Rushworth (*MP* 84). So, too, does the reasonably sensible Charles Musgrove (*P* 105). The curricle is neither good nor evil, but merely an indicator of a certain degree of youth, virility, and wealth. In Willoughby's case, the curricle is an evil, but only because he does not have the income to maintain it, a fact that Mrs. Jennings mentions as only one of his many extravagances (*S&S* 194).

Willoughby could, of course, save money by owning a gig instead and getting rid of one of his horses, but he no doubt knows the different impressions the two vehicles would create. Miss Denham, of the incomplete novel *Sanditon*, certainly knows. Status-hungry, she is "immediately gnawed by the want of a handsomer Equipage than the simple Gig" in which she and her brother travel, and she is embarrassed to see the groom leading it about (to cool down the horse after its exertions) in plain sight (*MW* 394). Likewise, Anne Elliot's sister Mary, prompted perhaps by "the Elliot pride," refuses a seat in Admiral Croft's gig. She will not "make a third in a one-horse chaise" (chaise was another term at the time for these open-seated, two-wheeled, roofless carriages), partly it seems because of the indignity of squeezing in and partly because of the nature of the carriage itself, which does not suit her ideas of the grandeur suitable to her station (*P* 90). The gig would, of course, have seated only two (Felton specifies that two-wheeled carriage seats were between 2 feet 10 inches and 3 feet 2 inches wide), but Admiral and Mrs. Croft hospitably make room for a third, and Anne gratefully and gracefully accepts their offer (*P* 91). As with so many of Austen's mentions of carriages, this incident elucidates the characters of all involved.

In both the instances just described, it is not the ownership of a gig that is condemned, but the attitudes of others toward the gig. However, there is some evidence that Austen considers a curricle a suitable accessory for a hero. Sir Edward Denham, another male character who seems destined for unsuitability, drives a gig (*Sand, MW* 403), as does the insufferable Mr. Collins of *Pride and Prejudice* (*P&P* 168). Mr. Darcy, however, drives a curricle (*P&P* 260), setting up the same contrast that Austen draws between Mr. Thorpe and Mr. Tilney.

There were other vehicles besides curricles and whiskies in the gig family. One of these was the tandem (*Sand, MW* 425), a variant of the dogcart. Dogcarts were two-wheeled carriages that seated four—two facing forward, two facing backward, with the pairs back to back. Beneath their joint seat was a box with louvered sides and a rear door that unlatched at the top. This compartment was for transporting hunting dogs—hence the name of the vehicle—with the louvers allowing the dogs to breathe en route. The name "tandem" simply meant that the carriage was pulled by two horses, one in front of the other, rather than side by side.

The sulky, not mentioned in Austen, was another two-wheeled, giglike carriage. It took its name from the fact that there was only one seat, and the driver could thus be alone, presumably sulking for some reason. The buggy was another sort of two-wheeled carriage, sometimes defined as a gig with a hood (*Clifford, MW* 43). The Irish car (*E* 374) was very much like a dogcart, but with the box turned ninety degrees, so that the passengers sat sideways with reference to the horse. The driver, too, sat sideways, which could be extremely precarious. It was developed, as its name implies, in Ireland, and Austen uses it with characteristic consistency in *Emma*, the one of her novels that makes the most dramatic use of Ireland and things Irish. *See also* Carriages and Coaches; Phaeton.

Gloves

Gloves (*Watsons, MW* 331, 336; *Sand, MW* 374; *S&S* 221; *P&P* 316; *E* 237; *P* 236) were an essential part of both men's and women's wear, worn by everyone with any pretense to fashion and even by servants who waited at table. They became associated with propriety and modesty. For women, they helped to preserve the pallid skin that was so highly prized. Gloves were worn outdoors, while dancing (*Col Let, MW* 157), and at evening parties (*Cath, MW* 213), but they were removed for dinner. Because they were such common items, and perhaps because they were also so personal—one has only to remember Romeo's speech outside Juliet's balcony to realize *how* personal—they were common "favors," or gifts, for guests at weddings and funerals.

The funeral gloves were black, often made of "shammy," the oil-tanned skins of chamois antelopes. Less exalted guests got "mock shammy," sheep or lambskin tanned in much the same way to imitate the more expensive leather. These funeral gloves were the only ones, for the period in question, that were black. In fact, few gloves were even made in bright colors, as the muted classical palette of the era called for light earth tones, pastels, and white.

Women typically wore long gloves, tied above the elbow to keep them from slipping down, though, as the anonymous author of *The Mirror of the Graces* (1811) hinted, women without arms that were "muscular, coarse, or scraggy" could push their gloves "down to a little above the wrists." The gloves were relatively free of ornament. Some white kid gloves had printed and painted designs on the back of the hand, or in imitation of a bracelet around the wrist, with the colors of paint being sometimes chosen to harmonize with other accessories like fans or shoes.

Preferred colors and materials were remarkably consistent through Austen's lifetime. Suede, kid, silk, and netting were favorite materials, with buff-colored suede, white kid, and "York tan"—an undyed suede—consistently leading in popularity. (Linen and worsted gloves were also common, but this was not because they were fashionable but because they were cheap.) Yellow and other pale colors were considered fine for daytime use but were banned as evening wear. One popular and rather unusual material for gloves was "chickenskin," not the skin of a chicken at all, but the skin of an unborn calf treated with almonds and spermaceti; these gloves were so thin and flexible that they were sometimes sold, to demonstrate their quality, bunched up inside a walnut shell.

Men wore short, wrist-length gloves in the same subdued range of colors as women—primarily tan, buff, yellow, and white (*Col Let*, *MW* 157). Like women, they wore York tans (*E* 200), chickenskin, white cotton (occasionally enlivened with a little discreet embroidery or a row of sequins at the wrist), kid, and doeskin. Woodstock gloves were especially fine and lightweight and were made of fawn skin. "Beavers" (*E* 200) were dark brown, like the fur of a beaver, and may have been made of felted cloth. Occasional machine-knitted gloves were seen, and cheap worsted gloves were available for purchase by the poor, but it is unlikely that Austen's fictional gentlemen would have worn these.

Prices varied widely according to the quality of the materials. The bankruptcy valuation of a Norwich milliner in 1785 gave the value of black worsted gloves—for funerals and mourning wear, no doubt—as 10d. a pair, but men's kid gloves, even in a damaged state, were worth 11s. a pair. Twilled cotton gloves were valued at 1s. Parson James Woodforde, without specifying the material, reported paying 2s. 2d. for a pair of gloves in 1784; later that year, he paid 2s. for a pair of riding gloves (presumably of some kind of leather). In London in 1795, while walking through the city, he stopped and bought a pair of gloves for 2s. These could hardly have been kid, much less a special material like chickenskin; they must have been made of an inferior leather or

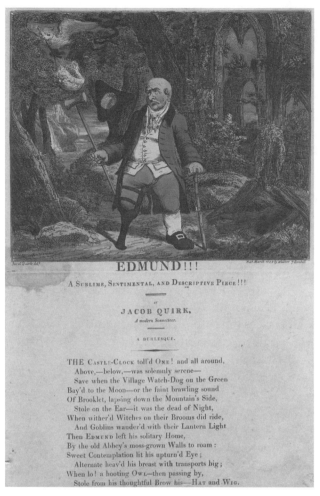

EDMUND!!!

A Sublime, Sentimental, and Descriptive Piece!!!

BY

JACOB QUIRK,

A modern Sonneteer.

A BURLESQUE.

THE Castle-Clock toll'd One! and all around,
   Above,—below,—was solemnly serene—
Save when the Village Watch-Dog on the Green
Bay'd to the Moon—or the faint brawling sound
Of Brooklet, lapsing down the Mountain's Side,
   Stole on the Ear—it was the dead of Night,
When wither'd Witches on their Brooms did ride,
   And Goblins wander'd with their Lantern Light
Then Edmund left his solitary Home,
By the old Abbey's moss-grown Walls to roam:
Sweet Contemplation lit his upturn'd Eye;
   Alternate heav'd his breast with transports big;
When lo! a hooting Owl—then passing by,
   Stole from his thoughtful Brow his—Hat and Wig.

Edmund!!!, Jacob Quirk, 1808. Austen was apparently not the only one making fun of the Gothic in her day. Here, a classic picturesque landscape, complete with ruined Gothic abbey, forms the backdrop to a parody of Gothic literature. The poem employs many of the stereotypical trappings of the Gothic and the picturesque, including tolling bells, moonlight, a "Brooklet, lapsing down the Mountain's Side," goblins, witches, and "the Abbey's moss-grown Walls." Courtesy of the Lewis Walpole Library, Yale University. 808.3.0.3.

of cotton. He does not say what kind of shop (*E* 199–201) sold him his London gloves, but it could have belonged to a perfumer, a breeches maker, a milliner, a dressmaker, or a specialist glover, all of whom retailed gloves. Examples of gloves may be seen in the illustrations *Monstrosities of 1799* and *Progress of the Toilet.—Dress Completed* (both in the article on Clothing). *See also* Clothing.

Gothic

The word "Gothic" could apply to several different types of art and expression, but it was principally an architectural style and a literary genre. In architecture, it meant a return to medieval or quasi-medieval forms, including pointed windows, pointed arches, asymmetrical design, and castlelike towers. At first, genuine Gothic ruins such as abbeys (*NA* 141) were embraced by the picturesque movement, and then the wealthy began to build neo-Gothic structures, beginning with garden follies, faux ruins, and guesthouses, and proceeding to sizable mansions. One of the smaller buildings in this style was Blaise Castle, not really a castle at all but an exotic cottage retreat and not ancient as John Thorpe implies but thoroughly eighteenth-century, as Austen's readers would have known. Austen herself was acquainted with several buildings in the Gothic style, including Adlestrop Park, which belonged to her mother's family, and the marquis of Lansdowne's Southampton castle, which stood very near the house she shared with her brother Frank's family in the early nineteenth century.

Flourishing alongside the interest in Gothic architecture was the interest in Gothic literature. The trend began with Horace Walpole's *Castle of Otranto* (1764), which in its first edition purported to be a translation of an original medieval work; in the second edition Walpole confessed his authorship. It possessed all the hallmarks of the Gothic genre: a medieval setting (often in Italy), a tyrannical parent (or stepparent, or guardian), damsels in distress, a noble hero, Catholic clergy and ritual, a supernatural or apparently supernatural occurrences, and archaic-sounding language. A typical passage, in which an execution is fortuitously forestalled by the revelation of a birthmark, reads:

> "What!" said the youth; "is it possible that my fate could have occasioned what I heard? Is the princess, then, again in thy power?"
>
> "Thou dost but remember me of my wrath," said Manfred; "prepare thee, for this moment is thy last."
>
> The youth, who felt his indignation rise, and who was touched with the sorrow which he saw he had infused into all the spectators, as well as into the friar, suppressed his emotions, and putting off his doublet, and unbuttoning his collar, knelt down to his prayers. As he stooped, his shirt slipped down below his shoulder, and discovered the mark of a bloody arrow.
>
> "Gracious Heaven!" cried the holy man, starting, "what do I see? It is my child, my Theodore!"
>
> The passions that ensued must be conceived; they cannot be painted. The tears of the assistants were suspended by wonder, rather than stopped by joy. They seemed to inquire into the eyes of their lord what they ought to feel. Surprise, doubt, tenderness, respect, succeeded each other in the countenance of the youth. He received with modest submission the effusion of the old man's tears and embraces; yet, afraid of giving a loose to hope, and suspecting, from what had passed, the inflexibility of Manfred's temper, he cast a glance towards the prince, as if to say, Canst thou be unmoved at such a scene as this?

This passage, with its secret identities, its stilted, faux-antique dialogue, and its exotic forays outside Protestantism, has much of what appealed to the readers of the Gothic.

The Gothic genre was further developed and, most would agree, mastered, by Ann Radcliffe (1764–1823), whose novels featured all the standard elements. Her works were of epic-length, peppered with her own poetry, and full of descriptions of Italian and French countrysides that she had never personally seen. Full of assassins (*NA* 167), banditti, and leering, powerful men, her books offered a taste of the supernatural but always explained the apparitions logically in the end, bringing them back into the realm of the ordinary. Austen refers to several of Radcliffe's works in her own novels, most notably in *Northanger Abbey*, which is a prolonged parody of the Gothic style. R. W. Chapman quotes a particularly relevant passage from Radcliffe's *Romance of the Forest* (1791), in his edition of *Northanger Abbey*, a passage in which a young woman discovers a mysterious document. Austen makes an indirect reference to this passage, or at least to passages of its kind, when Catherine Morland discovers the laundry bill in the cabinet in her room in the abbey. She also parodies the genre in Henry Tilney's mock-Gothic narrative of Catherine's future adventures within the abbey (*NA* 158–160).

A direct reference to Radcliffe's masterwork *The Mysteries of Udolpho* (1794) occurs earlier in *NA*, when Catherine refers to "such weather . . . as they had at Udolpho, or at least in Tuscany and the South of France!—the night that poor St. Aubin died!—such beautiful weather!" (*NA* 83). Yet Catherine is wrong on at least two points; the character who dies is St. Aubert, not St. Aubin, and St. Aubert dies at "about three o'clock in the afternoon," on a day marked by a bright morning sun and pure air. Catherine, lingering miserably inside on a rainy day in Bath, might indeed be thinking of this sunshiny fictional day, but she specifically mentions the weather at night. Perhaps, as Chapman believes, she means the weather on the night of that same day, but Radcliffe offers little description of that night, except to say that it was dark, with an "effulgent planet" setting in the sky over some woods. Perhaps Catherine instead means the weather on the night *before* "poor St. Aubin died." On that night, Radcliffe mentions "the silver whiteness of the moon-light" and

> the heaven, whose blue unclouded concave was studded thick with stars, the worlds, perhaps, of spirits, unsphered of mortal mould. . . . The still air seemed scarcely to breathe upon the woods, and, now and then, the distant sound of a solitary sheep-bell, or of a closing casement, was all that broke on silence. Elevated and enwrapt, while her eyes were often wet with tears of sublime devotion and solemn awe, she continued at the casement, till the gloom of mid-night hung over the earth, and the planet, which La Voisin had pointed out, sunk below the woods.

This is a far more descriptive passage than either of the others and more likely to have made an impression on Catherine. However, the interesting thing is that, no matter which of the three passages is intended, Catherine has still read sloppily. She has possibly mistaken the time of day at which the character dies, certainly gotten his name wrong, and chosen a nighttime reference for her wish that the daytime weather would improve. It is impossible to believe that in all Jane Austen's reading she could find no more appropriate literary allusion to clear weather. It is equally unlikely, though she sometimes slightly misquotes literary works in her letters, that she could have entirely mistaken the name of a character who inhabits a significant fraction of a well-known novel and who shares his last name with the heroine. The mistakes here are not Austen's, but Catherine's, and they reflect her inability at this point in her development to select and draw proper judgments from her reading. She remembers only part and misapplies the rest, foreshadowing her obtuseness at the abbey.

The Gothic novel took an entirely different turn in the hands of Matthew Lewis (1775–1818), who wrote *The Monk* in 1796 at the age of nineteen. Where Radcliffe explains away apparently supernatural events, Lewis not only allows them to be magical but positively revels in them, right down to the ending, in which the villain Ambrosio, who has not only threatened the innocent heroine but actually raped and then murdered her, is confronted by the Devil himself:

> As He said this, darting his talons into the Monk's shaven crown, he sprang with him from the rock. The Caves and mountains rang with Ambrosio's shrieks. The Dæmon continued to soar aloft, till reaching a dreadful height, He released the sufferer. Headlong fell the Monk through the airy waste; The sharp point of a rock received him; and He rolled from precipice to precipice, till bruised and mangled He rested on the river's banks. Life still existed in his miserable frame: He attempted in vain to raise himself; His broken and dislocated limbs refused to perform their office, not was He able to quit the spot where He had first fallen. The Sun now rose above the horizon; Its scorching beams darted full upon the head of the expiring Sinner. Myriads of insects were called forth by the warmth; They drank the blood which trickled from Ambrosio's wounds; He had no power to drive them from him, and they fastened upon his sores, darted their stings into his body, covered him with their multitudes, and inflicted on him tortures the most exquisite and insupportable.

Ambrosio's death takes seven full days to accomplish, during which time he is also torn apart by eagles, tortured by thirst as he hears but cannot reach a nearby river, blinded, and finally drowned in a flood. This almost self-parodically violent novel, which is fairly shamelessly pornographic in parts, was wildly notorious and earned its author the hated sobriquet of "Monk" Lewis. It exemplified the darker side of the eighteenth-century Gothic and justified its excesses on the grounds that, because the villain was punished in the end, morality was served. *See also* Architecture; Gardens and Landscape; Picturesque; Reading.

Great Mogul

The Mogul (or Mughal) emperors ruled much of India, plus areas to the north of the Indian subcontinent. They were Muslims of varying religious enthusiasm who tended to take multiple wives. Austen refers to a wife of the Great Mogul as a "Sultana" (*J&A, MW* 9), although this was a term more closely associated with the wives of Ottoman sultans. The harems and palace politics of the Muslim world had long been a fascination in the West. John Dryden, for example, composed a play in the seventeenth century based on a coup by a younger son of Shah Jahan (the builder of the Taj Mahal). This younger son, Aurangzeb, rose to power in an atmosphere of intrigue, sexual scandal, and murder. Travelers and readers in Britain saw the Mogul empire through two filters: that of the East India Company, which was increasingly powerful in the region, and that of the legends and anecdotes about concubines, eunuchs, poisonings, fratricide, and fabulous wealth that were recounted in histories, travel writings, novels, and plays.

Greek and Latin

While French and Italian were considered appropriate languages for young women to learn, Latin and Greek were traditionally the province of men. It was thought, in the first place, that women had no natural talent for Latin and Greek. Furthermore, these classical languages were deemed too demanding for women, and it was said that the intensive study required in this field would strain the frail female constitution to the breaking point, possibly rendering the female scholar incapable of bearing children. In any case, knowledge of the classics, especially Greek, which was too demanding even for many men, was thought to make women unattractive to the opposite sex, who did not like to think that their wives might possibly know more about Horace or Homer than they. This is not to say that women never studied the classics. Some, of course, did. However, they faced stigmatization as "bluestockings," women who could not manage to keep up a decent appearance of fashion because they were too concerned with the life of the mind.

Lady Jane Grey, a cousin of Mary I, Elizabeth I, and Edward VI, lived during a brief exception to this long-standing rule. Noblewomen during the time of Henry VIII were often encouraged to become extremely well educated, and Lady Jane Grey, who had an exceptionally unhappy home life, even by the ruthless standards of her day, found some solace in her studies. A quiet, religious, intelligent girl, she is remembered chiefly for her erudition, her forced marriage, and her execution after having been used as a pawn to oust Mary I from the throne. Austen, another brilliant Jane, cannot seize upon the marriage or the execution for comic effect, so she uses the erudition as her source of humor in her *History of England* (*MW* 141, 144). It was a joke that would have been well received in Austen's time, when women who knew Greek were treated not with admiration but with suspicion and were advised by their best friends to hide their knowledge with care.

Gypsies

Gypsies (not known widely by their preferred name of "Roma" till long after Austen's time) had been in Britain for hundreds of years. However, like Jews, they had for much of their history been marginal people, residing in England at the pleasure of the government. In 1530, the government ceased to be pleased by their presence and ordered them to leave.

In theory, further Gypsy immigration was banned, all Gypsies currently resident in England were to leave, and any Gypsies remaining could be put to death. In practice, this order was not assiduously enforced. Gypsies who were caught were generally deported rather than executed, and the government never came close to expelling them all. There were perhaps as many as 10,000 still in the country during Elizabeth I's reign, and periodic laws aimed at repressing their activities continued to be passed until 1908.

The Gypsies (*Evelyn*, *MW* 189; *E* 333–336), however, were determined to stay. Beginning in the sixteenth century, there are records of Gypsy baptisms in parish churches, and in Jane Austen's lifetime they show up in contemporary prints. Here, the iconic symbols of Gypsy life seem to be ragged clothes, an old woman wearing a head scarf, and a campfire; the Gypsies themselves appear to be cheerful, perhaps because they are often getting the better of their English associates. There was a clearly delineated picture in the English mind of Gypsies as thieves, fortune-tellers, and tricksters. Gypsy communities therefore knew that if unexpected trouble arose in the village near their camp, they would be blamed. When trouble occurred, they moved on quickly (*E* 336).

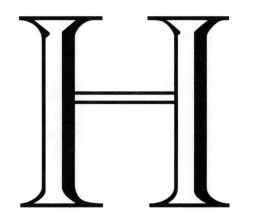

Hair

Hairstyles in Austen's childhood required enormous maintenance and were usually extremely uncomfortable. Women in the 1770s and 1780s wore their hair tall and powdered, which required the hair to be frizzed and built up on pads. In the 1770s hair was so tall that it attracted much comment and criticism. The hair, once styled, was greased with pomatum and then powdered with white or gray hair powder. This was a messy process, and the woman being powdered would wear a protective gown while her maid or hairdresser performed the task. Then she did all she could not to disturb the hairstyle for days or weeks, sleeping with a bag over the coiffure to protect it. Not surprisingly, women's heads itched like fury and served as perfect havens for vermin. Examples of this bouffant style may be seen in the illustrations *A Master Parson with a Good Living* (Clergy) and *The First Interview of Werter and Charlotte* (Reading), among others.

Men shaved their heads or wore their hair (*Harley, MW* 40; *L&F, MW* 93; *P* 142) extremely short in order to facilitate the wearing of wigs, which were also powdered (*Watsons, MW* 353, 357; *P* 20). Wigs (*MP* 189) came in a dazzling array of styles, some of which gave clues to the wearer's profession. Clergymen tended to favor one sort of wigs, physicians another, army officers still another. Naval officers did not wear wigs; it was too easy to lose them at sea (*P* 20).

The general revolution in fashion in the 1790s, however, altered hairstyles as well. Young men abandoned their wigs and began growing their own hair long and wearing it unpowdered. Portraits from this period of Robert Southey, Samuel Taylor Coleridge, and Napoleon all show them with long, flowing locks. Then, in a vogue for all things classical, men cut their hair short again. This time, they did not opt for the closely shorn look adapted to the wearing of wigs but for a layered cut reminiscent of the hairstyles seen on Greek statues and busts of Roman emperors. This style, called the "Titus" or the "Brutus crop," remained in fashion for the remainder of Austen's life. Southey, who in the mid-1790s sported long hair, was painted in 1804 wearing a Titus cut.

Some men still retained the powdered wig. The style was still considered essential for servants in livery (*Watsons, MW* 322; *MP* 189), for example, perhaps because the wig and powder entailed extra expense and thus added to the magnificent statement of disposable income represented by a liveried footman. Older men were generally reluctant to abandon wigs, and many of them never adopted the new fashion. Barristers were still required to wear them, and physicians preferred to do so, as it added to their presence and authority. The physician in the illustration *Jack, Hove*

Down (Spectacles), for example, retains his wig, along with his old-fashioned style of dress: buckled shoes, breeches, frock coat, and tricorne hat. However, such men were in the minority, and a tax on hair powder in the late eighteenth century, replaced in the early nineteenth by a flat fee for a "powdering license," helped hasten the demise of the powdered wig.

Women, no doubt with great relief, also adopted a simpler and more natural style of hairdressing. Abandoning pads and powder, their hair (*Evelyn, MW* 184; *Cath, MW* 204; *S&S* 60, 98, 135, 329) was cut short at the front, arranging this hair into short curls (*Sand, MW* 390; *NA* 15, 27, 52; *MP* 296–297) to frame the face. The rest, also kept relatively short, was curled and gathered at the back of the head by bandeaus and fillets of ribbon. These thin headbands reminded them of the hairstyles seen in Greek and Roman statuary. A few women, bolder than the rest, adopted a female version of the Titus cut; the woman in the illustration *Progress of the Toilet.—Dress Completed* (Clothing), for example, has dressed her hair this way. Other extremely fashionable women cut their hair very short and wore various styles of attractively curled wigs. In 1802, for example, Lady Stanley wrote to a friend, explaining,

> I have cut off my tail [the hair at the back of her head] for comfort, and as my front hair is always coming out of curl in the damp summer evenings, and as I find everybody sports a false toupee, I don't see why I should not have the comfort of one too. I wish to be as fashionable and as deceiving as possible.

A particularly unpleasant depiction of this fashion is shown in the illustration *A Maiden Ewe, Drest Lamb Fashion* (Clocks and Watches). Most women, however, seem to have kept their own hair. The standard coiffure (*S&S* 249; *MP* 360–361) remained short curls or wisps in front and hair of medium length gathered at the back, often covered indoors by a cap and outdoors by a bonnet or hat.

The simpler styles, however, did not do away with the hairdresser (*NA* 20; *E* 323). Women still needed to have their hair cut and, for special occasions, arranged. Men went to barbershops (*E* 205, 212) or had their servants shave them and dress their wigs at home (*P* 32), but in the case of women, hairdressers paid house calls. Writing from London in 1813, Jane told Cassandra that "Mr. Hall was very punctual yesterday & curled me out at a great rate. I thought it looked hideous, and longed for a snug cap instead, but my companions silenced me by their admiration." In August 1805, the same Mr. Hall had come to Edward's house at Godmersham to dress Elizabeth's and Jane's hair and to give lessons to Elizabeth Austen's lady's maid. He charged 5s. for each time he dressed Elizabeth's hair, 5s. for each lesson, and only 2s. 6d. for dressing Jane's hair. Apparently he had given Cassandra a similar discount when she visited Godmersham, for Jane remarked drily, "He certainly respects either our Youth or our poverty." It was common to join forces in this way and have a hairdresser arrange the hair of all the ladies in a household at once, especially if a ball or other important social event were imminent. In 1782, the local squire's wife asked Parson Woodforde's niece Nancy to her house, and the two ladies had their hair done at the same time:

> Mr. Custance sent after Nancy this morning to spend the Day with Mrs. Custance and to have her Hair dressed by one Brown, the best Ladies-Frisseur in Norwich. . . . Nancy returned home about ½ past 9 o'clock this Even', with her head finely dressed of [*sic*] but very becoming her. Mrs. Custance would not let Nancy pay the Barber, but she paid for her and it cost no less than half a guinea. Mrs. Custance gave the Barber for dressing her Hair and Nancy's the enormous sum of one guinea—He came on purpose from Norwich to dress them. Mrs. Custance (God bless her) is the best Lady I every [*sic*] knew.

The cost of a hairdresser, as Woodforde noted, could be substantial,* and for ordinary occasions women had their hair done by their maids (*P&P* 344; *E* 134, 324). Good hairdressing skills were therefore an important recommendation for a lady's maid.

Hair that did not possess a natural curl was curled artificially (*E* 134) by being twisted or rolled and wrapped in paper (*Watsons, MW* 322). The curling papers were cut 4 inches square and then again along the diagonal, then wrapped around the tightly curled hair and twisted so that they would remain in place until removed. When all the thin sections of hair had been rolled and wrapped, wrote London hairdresser James Stewart in 1782, "they look like regular rows of trees." Next the hairdresser took a heated curling iron, known as a toupee iron, that could open rather like a pair of scissors. He pinched the paper between the two sides of the iron, taking care not to touch the hair directly, and held them there until the paper began to smoke. The paper was unwrapped and the curl pinned to the side of the head, and the hairdresser moved on to the next curling paper. Jane had naturally curly hair, at least in front, for she wrote in December 1798,

> I have made myself two or three caps to wear of evenings since I came home, and they save me a world of torment as to hair-dressing, which at present gives me no trouble beyond washing and brushing, for my long hair is always plaited up out of sight, and my short hair curls well enough to want no papering.

She would not, therefore, have needed much help from a servant.

Some women wore caps for evening social occasions, but others merely

---

*Woodforde, by way of comparison, typically paid his barber only a shilling for a shave, and paid his manservant 2s. 6d. every three months for the dressing of his wigs. Even a shave and the dressing of his wig combined cost him only 1s. 6d. in London.

[Hairdressing], 1787. A lady and her maid watch nervously as the professional hairdresser applies a hot iron to her curling papers. Courtesy of the Lewis Walpole Library, Yale University. 787.2.3.1.

Curling iron. From the author's collection.

arranged their hair attractively, binding it up with ribbons or pins and adorning it with flowers (*NA* 71), strings of beads (*NA* 56), or twists of satin decorated with spirals of beads or pearls. A woman with beads strung through her hair may be seen on the left in the illustration *How to Pluck a Goose* (Cards). Sometimes a thin braid (*NA* 118) could be pinned over the front of the head to serve as a bandeau in place of a ribbon, or it could be wrapped around the chignon at the back. Ornaments were held in place by combs or pins (*S&S* 121); the combs themselves were often quite decorative, and the more expensive ones were jeweled.

The "queer fashion" to which William Price refers (*MP* 235) cannot be determined with any accuracy, as the year in which that part of *Mansfield Park* takes place is not clear. Critics disagree as the whether the main action of the novel is set in 1808–1809, 1812–1813, or some other year entirely. It is not even clear, in this instance, whether the fashion in question is for morning or evening. Austen may have left the exact style deliberately vague to avoid dating the novel too much, just as she does not specify the hairstyle worn by Jane Fairfax that Frank Churchill pretends to find "outré" (*E* 222). *See also* Hats.

Hats

The typical man's hat (*MW* 445; *NA* 157, 177) when Austen was born was the cocked hat. This was a felt hat, usually black, with a low round crown and a wide brim that was turned up either on three sides to make a triangle (a tricorne) or in the front and back to make a semicircle (a bicorne). As tricorne hats came to seem increasingly old-fashioned, gentlemen at first took to the chapeau bras, a bicorne that could either be worn or folded and carried under the arm. All of these hats might be decorated with a cockade (*Watsons, MW* 326), a small decoration made of ribbons or feathers, frequently worn by military men, by revelers at weddings, and by crowds at election time (in which case the colors of the ribbons would identify whose supporters they were).

Riders wore a tallish cylindrical hat with a hard crown and a medium-wide brim of the kind seen in the illustration *A Meeting at Margate* (Clothing). This hat, which over time would lose some of the width on its brim and become the top hat, was widely adopted for use throughout the day. This was consistent with a general trend toward the wearing of sporting attire for all purposes. By 1800, the round hat had triumphed over the tricorne and bicorne everywhere except on military officers and very old-fashioned gentlemen.

Women, especially married women or women of an age to be considered unmarriageable, wore caps (*Cath, MW* 207; *Watsons, MW* 323; *MP* 204) on all occasions. These were usually mob caps (*MP* 146) or biggins, which were similarly soft and made of cloth such as cambric or muslin (*NA* 28). They both had a rounded shape with a frill of some kind around the edge; mob caps were generally a little smaller than biggins and might have strings to tie under the chin or lappets—panes of cloth, often decorated in some way, that fell down to each side of the cap. Such caps may be seen in various illustrations in this book, including the illustrations *A Christening* (Clergy) and *Progress of the Toilet.—The Stays* and *Progress of the Toilet.—Dress Completed* (both in the article on Clothing). Both of these caps were appropriate for "morning" as it was understood in Austen's time—that is, from rising until dinner at anywhere from 3:00 to 6:30 P.M.

In the evening, smaller, more decorative caps were generally worn, made of finer materials and sometimes in fanciful shapes. Austen, for example, briefly adopted a "Mamolouc cap," a fezlike headdress worn in honor of Nelson's victory at the Battle of the Nile, and in December 1798 she was trimming an evening cap with "silver" (silver ribbon or braid) and a coquelicot feather. (Coquelicot—see *NA* 39—was a deep shade of red.) There was also a vogue for turbans (*NA* 217), which ranged in size from small to voluminous, and which were either created on the spot by winding fabric around the head or purchased already folded and shaped and ready to wear. Two of these may be seen in the illustration *How to Pluck a Goose* (Cards).

Outdoors, women wore hats (*Cath, MW* 202; *Sand, MW* 389; *NA* 39, 84, 165; *S&S* 272; *P&P* 6; *MP* 408; *P* 142) or bonnets (*F&E, MW* 4; *Cass, MW* 45; *Cath, MW* 211; *Sand, MW* 381; *NA* 71, 104, 161, 165, 177; *S&S* 272; *P&P* 72, 219, 221; *E* 173, 355, 358). The technical difference between them was that hats had a brim all the way around, while bonnets had no brim in back, or only the barest hint of a brim. Hats and bonnets came in many styles and were made of many materials. Hats and bonnets for walking outdoors, for example, could be soft and made of muslin, beaver, or velvet; or, quite commonly, stiffer and made of straw

(*Sand, MW* 389; *NA* 161) decorated with sewn-on or pinned-on ribbons. In a letter of May 1801, Jane mentions both "Bonnets of Cambric Muslin" and bonnets of "white chip" (willow fiber).

There were also indoor hats for evening wear that might be made of silk, satin, or crepe. For the first decade of the nineteenth century, small veils were common on hats, but afterward they fell out of fashion. Hats and bonnets were usually worn tilted back a little on the head so that the face was not entirely hidden, but the "close bonnet" (*MP* 49, 51) mentioned by Mary Crawford had a soft fabric crown and a very deep, almost tubular brim and would have revealed almost nothing of the face unless the wearer was facing one directly. Seen from the side, the wearer's head looked rather like a tilted cupcake. Hats and bonnets were fairly small at the beginning of the nineteenth century, broadening in about 1804 to 1807, flattening for the next few years, then growing tall and narrow toward the end of Austen's life (see the illustration *A Fashionable Belle* (Clothing). Some were shaped like truncated cones and worn on a slant, with the hair peeking out through a hole in the back; others were bonnets with brims that sloped away on the sides to reveal the lower half of the face; some were flexible straw hats tied under the chin with wide ribbons; some imitated the round hats worn by men, reinterpreting them in straw, lace, and ribbons. A "witch's hat" from 1809 is little more than a flat circle of white chip; the sides have been pushed toward each other by a band of ribbon, forcing the circle to poke out a little at the front and back, and keeping the hat on the woman's head. The front has been decorated with flowers. Perhaps this is the sort of hat that John Thorpe says makes his mother "look like an old witch" (*NA* 49).

Hats and caps could be made at home, but they were more commonly purchased (*Sand, MW* 381) from milliners (*Cass, MW* 44; *Watsons, MW* 323; *NA* 44; *P&P* 219), who sold relatively plain headgear, fully trimmed headgear, and materials such as lace

A Bonnet Shop, Thomas Rowlandson, 1810. At "Mrs. Flimsy's Fashionable Warehouse," a variety of straw hats and bonnets hang from the ceiling while a saleslady flatters a customer and a group of milliners trim more hats. Courtesy of the Lewis Walpole Library, Yale University. 810.5.15.1.

and ribbon. The customer could select a cap, for example, and either wear it as it was or take it home and decorate it to suit her own taste (*S&S* 272; *P&P* 6). She could add ribbons in various colors, beads, or feathers. In the late 1790s, artificial fruit and flowers were all the rage, and Jane commented on this fashion while she was staying in Bath in June 1799:

> Flowers are very much worn, & Fruit is still more the thing.—Eliz: has a bunch of Strawberries, & I have seen Grapes, Cherries, Plumbs & Apricots—There are likewise Almonds & raisins, French plumbs & Tamarinds at the Grocers, but I have never seen any of them in hats.

Hats could be stored individually in the wide cylindrical bandboxes (*P&P* 221; *MP* 379) provided by the milliner, or collectively in some sort of larger trunk or box (*NA* 165). Examples of bandboxes appear in the illustration *Progress of the Toilet.—Dress Completed* (Clothing).

Heraldry

As Jane Austen makes very few references to heraldic devices, it is unnecessary to present a detailed explanation of coats of arms (*P* 4) and the complicated rules for their construction. It is sufficient to point out that armorial bearings consisted of the actual coat of arms (the shield), on which one or more colored areas were decorated with charges (pictures of animals, flowers, geometric shapes, etc.). Above the shield was often a helmet with a decorative and symbolic crest, and descending from the helmet, behind and around the shield, was a drapery of leaves or cloth known as mantling. This was usually red and white but could be of other colors and could have an ermine lining for earls and above. The mantling was attached to the helmet by a wreath or coronet, depending on the rank of the person displaying the arms; a typical wreath appeared to be made of fabric twisted into six bunches in alternating colors. Coronets (*L&F, MW* 91) were crowns banded with ermine at the bottom whose decorations indicated rank: a baron's arms would display a coronet with four silver balls; a viscount's would show nine small silver balls; an earl's would have five balls and four gold strawberry leaves; a marquess' would have three leaves alternating with two balls; and a duke's would show five strawberry leaves. (For an example of a coronet, see the coach in the illustration *The Pacific Entrance of Earl-Wolf, into Blackhaven* [Landau].) A family motto (*P* 4) was often written on a scroll at the bottom of the arms, sometimes in English, sometimes in Latin or French. This entire collection of pictorial devices was sometimes known as an "achievement" (*MP* 86), particularly if it were granted for some specific act of bravery.

With royal permission, arms bearers could attach special additional devices to their arms. These additional devices could include augmentations

(*P* 294) to the crest and supporters (figures of animals or people who stood to one or both sides of the coat of arms). The arms of city corporations often had supporters, as did certain individuals, including the monarch himself; Queen Elizabeth I's arms, for example, had a lion and a dragon as supporters. An example of an augmentation is the "bloody hand" of Ulster, originally used as a badge by the baronets sent into Ulster by James I and by Austen's time an indicator of baronetcy in armorial bearings.

Those with family arms displayed them in various places. The arms might appear as a decoration in the home on stained glass windows, silver serving dishes, custom-painted china, and furniture. The arms also customarily appeared on the door panel of the family coach (*L&F*, *MW* 91; *P* 106).

Hobbies

Women of the gentry and nobility had a great deal of free time and found numerous ways to fill it. As Mr. Bingley notes, all the women of his acquaintance "paint tables, cover skreens and net purses" (*P&P* 39), and while Mr. Darcy disagrees that these skills can be considered "accomplishments," many women no doubt considered their time very well spent. Then as now, skill in artistic endeavors varied greatly, and some efforts were exceedingly clumsy (*MP* 152); Cassandra Austen's famous sketch of Jane is a very good example of an artistic failure. Those women who excelled (*S&S* 234–235), however, had to be careful not to pretend to professionalism. It was important that skills remain private, used primarily for the entertainment of one's family, gifts to one's friends, and the adornment of the home.

Many crafts were designed to imitate other materials or to emulate more professional productions. Artificial flowers (*MP* 14) were made of lamb's wool, and gold or gold-edged paper (*MP* 14; *P* 134) was cut into thin strips, rolled (*S&S* 145), and glued onto boxes and baskets in imitation of the lacy wirework known as filigree (*S&S* 144–145). Imitation medals were made of cardboard and gold leaf, while imitation coral was made of painted branches. A vogue for Japanese and Chinese art spurred many women to create folding screens like the ones found in Asian homes. The screens, covered with embroidery, printed maps, painted pastoral scenes, or découpaged cutouts from popular prints, were used to shield parts of the room from the heat of the fireplace. There were wooden screens, screens of fabric mounted in wooden frames, and screens in which the fabric was replaced by imported wallpaper. They might be made to stand on the floor or, in smaller versions, to hold in the hand like a hand-mirror. These hand-screens could be used an individual to keep the face, or another part of the body, protected from the fire's warmth.

From about the time of Austen's birth, there was a growing interest in transparencies (*MP* 152), publicly exhibited scenes painted on glass and lit by a "magic lanthorn," a bright light source such as an Argand lamp. In some exhibits, the transparencies formed the background, and figures in silhouette could be made to move across the lighted background, acting out various scenes. At other times, the transparency was a popular satirical print, perhaps poking fun at some government figure or ridiculous fad. Nighttime celebrations, such as the entertainments provided at city pleasure gardens, often featured transparencies along with other light-based spectacles such as illuminations and fireworks. Hobbyists attempted to re-create the experience at home by laying a print under glass and tracing the image onto the front of the glass, then hand-coloring the picture and illuminating it from behind. Jane wrote in 1800 of visiting Oakely Hall, where she "admired Mr Bramston's Porter & Mrs Bramston's Transparencies."

Some women painted furniture, as Mr. Bingley implied, but others took an easier route. They took popular prints, cut out the bits they liked, and varnished these onto tables and trays in imitation of Japanese lacquerwork. Women and children alike might create sculptures in wax—clay was too professional—or make trays, boxes, and needle cases out of strings of beads. Some made pictures out of seashells or hair; others worked in papier-mâché or even seaweed. Mrs. Lybbe Powys, an Austen connection, was fond of carving cherry pits. Many women took to "knotting," a craft that involved making trim with raised knots out of silk or metal thread. The knotted borders ended in loose threads that were then tied in larger knots to make fringe. Claire Wilcox, in her book on handbags, offers a description of this craft that seems to explain succinctly why it appealed to Lady Bertram (*MP* 179): "Knotting was a graceful occupation and did not require a great deal of concentration." *See also* Sewing.

Hobbyhorse

The hobbyhorse was both a toy and an element of traditional dance before it acquired another meaning, the one that Austen uses in her works. By the sixteenth century, the hobbyhorse was an established feature of morris dancing, a festive seasonal dance performed in many English towns. Along with a fool and a lord and lady (or Robin and Marian), the hobbyhorse was one of the peripheral characters associated with the dance. From about the same time, a hobbyhorse could also mean the child's toy— a stylized horse head on a stick that a child could pretend to ride by running with the stick between his legs. Over time, however, "riding a hobbyhorse" came to have another meaning, that of following a favorite pursuit or "hobby."

One's "hobbyhorse," therefore, became one's pet project, and the phrase often had connotations of obsession or of unhealthy enthusiasm for the object or endeavor. Thus, General Tilney says of his garden, "If he had a hobby-horse, it was that" (*NA* 178). With his characteristic false self-deprecation, he implies that perhaps he loves his garden too much, hoping of course to be told just the opposite. Austen's authorial voice, speaking more straightforwardly in *Sanditon*, says of Mr. Parker that the development of Sanditon as a seaside resort "was his Mine, his Lottery, his Speculation & his Hobby Horse; his Occupation his Hope & his Futurity" (*Sand, MW* 372). Her tone—mild contempt but not outright condemnation—is absolutely consistent with the way the phrase was used in her day. She speaks as one who views fanatic devotion without sharing it.

Holidays

Austen mentions three major holidays in her works: Easter, Michaelmas, and Christmas. These, as it happens, were three of the four principal seasonal holidays that served as markers for the passage of the year. Easter was associated with the spring, Michaelmas with the fall, and Christmas with the winter. The fourth holiday was Whitsuntide, associated with summer. Of all of these, Easter (*P&P* 62; *MP* 69, 359, 430; *E* 79) was the most solemn religious holiday. It therefore seems appropriate that it appears most frequently in Austen's most religious work, *Mansfield Park*. The references to it make little direct reference to the religious significance of the holiday, but Austen's choice is not accidental; the period before Easter that Fanny spends with her birth family in Portsmouth takes the form of asceticism, resistance to temptation, and, finally, a symbolic resurrection as Edmund rescues her and carries her off to the comparative heaven of Mansfield (*MP* 423). Henry Crawford and Maria Rushworth, on the other hand, spend it in idle socializing and moral decay (*MP* 434). Mary Crawford sees the holiday merely as the date at which she will trade one fashionable home for another, and she is, at this of all times, relieved that no one can tell by his clothing that Edmund is a clergyman (*MP* 416). The chief reference to Easter as a specifically religious occasion occurs, appropriately enough, in reference to Edmund's clerical duties (*MP* 226). Elsewhere in Austen's works, Easter is principally a time spent quietly with one's family (*S&S* 279; *P&P* 170; *E* 95). The only clergyman who actually delivers an Easter sermon is Mr. Collins (*P&P* 172).

Several folk traditions centered around Easter. Though these varied from one village to another, colored eggs were already firmly associated with the holiday. Dyed with cochineal or logwood, they were given in some places to children only and in other places to adults and children alike. The eggs given by wealthy families might be gilded. In some places, children dissolved candy or sugar in water. In Warwickshire, on Easter Monday, the children "clipped" (embraced) the local churches, standing with their backs against the church's exterior walls, holding hands, until they made a complete chain around the building. In some places, religious plays or comic mummer's plays were performed. Dorsetshire had boys' processions on Easter Eve, while in Twickenham and other places, penny loaves of bread were hurled from the church tower and gathered up by the children. In 1790, a correspondent to the *Gentleman's Magazine* informed its readers that in Harrowgate,

> On Easter Sunday, as soon as the service of the church is over, the boys run about the streets, and lay hold of every woman or girl they can, and take the buckles from their shoes. This farce is continued till the next day at noon, when the females begin, and return the compliment upon the men, which does not end till Tuesday evening.

The buckles had to be ransomed from their captors. A similar custom, in which the sexes engaged in mock combat, was "lifting" or "heaving." On Easter Monday, men would lift any woman they could find, holding her parallel to the ground, and hoisting her up three times in quick succession. On Easter Tuesday, women reversed the roles and lifted men. A 1784 description of the practice in England's northern counties called it "a rude, indecent, and dangerous diversion, practised chiefly by the lower order of people." Prohibitions of lifting, proclaimed by town bellmen, apparently had not managed to suppress the game.

Michaelmas (*Sand, MW* 377, 378; *S&S* 216; *P&P* 3; *MP* 189; *E* 75; *P* 142), September 29 (*P* 48), was an important date for legal purposes, though not a significant religious festival. Its religious role was largely as an arbitrary date on which many churches offered communion. Contracts often began and ended on Michaelmas, and, in some regions, servants' terms of employment customarily began on that date. Accordingly, Austen uses it in many cases as the date for the beginning or ending of leases (*P&P* 336; *MP* 405; *P* 33). Predictions of people being married by Michaelmas may simply indicate the passage of time, but perhaps the date is chosen for its associations with new enterprises and new legal arrangements (*S&S* 292, 293, 374).

Of all the holidays, Christmas (*Watsons, MW* 350; *NA* 118; *S&S* 112–113; *P&P* 153, 238; *MP* 255, 288, 434; *E* 79, 115; *P* 206) is the one most frequently mentioned. This seems perfectly natural today, when Christmas is the most commercialized and most sentimentalized of all Christian holidays, but it must be recalled that many of our modern associations with Christmas are the legacy of the Victorian era, and especially of the popularization of Christmas celebrations by Charles Dickens and others. In Austen's time, Christmas was viewed as a holiday in decline, a fairly old-fashioned holiday celebrated for the sake of children rather than adults. Nonetheless, some of the "gaieties which that season generally brings" (*P&P* 117) were still observed. Family members reunited (*LS, MW* 246; *NA* 33; *P&P* 139, 383; *E* 7, 40; *P* 134), children returned from boarding schools or universities (*MP* 21; *P* 129, 133), friends were invited to dinner parties and dances (*S&S* 44, 152; *MP* 252; *E* 108; *P* 163), and, given that the weather outside was generally unpleasant (*E* 115, 138), people played indoor games like hunt the slipper, blind-man's buff, and word games (*E* 372). Indoor theatricals were staged (*MP* 126–127) at Steventon parsonage as well as in more spacious homes. The men and boys might venture out to do a little hunting, if the weather were clear; Jane's oldest brother, James, wrote a poem on the subject to his son, uttering the wish that "may no frost your sport prevent" and that the weather would prove "hazy, mild & kind for scent."

Traditional foods included brawn (a kind of preserved pork—see *P* 134) and plum pudding (made not with plums but with raisins or currants). James Austen's poem on hunting also mentions "mince pies" at Christmas. Houses were decorated with holly and other green foliage. At church, a special sermon was delivered, and communion was offered. Children and adults alike might sing Christmas carols or watch mummers' plays. People went wassailing, and in some towns, morris dancers performed. Charity was distributed by those who could afford to do so; Parson Woodforde, in 1793 (a particularly hard year with regard to food prices), invited several poor people to dine at his house and sent dinners to others, giving all the recipients a shilling in addition to the food. Christmas gifts were not given on the scale that they would be in later years, but tips were distributed to certain people—Woodforde paid the local church-bell ringers at this time—and upper servants, who had influence over the choice of purveyors for household goods, received ample "Christmas boxes" by way of thanks from local merchants. All in all, the holiday was a happy, social time.

Horses

Horses (*L&F*, *MW* 107; *NA* 53, 66; *S&S* 52, 96; *P* 13, 43) were the engines of the preindustrial world. They were the sports cars, the exercise machines, the trains, the tractors, the buses, the generators, and the race cars all in one package of muscle and hair on four thin legs. They pulled the carts that hauled goods from one town to another and that carried the new-mown hay out of the fields (*MP* 58). They pulled the plows and harrows and hauled barges along England's new canals. They were essential to many types of hunting and, it was thought, preserved health. They certainly also made it faster to get from one place to another.

England had a number of horse breeds. Just as landowners were beginning to take an interest in improving their stocks of sheep, cattle, and pigs, so, too, they began to breed horses with the intention of promoting certain characteristics. They bred "Great Horses," the ancestor of the Shire horse, and heavy black horses descended from horses imported from Flanders and Holland. Oldenburg coach horses were imported from the Continent as well and bred with native stock. Cobs were among the "road horses" (*NA* 76; *MP* 37) that served the needs of mounted business travelers, while hackneys made such good riding horses that they were widely adopted by cavalrymen. Horses in Herefordshire, according to an account in the *Gentleman's Magazine* from 1819, were skinnier than most. "It is the habit of the country," wrote a correspondent, "to consider horses not in a fit condition for work, if too fat; and for this reason, saddle-horses, though not suffered to have an ugly leanness, are of more bony contour than the London horse with his mole-like rotundity and sleekness." The finest horses, according to many, were the thoroughbreds that populated the racecourses and some of the finest hunting stables in England.

Horseback riding (*Cath, MW* 206; *LS, MW* 285; *Watsons, MW* 331, 345; *NA* 35, 56, 73, 175, 195; *S&S* 65, 86, 359; *P&P* 9, 30–31, 49; *MP* 27, 35–36, 62, 69, 148, 334; *E* 29, 191, 243, 244, 317, 359, 363, 367, 394) was considered to be exceptionally good exercise, especially for ladies. *The Mirror of the Graces* (1811) recommended it in order to foster and maintain beauty:

> If a girl wishes to be well-shaped and well-complexioned she must use due exercise on foot. Horseback is an excellent auxiliary, as it gives much the same degree of motion, with double the animation, in consequence of the change of air and variation of objects.

John Lawrence, writing in 1796, similarly approved of riding, but on the grounds of health rather than beauty:

> This salubrious exercise . . . is peculiarly adapted to debilitated and consumptive habits, and the lax fibre; for it tends to the increase of substance, which the labour of walking has, in general, the effect to abrade. . . . It is, perhaps, the only effectual remedy for habitual costiveness and wind.

This, with the exception of the "wind," on which topic Austen naturally maintains a discreet silence, might have been lifted from the health records of Fanny Price (*MP* 27, 69–70, 95), who responds poorly to walking but well to riding and whose constitution is certainly "debilitated." Horseback riding as a prescription for health is also mentioned in one of Austen's juvenile works (*Col Let, MW* 153).

Women, therefore, as well as men, took riding lessons. These might take place outdoors, as Fanny Price's and Mary Crawford's do (*MP* 66–69), or in a riding ring in a town. A good riding horse needed to be calm, particularly if it was intended to carry a lady (*S&S* 58–59; *MP* 37); when carrying a lady, it also needed to be accustomed to a sidesaddle (see the illustration *The Charms of a Red Coat* [Army]), as women did not ride astride. Riding manuals emphasized that "a woman's limbs are unsuited to cross-saddle riding, which requires length from hip to knee, flat muscles and a slight inclination to 'bow legs!'" The sidesaddle made it harder

Taking an Airing at Brighton, Isaac Cruikshank, 1805. The fashion for "Donkies" is satirized. Courtesy of the Lewis Walpole Library, Yale University. 805.10.21.1.

to control a horse. Riding accidents (*Lesley, MW* 113) were uncommon, except in the hunt, but they did occur, as in 1804, when Mrs. Lefroy, a good friend of Jane's, was killed in a riding accident.

For a time in the early nineteenth century, there was a fashion among women for riding donkeys (*E* 356). A song performed at Astley's Royal Amphitheatre in 1805 mocked the trend:

> When fashion proves to all mankind, High priestess of the age, sir,
> What curious whims in life we find, Both on, and off the stage, sir.
> In short, each fav'rite has its day, Cats parrots, dogs, and monkies;
> But now o'er all that bears the sway, O lord it is the Donkies!
> O, the little Donkies, the pretty gentle Donkies!
> Both here and there, and ev'ry where, The rage is now the Donkies!

A print from that year (see illustration) shows three ladies riding donkeys that do not appear especially gentle. One lady has been thrown off, and a second asks the footman walking behind to "Whip my Ass John Whip it well."

Not all horses were trained as saddle horses. Many were trained to pull carriages and carts (*Watsons, MW* 322, 339; *Sand, MW* 364; *NA* 45–46,

64; *S&S* 12, 324; *P&P* 67; *P* 13, 35, 106, 114–115; *E* 20, 112, 126, 189, 233, 306, 353, 357, 475). To the upper, and to some extent the middle, classes, they were essential for travel of all kinds. Economic class was an issue, for carriages and carriage horses were taxed by the government on a sliding scale that charged progressively steeper penalties for owning more horses. There was a similar tax on saddle horses, but none on farm horses, which were essential to the work of the nation. The existence of the tax makes all the more humorous the list of horses kept by a character in one of Austen's juvenile works: "six Greys, 4 Bays, eight Blacks & a poney" (*Clifford*, *MW* 43).*

To avoid the expense of keeping, feeding, and paying the tax on horses, some people refused to keep them altogether (*MP* 62; *E* 213); they kept a simple carriage like a chair, hiring horses from the local inn as needed (*Watsons*, *MW* 323; *MP* 35). Innkeepers were the most common source for hired or "post"-horses (*Sand*, *MW* 406; *S&S* 311; *P&P* 351; *E* 197), as they had enjoyed a monopoly on the rental of such horses until late in the eighteenth century. Travelers passing through town and needing to continue swiftly on their journeys could opt to hire post-horses rather than waiting to "bait" (or rest) their own. Pulling a carriage was hard work, especially uphill (*MP* 189–190), and horses needed to stop periodically for rest (*L&F*, *MW* 90; *NA* 116; *P* 95, 117). The day after a long or late journey, they would also need to remain idle (*Watsons*, *MW* 340, 341). John Thorpe's casual dismissal of this necessity (*NA* 47–48), as well as his generally abysmal coachmanship (*NA* 44, 62, 88–89), adds to Austen's characterization of him as incompetent and insensitive.

Some horses did double duty, serving as both farm horses and as carriage horses. The Bennets in *Pride and Prejudice* employ this strategy, which is why Elizabeth is not permitted to take the family carriage to Netherfield (30–32). This is a case of art imitating life, as the Austens at Steventon were in precisely the same situation. The horses were primarily used for plowing and similar tasks, and only when this work was done and the horses adequately recovered from their labors could they be used to pull the family carriage. When the Austens moved to Bath in 1801, they tried to reduce expenses and sold the carriage, just as the Dashwoods were forced to do in *Sense and Sensibility* (26).

Keeping saddle or carriage horses entailed a good deal of care and expense. In addition to the taxes on them, horses frequently got sick (*Cath*, *MW* 222; *NA* 172; *MP* 59, 118; *E* 383) and needed medical care. They

---

*Horses were typically identified at this time by their color, rather than by their breed. This was because, after temperament and health, the most important characteristic of a horse was its color. People liked to match their carriage horses, for carriages that required more than one horse to pull. The marchioness of Lansdowne had a carriage pulled by six or eight ponies in which each pair was a bit darker and larger than the one ahead of it. Therefore, the "chestnuts" of *NA* 85 are not nuts but chestnut-colored horses.

Rowlandson Etching, 1790, detail. A country blacksmith shoeing a horse. Courtesy of the Lewis Walpole
Library, Yale University. 790.6.20.1.

required a staff of grooms (*MP* 118) to curry and ride them, to clean the stables (*P&P* 251; *MP* 191; *E* 179, 252), and to accompany employers on rides; coachmen to hitch them to the carriage and direct their movements; and farriers (*NA* 172) to shoe them. They had to be given periodic medical checkups, of a sort; in an age that still believed in routine phlebotomy, they were bled once a year to keep them healthy. When they were taken away from home, stables had to be found and rented for them (*MP* 193). Saddlers (*MP* 8) had to be paid to make and repair their tack. They had to be trained (*S&S* 233), if bred at home, or shopped for carefully and purchased. Of course, not all horse purchases were difficult. Parson Woodforde took a horse home for a "test drive" in March 1794, and his description offers an interesting look at how a gentleman of Austen's time evaluated a carriage horse:

> I am to give Gould for the Horse 15. Guineas if I liked him on trial. He is of a dark Chestnut Colour, very compact make, of the Suffolk kind, short body, handsome forehand, just the height for our little Curricle, hog mane, short dock Tail, which at present is by no means bad, he goes a little limping at first setting out. His Age I apprehend to be about 8. Years. His name is Punch.

Woodforde did indeed like Punch and bought him the same day.

Some horses were kept not for the sake of transportation or labor but for sport. Hunting fox, deer, or hare required the use of horses, and Georgian sportsmen, always serious about their hunting, were intent on finding and breeding the best hunters (*Cath*, *MW* 222; *LS*, *MW* 254, 283; *NA* 76; *S&S* 91, 194, 379; *MP* 37, 229, 237, 241, 342). Women were far less likely than men to engage in this sort of riding, but there were daring souls like Laetitia, Lady Lade, wife of Sir John Lade, a friend of the Prince of Wales. She was nationally famous in the 1780s and 1790s and lived until 1825; she is probably the subject of a 1794 engraving in *The Sporting Magazine*, which bears the caption, "a lady of rank and fortune, leaping over a five-barred gate in the neighbourhood of Windsor, and who may frequently be seen with his majesty's hounds during the hunting season." In November 1796 she was declared "the first horsewoman in the kingdom, being constantly one of the only five or six that are invariably with the hounds."

Horses were also raced. This was a sport that appealed to the propensity of Georgian men to gamble recklessly. Some of them raised racehorses, some bought racehorses, and others merely bet their inheritances on the outcomes of celebrated matches between renowned animals. There were race meetings at Newbury, Newmarket, Epsom, Salisbury, Doncaster, and Ascot. Newmarket was the most prominent of these sites, with seven race meetings a year at the end of the Regency. Winchester had a normal

Racing, Thomas Rowlandson, 1812. Courtesy of the Lewis Walpole Library, Yale University. 812.0.35.

racecourse and one for steeplechase; an announcement of a race to be held on St. Swithin's Day, 1817, prompted her to write or dictate her last poem on the amusing conflict of spirit between a saint's day and a loud-talking, hard-drinking, heavy-gambling race day (*MW* 451–452).

The period from about 1750 until Austen's death in 1817 was one of the golden ages of horse racing. An act of 1740 to set minimum prizes of £50 per race and to regulate horses' weights began the regulation and standardization of the sport. The Jockey Club was founded in 1752 at Newmarket to set rules for racing colors, pedigrees, and the racing calendar; it eventually gained control over all organized racing in England. Tattersalls (*P* 8), an auction house specializing in horses, was founded about twenty years later at Hyde Park Corner in London. Thereafter, a host of famous races was established: the St. Leger in 1776, the Oaks in 1779, the Derby in 1780, and the Ascot Gold Cup in 1807.

Different types of races (*Cath, MW* 199, 240; *NA* 66; *MP* 48, 59) were run, each with its own different style of matching horses and awarding prizes. Many races were two-horse affairs, with the prize being the statutory £50, a piece of plate, or a hogshead of claret. One unusual trophy was the Whip, a Newmarket prize said to have belonged to Charles II that eventually added hairs from the mane and tail of Eclipse, a phenomenally famous racehorse. The typical race length in all these cases was four miles.

From 1791, there were handicaps with three or more horses entering, with each horse carrying a different amount of weight. By the 1780s, some race meetings had adopted the system of weight-for-age, with five-year-old horses carrying 8 stone 2 pounds (114 lbs.), six-year-olds carrying 8 stone 11 pounds (123 lbs.), mares 3 pounds, and older horses 9 stone 5 pounds (131 lbs.). Still another method of handicapping was weight-for-size or give-and-take, in which bigger horses got more weight to carry.

Clever trainers learned to cheat the system by teaching the horse to stand with its feet apart to make the measuring rod on its withers drop a little lower. When race organizers fixed this problem by marking standard positions for the horses' feet, trainers countered by hitting the horses repeatedly on the withers. The horses learned to flinch downward when touched on the withers, and responded in this way when touched with the measuring rod.

The traditional method of running a race, as stated above, was a head-to-head "match" between two horses. Each owner put down a stake, and the winner took both his stake and the loser's. By the beginning of the nineteenth century, however, successful owners wanted to win more, and this led to the invention of the sweepstakes, in which a larger field competed. This method of entry increased the winnings and therefore the public interest in each race. The trend was clear; by 1807, there were 189 matches, 269 races for a piece of plate, and 263 sweepstakes. The interest in matches, however, did not die away immediately. A match in 1799 between two celebrated horses, Hambletonian and Diamond, had a 3,000-guinea purse and an estimated 200,000 to 300,000 worth of side-betting. Hambletonian's owner was so sick with tension that he had to leave the field, but his horse, ridden by the brilliant jockey Frank Buckle, won by half a neck.

As the period went on, several trends became clear. Horses were getting larger and, more and more, were becoming sprinters. The 4-mile standard race, which had packed most of its excitement into the last quarter-mile, shortened to 2 miles or even 1 in some cases. Another trend was the increasing reliance of owners on professional jockeys; still another was toward the racing of younger and younger horses. The first race for three-year-olds was held at Doncaster in 1776 over a distance of 2 miles. Reduced to a distance of 1 mile 6 furlongs 193 yards, this race was named the St. Leger in 1778 after one of its organizers. The Oaks, founded in 1778 and named for an inn owned by the earl of Derby, was another race for three-year-olds; another race founded near the same time was run over a mere mile-long course (*Watsons*, *MW* 339), raised to 1½ miles in 1784, and named the Derby. By 1797, 48 racehorses were two years old, 161 three years old, 122 four years old, and 262 five years old.

A race day was an exhilarating and sometimes dangerous event. Rowdy crowds of all classes gathered around the tracks, with no barriers between themselves and the horses. They diced, played cards or EO (the ancestor of roulette), and watched cockfights and boxing matches. Sometimes they attended dances. Pickpockets roamed through the throngs looking for easy marks and trying to avoid notice; if spotted, they were usually ducked, beaten, or shaved.

The horses, meanwhile, having trained for months in heavy blankets and having been given emetic to purge them, looked, as one spectator put it, "like toast racks." They were not only bony; their ears had been cropped, and their tails docked. If they were particularly good runners, they were at risk from dishonest men who might try to poison them. Even if they ran their best, they might not win if it were a "crimp" match, fixed beforehand by the owners who hoped to cash in on side bets. *See also* Animals; Carriages and Coaches.

Housework

Though women of Austen's class were not solely responsible for housekeeping (*L&F, MW* 107), as they almost always had servants to do the dirtiest and most onerous jobs (*NA* 184), they often engaged in household tasks. They had to know something about, even the chores they did not perform personally, as they had to superintend the work of the servants (*P* 6–7). The quality of a woman's housework—whether it was performed on behalf of her husband, her children, an unmarried brother or uncle, or anyone else—was the principal standard by which her worldly usefulness was judged (*P* 43). If she failed as a housekeeper, she failed as a woman.

To succeed, she had to be frugal, efficient, cheerful, creative, and competent. She also had to master several different sets of skills, including cooking, cleaning, laundering, gardening, dairying, and needlework. Of these, cooking and needlework are discussed in greater depth in other articles within this book. These skills are therefore addressed below principally as they affected the work and rhythm of the household, rather than in terms of the tools they required or the actual techniques used. The specific division of labor between a woman and her servants, moreover, varied from household to household, and the types of tasks typically performed by each sort of servant are discussed fully in the article on servants. Here we look at the work performed and how it was managed, rather than at the specific individual assigned to perform it.

Many of Austen's women, as Maggie Lane points out in *Jane Austen and Food*, are failed housekeepers. Mrs. Elton is extravagant, always "doing too much, and being too careless of expense" (*E* 283). Mrs. Norris has the opposite fault; her greed and stinginess are symptoms of frugality run mad. Mrs. Price does everything wrong; she's sloppy, a poor manager of servants, lazy, and querulous (*MP* 372, 439). There are several concrete examples of her incompetence, but Austen also sums up the case, making it clear exactly where Mrs. Price has gone wrong:

> Her days were spent in a kind of slow bustle; always busy without getting on, always behindhand and lamenting it, without altering her ways; wishing to be an economist, without contrivance or regularity; dissatisfied with her servants, without skill to make them better, and whether helping, or reprimanding, or indulging them, without any power of engaging their respect. (*MP* 389–390)

However, not all of Austen's female characters are bad at running a household. One suspects that Elizabeth and Jane Bennet will have no difficulties in that department; nor will Fanny Price, Elinor Dashwood, Anne Elliot, or Emma Woodhouse. Emma, indeed, is already an accomplished housekeeper, considerate of her guests, aware of the contents of her storerooms, and never, so far as the reader can tell, in conflict with her servants. Of all the heroines, the two most likely to have difficulties after their marriages are the two romantics, Catherine Morland and Marianne Dashwood. In Marianne's case, she will have the sensible Colonel Brandon's advice, and in Catherine's, though her mother predicts she will "make a sad heedless young housekeeper to be sure," this warning is followed by "the consolation of there being nothing like practice" (*NA* 249).

Several of the minor characters, too, appear to be in good control of their households. Mrs. Grant does better. The only complaints about the running of her home come from Mrs. Norris and from Dr. Grant, and Mrs. Norris' criticism of Mrs. Grant's expenditures can be dismissed as stemming from her stinginess, while Dr. Grant is acknowledged by nearly all of *Mansfield Park*'s characters to be unreasonably hard on his wife. Mrs. Collins, too, seems to be doing a good job of keeping house for an irritating husband (*P&P* 216–217, 228). The Bateses get by on charity, a tiny income, and a good deal of penny-pinching, and they can afford only one servant, but they appear on good terms with this maid-of-all-work, and Miss Bates' flaws are conversational, not domestic.

She is certainly well acquainted with cooking, as she would have to be in a one-servant household. Large homes had at least one cook (*P&P* 44, 65), sometimes more, as well as kitchen boys and scullery maids to do the less complex tasks. The running of a kitchen involved acquiring food, whether from the garden, the farm, or shops; the preliminary preparation of food, such as skinning rabbits or plucking and gutting chickens; the careful maintenance of the kitchen fire at the proper temperature for each types of food; and the scouring of dishes, pots, and pans after the meal was over. Whoever did the cooking had to be acquainted with basic methods of food preparation, including the making of simple sauces and gravies, the storage of perishable foods such as eggs and butter, and the cooking of meat over an open flame (*Lesley, MW* 112–113; *Watsons, MW* 360). She needed to know how to make butter and cheese (*MP* 104), how to brew beer, and how to make wine. In the Austen household at Steventon, Mrs. Austen made all the butter, cheese, bread, beer, and wine, and as an adult Jane Austen also made both gooseberry and currant wine. When the Austen women moved to Southampton after Jane's father's death, Mrs. Austen cured hams, made preserves, and brewed spruce beer and orange wine.

It is noteworthy that Mrs. Austen made her own bread. Bread was baked in many homes, but the practice was far from universal, and many people bought their bread from professional bakers. Of course, each home ran according to its own plan. In Parson James Woodforde's house, although he had his niece Nancy to act as housekeeper, it was Parson Woodforde himself, or a male surrogate, who brewed the household's beer. "Busy all Day," he wrote on July 7, 1785, "shewing Briton [his new manservant] the method of brewing. It made me rather cross—Ironing being also about." His niece was hardly idle, though. His diary frequently notes her efforts at confectionery: "Nancy very busy all the morning in making Cakes, Tarts, Custards, and Jellies," "Nancy very busy this morning in making some Rasberry Jam and red Currant Jelly. She made to day about 8 Pd. of Currant Jelly and about 9 Pound of Rasberry Jamm." Preserving would have been hot, uncomfortable work.

Cleaning, too, was extremely laborious. Many cookbooks of the day include recipes for cleaning solutions, and *The Toilet of Flora* (1775), a volume devoted mostly to the preparation of cosmetics, also instructs women how to remove rust, urine, ink, pitch, turpentine, and oil stains. Directions are given for cleaning gold and silver lace, tapestry and carpets (*NA* 163; *MP* 439, 440), and velvet. The anonymous author's directions for cleaning a Turkish carpet is brief, but it evokes the large amount of labor involved in cleaning a single object:

To clean Turkey Carpets.

To revive the colour of a Turkey Carpet, beat it well with a stick, till the dust is all got out, then with Lemon Juice or Sorrel Juice take out the spots of ink, if the carpet is stained with any, wash it in cold Water, and afterwards shake out all the Water from the threads of the carpet, and when it is thoroughly dry, rub it all over with the Crumb of an hot White Loaf, and if the weather is very fine, hang it out in the open air a night or two.

Eliza Haywood's *A New Present for a Servant-Maid* (1771) includes recipes for rust preventatives and cleansers and lists a daunting number of tasks to be undertaken in a single day by a housemaid. According to Haywood, she should rise early, clean out all the hearths and light the fires, clean the locks on the house's doors with an oily rag and then with "rotten-stone, or white brick," and sweep all the carpets. Then she ought to "brush and clean the window curtains, and with a broom sweep the windows, and behind the shutters." She must dust the picture frames, wainscoting, china, and stucco work with a bellows or a soft cloth, then rub down the wainscot and windows and dust the chairs. Next she should sweep the stairs, "throwing on the upper stairs a little wet sand, which will bring down the dust, without flying about," dust the ceilings, and wash the stairs. All this was to happen before her employers woke up.

When the family is up, she should set open the windows of the bed-chambers, and uncover the beds to sweeten and air them; which will be a great help against bugs and fleas. In making the beds, she ought to begin with that first

MISERIES of HUMAN LIFE.

Miseries of Human Life, George Woodward and Thomas Rowlandson, 1807. A charwoman scrubs the floor and cleans the fireplace. Courtesy of the Lewis Walpole Library, Yale University. 807.10.9.1.

aired, taking off the several things singly, and laying them on two chairs, without letting them touch the floor. She should shake the beds well every day, and if there be a matrass, let her turn it at least once a week. The cleaning of the head of the bed, the vallances and curtains, with a brush or whisk, is not to be omitted; nor sweeping clean all behind and under the bed-steads. . . . By thus keeping a constant method, her business will be a pleasure instead of a fatigue.

Haywood's optimism aside, it sounds like a rather fatiguing routine already. But the housemaid's chores were not yet finished. She still had to scour the floorboards with "a little hard brush, and then with a clean cloth, mop the floors, clean the tea-board, wash the silver, and scrub the china with soft sand and water before soaping and boiling it. Then there was the furniture to be waxed and cleaned and the candlesticks to be polished. Someone, even if it was not Haywood's industrious housemaid, had to perform these tasks, or work very much like them, in most of Austen's fictional households.

Then there was the care of clothing, a very serious business in the days when all clothing was made carefully by hand. No one discarded clothing lightly, and even then it was not tossed into the trash but sold as second-hand clothing to the poor. Stains were therefore given careful treatment, and rips were mended. The washing of clothes was also more arduous, since there were no washing machines, not even the hand-operated ones of the later nineteenth century. In larger households, there was a special room or even a separate building devoted to the washing of clothes. A large cylindrical structure was divided into two parts, with a large lidded tub above and a fireplace below. The laundry maid would build a coal fire in the fireplace base and pump water into the upper portion; an excellent picture of a pump located conveniently close to the tub can be found on the Lewis Walpole Library's Web site (call no. 807.7.10.1). Some households pumped the water and allowed it to settle for a few days before using it; others, whose well or other water source yielded hard, mineralized water, might soften it first by using chalk or a mixture of ashes and un-slaked lime. Haywood advises dipping the clothes in warm water, soaping them with a "wash ball" (a lump of often homemade soap, the cousin of

How Are You Off for Soap, Elmes, 1816. The man in the washtub is obviously fanciful, but the rest of the scene is true to life. The laundry maid, Betty, has a pile of dirty laundry in a basket on the floor and two tubs of clothes soaking in water on the table. A cake of soap lies in a bowl between the tubs. At the left-hand side of the room is a brick oven with a washtub built on top of it. A fire was lit in the oven, using the coal scuttle and shovel seen to the right of the oven, and the maid filled the tub above with water, often using a pump built into the wall above the tub, though such a pump is not visible in this particular illustration. She agitated the hot, wet laundry using a paddle, the handle of which can be seen sticking out of the tub. She has the windows of the laundry house open, as washing clothes was hot work. Courtesy of the Lewis Walpole Library, Yale University. 816.6.21.1.

the "breeches ball" of *NA* 172), and agitating them between the hands. "After that let them lie in hot water till next morning; then wash as usual, and there will be no occasion for more soap till the second lather." Washing "as usual" involved boiling in the big heated tub and stirring the clothes with a paddle. Then the garments were wrung out and spread in the sun to dry (*Sand, MW* 384), not only because the sun was warm but because the sunlight helped to bleach the white linen.

Smaller households could not afford a laundry maid. These homes employed a variety of tactics to get the washing done. Sometimes the washing was sent out (*S&S* 249); sometimes specialized laundresses (*P* 193) came to the house at regular intervals to wash the clothes. Parson Woodforde used the latter strategy, having his laundry done in one great burst every three weeks. He was not unusual in having such a long interval be-tween laundry days; given the fuel, the labor, and the soaking, boiling, and drying time required to do laundry, it was a mammoth task that required group labor for an entire day. It could not be done casually or frequently.

Clothing required other care as well, and this work, too, was the province of women. Women in working-class families made their own clothes and might also spin flax or wool. Women in the gentry and the aristocracy seldom made their own clothes, but they sewed clothes for the poor and did decorative needlework. Their servants had more onerous tasks: airing, brushing, and mending their employers' clothes, as well as removing stains and laying out morning and evening ensembles.

All the preceding work was done principally or entirely indoors, but women had other work that was done outside. In farming families, women might help with the harvest or the sowing. In most homes, gentry and working-class alike, they had charge of the dairy (*P&P* 163; *MP* 104), the poultry-yard (*P&P* 163; *MP* 104), and the kitchen garden. Here, their tasks included weeding, sowing, harvesting, milking, cheese making, but-ter making, feeding chickens or other fowls, and gathering eggs. In the dairy, according to cookbook author Charles Millington, daily labor in-cluded not only the gathering and the processing of milk but also the scrupulous care and cleaning of the dairy utensils:

> They should be well washed every day in warm water, and afterwards rinced in cold, and must be entirely cool before they are used. If, however, any kind of metal vessels are improperly retained in the dairy, they must be scalded every day, and well scrubbed and scoured.

Mrs. Austen superintended the dairy at Steventon, though she does not seem to have done the actual work. She also gardened enthusiastically all her life, digging her own potatoes and wearing a laborer's green frock. Jane, too, was an avid gardener, although her tastes seem to have run more to flowers than to potatoes. Even so, she reported at various times, with an accountant's eye for detail, on the produce of the family's fruit trees and garden. *See also* Fire; Food; Gardens and Landscape; Sewing.

Hunting

Hunting (*Watsons, MW* 360; *S&S* 32, 43, 91–92, 214–215, 379; *P&P* 374; *P* 55, 58, 83, 217) customarily began in the morning (*Watsons, MW* 347; *MP* 191; *P* 37), just after or just before breakfast. Earlier in the eigh-teenth century, it had begun quite early in the morning, beginning well before breakfast, but by the turn of the nineteenth century, gentlemen were willing to sleep in a little, eat a substantial meal, and then head out with dogs and guns. A few zealous men still got up early enough to see sleeping hares tracked to their forms (dens), but even the enthusiastic

The Breakfast: Symptoms of Drowsiness, Henry Bunbury, 1800. Hunters meet for an early-morning breakfast before heading out with guns and dogs. Courtesy of the Lewis Walpole Library, Yale University. 800.0.11.

hunter Peter Beckford, author of *Thoughts on Hunting in a Series of Familiar Letters to a Friend* (1781), remarked that he "thought hare-hunting should be taken as a ride, after breakfast, to get us an appetite to our dinner." Parson James Woodforde, who liked a hare hunt himself, went "Soon after breakfast" and liked to stay out for several hours. James Edward Austen-Leigh, Jane's nephew, remembered that Jane's brothers "usually took their hasty breakfast in the kitchen" before setting out. The best sort of weather (*LS, MW* 254; *Watsons, MW* 357; *S&S* 167) for hunting, according to Beckford, was "warm without sun," and the dogs tended to pick up scent best if the air and ground were moist without being wet. Beckford also noted that the English climate did not provide many days with perfect conditions, so avid hunters must have been especially disappointed if forced by circumstances to miss going out with their guns on such a day.

Most hunting took place in the autumn, when certain migratory birds were in season and, most importantly, when the harvest had been brought in. Some types of hunts could range unpredictably over vast swaths of terrain, taking horses and dogs through woods and fields. Cleared fields were easier to ride through and also had nothing left to be damaged by the horses' hooves, as James Austen made clear in a poem written for his son. It was perfectly all right, he wrote, to hunt "When corn is housed, & fields are clear, / And Autumn's various tints appear." But, he cautioned,

> . . . when the wheat is higher grown
> And pease and beans and barley sown,
>   And fences made up tight,
> To gallop all the country over
> And cut up saintfoin, grass, & clover,
>   Is neither fair nor right.

Men spent the spring and summer preparing for the hunting season by breeding and training large packs of dogs and exercising and training their horses. Then, on September 1 (*Mount, MW* 41; *P&P* 318; *MP* 114), the partridge season opened, and men all over England, especially in prime hunting regions like East Anglia and Northamptonshire, surged into the field, hoping to bring home heavy bags. Parson Woodforde described the sound of this masculine holiday in 1794: "This being the first Day of Partridge shooting, Guns from all Quarters of Weston were heard, Morn' & Afternoon." September, too, was Peter Beckford's preferred starting month for foxhunting (*Watsons, MW* 333). Hunting was forbidden on Sundays and Christmas, and certain stratagems, such as the use of snares to catch hares, were forbidden. By February, the season was over (*NA* 209; *P&P* 180; *P* 216).

Not everyone hunted. It was primarily the pastime of the nobility, the gentry, the portion of the merchant class wealthy enough to own some country land, and the guests of the above groups. The legal requirement was that the hunter own land worth £100 a year; once this plateau was reached, he could not only shoot on his own land but depute or invite others to do so. After 1784, hunters were also required to take out a certificate and pay an annual fee of three guineas, and many of Jane's relatives did so. Blood sports were, later in the nineteenth century, to become disreputable activities for clergymen, but the eighteenth century was rich in "hunting parsons," as they were called. Austen's life, bridging these two different worlds, brought her into contact with both kinds of clergymen—those who hunted and those who did not. Among those who did were her oldest brother, James, his friend Fulwar Fowle, and another of her brothers, Henry, who became a clergyman rather late in life. Among those who did not was her father.

A shooting party (*NA* 66) of any size included one or more servants who helped in various ways. Gamekeepers (*MP* 114) managed the land in its capacity as a refuge for game, patrolling for poachers (*MP* 115) and learning where certain types of animals liked to make their dens. They might also help the younger members of the family learn to shoot. Some gamekeepers, however, were purely nominal; they were friends of the lord or lady of the manor (*S&S* 33; *P&P* 15, 337) who had been given a "dep-utation" (*P* 22) as gamekeepers in order to legally qualify them (*MP* 115) to hunt.

"Whippers-in" were the inferior members of the staff in a large party, such as a foxhunt. Their job was to supervise dogs (*MP* 115) and keep them to their task. Their most important job was to keep the dogs from killing the fox until the gentry could be "in at the kill" and then to keep the dogs from tearing the fox to pieces. Two whippers-in were generally used: one in the front of the pack, one at the rear. When not on duty during the hunt, they assisted in the training of young dogs.

Whippers-in were subordinate to the huntsman (*NA* 66), who managed the entire hunt, supervising the finding of a fox, observing the overall discipline of dogs, and making sure that all the genteel hunters kept up with the group. A distinction was made between huntsmen and whippers-in, as revealed by the way they were addressed: huntsmen were called by their last names, whippers-in by their first. According to Peter Beckford, a good huntsman

> should be young, strong, active, bold and enterprising; fond of the diver-sion and indefatigable in the pursuit of it: he should be sensible and good-tempered; he ought also to be sober: he should be exact, civil, and cleanly; he should be a good horseman and a good groom: his voice should be strong and clear; and he should have an eye so quick, as to perceive which of his hounds carries the scent when all are running; and should have so excellent an ear, as always to distinguish the foremost hounds when he does not see them: he should be quiet, patient, and without conceit.

In exchange for all these virtues, the huntsman was entitled to tips, called "field money," whenever a fox was killed.

Grooms also went along to tend to the horses, and footmen might go as well, to attend to any needs that the gentlemen might have when they stopped to rest. Some hunters who shot at birds took a "loader," who did the tedious business of loading one gun while the other was in use. Others used "beaters," who tramped around and made noise to flush animals out of cover. Parson Woodforde went to a large hare hunt in November 1789, where his was one of twelve greyhounds in the field; he guessed there were as many as a dozen beaters mounted on horseback to drive the hares toward the dogs. Some hare hunters, rather than paying a game-keeper to find quarry, paid shepherds to keep an eye out for hares. At some gatherings, a shilling was collected from each hunter for each hare found, and Beckford thought this was excessive. He agreed that hare-finders should be paid, if only to keep them from poaching the hares themselves, but, he said, "hare-finders often are too well paid. I have known them frequently get more than a guinea for a single hare."

Children began to hunt at a fairly young age. James Edward Austen-

Leigh began at fifteen, Henry Austen at fourteen. Francis began to hunt at seven, on a pony named Squirrel that he bought with £1 11s. 6d. of his own money; it seems unlikely that he would have been permitted to ride with the local foxhunting pack, the Vine Hunt, at such a tender age, but Jane makes the fictional Charles Blake a hunter at the age of ten (*Watsons, MW* 331). Perhaps Francis began with less demanding riding, advancing later to grown-up hunts.

Guns and Dogs

First and foremost, a hunter needed a gun. Guns (*MP* 181), however, had several deficiencies in the late eighteenth century. They took a long time to load, as powder needed to be measured into the muzzle with a powder horn, and then flannel wadding and lead shot had to be rammed in after the powder. If the barrel of the gun were already hot from previous shots, the powder might explode as soon as it was poured; this was one reason that multiple guns tended to be used by a single hunter. Sometimes the unintended ignition would take place immediately, perhaps lighting the powder in the horn as well; at other times, it took place when the ramrod was still in use, sending the ramrod flying like a javelin. If all went well, the powder was lit properly by a flint, which made a spark that ignited a small amount of powder placed in a "pan" connected to the barrel.

Even if this proceeded smoothly, however, the hunter's worries were not at an end. He might have miscalculated the amount of powder needed, resulting in a shot that was too weak or too strong; in the latter case, the gun might explode in his hands. The lead shot was not always perfectly round, which meant that it often flew irregularly. It also left the gun a little late, due to the time it took the powder in the pan to ignite and set off the main explosion through a touchhole; though the delay was perhaps as little as a tenth of a second, this could make a difference in the hunter's ability to get off an accurate shot. Furthermore, the gun itself was not especially accurate and required a long barrel to compensate for its deficiencies. The normal minimum length was 40 inches, making it heavy and unwieldy.

The 1780s brought significant improvements to the gun. New methods of making lead shot improved its shape, and London gunsmith (*P* 240) Henry Nock invented a breech plug in 1787 that caused powder to ignite more predictably and powerfully. The combined effects enabled 10 inches to be shaved off the barrel length, making the hunting gun a very different and much more reliable weapon. Another innovation was the detonator, introduced in 1807, which ignited the powder without delay, but it was some time before this invention would be widely adopted; many hunters had grown used to the brief hesitation before the main powder charge was lit, and they found it difficult to adjust their aim to account for the faster ignition. Accordingly, both types of guns were to be found in the field in the last years of Austen's life. Also during her lifetime, a gradual shift from single-barreled to double-barreled guns was being made. Early double-barreled guns were especially prone to barrel explosions, and in the 1780s many hunters still considered them dangerous novelties, but as reliability improved, their popularity increased. Some of the finest double-barreled shotguns (*P* 240) were produced by Joseph Manton, who patented several improvements, and his brother John Durs Egg, a Swiss-born gunsmith, made some very fine flintlocks.

Improvements in the gun led to shifts in the types of dogs (*P* 43, 59) used in the field. With the old, heavier guns, it had been nearly impossible to shoot a flying bird, and the preferred dog was therefore a pointer (*S&S* 42, 44, 72, 330), which would seek out a sitting bird and silently indicate its position to the hunter; meanwhile, the frightened bird would remain very still, hoping to fool the dog into moving away, but inadvertently presenting itself as a perfect target to the hunter, who would stealthily approach and shoot the bird as it sat, or just as it rose. Shorter, lighter guns made this sort of hunting unsportsmanlike, and the gentlemanly approach was now to flush the birds and shoot them on the wing. Accordingly, pointers grew less popular and were replaced to some extent by retrievers, who need do nothing more than fetch the slain birds. Pointers, however, remained popular and could be trained to retrieve as well as to find game.

Setters performed much the same tasks as pointers but were believed to have more stamina. Although some red and black-and-tan setters existed by the early nineteenth century, most were white with liver-colored spots. Springer and cocker spaniels, distinguished from each other mostly by size, became increasingly important; their main task was to flush birds from cover. Newfoundlands, not always black at this time in history, were originally bred in Canada as fishermen's helpers. They were trained to retrieve people and objects that fell overboard and to swim ropes and nets to specified locations. Their instinct for retrieving appealed to English hunters, who made use of them in field sports (*Gen Cur*, *MW* 73; *NA* 212).

For foxhunting, foxhounds (*Watsons*, *MW* 337; *P&P* 20) were the favorite dogs. They were increasingly popular; Austen neighbor William Chute, master and founder of the Vine Hunt, switched from harriers to foxhounds in the 1790s. In 1800, owners began to keep centralized records of the genealogy of these dogs, enabling a more organized and efficient breeding program. Hares were hunted with either harriers or greyhounds. Several Austen neighbors kept packs of harriers, and one neighbor had a small pack of beagles. Town packs of harriers were also owned in some places for the use of less genteel hunters, who kept the dogs in individual houses and assembled them as necessary for the hunt. James Austen kept a pack of harriers at one time, when he was a newly minted curate, but this was considered somewhat extravagant, given his fairly low income at the time.

Peter Beckford was an avid dog breeder and included plenty of notes about breeding, care, and training in his *Essays on Hunting*. He recommended clean, spacious kennels and an exercise yard with trees for shade and pissing posts to keep the dogs from damaging the trees with their urine. The pack should be of uniform size and roughly uniform speed, composed of fifteen to thirty "couple"—that is, thirty to sixty dogs—and relatively young. He advised against hunting any one dog for more than five or six seasons. He fed his dogs mostly on barley and oatmeal, with "flesh" such as horsemeat and sheep's feet rationed out in fairly small quantities. Not all the hounds would hunt on a particular day, but each dog should be hunted enough to keep it in good practice. He estimated, "Forty couple of hunting hounds will enable you to hunt three, or even four, times in a week."

Beckford offered a great deal of advice to prospective pack owners about canine illnesses and injuries such as mange, distemper, worms, foot problems, muscle strains, and snakebite. He also described the form of the perfect hound:

> Let his legs be straight as arrows; his feet round, and not too large; his shoulders back; his breast rather wide than narrow; his chest deep; his back broad; his head small, his neck thin; his tail thick and brushy; if he carry it well, so much the better.

Breeding was to be done selectively, with not only the dog's appearance but also its hunting ability taken into consideration. Dogs permitted to breed should be stout, tender-nosed, and focused on hunting without babbling or skirting (barking for no good reason, or straying away from the pack). Each litter of new puppies was customarily given a set of names that all began with one letter; some of Beckford's suggestions for the letter "F" are Factious, Fervent, Finder, Firebrand, Flyer, Foamer, Faithful, Famous, Fashion, Frisky, and Funnylass, but, oddly enough, not Folly (*S&S* 214–215).

The huntsman, if there was one, taught young dogs (*P* 83) to hunt. It was important to teach them to seek the right quarry. They were, for example, specifically taught to avoid flocks of sheep at the command " 'Ware [beware] sheep!" or " 'Ware mutton!" Dogs who stubbornly refused to learn this lesson, he said, were sometimes tied to a ram to make them well and truly afraid of sheep, "but that is breaking them with a vengeance; you had better hang them." Beating dogs was the standard method of disciplining them, and Beckford does not break ranks with his contemporaries on this score. To train foxhounds to ignore hares, for example, he suggests placing them in a kennel with a hare and having the whippers-in simultaneously beat the dogs and scream at them every time they offer to chase the hare: "upon this occasion they cannot cut them too hard, or [be]rate them too much."

Any dog, in theory,* could be used for ratting (*P* 219)—the extermination of rats in barns—but terriers (*NA* 53, 212) were considered especially good at this job and at eliminating other kinds of vermin. Ratting was not really hunting as such. It was too informal, too confined in area, and too utilitarian to be much more than a particularly exciting farm chore, but, such as it was, it was considered great fun, especially at times of year when other sorts of hunting were not permitted. Parson Woodforde hired a professional rat-catcher in 1783, but his diary makes clear that he joined in the pursuit:

> We caught and killed about 3 Dozen of Rats in the Barn before Dinner to day—3 old female Rats with their young ones—2 old dog Rats and some half grown.

Ratting was most closely allied not to other types of hunting but to the sorts of blood sports, such as cockfights and dogfights, to which Englishmen had long been addicted.

The dogs were, in theory, supposed to stay out of the way of the horses' hooves, but Beckford thought that it ought instead to be the other way around:

> It is too much the custom, first to ride over a dog, and then cry, *'ware horse!* Take care not to ride over your hounds: I have known many a good dog spoiled by it. In open ground, caution them first; you may afterwards ride over them, if you please; but, in roads and paths, they frequently cannot get out of your way: it surely, then, is your business, either to stop your horse, or break a way for them. . . . good sportsmen seldom ride on the line of the tail hounds.
>
> An acquaintance of mine, when he hears any of his servants say *"ware horse!"* halloos out, " *'ware horse! 'ware dog!* and be hang'd to you!"

The horses (*MP* 229, 237, 241) required almost as much training as the dogs and were very highly valued. Even the sensible Edmund Bertram would rather give up his one all-purpose riding horse than either of his hunters (*MP* 37).

Types and Methods of Hunting

There were two principal types of hunts—hunts that moved and hunts that took place in a relatively fixed location. In the first category were hunts for fox (*MP* 237), rabbit, hares, and deer, where the enjoyment of the chase came from speed on horseback (*NA* 66) and from outwitting the native guile of the fleeing quarry. In this type of hunting, it was essential

---

*Except, of course, for Lady Bertram's pug (*MP* 10, 13, 20, 74, 179, 333), a singularly useless animal for which Austen clearly has no patience.

Rowlandson Etching, 1790, detail. Greyhounds pursuing a hare. Courtesy of the Lewis Walpole Library, Yale University. 790.6.20.1.

to maintain the goodwill of one's neighbors, for they had to grant permission for the hunt to cross their land, and they had to be repaid in case of damages to crops or livestock. This had not always been the case in Austen's lifetime but was decided in a closely watched legal battle between the earl of Essex and his half brother. The 1808 decision gave greater control to landowners, as opposed to hunters and in some cases led to friendly bribery, such as sponsoring a ball or inviting more people into the hunt, simply to keep the neighborly peace.

Foxhunting was justified by its proponents on the grounds that it rid the countryside of poultry-destroying vermin, but in areas with especially large and clever populations of foxes, such as Jane Austen's own Hampshire, care was taken not to destroy all these "vermin," for fear of destroying all the sport as well. Stag hunting, which, like foxhunting, involved swift, thrilling chases over varied terrain, was rapidly decreasing in popularity, mostly due to the diminishing number of deer. Only the richest landowners could afford to maintain deer parks (*Mount*, *MW* 41), and newly prosperous men with an interest in taking up hunting could not begin their hobby by pursuing deer. Instead, they turned to hare hunting, which could be accomplished with a relatively small pack of dogs. Hares were also easier to catch than foxes, especially since hunters pursued them not on foot, as in later years, but on horseback. Hares tended to flee in a circle, or to double back over their own paths, which confused the dogs to some extent but also meant that the hares covered less ground than did a fox. Hares also tended to hide or lie still, making it easier for the dogs to catch them too quickly, and the practice of some huntsmen of beating the bushes until a hare popped out meant that the dogs had little trouble in finding the hare. If the huntsman were not careful, the dogs would simply fall upon the hare the moment it appeared, and the sport would be over. The point was to give the hare enough of a head start that the contest was considered reasonably fair to the hare and a worthwhile challenge for the dogs.

Birds (*NA* 66; *P&P* 337) were hunted differently. They were rarely shot from horseback, and they were not pursued. Instead, hunters had either to find them where they nested or to wait for them to land. Birds such as partridges, pheasants (*MP* 181), woodcock, and snipe were hunted according to the first method. A party of hunters would go out with a handful of dogs, guns, loaders, and so forth, and set up at the edge of a likely field or covert (the latter was a thicket of bushes or similar covering in which birds might be hiding—see *S&S* 45). Dogs would be sent to point out or flush out birds, which would then be driven upward, with all the hunters present taking quick aim and blasting away in an enormous roar of gunfire. The English method of shooting, predicated in part, no doubt, on the weight of the gun, was to raise the gun at the very last moment and take aim in an instant. Keeping continuous aim while waiting for a bird to rise, it was thought, tired the eyes and reduced hand–eye coordination.

While large shooting parties did take place, it was equally common to see one or two men out with a single servant and one or two dogs, moving from field to field in quest of game. The hunters strove for balance, seeking enough birds to justify their day's shooting, but not so many that the overall population of birds diminished over time (*MP* 181). Preservation of game (*P* 43), by destroying predators, controlling the number of birds shot, and savagely prosecuting poachers, was a chief concern. The steel trap that breaks Lucy's leg in *Jack & Alice* was probably set out to deter poachers (*J&A*, *MW* 22).

Ducks, unlike partridges or pheasants, were lured to the hunter rather than tracked to their nests. Some hunters, especially those who hunted and sold wild ducks for a living, used decoys—not the carved wooden decoys of later years, but a cornucopia-shaped tube of pipes, surrounded by netting, with its wide end facing the ducks and its narrow end facing the hunter, who controlled a net at the narrow end. A reddish dog, resembling a fox, was sent into the water and swam into the wide end of the decoy, and the ducks followed, thinking they were driving a fox away from their nests. When the ducks were bunched together at the narrow end of the decoy, they were deliberately startled, whereupon they flew into the hunter's net. Alternatively, tame ducks were released onto the pond and lured up the pipe with whistles and food, and, when the wild ducks followed, they were chased to the narrow end by men or dogs. Shooting ducks by wading through ponds and marshes, with the dirt and damp this entailed, was considered "by no means gentlemanly" and even dangerous to the health, according to *The Shooter's Guide* (1809). *See also* Horses.

Hymen

Hymen (*MP* 440; *E* 308) was the Greek god of marriage. He was a relatively minor god, not meriting a seat on Olympus with the main pantheon, but he was important to women, who were taught that marriage was the whole purpose of their existence. Occasionally, he was celebrated in verse, as he was, centuries later, in Edmund Spenser's "Epithalamion" (1595), with its revelers approaching the bride:

> *Hymen iô Hymen, Hymen* they do shout,
> That even to the heavens theyr shouting shrill
> Doth reach, and all the firmament doth fill, . . .
> And evermore they *Hymen Hymen* sing,
> That al the woods them answer and theyr eccho ring.

Another reference to Hymen is found in John Milton's "L'Allegro" (1645):

> There let Hymen oft appear
> In saffron robe, with taper clear,
> And pomp, and feast, and revelry,
> With masque, and antique pageantry . . .

Austen's contemporaries, like Spenser's and Milton's, found classical times to be a fascinating golden age. Some of the traditions of ancient Greek and Roman weddings would have been familiar to well-educated people of Austen's day, including the Roman tradition of dressing the bride in yellow or "saffron" robes (*E* 308). Mrs. Elton, always anxious to prove herself a worthy member of the gentry, drops this reference, as she drops so many others, to assure her listeners that she is a woman of culture and fashion.

I

Illegitimacy

Illegitimate birth (*L&F*, *MW* 77, 106; *E* 481) carried two sets of penalties—legal/financial and social. Financial penalties might be severe or nonexistent, depending on the disposition of the father of the child. If he chose to abandon his responsibilities, there was little that the mother could do, especially if she were poor and he were rich. In such a case, she was likely to be dismissed from her job anyway and have little to show for it except the enmity of the embarrassed man. If she and the father were both working-class, she might very well name him to the local magistrate in the hope of forcing him either to marry her or to support her and the child; magistrates also often tried to force women to name the fathers of illegitimate children, as they could then force the father to provide financial support, rather than accepting the child's maintenance as an addition to the burden of parish "poor relief."

Mothers were not always willing to name a child's father, either because he was married or for some other reason. Parson James Woodforde recorded the baptism of such a child in December 1786:

> I privately named a spurious Child of one Mary Parker's this morning by name John. The Fathers Name I could not get intelligence of.

In general, fathers, especially fathers who could "do better" than to marry an impoverished lover, were expected to provide some sort of discreet maintenance for their "natural" children (*S&S* 66; *E* 22–23, 62, 393). They could send them to be raised by another family, for instance, or pack mother and child off to a place where they would not be taken notice of, or simply slip the mother funds now and then for the child's feeding and education. Some fathers were much more generous, taking their bastard children into their homes, mentioning them in their wills, and providing substantial support. Lord Chesterfield's famous letters on personal conduct were written, for example, to an illegitimate son.

If the father did not specifically provide for his child, however, the child had no legal right of inheritance. There were also social consequences for bastardy that only very high social status on the part of the father could mitigate. Illegitimate birth was a social stain that, in the absence of lofty parentage or significant fortune, was a serious impediment to marriage within one's class. The burden weighed differently on sons and daughters. Sons, who would have been able to inherit if they had been born in wedlock, had a stronger sense of financial loss; for daughters, however, the whispering among other women, the consciousness of one's origin, and the effect on marriageability would have been more painful.

Income

Incomes varied widely by profession, rank, and luck. It was generally true that working-class incomes rose over Austen's lifetime but that their real value fell over the same period due to inflation. Rising agricultural prices over the same period tended to favor large landowners and clergy whose income was derived from tithes (but not clergy who were paid a flat fee specified by contract). For the purposes of rough comparison, the following is a list of some real and fictional incomes.

Real Incomes

£5 5s.	Wages paid to Parson Woodforde's maid Betty Dade for the year 1789–1790
£10	Wages paid to Parson Woodforde's manservant Ben Leggatt for the year 1789–1790
£18–£20	Annual wages of a coachman, 1790s
£54 12s.	Henry Austen's salary as curate of Chawton, 1818; see *S&S* 276
£100–£150	Estimated value of about 3,000 of England's parish livings
£192	Charles Austen's income in 1814 as a half-pay naval captain
£200	Mr. Austen's income from two parishes in the 1770s
£230	Francis Austen's income in 1814 as a half-pay naval captain
£300	Income of Jane's oldest brother, James, a clergyman, at the time of his first marriage in 1792; £100 of this came from the bride's father
£600	Mr. Austen's income from two parishes c. 1801; he also had income from his farm
£1,100	James Austen's income later in his career, when he held the livings of three parishes
£2,000	Annuity granted to James Leigh-Perrot, Mrs. Austen's brother, in lieu of his share of the estate of his relative Mary Leigh; he also had income from other sources
£2,000	Annual income of Mrs. Knight, Edward Austen's adoptive mother, when she resigned the house at Godmersham to him in 1799

Fictional Incomes from Austen's Works

£100	Dowry income for Lydia Bennet (plus her part of her inheritance—*P&P* 302)
£200	Clergyman (*Gen Cur, MW* 73)
£350	Income considered too small to live on, by Elinor Dashwood and Edward Ferrars (*S&S* 369)

£400	James Morland's future living (*NA* 135); "An estate of at least equal value, moreover, was assured as his future inheritance."
£600	Mrs. Norris, in widowhood (*MP* 29–30)
£700	Edmund Bertram (*MP* 226)
£800–£900	Tom Musgrave (*Watsons, MW* 328)
£1,000–£1,200	Income promised to Edward Ferrars if he will marry the Hon. Miss Morton (*S&S* 224, 266)
£1,000	Mr. and Mrs. Norris (*MP* 3)
£1,800–£2,000	Marianne's "competence" (*S&S* 91–92)
£2,000	Colonel Brandon (*S&S* 70, 196, 292)
£2,000	Mr. Bennet (*P&P* 28)
£4,000	Henry Crawford (*MP* 118)
£4,000–£5,000	Mr. Bingley (*P&P* 4, 348)
£10,000	Mr. Darcy (*P&P* 10, 338, 378)
£12,000	Mr. Rushworth (*MP* 40)

Income could come from a variety of sources. For clergymen, it could come from tithes (a proportion of the produce of the parish) or from fixed payments agreed upon between the parish and previous holders of the living. Some clergy were curates, paid a stipend by the real holder of the living to perform its day-to-day duties. Income could also come from land (*Sand, MW* 401; *NA* 122), whether farmed by oneself or rented out to tenants, and from what Austen calls "funded" money (*Sand, MW* 401; *NA* 122)—money set aside in safe government investments at a fairly low rate of interest, usually about 5 percent per annum (*S&S* 12; *P&P* 106). Thus, Edward Ferrars and Elinor Dashwood, who between them have £3,000 to invest, plus a £200-per-year living at Delaford, can expect to make £350 a year (*S&S* 283, 369). Captain Wentworth, with £25,000 in prize money (*P* 248), can expect to yield £1,250 per year. An annuity (*S&S* 10–11) was not the same thing as funded income (*Sand, MW* 401). It lasted for a specified period, usually the lifetime of its recipient (*S&S* 4), and then the principal reverted to someone else.

Inns

Jane Austen traveled a great deal within England and was well acquainted with inns (*H&E, MW* 38; *First Act, MW* 172–174; *Evelyn, MW* 191; *NA* 104; *P&P* 260; *MP* 412, 446; *P* 98, 99, 111, 122). Sometimes, she dined at them only while horses were "baited" (allowed to rest—see *NA* 156) or exchanged. For example, she dined at Dartford's Bull and George in October 1798 and at a different inn in the same town, the Bull, in 1808. At other times, she stayed in inns, although, like many genteel travelers, she preferred to stay with friends for short visits or to rent lodgings for longer stays. Staying at London's Bath Hotel in June 1808, she found it "most uncomfortable quarters—very dirty, very noisy, and very ill-provided." A contemporary, Parson Woodforde, was likewise disappointed with his inn accommodations (*NA* 76) on many occasions. Staying at London's "Bell Savage" inn in 1782, he found the owners "civil" and the inn itself "a very good House," but he was plagued by bedbugs and woke to find himself covered with bites. Staying there again in 1786, he was "Very much pestered and bit by the Buggs in the Night," awakened at 4:00 A.M. by the bedbugs on the next night, and on the third night gave up and slept in a chair to avoid the mattress.

As an occasional visitor to Bath and a resident of the town from 1801 to 1806, Austen would have been familiar with the Bear Inn, demolished in 1806 to make way for the construction of Union Street, and the White Hart Inn (*P* 216, 220, 223, 229), which stood in Stall Street across from the Pump Room. It was generally considered the best inn in Bath. Foreign visitor Louis Simond stayed there in 1815, offering a detailed description of the services provided:

[T]wo well-dressed footmen were ready to help us alight, presenting an arm on either side. Then a loud bell on the stairs, and lights carried before us to an elegantly furnished sitting room where the fire was already blazing. In a few minutes a neat-looking chambermaid, with an ample white apron pinned behind, came to offer her services to the ladies and show the bedrooms. In less than half-an-hour five powdered gentlemen burst into the room with three dishes, etc., and two remained to wait. Our bill was £2 11s. sterling, dinner for three, tea, beds and breakfast. The servants have no wages—but depending on the generosity of travellers they find it to their interest to please them. They (the servants) cost us about five shillings a day.

Parson Woodforde, too, found the amenities at the White Hart pleasing. He stayed there much earlier than Simond, visiting Bath in 1793 and finding the White Hart "a very good, very capital Inn, everything in stile." This establishment did not, however, call itself a "hotel" (*Sand, MW* 378, 384, 401, 406, 413, 422, 425; *P&P* 117, 295; *P* 221), a term just coming into use in the last quarter of the eighteenth century. A hotel was really just a glorified inn, implying, by its use of a French-derived name, that it was fashionable and well equipped. The real-life White Hart appears in two of Austen's novels, and another White Hart—a fictional one this time—appears in the incomplete novel *The Watsons* (*MW* 321, 323, 325).

In Lyme (*P* 95), Austen might have been acquainted with the Golden Lion and the Three Cups, described in an 1810 guide to the city as "respectable Inns" renting rooms "on easy terms." In Southampton, where she lived for a few years early in the nineteenth century, she would certainly have known the Crown (*MP* 400, 406), a respectable inn on High

Street that tended to attract naval officers. Her aunt Mrs. Lybbe Powys stayed there in 1792 and had "an elegant dinner" but thought the place a little dirty. As with the White Hart, there is both a real Crown (Southampton) and a fictional one (Highbury—see *E* 193, 195, 197, 244, 250–254, 319, 382–383) to be found in Austen's work.

Inns provided a variety of services other than the overnight accommodation and daytime feeding of travelers (*H&E, MW* 38; *S&S* 160; *P&P* 222). There was no inn in Steventon, where Austen grew up, but there was an inn south of town where the main road intersected with one leading to Winchester. This inn, the Wheatsheaf, was where the Austens picked up their mail; innkeepers often performed this service for local residents. Innkeepers also hired out their large rooms for balls (*Watsons, MW* 327; *E* 197, 250–254, 319) and their smaller rooms for gatherings of men's clubs (*Watsons, MW* 325; *E* 197) and local officials (*E* 456). Austen attended balls during the winter months at an inn in Basingstoke, for example. Working-class wedding parties might also go to an inn for the postnuptial festivities. Inns were required at times to billet troops, a service that innkeepers reluctantly provided; they were more enthusiastic about their usual service as postmasters, which brought in customers and, for a number of years, gave them a monopoly on the rental of post-horses (*Watsons, MW* 323; *E* 197). Regularly scheduled coach services also tended to pick up passengers and drop them off at inns (*S&S* 354); most inns had an arched entrance to allow the carriages and horses to be brought into a courtyard (*H&E, MW* 38; *L&F, MW* 90–91, 108; *P* 105) and led to the attached stables.

The typical innkeeper (*Watsons, MW* 336; *NA* 45; *E* 255–256, 322) unloaded his or her guests outside (see illustration in article on Carts and Wagons), leading them into a receiving hall (*Watsons, MW* 326–327) and sending a maid (*P&P* 241) with a candle to lead them up the main staircase to their rooms. Most inns were more than one story tall, with balconies on the upper floors overlooking the central courtyard. Meals were taken in a dining room (*P&P* 219; *P* 104), which was usually located downstairs; there might also be a coffee room and some small sitting rooms identified by name, such as the Sun, the Lion, or the Paragon (*First Act, MW* 172). Gentlemen almost always took a private sitting room, and ladies always did so, but ordinary stagecoach passengers would not normally have done so. Pedestrians and passengers from the cheap stage wagons were only reluctantly admitted, given the worst food, and forced to eat in the kitchen. Karl Philipp Moritz, traveling in England in 1782, was shown this sort of rudeness. After pressing his case, he was permitted to dine on a tough fowl and sleep two to a bed with a drunk who kept his boots on, and this entertainment cost him nine shillings, an outrageous sum under the circumstances.

A well-run inn would know the scheduled arrival times of coaches that

Shewing a Good Figger of a Horse, North, 1806. A horse is inspected outside the Ram Inn, whose porte cochere into the inn yard can be seen at the right, with a post chaise in the archway. This passage would have led to a central courtyard, stables, and storage space for carriages. Courtesy of the Lewis Walpole Library, Yale University. 806.0.40.

stopped to bait or change horses and would have servants ready to take the passengers' hats and coats, waiters (*NA* 156; *P&P* 220; *P* 105, 193) at hand to serve dinner, and cold meat, cheese, and pastries ready for consumption. The price paid for this hospitality (*Sand, MW* 378) varied by location and quality of service, but tips to the staff (*P* 144) always accounted for a large proportion of the bill. Parson Woodforde, staying at the Angel Inn in the Strand in 1786, paid £3 4s. 6d. to the innkeeper for lodging from October 6 to October 10, plus 12s. 6d. to the "very civil" servants. *See also* Alehouse; Carriages and Coaches; Travel.

Insanity

Mental illness (*Evelyn, MW* 188) was of great concern in the late eighteenth century, not only because madness was supposed to be on the increase (a phenomenon blamed on the cult of sensibility—see *L&F, MW* 99) but also because people were growing uncomfortable with the way the mentally ill were treated. Few positive remedies could be offered to the insane, and care consisted mostly of warehousing the patients, who were little more than prisoners, in frightful conditions. For much of the eighteenth century, London's most famous mental hospital, the Bethlehem Hospital (or "Bedlam," for short) had been a popular tourist attraction. Visitors could pay a small fee to watch the madmen run through their various caprices, and for a long time, no one saw much harm in this.

By Austen's day, the mood was changing. London had a second mental hospital, St. Luke's, founded at midcentury on more humane principles, and many provincial towns were building similar facilities. There was an increasing feeling that insanity was no one's fault, simply "the most dreadful of all human calamities," in the words of conduct-book author John Gregory. The mad should be treated gently and with patience.

What occasioned this change of mood is uncertain, but several events and developments might have been responsible. There was, on the whole, a shift away from the Puritan perception that madness was a form of divine vengeance for sin and a shift, in this as in many other fields, toward a rational and scientific explanation. In addition, the same fashionable respect for deep feeling that some critics saw as creating lunatics made excesses of emotion more palatable and less worthy of punishment. A third influence may have been the growing awareness of abuses of the system, particularly as they affected women. It was, for much of the eighteenth century, perfectly legal for a man to lock his wife in a private madhouse with absolutely no medical evaluation or oversight, simply because he was angry with her or wished to take a mistress without interference. This state of affairs was increasingly widely deplored and formed the basis of Mary Wollstonecraft's unfinished novel, *Maria or the Wrongs of Woman* (1798). A fourth influence may have been the madness of George III, who suffered from a period of serious mental illness in 1788–1789 and recovered, supposedly thanks to the treatment offered by his doctor, Francis Willis.* This may have encouraged people to think of mental illness as treatable and to publicize the issue.

In literature, madness had been a popular topic since at least the time of Shakespeare, whose *King Lear* and *Hamlet* contain long speeches imitating the gibberish spoken by the mentally ill. Austen was familiar with both these plays and perhaps with poetry, such as Thomas Mozeen's "The Bedlamite" (1762), which attempted to capture the apparently nonsensical flow of insane chatter:

> Give me the reward,
> Give me the reward;
> And fill the goblet high:
> I now the traitor spy;—
> Tread soft and fair,
> All light as air,

*He relapsed in 1811, prompting Parliament to name the Prince of Wales as his regent; George III never recovered from this second illness and died in 1820.

> 'Tis my belief,
> Yon plaintain leaf
> Conceals him from your eye.
>
> 'Tis a Spaniard on my life!—
> Tawny face—bloody knife!—
> But let the bells merrily ring;
> We have store of great guns,
> And fine Chelsea buns,
> And the burgundy runs . . .

Austen's only depictions of madness are comic, and, like most of her Juvenilia, they are parodies of the literary efforts of others. Her madwoman's speech in *Love and Freindship* could be read as a parody of Mozeen, Shakespeare, or any of the other previous authors who had made an attempt to re-create this sort of monologue:

> 'Talk not to me of Phaetons . . . —Give me a violin—. I'll play to him & sooth him in his melancholy Hours—Beware ye gentle Nymphs of Cupid's Thunderbolts, avoid the piercing Shafts of Jupiter—Look at that Grove of Firs—I see a Leg of Mutton—They told me Edward was not Dead; but they deceived me—they took him for a Cucumber—' . . . For two Hours did I rave thus madly and should not then have left off, as I was not in the least fatigued, had not Sophia who was just recovered from her swoon, intreated me to consider that Night was now approaching and that the Damps had begun to fall. (*MW* 100)

Indeed, this passage could hardly be told from Mozeen's, if set typographically as verse and given a few rhymes. What marks it as parody is not the character's subject matter but the end of the episode, in which the supposedly mad character can switch off her ravings at the mention of approaching discomfort.

Italian

Italian was the second-most fashionable foreign language for women to study. The first was French, and Italian was a distant second in popularity. Even middle-class women picked up some French here and there, but it was far less common for an Englishwoman (or man) to master Italian. It remained the province of the aristocracy, the upper gentry, and serious music enthusiasts. The use of Italian therefore indicated either true study and dedication or affectation and a desire to seem fashionable.* Anne Elliot serves as an example of the first set of motives. As a baronet's daughter, she has had an excellent education that includes enough Italian for her

---

*An exception is when the Italian appears in a musical context; as knowledge of music was considered essential for a well-educated young woman, ignorance of the terms used in music was a sign of vulgarity (*Lesley, MW* 130).

to translate a song, as it is sung, "into clear, comprehensible, elegant English" (*P* 186). Yet, always modest, she does not parade her knowledge and insists, "I do not pretend to understand the language. I am a very poor Italian scholar." She also has a real justification for knowing and using Italian; as a good musician herself and an enthusiastic spectator of others' performances, she has a reason to be acquainted with Italian lyrics and with the musical directions given in Italian on sheet music. (Austen's reference to crying "*con amore*," *MP* 282, reads almost as a musical instruction.)

Standing in opposition to Anne is Mrs. Elton, who uses one Italian phrase, repeated as ostentatiously and as frequently as possible. Austen uses a number of details to characterize Mrs. Elton, but among the most telling is this woman's return to "caro sposo" (dear husband—see *E* 279, 302, 356), without any other Italian phrase being trotted out for public admiration. So eager is she for glory that surely she would exhibit a second Italian phrase, if she had one at her command. Clearly, then, she knows only the one expression, but she wants credit for knowing the language, because it solidifies her claim to gentility. Such ambitions were derided in *The Mirror of the Graces* (1811), whose anonymous author sniffed,

> Were girls of the plebeian classes brought up in the praiseworthy habits of domestic duties; had they learned how to manage a house, how to economize and produce comfort at the least expence at their father's frugal yet hospitable table; we should not hear of dancing-masters and music-masters, of French and Italian masters; they would have no time for them.

Austen, too, found the acquisition of Italian as an "accomplishment," as a means of self-display, annoying and wasteful. Miss Stanley, who serves as a foil to the heroine of Catharine or the Bower, has just spent twelve years "which ought to have been spent in the attainment of useful knowledge and Mental Improvement" studying "Drawing, Italian and Music." Austen has nothing against accomplishments per se; what she objects to is the neglect of reading in pursuit of fashion (*Cath, MW* 198). Knowledge of Italian is perfectly acceptable if it caps a splendid and well-rounded education; it is contemptible if it is made to substitute for "useful knowledge."

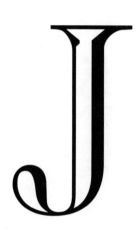

Jewelry

Almost every woman, even poor women, owned some form of jewelry (*P&P* 378). It came in a wide variety of materials, with most of the items falling into the categories still worn today: earrings, necklaces, bracelets, and so on. However, some types of jewelry were worn in different ways than today, and some have become rarities or fallen out of fashion altogether.

The most popular materials for jewelry, for those who could afford them, were diamonds and pearls. Diamonds (*Lesley, MW* 137) appeared in almost every category of jewelry, and, though some were rose-cut, most were brilliant-cut, with brilliant-cut diamonds increasing in popularity. (A rose-cut diamond is usually circular in shape, and the facets on its top come to a shallow point. A brilliant-cut diamond's top is shaped like a truncated pyramid, with a flat surface, or "table," at the summit.) Most diamonds at this time came from India and other parts of Southeast Asia, as the vast diamond deposits in South Africa and South America had yet to be discovered. As diamonds were so expensive, substitutes, known as "paste," were already in existence. Fake diamonds were manufactured from glass, iron pyrite (marcasite), and rock crystal. The best paste jewels, made of leaded glass, were much in demand from the early nineteenth century onward.

Pearls (*NA* 68–69; *S&S* 221; *E* 292, 324), like diamonds, could be simulated; false pearls sold for about one-fifth the price of real ones. However, women could also invest in seed pearls, small pearls that were strung in decorative arrangements and that were less expensive than large, round pearls. Matching sets of jewelry, comprising two to four harmonious pieces, were common, and it was a set of this kind that the local squire's wife gave to Parson James Woodforde's niece in 1781. "Mrs. Custance," Woodforde wrote in his diary, "gave Nancy a Pearl necklace and Pearl Chain to hang from the Necklace, a Pr of Pearl Earrings and another Pr of Ear-rings." The lucky Nancy's necklace, like most pearls sold on strands, were probably strung by a woman. Many women were employed as pearl-stringers, either in jewelers' workshops or in their own homes as a cottage industry.

Colored stones were less popular than diamonds, but they were also cheaper. A common method of setting them was to surround one large colored stone with a rim of small diamonds or pearls. Like diamonds, they were increasingly set with open "collets," the metal cups in which jewels rest. The open-backed collet allowed for more light to pervade the jewels. (Paste jewels, however, were an exception to the trend; they were usually set in closed collets with a bright foil backing to increase their sparkle.)

Colored stones, including amethyst, garnet, carnelian, agate, sapphire, emerald, topaz, and onyx, increased somewhat in popularity after the 1790s, but they were never as desirable as pearls and diamonds—not a surprising preference, perhaps, in light of the period's love affair with the color white.

Rich women tended to favor the more expensive end of this spectrum, such as sapphires and, until the discovery of a large deposit ruined their value, amethysts. Middle-class and working-class women had access to a variety of cheaper substitutes, including Wedgwood jasper ware cameos, tortoiseshell, ivory (*P&P* 221), jet, enamel, mother-of-pearl, brass, and stamped metal. Beads of steel faceted like gems and riveted to a back plate were, for a time, fashionable among all classes. The "cut steel" beads typically had fifteen facets and were found on a remarkable variety of products, from buckles to sword hilts. They remained well regarded throughout Austen's lifetime, but, starting in the 1810s, the Birmingham and Woodstock trade in such items was gradually siphoned off by the French. Gold (*P&P* 221) was always popular, sometimes as a uniform surface, sometimes rendered in various colors or textures for contrast; those who could not afford real gold had to make do with gilt, brass, or pinchbeck.

Gilding could be accomplished in at least two different ways. The more reliable of the two was to cover the item in nitrate of mercury, then dip it in a mixture of gold and mercury and heat the surface to fix the gold in place. It took skill to do properly and exposed the unfortunate jeweler to mercury poisoning and an early death. The less reliable method involved simply dipping the object in a gold solution, which yielded a less durable layer. Women who could not afford even a thinly applied layer of proper gilding had to make do with pinchbeck, a zinc-copper alloy invented in the early eighteenth century.

Jewelry made of hair was surprisingly popular. Sometimes the hair was merely a component; sometimes the entire piece of jewelry was composed of hair. The most common use of hair was as a decorative and sentimental addition to a traditional piece of jewelry. A piece of clipped hair might be placed in a locket, for example, but much of the jewelry that made use of hair did not allow for the removal of the hair. Instead, a special piece of jewelry—a ring, a brooch, or a pendant, for example—would be commissioned from a jeweler, who would use the hair as part of a picture or a pattern. The hair might be woven or braided and placed under a lid of crystal, visible through the transparent covering, or it might be used pictorially, as in one piece where the golden hair has become a sheaf of wheat, the seed stalks formed by minute droplets of gold. Hair jewelry was sometimes a love token, as it is in *Sense and Sensibility* (98, 135), but its most common use seems to have been in mourning jewelry, especially mourning rings that were provided for in the deceased's will and distributed to friends and family as a means of remembrance.

More valuable pieces of jewelry were also left as bequests (*Lesley, MW* 120–121, 137; *NA* 68–69; *E* 479), especially from women to their daughters or to favored servants. Jewelry was a woman's most liquid asset and was thought of very much in those terms. It sometimes had sentimental associations, true; it was pretty, yes; but first and foremost, it was valuable. Princess Caroline, wife of the prince regent, lived off her wedding jewels when her allowance from her husband proved inadequate, and many a woman (and man) sold jewels to pay gambling debts. Because their appeal was aesthetic and financial, women had few qualms about taking the gems out of their settings and rearranging them in fashionable new ways (*S&S* 220; *E* 479). There was little interest in preserving antique settings, particularly as gem cutting had greatly improved in the last century or two, and family heirlooms could look very dull next to new, brilliant-cut specimens.

People could afford to be more sentimental about jewelry that featured portrait miniatures of loved ones, and there was a great interest in all sorts of pieces that featured faces. Cameos showing family members, famous men, or classical figures were extremely popular, as were pendants, chatelaines, rings, lockets, and other pieces featuring hand-painted miniatures. The more expensive examples, following the prevailing taste, might be surrounded by a rim of small diamonds. One curious variation on the theme was the "eye" portrait, a detailed rendering of one of the lover's eyes, that could be found on a pendant, brooch, clasp, or ring. The wearer could see the eye and recognize his beloved, but nosy companions need never know the identity of the woman to whom the eye belonged.

Most types of jewelry popular in Austen's time would be perfectly recognizable today. There were necklaces, brooches (*Sand, MW* 374, 390), and bracelets, the last of these typically sold in pairs. There were rings (*Sand, MW* 390; *NA* 122; *S&S* 135; *P&P* 316, 317) of all kinds, from diamond rings to rings that bore gems engraved with classical designs. Lockets or pendants hung from necklaces or from a ribbon (*MP* 254) tied around the neck. Necklaces (*MP* 257–258, 261, 263, 271, 274) themselves might be in the form of a rivière—a sequence of stones in graduated sizes—or several large stones, cameos, or similar items connected by festoons of pearls, stones, beads, or chain links.

Earrings (*S&S* 226) fluctuated in size over time, growing quite long in the late 1790s, contracting again, passing out of favor entirely for a heartbeat in 1807, then returning for both morning and evening wear and gradually increasing in size again in the 1820 and 1830s. The typical earring had a top, backed by the wire hook that passed through the pierced ear, and one or more pendant drops. The girandole, a style that featured three drop pendants, was extremely popular. Others had tassel chains or came in the form of hoops or loops.

While earrings and necklaces still seem quite ordinary, other pieces of

jewelry would seem odd if worn today. Men were fond of jeweled shoe buckles and also wore "stock buckles" to fasten the backs of their cravats. In the evenings, women might wear armlets high on their upper arms, just below their short sleeves. A tremendous amount of jewelry was also worn in the hair (*E 479*), including combs, jeweled fillets for tying the hair near the back of the head, and aigrettes (feather-shaped brooches for the hair). Some wore tiaras or their close cousins, diadems. Others wore Eastern-inspired turbans decorated with brooches called "sultanas."

Men and women alike wore chatelaines. The chatelaine, whose name came from the ring of keys worn from the belt of a medieval great lady, was a ribbon connected to the belt by a hook and weighted at the end by a decorative item of some sort. In many cases, this was a watch, but it might equally be a portrait miniature, a cameo, a seal, or a locket. Gentlemen sometimes wore a fob that hung from the waist and held several seals—implying, perhaps, as the chatelaine's keys did, that he had a great deal of responsibility and thus needed multiple ways of sealing his letters. These clusters of seals can often be seen in contemporary prints. The lady in the illustration *The Successful Fortune Hunter* (Marriage) wears a host of trinkets suspended from her sash, including seals and a watch or chatelaine; her husband-to-be likewise wears items hung from his waist, including what is probably a bunch of seals. *See also* Clothing.

Jews

Design for a cut-steel chatelaine. From a sketch in Matthew Boulton's pattern books, Volume B.

There are few references to Jews in Austen's work, which is not entirely surprising. In the first decades of the nineteenth century, the entire Jewish population of England was only about 12,000 to 15,000, and the one major eighteenth-century controversy relating to Jews, a proposed Naturalization Bill that would have provided a few wealthy foreign-born Jews with the opportunity to become citizens, had been laid to rest in the 1750s. English Jews led a comparatively peaceful life in England, separatist in some places and at some levels of society, entirely or nearly entirely assimilated at others. The exact level of anti-Semitism is hard to define, but it seems to have been no worse than in most places on the Continent, and Jews suffered no more impediments to education or public service than did any other non-Anglicans, including Catholics and Dissenters. Most of the English, then, knew Jews at a distance—as isolated celebrities, like the Jewish boxer Daniel Mendoza, or as crudely drawn "types" in literature, drama, song, theology, and political rhetoric.

Stereotypes were widespread, as they were about every "foreign" group: Gypsies, Scots, Frenchmen, and so on. Stereotypes about Jews fell into several categories. There was the image of Jew-as-peddler, which had a great deal of truth behind it. Working-class Jews were concentrated in several trades, including the sale of citrus fruit, spectacles, pencils, sealing wax, slippers, cheap framed pictures, and other specific types of small goods. Jewish peddlers traveled the countryside selling buckles, watches, watch chains, jewelry, buttons, and snuffboxes. However, the trade most associated with Jews and the one most often used in prints and songs to typify them was the trade in secondhand clothes. The nerve center of this business was Rag Fair, an open-air clothing market near Tower Hill in London, which was heavily populated by Jews.

The second major stereotype about Jews was that they were dirty, poor, and criminal. It was true that the vast majority of Jews in England were poor, and it was also true that these poor Jews sometimes tended to wind up in court, often on charges of receiving stolen goods. However, like most stereotypes, this was an exaggerated view that did not take into account the law-abiding poor and the middle class and that further fed on the lingering lies that had circulated about Jews from the Middle Ages. The Jews were so dirty, it was said, that they caused epidemics to erupt; they blasphemed; they killed Christian babies; they thought it virtuous to defraud Christians. These old fables were far from dead. An anonymous correspondent to the *St. James Chronicle* wrote in 1804 that "the followers of Moses are the most nasty and filthy people under the canopy of heaven" and that they ought to be confined to ghettoes.

Paradoxically, a third common stereotype about Jews was that they were all fabulously rich, that they controlled the international stock markets, and that their dirty money would be the undoing of England. The English, an enthusiastically capitalist people at this point, felt that the Jews were greedy to an unseemly degree (though it was only the *degree* of their thirst for wealth that was at issue, as everyone acknowledged that money was good and that more money was better). This stereotype was fed by the highly visible example of a few rich Jews, including Samson Gideon (1699–1762), a stockjobber and loan contractor whose genius for finance ensured his quick rise as an adviser to the government. At one point, his personal fortune was £350,000. Gideon met with a great deal of resentment, particularly during the fight over the Jewish Naturalization Bill, which did not affect him as a native-born Anglo-Jew. Like many wealthy Jews, he was largely assimilated into English culture, and his children were baptized as Anglicans. He was succeeded in the popular imagination by Benjamin (1755–1808) and Abraham (1756–1810) Goldsmid, brothers who began contracting government loans in 1795, and by Nathan Meyer Rothschild, a noted financier of the 1810s and 1820s.

Overall attitudes toward the Jews varied. Some people adhered more to

[Lilliputian Figures], 1799, detail. The stereotypical image of the rich Jew, disappointed because he had a bad day at the Exchange. Courtesy of the Lewis Walpole Library, Yale University. 799.7.12.4.

one stereotype; others embraced all or part of all the popular myths. At one end of the spectrum was William Cobbett, author of *Rural Rides*, who saw Jews as the antithesis of the idealized country life he so admired. He subscribed to an unusually long and vicious catalog of canards and particularly resented the ability of wealthier Jews to purchase country estates. At the other end of the spectrum were well-educated and relatively tolerant members of the ruling class, Whiggish in their politics, who saw the criminal behavior of urban Jews as evidence of their poverty, not their immorality. Some popular songs and plays pointed to the image of Jews as greedy and questioned whether the rest of the English were not just as fond of money; one song asked, in the stereotypically accented English of the stage Jew, whether a purse full of money, dropped on the ground, would not be picked up just as quickly by an Englishman as by a Jew. Others defended Jews from different motives; they believed in millenarian prophecies that dictated that the Jews must be converted before Christ could return. Therefore, they reasoned, the Jews must be welcomed, shown the superiority of Christianity, and brought to Christ. To facilitate this, the Jews must be freed from legal disabilities and fully assimilated. To this argument, anti-Semites responded that the Jews had brought their own punishment upon themselves and that helping them in any way was acting in defiance to the will of God.

This is a brief and highly simplified version of an incredibly complex social picture, and yet Austen's presentation is still simpler. She refers to only one of the aforementioned stereotypes, and she puts the relevant words, "rich as a Jew" (*NA* 63, 96), into the mouth of an entirely unsympathetic character, John Thorpe. All we can know, then, is that she did not approve of this particular viewpoint. The voicing of it, like so much else about Thorpe, is evidence of his vulgarity. Whether she espoused the conversion of the Jews, nursed suspicions that they were criminal, hoped for tolerance, or even thought about them much at all is unknown.

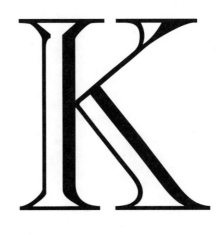

Keys and Locks

Not very long before Austen's birth, locks and the keys that opened them were fundamentally the same as they had been in the Middle Ages: extremely simple and rather easy to pick. However, in the late eighteenth and early nineteenth centuries, an increasing interest in all things mechanical resulted in significant improvements to the locks found on doors. The first important development was the "one-lever lock," in which the key slid a lever or tumbler back and forth between two positions: locked and unlocked. The problem with this type of lock was that the tumbler could be circumvented simply by pushing it higher than intended, either with the key or with some other thin object.

Later, multiple-lever locks were invented. Locksmith Robert Barron patented the world's first double-action tumbler lock in 1778; this type of lock could not be opened if the key were the wrong size, as it had tumblers protected by stops, or "shoulders," above and below. Additional refinements followed, and Barron eventually introduced a lock with six double-action levers, allowing for increasingly complex keys. Even this design was superseded in 1784, when Joseph Bramah, a locksmith contemptuous of his rivals' attempts to thwart thieves, invented a hollow, cylindrical key that was extremely hard to simulate with the tools then available to thieves.

Locks in Austen's novels never reach the next level of sophistication, for the next significant advance in security was not introduced until 1818, the year after her death. (This next generation of locks was designed by Jeremiah Chubb, whose locks had an internal revolving barrel that sealed off the keyhole, making it impossible to use any tools or false keys.) Most likely, the door locks (*NA* 159, 192, 193, 223; *MP* 73, 177) in her books resembled those so often seen in contemporary prints and drawings—boxlike brass inserts near the doorknob, visible from both sides of the door, with a large keyhole. The keys (*MP* 73, 98) that fitted these locks had fairly simple flanges and notches, connected by a long, thin shaft to a ring, usually round or oval, from which the key was suspended. Unlike the openings for key rings today, which are frequently only a few millimeters wide, these holes at the tops of keys were comparatively large, but this area of the key, and even the rest of the key as well, would sometimes be decorated with scrollwork or other ornamental devices. What is certain is that an interior door in a comfortable home would never have been secured by a padlock, as Henry Tilney suggests in his mock-Gothic narrative to Catherine Morland (*NA* 159); the clumsy padlock is being used purely for its medieval associations. The type of door lock that *was* used is depicted in the illustrations *A Shrewed Guess* (Clothing) and *Nobody's Song* (Servants).

Locks on furniture (*L&F*, *MW* 95–96; *NA* 163, 169, 173) tended to be smaller and might, especially in the case of expensive items, be highly decorative. Since personal possessions were fewer then than now, and since each item tended to be proportionally more costly, a wide array of objects carried locks. Chests that held fine linen, small boxes that held expensive tea and sugar, cabinets and desks that concealed important documents such as letters and legal papers, display cabinets for collections of rocks or beetles, and ornate miniature chests for jewelry might all bear locks. The keys (*L&F*, *MW* 95–96; *NA* 168, 169) for all these items might be held by a trusted servant, but one or more might be suspended from a chatelaine, a piece of jewelry that hung from the waist. Named for the medieval lady of a castle, who wore a large ring of keys, the chatelaine might also contain a watch or a miniature portrait.

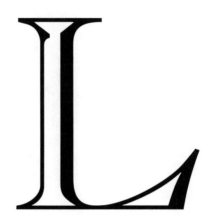

Landau

The landau (*Clifford, MW* 43), named after the German town in which it was invented in 1757, was simply a coach with a convertible top. It had four wheels, a box for the driver, and seats facing forward and backward. Its leather top divided in the middle and could be folded down, half toward the back of the coach and half toward the front. The window sash was then slid downward into the door, completing the transformation. When the top was erected, the landau looked almost exactly like a standard coach and provided protection from the elements; when the top was down, the occupants could enjoy pleasant weather and an improved view. It was not a perfect vehicle; the blackened and oiled leather hoods could be greasy and strong-smelling, and they never seemed to lie flat enough. However, the versatility of the landau, which could be used day or night, in good weather or bad, made it popular, and variations on the theme soon appeared.

One of these was the landaulette (*Clifford, MW* 43; *P* 250) or demi-landau, which corresponded to the chariot in the same way that the landau corresponded to the coach. In other words, it had four wheels, a box, and one seat that faced forward and held three people, the difference from the chariot being that the hood could be folded. Another variant was the barouche-landau (*E* 274, 343), which purported to have features of both the barouche and the landau. It was not a popular innovation. *See also* Carriages and Coaches.

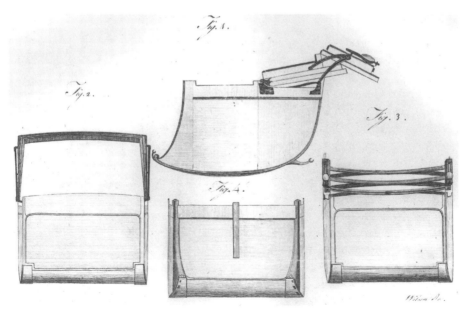

Landaulet, from William Felton's *Treatise on Carriages,* 1796. Library of Congress.

The Pacific Entrance of Earl-Wolf, into Blackhaven, 1792. This illustration is of no use with regard to horses or coachman, since they have been replaced for the purposes of political satire, but it shows a clear picture of a landau with both its roof sections folded down. The carriage body is pale green with gold trim; the wheels and hammer-cloth are red. Note the earl's coronet on his head and on the landau's door. Courtesy of the Lewis Walpole Library, Yale University. 792.1.20.1+.

Law

Lawyers (*Sand, MW* 401; *NA* 205; *S&S* 269; *E* 79, 116, 137, 214; *P* 9–11, 20) were educated (*P&P* 200) first at the universities and then in the Inns of Court, a collection of London buildings devoted to the study of law. Consisting of Lincoln's Inn, Gray's Inn (*Sand, MW* 389), the Inner Temple, and the Middle Temple, the Inns of Court were home to barristers, who ate their meals in the Inns and, when training was complete, approved of new members by calling them to the bar. They kept their numbers small; there were usually only a few hundred barristers at any one time in eighteenth-century England.

Most legal business, such as drawing up contracts, arbitrating disputes, passing bills for turnpikes or enclosures, arranging mortgages, and so on, was done by attorneys (*Watsons, MW* 348–349; *P&P* 28, 37; *MP* 34; *E* 183), with the assistance of clerks (*P* 32). Attorneys could be quite young. Parson James Woodforde, in 1785, entertained "Mr. Walker an Attorney," who was "about 18 Years of Age." Attorneys, also known as solicitors (*Sand, MW* 389), had far less social status than barristers. Indeed, the entire legal profession, though considered gentlemanly as a whole (*S&S* 102–103; *MP* 91, 94), was viewed with largely unjustified suspicion and resentment, then as now. Portrayals of lawyers in popular entertainment were usually negative; Gay's *Beggar's Opera* listed the ways in which foxes, whores, and relatives could steal one thing or another from a man, then concluded that a lawyer was the worst of them all:

> . . . It ever was decreed, sir,
> If lawyer's hand is fee'd, sir,
> He steals your whole estate.

The greedy lawyer was a stock stereotype, as was the lawyer devoid of all human feeling. *The Clandestine Marriage*, a play by David Garrick and George Colman the elder, included a conversation between two lawyers, one of whom reveals how little he cares about his client's welfare:

FLOWER. A pretty decent gaol-delivery!—Do you expect to bring off Darkin, for the robbery on Putney-Common? Can you make out your *alibi*?

TRAVERSE. Oh, no! the crown witnesses are sure to prove our identity. We shall certainly be hanged: but that don't signify.

The Five Alls, John Kay, 1788, detail. A barrister making an argument. Courtesy of the Lewis Walpole Library, Yale University. 788.0.2.2.

As the audience knew, being hanged certainly "signified" for the prisoner, if not for the lawyer who lost the case.

Lawyers were, however, reasonably well compensated for their trouble, and this no doubt allowed them to absorb at least some of the ridicule with good humor. A lawyer could make as much as two guineas a day, and his work brought him into contact—business contact, at least, if not always social contact—with some of the most eminent men in his region (*P* 18–19). If he had good manners and a decent income, he might even marry well; Jane's great-uncle, Francis Austen, made himself a fortune through his legal career and two advantageous marriages. He might also rise to become a justice of the peace, a local magistrate administering various kinds of criminal cases in his parish, although this job required property ownership and was more likely to be held by a wealthy man who learned his law on the job than by a skilled lawyer with little property (*E* 100). Eminent barristers could rise to become judges (*P&P* 52–53), and some of these judges became quite famous. A few ascended to the post of lord chancellor; others, to peerages.

Lawyers were skilled at navigating the complex jungle of English law, which was choked with recent legislation and obsolete medieval artifacts. Many laws were not enforced at all, while others were enforced so selectively that the court system was frequently accused of political or class favoritism. Some regions were ruled by centuries-old manorial courts (*MP* 82), and entirely different legal systems existed side by side. Canon law nominally governed marriage, though this branch of the law was increasingly insignificant; common law dealt with criminal infractions, debts, credit, and contractual disputes; chancery law involved trusts, wardship, and a good deal of litigation over property.* Areas of influence overlapped and competed, and within the common law there were further subdivisions. King's Bench was devoted to crimes and breaches of the peace, Common Pleas to civil cases, and Exchequer to debts owed to the crown.

Lighting

Artificial lighting was a convenience and, to a very great extent, a sign of affluence and status. This was because good-quality lighting was expensive in itself (*Col Let*, *MW* 156–157) and was, in addition, subject to taxes. Furthermore, the use of large numbers of candles required a substantial outlay in candlesticks and a further expenditure in servants to keep the wicks trimmed and to replace the candles as necessary. Large-scale nighttime illumination, then, remained the province either of commercial enterprises such as pleasure gardens and theatres or of the wealthy. Naturally, this meant that considerable illumination appealed to those eager to display their prosperity, and the result was a creeping inflation of mealtimes. Dinner at noon and supper in the early evening, followed by a similarly early bedtime, was by Austen's time replaced by a dinner in the late afternoon or early evening, a still later tea, and a supper (if one still ate supper at all) at perhaps ten o'clock, when artificial light was absolutely essential even in summer. This fashion, set initially at the highest socioeconomic levels, was enthusiastically imitated by all who could afford it, and the result was an increased consumption of lighting materials. By 1784, Prime Minister William Pitt estimated that the average family consumed thirty pounds of tallow candles per year.

These materials fell into two major classifications, with numerous subclasses. The first, candles (*Watsons*, *MW* 327, 336; *S&S* 144; *NA* 187; *MP* 108, 182, 184, 379, 381, 382, 439; *E* 253, 290, 329), fell into two principal groups—tallow and wax. Tallow candles, a by-product of beef and mutton production, could be made en masse by tallow chandlers, who rendered cow and sheep fat and solidified it in molds. Alternatively, it could be made at home by frugal housewives who saved the drippings from their beef roasts, but it is unclear how many women were willing to engage in this time-consuming and messy process. Tallow candles had numerous dis-

---

*Chancery cases, because they often involved large estates and therefore large fees, could be extremely lucrative. An 1803 satirical print, entitled *Temptation for Lawyers*, shows a crowd of lawyers rushing toward a large scroll that is held by two devils and entitled "A Suit in Chancery."

advantages: they did not consume their wicks and thus needed to be trimmed about four times an hour to keep the flame from guttering; they produced bad-smelling and sooty smoke; they melted at a fairly low temperature and thus burned up quickly in warm weather. Parson James Woodforde was no doubt speaking of a tallow candle when he wrote in his diary, "Very ill indeed today having had a very indifferent night of rest last night, owing to the night candle filling the room in being so long going out with intolerable smoke and stink."* The advantage of tallow candles was their cost; even the good ones cost less than beeswax candles, which were truly a luxury item (*E* 300). Beeswax smelled better, burned at a higher temperature, and thus consumed its wick more completely, necessitating less trimming and supervision. (It may have been either a beeswax or a tallow candle that Catherine Morland "snuffed" in *NA* 169–170—snuffing was trimming off the ashy part of the wick—but it is hard to imagine the general admitting mere tallow candles into his home.) The next improvement in candle making occurred just after Austen's death, in the 1820s, when stearine wax candles, which burned at an even higher temperature, were invented by the French.

At the opposite end of the spectrum from beeswax were rushlights, used only by those who could afford nothing better. These were rushes dipped in fat and set alight; they provided adequate illumination, but they burned at almost a right angle to the wall, and as they burned, they dripped hot grease onto the floor. Even the miserly Mrs. Norris would not have stooped to such measures (she probably cadged beeswax candles from Sir Thomas' pantry instead).

Sir Thomas and Austen's other well-to-do characters no doubt owned a number of candlesticks. These had historically been single-candle holders, usually made of turned brass, but increasingly, because of the status conferred by brilliant illumination, they held multiple candles and were made of new materials, such as Sheffield plate (silver-clad copper) and glass. They were also increasingly cast rather than turned, with a hollow stem through which wax or tallow remnants could be removed. Candlesticks, like most domestic objects, were often interpreted in the prevailing artistic style of the day, which meant that many of the new Sheffield plate candlesticks had neoclassical lines. Single candlesticks can be seen in the illustration *A Hitt at Backgammon* (Games), and mirrored wall sconces are shown in several illustrations, including *A Master Parson with a Good Living* (Clergy) and *A Master of the Ceremonies Introducing a Partner* (Dance).

The other majority category of interior lighting was the oil lamp (*NA*

*Not everyone found the smoke produced by candles to be a disadvantage; Jonathan Swift, early in the eighteenth century, complained that servants tended to amuse themselves by using the tallow smoke of a candle held high to write their names on ceilings.

88, 159, 160, 190; *E* 231), and this, like the candle, came in many forms. It had at least two advantages over candles: long burning times and low cost. The basic form of the oil lamp was a dish or tube, in various shapes, holding both a thick wick and a reservoir of oil, usually fish oil. Like tallow, this stank and smoked, and the wicks, like those in tallow candles, needed to be fussed over almost constantly. This was less of a problem in commercial settings than in the home; the great pleasure gardens at Vauxhall and Ranelagh could no doubt simply hire people to trim the wicks as needed, and outdoors the problems of odor and smoke were minimized. Theatres, too, sometimes used vast numbers of oil lamps; the King's Theatre, Haymarket, had 2,000 of them during the 1781–1782 opera season. Theatres generally had a designated lamp tender who lit and maintained the lamps, but indoors, in private homes, it was clear that a better solution was required.

One invention that presented itself during Austen's lifetime was the Argand lamp, designed by Swiss physicist François-Pierre Aime Argand (1750–1803). His innovation, demonstrated in 1782, was a hollow wick that created a circular flame and increased airflow in and around the wick. His lamps were bright and easy to maintain, but they were also expensive, and they remained a luxury novelty item. The affordable, efficient solution, gaslight, was in the first stages of its development during Austen's lifetime, but it would not be brought into homes until after her death; improvements in the oil used in lamps, in the form of whale oil and paraffin, would also wait for general adoption until later in the nineteenth century. In the meantime, candles remained the standard form of interior illumination.

Lodgings

People who traveled in Austen's time stayed in inns if they were merely stopping for a night or two, or with friends if they had friends in the area. If they had no friends or family near their destination, however, they took lodgings (*Mount, MW* 41; *Cath, MW* 203; *LS, MW* 294; *Sand, MW* 402, 407; *NA* 19, 91, 102, 138; *P* 122, 149, 154, 170). Lodgings were fully furnished homes (*Evelyn, MW* 180; *NA* 76; *S&S* 26; *MP* 245; *E* 317) of varying size and location and might be found in almost any town in England. They could also sometimes be found in the country, as the private estates of impoverished owners who found themselves forced to move somewhere cheaper (*S&S* 194; *P&P* 3, 310; *P* 18–19, 22, 32) or who simply chose to live elsewhere (*MP* 295).

Price varied greatly by location. London lodgings (*LS, MW* 296; *S&S* 230; *P&P* 295; *MP* 394), especially on the fashionable West End, were by far the most expensive. Bath was a good deal cheaper, thanks to the town's recognition of the importance of tourism. Prices for lodgings there had been regulated since before Austen's birth. By 1800, a furnished room rented for 10s. 6d. a week in season, 7s. 6d. out of season; a servants' room was 5s. 6d., threepence less in the off-season. Enforcement of the regulations declined somewhat after 1800 and later allowed landlords to charge more for lodgings with especially good furnishings, but the point was that Bath was doing its best to keep prices reasonable. They were more than reasonable at Lyme (*P* 97), which had, according to an 1810 guide, "several genteel lodging-houses, facing the sea, and each possessing a small plat before it, neatly railed in." According to the same guide, rates were "not merely reasonable, they are even cheap."

The quality of the furniture (*P* 22) and rooms also varied. The better lodging houses in Bath offered attractive tables and chairs, mirrors, fire screens, candlesticks, and good-quality beds and mattresses. They had indoor water closets, fashionable wallpaper, parlors, dining rooms, dressing rooms, large bedrooms for the family, and small garret apartments for the servants. However, not all lodgings came up to this standard. Austen, who had stayed in many rented lodgings by the time she wrote *Persuasion*, no doubt spoke from experience when she mentioned "the deficiencies of lodging-house furniture" (*P* 98).

Those who could not afford to rent an entire house and hire a temporary local staff of servants (*Sand, MW* 414)—or those who simply didn't want the bother—stayed instead in boardinghouses, in which they rented a room or suite of rooms and took their meals. These were sometimes also referred to at the time, confusingly, as lodging houses, but they were quite different from whole houses rented to one client. The "Lodgings to let" in *Sanditon* (*MW* 383) are probably actually boardinghouse rooms; as boardinghouses were less fashionable than lodgings, this less desirable form of housing would be in keeping with Austen's general description of the town as a substandard resort.

Joseph Farington stayed at a so-called lodging house in Bath in 1800 and recorded the evening schedule: the ladies retired from the general dining room at about 5:30, and the gentlemen left about an hour later, "that it may be prepared for Tea at 7." After tea, the lodgers who wished to do so played cards together, just as they might have done at a private home. They were served supper at 10:00 and went to bed at about 11:00; the rules stated that they were all to vacate the dining room by 11:30. The provision of public meals makes it clear that this was a boardinghouse, not private lodgings. Another Bath lodger, Ellen Wilson, wrote enthusiastically of her boardinghouse in 1794:

> Having been a fortnight in our lodgings to day we discharged them. . . . We have been most comfortably situated. . . . we were supplied with excellent eatables at breakfast, even an elegant dinner, never less than two good dishes & a pudding or tart, generally a remove besides. Bread & butter with our tea in an evening & some cold meat at supper. Wine, tea & sugar we provided for ourselves. Our candles were charged to us.

She was fortunate in having enough money for decent accommodation; boardinghouses for poor laborers were a good deal less savory. In these dirty establishments, men and women who were strangers to each other slept in the same crowded rooms, and theft was a frequent problem. Some rented space by the night or by the hour to prostitutes and their clients. Running a boardinghouse, which in any case brought strangers into one's home, was never considered a perfectly admirable occupation, and in some cases could be downright disreputable (*E* 275–276); it makes perfect sense that Austen should turn Mrs. Younge, Miss Darcy's unethical former governess, into a woman who "maintained herself by letting lodgings" (*P&P* 322). The worst boardinghouses, according to John Glyde, were home to "the dangerous classes," and perhaps because of this unsavory reputation, they became less popular in certain parts of the country, including Bath, over the course of Austen's lifetime.

Just as today, the quality of rented lodgings varied widely. Staying in Lyme in September 1814, Jane wrote to Cassandra that nothing could "exceed the inconvenience of the Offices, except the general Dirtiness of the House & furniture, & all it's Inhabitants." In 1799, she had also found dirt in the Austens' lodgings at 13 Queen Square, Bath. She wrote to Cassandra that they had been in town "just long enough to go over the house, fix on our rooms, & be very well pleased with the whole of it." Her description reveals the natural tendency of people in a vacation house to choose rooms with the least possible offense to anyone and to criticize the storage arrangements:

> We are exceedingly pleased with the House; the rooms are quite as large as we expected. . . . Eliz: has the apartment within the Drawing room; she wanted my Mother to have it, but as there was no bed in the inner one, & the stairs are so much easier of ascent or my Mother so much stronger than in Paragon as not to regard the double flight, it is settled for us to be above; where we have two very nice sized rooms, with dirty Quilts & everything comfortable. I have the outward & larger apartment, as I ought to have; which is quite as large as our bed room at home, & my Mother's is not materially less.—The Beds are both as large as any at Steventon; & I have a very nice chest of Drawers & a Closet full of shelves—so full indeed that there is nothing else in it, & should therefore be called a Cupboard rather than a Closet I suppose.

Her mention of the quilts is consistent with what is known about lodgings in Bath. Linen was usually provided by the owner of the building. Food and meals, however, were not, and a lodger's first errand was usually to the market to stock the pantry.

A humorous poem by John O'Keeffe, written in 1791 and published in 1834, described the condition of a set of lodgings and the state of mind of their landlord. *I Want a Tenant: A Satire* first tells, in the landlord's voice, of the woes of getting lodgings ready to rent. There are difficulties with workmen, everything remains half undone, and the landlord is troubled day and night by people wanting to see the house (*P* 24). Eager to be making money off his property, he describes everything in the most favorable terms possible and promises to make all sorts of improvements if they will only sign a long lease:

A handsome dining-parlour, sir;
Nice shade from those two rows of fir:
Round here I mean to plant some box;—
See, ma'am, the doors have all brass locks.
A smartish marble I'll put round
This chimney-piece, that I'll be bound.
And then the chimneys do not smoke:
I bought some pots—but they were broke;
Though, should they smoke, I'll take no rent,
My wish is but to give content.

After he gets a tenant, he ignores the smoking chimneys, the flimsy locks, the bare garden, and the lack of wallpaper in the garret, laughingly telling another speaker (his wife, perhaps) that, as the tenants have signed their lease, he will do as he likes.

Lodgings could be rented, as in O'Keeffe's example, by personal inquiry (*Sand, MW* 411, 414). A renter might ask around among friends and acquaintances, and a landlord might advertise in the newspapers (*P* 15). Bath, where renting lodgings was a major local business, had a register office and circulating libraries where available lodgings were listed. In Bath, high turnover meant that something interesting was nearly always available (*NA* 73, 238); one visitor claimed that it was necessary to walk around the town for only five or ten minutes in order to find suitable lodgings. He exaggerated somewhat; it took the Austens a great deal longer to find something they liked and could afford when they moved to Bath in 1801.

London

To those of us growing up in industrialized countries with major urban areas almost commonplace, the dominance of London (*Clifford, MW* 43; *L&F, MW* 89, 90, 92; *Lesley, MW* 112, 122; *LS, MW* 271; *Sand, MW* 373, 378; *NA* 113, 220; *S&S* 107, 311, 318; *P&P* 82, 116, 126, 201, 275, 282–283, 293, 295, 298, 299, 319; *MP* 8, 58, 193, 203, 360, 381, 420, 426; *E* 16, 17, 91, 169, 216, 306, 316, 318; *P* 13, 14, 105, 250) during Jane Austen's lifetime is hard to grasp at an intuitive level. London ruled everything—art, shipping, shopping, music, society (*S&S* 171), entertainment (*NA* 78; *P&P* 129), and fashion. Most of the news in provincial newspapers was culled from London's press. Most publishers were located in London (*NA* 112). The best girls' schools, it was thought, were

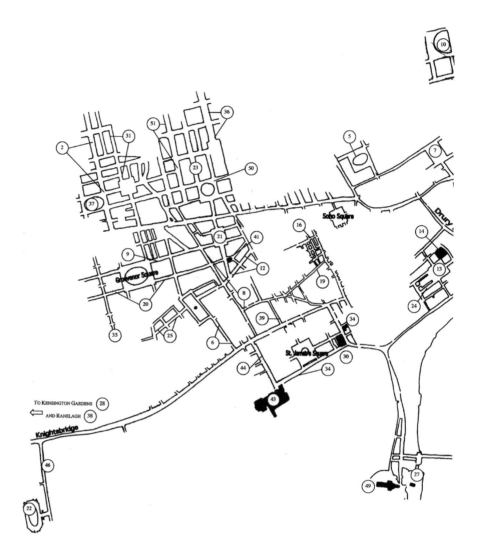

Map of London.

A city the size of London, even as it stood in the early nineteenth century, is hard to reproduce on a page this size. Either a sense of the city's true size is lost, or the reader becomes unable to locate the relevant sites mentioned by Austen. I have chosen to emphasize Austen's details rather than to attempt to show the overall size and shape of the metropolitan area. This is therefore an extremely simplified map, intended to show relative location only.

Readers interested in detailed contemporary maps without the size constraints of this volume may wish to examine my bibliography, under the headings "Time and Space" and "Web sites," for useful resources. A few sites are included as landmarks or because they are sites mentioned in other articles within this book.

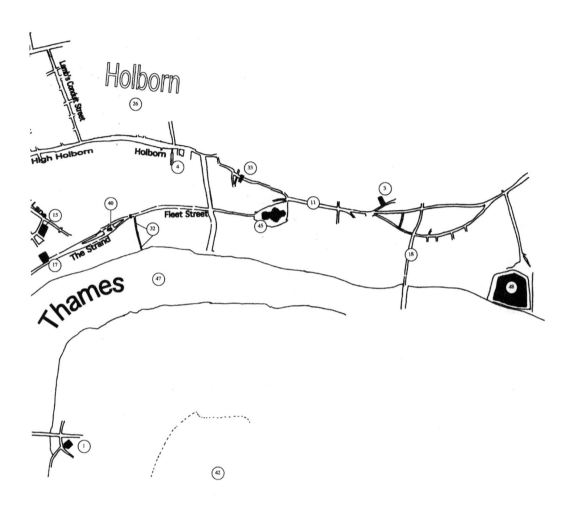

	London Sites	**Notes**
1	Astley's Royal Amphitheater	*E* 471, 472, 481 *See also* Entertainment.
2	Baker Street	*MP* 49
3	Bank of England	*NA* 113
4	Bartlett's Buildings	The Steele sisters lodge here in *S&S*; its easterly location was very unfashionable (*S&S* 217, 230, 277).
5	Bedford Square	*MP* 434
6	Berkeley Street	Mrs. Jennings has her house here (*S&S* 170, 171, 177, 217, 229, 294).
7	Bloomsbury Square	*Cass, MW* 46
8	Bond Street	*Cass, MW* 44; *S&S* 115, 164, 183, 204, 326; *E* 56

(*continued*)

	London Sites	Notes
9	Brook Street	*Cath*, *MW* 202
10	Brunswick Square	Home of John and Isabella Knightley (*E* 9, 46, 102–103, 386, 393, 420, 429, 435).
11	Cheapside	*P&P* 37 A street through London's commercial district; see Gracechurch Street, below.
12	Conduit Street	Site of the Middletons' house (*S&S* 170, 217, 223, 231).
13	Covent Garden	Site of the Bedford Coffee House (*Watsons*, *MW* 356; *NA* 96) and a busy vegetable market.
14	Covent Garden Theater	*L&F*, *MW* 109
15	Drury Lane Theater	*S&S* 330
16	Edward Street	*LS*, *MW* 252; *P&P* 322
17	Exeter Exchange	Like the Tower, Exeter Exchange had a menagerie of wild beasts (*S&S* 221).
18	Gracechurch Street	*P&P* 152, 219, 288, 295 The home of Mr. and Mrs. Gardiner, Elizabeth Bennet's uncle and aunt. The street was located in the City of London—that is, the old central city, now a commercial district—and its association with trade made it decidedly ungenteel.
19	Great Pulteney Street	John Broadwood's pianoforte company was located here.
20	Grosvenor Street	Mr. Bingley's brother-in-law Mr. Hurst has a house here (*P&P* 116, 147).
21	Hanover Square	*S&S* 110, 301
22	Hans Place	One of Henry Austen's addresses in London, so far west that Jane spoke of walking "into town" when she stayed there. Hans Place was a long octagonal plaza with an oval garden in the center, just a block west of Sloane Street and a few blocks south of Knightsbridge.
23	Harley Street	The house rented by John and Fanny Dashwood is here (*S&S* 230, 231, 248, 254, 257, 273, 282).
24	Henrietta Street	Henry Austen and his wife, Eliza, lived at No. 10 above his bank, and Jane sometimes stayed there.
25	Hill Street	Home of Admiral Crawford (*MP* 300).
26	Holborn	*L&F*, *MW* 89; *S&S* 217, 286 A region of northern London that includes Bartlett's Buildings and the Inns of Court, among other sites.
27	House of Commons	*Cath*, *MW* 197; *P* 8
28	Kensington Gardens	*S&S* 271, 274–276 *See also* Public Places.
29	King's Theater, Haymarket	London's Italian opera house. *See also* Opera.
30	Little Theater	*P&P* 319 *See also* Theater.
31	Manchester Street	
32	Middle Temple Street	William Walter Elliot, in his early years, lived in the Temple (*P* 199).
33	Newgate	*L&F*, *MW* 89, 97
34	Pall Mall	*S&S* 199 Edward Ferrars lodges here for a time (*S&S* 275).
35	Park Street	Site of Mrs. Ferrars' home (*S&S* 131).
36	Portland Place	*F&E*, *MW* 8, 9
37	Portman Square	*Lesley*, *MW* 123, 128, 135; *S&S* 153

London Sites	Notes
38 Ranelagh	*Cath, MW* 204
	See also Public Places.
39 Sackville Street	*Col Let, MW* 162; *S&S* 220
40 St. Clement's Church, Strand	*P&P* 318
41 St. George's Church, Hanover Square	*MP* 416
42 St. George's Fields	*NA* 113
43 St. James's Palace	*P&P* 18
44 St. James's Street	*S&S* 290
45 St. Paul's Cathedral	
46 Sloane Street	Henry Austen lived for a time on Sloane Street.
47 Thames	*P* 32
48 Tower of London	*NA* 113
49 Westminster Abbey	
50 Wigmore Street	*LS, MW* 245, 246, 273
51 Wimpole Street	Site of the Rushworths' London house (*MP* 394, 423, 438, 439).

there as well (*L&F*, *MW* 78; *E* 164). London's population dwarfed that of any other city. In 1801, the population of England was about 8,500,000. London accounted for 900,000 of these people, almost twice the total of the next largest six cities combined.* Nothing encapsulated the position of the metropolis more than the fact that "going to town" almost always meant going to London (*J&A*, *MW* 17; *Lesley*, *MW* 131; *Cath*, *MW* 197, 201, 207; *LS*, *MW* 249, 251; *S&S* 110, 114, 325, 359; *P&P* 67, 141, 147, 211, 238, 293, 378; *MP* 38, 284, 425; *E* 79, 116, 308).

This is not to say that everyone approved of London. In fact, it was intellectually fashionable to think otherwise, and it had been so for many years. London offered too much distraction (*MP* 234) and too many temptations, or so the saying went. It was not as pure and simple as life in the country, and hadn't life in the country been celebrated by the ancient Romans? London was expensive. It lured women into its bow-windowed shops and men into its dens of iniquity. Mrs. Austen, Jane's mother, agreed with those who criticized the city. After a visit, she concluded, "It is a sad place. I would not live in it on any account; one has no time to do one's duty to God or man."

Jane herself had mixed feelings. On the one hand, she loved country life and appears to have despised women who aspired to nothing more than a large house in London's rapidly expanding, fashionable West End. On the other hand, she often visited her brother Henry in London and soaked up all the pleasures that the city afforded to a woman of her class—principally shopping and the theatre. In her Juvenilia, she mocked those who

*Manchester, Liverpool, Birmingham, Bristol, Portsmouth, and Bath, which had a combined population of about 500,000.

uttered parroted condemnations of London by placing in the mouths of some of her characters the kind of highly literary, conventional attacks on the capital that appeared in sermons and moral tracts (*Lesley, MW* 120). Here, it is a "hot house of Vice" (*Cath, MW* 239) and a home of "insipid Vanities and idle Dissipations" (*L&F, MW* 78). Isabella Thorpe echoes the same sentiments in the language of romances rather than the language of sermons (*NA* 120), but we are still meant to hear the threadbareness of her language. Edmund Bertram's assessment is more measured: "We do not look in great cities for our best morality. It is not there, that respectable people of my denomination can do most good" (*MP* 93). Fanny Price, similarly, is "disposed to think the influence of London very much at war with all respectable attachments" (*MP* 433). Yet Austen understands perfectly that people like to get into town and have a little fun, and she does not condemn this impulse (*S&S* 155–156; *P&P* 151). Overall, her opinion of London seems to have been summed up by the old saw, "It's a nice place to visit, but I wouldn't want to live there."

For shoppers, London was a foretaste of heaven. The newest fashions made their debut in the metropolis (*Cath, MW* 207) and only slowly worked their way outward to the countryside, so a woman who visited London could gain an advantage over her provincial friends. She could also shop in a wider variety of stores (*S&S* 164, 182, 220–221, 326; *P&P* 43), almost all of which had a wider selection than the average shop in a middling-sized town. London had china showrooms, huge bookstores, and "warehouses" (*P&P* 288)—large shops—selling every conceivable kind of ribbon, lace, calico, or silk. It had the best hairdressers (*E* 205) and the best makers of musical instruments, including the famous John Broadwood from whom Frank Churchill buys Jane Fairfax's pianoforte (*E* 215, 323). Men and women alike saved up their specialized shopping, sometimes for a whole year, and did it all at once in London. If they could not get to London themselves, they asked friends or relatives who were going to do their shopping for them (*F&E, MW* 4). Jane often bought things for Cassandra when she was in town, writing to inform her of what purchases she had made and to request authorization for other items.

The prime season for being in London (*MP* 295) was the winter (*J&A, MW* 17; *Cath, MW* 202; *S&S* 110, 150, 214; *P&P* 117, 238), when Parliament was in session (*Cath, MW* 197) and therefore drawing the most illustrious society into town. The principal theatres, Covent Garden and Drury Lane, were open then, and wealthy and titled women gave their best parties. The season extended into spring (*LS, MW* 251; *MP* 20; *E* 259, 308; *P* 7) as far as Easter, but at that point most people went back to their country homes for the holiday.